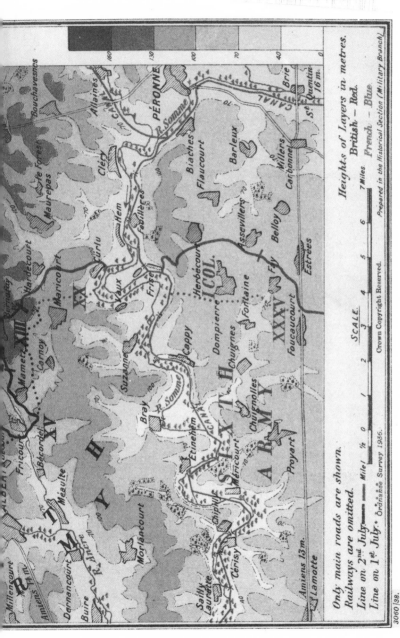

Heights of layers in metres.

British — Red.

French — Blue.

Prepared in the Historical Section (Military Branch).

Only main roads are shown.
Railways are omitted.
Line on 2nd July.
Line on 1st July.

SCALE.

Crown Copyright Reserved.

Ordnance Survey 1936.

3060/38.

HISTORY OF THE GREAT WAR

MILITARY OPERATIONS

Ordnance Survey, 1938.

MARK I. TANK (Male)

Length—26 feet, 5 inches.
Main Armament—Two 6-pdr. Hotchkiss Q.F.
The Tank is fitted with a hydraulic
stabiliser, or tail.

HISTORY OF THE GREAT WAR

BASED ON OFFICIAL DOCUMENTS

BY DIRECTION OF THE HISTORICAL SECTION OF THE
COMMITTEE OF IMPERIAL DEFENCE

MILITARY OPERATIONS

FRANCE AND BELGIUM, 1916

2ND JULY 1916 TO THE END OF THE BATTLES OF THE SOMME

COMPILED BY

CAPTAIN WILFRID MILES

(late Durham Light Infantry)

WITH A PREFACE BY

BRIGADIER-GENERAL SIR JAMES E. EDMONDS

C.B., C.M.G., Hon. D.Litt. (Oxon.), R.E. (Retired), p.s.c.
Director of the Historical Section (Military Branch)

MAPS AND SKETCHES COMPILED BY

MAJOR A. F. BECKE

Hon. M.A. (Oxon.), R.F.A. (Retired)

THE IMPERIAL WAR MUSEUM
Department of Printed Books

In Association With
THE BATTERY PRESS
Nashville

Originally released 1938

Published jointly by
**The Imperial War Museum, London
Department of Printed Books
ISBN: 0-901627-76-3**
and
The Battery Press
P.O. Box 3107, Uptown Station
Nashville, Tennessee 37219

Nineteenth in The Battery Press Great War Series
1992
ISBN: 0-89839-169-5

Printed in the United States of America

D
521
H573
1992
V.2

INTRODUCTION

By

Dr. G. M. Bayliss

The Keeper, Department of Printed Books, Imperial War Museum

I am pleased to introduce this volume, one of a series of reprints of British official histories of military operations in the First World War. For some time I have hoped to make this invaluable source more widely available to students of the Great War; this has now been made possible by co-operation between the Imperial War Museum and Battery Press.

The original editions in the series were produced by the Historical Section of the Committee of Imperial Defence; the first appearing in 1922 and the last in 1949. Apart from Her Majesty's Stationery Office, two commercial publishers were also involved: Macmillian put their imprint on several volumes and Heinemann was responsible for the account of the Gallipoli Campaign. Due to the number of full-colour maps, costs of production were high and this has served to limit later attempts to reprint the series, which have foundered after the publication of text only volumes.

Battery Press, in conjunction with the Imperial War Museum's Department of Printed Books, have taken up the reprinting challenge. In order to make the project viable, we have also decided not to reprint the expensive map volumes. However, readers who wish to obtain copies of any maps in the series are welcome to contact the Imperial War Museum library for further assistance. Since no complete and accurate list of the series exists, the following represents an attempt to remedy this deficiency.

Constantinople
Edmonds, Brig. Gen. Sir James E.
> The Occupation of Constantinople 1918-1923. (Draft provisional history, prepared in 1944 but not printed. It is the intention of Battery Press to produce an expanded version in cooperation with the Imperial War Museum).

East Africa
Hordern, Lt. Col. Charles
> East Africa: Vol. I. August 1914-September 1916 [based on a draft by Major H. Fitz M. Stacke]. London: H.M.S.O., 1941.
> East Africa: Vol. II. [Never published; draft chapters exist in the Public Record Office, London].

Egypt and Palestine
MacMunn, Lieut. Gen. Sir George and Falls, Captain Cyril
> Egypt and Palestine: [Vol. I] From the outbreak of war with Germany to June 1917. London: H.M.S.O., 1928. Accompanying map case.

Falls, Captain Cyril
> Egypt and Palestine: [Vol. II] From June 1917 to the end of the War. Parts I and II. London: H.M.S.O., 1930. Accompanying map case.

France and Belgium
1914
Edmonds, Brig. Gen. Sir James E.
> France and Belgium 1914: [Vol. I] August-October. Mons, the retreat to the Seine, the Marne and the Aisne, August-October 1914. London: Macmillian, 1922 (2nd. ed. 1925; 3rd. ed. 1934). Accompanying map case. [Addenda and Corrigenda to '1914' Vol. I issued with the '1918' Vol. II]. Text volume only reprinted by Shearer Publications, Woking, Surrey, 1984.

Edmonds, Brig. Gen. Sir James E.
> France and Belgium 1914: [Vol. II] Antwerp, La Bassée, Armentiéres, Messines, and Ypres, October-November 1914. London: Macmillian, 1925. Accompanying map case. [Addenda and Corrigenda issued with '1915' Vol. I and '1915' Vol. II].

1915
Edmonds, Brig. Gen. Sir James E. and Wynne, Capt. G. C.
> France and Belgium 1915: [Vol. I] Winter 1914-15: Battle of Neuve Chapelle: Battle of Ypres. London: Macmillian, 1927 Accompanying map case. [Addenda and Corrigenda issued with '1915' Vol. II and

'1916' Vol. I, '1918' Vols. I and II].

Edmonds, Brig. Gen. Sir James E.
France and Belgium 1915: [Vol. II] Battle of Aubers Ridge, Festubert, and Loos. London: Macmillian, 1928. Accompanying map case.

1916

Edmonds, Brig. Gen. Sir James E.
France and Belgium 1916: [Vol. I] Sir Douglas Haig's command to the 1st July: Battle of the Somme. London: Macmillian, 1932 Accompanying appendices volume and map case. [Addenda and Corrigenda to '1916' Vol. I issued with the '1918' Vol. II]. Text volume only reprinted by Shearer Publications, Woking, Surrey, 1986.

Miles, Captain Wilfrid
France and Belgium 1916: [Vol. II]. 2nd July 1916 to the end of the Battles of the Somme: preface by Brig. Gen. Sir James E. Edmonds. London: Macmillian, 1938. Accompanying maps and appendices volume.

1917

Falls, Captain Cyril
France and Belgium 1917: [Vol. I]. The German retreat to the Hindenburg Line and the Battle of Arras: preface by Brig. Gen. Sir James E. Edmonds. London: Macmillian, 1940.

Edmonds, Brig. Gen. Sir James E.
France and Belgium 1917: [Vol. II] 7th June-10th November: Messines and Third Ypres (Passchendaele). London: H.M.S.O., 1948. [Volume begun by Cyril Falls and G. C. Wynne completed and edited by Edmonds].

Miles, Capt. Wilfrid
France and Belgium, 1917: [Vol. III] The Battle of Cambrai; preface by Brig. Gen. Sir James E. Edmonds. London: H.M.S.O., 1948.

1918

Edmonds, Brig. Gen. Sir James E.
France and Belgium 1918: [Vol. I]. The German March offensive and its preliminaries. London: Macmillian, 1935. Accompanying appendices volume and map case. [Addenda and Corrigenda '1918' Vol. I issued with Vol. II].

Edmonds, Brig. Gen. Sir James E.
France and Belgium 1918: [Vol. II]. March-April: continuation of the German offensives. London: Macmillian, 1937. Accompanying map case. [Special addendum to '1918' Vol. II. Further Addenda and

Corrigenda issued with '1917' Vol. I and '1918' Vol. III].

Edmonds, Brig. Gen. Sir James E.
France and Belgium 1918: [Vol. III]. May-July: the German diversion offensives and the first Allied counter-offensive. London: Macmillian, 1939.

Edmonds, Brig. Gen. Sir James E.
France and Belgium 1918: [Vol. IV]. 8th August-26th September: the Franco-British offensive. London: H.M.S.O., 1947

Edmonds, Brig. Gen. Sir James E.
France and Belgium 1918: [Vol. V]. 26th September-11th November: the advance to victory. London: H.M.S.O., 1947

Gallipoli
Aspinall-Oglander, Brig. Gen. C. F.
Gallipoli: Vol. I: Inception of the campaign to May 1915. London: William Heinemann, 1929. Accompanying maps and appendices volume.

Aspinall-Oglander, Brig. Gen. C. F.
Gallipoli: Vol. II: May 1915 to the evacuation. London: William Heinemann, 1932. Accompanying maps and appendices volume.

Italy
Edmonds, Brig. Gen. Sir James E. and Davies, H. R.
Italy, 1915-1919. London: H.M.S.O., 1949.

Macedonia
Falls, Captain Cyril
Macedonia: [Vol. I] From the outbreak of war to Spring 1917. London: H.M.S.O., 1933. Accompanying map case.

Falls, Captain Cyril
Macedonia: [Vol. II] From the Spring of 1917 to the end of the war. London: H.M.S.O., 1935. Accompanying map case.

Mesopotamia
Moberly, Brig. Gen. F. J.
The Campaign in Mesopotamia 1914-1918. Vol. I: London: H.M.S.O., 1923. Vol. II: London: H.M.S.O., 1924. Vol. III: London: H.M.S.O., 1925. Vol. IV: London: H.M.S.O., 1927.

Persia
Moberly, Brig. Gen F. J.
Operations in Persia, 1914-1919. Confidential edition. London: H.M.S.O., 1929. Public edition. London: H.M.S.O., [in association

with the Imperial War Museum], 1987.

Rhineland
Edmonds, Brig. Gen. Sir James E.
> The Occupation of the Rhineland, 1918-1929. Confidential edition. London: H.M.S.O., 1944. Public edition, with introduction by Dr. G. M. Bayliss. London: H.M.S.O., [in association with the Imperial War Museum], 1987.

Togoland and the Cameroons
Moberly, Brig. Gen F. J.
> Togoland and the Cameroons, 1914-1916. London: H.M.S.O., 1931.

OTHER RELATED VOLUMES

Order of Battle of Divisions
Becke, Major A. F.
> Order of Battle of Divisions. Part 1: The Regular British Divisions. London: H.M.S.O., 1935. Part 2A: The Territorial Force Mounted Divisions and the 1st-Line Territorial Force Divisions (42-56). London: H.M.S.O., 1936. Part 2B: The 2nd-Line Territorial Force Divisions (57th-69th) with the Home Service Divisions. (71st-73rd) and 74th and 75th Divisions. London: H.M.S.O., 1937. Part 3A: New Army Divisions (9-26). London: H.M.S.O., 1938. Part 3B: New Army Divisions (30-41) and 63rd (R.N.) Division. London: H.M.S.O., 1945. Part 4: The Army Council, G. H. Q's, Army and Corps, 1914-1918. London: H.M.S.O., 1945.

Principal Events
Committee of Imperial Defence, Historical Section
> Principal events 1914-1918. London: H.M.S.O., 1922.

Transportation on the Western Front
Henniker, Col. A. M.
> Transportation on the Western Front 1914-1918; with introduction by Brig. Gen. Sir James E. Edmonds. London: H.M.S.O., 1937. Accompanying case of maps.

PREFACE

THIS volume concludes the account of the Battles of the Somme, 1916, begun in its predecessor, " 1916 " Volume I. The preliminaries of that great Franco-British offensive, and the plans and preparations culminating in the events of the 1st July, when the great assault was launched, have been described in the earlier volume. There, also, will be found three explanatory chapters dealing with the expansion and reorganization of the British Expeditionary Force between August 1914 and July 1916, and with the building-up in France of the great establishments required for the maintenance of an Army which numbered, including the units on the lines of communication, one and a half million men. A fourth chapter described the administrative system and what may be called the domestic conditions of the battle, which must be borne in mind throughout its course.

The delay which has occurred in continuing the account of the battles was explained in the Preface to " 1918 " Volume I. Two teams had been working on the history of the Western Front, one beginning on 1914 and the other on 1918 ; owing to the reduction of the staff for reasons of economy, this arrangement had to cease, and it was not until the volumes on Gallipoli, Egypt and Palestine, and Macedonia were completed that officers became available, Captain W. Miles then taking up 1916 and Captain C. Falls 1917, whilst I myself dealt with 1918.

In the following pages the course of the Somme offensive is traced from the conclusion of the first day's fighting to the dying down of the struggle in November. Chapters are devoted to a brief account of the Chantilly Conference which, in that month, outlined the future strategic plans of the Allies ; to a summary of events upon the remainder of the British front, where active trench warfare was maintained throughout the Somme offensive ; and to a

description of the transportation problems which confronted the British Armies in France at this time. A final
chapter reviews the plans for the Allied offensive on the
Somme 1916 and considers the tactics employed, which
were based upon the French faith in the power of the
heavy artillery ; [1] it reveals the special difficulties of the
British commanders and the efforts made to overcome them.

The Chantilly Conference will be treated at greater
length in " 1917 " Volume I., as also the circumstances
which led up to the supersession of General Joffre by
General Nivelle in the command of the French Armies on
the Western Front. Mention of other events of November
and December 1916—the death of Franz Joseph, Emperor
of Austria, the Lansdowne " Peace Memorandum ", the
Peace Notes of the Central Powers and that of President
Wilson which followed—has been relegated entirely to the
next volume.

There being no open flank on the Western Front, Sir
Douglas Haig's plan for the Somme offensive, as originally
conceived and approved by the War Committee of the
Cabinet, was to break through the German defences and,
having thus made an internal flank, to roll them up northwards from flank and rear. In view of the tactics adopted
in 1916, with the resources then available, this proved an
impossible task.[2] The British artillery, admittedly insufficient for the purpose, and possessing an even less
density per mile of front than that of the French, certainly
played great havoc with the enemy's positions, which were
much more than mere fieldworks after the labour bestowed
on them for the better part of two years. The British
gunners inflicted very heavy losses upon his troops, and at
times extended them to the utmost limit of endurance ;
but they could never count upon overcoming the machine-
gun defence, while their efforts—without gas shell—to
neutralize the enemy batteries were only partially successful. They were rarely able to silence temporarily even
half of those in action. Under these conditions the impetus

[1] After a search for a doctrine during 1915, General Joffre had fallen
back on the Napoleonic dictum, " C'est l'artillerie qui prend les places, et
" l'infanterie ne fait qu'aider ". (Correspondance 25 octobre 1793.)

[2] General Krafft von Dellmensingen, who planned Caporetto, in his
exhaustive treatise on the break-through (" Der Durchbruch ") rightly
regards the operation as " the attack form of superior numbers " : it
requires " unlimited resources of men, apparatus, industrial facilities, raw
" materials, food supplies and money " : and with the relative means
available on the Western Front " a rapid break-through by sheer force
" was unobtainable ".

of the infantry assault could never be maintained long enough to achieve a " break through ". Owing to lack of numbers, fresh divisions were never at hand either to complete the operation or to obtain a surprise " break-through " at some other less well-guarded front—for which latter purpose additional artillery would also have been required. The consequent slowness of the advance which set in after every forward step, gave the enemy the respite he needed to prevent the collapse of his resistance. Possibly by following more closely the classic methods of siege warfare, with its parallels, saps and approaches, and by a greater use of mining, the same results—but no more—might have been achieved at less cost in life. The Germans in 1916, however, were undoubtedly more skilled in and better equipped for siege and trench warfare methods, except in tunnelling, and the British might have fared worse. In the result, the number and ballistic properties of the guns and the stock of ammunition dictated the form and imposed the limits on the battle, and to this extent it was an artillery battle ; yet as it was the infantry which provided movement, the narrative perforce deals mainly with the action of that arm. Periods of fair weather prevailed during the summer months and in the early autumn, but, generally speaking, the elements were on the side of the defender, on certain occasions in decisive fashion.

Briefly, the intention was first to capture the enemy's defences on the line Montauban—Pozières—Serre, and to overrun his immensely strong first defensive system along the whole front of attack, as well as his 2nd Position on the ridge from Pozières to the Ancre and thence up the slopes in front of Miraumont to a point opposite Serre. Then, by a wheel eastward, it was hoped to break through the 2nd Position on the high ground from Bazentin le Grand to Pozières, as a preliminary to securing the Ginchy —Bazentin le Grand plateau. This accomplished, the capture of the German 3rd Position, which lay along the reverse slope in front of Flers and Le Sars, would place the British right in the vicinity of Bapaume and prepare the way for an advance northward, in order to roll up the German lines south of Arras. Since the preoccupations of the French caused by the German attack on Verdun prevented their Armies from playing the main part in the battle, as originally intended, the British right flank, from the outset, could only be covered by the French XX. Corps north of the Somme. Astride the river the rest of the

Sixth Army, of the Groupe d'Armées du Nord under General Foch, was to capture the three German defensive systems as far south as the Amiens—St. Quentin road, and then, by advancing eastward and north-eastward, to take its share in the exploitation of success.

The results of the 1st July may be said to have determined the future course of the offensive, if not, indeed, to have supplied the answer as to whether a rupture of the German front was possible in 1916. At the end of the first day of battle the French astride the Somme and the British right next to them, had carried the German front system, but little or nothing had been won by the British centre and left. This want of success, as a whole, seemed for a time to rob the higher commanders of their self-confidence. Lacking the resources to renew the attack along his whole front from Maricourt to Serre, Sir Douglas Haig concentrated upon exploiting the success of his right which, unfortunately, had its junction with the French in the shoulder of a salient, a cramped position unfavourable for offensive action. Hence during the twelve succeeding days, the efforts of the British to establish themselves within assaulting distance of the German 2nd Position on the main ridge from Longueval to Bazentin le Petit received little aid from their Allies. The dawn attack of the 14th July broke into this position, but only on a front judged too narrow for exploitation. Operations were then continued with the object of driving the Germans completely from the main ridge and improving the situation at the junction with the French. Farther west, in the meantime, the Fricourt salient had been reduced and, by the capture of Pozières, the crest of the ridge approached. Before the beginning of August, however, Sir Douglas Haig had been obliged to accept the conditions of a " wearing-" out battle " ; but he hoped that by the middle of September the resistance of the enemy would be so much reduced that a powerful assault might break through. During the intervening weeks repeated endeavours, not wholly successful, were made to capture the fortified localities—Leuze and Bouleaux Woods, the Quadrilateral, Guillemont, Ginchy, Delville Wood (where the S. African memorial stands)—in front of that part of the German 3rd Position which covered Morval, Lesboeufs, Gueude-court and Flers. On the left flank smaller forces were engaged in an advance towards Thiepval, both north-westward from Pozières, and from the south ; the fighting

was of a most desperate character, and even Australian
troops could make but small progress.

On the 15th September the great attack in which tanks
were used for the first time failed to force a way through
the German defences and so permit the waiting cavalry to
come into action ; although the British employed all their
available means they could do no more than secure a portion
of their immediate objectives. Before the end of the month
other local successes were won ; Lesboeufs and Gueudecourt
were captured in the Battle of Morval, when, after Combles
fell, the French were at last able to lend close assistance on
the right by advancing due northward instead of north-
eastward. On the other flank Thiepval was taken, but the
struggle persisted on the heights south of the Ancre, which
had become the battle ground of the Canadians. It was
then too late in the year to embark upon any extensive
plan for the advance eastward beyond the river which the
Commander-in-Chief had kept in view. The Germans had
been driven from the uplands between the Péronne—
Bapaume road and the river Ancre ; it was therefore on
the lower ground lying beyond, in the autumn rain and
mud and fog, that the British continued the battle of
attrition. Indeed, it had become a battle of attrition such
as General Joffre had expected and desired from the moment
when, as a result of the German attacks at Verdun, it grew
manifest that the British must play the principal rôle in
the Somme offensive. At length, after the German salient
astride the Ancre had been reduced and the strong Beaumont Hamel position captured in the Battle of the Ancre,
the operations came to an end. The last attack, on the
18th November, was made in the first snowstorm of winter.

On certain occasions General Joffre intervened in an
endeavour to induce Sir Douglas Haig to attempt more
than he was in a position to perform, the object of the
French generalissimo being to preserve, whatever the
circumstances, the original broad front of attack. Thus
he urged a renewal of the assault along the whole British
front after the partial success of the 1st July ; he tried to
hurry on the great British attack of the 15th September ;
and in the middle of October, when the weather threatened
to put an end to major operations, he tried to insist upon
another British effort to reach the line Bapaume—Achiet
le Petit.

At times, when the British efforts seemed to have failed
or to have come to a standstill, the French on the British

right departed from their rôle of right flank guard and
initiated almost independent operations.   These, it seemed,
could hardly lead to important strategic results but merely
to driving back the Germans a short distance, or to the
creation of a small breach.   General Foch had warned his
corps commanders that " the fundamental intention of the
" Somme offensive should be to support the British forces
" operating in the north, whilst our offensive in the south
" is secondary and subordinate to the results already
" obtained in the north ".   But, in spite of this and the
loyalty of General Foch and Sir Douglas Haig to each
other, the battle, after the first day, tended to be fought
in two sections, at any rate as regards time.   A single
command was required, but in 1916 national feeling prevented the flank guard being placed under the commander
of the main force.   In August 1918, when General Debeney's
Army was put under Sir Douglas Haig, it was to be otherwise.   One German critic, General Kabisch (in his " Somme
" 1916 "), goes so far as to say, " If Haig had found in
" Foch the understanding and willing support for his
" conduct of the battle which he had the right to expect
" as the commander of the major part of the attacking
" Entente Armies, Joffre would not have had so constantly
" to complain of dispersion of effort."

The true achievement of the British in the Battles of
the Somme 1916 has never been generally recognized,
except by our foe.   For the first six months of the year
Sir Douglas Haig had kept his Armies engaged in active
trench warfare, and in March he had relieved the French
of over twenty miles of front.   Bound by his instructions
from Lord Kitchener, which laid down that " the closest
" co-operation of French and British as a united Army
" must be the governing policy ", and pledged to loyal
collaboration with an Ally to whose tactical methods he
could not do otherwise than conform, he was obliged to
launch his offensive before he considered that his forces
were fit and ready to do so, and in a region and under
conditions which were not of his own choosing.   His
amateur Army—for such it must be regarded in comparison with Continental standards—was committed to the
attack of semi-permanent fortifications constructed and
held by a professional Army ; yet it bit deep into these
positions and inflicted upon the enemy a moral and material
loss from which he never fully recovered.   There was certainly heavy loss of life, but not an inadequate result.

To realize the condition to which the German Army was reduced by the battering which it received on the Somme in the offensive of which the British bore the brunt, German regimental histories and the published diaries and reminiscences of German combatants must be read. They are full of the horrors of " the Hell of the " Somme " and of the " material battle ". There is general agreement that the troops never again fought so well, an opinion which is strengthened by definite statistical proof that in later years they gave way before they had suffered such heavy casualties. It will be sufficient to draw attention to the admissions in the recently published Volume XI. of the German Official History. This volume opens at the date on which General von Falkenhayn was relieved, nominally because he had not foreseen that Rumania would enter the War, but actually on account of his failure at Verdun and on the Somme.[1]

The situation when Field-Marshal von Hindenburg took over the duties of Chief of the General Staff is described as " the most serious crisis of the War ". In spite of this crisis and the drain on German man-power, it was decided that the last man who could be spared must be sent against Rumania, " because a tactical success is " necessary to encourage both the Nation and the Army ".[2] Although unrestricted U-Boat warfare offered good prospects, the decision was made to refrain from it for the moment and, " until forces were available sufficient to " deal with any eventualities which might arise ", on the grounds that such radical action might bring certain hitherto neutral Powers into the War. On the 2nd September O.H.L. issued an order " for the complete " cessation of the attack on Verdun ", and on the 4th for that front to give up to the Somme four divisions and 18 heavy batteries in exchange for two tired divisions.

---

[1] Rumania declared war on Austria-Hungary on 27th August. "Serious " sounding news from Bukarest " had led Falkenhayn at the end of June to strengthen the Bulgarians. On 14th July O.H.L. issued preliminary instructions to Mackensen's Group " for the case of Rumania breaking " loose " and arrangements for Austro-Hungarian co-operation were made. On 2nd September, that is only six days after declaration of war, Mackensen crossed the frontier and struck, capturing at Tutrakan 28,000 Rumanians and over 100 guns, and finding about 7,000 dead and wounded.

[2] From the Western Front were sent 1 division (without mountain equipment) from the Alsace front, 1 (the Alpine Corps) from the reserve on the Verdun front, and 1 from the Flemish coast. But, including 7 whose formation Falkenhayn had already ordered in July–August, 22 new divisions were formed, so that during September the total on the Western Front rose by 11.

At a Conference of the chief General Staff officers of the Groups and of the Armies on the Western Front, held by Hindenburg-Ludendorff at Cambrai on the 8th September, General von Kuhl (C.G.S. of Crown Prince Rupprecht's Group) drew a dismal picture of the situation on the Somme : the divisions could not as a rule be kept in the battle for more than 14 days : this meant that, on the average, a fresh division was required every day : divisions had therefore to be put in twice, even three times, with insufficient time between their tours of service for rest and training : " the quality and number of the reinforcements " were on the decline, but this was also the case with the " French ". Nevertheless, Kuhl did not recommend a retirement whilst the fighting continued, " as a retreat in " the midst of a battle is difficult and dangerous ". The situation before Verdun was depicted in blacker colours : " no positions, the men are lying in shell-holes, no work " possible under hostile fire ".

O.H.L. could do no more than order the construction, as insurance against a mishap, of the rear lines known to us later as the Hindenburg and Michel Lines, the formation of the last batch of new divisions, and the better organization of munitions supply.

" The month of September brought the heaviest losses " of the whole battle ", and Crown Prince Rupprecht reported that the reinforcements sent " had not even " covered one-tenth of requirements ". Finally, by the end of November, " what still remained of the old first-" class peace-trained German infantry had been expended " on the battlefield ".

The battle having come to an end, some officers urged a retirement to the Hindenburg Line ; but on the 11th December Ludendorff declared to General von Kuhl that the line " was only a safety precaution, and a retirement " to it was not intended ". On the 9th January he told the *Reichskanzler*—as an argument for the introduction of unrestricted U-Boat warfare—" we must spare the troops " a second Somme battle ", yet on the 21st January he repeated " retirement is not intended except in case of " necessity " A week later Crown Prince Rupprecht's Group informed him that the present positions were bad, the troops worn out : " it is questionable whether they " are still in a condition to stand such defensive battles " as the Somme 1916, and it would be better to go back " to the Hindenburg Line ". On the 4th February the retirement to the Hindenburg Line was ordered, in the name of the Kaiser, for the reasons given by Crown Prince Rupprecht's Group. Thus the retirement was not ordered by Ludendorff as a strategic measure, but forced on him as a tactical measure by the staff of the fighting troops.

It is not too much to claim that the foundations of the final victory on the Western Front were laid by the Somme offensive of 1916. The cost to the flower of the Empire's manhood was very great, but the British losses were not so heavy as those suffered by the Germans with whom they were engaged. In spite of the careful and accurate calculations made at the time by the British Intelligence Branch, there is a general belief that Sir Douglas Haig's troops at the Somme suffered far more heavily than their opponents. This belief has been voiced by great rhetoricians in such phrases as : " in all the " British offensives the British casualties were never less " than 3 to 2, and often nearly double the corresponding " German losses ",[1] and in the still wilder one, that on the Somme " our losses were twice as great as those we " inflicted ".[2] Both statements may be traced, in part, to the error of accepting figures issued by the German Government in order to keep from the German public the truth concerning the terrible losses sustained by their Armies.

Until the Battles of the Somme were well in progress, casualty lists (*Verlustliste*) were regularly published in Berlin, with some weeks' delay, which gave the names, regiments and other particulars of the fallen. After 18th February 1915, the locality was not given, nor after 9th June 1915, the date. It was possible, however, from the 1916 lists to discover the losses of the units and divisions known to have been engaged in a particular battle. Then an important change was made. To use the words of Sir Charles Oman, who during the War was charged with the investigation of the enemy casualty lists, " in the first " days of December 1916, the Berlin office suddenly ' shut " ' down ' and published no more regimental lists. The " reason was obvious—the total was getting too ghastly, " and the information afforded to the Paris or London " calculators was too valuable. From 6th December on-

---

[1] " The World Crisis " (abridged and revised edition), by Winston S. Churchill, p. 548.
[2] " War Memoirs of David Lloyd George ", vi., p. 3414.

" ward the system adopted was to publish every day only
" alphabetical lists of individuals from A to Z, with no
" indication of the unit to which any man belonged ".[1]
Thus those who fell on the different fronts were mixed
together. After the latter part of October, allowing for
the lag in publication, no further counting of regimental
losses was possible.

Making a suitable allowance for November, Sir Charles
Oman came to the conclusion that in the Battles of the
Somme the losses of the two sides, the combined French
and British and the German, were " almost exactly the
" same ", about 560,000. Proceeding from quite different
data, I calculated in 1932 that the losses were around
600,000, the French and British slightly over that figure,
and the German slightly under it.[2]

From the figures now available in the German Official
History it appears that both calculations, from the desire
of the compilers not to overstate their case, had erred in
underestimating the German casualties. These were, as
the British Intelligence at the time averred, actually
greater than those of the Allies. There is still no full
and clear statement from the German side, such as the
French and British have published, partly no doubt from
lack of accurate returns. The German historians seem
to be torn between two conflicting sentiments : first a
desire to show how heavily their troops suffered before
they gave up ground, and, secondly, a determination
to assert that they did not suffer as severely as their
opponents.

The figures given in the German Official History are,
however, sufficient to demonstrate the approximate totals.
In dealing with German casualties for the purpose of comparison, it has always been asserted in the British Official
History that, as the Intelligence discovered, the totals
published did not include the less seriously wounded who
were treated in the hospitals of their corps area. This is
now admitted. The German Official History (Vol. XI., p. 41)
states " the great losses of the summer of 1916 since the
" beginning of the year, *without the wounded whose recovery*

---

[1] "The German Losses on the Somme (A Correction to the *World Crisis*)",
by Sir Charles Oman (in *The Nineteenth Century and After*, May 1927).
About the end of November 1918, that is after the Armistice, the unit,
company and date again appeared in many cases, and from the 1st January
1919 almost invariably. The casualty lists had fallen so much behind that
they continued to appear until 14th October 1919.
[2] The calculations are given in " 1916 " Vol. I., pp. 496-7.

" *was to be expected within a reasonable time* (the italics are
" mine) amounted to a round figure of 1,400,000, of whom
" 800,000 were between July and October ". For the
Somme, the German Official History puts the casualties,
excluding the 7-days' bombardment, at " about 500,000 ".[1]
According to German statistics, the less seriously wounded
amounted to from 27 to 33 per cent : thus an average of
30 per cent must be added. This gives a gross total for
comparison not of 500,000, but 650,000, plus, say, 10,000
in the preliminary bombardment, total 660,000.

As a check on this, the *Zentral Nachweiseamt*, the
Casualty Enquiry Office which cleared up the casualties
after the War,[2] has given the *gross* Somme losses for July
to October as 582,919 ; for November the Official History
gives the *net* losses as 45,000, or, say, 58,500 gross. Thus,
the total to the end of November comes to 641,419.[3] And
over 40,000 prisoners, some of whom, however, died in
captivity, are not included ; nor are the still unaccounted-
for missing ; so the grand total by this method is about
680,000, which is no doubt closer than the round figures
of the Official History.[4]

[1] The losses (*Verluste*) in officers and men, not distinguishing between
killed and wounded and no doubt, according to custom, excluding missing,
from 1st July are given by divisions in tables, but, somewhat strangely,
are not added up. They amount to 465,181. No hint of the losses in the
bombardment—except that one division had to be relieved—or the
casualties of the Corps and Army troops is given, so 500,000 is well under
the mark.

[2] 497,000 German casualties were reported to it after the Armistice
and, for accuracy, some part of them should be assigned to the Somme.

[3] Sir Charles Oman, with figures which cannot be over the mark, found
the infantry losses alone were 510,000.

[4] One German divisional commander has written (see p. 229) that the
official casualties of his division from 24th July to 9th August were 187
officers and 8,110 other ranks (no British division reached such a total in
one tour of service), but he thinks they " were still heavier ".

The official practice of minimizing losses began in 1914. A battalion
medical officer (*III./49th Regiment* of the *II. Division* of the *II. Corps*
of Kluck's Army) Dr. W. Jacobson, has written in his Memoirs (published
in Belgium as " En Marche sur Paris ") that after a fight near Montdidier
on 7th October 1914, when the regiment (not the battalion) was reduced
to 3 officers and hardly 350 unwounded men " A notre grand étonnement,
" nous constatons que, dans les listes des pertes ne figuraient plus qu'un
" tiers de celles-ci, et que les autorités, au hasard, enlevaient des noms
" de nos consciencieux rapports. Nous en conclûmes tous que ce n'étaient
" pas des erreurs fortuites ; on procédait de la même manière avec les
" autres régiments. Pour évaluer les pertes effectives, le Ministère les
" portait expressément à la connaissance du public en les diminuant très
" sensiblement."

That there was a serious difference between the totals of " the con-
" scientious reports " of the medical authorities and the Army returns
is admitted in the German Official History, Volume XI., p. 407, footnote,

The unadjusted gross Allied figures to 30th November are, British 419,654 (from which at least 5 per cent should be deducted for absentees at roll call who subsequently returned) and French, 204,253.[1] This makes a gross total of 623,907, which includes prisoners and missing, to the German 680,000. A perusal of the German and British regimental histories leaves no doubt whatever on the mind as to which side, after the 1st July, suffered the heavier punishment. In the many illuminating extracts from the German regimental histories given in the footnotes of this volume will be found ample evidence of extraordinary heavy casualties, with companies reduced to 25 men, battalions to a hundred, and regiments (of 3 battalions) to 250 during one tour of service. The struggle became a grim test of endurance, in which the gallantry, on both sides, was unsurpassed.

When opponents are equally matched the losses of the attackers are expected to be less than those of the defenders (this was clearly shown in the varying fortunes at Verdun). That the disproportion at the Somme was not greater must be ascribed to the insufficient number of heavy howitzers possessed by the British ; to the inadequate training of the troops ; to the unevenness in the fighting value of the different divisions ; to faulty tactics, as exemplified by the terribly heavy losses, over 57,000, on the first day of assault ; and to the failure of the commanders of the higher formations to consult, or accept the views when offered of the forward

---

in reference to the Russian campaign in 1916. The medical reports repeatedly give considerably higher figures than the Army returns. According to the former, the figures on page 566 of Volume X., taken from the Army returns, required to be raised : to about 225,000 (instead of 140,000) for the total losses from January to August, of which 140,000 (instead of 85,000) were due to the Brusilov offensive. These enormous (*gewaltig*) differences have so far not been capable of explanation ; they are partly due to the incompleteness of the Army returns. "The figures of the " medical report are regarded as the more accurate."

In " 1914 " Volume II., p. 444, in describing the First Battle of Ypres, I pointed out that the losses returned by Winckler's Guard Division were very considerably less than the sum of the regimental casualties.

There seems therefore to have been several sets of figures : the regimental founded on the roll call and medical returns ; the divisional (omitting the less-seriously wounded) ; the Army (imperfect, possibly including only divisions, not corps and Army troops) ; and the War Ministry lists issued to the public.

It is expected in the course of time by the addition of the totals of the nominal lists given in the Rolls of Honour in the regimental histories to prove conclusively—as a partial examination indicates—that the German losses in dead were about double the number officially stated.

[1] Total of returns rendered every 5 days, published in 1936 ; the previous adjusted total had been 194,451.

leaders. Had it not been for the first day's unnecessary slaughter, when the heavier losses might reasonably have been expected to have befallen the defenders—in prisoners if not in other classes—the relative casualties would have shown a greater disproportion.

A word may here be added on the subject of the subsidiary engagements which were so often judged to be necessary preliminaries to the main attacks or became the inevitable consequences of them. Although the assaults against a local objective failed time after time, each attempt nevertheless played its part in loosening the grip of the defenders so that ultimate success was made possible ; each was a microcosm of the " battle of attrition " into which the whole Somme offensive developed.

This volume has been compiled by Captain Wilfrid Miles. Since the account of continuous fighting, which extended over five months on the fronts of two British Armies, might well have occupied more than the one volume allotted to it, style, arrangement and treatment have had to conform strictly to the limitations of space. It has been necessary to concentrate upon those operations which derive particular importance from the circumstances in which they were initiated, or from the tactics employed, the objectives aimed at, and their instructional value. For instance, the efforts to exploit such success as was gained in the great assault of the 1st July, the night assembly and the dawn attack of the 14th July, the plans for the mid-September offensive, and the Battle of Flers—Courcelette in which tanks were in action for the first time, all deserved to be described in as great detail as space would permit. The result has been that the accounts of the subsidiary actions which were undertaken in the period from the middle of July until the middle of September have had to ber uthlessly compressed, and this applies equally to the story of the fighting in the later autumn, with the exception of the account of the Battle of the Ancre. Similarly the note on " The Evolution of the Tank ", at the end of Chapter IX., would have been written at much greater length had space allowed ; but a broad outline had to suffice. It is regretted that no mention could be made of all who in some degree or other contributed to the production of the new arm.

The documents selected for printing as Appendices are contained in a separate volume, together with the maps.

Separate " Orders of Battle " volumes are now in course
of publication, but abbreviated orders of battle of the
British and German divisions engaged are inserted in the
Appendix Volume, since the reader may find them useful
for quick reference.

The draft narrative was sent to over fifteen hundred
combatant officers who served in the Somme offensive,
and the compiler is very greatly beholden to those who
have sent additional information and explanations of points
which were obscure, or have indulged in constructive criticism which it is always a satisfaction to receive. The
Branch could not dispense with their assistance. As regards
the chapters dealing with the operations of the Canadian
Corps, Colonel A. Fortescue Duguid, D.S.O., Director of
the Historical Section of the Department of National
Defence, Ottawa, not only supplied his own comments,
but was also good enough to obtain those of many other
Canadian officers. Dr. C. E. W. Bean, M.A., LL.D., the
Australian Official Historian, has read in draft those
chapters concerned with the operations in which Australian
troops were engaged ; his comments have supplemented
the considerable assistance derived from his own volume
" The A.I.F. in France, 1916 ".

The published volumes of both the French and German
Official Histories now cover completely the period of the
Somme offensive 1916 and contain practically all that is
required—certainly much more than can be used—for the
French and German share. Nevertheless, General Halb-
wachs, the head of the *Service Historique* of the French
General Staff, and his successor, General Blin, kindly read
and commented upon the final draft ; and the *Kriegsgeschichtliche Forschungsanstalt des Heeres* (now in charge
of the German Official History in place of the *Reichsarchiv*)
has lent ready assistance with information on various points
as they arose.

Captain G. C. Wynne has helped in the translation of
German accounts. Mr. A. W. Tarsey and other members
of the staff of the Historical Section (Military Branch)
have assisted in checking various statistics and verifying
points of detail. The compiler is much indebted to Mr.
W. B. Wood, M.A.(Oxon.) and to Lieut.-Colonel H. G.
de Watteville, C.B.E., M.A.(Oxon.), *p.s.c.*, R.A. (retired),
both of whom read the final draft and gave him the benefit
of their comments.

Some officers who have not seen the draft or proofs may be in a position to offer criticism or to suggest additions to the narrative. If so, I shall be very grateful if they will communicate with the Secretary of the Historical Section, Committee of Imperial Defence, Audit House, Victoria Embankment, London, E.C.4.

J. E. E.

September 1938

NOTES

THE location of troops and places is written from right to left of the front of the Allied Forces, unless otherwise stated. In translations from the German the order given is as in the original; otherwise enemy troops are enumerated like the British. Where roads which run through both the British and German lines are described by the names of towns or villages, the place in British hands is mentioned first, thus : " Albert—Bapaume road ".

To save space and bring the nomenclature in line with " Division ", " Infantry Brigade " has in the text been abbreviated to " Brigade ", as distinguished from " Cavalry Brigade " and " Artillery Brigade " ; and " Regiment " similarly means " Infantry Regiment ".

The convention observed in the British Expeditionary Force is followed as regards the distinguishing numbers of Armies, Corps, Divisions, etc., of the British and Allied Armies, *e.g.* they are written in full for Armies, in Roman figures for corps, and in Arabic for smaller formations and units, except Artillery Brigades, which are Roman ; thus : Fourth Army, IV. Corps, 4th Cavalry Division, 4th Division, 4th Cavalry Brigade, 4th Brigade, IV. Brigade R.F.A. ; but for artillery brigades with numbers higher than one hundred, Arabic figures are used.

German formations and units, to distinguish them clearly from the Allies, are printed in italic characters, thus : *First Army, I. Corps, 1st Division.*

The usual Army abbreviations of regimental names have been used : for example, " 2/R. West Kent " or " West Kent " for 2nd Battalion The Queen's Own Royal West Kent Regiment ; K.O.Y.L.I. for the King's Own Yorkshire Light Infantry ; K.R.R.C. for the King's Royal Rifle Corps. To avoid constant repetition, the " Royal " in regimental titles is sometimes omitted. To economize space the 63rd (Royal Naval Division), the 14th (Light) Division, etc., are usually described by their numbers only.

First-line and Second-line Territorial Force units are distinguished by a figure in front of the battalion or other number, thus : 1/8th London, 2/8th London, 1/3rd London or 2/3rd London Field Company R.E. Where two (Territorial or Service) battalions have been amalgamated the numbers of both are shown thus : 4th/5th Black Watch, 10th/11th Highland L.I. The Yorkshire Regiment is called by its ancient name " The Green Howards ".

To save space, Australian and Canadian brigades, when their identity is unmistakable, are sometimes referred to by their numbers only : thus, " 4th Brigade " instead of " 4th Australian Brigade."

Abbreviations employed occasionally are :

B.E.F. for British Expeditionary Force ;

F.O.O. for Forward Observing Officer ;

G.A.N. for Groupe d'Armées du Nord ;

G.H.Q. for British General Headquarters ;

G.Q.G. for French Grand Quartier-Général (usually spoken " Grand Q.G. ") ;

O.H.L. for German *Oberste Heeresleitung* (German Supreme Command). *N.B.*—" G.H.Q." in German means Grosses Haupt-Quartier, that is the Kaiser's Headquarters, political, military and naval, as distinguished from O.H.L.

The spellings of " lacrymatory " and " strongpoint " are arbitrary, and were selected as being shorter than the usual ones.

Officers are described by the rank which they held at the period under consideration. To save space the initials instead of the Christian names of knights are generally used.

The German pre-war practice of writing the plain name without " von ", when it is applicable and no rank or title is prefixed, has been adopted, *e.g.* " Falkenhayn " and not " von Falkenhayn ".

In July all the belligerents were reckoning in " summer " time. It ended for British, French and German alike at midnight 30th September/1st October. Thus German time was one hour ahead of British time throughout, but it has been corrected in the narrative to our standard except when " German " time is specifically mentioned.

MAPS AND SKETCHES

A LAYERED Sketch of the Somme battlefield (Sketch A) is placed at the beginning of this volume. In " 1916 " Volume I. a layered general map of the battlefield (scale 1/40,000) was given, as well as a squared map of the same area and scale. These two maps have not been repeated.

For the fighting up to the opening of the Battle of Flers—Courcelette on the 15th September it has not been found necessary to provide any maps ; all the information is given on thirty-two page-size sketches which are bound in the text volume in their appropriate places.

To illustrate the battles from the 15th September until the conclusion of the Battles of the Somme in November 1916, six maps and eleven sketches are provided.

A special page-size sketch is given to show the route and fate of each tank which took part in the XV. Corps attack on Flers on the 15th September, when tanks went into action for the first time ; and a photograph of a Mark I. tank, which was found among the war records in this Branch, is reproduced as a frontispiece to this volume.

To assist readers to appreciate the progress made during the prolonged and extensive Battles of the Somme, six general situation sketches of the battle front are included. These situation sketches illustrate both the advance made after the opening of the offensive and the actual progress made during the month which the situation sketch illustrates. A sketch placed at the end of the volume shows the line held by the B.E.F. in France and Belgium at the close of the year, as well as the general result of the Somme fighting.

The spelling of the place-names on the 1/80,000 French map and on the 1/20,000 Belgian survey has been followed.

All the maps and sketches issued with this volume have been drawn for reproduction by the late Mr. J. S. Fenton, late R.E., the senior draughtsman of the Branch. It is with

xxiii

the greatest regret I have to record that Mr. Fenton died in harness during June 1938. For nearly fifteen years Mr. Fenton has worked on drawing maps for this Branch ; his rapidity of work, the skill with which his finished drawings were produced, his zeal and willingness, his knowledge of the history of the War, and of the map collection, and his cheery personality will always be remembered by those who worked in close contact with him.

A. F. B.

CONTENTS

CHAPTER I

CHAPTER II

CHAPTER III

CHAPTER IV

CONTENTS

CHAPTER IX

CHAPTER X

CHAPTER XI

CHAPTER XII

CHAPTER XIII

CHAPTER XIV

CHAPTER XV

CHAPTER XVI

CHAPTER XVII

CHAPTER XVIII

CHAPTER XIX

CHAPTER XX

CHAPTER XXI

TABLE OF APPENDICES

(In Separate Volume)

SKETCHES AND MAPS

SKETCHES

(*Bound in Volume*)

MAPS

(*In Appendices Volume*)

LIST OF BOOKS

TO WHICH MOST FREQUENT REFERENCE HAS BEEN MADE

BAVARIAN OFFICIAL ACCOUNT : " Die Bayern im Grossen Kriege 1914–1918 ". (Munich : Verlag des bayerischen Kriegsarchivs.)

This volume records the achievements of the Bavarian troops in all theatres throughout the war. It contains a short but useful summary of the operations of the Bavarian divisions on the Somme in 1916.

FALKENHAYN : " Die Oberste Heeresleitung 1914–1916 in ihren wichtigsten Entschliessungen ". By General Erich von Falkenhayn. (Berlin : Mittler.)

FRENCH OFFICIAL ACCOUNT (F.O.A.) : " Les Armées françaises dans la Grande Guerre ", compiled in the État-Major de l'Armée, Service Historique. (Paris : Imprimerie Nationale.)

Tome IV. volume ii, with three " annexes " containing documents, and a case of maps, covers the Verdun fighting during the period 1st May–3rd September and the Somme offensive up to the 3rd September.

Tome IV. volume iii, with four " annexes " of documents and a case of maps, continues the operations at Verdun up to the end of 1916 and the Somme offensive to its conclusion in November.

GALLWITZ : " Erleben im Westen 1916–1918 ". By General Max von Gallwitz. (Berlin : Mittler.)

General Gallwitz was appointed to command the German Second Army, facing the French south of the Somme, on 16th July 1916, the First Army, north of the river, also coming under him. At the end of August he reverted to the command of the Second Army alone. He was a very capable commander and his book is both well written and full of valuable information.

GEHRE : " Die deutsche Kraftverteilung während des Weltkriegs ". By L. Gehre. (Berlin : Mittler.)

Contains a large coloured diagram on squared paper showing, under the various fronts and Armies, the German strength in divisions on the 15th and last days of every month of the war.

GERMAN OFFICIAL ACCOUNT (G.O.A.) : " Der Weltkrieg 1914 bis 1918 : Die militärischen Operationen zu Lande", compiled by the " Kriegsgeschichtliche " Forschungsanstalt des Heeres. (Berlin : Mittler.)
Volume X covers the plans, events, and operations of 1916 on all fronts up to the change in the High Command (supersession of Falkenhayn by Hindenburg-Ludendorff) at the end of August.
Volume XI. continues the narrative up to the beginning of 1917.

GERSTER : " Die Schwaben an der Ancre ". By M. Gerster. (Heilbron : Salzer.)
This is the story of the 26th Reserve Division in the sector astride the Ancre which it held from the end of September 1914 to October 1916. Some units were engaged later in the Battle of the Ancre.

HINDENBURG : " Out of my Life ". By Marshal von Hindenburg. (English translation, Cassell & Co.)

JOFFRE ii. : " Mémoires du Maréchal Joffre ". (Paris : Librairie Plon.)
The Marshal's memoirs are in two volumes and the period of the Franco-British offensive, 1916, forms the concluding part of the second volume.

KUHL : " Der Weltkrieg 1914–1918 ". By General von Kuhl. (Berlin : Kolk.)
General von Kuhl's commentary occupies two large volumes. He was Chief of the Staff to Crown Prince Rupprecht who, from the end of August 1916, commanded the Group of Armies opposed to the British and French on the Somme.

LUDENDORFF : " Meine Kriegserinnerungen 1914–1918 ". By Erich Ludendorff. (Berlin : Mittler.)

OEHMICHEN : " Essai sur la doctrine de Guerre des Coalitions. La Direction de la Guerre " (November 1915–March 1917). By Colonel Oehmichen. (Paris : Berger–Vrault.)
An authoritative work, based on official documents, dealing with the general direction of the war by General Joffre. The author was one of the two officers detailed in December 1915 to organize a section of the 3rd Bureau (Operations) of the General Staff to co-ordinate the Allied operations.

PALAT xi. : " Bataille de la Somme ". By General Palat. (Paris : Berger-Levrault.)
The eleventh volume of a valuable unofficial account of the French operations on the Western Front.

" REGT. No. . . ." These are references to the war histories of German regiments. The volumes vary in length and value : some give detailed accounts of the operations with extracts from the reminiscences of combatants ; others merely reproduce the official war diaries. Some of the latter type have been superseded by fuller accounts.

RUPPRECHT : " Mein Kriegstagebuch ". By Crown Prince Rupprecht of Bavaria. Edited by E. von Frauenholz. (Munich : Deutsche National Verlag.)
Extracts from the diaries and papers of the Crown Prince in three volumes. A very valuable source and commentary.

SCHWARTE ii. : " Der deutsche Landkrieg ". Edited by Lieut.-General M. Schwarte. (Leipzig : Barth.)
A compendium of the war in 12 volumes. Volume II. covers the operations on the Western Front from the spring of 1915 to the winter of 1916–17.

SOMME–NORD : " Schlachten des Weltkrieges. Somme-Nord ". Issued by the Reichsarchiv in 1927. (Oldenburg : Stalling.)
Two parts.
An official monograph on the battle of the Somme in July 1916, north of the river, with a number of sketch maps.

WELLMANN : " Mit der 18. Reserve-Division in Frankreich ". By Generalleutnant a.D. Wellmann. (Hamburg : Berngruber & Hennig.)
General Wellmann gives a very frank account of the fighting in which his division was engaged at Pozières, July–August 1916.

WENDT : " Verdun 1916 ". By Hermann Wendt. (Berlin : Mittler.)
An examination of General von Falkenhayn's strategy in 1916, with a number of new documents and statistics furnished to the author by the French and German military authorities.

WÜRTTEMBERG OFFICIAL ACCOUNT : " Die Württemberger in Weltkriege ". By Lieut.-General Otto von Moser. (Stuttgart : Bellsen.)

Note :
" 1914 " Vol. I. The Official History of the Great War, Military Operations, France and Belgium, Volume I. (3rd Edition) (first part of 1914) ;
" 1914 " Vol. II. Do. do. Vol. II. (close of 1914) ;
" 1915 " Vol. I. Do. do. Vol. III. (first part of 1915) ;
" 1915 " Vol. II. Do. do. Vol. IV. (close of 1915) ;
" 1916 " Vol. I. Do. do. Vol. V. (first half of 1916) ;
" 1918 " Vol. I. Do. do. (first part of 1918).
" EGYPT & PALES-\ Volumes I. and II. The Official History of the
    TINE " / Great War, Military Operations.
" MACEDONIA ", Volumes I. and II. The Official History of the Great War, Military Operations.
" THE WAR IN THE AIR ", Vol. II. The Official History of the Royal Air Force in the Great War (1916).

CALENDAR OF PRINCIPAL EVENTS

Mainly extracted from "Principal Events 1914–18" compiled by the Historical Section of the Committee of Imperial Defence, London. His Majesty's Stationery Office. 10s. 6d. net. The dates of the Somme battles are taken from the British official List of Battles and Engagements.

	Western Theatre.	Other Theatres.	Naval Warfare and General Events.
		JULY 1916	
2nd.	Somme—Battle of Albert continues (began 1st July). French attack south of Somme continues (began 1st July, ends 9th July): Flaucourt plateau occupied. Verdun—German offensive continues (began 21st February).	*Russia*: Brusilov offensive continues (began 4th June). Evert attacks at Baranovichi. *Italy*: Italian counter-offensive in Trentino continues (began 16th June).	
3rd.			Russia and Japan conclude treaty on future policy in Far East.
4th.		*Russia*: Brusilov drives Austrians over river Stochod.	
7th.		*East Africa*: Tanga occupied by British forces.	Mr. D. Lloyd George succeeds Lord Kitchener as Secretary of State for War.
9th.		*Russia*: Battle of Baranovichi ends.	
11th.	Verdun—German order for "strict defensive".		Seaham harbour shelled by German submarine.
13th.	Somme—Battle of Albert ends.		
14th.	Somme—Battle of Bazentin Ridge begins.		
15th.	Somme—Battle of Delville Wood begins.	*Russia*: Brusilov attacks on the upper Styr.	
17th.	Somme—Battle of Bazentin Ridge ends.		
19th.	Action of Fromelles.	*Egypt*: Turkish offensive against the Suez Canal begins.	
20th.	Somme—French attack against Villers Carbonnel-Maurepas.		

CALENDAR OF PRINCIPAL EVENTS—*(continued)*

Western Theatre.	Other Theatres.	Naval Warfare and General Events.
	JULY 1916—*(continued)*	
23rd. Somme—Battle of Pozières Ridge begins.	23rd. *Italy*: Italian counter-offensive in Trentino ends. *Russia*: Russian advance on Riga front.	
	25th. *Balkans*: Reconstituted Serbian Army in action on Macedonian front.	
	28th. *Russia*: Brusilov's forces enter Brody.	
30th. Somme—French attacks against Cléry–Maurepas.		
	AUGUST 1916	
1st. Verdun—German attack at Souville and French counter-attack.	4th-5th. *Egypt*: Repulse of the Turks at Romani.	
	6th. *Italy*: Sixth Battle of the Isonzo begins.	
7th. Somme—French attacks south of Maurepas (end 11th).	9th. *Italy*: Capture of Gorizia (Sixth Battle of the Isonzo). *Balkans*: Battle of Doiran (Allied offensive) begins.	
	10th. *Russia*: Brusilov's forces enter Stanislau.	
12th. Somme—French attacks, Cléry–Maurepas (end 18th).	15th. *Russia*: Heavy fighting north of Halicz. Brusilov's centre held.	
	17th. *Italy*: Sixth Battle of the Isonzo ends. *Russia*: Front of the Central Powers stabilized, but heavy fighting continues into September.	

24th. Somme—French capture Maurepas.

20th. *Balkans* : Battle of Florina (Bulgarian counter-offensive) begins.
21st. *Balkans* : Battle of Doiran ends.
Balkans : Battle of Florina ends.

28th. *Rumania* : Rumania invades Transylvania.
Mesopotamia : General Sir S. Maude becomes Commander-in-Chief.

27th. Rumania declares war on Austria-Hungary.
28th. Germany declares war on Rumania. Italy declares war on Germany.
29th. Hindenburg-Ludendorff succeed Falkenhayn at O.H.L.
30th. Turkey declares war on Rumania.

SEPTEMBER 1916

1st. Bulgaria declares war on Rumania.
2nd. Largest airship raid (14 Zeppelins) on London. One destroyed.

2nd. *Rumania* : German and Bulgarian forces invade the Dobrudja.

3rd. Somme—Battles of Delville Wood (see 15th July) and Pozières Ridge (see 23rd July) end. Battle of Guillemont begins. French attacks (end 15th) : Bouchavesnes captured (12th).
4th. Somme—French attacks south of Somme (end 6th) : Soyécourt captured.
6th. Somme—Battle of Guillemont ends.
9th. Somme—Battle of Ginchy.

4th. *East Africa* : Dar es Salaam surrenders to British forces.

10th. *Rumania* : Silistra (Dobrudja) occupied by German and Bulgarian forces.
14th. *Italy* : Seventh Battle of the Isonzo begins.

CALENDAR OF PRINCIPAL EVENTS—(continued)

Western Theatre.	Other Theatres.	Naval Warfare and General Events.
	SEPTEMBER 1916—(continued)	
15th. Somme—Battle of Flers-Courcelette begins. French attacks south of Somme (end 18th): Berny, Deniécourt, Vermandovillers captured (17th).	18th. Italy: Seventh Battle of the Isonzo ends.	19th. Allied blockade of Greek Macedonian coast begins.
22nd. Somme—Battle of Flers-Courcelette ends.		23rd. German airship raid on East Coast and London. Two Zeppelins destroyed.
25th. Somme—Battle of Morval begins. French attacks (end 28th): Rancourt captured (25th) and Frégicourt (26th).	26th. Rumania: Battle of Sibiu (Hermannstadt) begins.	
26th. Somme—Battle of Thiepval Ridge begins.		
28th. Somme—Battles of Thiepval Ridge and Morval end.	29th. Rumania: Battle of Sibiu ends. Rumanian invasion of Transylvania checked.	
	OCTOBER 1916	
1st. Somme—Battle of the Transloy Ridges begins. Battle of the Ancre Heights begins.		
7th. Somme—French attacks towards Sailly-Saillisel.	7th. Rumania: Battle of Brasov (ends 9th). Rumanians retreat to Transylvanian frontier.	

xlii

9th. Italy: Eighth Battle of the Isonzo begins.

10th. Somme—French attacks south of Somme against Ablaincourt, Bois de Chaulnes (end 21st).

12th. Somme—French attacks towards Sailly-Saillisel (end 18th).

12th. Italy: Eighth Battle of the Isonzo ends. Balkans: Allied Monastir offensive opens.

18th. Somme—Battle of the Transloy Ridges ends.

22nd. Rumania: Constanza (Dobrudja) captured by German and Bulgarian forces.

23rd. Somme—French attacks towards Sailly-Saillisel (end 27th).

24th. Verdun—Successful French offensive: Fort Douaumont recaptured.

26th. First German destroyer raid in Straits of Dover (26th/27th).

29th. Sherif of Mecca proclaimed "King of the Arabs".

31st. Italy: Ninth Battle of the Isonzo begins.

NOVEMBER 1916

1st. Verdun—Fort Vaux reoccupied by French. Somme—French attacks, St. Pierre Vaast Wood–Saillisel (end 14th).

4th. Italy: Ninth Battle of the Isonzo ends.

5th. Germany and Austria proclaim an "Independent State of Poland".

7th. Somme—French attacks south of Somme: Pressoire, Ablaincourt captured.

xliii

CALENDAR OF PRINCIPAL EVENTS *(continued)*

Western Theatre.	Other Theatres.	Naval Warfare and General Events.
	NOVEMBER 1916—*(continued)*	
11th. Somme—Battle of the Ancre Heights (see 1st October) ends. 18th. Somme—Battle of the Ancre begins.	16th. *Rumania* : Second Battle of Târga-Jui (ends 17th). Austro-German forces enter Wallachia.	15th. ⎱ Inter-Allied Conference in Paris. 16th. ⎰ Inter-Allied Military Conference at Chantilly.
18th. Somme—Battle of the Ancre ends. End of the Battles of the Somme.	19th. Allies enter Monastir (see 5th October).	21st. Death of Emperor Franz Joseph of Austria. Succeeded by Archduke Karl.
		23rd. Greek Provisional Government (M. Venizelos) declares war on Germany.
		27th. German airship raid on East Coast.
		28th. First German aeroplane raid on London.
	DECEMBER 1916	
	3rd. *Rumania* : Bucharest evacuated. Rumanians retreat into Moldavia.	1st. Last meeting of War Committee of British Cabinet.
	6th. *Rumania* : Bucharest entered by German forces.	4th. Mr. Asquith, Prime Minister, resigns.
		7th. Mr. Lloyd George becomes Prime Minister.

9th. British War Cabinet Formed.

12th. Reorganization of French Cabinet. General Nivelle succeeds General Joffre as Commander-in-Chief. Peace Note of Central Powers presented to Ambassadors of U.S.A.

18th. President Wilson issues his circular Note suggesting peace negotiations.

19th. British Government decides for National Service.

22nd. Ministries of Food, Pensions and Shipping formed.

30th. Allied Governments reject German peace proposals.

11th. *Balkans* : Battle of the Cerna and Monastir (see 5th October and 19th November) ends.

15th. *Egypt* : British advance into Sinai begins.

21st. *Egypt* : El Arish (Sinai) occupied by British forces.

23rd. *Egypt* : Affair of Magdhaba (Sinai)

15th. Verdun—New French attack succeeds.

18th. Verdun—French offensive ends.

CHAPTER I

THE SOMME

2ND–6TH JULY 1916

THE BATTLE OF ALBERT (*continued*) [1]

(Sketches A, 1, 2, 3, 4, 5, 6)

SITUATION AT NIGHTFALL, 1ST JULY

FOLLOWING a seven days' bombardment, the great assault Sketch A. on the 1st July had been delivered by eleven British divisions along a front of over fourteen miles from Montauban to Serre. Farther north, portions of two other divisions had launched a subsidiary attack upon the Gommecourt salient. More than 57,000 casualties had been suffered, and on two-thirds of the front the gallantry and devotion of the troops had proved of little avail : by the evening there stood revealed the true character of the task which confronted General Rawlinson's Fourth Army.

Yet a substantial success had been won upon half the total frontage of the Allied attack ; for the French astride the Somme, and the British between Maricourt and Fricourt had driven the enemy from his front position. In this area at least he had lost heavily in killed, wounded and prisoners, much of his artillery had been destroyed, and considerable disorganization had set in. Moreover, behind the seven German divisions of the *Second Army* which had faced the Allied attack there were only four, whereas each of the five British corps engaged in the main offensive had available one comparatively fresh division ; there were two divisions in Fourth Army reserve ; and two more at the disposal of

---

[1] The official name " The Battle of Albert " covers the whole of the fighting front during the period 1st–13th July.

G.H.Q. not far from the battle front.[1] The French, who attacked with five, had six fresh divisions in hand.

On the British right, where the enemy had not been expecting an attack, and the bombardment, with good observation, proved particularly effective, the success of the XIII. Corps was complete.[2] The corps was in touch with the French south of Bernafay Wood, and held Montauban with observation into Caterpillar Valley.[3] Next on the left, in the XV. Corps,[4] the 7th Division was in possession of Mametz, but had been obliged to throw back a flank facing Fricourt which had defied the efforts of the 21st Division. North of that village, the 21st Division held some thousand yards of the German front line and had penetrated to about the same distance ; but it had almost twice as far still to go in order to reach its objective for the first day, namely Quadrangle Trench, close to Mametz Wood which lay just in front of the German 2nd Position.

Farther north there had been no surprise. The enemy's artillery was unsubdued and his wire nearly intact when the assault was launched across No Man's Land, in most places far too wide and exposed to the deadly fire of machine guns undamaged by the British bombardment. Small detachments, with great courage and enterprise, had fought their way far into the enemy's lines, there to be overwhelmed or forced to withdraw ; only a few narrow lodgments in the German front were retained.

In the III. Corps,[5] which had as its objective a line beyond Contalmaison and the German 2nd Position from Pozières to Mouquet Farm, one party of the 34th Division held a footing on the extreme right next to the XV. Corps, and another was in Schwaben Höhe, where the great mine

---

[1] In addition, three cavalry divisions were concentrated between Albert and Amiens.
[2] XIII. Corps (Lieut.-General W. N. Congreve) :
  30th Division (Major-General J. S. M. Shea) ;
  18th Division (Major-General F. I. Maxse) ;
  in reserve, 9th Division (Major-General W. T. Furse).
[3] Marked in Sketch 1 by Caterpillar Wood.
[4] XV. Corps (Lieut.-General H. S. Horne) :
  7th Division (Major-General H. E. Watts) ;
  21st Division (Major-General D. G. M. Campbell) with 50th Brigade attached ;
  in reserve, 17th Division (Major-General T. D. Pilcher) less 50th Brigade.
III. Corps (Lieut.-General Sir W. P. Pulteney) :
  34th Division (Major-General E. C. Ingouville-Williams) ;
  8th Division (Major-General H. Hudson) ;
  in reserve, 19th Division (Major-General G. T. M. Bridges).

had been fired south of La Boisselle.[1] The X. Corps,[2] whose Sketch A.
task it was to secure the German 2nd Position from Mouquet
Farm to Grandcourt, had a small party of the 32nd Division
in Leipzig Redoubt—the German salient east of Authuille—
whilst the 36th Division was still clinging to a portion of
the German front line north of Thiepval. On the front of
the VIII. Corps,[3] which was to have formed the defensive
flank along the spur between Serre and Grandcourt, securing with its right some 2,500 yards of the German 2nd
Position, a party of the 4th Division maintained a footing
at the Quadrilateral, a small salient mid-way between
Beaumont Hamel and Serre. This party had to withdraw
on the morning of the 2nd July.[4]

The extent of the losses suffered was not known at
G.H.Q. on the evening of the 1st July ; but, whatever the
cost, there could be no relaxation of the British effort nor,
at this stage, any drastic change of plan. Sir Douglas
Haig wished the assault to be renewed as soon as possible
in order to wear down the enemy's resistance and to secure
a line from which to attack his 2nd Position.[5] At 10 P.M.,
therefore, General Rawlinson issued orders for the attack
to be continued " under corps arrangements as early as
" possible compatible with adequate previous artillery
" preparations ".

The XIII. Corps was directed to consolidate its gains Sketch 1.
and prepare to attack Mametz Wood in conjunction with
the XV. Corps : the XV. Corps to capture Fricourt village
and wood and push on to its original objective, linking up
with the III. Corps south of Contalmaison : the III. Corps
to secure La Boisselle and Ovillers, and then Contalmaison,
forming a flank between the two last-named villages : the
X. and VIII. Corps to carry the German front system and Sketch A.

[1] See " 1916 " Vol. I., pp. 374-5.
[2] X. Corps (Lieut.-General Sir T. L. N. Morland) :
    32nd Division (Major-General W. H. Rycroft) ;
    36th Division (Major-General O. S. W. Nugent) ;
    in reserve, 49th Division (Major-General E. M. Perceval).
[3] VIII. Corps (Lieut.-General Sir A. G. Hunter-Weston) :
    29th Division (Major-General H. de B. de Lisle) ;
    4th Division (Major-General Hon. W. Lambton) ;
    31st Division (Major-General R. Wanless O'Gowan) ;
    48th Division (Major-General R. Fanshawe).
    The 48th, which held the left of the corps front with one brigade, had
not attacked.
[4] See " 1916 " Vol. I., p. 449, f.n.
[5] Opposite the British front this position followed the high ground from
Guillemont to Pozières and thence passed over the ridge east of Thiepval
to Grandcourt on the Ancre ; beyond the river it continued due north in
front of Puisieux and Bucquoy.

1 July.   capture the intermediate line which ran in front of the 2nd
Position from the vicinity of Mouquet Farm to opposite
Beaucourt, and thence, beyond the Ancre, from Beaucourt
to Serre.

Thus General Rawlinson proposed to renew the attack
in his centre and on his left, where it had failed, refrain-
ing, for the time, from any exploitation of the success
Sketch 1. gained by his right. The XIII. Corps, however, could
hardly attack the German 2nd Position on the ridge
between Guillemont and Bazentin le Grand, reported by
the R.F.C. to be strongly held, unless the French covered
its flank.[1]

Lieut.-General Sir H. Gough, with three cavalry divisions
and other G.H.Q. troops, was to have exploited any break
in the German lines by passing through the gap and turning
northwards to " roll up " the enemy defence. He had now
gone to take command, under the Fourth Army, of the X.
and VIII. Corps in their renewed assault astride the Ancre.
From Army reserve the 12th Division (Major-General A. B.
Scott) was sent to the III. Corps to relieve the 8th Division,
and the 25th Division (Major-General E. G. T. Bainbridge)
moved to the X. Corps. To replace these two divisions,
General Rawlinson received the 23rd (Major-General J. M.
Babington) and 38th (Major-General Ivor Philipps) from
G.H.Q. reserve.

2ND JULY : OCCUPATION OF FRICOURT

After the first day of battle there followed a quiet night,
although, as mentioned below, at the junction of the British
and French the enemy delivered an unsuccessful counter-
attack in the early morning. The Germans seemed glad of
a respite, and throughout Sunday the 2nd July, a fine day
with bright sun and cool wind, were so inactive that the
British had no difficulty in reorganizing their divisions,
sending reinforcements and supplies across No Man's Land,
and pushing batteries forward. On this day, and for
several days after, there was little shelling of the areas
behind the British front : troops in reserve bivouacked and

---

[1] The congestion in the Maricourt salient was embarrassing both British
and French, and delayed concerted action. A French Sixth Army order
(8.30 P.M. 1st July) announced that the attack of the XX. Corps on the
intermediate line (including Hardecourt) would depend upon the British
attacking Trônes Wood and Bernafay Wood ; at 10.30 A.M. next morning
a further order simply instructed the corps to stand fast. F.O.A. iv. (ii.),
Annexes 1827, 1885. The operations of the French Sixth Army are
summarized in Note I. at end of Chapter.

SKETCH I.

THE SOMME, 1916.
SUNDAY, 2ND JULY.

fed from their cookers, horsed transport was on the move, 2 July. messengers on foot or motor-bicycle came and went, and carrying parties were busy, the whole composing an animated but almost peaceful scene. Air observers discovered little movement behind the German lines and few enemy machines were encountered. Bapaume was bombed with success by the R.F.C. in the afternoon.

In the XIII. Corps, the left of the 30th Division and the Sketch 1. right of the 18th, which were holding the Montauban ridge, had been attacked twice between 3 A.M. and 4 A.M. by four large infantry groups in close formation.[1] The noise of the German advance gave ample warning, and the batteries of the 30th Division put down a shrapnel barrage which stopped the enemy and caused him heavy loss. Only at the north-western corner of Montauban did a party of Germans succeed in closing and all were bombed and killed. The field batteries had been pushed up during the previous night, some to the old British front line, and the forward movement of the heavy artillery was begun. During the morning, the 30th Division field howitzers made an unsuccessful attempt to set Bernafay Wood on fire with thermite shells, of which 500 were used.[2] Later in the day, patrols found many German dead in the wood, and captured 18 men of the *51st Reserve Regiment*. Consolidation, reconnaissance, and the registration of targets proceeded under quiet conditions except for a heavy bombardment of Montauban and its vicinity.

Lieut.-General Horne, commanding the XV. Corps, had issued instructions during the night for the capture of Fricourt by the 17th Division,[3] whose advance was to link up with the 7th Division north of Mametz. Zero hour was fixed for 12.15 P.M. on the 2nd, following a bombardment of 75 minutes. Soon after the necessary orders had been issued, it was reported that a patrol of the 7th Division had entered Fricourt unopposed at midnight and that, in the

---

[1] This was part of a big night counter-attack by the *12th Reserve Division* (*VI. Reserve Corps* resting at Cambrai) and the *16th Bavarian Regiment* (*10th Bavarian Division*, also in reserve). The Bavarians and the *51st Reserve Regiment* attacked Montauban on two sides ; but the *38th Reserve Regiment*, which should have attacked the right of the 30th Division, lost direction, and, with the *23rd Reserve Regiment*, attacked the left of the French, also without success.

[2] The first trial of thermite.

[3] The 17th Division had been ordered to take over the front facing Fricourt held by its 50th Brigade, which had participated in the assault of the 1st July as right brigade of the 21st Division. Major-General Pilcher had relieved the 50th by the 51st Brigade (Br.-General R. B. Fell) during the night.

2 July. early morning, patrols of the 8/S. Staffordshire (51st
Brigade) had collected over a hundred prisoners of the *111th
Reserve Regiment.* There were so few signs of resistance
that at 8.50 A.M. Major-General Pilcher directed the 51st
Brigade to advance into the village without waiting for the
bombardment ; but the changing of orders caused considerable delay, and Fricourt was not entered until noon. There
was no fighting, and only eleven German stragglers were
rounded up.[1]

The movement continued behind a barrage, with
Bottom Wood as the final objective, slow progress being
made through the thick undergrowth and over the fallen
trees in Fricourt Wood where machine-gun fire caused
the 7/Lincolnshire some loss. At the end of the day, the
Lincolnshire and S. Staffordshire, reinforced by the
10/Sherwood Foresters, occupied old German trenches in
touch with the 7th Division on the right, and along the
north-eastern and northern faces of Fricourt Wood to
Fricourt Farm, connecting on the farther side with the
21st Division. Railway Alley was found to be well wired
and strongly held ; but after 11 P.M. bombers of the
Foresters fought their way in from the west and secured
200 yards of the trench.

Before daylight on the 2nd the ground in front of
Mametz had been reported clear of the enemy, and at
7.30 A.M. the 7th Division ordered the 91st Brigade (Br.-
General J. R. Minshull-Ford) to occupy White Trench and
Queen's Nullah. By eleven o'clock the 2/Queen's were in
possession, taking a few prisoners and a machine gun,
whilst the 8/Devonshire linked up with the 17th Division
by reaching Orchard Trench North, which led forward
from Bunny Trench. The new line was consolidated and
wired before dark. Meanwhile the 22nd Brigade had
advanced from the old German support line south-east of
Fricourt and cleared the trenches as far as the light-railway
cutting. Twenty-five prisoners were gathered in.

In the 21st Division, the left of the corps, the 62nd
Brigade (Br.-General C. G. Rawling), which had relieved
the 64th Brigade during the night, pushed out patrols
towards Fricourt Farm, capturing 75 prisoners and two
machine guns ; by 2 P.M. the 10/Green Howards were near

---

[1] Somme-Nord, after describing the successful defence of Fricourt on
1st July, states that the *111th Reserve Regiment* began to withdraw shortly
before midnight, under British artillery fire but undisturbed by British
infantry.

the trees called " Poodles ", and the battalion eventually 2 July. joined hands with the left of the 17th Division.

Thus the XV. Corps had reached, on the right, its objective of the previous day, and Fricourt village and wood had been captured.

In the III. Corps a night attack of the 19th Division against La Boisselle, planned to start at 10.30 P.M. on the 1st, did not take place : it proved impossible for the troops of the 57th and 58th Brigades to get forward in time over the shell-shattered ground littered with dead and all the débris of battle, or up the communication trenches congested by stretcher bearers and walking wounded. By dawn of the 2nd, only the 9/Cheshire (58th Brigade), which relieved the men of the 34th Division in the big crater (Schwaben Höhe), had arrived ; and it was then decided that the 58th Brigade (Br.-General A. J. W. Dowell) should attack alone at 4 P.M., as the 57th could not get into position by daylight.

Owing to the quiescence of the enemy, there was no difficulty in getting food, water and bombs across to the two lodgments in the old German line. As both were flanked by Sausage Redoubt, two companies of the 7/E. Lancashire (56th Brigade) were lent to the 34th Division to capture it. This they did in the afternoon, the Germans offering little resistance to a resolute bombing attack which began after an advance across the 500 yards of No Man's Land. The East Lancashire then entered the enemy trenches beyond the redoubt, occupying and consolidating a frontage of 1,000 yards. They sent back 58 prisoners, mostly hauled from dug-outs.

To deceive the enemy as to the point of the 58th Brigade attack, Ovillers was bombarded from 3.30 to 4 P.M., and the approaches thereto covered by a smoke screen released at zero hour. This ruse had the desired effect, for the Germans put a barrage round Ovillers and left La Boisselle alone. The assault was made across the open by the 6/Wiltshire and 9/R. Welch Fusiliers against the western end. With little loss the two battalions captured the German front trench and pushed on, the 9/Cheshire joining in on the right. Progress through La Boisselle involved the systematic searching and bombing of dug-outs and cellars ; but with the assistance of the artillery, which had good observation, the western half of the village was cleared by 9 P.M. and a line consolidated along a road just short of the church.

2 July.   Having relieved the 8th Division, a difficult and tedious
operation, during the night of the 1st/2nd July,[1] the 12th
Division could hardly be ready to renew the assault upon
Ovillers at dawn, as had been intended. The order was
therefore cancelled, and the day was devoted to very need-
ful reconnaissance and preparation.

Sketch A.   That the X. and VIII. Corps could carry the whole of
the German front position and then the intermediate line,
as required by Fourth Army orders, seemed out of the
question. After conferring with the corps commanders,
Lieut.-General Gough had reported as much to the Fourth
Army by telephone at 12.5 A.M. on the 2nd : he explained
the need for thorough reconnaissance and artillery preparation, but considered that an attack could be delivered on
the morning of the 3rd.

In the X. Corps it was not known definitely until the
early hours of the 2nd that the footing of the 36th Division
in the German front line north of Thiepval was still retained.
The divisional artillery placed a box barrage round it, and
in the afternoon the 107th Brigade sent a reinforcement of
360 men—collected from four different battalions—across
No Man's Land. Carrying parties followed and consolidation proceeded without interference until 6 P.M. From
that hour onwards the enemy made repeated bombing
attacks, all unsuccessful, on this position and at Leipzig
Redoubt.

The X. Corps handed over its frontage north of the
Ancre to the VIII. Corps, part of the 29th Division relieving
the troops of the 36th Division there ; and at dusk the
whole of the latter was relieved by the 49th from corps
reserve.[2]

Lieut.-General Snow, commanding the VII. Corps
which formed the right of the Third Army, was prepared,
with General Allenby's approval, to renew his attack at
Gommecourt,[3] should such action be required to ease the
situation elsewhere ; but G.H.Q. were informed that there

---

[1] The 8th Division had reported casualties amounting to 4,921 officers
and men. Its artillery did not hand over until the night of the 4th/5th,
the whole division then being exchanged for the 1st Division from the
First Army.
[2] On 1st and 2nd July the 36th Division lost over 5,000 officers and
men.
[3] See " 1916 " Vol. I., pp. 453 et seq. On 1st July the VII. Corps
had made a subsidiary attack upon the very strong Gommecourt salient
in order to divert enemy forces from the left flank of the main attack.
The troops had fought their way into the German position, but had not
been able to maintain themselves there.

was little prospect of success, and, when it became known **2 July.** that the attack of the VIII. and X. Corps was deferred, the VII. Corps reverted to active trench warfare.

Sir Douglas Haig, arrived at Fourth Army headquarters at 10.30 A.M. He said that there were sufficient reserves of men to replace casualties ; ammunition was the limiting factor, and he gave General Rawlinson particulars of the quantities available and in sight, desiring him to consider how best he could employ them.[1] Throughout the offensive, indeed, the control of ammunition expenditure remained of the greatest importance ; only by constant economies could the operations be continued. Moreover, owing to haste in manufacture and lack of skilled inspection, much of the ammunition, particularly the fuzes, was defective, so that full value could not be obtained from the bombardments.

The Commander-in-Chief was anxious to exploit the success gained by his right on the 1st July, concentrating on the Mametz Wood—Contalmaison sector with a view to reaching the German 2nd Position on the Longueval— Bazentin le Petit ridge. He appreciated that an advance from the line Montauban—Fricourt would take in rear the long line of enemy defences facing westward ; so, in his view, Thiepval should be attacked as a diversion, and north of the Ancre the enemy should merely be kept in anticipation of attack. At the same time, Sir Douglas Haig recognized the difficulties caused by the congestion in the Maricourt salient, and, without further discussion and arrangement with General Foch, he could hardly concentrate upon developing the success of General Rawlinson's right. In the circumstances, the commander of the Fourth Army was in favour of first improving the position of his centre and of securing Thiepval ; at noon he issued a short order for the X. and VIII. Corps, under General Gough, to attack the objectives already given them, the III. Corps, acting in close co-operation, to take Ovillers. Zero hour was to be 3.15 A.M. on the 3rd, following an hour's intense bombardment.

At 8.30 P.M., with Army approval, the XV. Corps **Sketch 2.** ordered an independent attack for 9 A.M. next morning ;

---

[1] Behind the ammunition echelons of field units there were 1,750,000 rounds of 18-pdr. and 85,000 of 6″ howitzer : the daily income from England was 70,000 of 18-pdr. and 6,000 of 6″ howitzer. From 24th June to 1st July the expenditure by the Fourth Army of 18-pdr. and 6″ howitzer ammunition had been 1,022,296 and 95,677 rounds respectively.

2 July. after a 20 minutes' bombardment, the 17th and 21st
Divisions, by an oblique advance, were to eliminate the
re-entrant they held and come up into the general line.
This advance would involve the capture of Bottom Wood
and Shelter Wood. Although these plans had Sir Douglas Haig's tacit
approval, he subsequently urged General Rawlinson to
activity in the Montauban area, and it was arranged to push
patrols into Bernafay Wood. After visiting General Gough,
the Commander-in-Chief gave instructions that the left
attack should be reduced to an assault by two brigades of
the X. Corps.

No directions or suggestions were received from Generals
Joffre or Foch. In the Montauban area the enemy was
obviously shaken, had expended most of his gun ammunition, and seemed to have exhausted the only infantry
reserves close at hand in an abortive night attack ; yet no
measures were taken, by combined action, to exploit the
success of the British right and French left. Between 10
and 11 P.M., however, Lieut.-General Kiggell, Chief of the
General Staff, speaking over the telephone for the Commander-in-Chief, had again impressed upon General Rawlinson the importance of exploiting this success. General
Rawlinson said that he had arranged to see General Foch
at 9 A.M. next morning with a view to securing French
co-operation ; his only doubt was whether the supply of
heavy howitzer ammunition was sufficient to deal with a
strong resistance if such should be offered. To this General
Kiggell replied that the Commander-in-Chief was prepared
to expend ammunition freely and employ his reserve
divisions in order to secure the German 2nd Position on the
Longueval ridge : he was asking the French Mission at
G.H.Q. to represent to General Foch the importance of
turning the present opportunity to account.

3RD JULY : FAILURE OF THE ATTACKS AT OVILLERS AND THIEPVAL

The morning of the 3rd July was dark for the time of
year, with high cloud ; but the weather continued fine until
the afternoon when there was a thunderstorm. Useful
information of the enemy's dispositions was obtained by
air reconnaissance, and German reinforcements were
observed moving on Bapaume and Péronne from the east
and south-east. The German aircraft were now active but

SKETCH 2.

THE SOMME, 1916.
3RD JULY.

Ordnance Survey, 1930.

BRITISH LINE.
Night 2nd/3rd July ————
Night 3rd/4th July ●●●●●●●
Brigade 56TH 27TH

M.V. ... Mash Valley.
S.V. ... Sausage Valley.

SCALE/R
Heights in metres.

YARDS 1000   0   1000   2000   3000   4000   5000 YARDS

3100/31. 3080/88

only over their own territory, where they checked some of 3 July. the British bombing raids.

At 2.55 A.M., twenty minutes before the general attack of the III. and X. Corps was timed to begin, General Gough informed the III. Corps by telephone that the X. Corps could not be ready before 6 A.M. : smoke would, however, be released, and half the arranged bombardment fired as for the original attack : more ammunition could not be spared, as the X. Corps would attack later.[1]

In the III. Corps the bombardment which preceded the Sketch 2. attack of the 12th Division against Ovillers opened punctually at 2.15 A.M. against the same targets as on the 1st July ; but two brigades of the 19th Division artillery now participated, firing upon the German lines north and south of the village. Rough assembly trenches had been dug, reducing No Man's Land at its widest from 800 to 500 yards. On the right, the 35th Brigade (Br.-General A. Solly-Flood) had the 5/R. Berkshire and 7/Suffolk in front, the 37th Brigade (Br.-General A. B. E. Cator) on the left, attacking with the 6/Queen's and 6/R. West Kent. The extreme left of the divisional front was held by a battalion of the 36th Brigade, which was to cover the flank of the attack by a discharge of smoke.

At 3.15 A.M., when the advance began, red rockets shot up from the enemy's front position and, in a moment, very severe fire from field and heavy batteries fell on the British assembly trenches, front line and communication trenches. Farther forward, in No Man's Land, the attacking waves were comparatively free from this shelling, but as they pressed on in semi-darkness, amid the dust and smoke, machine-gun fire gradually increased in volume from front and from both flanks. Yet all four battalions, finding plenty of gaps in the German wire, entered the enemy front trench, which appeared to hold only a few sentries. By the time the support line was reached, however, Germans were pouring out of deep dug-outs to counter-attack with bomb and bayonet.

Dawn broke, but observers in the British lines could see little : lowering masses of smoke obscured the action whilst the German machine guns rattled on without a pause. The whole of the West Kent had gone forward, with two companies of the 6/Buffs following in support ; in each of

---

[1] At noon a G.H.Q. order removed the VIII. and X. Corps from General Rawlinson's command, and constituted them the " Reserve Army " under General Gough.

3 July. the other three battalions one or two companies were still
held back, for hostile artillery and machine-gun fire now
almost prevented passage across No Man's Land. Even
after sun-rise little could be seen of the stormers, whilst on
the left flank the smoke, blowing back, was useless as a
screen. Of the men of the five battalions who had entered
the German position very few returned ; they fought until
their supply of bombs ran out and were then gradually
overwhelmed. By 9 A.M. the 12th Division reported total
failure with the exception of a footing gained on the outskirts of Ovillers, and, in the end, this was lost. The action,
which cost nearly 2,400 officers and men, was another
reminder that an assault upon a narrow front, without
adequate flank protection and lacking the element of surprise, was bound to result in a useless waste of life. For the
infantry to have reached the German trenches at all was an
outstanding feat of arms.

One company of the 9/Essex, which advanced in support
of the Berkshire, had lost its way and drifted to the right
towards La Boisselle, where it cut off 220 Germans and
handed over the prisoners to the 19th Division. Major-
General Bridges, commanding that division, had ordered
the 57th Brigade to come up on the left of the 58th, and at
2.15 A.M. the 8/N. Staffordshire, with bombers of the
5/S. Wales Borderers (Pioneers), had led the advance
between La Boisselle and the Albert—Bapaume road, the
10/Worcestershire covering the outer flank. Then at
3.15 A.M. both brigades attacked in order to complete the
capture of the village, to occupy a German trench 400 yards
beyond, and to link up with the divisions on either flank.
In the dim light there ensued fierce bombing and hand-to-
hand fighting, a regular " soldiers' battle ", until the
Germans were driven from La Boisselle, 153 of the *23rd*
and *110th Reserve Regiments* being made prisoner.

The defences of the village were still in good condition,
with a maze of deep dug-outs leading into each other.
Efforts to indicate by means of red flares that La Boisselle
was captured brought heavy retaliation from German
howitzers and mortars, and then a counter-attack from the
direction of Pozières was delivered against the 57th Brigade.[1] The supply of bombs ran short, and the enemy

---

[1] By the *190th Regiment* (*185th Division*), moving up to relieve the
110th Reserve (*28th Reserve Division*), which, according to regimental
accounts, was withdrawn by the end of the day, having lost 1,251 officers
and men.

gained the eastern end of La Boisselle, but reinforcements **3 July.**
of the 10/Warwickshire and 8/Gloucestershire were sent
forward, and the fight continued. In the end, the Germans
were held on a line running through the ruins of the church,
which represented a British gain of about one hundred
yards.[1] The 57th Brigade was then reinforced by a
battalion of the 56th, and after dark the 12th Division dug
a forward trench to connect its right with the flank of the
19th.

The 34th Division, still holding the right sector of the
III. Corps, had made three attempts, by bombing out from
its forward position, to link up with the 19th Division, but
failed to do so. When darkness fell, the 23rd Division
began the relief of the 34th, the 69th Brigade taking over
the captured trenches ; following the usual practice, the
artillery of the 34th remained in action.[2]

General Gough had intended to employ the 32nd and **2 July.**
49th Divisions (X. Corps) and the 48th Division (VIII.
Corps) in his Thiepval attack ; but when the scope of the
operation was reduced by the Commander-in-Chief to an
assault of two brigades, he called upon Major-General W. H.
Rycroft's 32nd Division to act alone. The first orders
had defined the divisional objective as a south-north line **Sketch A.**
from the eastern end of Leipzig Redoubt (east of Authuille)
to the " Wonderwork " on Thiepval spur, a frontage of
800 yards. The attack was to be made on the right
by the 14th Brigade—it had already relieved the 97th in
the tip of the Leipzig salient—and on the left by the 75th
Brigade (Br.-General N. F. Jenkins) attached from the
25th Division which was then moving into corps from
Army reserve.[3] The 75th Brigade had arrived in Aveluy
and Martinsart woods at 3.30 P.M. on the 2nd July, and

---

[1] After Lieut.-Colonel G. A. Royston-Pigott (10/Worcestershire) and
Major C. Wedgewood (8/N. Staffordshire) had been killed, and Lieut.-
Colonel R. M. Heath (10/R. Warwickshire) wounded, Lieut.-Colonel A.
Carton de Wiart (8/Gloucestershire) led the fight in person. He had lost
an eye in Somaliland, and an arm at " Second Ypres ", but he pulled the
pins from the Mills grenades with his teeth. For his " dauntless courage
" and inspiring example " he received the V.C. The same award was
made to Pte. T. G. Turrall (10/Worcestershire), who stayed out all day
beyond the village with a wounded subaltern, and brought him in after
dark.

[2] The losses of the 34th Division, 1st-5th July were reported as 6,811
of all ranks. On arrival in reserve, the shattered 102nd and 103rd Brigades
were exchanged for the 111th and 112th Brigades of the 37th Division.
The pioneer battalions were also exchanged. The 34th Division was re-
formed as originally constituted on 21st August.

[3] The 96th and 97th Brigades of the 32nd Division had suffered heavy
losses on 1st July.

2 July. preparations for the night advance and early morning
attack were hurried forward.

Notice of the reduction in the scope of the attack did
not reach X. Corps headquarters until 9.45 P.M. Not until
an hour later was Major-General Rycroft informed that
only his division would attack, and that his frontage was
increased from 800 to 1,400 yards to extend northwards as
far as Thiepval chateau on the south-western side of the
village. It was no easy matter to get the changed orders
to the 75th Brigade, whose battalions were beginning to
cross the Ancre by footbridges, in single file against a
stream of battle traffic ; new guides had to be provided and
new instructions passed on down to companies and platoons.
Br.-General Jenkins therefore felt obliged to ask for a
three hours' postponement of zero hour, and to this the
divisional commander was forced to agree. Unfortunately
3 July. there was hardly a battery telephone wire intact, and, as a
consequence, most of the batteries did not receive notice of
the postponement until they were half-way through the
preliminary bombardment for the original 3.15 A.M. attack ;
thus, for the later one, against a wider front, only half the
ammunition was available. The infantry, when it did
advance, got little support or protection from the artillery.

The attack of the 14th Brigade was nothing more than
an assault of two companies of the 15/Highland L.I. from
the tip of the Leipzig salient, where they had already
repelled several counter-attacks. At 6.15 A.M. they entered
the German front trench only to be driven out again, and a
second attempt also failed.

There was as little chance of success for the 75th Brigade
as there had been for the 12th Division three hours earlier.
In the centre, the 8/Border Regiment reached the shell
holes which marked the German front line, but was
eventually bombed out of them. Opposite the 11/Cheshire
on the right and the 2/S. Lancashire on the left the enemy
wire was still intact,[1] and the leading waves, which reached
it, were mown down by the German machine guns. Those
who did succeed in entering the German positions were
killed or captured, but some sixty of the Cheshire drifted
to the right and joined the Highland L.I. in the Leipzig
salient. It was obviously useless to continue the attack,
and the supporting lines, occupying shell-holes in No Man's

----

[1] Owing to a dip in the ground it could not be observed except by
periscope in the front line, and communication from the trenches to the
batteries was continually broken.

Land, were ordered to return as best they could.   Casualties
amounted to nearly eleven hundred of all ranks, including
Lieut.-Colonel R. L. Aspinall of the 11/Cheshire.[1]

During the night of the 3rd-4th, the infantry of the 32nd
Division was relieved by that of the 25th, the 75th Brigade
remaining in the line from which its attack had been
launched.[2]

The 9 A.M. advance of the XV. Corps was by no means Sketch 2.
undisputed.   In the 17th Division the 7/Border Regiment
(Br.-General Fell's 51st Brigade), which led the way, came
under machine-gun fire at once, and Railway Alley was not
occupied until 11.30 A.M.   The 7/Lincolnshire and bombing
detachments of the 8/S. Staffordshire and 10/Sherwood
Foresters had already been drawn into the fight.   One
company of the Border Regiment went on up the slope and
entered the western part of Bottom Wood where, for a time,
it was almost surrounded ; but when the 21st Division, on
the left, captured Shelter Wood, resistance on the brigade
front broke down completely, the Germans either yielding
or running away.   The Border Regiment, pressing on to
complete the capture of Bottom Wood, was forestalled by
the 21/Manchester (91st Brigade, 7th Division), which had
occupied the eastern end without fighting.   Two batteries
of the XIV. Brigade R.H.A. (7th Division) were then
brought up to Queen's Nullah, and began to cut the wire of
Mametz Wood defences, assisted by a howitzer battery
south of Mametz.   The gain of ground had cost the 51st
Brigade about 500 of all ranks.

The 1/Lincolnshire of the 62nd Brigade, advancing in
the 21st Division sector, was supported by the fire of the
brigade machine-gun company.   The German machine guns
caused some loss before the leading lines reached the edge
of Shelter Wood and the much smaller Birch Tree Wood,
just beyond it to the north-west.   Here a stubborn resistance was offered by large numbers of Germans who emerged
from dug-outs, so that the whole of the 12/Northumberland
Fusiliers, moving in support, was soon engaged.   Birch
Tree Wood was captured, but a strong bombing attack
from the right, which was only repulsed with difficulty,
delayed the entry into Shelter Wood.

Shortly after 11.30 A.M. it was reported from the air that

---

[1] The *1/99th Reserve (26th Reserve Division)*, which opposed this attack,
had no reserves and called upon the *8th Bavarian Reserve Regiment (10th
Bavarian Division)* for assistance.   A company of Bavarians was sent up.

[2] The 32nd Division reported 4,676 casualties for 1st-3rd July.

3 July. German columns could be seen moving forward from Contalmaison.   Thereupon Br.-General Rawling determined to
anticipate   the   enemy ;   using   the   13/Northumberland
Fusiliers, from reserve, to join in an enveloping movement
which was covered by Stokes mortar fire, he took Shelter
Wood without much further trouble.   At 2 P.M. a counter
attack against Bottom Wood and Shelter Wood was
repulsed, mainly by Lewis-gun fire, and the collection of
prisoners then continued.   Some six hundred officers and
men of the *186th Regiment* surrendered, and about two
hundred of the *23rd Regiment* and *109th*, *110th* and *111th*
Reserve Regiments were captured in the vicinity.[1]   On the
left, the 63rd Brigade (Br.-General E. R. Hill) formed a
defensive flank until definite junction was obtained with
the 34th Division (III. Corps) at Round Wood, south-east
of Scots Redoubt.

    The three divisions of the XV. Corps set about con-
solidating their new positions, also improving roads and
communications.   The Albert-Péronne light railway in
Caterpillar Valley became the principal line for the evacuation of the wounded.   Corps headquarters had received
many reports to show that on its front the enemy had
not yet rallied, and at 3 P.M. patrols found that Mametz
Wood and Quadrangle Trench were empty.[2]   Lieut.-General
Horne was averse to patrol action which might bring on an
engagement before he was prepared to accept it ;   but
about 5 P.M. he gave permission for the 7th Division to
occupy after dark a line on the southern edge of Mametz
Wood continuing along Strip Trench, Wood Trench and
the eastern end of Quadrangle Trench.   The 22nd Brigade,
in support, sent up the 2/Royal Irish and 1/R. Welch
Fusiliers for this purpose, but much time was lost owing to
a guide going astray, and daylight came before most of the
troops were ready to advance.   During the night, however,
a patrol of the Royal Irish fired on and dispersed a German
detachment which was bivouacking in Mametz Wood without precautions,[3] and then removed the breech-blocks of
two abandoned guns.   The patrol reported that Wood

---

[1] According to the German regimental accounts the *111th Reserve Regiment* (*28th Reserve Division*) lost 2,315 of all ranks, and the *III./186th
Regiment* (*185th Division*) over 700.   Thus these four battalions were
practically destroyed by the afternoon of 3rd July.   The 62nd Brigade
had under a thousand casualties in this operation.

[2] The annihilation of the *III./186th Regiment* left a gap which was not
closed until night.

[3] This was a company of the *55th Landwehr Regiment*, which, according
to German accounts, " made a premature retirement ".

Trench and Quadrangle Trench were certainly held ; but 3 July. not in any strength, according to the 17th Division, which had found no Germans in Peake Woods, half-way between the front line and Contalmaison.

It would appear that if the XV. Corps had encouraged more vigorous action on the afternoon of the 3rd, a hold on Mametz Wood could have been secured, and Wood Trench and Quadrangle Trench occupied. The last-named objective was taken on the morning of the 5th, but the others were to cost many lives and much precious time.

On the night of the 3rd/4th July, the 21st Division, less artillery, was withdrawn to rest, the 52nd Brigade of the 17th Division taking over its front.[1] The 38th (Welsh) Division, which had moved forward during the day came into corps reserve.

The divisions of the XIII. Corps spent the 3rd July in consolidation, the 27th Brigade (Br.-General S. W. Scrase-Dickens) of the 9th Division having relieved the 90th Brigade of the 30th Division in the Montauban salient during the previous night. Patrols ascertained that Bernafay Wood was still undefended—a few of the *51st Reserve Regiment* encountered there surrendered on summons—and Lieut.-General Congreve felt that the opportunity to gain ground could be ignored no longer. At 3.15 P.M., with Army approval, he ordered the 30th Division to occupy the wood.

After a twenty minutes' bombardment of the near edge, the 27th Brigade moved forward at 9 P.M. when the guns lifted their fire to form a barrage beyond. With only six casualties, the 6/K.O.S.B. and 12/Royal Scots covered 500 yards of flat open ground, entered the wood, and took possession of the whole of it, capturing 17 prisoners, three field guns and three machine guns.[2] The dense undergrowth made movement difficult in the dark and the two battalions took some time to reorganize ; but the farther edge of the wood and the eastern portion of Montauban Alley were consolidated, and incorporated in the XIII. Corps salient.

Patrols sent out eastward gathered that Trônes Wood was held by a number of machine-gun detachments, so Lieut.-General Congreve did not feel justified in attempting

[1] The casualties of the 21st Division from midnight 30th June to midnight 3rd July were reported as 4,663 officers and men.
[2] German accounts state that the *I.* and *III. Battalions* of the *51st Reserve* (*12th Reserve Division*) had been shelled out of the wood by the British artillery in the course of the day.

C

3 July. to seize it.   The Fourth Army, however, ordered the occupation of Caterpillar Wood, which had been reported empty by the R.F.C., and this was done by the 18th Division at 4 A.M. on the 4th.   The 10/Essex (53rd Brigade), which found five abandoned field guns, also took possession of a length of trench flanking the valley and the left rear of the wood.

Among the regimental officers of the XIII. and XV. Corps the events of the day accentuated the general feeling that the Germans on their front were beaten, and that a resolute advance might set them on the run, whereas every hour of delay increased the chance of meeting with stout opposition.   Without French co-operation, however, General Rawlinson was reluctant to push out from the sharp salient formed by the XIII. Corps position ; as it was, an awkward re-entrant had been created at the junction of French and British by the occupation of Bernafay Wood.

The outcome of General Rawlinson's meeting with General Foch on the morning of the 3rd was the arrival of the latter with General Joffre himself at Advanced G.H.Q. about 3 P.M. for the first personal interchange of views since the start of the offensive.   The French commanders objected to the weight of the British attack being directed against the Longueval—Contalmaison front : they wanted the main effort to be a renewed assault farther north— Pozières to Thiepval—where it had already failed.   General Joffre went so far as to order the British Commander-in-Chief to carry out this operation.

Sir Douglas Haig showed that his supply of gun ammunition was insufficient to enable him to press his attack with equal strength on the whole of the original front : he was obliged to concentrate his efforts upon one portion, doing all he could to hold the enemy elsewhere : the pulse of the battle clearly showed that a renewed attack on the front Longueval—Contalmaison promised the best results : from Pozières to Thiepval the defences were particularly strong and the German resistance was almost unshaken : the general object, to defeat the enemy, was not changed, but in the matter of tactical method he must be allowed to decide for himself : for the moment the southern half of the the front offered greater advantages, but later the situation might favour a decisive attack on Pozières and Thiepval.

As General Joffre still persisted in his view, although his only argument was that Sir Douglas Haig proposed to

SKETCH 3.

THE SOMME, 1916.
4TH JULY.

BRITISH LINE:
Night, 1st/2nd July. ————
Night, 1st/2nd July. ••••••
Proposed........ 53RD 27.TH

M.V. Mash Valley.
S.V. Sausage Valley.

SCALE

Heights in metres.

Ordnance Survey 1930.

3100/31. 3060/38.

3 July. depart from the original plan, the British Commander-in-Chief felt obliged to point out that he was responsible solely to his own Government, and must decline to pursue a tactical plan of which he did not approve. He emphasized his readiness to conform, as he had always done, to General Joffre's strategy, to this extent treating him as generalissimo of the Allied forces ; but he could go no further. General Joffre accepted this attitude, and the discussion closed with mutual assurances of friendship and goodwill. No definite arrangement was made, however, for French support of the British right, beyond the occupation of Hardecourt knoll (just north of the village of that name) which, the French generals said, was a matter for the local commanders to settle.[1]

As the result of a corps commanders' conference held in Sketch 2. the afternoon, a Fourth Army order was issued at 9.45 P.M. It announced that every preparation would be made for an attack on the German 2nd Position, Longueval—Bazentin le Petit : the first step was to advance the front line to assaulting distance, and dispose the artillery so that it could destroy the enemy defences. More specifically, the XIII. Corps was to secure Bernafay and Caterpillar Woods, which, as we know, it did in the course of the night ; the XV. Corps was to occupy Mametz Wood ; the III. Corps was to capture Contalmaison and establish itself upon a line Mametz Wood—far edge of Contalmaison—Bailiff Wood, and so westward north of La Boisselle.

The Reserve Army reverted to trench warfare, but was required to carry out raids and bombing attacks, supported by artillery barrages, in order to hold the enemy guns and infantry on its front : the X. Corps was to extend its two footings in the German front system.

4TH-6TH JULY : CAPTURE OF LA BOISSELLE

The weather, which had so far favoured the attackers, began to change during the night of the 3rd/4th July, when some rain fell. Heavy showers on the 4th culminated in a

---

[1] This interview is merely mentioned in a footnote (p. 237) by F.O.A. iv. (ii.), which states (pp. 237 and 243-4) that the results of 1st July prompted Foch to exploit the success gained south of the Somme ; on the morning of the 3rd he instructed General Fayolle to aim at securing the whole of the Flaucourt plateau in readiness to advance southward from the Estrées—Villers Carbonnel road (see Sketch 4) if eventually ordered to do so. The comparative failure of the Fourth Army on the first day appears to have caused a French lack of confidence in the success of further British efforts, and this feeling was heightened when it became known that Sir D. Haig was reducing his frontage of attack. " Il a donc fallu prévoir " cette éventualité et chercher ailleurs la solution."

4 July. thunderstorm which lasted all the afternoon ; the troops were soaked, the trenches filled with water, and the ground became inches deep in clinging mud which balled on the feet of horse and man.   The R.F.C. could not render much assistance, although some targets were registered and a useful reconnaissance of Mametz Wood was made.   No German machines crossed the British lines.

The three days, 4th to 6th July, were spent by the British and the left division of the French XX. Corps in making their preparations and endeavouring to improve their positions in readiness for the advance against Harde-court, Trônes Wood, Mametz Wood and Contalmaison, which was fixed for the 7th July.[1] Destructive and harass-ing fire was maintained by the artillery, many batteries being pushed forward.[2] In the repair and improvement of roads, a vital need, the engineers, including tunnellers, had the assistance of pioneers and infantry ; but supplies of road metal, and the rail and road transport to bring them up were strictly limited.   The problem of ensuring an adequate water-supply for the large numbers in the forward area was already difficult and threatened to become more so on the uplands between the Somme and the Ancre.[3]

The enemy shelled severely some parts of the front on the 4th July ; his only counter-attacks were made from 9.30 A.M. onwards by bombing parties against the 49th Division north of Thiepval and the 25th Division in the Leipzig salient.   None of these was successful, but at night two attempts of the 49th Division to account for some machine-gun nests near St. Pierre Divion likewise failed.

Sketch 3.   At 8.30 A.M. the III. Corps made an effort to complete the capture of La Boisselle, the 56th Brigade (19th Division) sending forward the 7/King's Own, which bombed up the trenches supported by the fire of machine guns and mortars. Slow progress was made against a very determined resist-ance, but by 2.30 P.M. the whole of the village, except a few ruins at its northern end, was in British hands.   In the XV. Corps the 17th Division made some advance along the trenches towards Contalmaison.   The XIII. Corps stood fast, but at night the 18th Division occupied unopposed

---

[1] See below.

[2] Their movements are difficult to trace, for the war diaries are not helpful.   The Carnoy—Fricourt valley was full of heavy guns on 6th July.

[3] To ease the strain on water-supply, and also upon the railways, which found the transport of bulky forage a great burden, the 1st and 3rd Cavalry Divisions (which had passed from G.H.Q. to Fourth Army reserve) were sent back to the Abbeville region.   The 2nd Indian Cavalry Division remained in the battle zone east of Amiens.

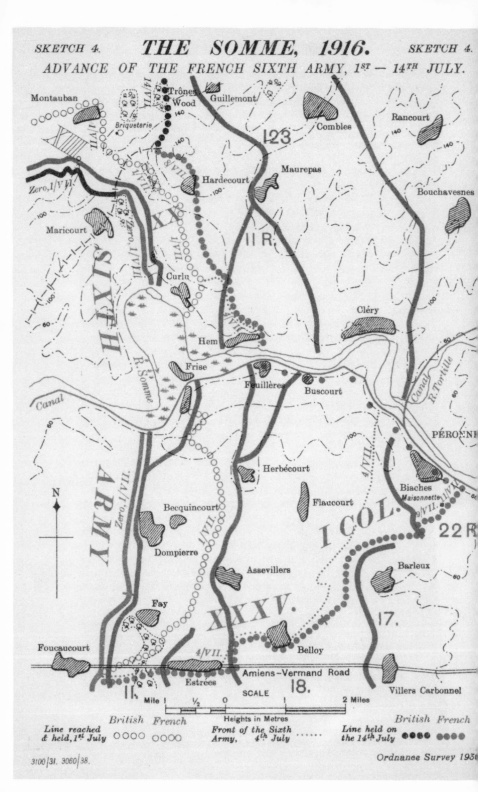

SKETCH 4.   **THE SOMME, 1916.**   SKETCH 4.

ADVANCE OF THE FRENCH SIXTH ARMY, 1ST — 14TH JULY.

Montauban

Trônes Wood   Guillemont

Briqueterie   Combles   Rancourt

Maurepas

Hardecourt   Bouchavesnes

Maricourt   II R.

Zero, 1/VII.   Cléry

Curlu

Hem

Frise

Feuillères   Buscourt

PÉRONNE

Herbécourt

Biaches
Maisonnette

Becquincourt   Flaucourt   I COL.   22 R

Dompierre   17.   Barleux

N   Asseviliers

XXXV.

Fay

Foucaucourt   Belloy

Estrées   Amiens—Vermand Road   18.   Villers Carbonnel

SCALE

Mile 1   ½   0   1   2 Miles

Heights in Metres

British   French   Front of the Sixth   British   French
Line reached   ○○○○ ○○○○   Army, 4th July ....   Line held on   ●●●● ●●●●
& held, 1st July   the 14th July

3100/31. 3060/38.   Ordnance Survey 1936

Marlboro' Wood, some five hundred yards up the slope beyond Caterpillar Wood.[1]

Hostile artillery action diminished on the 5th July, and 5 July. although the 49th Division, north of Thiepval, again had to repel bombing assaults, the general attitude of the enemy was quiescent, except when called upon to oppose an attack.

Lieut.-General Horne had planned a surprise advance at Sketch 5. midnight 4th/5th July, in order to secure the southern projection of Mametz Wood, Wood Trench, and Quadrangle Trench as far as Shelter Alley; but a heavy rainstorm hampered his preparations. The XV. Corps advance eventually took place at 12.45 A.M., after half an hour's bombardment. Favoured by the rain and darkness, the leading companies of the 2/Royal Irish and 1/R. Welch Fusiliers (22nd Brigade, 7th Division) and the 9/Northumberland Fusiliers and 10/Lancashire Fusiliers (52nd Brigade, 17th Division) crept up to within a hundred yards of the enemy position before zero hour. Then they charged in, securing Quadrangle Trench and Shelter Alley with prisoners of the *163rd* and *190th Regiments*. On the right, however, the Royal Irish were held up by uncut wire, counter-attacked and driven back. Although they made two more efforts, the German machine-gun fire was too severe, so neither Mametz Wood nor Wood Trench was gained. At night, the 38th Division (Major-General Ivor Philipps) completed the relief of the 7th Division.[2]

In the III. Corps, the 23rd Division had been ordered to assist the left of the XV. Corps in its 12.45 A.M. attack, improving its own position in front of Contalmaison and helping the 19th Division on the other flank at the same time. At 4 A.M. the 69th Brigade sent forward on the left bombing parties of the 9/Green Howards, and others of the 11/W. Yorkshire and 10/Duke of Wellington's advanced on the right at 6.45 A.M. Fighting in Horseshoe Trench was continuous until 10 A.M. when most of the ground won was lost to a strong counter-attack. The enemy came on again in the afternoon, and nearly the whole of the 69th Brigade was absorbed into the fight;[3] but soon after 6 P.M.

---

[1] Before next morning the 9th Division (Major-General W. T. Furse) completed the relief of the 30th Division next to the French. The 30th Division had suffered 3,000 casualties.

[2] From 1st-5th July, the 7th Division had lost 3,824 of all ranks.

[3] At a critical moment 2/Lieut. D. S. Bell (9/Green Howards) disposed of a German machine-gun detachment almost single-handed, for which exploit he was eventually awarded the V.C. He was killed a few days later.

5 July. Br.-General Lambert launched the 10/Duke of Wellington's and 8th and 9/Green Howards in an attack over the open which cleared both Horseshoe Trench and Lincoln Redoubt at its western end. On the other flank, ground was gained to the eastward but touch was not established with the 17th Division in Shelter Alley. About two hundred and seventy Germans were captured during the day. The 19th Division endeavoured to straighten out the re-entrant on the eastern side of La Boisselle, but the bombers of the 56th and 57th Brigades met with little success.[1] The arrival of the 1/Sherwood Foresters, lent by the 24th Brigade, (23rd Division) to reinforce, coincided with that of the *9th Grenadiers* (*3rd Guard Division*) for a like purpose, and practically no progress was made.[2] At night the 12th Division relieved the 57th Brigade in the La Boisselle sector.

Farther north, in the X. Corps area, the 25th Division endeavoured at 7 P.M. to improve its hold on the Leipzig salient, a company of the 1/Wiltshire (7th Brigade) obtaining a foothold in Hindenburg Trench, the German front position.

6 July. On the 6th July the enemy's bombardment became more general, and at night he shelled certain areas with tear gas. The re-entrant between the 23rd Division in Horse-

Sketch 6. shoe Trench and the 19th Division in La Boisselle was still occupied by Germans, so at 7.30 P.M. the 7/E. Lancashire (56th Brigade) tried to drive them out by bombing. This effort failed, but a direct assault over the open was completely successful, and three counter-attacks were afterwards repulsed. At night the 68th Brigade relieved the 69th in the 23rd Division sector, and the 12/Durham L.I. then occupied a trench, called Triangle Trench, running eastward from the Horseshoe.

4 July. When he called upon General Rawlinson about noon on the 4th July, the Commander-in-Chief had emphasized the importance of seizing Trônes Wood to cover the right flank of the attack upon the German 2nd Position, and of securing Mametz Wood and Contalmaison to cover the left. Afterwards, he had visited the commanders of the XIII., XV. and III. Corps in turn, urging them to pursue an

---

[1] The very gallant leadership of Lieut. T. O. L. Wilkinson, 7/L. N. Lancs., killed in action, was recognized by the posthumous award of the V.C.

[2] The *3rd Guard Division* was relieving the *28th Reserve Division* on the front Mametz Wood—Ovillers.

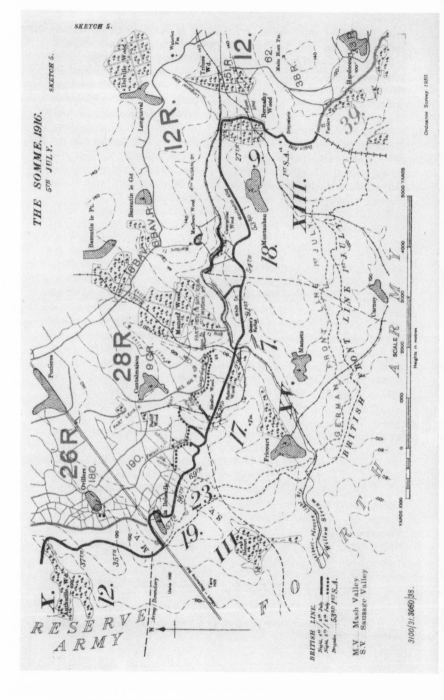

SKETCH 5.

THE SOMME, 1916.
5TH JULY.

BRITISH LINE:
Night, 1st / 4th July.
Night, 4th / 5th July.
Proposed 53RD 1ST S.A.

M.V. ... Mash Valley.
S.V. ... Sausage Valley.

Ordnance Survey 1930

3100/31.3060/33.

energetic and enterprising policy. A formal order issued 4-6 July. by G.H.Q. on this day recapitulated the immediate object- ives of the Fourth Army : [1] the Reserve Army was to be ready to attack Ovillers and the Leipzig salient, and also to prepare to renew the assault astride the Ancre, so that General Gough, at short notice, could act in combination with General Rawlinson as the latter progressed in his advance northwards.

General Foch had informed General Rawlinson on the Sketch 5. 4th July that the French XX. Corps would attack the knoll north of Hardecourt, and asked for simultaneous action by the British against Trônes Wood and Maltz Horn Farm.   Early on the afternoon of the 5th Sir Douglas Haig arrived at Fourth Army headquarters to confer with Generals Rawlinson and Gough ; it was then arranged that at 8 A.M. on the 7th the Fourth Army should extend its right to Maltz Horn Farm and Trônes Wood, whilst its centre and left attacked Mametz Wood and Contalmaison. The Reserve Army was to take Ovillers ; its left, in common with the Third and First Armies, to simulate an attack by the release of gas and smoke.[2]

On the 5th July G.H.Q. informed the Armies of the ammunition situation and the maximum amounts which could be allotted to them daily.   As regards the all import- ant 18-pdr. and 6-inch howitzer, these were 56,000 and 4,920 rounds, respectively, to the Fourth Army, and 14,000 and 880 to the Reserve Army, a very unsatisfactory state of affairs.   To augment General Rawlinson's artillery, the French lent four batteries of 120-mm. (long) guns, and a battery of 220-mm. howitzers, with an ample supply of ammunition.

On the morning of the 6th July, General Rawlinson Sketch 6. visited General Fayolle and arranged with him the details of the combined Hardecourt—Trônes Wood attack, which formed part of the operation to be carried out on the 7th. Later, the British commander, by letter, tried to reassure General Foch who understood that the British right would start from Bernafay Wood, leaving the French left, on the other side of the re-entrant, in the air.   In the same letter General Rawlinson mentioned that the French XX. Corps had been counter-attacked in Bois Favière, and that, as

[1] See page 19.
[2] These decisions were embodied in a formal order issued by G.H.Q. at 12.30 P.M. on the 6th.   The operation order of the Fourth Army was sent out at 9.45 P.M. on the 5th.

6 July. Germans were now in possession of its northern end, the Hardecourt—Trônes Wood attack was postponed until the 8th. This was being done at the request of General Balfourier (commanding the French XX. Corps) who wanted time to complete the capture of the wood ; General Rawlinson added that the British attack against Mametz Wood and Contalmaison would take place on the morrow, as arranged.[1] Before this letter arrived General Foch had left for Beauquesne, Advanced G.H.Q., to see Sir Douglas Haig. He informed the British Commander-in-Chief that all was in train for the combined attack next morning, and proceeded to discuss the subsequent action of the French left.[2] Sir Douglas Haig did not hear of the postponement of the Hardecourt—Trônes Wood attack until after General Foch had gone ; in any case, he could hardly do otherwise than agree to it.

On the 6th July the Chief of the General Staff addressed to the Fourth Army a memorandum on general policy : in view of British numerical superiority, and the evidence of confusion and loss of morale on the enemy side, any advantage gained must be followed up boldly ; it was probable that serious demoralization in the German ranks might supervene, " possibly to-morrow " ; according to Intelligence information there were now in the line from Hardecourt to La Boisselle only 15 German battalions, of which 11 had suffered severely in the last two days' fighting. Actually, 33 German battalions had been engaged on this front up to this date, and at least 40 fresh battalions were close at hand.[3] The three corps of the Fourth Army, with six divisions in the line and five more in support and reserve,

[1] Somme-Nord, pp. 125-6, states that the French attacked at 6 A.M. on the 6th and ejected the Germans from the northern end of Bois Favière, but were counter-attacked and expelled in their turn. French attacks at 12.30 P.M. and 2.30 P.M. failed.

According to F.O.A. iv. (ii.), pp. 246-7, the right division (11th) of the XX. Corps was prevented from joining in the attack of the 8th July owing to German counter-attacks north of Hem (see Sketch 4).

[2] Owing to his cramped communications north of the Somme, General Foch explained that he could not feed sufficient reinforcements to develop a movement eastwards against Maurepas (see Sketch A) until the British had taken the German 2nd Position (Longueval—Bazentin le Petit) and were ready to attack Guillemont. Meanwhile he would contribute counter-battery fire.

[3] The German front between the British right and La Boisselle had certainly been held by 15 battalions (*6th Bavarian Reserve Regiment, 62nd Regiment, 109th, 111th, 110th Reserve Regiments*) on 1st July ; but the troops subsequently engaged included the *12th Reserve Division* and parts of the *185th, 12th, 10th Bavarian* and *3rd Guard Divisions*, with the *163rd Regiment* (*17th Reserve Division*). In addition, the *183rd Division* was approaching the front.

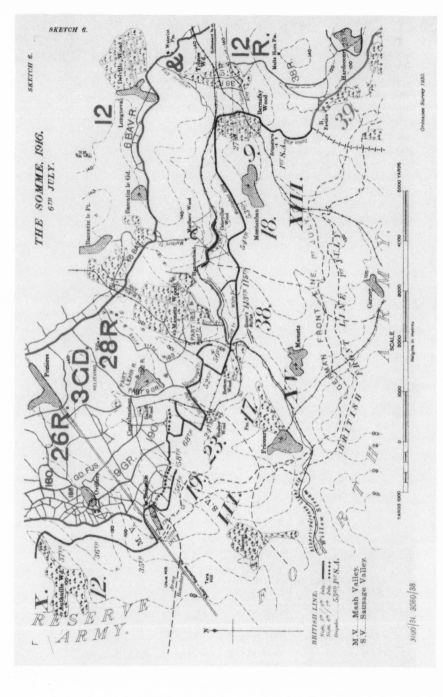

SKETCH 6.

THE SOMME, 1916.
6TH JULY.

BRITISH LINE:
Night, 3rd/4th July.
Night, 4th/5th July.
Brigade.   53RD Iᵗ S.A.

M.V....Mash Valley.
S.V....Sausage Valley.

Ordnance Survey 1930.

3100/31 3060/38

at the moment had a numerical superiority of more than two to one.

At midnight on the 4th/5th July the front of the Reserve Army had been extended to the right, the 12th Division in the sector opposite Ovillers passing from the III. to the X. Corps. The headquarters of the II. Corps (in G.H.Q. reserve) was placed under the Fourth Army, and the 3rd Division, on its way to the II. Corps from the Second Army, was transferred to the XIII. Corps. The Reserve Army received the 35th Division from Third Army reserve.[1] All the divisions originally in Fourth Army or G.H.Q. reserve had been drawn into the battle, and three more were arriving from other parts of the front. Only the 8th Division was being transferred elsewhere.

NOTE I

The French Operations, 2nd-6th July [2]

By the close of the 1st July General Fayolle's Sixth Army [3]— **Sketch 4.** XX. Corps (General Balfourier) north of the Somme next to the British, and I. Colonial Corps south of the river, with XXXV. Corps on its right—was in complete possession of the German 1st Position with the exception of Frise. Casualties were light, no reserves had been employed, 4,000 prisoners had come in, and the I. Colonial Corps was within assaulting distance of the German 2nd Position. It appeared that the Germans south of the Somme were withdrawing their artillery.

The causes of the inaction of the left division of the XX. Corps during the following days have already been explained. On the 5th July the 11th Division, on the right, captured the village of Hem ; the high ground to the north of it, which was also secured, fell into German hands again as the result of counter-attacks on the 6th and 7th.

South of the Somme, on the 2nd July the I. Colonial Corps and

---

[1] The order of battle, exclusive of cavalry, thus became :
  Fourth Army :
XIII. Corps : 3rd, 9th, 18th, 30th Divisions ;
XV.   ,,   : 7th, 17th, 21st, 38th Divisions ;
III. ,,   : 19th, 23rd, 34th Divisions ;
II. Corps (in reserve) : 8th Division, about to be exchanged with the 1st (First Army).
  Reserve Army :
X. Corps : 12th, 25th, 32nd, 36th*, 49th Divisions ;
VIII. Corps : 4th, 29th, 35th*, 48th Divisions and 31st Division (temporarily).
      * Earmarked as Army reserve.
[2] F.O.A. iv. (ii.), pp. 233-44.
[3] Under the direction of General Foch, commanding the G.A.N. (Sixth, Tenth and Third Armies from north to south).

XXXV. Corps captured Frise and broke into the German 2nd Position, taking Herbecourt ; but the attack on Assevillers failed. Next day the enemy offered little resistance to the occupation of Assevillers and Flaucourt—he had, indeed, withdrawn—and the French were then established on the Flaucourt plateau overlooking the " boucle " formed by the Somme in its turn north-westward at Péronne. On this day a vigorous pursuit of the enemy might have been undertaken, but General Fayolle still regarded the operations south of the Somme as of secondary importance, in spite of the message he had received from General Foch.[1] There was heavy fighting on the 4th before Belloy, and Estrées were taken, but Estrées was lost on the 5th when Belloy was held against a succession of counter-attacks. It was evident that the Germans had recovered themselves.

General Foch, however, had decided upon vigorous action both north and south of the Somme, enlarging the scope of the operations to the south by employing the Tenth Army (General J. Micheler) on the right of the Sixth. He proposed to use his reserves to exploit success wherever obtained.

NOTE II

The Germans during 2nd–6th July [2]

The success of the French and of the British right on the 1st July had created a serious situation on the front from the Amiens—Vermand road, south of the Somme, to the Albert—Bapaume road. That the French, so heavily engaged at Verdun, should be capable of a vigorous offensive prepared by such a powerful concentration of heavy artillery came as a great surprise. The heavy German casualties and the loss of ground on this and the following days were attributed, mainly, to overwhelming artillery fire. In asking for substantial reinforcements, General Fritz von Below, commanding the *Second Army*, especially mentioned artillery [3] ; he was told by O.H.L. that three divisions, 16 heavy batteries and three aeroplane flights were on their way to him. Fifteen heavy batteries were sent from the *Fifth Army* before Verdun.

Sketches 1, 4.
After the failure of the counter-attack against the junction of the British and French on the night of the 1st/2nd July, a new front was organized in the 2nd Position (Assevillers—Herbecourt—Hem —Maurepas—Guillemont—Longueval—Bazentin le Petit Wood), and a forward line thence through Mametz Wood to La Boisselle ; but this took time to establish and organize. General von Stein (whose *XIV. Reserve Corps*, with attached troops, held the front from the Somme to Gommecourt) would have counter-attacked between Montauban and Fricourt on the 2nd had there been two fresh divisions available ; but of his corps reserve the *10th Bavarian Division* had been used partly to reinforce and partly in the night counter-attack, and the *185th Division* had been called upon to

---

[1] See page 19, f.n.
[2] G.O.A. x., pp. 353-60, and Somme-Nord i. also Schwarte ii., Rupprecht, and Wendt.
[3] On 1st July he had lost 109 guns north of the Somme, and the whole of the *121st Division* artillery south of the river.

reinforce the fighting front and to occupy the new line. Of the *VI. Reserve Corps* (General von Gossler) in general reserve, the *12th Reserve Division* had taken part in the night counter-attack and the *11th Reserve Division*, on its way from Cambrai by rail, could not be available before the 3rd. At this time the only other reserves near were the *3rd Guard Division* (in Valenciennes, reserve of the *Sixth Army*) ; *183rd Division* (between Lille and Tournai, general reserve) ; and the *5th Division*, resting at St. Quentin after being relieved on the Verdun front.

General von Pannewitz, commanding the *XVII. Corps* south of the Somme, withdrew on the 2nd July after obtaining the consent of the *Second Army*. On hearing of this, General Falkenhayn, accompanied by Major-General Tappen, Chief of the Operations Section, went to St. Quentin, General von Below's headquarters. Falkenhayn laid it down that " the first principle in position warfare " must be to yield not one foot of ground ; and if it be lost to retake " it by immediate counter-attack, even to the use of the last man ". This was the subject of a special Army order issued next day. O.H.L. made General Grünert, Chief of the Staff of the *Second Army*, responsible for the voluntary retirement and replaced him by Colonel von Lossberg.[1]

By the 3rd July the new position between Longueval and Ovillers was held by a heterogeneous collection of units representing at least six divisions, besides attached troops. The whole fighting front was then organized into three " Groups " under three corps commanders : General von Quast, south of the Somme ; General von Gossler, Somme to Albert—Bapaume road ; General von Stein, thence to Gommecourt. The air forces, now augmented, were reorganized for distant and near reconnaissance, registration of artillery targets, air fighting, and bombing. The Germans, in fact, turned to good account the few days' respite accorded them. On the 5th July General von Below reported to O.H.L. that he was improving his defences and would hold on, deferring counter-attacks until the situation cleared : he anticipated further attempts to break through.

Crown Prince Rupprecht (commanding the *Sixth Army*) was anxious to help the defence by sending any reinforcements he could spare ; but several days elapsed before the Supreme Command abandoned its belief that the *Sixth Army* was threatened. Late on the 3rd July, however, the *183rd Division* was ordered to follow the *3rd Guard Division*, already sent to the *Second Army*, and Rupprecht was told to select another division to join the general reserve.

[1] G.O.A. (x., p. 355), remarks that Falkenhayn did not cancel the withdrawal although he knew of it in time to do so. Rupprecht states that Grünert's great offence was that he had foreseen the British attack against the *Second Army*, and asked for reinforcements accordingly ; these had been refused by O.H.L., who were convinced that the blow would fall on Rupprecht's *Sixth Army* (Arras—Armentières).

CHAPTER II

7TH–13TH JULY 1916

THE BATTLE OF ALBERT (*concluded*)

(Sketches A, 4, 7, 8, 9, 10)

7TH JULY : MAMETZ WOOD, CONTALMAISON, OVILLERS

BELYING the promise of the early morning, heavy showers set in on the 7th July, with a variable wind. Weather conditions were too bad to allow of much co-operation from the air. The trenches became knee-deep, in some places waist-deep, in clinging slime, and, under shellfire, collapsed beyond recognition. Movement was often an agony : men fainted from sheer exhaustion whilst struggling through deep mud ; in some localities a team of fourteen horses was required to bring up a single ammunition wagon. Under such handicaps, the advance of reinforcements and the circulation of orders suffered grave delay ; and on many occasions artillery barrages were called for in vain, so frequently did hostile bombardments cut telephone lines in the forward area where there had been no time to bury them.

The British right was waiting upon the French, who could not be ready until the 8th, so the XIII. Corps took no part Sketch 7. in the day's fighting. The failure to achieve the general objective—the occupation of Mametz Wood, Contalmaison, and Ovillers, thereby closing up to the German 2nd Position —was partly due to the defeat of a preliminary night attack. This operation aimed at securing favourable assault positions west of Mametz Wood and south of Contalmaison before the combined attack of the XV., III., and part of the X. Corps was launched at 8 A.M.

It was considered by the XV. Corps that the attacks

28

SKETCH 7.

THE SOMME, 1916.
7TH JULY.

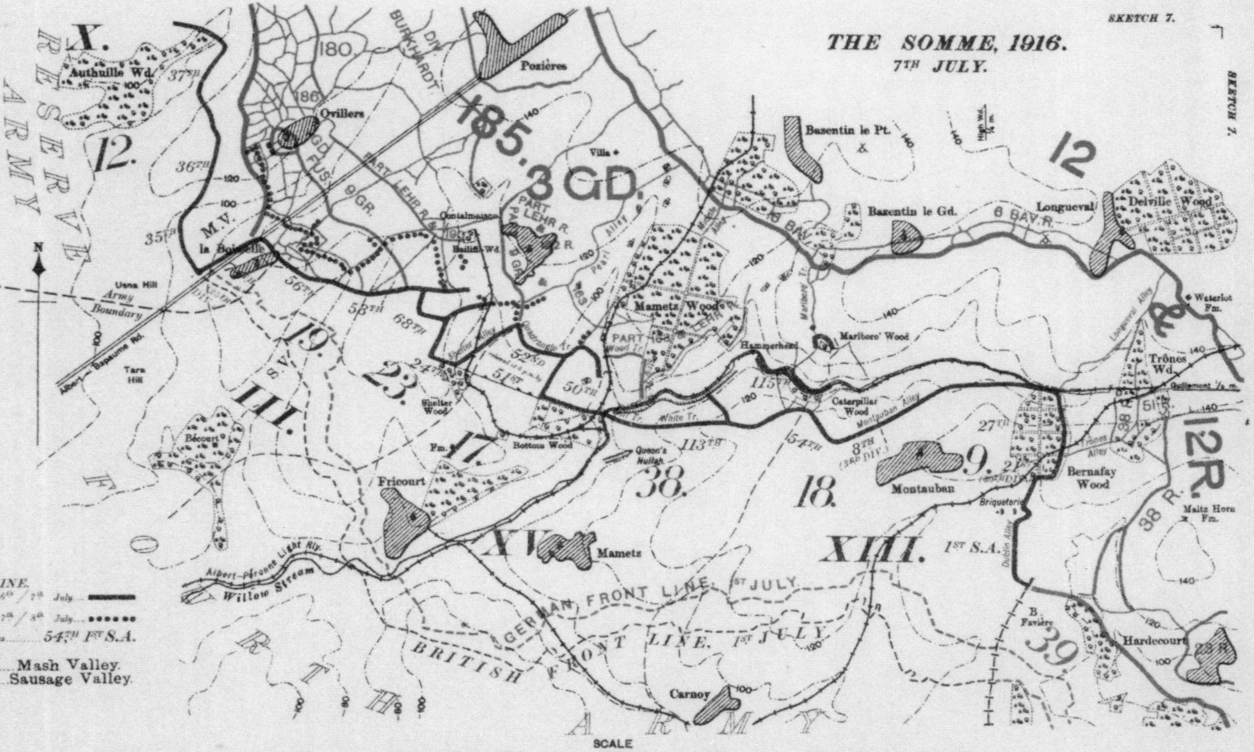

SCALE

Heights in metres

YARDS 1000

5000 YARDS

BRITISH LINE.
Night, 6th / 7th July.
Brigades. 54TH / 1ST S.A.

M.V.... Mash Valley.
S.V.... Sausage Valley.

3100/31. 3060/38.

Ordnance Survey, 1930.

upon Mametz Wood and Contalmaison would be greatly 7 July. facilitated if possession were first gained of the two German trenches which formed a re-entrant in the intervening valley : these were Quadrangle Support Trench (about 500 yards north of Quadrangle Trench) and that portion of Pearl Alley running forward from it. As the ground was quite open and it was very difficult for the artillery to range on Quadrangle Support—when entered it was found to be almost undamaged and the wire uncut—the 17th Division was ordered by General Horne to capture the two trenches by a night advance at 2 A.M. Major-General Pilcher and his subordinate commanders represented, in vain, that even if the trenches were captured they could not be held whilst under the cross-fire of the machine-guns in Mametz Wood and Contalmaison.

After a 35 minutes' bombardment which included Contalmaison and became intense for the last ten minutes, the attack was made at the appointed hour. Moving out when the guns quickened their rate of fire, the 9/Northumberland Fusiliers and 10/Lancashire Fusiliers of the 52nd Brigade (Br.-General J. L. J. Clarke), with the 10/Sherwood Foresters (51st Brigade) in support, soon found that the Germans were roused and ready. Flares and light-balls lit up the darkness, heavy rifle and machine-gun fire opened, and a defensive barrage came down. The leading waves of the Northumberland Fusiliers and the right of the Lancashire Fusiliers had been hindered in their advance by the many British shells which fell short ; when they reached the German wire they found it intact. They fell back, then tried again with no better fortune, and eventually withdrew as best they could. The left of the Lancashire Fusiliers, however, entered Pearl Alley—a shallow communication trench, lightly held—and some parties, drifting farther to the left in the dark and effecting something of a surprise, entered Contalmaison. Few in numbers, they were driven out by a counter-attack of the *Lehr Regiment* and bombers of the *9th Grenadiers*.[1] The hold on Pearl Alley was lost later.

The Germans then attempted to counter-attack from

[1] Originally the *Lehr Regiment* was a battalion maintained in peacetime as an instructional unit to which were drafted selected men from the whole Prussian Army, in order to ensure uniformity of training ; it ceased to be required for this purpose and became the Kaiser's bodyguard at Potsdam, being used to exhibit to him new equipment, drill, etc. Somme-Nord i., p. 175, states that the *9th Grenadiers* lost nearly the whole of one company in Contalmaison.

7 July. the eastern side of Contalmaison against the shoulder of the
salient held by the 17th Division.   They were driven off,
but fighting continued at close range until 7 A.M. and
greatly interfered with preparations for the main attack.

Provision had been made in the XV Corps artillery
orders to meet the contingency of a failure of the night
advance.   In that event the preliminary bombardment due
to be fired from 7.20 to 8 A.M. for the main operation was
to be continued for another 30 minutes, and all lifts and
movements were to be made half an hour later.   The III.
Corps, which had definitely ordered its assault to be delivered at 8 A.M., received notice at 6.15 A.M. that these
changes would be made in the XV. Corps programme, but
that General Horne had ordered the 17th Division to try
again for its preliminary objective at 8 A.M.

The whole front of attack had been heavily bombarded
during the afternoon of the 6th, and intense fire was opened
punctually at 7.20 A.M.   The Germans, now thoroughly
alert, placed a barrage upon the trenches from which the
night attack had started.   From Mametz Wood to Ovillers
their line was held by a new division [1] which had carried out
the relief with great difficulty and considerable loss owing
to the accuracy of the British artillery fire.

The corps order for the renewed attack had been
received by the 17th Division at 5.25 A.M., but great difficulty was experienced in preparing for it as telephone
communications forward of brigade headquarters could not
be relied on.   The 52nd Brigade was again employed,
Br.-General Clarke now detailing the 12/Manchester and
9/Duke of Wellington's ; but only two companies of the
Duke's could get forward in time. [2]   Even so, the attack
was a few minutes late in starting, with the consequence
that the barrage lifted from the German front trenches
before the troops were within assaulting distance. [3]
Machine-gun fire, most of it from Mametz Wood on the
right, cut down the first wave of the attack and the second
struggled forward to meet a like fate : in broad daylight
the two battalions had no chance of reaching Quadrangle
Support over bare and open ground.   The survivors were
brought back, Lieut.-Colonel E. G. Harrison of the Man-

---

[1] The *3rd Guard Division* with two regiments, *163rd (17th Reserve
Division)* and *183rd (183rd Division)*, attached.
[2] By some misunderstanding this battalion was told that the operation
was cancelled, and only received orders to proceed at 7.25 A.M.
[3] The XV. Corps artillery lifted from one trench to another, but the
infantry had been told to get as close as possible before each lift.

chester being wounded whilst superintending the with- 7 July.
drawal.   Only a few small posts remained out, and these
were engaged all day with the enemy's bombing parties.

Farther to the right the 7/E. Yorkshire of the 50th
Brigade (Br.-General W. J. T. Glasgow) had sent forward
its bombers to work up Quadrangle Alley which led back
into Mametz Wood from Quadrangle Trench.[1]   They were
driven back, and a company of the 6/Dorset, which
attempted to advance against the western face of Mametz
Wood, was caught by machine-gun fire from Strip Trench
and lost half its numbers.

The 38th Division attacked Mametz Wood [2] at 8.30
A.M., the 115th Brigade (Br.-General H. J. Evans) advancing north-westward across the valley from the line
Marlboro' Wood—western end of Caterpillar Wood.   Owing
to the high wind, smoke could not be used to screen the
movement, which was, however, well supported by trench-
mortar and machine-gun fire ;   but the 16/Welch and
11/S. Wales Borderers were soon held up by the machine-
gun defence.   Renewed attempts, after fresh bombardment, were made at 10.15 A.M. and at 3.15 P.M., the 10/S.
Wales Borderers reinforcing the attack ;   yet the Welshmen
could not get within 250 yards of the wood, owing to
enfilade machine-gun fire from higher up the valley to the
north.

The XV. Corps had ordered a renewed attack by both
divisions for 5 P.M.   Although rain and mud added to the
usual difficulties of communication, the artillery fulfilled its
part, but the 50th Brigade of the 17th Division could not
be organized in time.   The advance was therefore postponed until 6.30 P.M. and eventually began at 8 P.M. when
the Dorset and E. Yorkshire went forward, the 10th
Sherwood Foresters, of the 51st Brigade (Br.-General G.
F. Trotter) which had replaced the 52nd on the left,
attacking at the same time.   As they struggled through the
mud, the leading lines of all three battalions were smitten by
machine-gun fire from the front and from both flanks and
were caught by a hostile artillery barrage.   There was no
hope of success, so the operation was abandoned with a total
loss of nearly 400 officers and men.   The 115th Brigade of
the 38th Division was not ready in time to take advantage

[1] Mametz Wood had been bombarded at 5.30 A.M. with gas shell, not
yet available in the British Army, by a " groupe " of French field batteries.
[2] Defended by the *II/Lehr Regiment* (*3rd Guard Division*) and *II/163rd*.
The *III/16th Bavarians* (*10th Bavarian Division*), in support, is said to
have made a counter-attack.

of the bombardment, and Major-General Philipps eventually ordered the brigade to withdraw, two companies of the
17/R. Welch Fusiliers being left to hold the Marlboro' Wood
—Caterpillar Wood position.

Thus the XV. Corps, which was to have advanced its
line to the northern edge of Mametz Wood, had accomplished
nothing.

In the III. Corps the assaults of the 23rd and 19th
Divisions, fixed for 8 A.M., were not simultaneous. The
plans of the former division were upset by the failure of the
17th, in its night attack, to retain a hold on Pearl Alley
which the 24th Brigade was to have taken over and used
as a " jumping-off " trench. The 19th Division, on the
left, therefore started first, after waiting a quarter of an
hour.

Its objective was a trench running from Bailiff Wood
south-west and then west, and another which led towards
the north-eastern end of La Boisselle,[1] involving an advance
of some 600 yards on the right and half that distance on the
left. With patrols and bombers leading, the 9/Welch
(58th Brigade, Br.-General A. J. W. Dowell) and 7/King's
Own (56th Brigade, Br.-General F. G. M. Rowley) moved
forward behind a barrage, carrying out to the letter their
instructions to " approach the objective as near as possible
" before the bombardment lifts".[2] The British bombardment was accurate and effective, but owing to some mistake
in the timing the infantry ran into the barrage almost at
once, and considerable loss and disorganization ensued.
Fortunately communications held, so that the lines of fire
could be adjusted without much delay, and the advance
was restarted at 9.15 A.M. after reinforcement by the
6/Wiltshire of the 58th Brigade. The three battalions then
rushed the whole of their objective, capturing over 400
Germans belonging to six different regiments and five
different divisions.[3] The dead lay thick at the dug-out
entrances which seemed to show that those who had been
first to leave cover were caught by the British barrage.

[1] The village had been taken over by the 12th Division (X Corps,
Reserve Army) during the previous night.
[2] In the III. Corps the field artillery lifted back slowly 100 yards at a
time, different batteries being detailed to lengthen their range in succession.
[3] *185th, 190th* (*185th Division*) ; *110th Reserve* (*28th Reserve Division*) ;
23rd (*12th Division*) ; *95th* (*38th Division,* hitherto believed to be before
Verdun) ; *210th Reserve* (*45th Reserve Division,* believed to be at Messines).
Somme-Nord states that the trenches were flattened out by the British
bombardment and the defenders retired on Pozières, suffering heavy loss
and leaving their wounded behind.

Consolidation began forthwith, the infantry being heartened by the quick appearance on the scene, in spite of the mud, of the 56th Machine Gun Company. The 9/R. Welch Fusiliers (58th Brigade) was brought up to secure the right flank where there was no sign of the 23rd Division. This success had cost the two brigades less than 600 casualties, most of them wounded.

Next to the 19th Division the 68th Brigade (Br.-General H. P. Croft), of the 23rd Division, was to advance when the 24th Brigade came up on its right. Actually, in order to avoid running into the heavy artillery barrage which was to lift from the objective, Bailiff Wood, at 9.30 A.M., Br.-General Croft delayed the attack of the 11/Northumberland Fusiliers until 9.15 A.M. The Fusiliers started well and their leading companies reached the southern end of the wood, in the valley, capturing some Germans ; but here they were exposed to such heavy machine-gun fire from Contalmaison and from the north that they had to be withdrawn 400 yards. In an endeavour to link up with the 19th Division the 12/Durham L.I. was then brought forward to occupy a trench on the higher ground to the left, and this was done gradually under heavy fire.

The 24th Brigade which was to carry Contalmaison[1] had ordered the 1/Worcestershire and 2/E. Lancashire to advance from the vicinity of Shelter Wood when the 52nd Brigade, at 8 A.M., made its second attempt to secure Pearl Alley. Br.-General Oxley's orders, sent by runner to his battalions, were delayed in transit, and the movement of the troops, up trenches deep in mud and blocked by dead and wounded, proved very slow. Eventually, soon after 10 A.M., the Worcestershire deployed over the open and advanced from the southern end of Pearl Alley, the E. Lancashire coming forward on their left, from Shelter Wood, at the same time. In spite of the German machine guns the Worcestershire breasted the slope and forced their way into Contalmaison, clearing the ruins as far as the church after a struggle which lasted half an hour. Many prisoners were taken from dug-outs and two counter-attacks were repulsed,[2] but hand-to-hand fighting continued whilst the German gunners shelled the whole village indis-

---

[1] Held by the *II/9th Grenadiers* and *III/163rd Regiment*.
[2] The first delivered by one company of the *122nd Reserve* (*183rd Division*) and the second by another company and one of the *9th Grenadiers*. According to Somme-Nord the British batteries had wrought great havoc, and two companies of the *122nd Reserve* sent up as reinforcements dissolved in panic under artillery fire.

criminately. Meanwhile the advance of the East Lancashire on lower ground was much impeded by the mud and
a heavy rain-storm, and came under accurate machine-gun
fire from Contalmaison and Bailiff Wood. Little progress
could be made,[1] and the efforts of the 2/Northamptonshire
to support the East Lancashire in their efforts to reach
Contalmaison were of no avail. Amid the ruins of the village three companies of the Worcestershire carried on the
struggle throughout the afternoon but were obliged to fall
back when their supply of bombs and ammunition failed.

Lieut.-General Pulteney desired that a renewed assault
should be made upon Bailiff Wood and Contalmaison at
8 P.M., when the 17th Division was to advance again ; but
the deep mud, the heavy German barrage, and the absence
of fresh troops made the enterprise impossible. The 68th
Brigade established a line facing Contalmaison on the west,
in touch with the 24th Brigade in its positions south of the
village ; this was as much as could be done. The three battalions of the 24th Brigade had lost nearly 800 officers and
men, nearly half of them belonging to the Worcestershire.

In the Reserve Army, the X. Corps which was to attack
Ovillers at 8 A.M. was itself attacked before the hour of
assault. A heavy bombardment of the 49th Division front
near the Ancre lasted from 12.30 A.M. to 2.30 A.M., when
fire was concentrated upon the British lodgment north of
Thiepval and the communications to it. A furious onslaught, in which the Germans used the new light " egg "
bomb which could easily be thrown 50 yards, then took
heavy toll of the garrison, two companies of the 1/4th
K.O.Y.L.I. (148th Brigade) reinforced later by two of the
1/5th Battalion. Bombing parties of the 1/5th York &
Lancaster were then sent forward, but soon after 6 A.M. all
the survivors were obliged to withdraw to their old front
line. It was too misty for the artillery to help them except
by firing on its prearranged S.O.S. lines.[2] The enemy

---

[1] A shell which fell on battalion headquarters in Shelter Alley buried
Lieut.-Colonel G. E. M. Hill and his adjutant, and killed or wounded the
rest of the staff.

[2] The Germans had employed " storm troops " (see Note III at end of
Chapter) of the *185th, 15th Reserve* and *8th Bavarian Reserve Regiments.*
Such was the confusion of units on this day that the *10th Bavarian Division*
was broken up, and its commander, Major-General Burkhardt put in com-
mand of a composite division comprising the *8th Bavarian Reserve* (*10th
Bavarian Division*) ; two battalions of the *15th Reserve* (*2nd Guard Reserve
Division* ; *185th* and one battalion *186th* (*185th Division*). General Burk-
hardt took over the front between Ovillers and the Ancre from the *26th
Reserve Division.*

attacked at the Leipzig salient at 1.15 A.M., trying to rush 7 July.
the position, held by the 7th Brigade (25th Division), from
front and flanks. He was beaten off by the 1/Wiltshire,
assisted by field artillery fire, but there followed a bombing
contest which lasted for two hours and continued inter-
mittently until 5.30 A.M. Despite the confusion and tur-
moil an attack which had been already planned was carried
out by two companies of the Wiltshire which completed the
capture of the German front line in the Leipzig salient,
and held it, with the assistance of the 3/Worcestershire,
under a very severe bombardment.[1]

General Gough's orders were for the capture of Ovillers Sketch 7.
and then for an advance of 500 yards farther eastward,
linking up with the 19th Division (Fourth Army) at each
stage. There was to be an hour's preliminary bombardment, and arrangements were made for an extensive discharge of smoke in order to conceal the actual front of
attack. The first assault was to be delivered at 8 A.M. by
the 74th Brigade (Br.-General G. A. Armytage)[2] from the
south across the head of Mash Valley ; half an hour later
the 36th Brigade (Br.-General L. B. Boyd-Moss) would
come in from the west, starting from trenches dug in No
Man's Land 300 yards from the enemy and behind the crest
of the long flat slope which stretches westward to the
Ancre.

The smoke screen failed to act in the absence of sufficient
breeze and merely served to draw artillery fire ; but at the
appointed time, when the British guns were still bombarding
Ovillers, the 9/L.N. Lancashire and 13/Cheshire began the
advance of the 74th Brigade. They reached the first
German trench, where a pause was to be made, but so many
officers and N.C.O.'s of the leading companies had been hit
that, in the face of galling machine-gun fire, no further
movement developed. Stirred to action, the German artillery had already placed a heavy barrage on the assembly
trenches of the 36th Brigade where the losses of the 8/R.
Fusiliers, 7/R. Sussex and 9/R. Fusiliers totalled nearly
three hundred. Nevertheless, at 8.30 A.M., the attack was
made with fine determination close behind the British
barrage. After a furious melée Sussex and Fusiliers carried
the first three lines of German trenches at Ovillers, all of

---

[1] Two companies of the *Guard Fusiliers* (*3rd Guard Division*) and one
of the *185th Regiment* reinforced by four more were engaged. All suffered
heavy losses.
[2] 25th Division, attached 12th Division.

7 July. them deep in mud.   Many prisoners [1] were collected from
the dug-outs, for the rapidity with which the assault had
followed the lifting of the barrage had taken the enemy by
surprise.

To gain this footing in Ovillers, which had hitherto
resisted all attacks and was considered by the German
troops to be impregnable,[2] had cost the three battalions
over 1,400 in killed and wounded.   The survivors were too
few to hold the front position, so the shattered line of the
second German trench was consolidated, with outposts
beyond : as the 74th Brigade had not come on, nothing
more could be attempted.   Rain in the afternoon hindered
work and made more difficult the getting forward of supplies
and the evacuation of the wounded.   During the night
Major-General Scott linked up the forward lines of the two
brigades by an advance of the 8/S. Lancashire (75th
Brigade) which was unopposed.

During his visit to General Rawlinson in the afternoon,
when further attacks upon Mametz Wood were pending, Sir
Douglas Haig merely mentioned Pozières as the direction in
which the left of the Fourth Army should press.   When he
reached Reserve Army headquarters and learnt that only
a footing had been gained in Ovillers, he told General Gough
to complete the capture of the village as soon as possible
and join up at La Boisselle with the III. Corps.   In the
evening the Commander-in-Chief took measures to reinforce
the battle front.   He ordered the Anzac Corps, with the 1st
and 2nd Australian Divisions, from the Second Army to
G.H.Q. reserve in the Fourth Army area, the 4th Australian
Division to be held in readiness to follow ;   the 36th
Division to the Second Army ;   the 33rd Division from the
First Army to the II. Corps of the Fourth Army ;   and the
51st Division to G.H.Q. reserve, after it had been relieved
on the Third Army front.   The process of relieving battle-
weary divisions by exchange with formations from quieter
parts of the front was now in operation and continued until
the close of the offensive.

---

[1] Some of them belonged to the *186th Regiment*, holding the left of
Burkhardt's sector.   Somme-Nord states that the *Guard Fusiliers* were
in Ovillers, the *II Battalion*, with a company of the *180th Recruit Battalion*,
being in front of the village.   The Germans, having sustained very heavy
losses, are said to have retreated to a line passing through the ruins of the
church.

[2] So prisoners declared.   One who was no stranger to hard fighting
said " Galicia was bad, Verdun was worse, but this is the worst of all ".

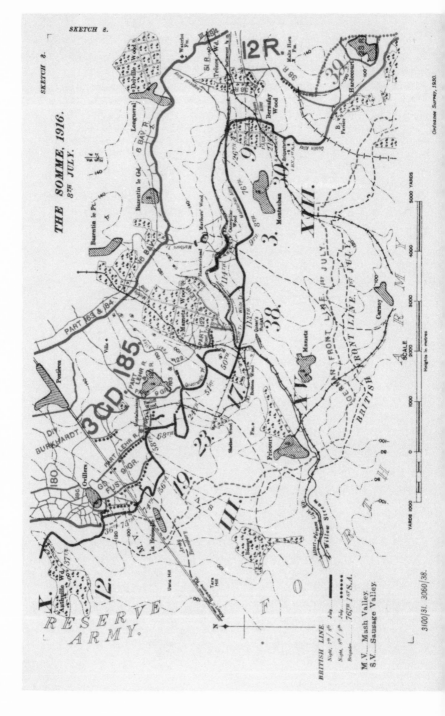

SKETCH 8.

THE SOMME, 1916.
8TH JULY.

Ordnance Survey, 1930.

BRITISH LINE
Night, 1ST / 2ND July.
Night, 8TH / 9TH July.
Brigade.
76TH 1ST S.A.

M.V. ... Mash Valley.
S.V. ... Sausage Valley.

SCALE
Heights in metres

3100/31. 3060/38.

8TH JULY : FIRST ATTACKS ON TRÔNES WOOD

After a wet night the 8th July was fine and warm, but mud still proved a hindrance to movement. The R.F.C. was active in reconnaissance and took a number of photographs ; many hostile aircraft could be seen but they made no attempt to cross the British lines. Of chief importance on this day is the advance of the British right, in combination with the French, and the fighting which ensued in the neighbourhood of Trônes Wood.

Facing Longueval, in the German 2nd Position, Trônes **Sketch 8.** Wood stretches down the southern slope of Caterpillar Valley [1] as far as the foot of its northern slope ; east of the wood the valley extends as a shallow trough to Guillemont, which was also in the 2nd Position. Thus the wood was commanded at close range both from the north and the east, and there was little chance of holding it whilst the enemy sat in Longueval and Guillemont. Captured it might be, at a price, but only by permission of the Germans could it be held.

The Allied attack, starting at 8 A.M., was to be in two stages. First the French would capture the trench, " Maltz Horn Trench ", covering the knoll north of Hardecourt, whilst the British secured the continuation of this trench as far as Trônes Wood and the southern half of the wood itself, " as far as the railway line ". So much, it was hoped, would be accomplished by 9.45 A.M. ; at an hour to be agreed upon by the divisional commanders concerned, the French would attack Hardecourt village and knoll and the British Maltz Horn Farm of which there remained only a few heaps of rubble. After some discussion Lieut.-General Congreve issued an order at 8 A.M., the hour at which the first assault was to be delivered, for the completion of the capture of Trônes Wood in the second stage.

The re-entrant at the junction of the two Armies presented a problem of its own. To make the attack truly " jointive ", as the French desired, the British would have to advance from La Briqueterie to Maltz Horn Farm across 1,100–1,500 yards of open fire-swept ground : opposite the French, No Man's Land was only 300 yards wide. It was therefore decided to secure the southern half of Trônes Wood as a preliminary operation, since part of the approach

[1] Running from Guillemont westward by Caterpillar Wood and then south-westward to Fricourt.

8 July. thereto from the southern part of Bernafay Wood was not exposed to view from Longueval, although it was commanded by Maltz Horn Trench. The attack on Maltz Horn farm and trench could then be made south-eastward across the shallow head of the Maltz Horn valley which was entirely hidden from the German 2nd Position.

In the early hours of the 8th the objectives were bombarded by the XIII. Corps heavy artillery and the batteries of the 30th Division, the 18th Division artillery firing on the southern edge of Longueval. The 2/Green Howards, of the 21st Brigade (Br.-General Hon. C. J. Sackville-West),[1] which formed up for the assault behind Bernafay Wood [2] moved through the wood at 7.15 A.M., being much impeded by fallen trees and thick undergrowth and subjected to considerable shell fire.

At 8 A.M. the leading company, with the battalion bombers, advanced from the eastern edge, covered by the fire of the 26th Brigade (9th Division) from the left flank. The way to Trônes Wood led across a slight crest, and when they had breasted this rise the assailants were shelled by two field guns, firing over open sights, whilst machine-gun fire from the wood began to do great execution among them.[3] The advance was checked, although attempts were made to bomb along Trônes Alley and so into the wood ; some men, in a gallant rush over the open, reached the edge, but they were not seen again. The Green Howards were now withdrawn, and the 2/Wiltshire was ordered to renew the attack at 10.30 A.M. ; the brigadier, however, secured a postponement until 1 P.M.

The French (39th Division of General Balfourier's XX. Corps) attacked at 10.5 A.M., and carried Maltz Horn Trench, the position of their flank being reported as opposite the farm, and exposed to machine-gun fire from Trônes Wood.[4] Thereupon Lieut.-General Congreve ordered the 30th Division to attack from La Briqueterie, so as to

---

[1] The brigade belonged to the 30th Division which had taken over the attack frontage next to the French.

[2] Bernafay Wood was held by the 9th Division.

[3] The edge of the wood was held by five companies of the *38th Reserve Regiment* (*12th Reserve Division*) with a number of machine-gun posts, some on platforms in trees. In support was the *51st Reserve Regiment*, and during the day the *III./184th* (*183rd Division*) was used to reinforce the troops holding the wood, which had not been organized for defence. The main line of resistance was now the 2nd Position.

[4] German accounts attribute the success of the French to heavy artillery fire : before the assault the *III./123rd Reserve* is said to have been reduced to 2 officers and 150 others.

cover the French left, and also to secure Trônes Wood : 8 July. Major-General Shea was told about 12.20 P.M. that this must be done even if he had to employ his whole division. Meanwhile a company of the Wiltshire had started from La Briqueterie, and, by means of a sunken road, gained the head of the Maltz Horn valley. Covered by artillery and machine-gun fire, it was then able to work its way down the slope into Maltz Horn Trench with little opposition, the Germans who were not killed or captured withdrawing to the farm.[1] A counter-attack was repulsed later, and the enemy then began to dig rifle pits on the reverse slope of the Hardecourt knoll, leaving the farm, a shell-swept heap, between the opposing lines. During the afternoon the Wiltshire company was reinforced by one of the 19/Manchester which arrived by the same route, and linked up with the French.

About 1 P.M. a fresh advance from Bernafay Wood had been attempted by the remaining companies of the Wiltshire, led by Lieut.-Colonel R. M. T. Gillson.[2] In spite of heavy losses, especially in officers, they managed to reach and then entrench a position along the south-eastern edge of Trônes. The wood itself presented an immense obstacle, for its undergrowth, which had not been cut for two years, formed dense thickets, and there was a chaotic tangle of trees and branches brought down by the bombardment. German communication trenches, and a few clearings through which ran light-railway tracks, formed the only easy lines of passage ; it was all but impossible to keep direction without a compass bearing. Whilst the German artillery shelled the south-eastern corner and the approaches to it, the Wiltshire dug a line facing north through the wood to protect their flank. Two companies of the 18/King's and one of the 19/Manchester, which had managed to come up, helped to consolidate the position ; and when darkness fell a further reinforcement arrived in the shape of the 18/Manchester of the 90th Brigade.[3] Major-General Shea had intended to relieve the 21st by the 90th Brigade after the capture of Trônes Wood : he now had no option but to

---

[1] The French had assisted this movement, as soon as they perceived it, by bombing northward up the trench.

[2] He was severely wounded by a sniper after the wood had been entered. An hour later Captain F. R. Mumford, the next senior officer, was killed and Lieut.-Colonel Gillson resumed command until 3.30 P.M., when he handed over to a subaltern.

[3] A shell which caught the headquarters of the 21st Brigade, 500 yards west of La Briqueterie, killed Lieut.-Colonel E. H. Trotter, 18/King's, and Lieut.-Colonel W. A. Smith, 18/Manchester.

8 July. order the 90th to renew the attack upon it before dawn next morning.

During the night the 3rd Division (Major-General J. A. L. Haldane) completed the relief of the 18th which had been in the line since the opening of the offensive and had lost over 3,400 of all ranks, the great majority being wounded.

In the XV. Corps, from 6 A.M. onwards, the bombers of the 50th and 51st Brigades (17th Division) had endeavoured to press forward from Quadrangle Trench and Pearl Alley ; but the enemy fought stubbornly in the trenches which were knee-deep in mud.   In spite of the most determined efforts little progress was made, and at 10 A.M. Major-General Pilcher was ordered by the corps to co-operate in the afternoon attack of the III. Corps by making a fresh attempt upon Quadrangle Support.   Later it transpired that Lieut.-General Pulteney had no such operation in view, so the 17th Division was called upon to attack alone. After a bombardment of 25 minutes, parties of the 7/E. Yorkshire, 7/Green Howards and 6/Dorset (all 50th Brigade), with bombers of the other two brigades, made another start at 5.50 P.M., but again without much success. The division was then called upon to gain a footing in Wood Trench to protect the left of the 38th Division which had received orders to attack Mametz Wood after dark.   Advancing at 8.50 P.M., a company of the Dorset secured two-thirds of the trench without much trouble, and then dug back to Quadrangle Trench.   The enemy did not interfere, but there was no sign of the Welshmen on the right.

In confirmation of verbal instructions given to Major-General Philipps by Lieut.-General Horne, a corps order issued at 1.40 P.M. had directed the 38th Division to secure the southern salient of Mametz Wood under cover of darkness, and be ready to push northward through the wood next day.   During the afternoon it was several times reported that the Germans had withdrawn, but Welsh patrols which went out to investigate drew heavy fire. The division fixed the time of attack for 2 A.M., ordering the 113th Brigade (Br.-General L. A. E. Price-Davies) to make it with one solitary platoon, which was provided by the 14/R. Welch Fusiliers.   Shortly after 3 A.M., however, the officer commanding this platoon reported that owing to the congestion in the mud-filled trenches his party had been obliged to take to the open, but even then found it impossible to reach the starting-point in the darkness over ground pitted with shell-holes and littered with loose wire.

The III. Corps ordered the 23rd Division to bomb 8 July. towards Contalmaison and to fill the gap of 400 yards which existed between the forward positions of the 24th and 68th Brigades. To attack up the trenches, however, proved almost impossible, for the mud was still so deep that many men stuck fast and could not extricate themselves without assistance. Patrols found the enemy alert in Contalmaison and Bailiff Wood despite persistent rumours that he had evacuated both localities. The 24th Brigade made another attempt to capture Contalmaison, using the two companies of the 1/Worcestershire which had suffered least on the previous day. Made in the evening, the advance was stopped by machine-gun fire and a heavy barrage. The 2/Northamptonshire was likewise checked on emerging from Peake Woods, half way between Shelter Wood and Contalmaison, to link up with the forward line of the 68th Brigade.

Of the 19th Division only the bombers had been engaged during the day, but at 6 P.M., after warning had been received from the air, a movement of German troops from Contalmaison towards Bailiff Wood was stopped by rifle and machine-gun fire. Later, an advance of the left was ordered, to co-operate with an attack of the 12th Division (X. Corps). The objective, nearly a thousand yards ahead, was a German trench which ran into the northern end of Ovillers, and this fell, after little opposition, to the 13/Royal Fusiliers, one of the two battalions of the 111th Brigade (34th Division) attached to the 56th as a step towards its relief. Consolidation proceeded, and during the night the 58th Brigade on the right was relieved by the 112th Brigade.[1]

The Reserve Army continued its efforts to complete the capture of Ovillers. From 3.45 A.M. onwards the 12th Division tried to bomb forward, but the troops were impeded, here as elsewhere, by the deep and clinging mud. The 36th Brigade at the edge of Ovillers had been reinforced during the night by the 7/E. Surrey (37th Brigade) and 9/Essex (35th Brigade), and by great exertions an advance of 200 yards into the ruins was made, with the loss, among others, of Major C. I. Ryan, commanding the Essex. From the valley to the south-east the 2/R. Irish Rifles and 13/Cheshire of the 74th Brigade, with the 8/S. Lancashire (75th Brigade) on the left, bombed forward up the communication trenches ; then, turning right, they secured the trench which ran towards Ovillers church.

[1] See page 13, f.n. 2, for the composition of the reconstituted 34th Division.

8 July.   At 8 P.M. the 74th Brigade renewed its attack, having received orders to capture the next German trench, the left portion of the objective attacked at the same time by the 19th Division as already related. A company of the 11/Lancashire Fusiliers advanced quietly and effected a surprise ; but by mistake, it pressed on to another trench, 600 yards ahead, meeting with little resistance and taking some prisoners. It reported by lamp-signal that the objective was secured, whereupon a company of the 2/R. Irish Rifles was sent forward to consolidate, and joined the Fusiliers in the forward trench which was under British artillery fire. When the situation became known the barrage was adjusted and the 13/Cheshire was despatched to occupy the trench which had been passed over.

A general impression prevailed among the troops that Pozières could have been entered on this night, or at any rate, Ovillers cut off from the rear : it is certain that the Albert—Bapaume road area, opposite the junction of the Fourth and Reserve Armies, was at this moment the most vulnerable part of the German defence. Here the enemy feared a break-through,[1] but such a situation had not been foreseen by the British, and they were not ready to exploit it. It must be admitted that the deep mud was all in favour of the defence.

Before morning the 14th Brigade of the 32nd Division had completed the relief of the troops of the 12th Division in Ovillers, and command of the sector passed to Major-General Rycroft.[2]   The line taken over was only a series of craters linked up by sapping, but good cover was found for the supports in the old German dug-outs.

Sir Douglas Haig, who visited both his Army commanders during the day, was chiefly concerned with the situation at Mametz Wood. General Rawlinson reported to him that the leading of some of the higher commands was unsatisfactory, with the result that the officers in question were soon afterwards replaced.

At 5.30 P.M. a Fourth Army conference of corps and corps artillery commanders was held to discuss the next operation, and also the attack on the enemy's 2nd Position, Longueval—Bazentin le Petit. General Rawlinson issued the operation order for the latter but left the date to be

---

[1] See Note II. at end of Chapter.
[2] The casualties of the 12th Division, since 1st July, amounted to 4,721 officers and men.

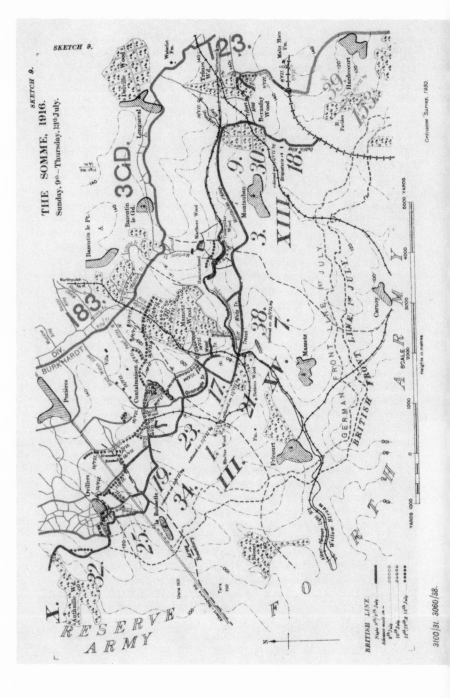

SKETCH 9.

THE SOMME, 1916.
Sunday, 9th — Thursday, 13th July.

SKETCH 9.

Ordnance Survey, 1930.

BRITISH LINE
Night 9th/10th July
Advances made on —
9th July
10th July
11th/12th & 13th July

SCALE

YARDS 1000   0   1000   2000   3000   4000   5000 YARDS

Heights in metres

3100/31. 3060/38.

fixed later, as it depended upon the preliminary operations and also upon the weather. He was determined not to launch the main attack unless conditions were sufficiently good to profit by the advantages of British superiority in the air.

9TH–13TH JULY

TRÔNES WOOD : CAPTURE OF MAMETZ WOOD : CAPTURE OF CONTALMAISON

From the 9th to the 13th July the weather was fine and grew cooler. Conditions now generally favoured offensive operations, but cases of " trench feet " had already occurred among men who had stood in mud and water, with little chance, for several days, of taking off their boots.

The R.F.C. was able to give more assistance to the heavy batteries in the registration of targets, and carried out bombing raids against railway centres, dumps, bivouacs, Sketch A. and headquarters in the area Cambrai—Havrincourt Wood (5½ miles S.E. of Beugny)—Bapaume—Le Sars—Le Transloy. On the 13th, British machines took advantage of low clouds to attack two trains approaching Cambrai and derailed one of them. Hostile craft made no attempt to cross the British lines, but displayed considerable activity in defence, so that there were many combats in the air.

In a series of visits to General Rawlinson and the three corps commanders of the Fourth Army Sir Douglas Haig discussed the plan of the Longueval-Bazentin attack. He was still insistent that Trônes Wood, of which only the southern extremity was held, should be secured to cover the right, and Mametz Wood and Contalmaison to cover the left, before the main attack was launched. It so happened that in these preliminary operations several days of hard and costly fighting did not achieve complete success ; yet, if the three localities had been included in the general attack against the German 2nd Position, they might, if stoutly defended, have disorganized the assault and destroyed its impetus before the main objectives were approached. Certain it is that some penalty had to be paid for the failure to take advantage of the opportunities which had offered themselves on this front immediately after the first day of the offensive.

The 30th Division renewed its attempts to secure Sketch 9. Trônes Wood at 3 A.M. on the 9th July, following a 40

9 July. minutes' bombardment by the right group of the divisional artillery and a portion of the corps heavy guns. The 2/R. Scots Fusiliers (90th Brigade) formed the right attack, which was completely successful, although the French did not move.[1] After reaching the centre of Maltz Horn Trench by a sunken road which led forward from La Briqueterie, the Fusiliers rushed the ruins of the farm with the loss of two men, and began to dig a trench along the western slope of the knoll, the French establishing a post in order to link up with the new British right. The Fusiliers also bombed northward up Maltz Horn Trench, and, after a brisk fight, captured 109 men of the *38th Reserve Regiment.* By 7 A.M. the whole trench as far as its intersection with a track leading to Guillemont from the eastern side of the wood, together with a strongpoint situated there, was in British possession. The 2/Wiltshire was then relieved.[2]

The 17/Manchester was to have advanced from Bernafay Wood astride the light railway at 3 A.M. to clear the centre and northern portions of the wood. Owing to the gas shelling of Bernafay Wood, the troops had to wear their respirators, of which the eye-pieces became misted by a drizzling rain; direction was lost, and it was not until after 6 A.M. that the leading lines emerged into the open. Yet only a few shots were fired at them, and, after a tiring and exasperating struggle among the undergrowth, shell-holes, and fallen trees, the Manchester reached the eastern edge of the wood about 8 A.M. There they joined hands with the Scots Fusiliers and pushed patrols northward. Except for a few nests of Germans, Trônes Wood was now in British hands.

It was not long to remain so. The enemy began a systematic shelling of the wood and its western approaches : from 12.30 P.M. onwards fire was concentrated from a large number of German batteries deployed on a huge crescent from Maurepas (east of Hardecourt) to Bazentin le Grand. Only the southern part of the wood, which was sheltered by the lie of the ground, escaped. On the eastern edge the 17/Manchester suffered severely,[3] and, as the left flank of the battalion was unsecured and a counter-attack appeared to be imminent, at 3 P.M. a withdrawal to Bernafay Wood was ordered. The movement was carried out at

[1] See Note I. at end of Chapter.
[2] See page 39.
[3] Both brigade and battalion orders directed that a line should be taken up 10 yards inside, but the interior of the wood offered no field of view or fire.

once, but the messenger sent to recall one party of 40 men was killed and the party remained at its post. The retirement caused the 18/Manchester to fall back on La Briqueterie, leaving one company in the south-eastern corner of the wood, and the Scots Fusiliers then withdrew from Maltz Horn Trench and blocked it at a point just clear of the wood.

At 3.30 P.M. German troops[1] advanced to attack westward against the whole front line from Maltz Horn Farm to the northern end of Trônes. Opposite the Scots Fusiliers and the company of the 18/Manchester the enemy was driven off with considerable loss by rifle and machine-gun fire, assisted by an effective French barrage in which the 149th Brigade R.F.A. took part. North of the Guillemont track, however, the Germans were able to penetrate to the western side of the wood, the only opposition coming from the isolated party of the 17/Manchester which resisted stoutly until it was overwhelmed. The enemy artillery shelled Bernafay Wood and caused considerable loss to the troops assembled there, but the counter-attack was not carried farther.

On hearing of the retirement of the 17/Manchester Br.-General Steavenson called upon the 16/Manchester, which attacked northward from the sunken road east of La Briqueterie at 6.40 P.M. The battalion had orders to gain the southern part of the wood and cover the left of the Scots Fusiliers in Maltz Horn Trench; this was accomplished with slight loss, for the enemy were unprepared for such a flank movement. Owing to the activities of the German bombers and of snipers in trees it was thought best to occupy a line outside the wood for the night, and the 16/Manchester dug in about 60 yards from its south-western edge.

Patrols which endeavoured to advance northwards through the wood during the night found progress scarcely practicable, although few Germans were met; but after a 10 July. preliminary bombardment the battalion, assisted by a company of the 4th S. African Regiment (9th Division), went forward at 4 A.M. on the 10th, moving in groups of twenty men. Many lost their way, but some went on through the wood unopposed and returned to report it

---

[1] The *II./182nd Regiment* (*123rd Division*) which was fresh, and portions of the *38th Reserve* and *51st Reserve* (*12th Reserve Division* already engaged). The *II./182nd* had been delayed between Ginchy and Guillemont by an artillery barrage called for by British air observers.

10 July. clear of the enemy.   Farther west, bombing parties occupied a portion of Longueval Alley which led back from Bernafay Wood to the German 2nd Position via the northern apex of Trônes.   There was fighting at a small redoubt [1] in the trench, known as " Central Trench ", which ran up the centre of the wood, and in the midst of the prevailing confusion a long chain of Germans advanced from the east, captured several patrols and reoccupied the western edge. By 8 A.M. only the south-eastern portion remained in British possession.

The remainder of the day was comparatively quiet, and at night the 90th Brigade was relieved by Br.-General 11 July. Hon. F. C. Stanley's 89th Brigade.[2]   At 1 A.M. on the 11th July the 20/King's took over Maltz Horn Trench from the Scots Fusiliers, the 2/Bedfordshire coming into the sunken road east of La Briqueterie.   All British troops having been withdrawn from the wood, the artillery opened on it at 2.40 A.M., the bombardment being described by the Germans as the fiercest and most destructive yet experienced.[3]   At 3.27 A.M. the 20/King's started to bomb northward along Maltz Horn Trench, killing 50 Germans and capturing two machine guns ; but the battalion did not reach the strongpoint, for, by mistake it stopped short at a fork in the trench.   Meanwhile the Bedfordshire advanced northeastward with the object of re-entering the wood, gaining its eastern edge, and joining hands with the King's at the strongpoint.   German machine-gun fire caused the two right companies of the Bedfordshire to swerve away to the right, so that they arrived at the south-eastern edge of the wood.   There they occupied the trenches after an attempt to work northward into their proper position had been checked by fire from the strongpoint.   The other two companies entered the wood between Trônes Alley and the light railway, captured 30 Germans, and took up a position with both flanks thrown back to the western edge.   Although patrols worked both northward and eastward, parties of the enemy still held out, and soon these were strongly reinforced from the direction of Guillemont.[4]

[1] Held by one German company which had not received the orders to evacuate the wood when the British bombardment began.
[2] The 90th Brigade had lost nearly 800 officers and men.   According to its regimental history the *II./182nd Regiment* lost, approximately, 620. It was withdrawn on 12th July.
[3] " Regt. No. 182."
[4] The *I./106th Reserve (123rd Division)* reinforced the *II./182nd* and part of the *III./51st Reserve* which had been holding on.

Fighting continued during the morning of the 11th July, both in the wood and in Maltz Horn Trench, but without decisive result. About noon, however, the Germans, who had received fresh reinforcements, cleared the northern portion of the wood, forcing one company of the Bedfordshire to withdraw to Bernafay Wood. This company came forward later to the wedge-shaped position, near Trônes Alley, which the battalion had now entrenched.

A piece of good fortune now befell the British. Orders for a counter-attack by two battalions of the *106th Reserve* were found on a German officer captured by the French in the afternoon. Informed of this about 6 P.M., the XIII. Corps ordered a barrage to be put down between Guillemont and Trônes Wood and the ground east of Guillemont kept under fire.[1] The 17/King's received orders to attack the wood at 10.30 P.M. when two companies, advancing from the sunken road east of La Briqueterie, entered it without opposition after overcoming one small post.[2] They took up a line along the south-eastern edge of the wood, wired it under the protection of a field artillery barrage, and dug in behind it.

On the 12th July a new line was dug to link up the posi- **12 July.** tion of the King's with that of the Bedfordshire on the left. The divisional engineers came up to help, and, although the thick undergrowth made the work difficult, by the dawn of the 13th a good wired trench of rather irregular trace had been completed right across the wood. At 8.30 P.M. on the 12th enemy attempts to advance upon Maltz Horn Trench and Trônes Wood from the east were discovered in time and checked by the fire of the British and French artillery.

As the offensive of the Fourth Army against the German 2nd Position had now been fixed for 3.20 A.M. on the 14th, the capture of Trônes Wood became of urgent importance. General Rawlinson therefore ordered the XIII. Corps to complete it " at all costs " before midnight of the 13th/14th July. In any case a fresh attempt demanded fresh troops, for the infantry of the 30th Division had lost over 2,300 of all ranks in the five days' fighting ; so, before the dawn of the 13th, the 18th Division (Major-General F. I. Maxse) came in. The 55th Brigade (Br.-General Sir T. D. Jackson)

[1] " Res. Regt. No. 106 " describes how British artillery fire delayed the assembly of the two battalions and inflicted heavy loss upon them. The counter-attack was never made, but some of the companies reinforced the Germans in the wood.

[2] The survivors of the *182nd Regiment* had anticipated their relief by moving back at 9 P.M., leaving only a few posts.

13 July. took over the positions in Maltz Horn Trench and Trônes Wood, and it was settled that a new attack should be made at 7 P.M. after a two hours' bombardment by the 30th Division artillery.

The fire of the batteries, intense for the last half-hour, was specially directed upon Central Trench and the area facing Longueval Alley. At the appointed time the 7/Buffs began to bomb along Maltz Horn Trench, but failed to reach the strongpoint, although several attempts were made in combination with advances over the open. A barricade was therefore erected within 20 yards of the work. Attacking from the trench across the wood the 7/R. West Kent lost direction amongst the undergrowth and fallen trees, whilst German posts in Central Trench opened deadly fire at close range. Nevertheless about 150 men, without officers, reached the eastern edge south of the Guillemont track. Unable to locate themselves in the darkness, they imagined that they had reached the northern apex and that the whole wood was in British hands; when dawn came the mistake was realized, but efforts to press on met with no success. Meanwhile the 7/Queens,[1] forming the left of the attack, had advanced across the open from Longueval Alley, to be met by the concentrated fire of rifles and machine guns, and systematic shelling of the German artillery which enjoyed the advantage of excellent observation from the Longueval ridge. The Queen's could not get within 100 yards of the wood, and when a renewed British bombardment which began at 8.45 P.M. was seen to be ineffective, they withdrew in the darkness bringing their wounded with them.[2] One small party which had bombed up Longueval Alley reached the apex of the wood and remained there throughout the night.

Soon after midnight the 18th Division informed the **14 July.** corps that the strongpoint in Maltz Horn Trench had not been taken; that the West Kent had disappeared into the wood, leaving behind them detachments of Germans who were still holding out; and that the attack from Longueval Alley had failed.

Thereupon Lieut.-General Congreve asked what the division proposed to do, seeing that the advance upon the German 2nd Position was due to start in three hours' time.

---

[1] No drafts had been received to replace the losses of 1st July, so the battalion, only 280 strong, was reinforced by a company of the 7/Buffs.

[2] Apart from the company of the Buffs, casualties amounted to 200, so that the Queen's ceased to exist as a battalion.

Major-General Maxse replied that he would send in the **14 July.**
54th Brigade (Br.-General T. H. Shoubridge) [1] to renew the
attack : he still hoped to get possession of Trônes Wood by
the time that the main assault began to make itself felt.
At 12.45 A.M. on the 14th July Br.-General Shoubridge was
informed by telephone that his brigade would attack the
wood before dawn and then hold its eastern edge as a
defensive flank to the attack of the 9th Division on Longueval.

After the failure of the 38th Division on the night of the **9 July.**
8th/9th July against Mametz Wood orders for an alternative plan of attack came into force.   At 11 A.M. on the 9th,
however, General Horne judged it expedient to place
Major-General H. E. Watts, G.O.C., 7th Division,[2] in
command of the 38th as a temporary measure.[3]   The new
commander, who knew the ground, issued fresh orders for
an attack which was to be made at 4.15 A.M. on the 10th
when, in contrast to the piecemeal efforts hitherto ordered
by the corps, the whole division was to be employed.

Mametz Wood is divided transversely by two straight **Sketch 9.**
rides and longitudinally by a third.   In July 1916 these
were not easy to recognize owing to the thick undergrowth
of hawthorn and briar, and to the effects of bombardment.
The wood, in fact, was in much the same state as Trônes,
with trees—oak, beech, and birch—still standing, and
many fallen trunks and broken branches to impede progress.   There was also a considerable amount of wire which
had been put up by the enemy during the respite allowed
him after the 1st July.   The rides and the light-railway
track were the only guiding lines, and German barrages
were put down frequently upon the transverse rides and the
southern approaches to the wood.

The first objective of the 38th Division was the first
transverse ride which cut off the narrow portion of the
wood ; also included was the odd-shaped eastern projection
called " Hammerhead ".   On the other flank, the 17th
Division was to secure Wood Support Trench, abreast of
the first ride.   The preliminary bombardment lasted 45
minutes, and smoke barrages, put down along the whole
front of attack, were thickened on the flanks ; Hammerhead

---

[1] Then in support near Maricourt, about two miles behind the front.
[2] In reserve, except its artillery which had remained to assist the 38th
Division.
[3] Major-General C. G. Blackader took over command of the 38th
Division on 12th July.

E

10 July. was shelled by trench mortars. A creeping barrage was provided by the 7th and 38th Division artilleries, all guns beginning to search forward at 4.15 A.M. " by short quick lifts " of about 50 yards every minute to just beyond the first " objective ", which the infantry was given two hours to reach and consolidate. At 6.15 A.M. the barrage would begin to search back towards the second objective, the second transverse ride, where it would rest until 7.15 A.M. At that hour it would lift and search back again, to pass on to the German 2nd Position at 8.15 A.M., when, it was calculated, the infantry should be in possession of the whole of the wood.

To receive their instructions brigadiers had to make the long journey to divisional headquarters,[1] so it was nearly midnight, 9th/10th July, when orders reached the battalions; and there remained none too much time to prepare for the assault. It was delivered from White Trench. On the right the 114th Brigade (Br.-General T. O. Marden) advanced with the 13th and 14/Welch in front, followed by the 10th and 15/Welch; the 113th Brigade (Br.-General L. A. E. Price-Davies), on the left, employed the 16/R. Welch Fusiliers with the 14/R. Welch Fusiliers in support. The longitudinal ride marked the boundary between the brigades, to each of which was attached a field company R.E., and a company of the 19/Welch (Pioneers).

A distance of nearly a thousand yards had to be covered. Midway, a drop of 50 feet into Caterpillar Valley preceded a steady rise of 400 yards to a bank which marked the edge of the wood.[2] As they scrambled down the slope in the early daylight the eight waves of advancing men were met by heavy rifle and machine-gun fire so that formation was soon lost, and officers led forward the groups nearest at hand. Under cover of the barrage the 114th Brigade quickly reached the edge of the wood and pushed on to the first ride just short of which the men scooped a trench as well as the tree-roots allowed. Hammerhead still held out, defying the most valiant efforts at capture.[3] On the left the 16/R. Welch Fusiliers, being a little late, lost the protection of the

---

[1] Near Morlancourt, six miles S.W. of Mametz Wood.

[2] The wood was held by the *II./Lehr Regiment* (*3rd Guard Division*) with the *III./122nd Reserve* (*183rd Division*) on the south-western side. Behind were the *II./184th* (also *183rd Division*) and *III./16th Bavarians* (*10th Bavarian Division*).

[3] Lieut.-Colonel G. D.'A. Edwardes, commanding the 13/Welch, was killed whilst organizing an attack upon it.

barrage and was smitten by heavy fire from the German 10 July.
trenches west of the wood. Rallied by its commander,
Lieut.-Colonel R. J. W. Carden who met his death whilst so
engaged, and reinforced by the 14/R. Welch Fusiliers, which
lost Lieut.-Colonel G. H. Gwyther severely wounded, the
battalion pushed on and reached the first objective. Heavy
fire came from the left and also from the right where Major
P. Anthony commanding the 15/Welch was killed. British
shells were bursting short [1] and for a time the situation was
an uneasy one.

Both Fusilier battalions appealed for support, and, as
all communications to the 113th Brigade were cut, the
commander of the 15/R. Welch Fusiliers, in reserve in
Queen's Nullah, sent up two companies and then followed
with the rest of his battalion. A gap which developed
between the two brigades was filled by the 10/Welch (114th
Brigade). This battalion, whose commander, Lieut.-
Colonel P. E. Ricketts, was twice wounded, also reinforced
the right near Hammerhead and sent further support to the
Fusiliers on the left. Here some hundred Germans, per-
ceiving themselves outflanked, came out of their trenches
en masse to surrender ; about seventy more gave themselves
up to the 123rd Field Company R.E., which was wiring the
first objective. Patrols failed to gain contact with the
enemy in front and everything seemed to favour a resumption of the advance : in fact at 4.50 and 5.10 A.M. two
battalion commanders asked for permission to go on, since
opposition, except for Hammerhead, appeared to have
ceased. It was, however, impossible to alter the artillery
programme, and the two hours allowed for the capture and
consolidation of the first objective afforded the enemy such
a respite that he thought better of evacuating the wood
completely.[2]

At 6.15 A.M., the time at which the infantry was due to
advance through the wider part of the wood in order to
assault the second ride an hour later, some delay occurred
in placing the companies to cover the enlarged front. When
a start was made it proved very difficult to keep close to

[1] Partly owing to bad fuzes and partly to many shells exploding by
percussion in the tree-tops.

[2] Orders to this effect had been written at 4.15 A.M. by the local
German commander. When the situation became known, however,
portions of the *122nd Reserve, 16th Bavarians* and *184th* were sent into the
wood and the *183rd Division* artillery put a barrage on its southern
approaches. Prisoners declared that Mametz Wood was practically
undefended from 1st-6th July ; obviously the half-hearted British attacks
from the 7th onwards induced the Germans to organize a strong resistance.

10 July. the barrage. Two companies of the 15/Welch, sent to clear Hammerhead and gain the right of the second objective, were counter-attacked and driven back; attempts to advance on the left were stopped by fire from Quadrangle Alley which ran parallel to the edge of the wood on that flank. Some men pressed forward, others drifted to the rear, and there were wild bursts of firing as the confused struggle continued amid the undergrowth and fallen trees.

All telephone wires had been cut. Most of the runners had become casualties; in one brigade the whole of them, 96 in number, were lost. Br.-General Price-Davies (113th Brigade) therefore went up into the wood to try to re-establish control, Lieut.-Colonel J. H. Hayes (14/Welch) taking command of the troops of the 114th Brigade on the right.[1] The barrage was brought back after some delay, and at 11.15 A.M. Major-General Watts despatched two battalions of the 115th Brigade hitherto held in reserve: the 10/S. Wales Borderers to the 114th Brigade and the 17/R. Welch Fusiliers to the 113th. Meanwhile the attempts to reorganize the confused mass of troops already in the wood had met with little success. Hammerhead continued to resist strongly until it was reduced by the fire of Stokes mortars; and the Germans holding a strongpoint, headquarters of a battalion of the *122nd Reserve*, only surrendered after the commander and his staff had broken out and escaped.

To this exhausting and indecisive combat came a turning point when, at 2.30 P.M. three companies of the 17/R. Welch Fusiliers, whose commanding officer, Lieut.-Colonel J. A. Ballard, had been wounded, arrived to cover the reorganization of the fighting front. At the same hour the 13/R. Welch Fusiliers was ordered to capture the whole of Wood Support Trench, which its bombers had already entered; bombers of the 50th Brigade (17th Division) had advanced from the western end and soon the Germans there surrendered. By this time Br.-General Marden had arrived, and he and Br.-General Price-Davies thereupon conferred with Lieut.-Colonel H. E. ap Rhys Pryce, G.S.O. 1 of the division, who had directed the movements of the reinforcements. It was decided to make a general advance which was begun at 4.30 P.M. by the 10/S. Wales Borderers —specially detailed to clear the Hammerhead sector— 15th and 14/Welch, and 13/R. Welch Fusiliers, the 13/

---

[1] By divisional order brigade commanders were forbidden to leave their headquarters, and not for some time was Br.-General Marden (114th Brigade) permitted to do so.

Welch following in support. As the movement progressed the 17/R. Welch Fusiliers and scattered parties of various battalions joined in, and after two hours of hard work and spasmodic fighting the wood was cleared to within 40 yards of its northern edge. The troops had required much leading to keep them in any sort of formation, and among the many officers who fell was Lieut.-Colonel O. S. Flower of the 13/R. Welch Fusiliers.

Machine-gun fire from a trench beyond the wood checked further progress in spite of the efforts of the 14/Welch and 17/R. Welch Fusiliers. A line two hundred yards inside the wood was therefore occupied, with flanks thrown back, conforming on the left to the light railway track. A decision to advance again at 8 P.M. was cancelled owing to the manifest exhaustion of the troops, who were in dire need of water. The withdrawal saved the troops considerable loss, for the German batteries shelled the edge of the wood at intervals throughout the night. Amid the trees the noise of the German bombardment was deafening; there were many false alarms, much indiscriminate firing, and some panicking of men to the rear. No counter-attack took place.[1] The new position was wired by the 123rd Field Company R.E., whilst the 124th and 151st Field Companies and the pioneers, worked on strongpoints behind the front.

In the early hours of the 11th July the 115th Brigade (Br.-General H. J. Evans) took over the line, the 11/S.W.B. and 16/Welch relieving the troops of the other brigades, **11 July.** which left four battalions in the wood in support and reserve. At 7.30 A.M. orders were sent to Br.-General Evans to clear the remainder of the wood; but after a personal reconnaissance in which he and his staff officers were wounded, he suggested that the wiser course would be to straighten out and consolidate the front. At 10.40 A.M. Major-General Watts replied by directing him to clear the wood entirely of the enemy.

An attack was arranged for 3 P.M. but interrupted telephone communications caused half an hour's delay.

[1] Over 400 prisoners of five different regiments had been captured, the defenders being reduced to 140 men of the *II./Lehr Regiment, II./184th,* and engineers. The various German headquarters had no clear knowledge of the situation : the *183rd Division* felt sure that the British had reached the northern edge of the wood which the *3rd Guard Division* thought was still in German possession. The *183rd Division,* having no reserves left, begged for reinforcements to retake the wood, but only one battalion was available, and that not until next morning. The only reinforcements received on the 10th were a company of the *77th Reserve (2nd Guard Reserve Division),* 120 recruits and two machine guns.

11 July. At 3.30 P.M. the British artillery ceased firing on the northern end of the wood, but kept a barrage round the edge to stop the advance of German reinforcements. The 11/S.W.B. and 15th, 10th, and 16/Welch encountered little opposition in their advance ; but it was found to be inadvisable to hold a line so far forward as to be under observation of the enemy in his 2nd Position. On the left bursts of machine-gun fire and a flame-projector attack forced the 16/Welch to fall back slightly, so the line occupied faced northward about sixty yards inside the wood with both the eastern and western edges held. At night, however, a heavy German bombardment rendered the trenches untenable, and a withdrawal was made to the former position.

12 July. Between dawn and 9 A.M. on the 12th July the exhausted Welshmen in the wood were relieved by the 62nd Brigade (Br.-General C. G. Rawling) of the 21st Division.[1] During the morning, patrols of the 10/Green Howards and 12th and 13/Northumberland Fusiliers encountered no organized resistance and finally cleared Mametz Wood of the enemy.[2] Under a heavy hostile bombardment the northern edge was then consolidated, the line being linked up on the right with the 7th Division and on the left with the 1st Division, which had just appeared on the battle front. Hundreds of German dead and 13 heavy guns were found in the wood ; and, just beyond it, two batteries of old French fortress guns from Maubeuge, on high " overbank " carriages.

It may here be added that the 62nd Brigade held Mametz Wood until relieved on the night of the 15th/16th July. Heavily bombarded with shrapnel, lacrymatory, high explosive, and gas shell it lost 950 officers and men in so doing.

9 July. In the III. Corps on the morning of the 9th July the 24th and 68th Brigades of the 23rd Division endeavoured to improve their positions south and west of Contalmaison.
Sketch 9. The 69th had been ordered to assault the village on the morrow, passing through the other brigades. Reports were

---

[1] At the same time the 7th Division had relieved the right of the 38th Division on the eastern side of the wood. The 38th Division was then drawn into reserve and sent to the Abbeville area, having lost nearly 4,000 of all ranks, among them seven battalion commanders.

[2] Somme-Nord i., p. 216, states that the condition of the defenders was so desperate that the evacuation of the wood was sanctioned and took place about midnight 11th/12th July. " The defence had cost countless " brave men."

current that the enemy seemed to be preparing a counter-attack from Contalmaison, and many casualties were caused by a bombardment of the trenches of the 68th Brigade which were shallow and full of men.   A number of Germans who then advanced were speedily disposed of by the British artillery and machine guns.

As a preliminary measure the 10/Duke of Wellington's (attached to the 24th Brigade) sent forward bombing parties which established, south of Contalmaison, a post from which machine-gun fire could sweep nearly the whole area.   Patrols of the 12/D.L.I. (68th Brigade) entered Bailiff Wood—a newly planted spinney of saplings only a few feet high—but could not stay there as it was still under the fire of the British artillery.   Br.-General Croft decided to seize the wood by an advance of two companies from the west at 6.15 P.M., but a German attempt at counter-attack delayed the movement.[1]   The barrage that had been ordered was duly fired, and, as the telephone wires were cut, it was impossible to provide another when the Durham L.I. went forward at 8.15 P.M.   Nevertheless the two companies fought their way with bomb and rifle and captured nearly the whole of the original objective of the brigade : Bailiff Wood and the trenches on either side of it.[2]   Only on the right was success not quite complete, and here the trench was barricaded, a counter-attack which soon followed being repulsed with loss.   The capture of the wood proved of great advantage in the following day's operation, for the Germans were no longer able to bring short-range enfilade fire to bear from the north.

Careful reconnaissance of the ground by the brigadier **10 July.** and the battalion commanders preceded the attack of the 69th Brigade at 4.30 P.M.[3] on the 10th July, and close co-operation with the artillery of the 23rd and 34th Divisions was arranged.   Br.-General Lambert assembled the 8th and 9/Green Howards in and near the northern part of Horseshoe Trench on a front of 1,000 yards, some 2,000 yards west of Contalmaison.   He sent two companies of the 11/W. Yorkshire 500 yards forward to Bailiff Wood with

---

[1] Somme-Nord i., pp. 193-4, speaks of a counter-attack delivered at 4.30 P.M. by parts of the *II.* and *III./183rd* west of Contalmaison to strengthen the weak line between that village and Pozières.   The advance melted away under fire, one battalion losing all its officers.

[2] Behind the wood were found four damaged field guns with 300 rounds of ammunition.

[3] Most of the various reports and orders give the time as such, but the 69th Brigade puts the hour of assault at 4.50 P.M.

10 July. orders to make a flank attack and join hands with the Green Howards at the north-western corner of the village.

The village and the trench in front of it were bombarded from 4 to 4.30 P.M., the batteries firing in enfilade from the south and quickening their rate to cover the infantry during its approach to within assaulting distance. Fire then swept in five short lifts from the trench west of Contalmaison to its eastern edge. A smoke barrage was to have been put down by 4-inch Stokes mortars in position 400 yards west of Bailiff Wood, but although the wind was favourable it proved impossible, in the time available, to carry up sufficient ammunition to produce an effective screen. The advance, was however, well covered by fire from all the machine guns of the division which enfiladed the flanks of the village and all approaches to it.

Moving out steadily in four waves, with searching and consolidating parties in rear, the Green Howards battalions were met by fire of all kinds, and, on the right, un-cut wire in front of a hedge caused some delay. Yet the trench in front of the village was carried, and the Germans broke back into the ruins. Going on, over ground broken by innumerable shell holes and intersected by wire, the Yorkshiremen, now in small groups, ran into the creeping barrage, so that the times of the lifts had to be advanced.[1] Soon Contalmaison was entered, and, although some Germans still fought stoutly, all resistance was overcome and the remains of the village were at last in British hands. The 8/Green Howards, reduced to five officers and 150 men, had the satisfaction of taking prisoner a force greater than its own : eight officers and 180 unwounded men of the *122nd Reserve Regiment*.[2]

The flank attack of the West Yorkshire companies was also successful. They caught with their fire the enemy retreating northward from Contalmaison, and joined hands with the Green Howards about 5.30 P.M. In all 280 unwounded prisoners, among them a battalion commander, and nine machine guns were taken. Unfortunately the buffer springs of many of the 18-pdrs. gave out so that the artillery could not take proper toll of the Germans in retreat.[3]

[1] Owing to the initiative of Br.-General D. J. M. Fasson, C.R.A. 23rd Division, this alteration was accomplished with very little delay.

[2] This regiment held the western part of Mametz Wood, Contalmaison, and the ground between. Six companies, with four of the *I./9th Grenadiers* were in the village and the trench outside.

[3] Somme-Nord i., pp. 206-7, describes Contalmaison under bombardment : " One dug-out after another collapsed, one machine gun after

Consolidation proceeded with the assistance of the 10/Duke of Wellington's, the remainder of the 11/West Yorkshire, and the 101st Field Company, R.E. Throughout the night a " box " barrage was maintained round Contalmaison. Towards 9 P.M. a strong body of the enemy advanced from the north, but was driven back by a party of bombers, and no further attempts to counter-attack were made. The 102nd and 128th Field Companies which started forward at dusk from the original German front line were stopped by a hostile barrage and then held up by the congestion of battle traffic; they did not arrive until the early **11 July.** morning of the 11th, but were able to do a good day's work.

Before noon on the 11th the relief of the infantry of the 23rd Division was completed by the 1st Brigade of Major-General E. P. Strickland's 1st Division.[1]

Between Mametz Wood and Contalmaison, where Quadrangle Support Trench had hitherto defied all attempts at capture, success was also obtained on the 10th July, but not until the village and part of the wood were in British hands. As no advance across the open was possible by day in face of the machine-gun defence, bombing attacks **9 July.** up the trenches had been made in the early morning and at noon on the 9th July ; but very little ground was won. The XV. Corps therefore ordered the 17th Division to try a surprise attack with the bayonet, and this was attempted at 11.20 P.M. by the 7/Green Howards (50th Brigade), and 8/S. Staffordshire (51st Brigade), both much reduced in numbers, assisted by bombers of the 7/Lincolnshire (51st Brigade). On the left the Staffordshire reached and occupied part of the trench, accounting for all its garrison ; but, being unsupported on their flanks, they were obliged to fall back, with the loss of 19 officers and 200 other ranks. The attack on the right, made by one company—actually only 40 officers and men—of the Green Howards, started four minutes later than that on the left. It broke down under intense fire, but was renewed with the support of one company of the 7/E. Yorkshire and one of the 6/Dorsetshire (both 50th Brigade). This attempt also resulted in failure and further attacks were stopped by order of the 17th Division.

" another was destroyed, the cellars of the château were full of wounded. " . . . Scarcely more than a hundred men escaped to the 2nd Position."

[1] The 69th Brigade lost 855 officers and men in the capture of Contalmaison. The total casualties of the 23rd Division, up to 10th July amounted to 3,485.

10 July.   When, however, Contalmaison fell during the afternoon
of the 10th parties of the 51st Brigade bombed their way
from the sunken road east of the village into Quadrangle
Support Trench, whilst others of the 50th Brigade got into
the eastern end and worked up Strip Trench into Wood Support.   Attacked from both flanks the Germans still resisted
stoutly, and it was only after stubborn hand-to-hand fighting
that the trench was cleared and the 17th Division was left
in possession of the objective which had cost it so dear.
Touch was then established with the 38th Division in Mametz
Wood and the 23rd Division in Contalmaison.   The relief of
the 17th Division by the 21st Division was carried out during
the night of the 10th/11th July, being completed by 4 A.M.[1]

Two of the three localities which Sir Douglas Haig
wished to have in his hands before the attack of the 14th
July were thus secured, and were now held by fresh, or
comparatively fresh, troops.

9-13   Meanwhile the X. Corps of the Reserve Army was still
July. fighting for Ovillers, slow progress being made against a
very obstinate defence.   In this maze of ruins, trenches,
dug-outs and shell-holes, the antagonists were at such close
quarters, that artillery could afford little assistance ; the
struggle was maintained with bomb, rifle, machine gun, and
trench mortar, and occasionally with the bayonet.   On the
western side of the village, the 15/Highland L.I., 1/Dorset-
shire and 2/Manchester (14th Brigade, 32nd Division) gained
a little ground on the 9th and 10th July, the 11/Cheshire
(75th Brigade, 25th Division) being engaged on the southern
edge, whence it launched a daylight attack on the 10th.
Farther to the right, the 8/Loyal N. Lancashire (7th Brigade,
25th Division) on this day tried to work forward from
the Albert—Bapaume road up a trench leading round to the
rear of Ovillers, but was repeatedly counter-attacked.   The
battalion repulsed the Germans in fine style, with some
assistance from the 3/Worcestershire (also 7th Brigade),
but could not make much progress.   At night the 2/R.
Inniskilling Fusiliers (96th, attached 14th Brigade) assaulted
over the open north-west of the village and improved the
situation in that quarter.   On the night of the 12th/13th
July, the 10/Cheshire (7th Brigade), 8th Border Regiment
and 2/S. Lancashire (both 75th Brigade) attacked from the
south-eastern and southern edges in co-operation with the

---

[1] The total casualties of the 17th Division, 1st-11th July, amounted to
4,771 officers and men.

96th Brigade advancing from the west. Considerable progress was made and a number of prisoners were captured.

NOTE I

The French Operations, 7th-13th July [1]

The ill success which attended the British efforts of the 7th and 8th July caused General Foch to keep the left of the French Sixth Army on the defensive. So long as Trônes Wood, Mametz Wood, and Contalmaison remained in German hands he saw no possibility of an Anglo-French advance. He wished to wait, in fact, until the British had broken through the German 2nd Position, Longueval—Bazentin le Petit—Pozières, and on the 9th July he instructed General Fayolle to remain on the defensive until this had been accomplished. " Pour le moment tout l'effort français va se con-" centrer au sud de la rivière."

Preparations were in hand for a big operation south of the Somme **Sketch 4.** where General Foch intended to press southward across the Amiens—Vermand road between Estrées and Villers Carbonnel, after Biaches and Barleux had been captured. Here also the preliminary operations did not go well. The attack of the 1st Colonial Corps, postponed from the 8th to the 9th July on account of the bad weather, resulted in stubborn fighting, and, although the German 2nd Position was broken through at Biaches and the village captured, there was failure before Barleux. The Colonials tried again without much success on the 10th when the XXXV. Corps failed in an enterprise east of Estrées.

NOTE II

The Germans during 7th-13th July [2]

Losses were serious on the 7th July, a day of heavy fighting. There was a lack of deep dug-outs in the 2nd Position, and the troops occupying it between Bazentin le Petit and Pozières suffered severely from the British bombardments directed by aeroplane observation. One battalion of the *122nd Reserve* lost 5 officers and 238 men in this way. Communications were impossible to maintain owing to the hostile artillery fire and at night *XIV. Reserve Corps* headquarters knew little of the actual situation : it was not even sure that a line still held between Contalmaison and Pozières. A proposed counter-attack with the *122nd Reserve* and *183rd Regiments* was postponed until next day.

Information was still lacking on the morning of the 8th, with the result that the counter-attack was cancelled. The commander of the *185th Division*, with units of four different divisions at his disposal, was placed in charge of the sector between the south corner

[1] F.O.A. iv. (ii.), pp. 245-253.
[2] G.O.A. x., p. 362, Somme-Nord i., Wendt, and regimental histories.

of Mametz Wood and Ovillers and ordered to fill the Contalmaison
—Pozières gap by the morning of the 9th.   The *I./122nd Reserve*
relieved the *I./Lehr Regiment* which had lost 618 officers and men in
Contalmaison.   Reinforcement was difficult under the pitiless fire of
the British artillery ; the troops were in a miserable state, lying in
mud and water with many wounded and sick among them.

During the next few days the hard-pressed infantry on this front
received as reinforcement about a hundred recruits per battalion,
and the *77th Reserve* arrived from the *2nd Guard Reserve Division*
in the Gommecourt sector.   The *7th Division* (Lieut.-General von
Armin's *IV. Corps*) was arriving from the *Sixth Army* and assembled
south-west of Bapaume, and the *8th Division* (also *IV. Corps*) was
expected at Cambrai on the 13th.   Between the 6th and 13th July
65 (gun and howitzer) heavy batteries were sent to augment the
artillery on the Somme.   Between these dates the aviation reinforcements comprised three artillery flights, two reconnaissance
flights and a bombing flight.

Sketch 9.   On the 12th July Falkenhayn expressed his uneasiness regarding
the Hardecourt—Trônes Wood position and urged Below to hold it,
since from this line both British and French attacks could be taken
in flank, should it become possible to deliver a counter-stroke.
Below preferred to counter-attack in the area south of the Somme,
where it was easier to concentrate artillery fire ; but five fresh
divisions were required for such an operation and there was no hope
of obtaining them.   The *Second Army* begged for more machine-gun
units, which were the mainstay of the defence.

On the 13th July all counter-attacks were cancelled and considerable reorganization of commands took place in anticipation of
a fresh British attack.   " Group Stein " (*2nd Guard Reserve Division*,
52nd Division, and *26th Reserve Division*) was allotted the front from
a point just short of Monchy au Bois to the Ancre ; from that river
southward to Longueval the line was to be held by " Group Armin "
(Burkhardt's division, *183rd Division*, and *3rd Guard Division*) ; and
" Group Gossler " (*123rd Division* and portions of the *12th Reserve
Division*, and *11th Reserve Division*) was to hold from Longueval
(exclusive) southward to the Somme.   The divisions as named were
very mixed in composition, consisting largely of units belonging to
other formations, for there was no time or opportunity to sort out
and reorganize, and very heavy casualties had been sustained.   In
addition to those already mentioned the *183rd Regiment* had lost
1,577 ; the *Guard Fusilier Regiment* 1,218 ; and the *9th Grenadiers*
(4th-16th July) 35 officers and 1,150 other ranks out of 65 and 2,767.

The most significant event on the enemy side during this period
was the termination of his Verdun offensive.[1]   On the afternoon of
the 11th July, after the assault towards Fort Belleville (north of
Verdun and barely a mile from the city) had, in effect, failed, Falkenhayn arrived at *Fifth Army* headquarters.   He at once ordered the
" strict defensive ", as the result of the serious situation on the
Somme, and numerous artillery units were at once withdrawn from
the Meuse and sent north.   So on this date was achieved the primary
object of the Allied offensive.

[1] See also " 1916 " Vol. I., pp. 53-5.

NOTE III

German Storm Troops [1]

As early as March 1915 the Prussian War Ministry ordered the constitution for special assault purposes of a new formation comprising two companies of engineers (for *Minenwerfer* and flame-projectors) and an *Abteilung* of artillery (twelve 3·7-c.m. guns). From this developed the first " storm battalion ", and further experience during the fighting of 1916 led to the establishment of one permanent " storm battalion " per German Army. This unit consisted of two (or three) infantry companies ; one machine-gun company ; one *Minenwerfer* company ; one " infantry gun " battery (four 3·7-cm. guns) ; and one flame-projector section. The number of battalions was increased gradually up to 17, all Army troops but allotted to divisions as required. They received their reinforcements from special *Ersatz* units at home. Meanwhile, in many infantry divisions, " storm companies " or " storm battalions " were formed from infantry personnel ; but they were not authorized by Army establishments. Some fought with credit on the Somme.

Judging by certain German orders, it appears to have been necessary, on occasion, to discourage the practice of leaving all the most desperate fighting to the " storm troops ". Crown Prince Rupprecht considered them a drawback, as the infantry were inclined to leave the whole work to them : as instructors for the infantry they were excellent, " but the view must not be allowed to arise " that one cannot attack without them ".[2] No such formations ever existed in the British or French Armies.

---

[1] Kindly supplied by the *Reichsarchiv*. The *Kriegsgeschichtliche Forschungsanstalt des Heeres* now has charge of the writing of the German Official History.

[2] Rupprecht ii., p. 51.

CHAPTER III

14TH JULY 1916

THE DAWN ATTACK AND THE BREAK INTO THE GERMAN SECOND POSITION [1]

(Sketches A, 10, 11)

PREPARATIONS

Sketch 10. ON the 8th July, when the Fourth Army had yet to secure the important preliminary objectives — Trônes Wood, Mametz Wood and Contalmaison — General Rawlinson issued a preparatory order for the attack against the German 2nd Position, to be launched, probably, at 8 A.M. on the 10th.[2] General preparations behind the battle front, similar to those which preceded the great assault of the 1st July, were begun without delay, the engineers and pioneers clearing roads and tracks and filling in old trenches, the artillery moving forward guns and ammunition. The new objective, as well as the German 3rd Position, was reconnoitred and carefully photographed from the air.

After discussion with his corps commanders and their senior artillery officers, General Rawlinson decided, in agreement with the whole body of infantry opinion, that the main attack should be made at dawn,[3] before there was sufficient light for the enemy machine-gunners to see very far. It was then settled that the XIII. Corps should attack the line Longueval—Bazentin le Grand village with two divisions, which were to form up in No Man's Land (some twelve hundred yards wide) under cover of darkness

---

[1] The official name " Battle of the Bazentin Ridge " covers the fighting, 14th-17th July, from the right of the Fourth Army to the river Ancre.

[2] Appendix 1.

[3] The moon was practically full (full moon at 3.40 A.M. on the 15th) and set at 1.28 A.M. on the 14th. (The times are " summer " time.)

about five hundred yards away from the enemy, and then advance to the assault. The XV. Corps, also with two divisions, was to attack against Bazentin le Grand Wood—Bazentin le Petit village and cemetery from a line following the northern edge of Mametz Wood (expected soon to be in British hands) where the distance to the German position was much less. An auxiliary attack on the left would be carried out by one division of the III. Corps.

General Rawlinson realized that, unless secrecy could be preserved up to the hour of assault, all might end in disaster ; but he felt justified in accepting the risk. The Commander-in-Chief, however, raised objections to the forming up of divisions in the dark and to the dawn attack. He considered that the troops lacked the necessary training and discipline, and that many of the staff officers were not sufficiently experienced, for such a task ; to move two divisions in the dark over a distance of nearly half a mile, form them up, and deliver an attack in good order and in the right direction at dawn, would be very difficult even as a peace manœuvre. In view of the distance between the front of the XIII. Corps and the German 2nd Position, with Caterpillar Valley intervening, he thought that the wisest course would be to attack first with the XV. Corps from the Mametz Wood line against the front Bazentin le Grand Wood—Bazentin le Petit Wood where No Man's Land was of much less width : the right flank could be secured by holding the spur north-east of Marlboro' Wood, and the III. Corps could protect the left by an advance to Contalmaison Villa and beyond : when all these objectives had been gained the XV. Corps could press eastward to clear the ridge towards Longueval whilst the XIII. Corps joined in from the south : the XV. Corps might make its first attack about two hours before dark on the 12th, then, if all went well, the XIII. Corps would be able to advance without undue risk at daybreak on the 13th against the Waterlot Farm—Longueval—Bazentin le Grand line.

Such a scheme certainly did not stake everything upon an initial surprise ; but it gave the enemy an opportunity to concentrate his artillery and reserves against a narrow frontage of attack, and presented the XV. Corps with the difficult task of changing direction in the dark between two phases of the operation.

By Sir Douglas Haig's direction, General Rawlinson held another conference at 2 P.M. on the 11th July. As a result, he could only report that he, his corps commanders

11 July. and their divisional commanders, were all strongly in
favour of the original plan, being quite confident that
it offered excellent prospects of success. Lieut.-General
Horne (XV. Corps), who as a rule saw eye to eye with Sir
Douglas Haig, was in perfect agreement with General
Rawlinson, being definitely averse to attacking in the
evening and without the support of the XIII. Corps on
his right.

The Commander-in-Chief remained unconvinced, and
decided, on the 11th July, that the XV. Corps should make
the initial attack, with such additional troops as might be
required to secure its right flank. He directed that the
XIII. Corps should prepare, as supporting points, a series
of trenches or small works on the southern slopes of the
Longueval—Bazentin ridge ; push patrols towards the
enemy position in co-operation with the attack of the XV.
Corps ; and be ready to assault if opportunity arose. He
did not expect that such an opportunity would arise ; and,
if the XIII. Corps did not attack, the XV. Corps, after
capturing the two Bazentin woods and Bazentin le Petit
village, was to turn eastward, taking the trenches opposite
the XIII. Corps in flank and reverse. Then, if not before,
the XIII. Corps would make its weight felt.

The bombardment began on the 11th.[1] In addition to
counter-battery work, and the shelling of the fronts of
attack, the artillery of the XIII., XV. and III. Corps was
directed to fire at night upon the villages and woods in rear
and the lines of approach to them, particularly Waterlot
Sketch A. Farm, Flers, High Wood, Martinpuich, Le Sars and
Bapaume. The Reserve Army was to deal similarly with
Pozières and Courcelette, and the French batteries with
Guillemont, Ginchy and Waterlot Farm. Some anxiety
prevailed regarding the state of reserves of heavy howitzer
ammunition, so the number of rounds allotted per day for
the two days' bombardment had to be strictly limited :
25 per 15-inch ; 50 per 9·2-inch ; 110 per 8-inch ; and
250 per 6-inch. Two thousand rounds per field gun were
brought up, and many batteries were pushed forward to the
slopes behind Montauban. As the supremacy of the R.F.C.
denied to the enemy any observation from the air, it was
possible to bring up ammunition continuously by night and
by day ; and such immunity was of particular value, for,
owing to the state of the ground, wagons could only proceed
at a slow walk, taking five or six hours for the round journey

[1] Appendix 2.

between the forward dumps and the guns.   On the evening **11 July.**
of the 11th July Lieut.-General Horne reported that the
wire-cutting could not be completed before the 14th, and at
10.45 P.M. the attack was fixed by the Fourth Army for that
day—the French National Fête Day—an additional allotment of ammunition being made to cover the extended
period of preparation.

During the five days which preceded the assault only a
few rounds from a long-range gun fell near the field batteries
of the XIII. and XV. Corps, whose positions were, for the
most part, in the open.   Dumps of all kinds of battle
stores were formed by night in Caterpillar Valley, under
cover of an outpost line, and remained in daylight between
British and Germans, unprotected and undiscovered.   As
no German aircraft came over, these dumps were secure
from air observation ; and the enemy's artillery inferiority
led him to reserve his fire until an attack appeared to be
imminent, when it was chiefly employed in protective
barrages.

The divisions of the XIII. and XV. Corps proceeded
with their preparations on the lines of General Rawlinson's
original plan, in the general hope that the sanction of
G.H.Q. would yet be obtained.   The commander of the
Fourth Army was satisfied that the arrangements made by
the 9th Division (Major-General W. T. Furse) and the 3rd
Division (Major-General J. A. L. Haldane) for the night
approach and dawn attack of the XIII. Corps were thorough **12 July**
and complete, and would ensure surprise and success.   He
therefore wrote a private letter to Sir Douglas Haig, which
was received early on the 12th, and at 8 A.M., Major-
General A. A. Montgomery (Major-General General Staff
Fourth Army) made a final appeal on the telephone to
General Kiggell, the Chief of the General Staff.

The Commander-in-Chief replied to General Rawlinson
that he was now prepared to agree to the Fourth Army
plan, and was sending General Kiggell to convey his
decision.   He sanctioned the attack of both XIII. and XV.
Corps at dawn, on condition that the supporting points
which had been mentioned were constructed by the XIII.
Corps on the slope of the ridge, and the flanks secured by
holding in strength Trônes Wood and Mametz Wood.   By
this time most of the latter was in British hands and the
fight for Trônes was still proceeding.   The Commander-in-
Chief was further influenced by the report of his Artillery
Adviser, Major-General J. F. N. Birch, who pointed out

F

12 July. that the guns were doing well ; that the dug-outs in the German 2nd Position, if any existed, could not be so deep and elaborate as those in the 1st Position ; that on the Montauban front the British obviously held the upper hand and that a dawn attack would leave plenty of daylight to exploit the success.

At 5 P.M. on the 12th the final order was issued for the infantry assault to take place at 3.25 A.M. on the 14th July. As a further measure to ensure surprise it was to be preceded by only five minutes' intense bombardment of all available guns of the XIII. and XV. Corps. The Fourth Army had originally ordered the usual half an hour's intense bombardment before the assault ; but it was pointed out by the artillery commanders of the 9th and 3rd Divisions (Br.-Generals H. H. Tudor and E. W. M. Powell) that this procedure practically warned the enemy to get ready and put down his protective barrages : steady wire-cutting and destruction of strongpoints could be spread over several days, but the intense bombardment should be simultaneous with the infantry advance. A further innovation concerned the creeping barrage which preceded the infantry advance. In order to avoid the danger of short bursts being caused by trees and buildings, only H.E. shell (18-pdr., 4·5-inch and medium howitzers) with delay fuzes were to be used. This type of barrage proved so satisfactory, and so easy for the infantry to follow, that, except to meet special conditions, few barrages consisting solely of shrapnel were ever fired again. It will be noticed that the preparatory measures now adopted differed considerably from those for the original assault in broad daylight on the 1st July, when the views of the French had to be taken into account.

As finally settled, the first objective was the enemy's front and second trenches from the south-west corner of Delville Wood, through the centre of Longueval, the southern ends of Bazentin le Grand village and wood, and the south face of Bazentin le Petit Wood. The second objective was a line embracing Delville Wood, the remainder of Longueval and Bazentin le Petit wood and village. On the left flank, the III. Corps was to secure Contalmaison Villa at the earliest possible moment.

The three cavalry divisions were to be ready to move at 4 A.M., their first objectives being : 2nd Indian Cavalry Division, High Wood ; 1st Cavalry Division, Leuze Wood (1,000 yards east of Guillemont) ; 3rd Cavalry Division,

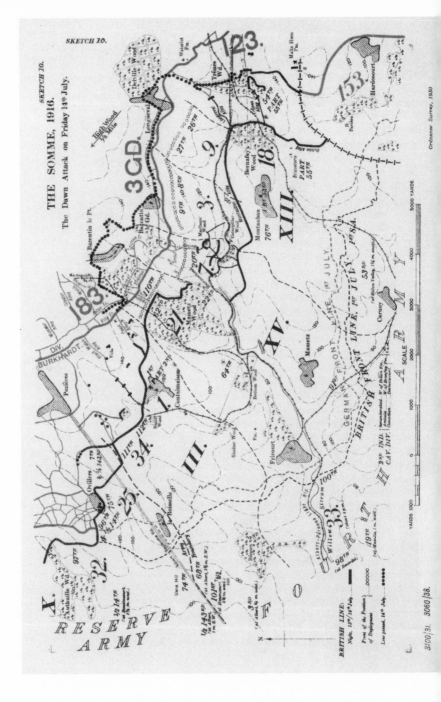

SKETCH 10.

THE SOMME, 1916.

The Dawn Attack on Friday 14th July.

BRITISH LINE:
Night, 13th/14th July. ▬▬▬▬
Front of the Position of Deployment. ००००००
Line gained, 14th July. ●●●●●●

SCALE

1000   0   1000   2000   3000   4000   5000 YARDS
YARDS

Ordnance Survey, 1930.

3100/31.   3060/38.

Martinpuich.[1] General Rawlinson attached great importance to the seizure of High Wood which lay on the crest of
the ridge some two thousand yards north-west of Longueval; 13 July.
by a memorandum [2] dated the 13th, he placed the 2nd
Indian Cavalry Division under the orders of the G.O.C.
XIII. Corps for this operation. The other two cavalry
divisions he kept under his own hand, for he relied upon
receiving such information from the corps and from the air
as would enable him to decide when to send them forward
and launch them to the attack.

In the preliminary order, issued on the 8th July, General
Rawlinson had assumed that his XIII. Corps would have
the co-operation of the French XX. Corps attacking south
of Guillemont. The French decision to remain on the
defensive [3] was a great disappointment to him, and, moreover, created a very unsatisfactory situation, seeing that
the gap between the French left and Delville Wood was
covered by Trônes Wood, the fight for which was still in
progress.   The local French commanders, in any case, were
convinced that the dawn assault of the Fourth Army stood
no chance of success, carried out, as it would be, after a
night approach and with far less artillery preparation and
support than they judged necessary.

THE ASSEMBLY BY NIGHT

The attack against the German 2nd Position was to be Sketch
carried out by the 9th and 3rd Divisions of the XIII. Corps, 10.
and the 7th and 21st of the XV. Corps.[4] The position of
the two former divisions, extending from the north-west
corner of Bernafay Wood to Marlboro' Wood, necessitated
an advance of 1,200 yards in order to reach Delville Wood—
Longueval—Bazentin le Grand ; most of this ground was
to be crossed in the dark, in order to assemble the troops
close to the German line.   From the front, Marlboro' Wood
—north face of Mametz Wood, the 7th and 21st Divisions
had only 600–350 yards to traverse before attacking Bazentin
le Grand Wood, Bazentin le Petit wood and village and
the cemetery 500 yards east of the village. Everywhere,
except on the extreme left in front of Mametz Wood, where
the ground was flat, the first advance would be uphill.

On the right, as we know, the 18th Division was to
establish a defensive flank along the eastern edge of Trônes

---

[1] Appendix 3.   [2] Appendix 4.   [3] See Note I., Chapter II.
       [4] See Appendix 5 for XIII. Corps Operation Order.

Wood, linking up with the 9th Division and, near Maltz Horn Farm, with the French.   The French XX. Corps was prepared, if required, to assist the holding of the defensive flank by putting down an artillery barrage along its entire length.   On the left of the attack, the 1st Division (III. Corps) was, similarly, to form a flank in the communication trench called Pearl Alley, and this was to be extended by seizing Contalmaison Villa ; connection was to be made with the XV. Corps at the south-western corner of Bazentin le Petit Wood.   In pursuance of this plan, the 1/Black Watch (1st Brigade, 1st Division) seized Lower Wood (just **13-14** north of the north-west corner of Mametz Wood) at 10.45 **July.** P.M. on the 13th, and Contalmaison Villa at 3.45 A.M. on the 14th.   Thus, as the repeated attacks of the 18th Division were engaging the attention of the Germans in Trônes Wood, both flanks were more or less secured.

The great problem was whether the six assaulting brigades, over 22,000 men, of the divisions detailed for the dawn attack, with their supporting troops, could be assembled in the darkness and formed up within 500 yards of the enemy, not only without confusion but without the alarm being raised.   There were anxious moments at G.H.Q. and at Fourth Army headquarters until successive reports brought news of the undisturbed assembly of the various divisions ; but this anxiety bore no comparison with the mental strain imposed on the brigade staffs, few of which boasted one trained staff officer, and on the engineer officers who arranged the details of the deployment.

Every possible precaution had been taken to ensure secrecy ; it was known that the enemy possessed means of **13 July.** overhearing telephone conversations, and there was danger that he might have received some hint.   On the morning of the 13th came the discovery that he had been tapping the telephone communications of the 62nd Brigade ; accordingly, at 9 P.M. that night, after a verbal warning of its purpose had been given, a bogus order stating " opera- " tions postponed " was telephoned to companies of the brigade in the front line.   It is possible that the ruse succeeded, for there was hardly any hostile machine-gun and rifle fire until the British were almost in position ; it is certain that the enemy made not the slightest attempt, by patrols or raiding parties, to ascertain if all was normal on his front.   When questioned about this want of enterprise, officer prisoners stated that the failure to push out recon- noitring parties was due to there being no reliable N.C.O.'s left to lead them : in the German Army this was not 13 **July.** officers' work.

In the 9th Division (Major-General W. T. Furse), the 26th Brigade (Br.-General A. B. Ritchie) and the 27th Brigade (Br.-General S. W. Scrase-Dickens) were detailed to lead, with the South African Brigade (Br.-General H. T. Lukin) in reserve.[1] The 26th Brigade was to assemble on the northern slopes of Caterpillar Valley, with its left at the Montauban—Longueval road.[2] The 8/Black Watch and 10/Argyll & Sutherland Highlanders were to lead the advance. To cover the assembly of the brigade, four platoons with Lewis guns were pushed forward on the night of the 13th July to form a screen, some two or three hundred yards from the enemy, on the crest of the ridge south of Longueval, occupying a line of shell-holes, made for the purpose by 6-inch howitzers. This covering detachment was followed by the brigade-major and the two adjutants, with 24 markers from each of the two battalions, the Black Watch party proceeding to the Bernafay Wood—Longueval road and the Argyll & Sutherland to the Montauban—Longueval road.[3] These roads, running almost parallel, marked the respective left flanks of the two battalions. Each battalion was to be formed in columns of two companies, each company in open column of platoons in single rank, with 70 yards between platoons. Thus there were eight lines or waves. The markers were therefore halted in threes, at about 70 yards' distance, the front being 500 yards from the enemy : as each three was posted on the road, two markers were sent to the right at right angles from it with two tapes, each 150 yards long, which were laid in succession to mark the front of the waves (platoons).[4] After midnight the two battalions moved forward into No

[1] The South African Brigade, consisting of the 1st (Cape Province), 2nd (Natal and Orange Free State), 3rd (Transvaal and Rhodesia), and 4th (Scottish regiments in S.A.) South African Infantry was raised by the Union of South Africa, on the successful conclusion of the campaign in German South-West Africa, to represent the Union on the Western Front. Numbering 160 officers and 5,648 other ranks, it arrived in Egypt early in November 1915 ; it was employed against the Senussi, January-February 1916, and disembarked at Marseilles on 23rd April. After training in the trenches it went, on 14th May, to the 9th Division, where it took the place of the 28th Brigade, temporarily broken up.

[2] Whilst the brigade was forming up, the right was guarded by a machine-gun post in shell-holes, and when the advance began part of the original covering party remained to watch this, the Trônes Wood, flank.

[3] The front of deployment is shown on Sketch 10.

[4] An engineer " tape " is a stout white canvas band an inch wide and 50 yards long. On the day previous to the attack there was a frantic hunt to find sufficient of them, as a great quantity had been " mislaid ".

13-14
July.
Man's Land by companies in single file, crossing the road from the southern edge of Bernafay Wood to Montauban at 12.25 A.M.   They made for the roads on which their left markers had been placed, and each platoon, as it reached its marker, wheeled to the right and marched along its tape.

The assembly of the brigade, carried out in silence and without the least hitch, was completed by 3 A.M.   Caterpillar Wood had been heavily shelled on the previous night, so severely as to give the impression that the enemy had heard of the date originally fixed for the assault but not of the postponement, and the working parties carrying up battle stores into the valley had suffered heavy loss thereby. Except for a little shelling, all was quiet on the night of the 13th/14th whilst the markers were being posted, and this firing died down before the Black Watch and Argyll & Sutherland arrived.   A section of the 26th Mortar Battery followed each battalion.   The 7/Seaforth Highlanders, with two sections of the 26th Machine Gun Company, was in support in Montauban Alley ; and the 5/Cameron Highlanders, with the remainder of the brigade trench mortars and machine guns, was in reserve south of Montauban. The total casualties in the 26th Brigade during the period of assembly were one officer (who subsequently died) and six men wounded.

Lacking two such conveniently placed roads to assist its assembly, the 27th Brigade, on the left of the 26th, employed a somewhat different method, following the plan of the 76th Brigade (3rd Division) which, originally, was to have assembled in the same area.   After putting out a covering detachment of one platoon at 11 P.M. a tape (or rather a series of 50-yard tapes) a thousand yards long was used as a directing line.   It was laid out by the brigade-major with an officer and two N.C.O.'s of the 90th Field Company R.E., very accurately on a compass-bearing, the far end of the tape being about four hundred yards from the enemy. The operation took 45 minutes.   From this central tape transverse tapes to mark the fronts of battalions and platoons were set out at right angles by the " field level ",[1] and checked by officers pacing along the Montauban— Longueval road on the right flank, also by a bearing taken on the other flank.   Markers were then put out.

The assembly of the 27th Brigade was carried out in two

[1] A Service instrument formed of three pieces of wood which can be jointed together to lay out angles in the field.   For setting out vertical angles it is graduated and provided with a spirit-level and plumb-bob.

stages, the first being a movement to the near end of the 13-14 tape on the lower slopes of Caterpillar Valley, which were July. well out of sight of the German 2nd Position. Passing by the western end of Montauban in column of route, the brigade arrived at 12.30 A.M. and formed up in mass : the 11/Royal Scots and 9/Scottish Rifles in front with all four companies in line in column of platoons in single rank ; the 12/Royal Scots immediately behind, with the 90th Field Company R.E. on its right and a company of the 9/Seaforth Highlanders (Pioneers), on its left. At 1.45 A.M. the 11/Royal Scots moved forward along the central tape to its final position, the 9/Scottish Rifles and 12/Royal Scots following at 2.10 A.M. ; then each battalion re-formed with its platoons in open column at 70 yards' distance, thus providing four waves with a total depth of eight waves in the brigade. Trench mortars and machine guns were in rear, and the 6/K.O.S.B. provided carrying parties.[1] The assembly, like that of the 26th Brigade, was completed without untoward incident and at the cost of only five casualties, one of them, however, being Lieut.-Colonel H. L. Budge of the 12/Royal Scots, killed by a fragment of shell.

The infantry of the 3rd Division had relieved the 18th Division on the Montauban ridge during the nights of the 7th/8th and 8th/9th.[2] It proceeded to establish a night outpost line nearly a thousand yards ahead along a sunken road which ran almost parallel to, and about two hundred and fifty yards in front of, the German 2nd Position. From this line active patrolling was carried out, the troops of the 3rd Division thoroughly establishing their predominance over the enemy ; but he continued to work on his wire and the long grass made it impossible at many points to see the state of this obstacle.[3] On the nights of the 11th/12th and 12th/13th three communication trenches were dug forward into Caterpillar Valley ; and an old German trench within two hundred yards of the enemy was deepened and improved under cover of a series of piquets put out at 10.30 P.M. on the 13th.

---

[1] The battalion carried up material throughout the 14th, often through heavy barrages, and at night, when hungry and exhausted, was put into the fight at Longueval.

[2] See Appendix 6 for 3rd Division Operation Order.

[3] Artillery observation was conducted through periscopes by officers who lay out among the tall thistles between the sunken road and the wire, as most of the latter, viewed from the Montauban ridge, was behind the crest.

The 8th Brigade (Br.-General E. G. Williams) and 9th Brigade (Br.-General H. C. Potter) were assembled and deployed in lines of platoons, with a long tape as directing axis, in practically the same way as the 27th Brigade which, as already mentioned, had adopted the 3rd Division method. The front of deployment was marked generally by the sunken road, 250 yards from the German trenches ; to this line the leading battalions advanced up the slopes of the valley at 12.25 A.M., and were assembled by 1.45 A.M., with one wave beyond the road, the only casualty being one man wounded. Three quarters of an hour earlier three deserters from the *Guard Fusiliers* had given the important information that an attack was not expected by the enemy. The 8th Brigade placed the 8/East Yorkshire and 7/Shropshire L.I. in the front line ; the 1/Royal Scots Fusiliers, to which were attached four machine guns and four Stokes mortars, in support ; and the 2/Royal Scots, with four machine guns, in reserve.[1] In the 9th Brigade the 13/King's with four machine guns and the 12/West Yorkshire with two machine guns were to lead ; the 1/Northumberland Fusiliers with four machine guns to follow in support ; and the 4/Royal Fusiliers to remain in reserve. Two Stokes mortars accompanied each assault battalion. Each brigade was allotted a section of the 1/1st Cheshire Field Company R.E. ; to the 8th, also, one company of pioneers (20/K.R.R.C.) ; and to the 9th, for fortifying Bazentin le Grand, the 56th Field Company R.E. (less two sections) and 1½ companies of pioneers. The 76th Brigade (Br.-General R. J. Kentish) and the rest of the engineers and pioneers were in reserve in the old German trenches south of Montauban.

The 7th Division had enjoyed barely five days' rest from the battle, not time enough to absorb the large drafts which it required to fill its depleted ranks.[2] During the night of the 11th/12th July it had relieved the 38th Division on a line in rear of Marlboro' Wood (held by outposts) extending to the eastern side of Mametz Wood. Two companies of the 9/Devonshire (20th Brigade) occupied covering trenches 200 yards in front of Caterpillar Wood, since the wood itself was untenable owing to shell-fire.

The 20th Brigade (Br.-General C. J. Deverell) was

---

[1] For 8th Brigade orders and instructions see Appendices 7, 8, 9.

[2] The 20th Brigade received some fourteen hundred reinforcements, wearing the badges of many different regiments, whilst actually on its way to the trenches.

detailed to lead the attack, and, on the afternoon of the 13th, the 2/Gordon Highlanders, then in support, seized the opportunity during a quiet period to push forward to the Hammerhead to which it was to have moved at night. Here the battalion dug in.   At 10 P.M., when outposts had been placed in position, the assaulting battalions, 2/Border Regiment and 8/Devonshire, were led forward in Indian file by brigade staff officers, first up communication trenches and then over open ground broken by trenches and wire, passing through the two companies of the 9/Devonshire which were then withdrawn into reserve.   A bank on which grew young trees formed the front of deployment, which was marked on the flanks by a large bush and by Flat Iron Copse (on the left boundary of the division); nevertheless it was further defined by tapes.   It lay only 500 yards from the general line of enemy trenches, and less from the salient known as " The Snout " ; but the latter had been heavily shelled by a 7th Division heavy trench-mortar battery and did not seem to be occupied.   Its deep dug-outs had, in fact, been destroyed. One section of Stokes mortars was to be in close support of the advance, the remainder of the battery being with the Gordon Highlanders.   No machine guns were to be taken forward until they could go straight into action on the farthest objective.

Before 2 A.M. the 20th Brigade, with the 95th Field Company R.E. and two companies of the 24/Manchester (Pioneers) attached, was in position, with very few casualties and without telephone communication between the troops and brigade headquarters having suffered the least interruption.   The 22nd Brigade (Br.-General J. M‘C. Steele) with the 54th Field Company R.E., in support, was assembled in Mametz Wood ; in reserve, south of the old British line near Carnoy, was the 91st Brigade (Br.-General J. R. Minshull-Ford), with the 1/3rd Durham Field Company R.E. and the remainder of the pioneers.

The assault of the 21st Division was to be delivered by the 110th Brigade (Br.-General W. F. Hessey), to which was attached one battalion of the 64th, the 1/East Yorkshire.   On the night of the 12th/13th the 110th Brigade had been relieved on the Mametz Wood front and withdrawn to the vicinity of Bottom Wood, north-east of Fricourt.   The line chosen for its deployment was 100 yards outside the northern edge of Mametz Wood, its right extending across the open to a path north of

13-14 July.

Hammerhead, and lay some four hundred yards from
the enemy. In the front line were to be the 6th and
7/Leicestershire, each with a Stokes mortar attached, and
one company of the 8/Leicestershire—the remainder of this
battalion was in support—with the 9/Leicestershire and
1/East Yorkshire in reserve. The task of the 110th
Machine Gun Company was to cover the left flank of the
advance. The 6/Leicestershire moved up via the eastern
edge of Mametz Wood and the 7th and 8th by the light
railway, where Lieut.-Colonel W. Drysdale of the 7th was
wounded. By 2.35 A.M., in spite of shell-fire—directed not
on them but on Mametz Wood—the battalions were formed
in four lines on the tapes already laid out by the 98th
Field Company R.E. Owing to uprooted trees and other
obstacles, only the fourth line of the 6/Leicestershire could
be placed inside the wood, although the last three lines of
the 7th were hidden there.

All six assaulting brigades of the XIII. and XV. Corps,
therefore, had been formed up within four or five hundred
yards of the enemy with hardly the loss of a man. Except
near Mametz Wood, nothing more serious than an occasional
field-gun shell had come over. The outposts covering the
deployment had been untroubled by fire or flares, and had
not sighted a single hostile patrol.

Some of the battalions sought to get even closer for
their spring, the difficulty, indeed, being to keep the troops
back. The 8th Brigade began creeping forward at 2 A.M.,
gaining twenty yards every fifteen minutes, so that by
3.15 A.M. the leaders were only 120 yards from the German
trenches. The 9th Brigade pushed on in the same way, and
at 3.20 A.M., when the five minutes' intensive bombardment
began, it was only fifty yards from the enemy position.
The other brigades waited until this moment when the
leading waves crawled forward as far as possible, a few
casualties being suffered from British shells falling short.

In addition to the operations intended to secure the
flanks, carried out on the right by the 18th Division at
Trônes Wood and on the left by the 1st Division near
Contalmaison, throughout the night the 25th and 32nd
Divisions of the X. Corps (Reserve Army) had continued
their attempts to complete the capture of Ovillers, and the
49th Division to improve its position in the Leipzig salient.

At Ovillers, the 3/Worcestershire (7th Brigade, 25th
Division) advanced along the trench beyond the Albert—
Bapaume road in a fresh endeavour to close in upon the

village from the north-east. Attacking from the south-east, the 10/Cheshire (7th Brigade) could make little progress; but on its left the 8/Border Regiment (75th Brigade of the same division) gained some ground and the 1/Dorsetshire (14th Brigade, 32nd Division) did likewise on the western side. North-west of Ovillers, troops of the 96th and 97th Brigades (32nd Division) launched bombing attacks and slightly improved their positions.

At 3 A.M. on the 14th July, 25 minutes before the **14 July.** Fourth Army assault, the 4th and 48th Divisions of the VIII. Corps discharged smoke from their fronts north of the Ancre, during an intense bombardment from the 4th Division front lasting from 2.25 A.M. to 3.30 A.M. These operations succeeded, to some extent, in diverting German attention from the front of the main attack.[1]

CAPTURE OF TRÔNES WOOD

Whilst the brigades of the 9th, 3rd, 7th and 21st Divisions lay out in the misty night ready to storm the German 2nd Position, the right of this great assembly of men barely 300 yards from the western edge of Trônes Wood, preparations were in hand to complete the capture of the wood. This task was not entirely accomplished until six hours after the main attack had started, but the German defenders were so absorbed in the struggle that the advance of the four divisions met with no interference from the right flank.

As we know,[2] soon after midnight on the 13th/14th July, the 54th Brigade of the 18th Division had been ordered up to make a last desperate attempt to secure the wood. Time was too short for reconnaissance, the attack would have to be made in the dark, and the advancing troops were bound to stumble upon nests of Germans whose whereabouts would not be disclosed until they opened fire at close range. Br.-General Shoubridge, therefore, considered that only the simplest plan could succeed: he decided to sweep straight through the wood from south to north, establishing a defensive flank along the eastern edge as the attack progressed.

The two battalions of his brigade nearest to hand had naturally to be employed; these were the 12/Middlesex which was to lead the way through the wood, and the 6/Northamptonshire whose task would be to clear up in

[1] Somme-Nord ii., p. 6.   [2] See page 49.

the wake of the advance and establish the defensive flank. The other two battalions, 11/Royal Fusiliers and 7/Bedfordshire, were held in support.

Owing to the difficulties of communication, Lieut.-Colonel F. A. Maxwell,[1] commanding the Middlesex, was placed in control of the whole attack. By 2.30 A.M. the Northamptonshire were formed up ready in the sunken road east of La Briqueterie, but only one company of the Middlesex was in position. The other companies, which had earlier been placed at the disposal of the 55th Brigade, were much scattered ; one in Dublin Trench—south of Dublin Alley—one in Bernafay Wood, and one on its way to La Briqueterie. There was no time to lose, for dawn was on the point of breaking, so Colonel Maxwell decided to exchange the rôles of the two battalions, the Northamptonshire to attack, and the Middlesex to clear up and form the defensive flank.

By 4.30 A.M., over an hour after the main attack had started, the Northamptonshire, in artillery formation, had covered the thousand yards of open ground under a violent barrage, mostly of 5·9-inch shell, and entered the south-western edge of Trônes Wood. The redoubt in the southern part of Central Trench resisted stoutly, but, after being surrounded on three sides, the work was rushed in the most gallant manner about 6 A.M., some fifty Germans being killed. In scattered groups the advance continued, but direction was lost amid the dense undergrowth. Like the West Kent before them, the Northamptonshire mistook a projection on the eastern edge of the wood for the northern apex, and halted at this point,[2] lining the eastern edge between the railway and the strongpoint on the Guillemont track.

It was 8 A.M. before the greater part of the Middlesex had been collected and had moved into the wood ; and, as no satisfactory news had been received from the Northamptonshire, Colonel Maxwell went forward himself. He lost his way at first among the maze of shell-holes, fallen trunks, and undergrowth, an accident which was not without influence on his final plans. In the trenches about the

---

[1] An Indian cavalry officer who had won the V.C. in South Africa, where he was afterwards A.D.C. to Lord Kitchener. He was killed on 21st September 1917 during " Third Ypres ", whilst commanding the 27th Brigade (9th Division).

[2] A different point to that reached by the West Kent, which was south of the Guillemont track. On the sketch these two points on the eastern side of the wood do not appear so prominent as they are on the ground.

south-eastern corner of the wood he found scattered groups of the 7/R. West Kent which had been there all night, and also stray parties of the Northamptonshire and Middlesex. All sound of fighting had now ceased. A reconnaissance northward through the wood revealed no trace of the majority of the Northamptonshire, so Colonel Maxwell resolved to start the attack afresh with the men he had at hand, tired as they undoubtedly were.

He collected and reorganized all the troops available in the south-eastern corner of the wood, detailing one company of the Middlesex to attack the strongpoint on the Guillemont track in conjunction with the 7/Buffs (55th Brigade) still in occupation of Maltz Horn Trench. His plan was to form a continuous line, east to west across the wood, and then to advance northward. First he detailed an officer to march, on a compass bearing, due west from the south-eastern corner of the wood, followed by the men in single file. When the officer reached the western edge the whole line was turned to the right, and the advance, almost shoulder to shoulder, began.

The men would insist upon making for any gap where they could see the light through the trees, and it was only by constant use of the compass, and frequent halts to readjust the line, that the true direction could be maintained. Snipers up in the trees and hidden in the undergrowth worried the advance which at one stage looked as if it might cease altogether, for the strain on the troops was very great. Colonel Maxwell then ordered them to fire into the tangle ahead as they went forward, and after this there was no more holding back. Near the point where the light railway entered the wood on its western side a machine-gun post was encountered. The whole line halted whilst Colonel Maxwell, with 70 men, surrounded and rushed the post, killing the Germans and capturing the machine gun. The advance was then resumed.

Steady pressure told, and by 9.30 A.M.—long after the main attack had gained its objectives—the northern apex of the wood was reached.[1] The Germans who had retreated northward through the wood broke out eastward, streaming across the open in order to gain their 2nd Position at Guillemont. As they did so they suffered considerable loss

[1] Sergt. W. E. Boulter, 6/Northamptonshire, had advanced alone at a critical moment in the face of heavy fire and bombed a German machine-gun detachment from its lair. For this gallant and valuable service, performed after he had been wounded in the shoulder, he was awarded the V.C.

from the fire of the Middlesex and Northamptonshire, now
lining the eastern edge, and also from that of the 7/Buffs
who, with the assistance of the Middlesex company, had
taken the strongpoint on the Guillemont track about
9 A.M.[1]

Preparations were made to consolidate a defensive front
facing Guillemont outside the eastern edge of the wood by
linking up a line in the maze of shell-holes with which the
ground was covered.   Over four hundred and fifty casualties had been added to the heavy price already paid for
Trônes Wood, which presented a dreadful sight of British
and German dead and wounded, many caught by fallen
trees.

During the afternoon there were signs of preparation
for a counter-attack, and at night the eastern part of the
wood was kept under heavy fire; but the German infantry
made no advance.

THE DAWN ASSAULT AND THE EVENTS OF THE DAY

At 3.20 A.M. the whole sky behind the waiting infantry
of the four attacking divisions seemed to open with a great
roar of flame.   For five minutes the ground in front was
alive with bursting shell, whilst the machine guns, firing on
lines laid out just before dark on the previous evening,
pumped streams of bullets to clear the way.   When the
barrage lifted at 3.25 A.M. the leading companies of the
8/Black Watch, 10/Argyll, 11/Royal Scots, 9/Scottish
Rifles, 8/East Yorkshire, 7/Shropshire L.I., 13/King's,
12/West Yorkshire, 2/Border Regiment, 8/Devonshire, and
6th, 7th and 8/Leicestershire—all New Army battalions
except the Border Regiment—rose and advanced through
the ground mist at a steady pace.   There was just light
enough to distinguish friend from foe.   Surprised by the
shortness of the intensive and most effective bombardment, by the deployment of the stormers so near in the
dark, and by the creeping barrage of high-explosive, the
enemy made but a feeble and spasmodic resistance to

---

[1] " Res. Regt. No. 106 " states that the British first got into the
southern corner of the wood and rolled up the defence of " South Central
"Trench " by taking it in front and rear.   The defenders of the wood
had to withdraw to the railway, but suffered heavy loss in so doing ;
finally, at 8 A.M. the order was given to withdraw from the northern part
of the wood.   The fighting is said to have cost " much German blood ",
the *I./106th Reserve* being reduced to 152 and the *II. Battalion* to 138 of
all ranks.

the first onslaught.[1] The leading British wave reached the
German wire before a shot was fired, and in the hostile
trenches the only serious opposition came from men who
rushed from dug-outs and shelters after the first waves had
passed to engage those which followed. The enemy counter-
barrage, when it came down a little later, fell in Caterpillar
Valley behind the assaulting troops.

On the right the 26th and 27th Brigades crossed two
lines of wire, although the obstacle had, in places, to be cut
through by hand. The 10/Argyll experienced most
trouble, but its left company broke through and gave flank
assistance to the others. Two lines of trenches were then
carried by the four battalions, the only delay occurring on
the front of the 9/Scottish Rifles in the salient at the southern
end of Longueval. Here the advance was held up until the
flank movement of a party of Royal Scots cleared the
opposition away. Pressing on, whilst the support battalions
came up to begin the work of consolidation, the leading
troops were soon engaged in a fierce struggle amid the ruins
of Longueval. By 10 A.M. the Scots had captured all their
immediate objectives, including the edge of Delville Wood,
except the northern part of Longueval and a strongpoint
at its south-eastern end. The latter held out till 5 P.M.
when it was taken with the aid of the 7/Seaforth and
5/Cameron Highlanders. Waterlot Farm—really a sugar
refinery—in the German 2nd Position, should have been
secured as an advanced post, but it proved impossible to
get so far in the face of the fire of machine guns and
snipers ; parties of the Seaforth and Camerons therefore
occupied Longueval Alley, where they were in touch with
the 18th Division.

About 6.30 A.M. misleading messages reporting the capture of the whole of Longueval had been received by the
9th Division from both attacking brigades.[2] However, what
had been won was consolidated, and strongpoints completed by the engineers before the enemy began to react.
A large store of bottled mineral water found in the village
relieved all anxiety regarding the supply of water for the
troops.

[1] Somme-Nord ii., states that the *II./16th Bavarian Regiment* in
Longueval had been warned to be in a state of readiness, and had four
strong patrols out : one ran into a British patrol, two returned without
discovering anything, the fourth was not heard of again.

[2] According to 9th Division operation orders Delville Wood was to
be attacked from the west after the village and Waterlot Farm had been
secured.

When the battalions of the 3rd Division reached the enemy position, the 8th Brigade found the front belt of wire hardly cut and the second not damaged at all. Here the attack was held up until the brigade-major, with a company of the 2/Royal Scots and a machine gun, broke in on the left next to the 9th Brigade and began to bomb down the German front line. The troops lying outside the wire were then able to break through or pass over it, and the German trenches were soon overrun. The 9th Brigade, in whose sector the wire, sited on a forward slope, had been destroyed, rushed upon the defenders who fought desperately until overcome.[1] In spite of machine-gun fire which opened from the houses in Bazentin le Grand as the troops topped the ridge, the brigade gained possession of the trenches ; and, after trench mortars had been brought into action, the 1/Northumberland Fusiliers passed through and captured the village. Major W. D. Oswald, 12/West Yorkshire, had been killed ; Lieut.-Colonel A. St. H. Gibbons, 13/King's, mortally wounded ; and Lieut.-Colonels R. E. Negus, 7/Shropshire L.I., and B. I. Way, 8/East Yorkshire, wounded.

The 8/Devonshire and 2/Border Regiment of the 20th Brigade, leading the 7th Division assault, captured the German front line at the moment when the artillery lifted. Here the enemy wire and trenches had been completely destroyed by the bombardment, and the Germans in the Snout all killed. The assaulting companies moved straight on to the second line, which was entered, with little loss, simultaneously with the lift of the barrage at 3.35 A.M. Large numbers of Germans were seen retiring up the slope towards High Wood, but they came under the fire of rifles and machine guns, and few of them reached its shelter. The 20th Brigade then lay down and waited until 4.25 A.M., when the barrage lifted off Bazentin le Grand Wood which in its turn was quickly cleared, a line being established beyond it. Thus the final objective of the brigade was occupied exactly to scheduled time. Consolidation proceeded whilst the 22nd Brigade, with the 2/R. Warwickshire leading, passed through to continue the attack. This battalion, covering the advance of the 2/Royal Irish on Bazentin le Petit, approached the southern edge at 6.30 A.M. An hour later, the Irishmen, with the very opportune assist-

---

[1] A sentry of the *I./16th Bavarian Regiment* holding Bazentin le Grand, reported at 2 A.M. that the British were close up to the wire ; two light-balls were fired and the report was confirmed. The battalion then stood to arms. Somme-Nord, ii.

ance of the 6/Leicestershire (110th Brigade),[1] on the left flank had secured the village. The headquarters staff of the *16th Bavarian Regiment* and over two hundred men were captured here. About 8.30 A.M., however, the Royal Irish were driven out of the northern part of Bazentin le Petit by a counter-attack ; but they held on to the cemetery on the eastern side. Reinforced by the 2/Gordon Highlanders (20th Brigade), the Irishmen subsequently recaptured what they had lost, and the whole village was consolidated in time enough to ensure the defeat of further counter-attacks.

The leading waves of the 110th Brigade (21st Division, left of the XV. Corps) began to enter the enemy's front trenches almost as the guns lifted ; only the centre of the left battalion was held up. Here for twenty minutes machine-gun fire checked the stormers, but parties of the successful companies worked inwards and captured the guns, the commander of the 8/Leicestershire, Lieut.-Colonel J. G. Mignon, being killed whilst leading his bombers. The second line was taken, without much resistance, by 4 A.M., when touch was established with the 1st Division (III. Corps) on the left, and the Leicestershire battalions pushed on to occupy Bazentin le Petit Wood. The wood was taken with little fighting, except at the north-western corner, where the Germans held out all day, two company commanders who knew the situation being wounded before their plans to capture it could be carried out. A flank facing east was formed to stop German fugitives fleeing westward from the front of the 7th Division.

About 6 A.M., before Bazentin le Petit village had been entered by the troops of the 7th Division, the 6/Leicestershire moved forward and secured the northern part, joining hands there with the 2/Royal Irish. After handing over their portion of the village, the Leicestershire consolidated a line from its northern extremity to the north-eastern corner of Bazentin le Petit Wood ; and when the Royal Irish were counter-attacked and driven back, the Leicestershire also fell back, for a time, to the wood.

Field artillery of the 7th Division was brought forward in the course of the morning to Caterpillar Valley, and the 1/3rd Durham Field Company R.E., with the pioneers, set

[1] The road through the village was the divisional boundary, but most of the houses lay east of it. On Sketch 10 the boundary line between the 20th and 110th Brigades should therefore run round the western side of the village.

G

to work to improve the tracks across the valley in order to facilitate the bringing up of ammunition and supplies. Contrary to the divisional custom of not sending up the R.E. until night, the 54th Field Company was ordered to Bazentin le Petit and the 95th to Bazentin le Grand Wood before noon. Both village and wood were strongly consolidated.

Thus the British were on the main Ginchy—Pozières ridge at one bound : forty-two German officers, including two regimental commanders and their staffs, and 1,400 men had been captured, and German dead and wounded lay thick in and around the captured positions. Far more execution could have been done had the infantry made better musketry practice on the retiring enemy ; in many units the men, owing to lack of training, could not be depended upon to hit anything even at 300 yards ; in despair, officers took up rifles and picked off fleeing Germans until the machine guns could be brought forward

When the reports of success arrived in the General Staff room at Fourth Army headquarters—the capture of the German 2nd Position on a front of 6,000 yards ; Contalmaison Villa, Bazentin le Grand village and wood, Bazentin le Petit village and wood, all (actually half) Longueval and the whole of Trônes Wood in British hands ; counterattacks beaten off ; the enemy surrendering freely—a message was sent over the telephone to General Balfourier, commanding the French XX. Corps on the British right. Captain Sérot, his liaison officer with the Fourth Army, spoke with soldierly brevity : " Ils ont osé ; ils ont réussi ". To this came the unexpected rejoinder, " Alors, le général " Montgomery ne mange pas son chapeau ". The explanation of this phrase is of particular interest. On the 12th and 13th July Fourth Army headquarters had been called up on the telephone repeatedly by the French Sixth Army and implored not to carry out the attack, which was regarded as sheer madness. Finally, about 6 P.M. on the 13th, Captain E. L. Spears, the British liaison officer, had come over from General Balfourier—a much-beloved old gentleman, who still affected the Second Empire cut of French uniform with wide red trousers—bearing a message which pointed out that a night approach with a view to a dawn attack was quite impossible for such inexperienced troops. Thereupon Major-General Montgomery had said to Captain Spears, little thinking his message would be repeated verbatim, " Tell

" General Balfourier, with my compliments that if we are
" not on Longueval ridge at eight to-morrow morning I
" will eat my hat ".

In Longueval and on the edge of Delville Wood fighting
continued all day under a heavy hostile bombardment, the
26th and 27th Brigades of the 9th Division becoming much
reduced in numbers and very exhausted. Twice, at 7 A.M.
and again at 4 P.M., the XIII. Corps reported that the whole
of Longueval was captured, and twice, at 10.52 A.M. and
4.30 P.M., it had to reduce the success claimed to the southern
half of the village where the 1st S. African Regiment, from
the South African Brigade in reserve, entered the fight.
Longueval and Delville Wood were undoubtedly the most
difficult to secure of all the day's objectives ; and once the
advance had progressed beyond Trônes Wood provision had
to be made for the protection of the open right flank. It
would seem that, apart from the question of special artillery
measures, two brigades with another in reserve could not
deliver an attack of sufficient weight and impetus to drive
right through wood and village, clear them of Germans,
and consolidate them.[1] As it happened, the successful
resistance of the Germans in this locality [2] made the XV.
Corps and the Fourth Army reluctant to countenance a
more enterprising policy farther west.

The 7th Division (right of the XV. Corps) and the 3rd
Division (left of the XIII. Corps) were fit and ready to go
on, but orders had been given not to advance beyond the
objectives already taken. Before 10 A.M. all opposition on
this front appeared to have melted away. The day was
fine, the ground open and easy for movement. Several
senior officers, including Br.-General H. C. Potter (9th
Brigade) and Lieut.-Colonel C. A. Elliott (C.R.E. of the
3rd Division), walked forward up the slope towards High
Wood. Not a shot was fired at them, they saw no Germans,
and they did not notice any defensive works. Major-
General Watts, commanding the 7th Division, proposed to
send through his reserve brigade, the 91st, to High Wood ;
but he was instructed by the corps to leave this operation
to the cavalry which, as will be related, did not arrive upon

[1] By contrast it will have been noted that the 7th Division, attacking
upon a narrower front, used troops of a fresh brigade to assault the final
objective.
[2] In Longueval the *II./16th Bavarians* was reinforced during the day
by the *II./26th Regiment* (*7th Division*) and a battalion of the *99th Reserve
Regiment*.

the scene until many hours later.[1] The commander of the 3rd Division, Major-General Haldane, had intended to use his reserve brigade, the 76th, " for pursuit ", but the Army ordered it to be kept in hand to deal with counter-attacks.

It was in the highest degree unfortunate that, at a moment when fresh troops were at hand to maintain the impetus of the advance, such a delay should have been imposed by higher authority. Responsibility might well have been delegated to the divisional commanders, both experienced and capable leaders, who were in the best position to know what could, and what could not, be done. There was no lack of troops to cope with any unforeseen emergency, for the head of the 33rd Division had already reached Montauban. Obviously the infantry should have been encouraged to exploit its success to the uttermost, since the more progress it made through the German defences the more favourable would be the conditions for the cavalry when, and if, mounted troops were able to come through. Every hour was precious. At this juncture it might have been possible—at least the attempt was worth making—not only to occupy High Wood, but to take up and hold a position, in its vicinity along the ridge, which would threaten the envelopment of Pozières on the left and Delville Wood on the right. Yet High Wood was not to pass completely into British hands until after two whole months of bitter and costly fighting.

At 8.50 A.M. Lieut.-General Horne, commanding the XV. Corps, settled on his further plan : the 7th Division was to relieve the troops of the 2nd Indian Cavalry Division at High Wood, as soon as the latter were established there ; the 21st Division to move northwards and clear the enemy communication trenches between Bazentin le Petit and the light railway to Martinpuich, in order to facilitate the capture by the III. Corps of the German 2nd Position between the corps boundary and Black Watch Alley. This Lieut.-General Pulteney had agreed to undertake. Arrangements were then made between the 21st Division

---

[1] The 2nd Indian Cavalry Division, which was intended to secure the High Wood locality if opportunity arose, was placed under the XIII. Corps (Appendix 4). Nevertheless, the commander of the Secunderabad Cavalry Brigade, which was in front, had been instructed by his division (Appendix 10) that both the XIII. and XV. Corps had a call upon him ; he himself was to be at 3rd Division headquarters with liaison officers at the headquarters of the other divisions of the XIII. Corps, and the 7th Division (XV. Corps). As will be seen, the brigade did not begin to cross the old British front line until the evening.

(XV. Corps) and the 1st Division (III. Corps) for a combined operation at 2.30 P.M., when the 34th Division was to push forward strong patrols towards Pozières.

At 7.40 A.M. the XIII. Corps had ordered forward the 2nd Indian Cavalry Division from its place of assembly around Morlancourt (4 miles south of Albert). The division moved at 8.20 A.M., but its progress across slippery ground cut up by trenches and pitted with shell-holes proved very slow : it was well past noon when its advanced guard, the Secunderabad Cavalry Brigade (Br.-General C. L. Gregory) with attached troops,[1] arrived in the valley south of Montauban. As it had not appeared by 12.15 P.M. the Fourth Army sanctioned the advance of the 7th Division to High Wood ; but it was known at XV. Corps headquarters that the fight for Longueval was not yet over, and Lieut.-General Horne therefore postponed further action until the village should have been secured. For the same reason, the XIII. Corps was now holding the cavalry back, so that the Secunderabad Brigade, on arrival at its rendezvous near Montauban, did no more than push out patrols to keep in touch with the situation.

Neither did the combined attack of the 21st and 1st Divisions materialize. The former had been unable to expel the enemy from the north-western corner of Bazentin le Petit Wood, and was suffering a good deal from the fire of the German batteries. The attack was therefore postponed from 2.30 P.M. to 4.30 P.M., but at 3 P.M. came a heavy German counter-attack against the village and the northern face of the wood. The infantry of the 21st Division was now so reduced in numbers—the 62nd Brigade could only muster 1,200 rifles—that all idea of further offensive movement was abandoned, the III. Corps deciding that the 1st Division could not act alone.

Earlier in the afternoon artillery forward observing officers and others had reported that large numbers of Germans were leaving Pozières, so it seemed possible that the village had been evacuated. Orders were therefore issued for all artillery to cease firing on it at 6 P.M., when strong patrols of the 34th Division went forward to reconnoitre. They were able to reach the trenches just south of the village, but could go no farther and were soon driven back. In the meantime the 21st Division had continued the fight for the north-western corner of Bazentin le Petit

---

[1] One squadron Canadian Cavalry Brigade, one field troop R.E , two armoured cars.

Wood, which was not entirely cleared of the enemy until 7 P.M., and even then he clung to a machine-gun post fifty yards beyond the edge.

At 3.10 P.M. an erroneous report announcing the capture of the whole of Longueval reached the XV. Corps—it was the same report that the Fourth Army received at 4 P.M.—and at 3.30 P.M. Lieut.-General Horne informed the XIII. Corps that the 7th Division would therefore advance upon High Wood at 5.15 P.M. : he asked that the cavalry might cover the right flank. It was not, however, until 5.40 P.M. that Br.-General Gregory received orders, issued by the XIII. Corps, to take his brigade to Sabot Copse, in the valley south of Bazentin le Grand Wood, where it arrived at 6.25 P.M.[1] Also, it was long after 5 P.M. when the orders for the movement reached Br.-General Minshull-Ford's 91st Brigade, the reserve of the 7th Division, which now lay east of Mametz Wood. The brigade was told that it would be supported on the left by the leading brigade of the 33rd Division, which was to pass through the 21st, and that the barrage was timed to lift at 6.15 P.M. To reach the position of deployment, with the left of the brigade at Bazentin le Petit cemetery, by that hour was impossible, and the leading battalions, 2/Queen's and 1/South Staffordshire, had barely arrived there by 6.45 P.M. The cavalry was ready on the right, one squadron each of the 20th Deccan Horse and 7th Dragoon Guards in front, but nothing could be seen of the 33rd Division on the left, so the South Staffordshire had to provide their own protection on that flank.

Thus, at about 7 P.M., began the advance towards High Wood, which stood nearly three-quarters of a mile away to the north-east on a ridge beyond a slight dip of open ground. The wood was almost untouched by shell-fire.

A machine gun in Delville Wood opened on the cavalry, but was silenced by an airman ; a little fire came from riflemen hidden in the crops near High Wood. Machine-gun fire from the high ground beyond their left somewhat delayed the South Staffordshire ; but the two battalions, which gathered in some prisoners and passed two abandoned field guns, entered the wood almost together. Few Germans were found in it ; the great difficulty was to force a passage through the thick undergrowth. The northern angle of the wood, defended by a trench,[2] was not cap-

---

[1] On arrival it passed from the command of the XIII. Corps to that of the XV. Corps.

[2] Part of a new " Switch Line ". See Note at end of Chapter.

THE SOMME, 1916: 14th July.

Sketch II.

Compiled in the Historical Section (Military Branch).
3060/38.

Crown Copyright Reserved.
Scale of Miles.

Ordnance Survey 1936.

Line at night
British - Red
French - Blue
Germans - Green

tured, a line being consolidated across the middle and up the eastern edge. The enemy was not cleared from the western side. Soon the 1/3rd Durham Field Company R.E. arrived and proceeded to construct strongpoints at the eastern and southern angles ; again and again the sappers had to pick up rifles and assist the infantry to repel counter-attacks.

The advanced squadrons of the 7th Dragoon Guards and Deccan Horse had reached the high ground between Delville Wood and High Wood where they came under shell-fire from the direction of Flers (1½ miles E.N.E. of High Wood) beyond the ridge. There was some sniping, but an enemy barrage which was put down dropped in a valley behind the horsemen. The 7th Dragoon Guards charged some infantry and machine gunners in the crops, killed a number with the lance, and captured 32, whilst a German machine gun near Longueval was silenced by the cavalry machine guns before it had done much damage. At 9.30 P.M., when it had grown too dark for mounted action, the squadrons took up a line from near Longueval to the southern corner of High Wood, a convenient bank beyond a rough road providing cover for the horses.

The two other brigades of the 2nd Indian Cavalry Division, which had not left their rendezvous, were sent back to bivouac ; the 1st and 3rd Cavalry Divisions, had remained all day in their bivouacs around Buire sur Ancre (4 miles south-west of Albert) and Daours (10 miles south-west of Albert) without receiving any orders to move. The 33rd Division does not appear to have received any orders to support the 7th Division ; its own orders, issued at 6.25 P.M., were for an attack through the 21st Division next day. At 7.30 P.M., however, Br.-General A. W. F. Baird, commanding the 100th Brigade which was in front, went to the headquarters of the 91st Brigade, where he learnt that assistance was expected. Acting on his own responsibility, he sent up the 1/9th Highland L.I. (Glasgow Highlanders) and the 1/Queen's, which filled the gap in the front between High Wood and Bazentin le Petit.

Thus in this part of the field the day's fighting came to an end, although there were some encounters in the wood during the night. At Longueval the South Africans, in the face of the German machine guns, were still striving to get forward through the ruins.   Sketch

The position on the ridge, won at the cost of over 9,000 11.

officers and men killed, wounded and missing,[1] formed a
blunt salient, some 6,000 yards wide, in the British line.
At the right shoulder of this salient Delville Wood and the
northern part of Longueval, still uncaptured, provided a
covered approach for enemy counter-attacks from the
direction of Flers ; so, until these localities were secured
they would embarrass the left of any Allied assault eastward
upon the German 2nd Position south of Waterlot Farm.
From the left shoulder on the north-western side of Bazentin
le Petit Wood, a movement along the German 2nd Position
towards Pozières might enable the British to close in upon
that village from three sides. Such a situation clearly
demanded a renewed effort upon the part of the whole
Fourth Army, although German counter-attacks, seeing
that reinforcements were arriving, were bound to ensue.

At Ovillers,[2] the 10th Cheshire had attempted a daylight
advance, only to be checked by the fire of machine guns at
close range, and the 1/7th R. Warwickshire (143rd Brigade,
attached from the 48th Division), which afterwards
attempted to extend the success of the 3/Worcestershire,
likewise failed. The Cheshire tried again at 11 P.M., but,
after securing their objective, were obliged to withdraw on
account of the heavy losses they sustained. Preparations
for a fresh assault were made without delay.

NOTE

The Germans on 14th July [3]

The German official history states that the British, by their
surprise attack at dawn, " evidently meant to smash a way through ".
Other accounts claim that a complete surprise was not achieved,
and that the first onslaught only penetrated at a few points ; but
the parties which did get in worked right and left, rolling up the
defence, " which they had not done on the 1st July ". The
struggle was a severe one, and very heavy losses were sustained ;
among the captured were the commanders and staffs of the *Lehr*

[1]
XIII. Corps	9th Division	1,159	
	3rd ,,	2,322	9,194
XV. Corps	7th Division	2,819	
	21st ,,	2,894	

Three battalions of the 110th Brigade (21st Division) give their casualties
for the period 14th-17th July, inclusive, but most of these were incurred on
the 14th.

[2] See page 75.

[3] G.O.A. x. p. 363, Somme-Nord ii., and regimental histories.

Regiment and the *16th Bavarian Regiment*, and of the *I./91st Reserve* and *III./16th Bavarians*. On this day, the *16th Bavarians*, which had all its three battalions in the front line, lost nearly 2,300 officers and men.

General Sixt von Armin, who took over command of the front between Longueval (inclusive) and the Ancre at 9 A.M., was faced with a critical situation : " there were no rear positions, no switches, " no communication trenches ", and the artillery had suffered severely. He ordered all troops to hold on where they were and proceeded to organize a defence in depth. At the moment of attack the *7th Division* (of his own IV. Corps) was arriving to relieve the *183rd Division* in the Bazentin le Petit Wood—Pozières sector ; its three regiments, *26th*, *27th* and *165th*, were put in to reinforce the whole front which had been attacked, including Longueval, and to occupy a second line in rear. Units of the *185th, 17th Reserve, 26th Reserve*, and *3rd Guard Divisions*, and some companies of the *55th Landwehr Regiment* (Army troops), which were out at rest, were sent up for the same purpose. Thus, although the equivalent of fourteen battalions reinforced the fighting front, the German formations were as much intermingled as ever.

West of Longueval the Germans rallied on their second line, now the " Switch Line ", a new trench which, following the reverse slope of the ridge, extended from the Flers defences, south of that village, to the Albert—Bapaume road, cutting through the northern part of High Wood. This trench was improved and wired during the night of the 14th/15th July.

The appearance of the British and Indian cavalry near High Wood [in the evening] gave rise to alarmist reports at corps and Army headquarters : " The British had broken through northwards " between Longueval and Pozières, and by 9.40 P.M. [8.40 P.M. British time] " had reached the line Flers—High Wood—Martin- " puich, and were still advancing ". At night, therefore, Below placed all reserves—*8th Division* (Armin's *IV*. Corps), *5th Division* from the general reserve at St. Quentin, *24th Reserve Division*, now beginning to enter the line south of Longueval, and *8th Bavarian Reserve Division* south of Péronne—under Armin, who was given orders to bring to a standstill the British who had broken through, and to counter-attack as soon as the situation allowed. Before anything could be done the true state of affairs was ascertained, and Below then gave instructions that a big counter-stroke need not be attempted ; and he brought the *5th Division* and *8th Bavarian Reserve Division* back into general reserve.

CHAPTER IV

THE SOMME

15TH–22ND JULY 1916 [1]

(Sketches A, 11, 12, 13, 14)

THE FOURTH ARMY, 15TH–17TH JULY

LONGUEVAL AND DELVILLE WOOD, HIGH WOOD AND THE SWITCH LINE, POZIÈRES

AT 9.45 P.M. on the 14th July General Rawlinson issued an order for the resumption of operations next morning : the successes gained were to be exploited, and the capture of the previous day's objectives completed, full advantage being taken of the confusion and demoralization of the enemy : the cavalry divisions were to remain in their bivouacs ready for action. By the morning of the 15th, however, the Germans, with reinforcements arriving, had sufficiently recovered to oppose stoutly every new advance on the front of the Fourth Army, although their plan to counter-attack and regain the line Longueval—Bazentin le Petit miscarried.[2]

British supremacy in the air was not to be challenged seriously for some time to come ; but weather conditions began to handicap the offensive by hindering aeroplane observation of artillery fire. The 15th July was misty and overcast until the evening ; persistent rain set in on the

---

[1] Officially the " Battle of Bazentin Ridge ", 14th-17th July, includes amongst its " tactical incidents " the capture of Longueval ; but the fighting in Longueval, which continued long after the 17th, cannot be treated as distinct from that in Delville Wood. The official " Battle of " Delville Wood ", too, covering the period 15th July-3rd September, is not really a separate operation and will be described in conjunction with the course of events on either flank.

[2] See Note II. at end of Chapter.

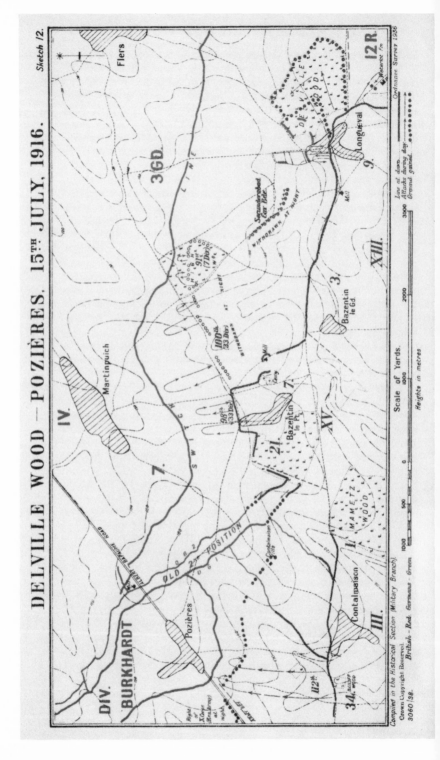

DELVILLE WOOD – POZIÈRES. 15TH JULY, 1916.

Sketch 12.

Scale of Yards.

Heights in metres

Compiled in the Historical Section (Military Branch).
Crown Copyright Reserved.
3060/38.
Ordnance Survey 1936

British – Red. Germans – Green.

Low at dawn.
Attacks during day.
Ground gained.

afternoons of the two succeeding days, making movement 15 July. difficult over the heavy ground. On the 15th, moreover, the Fourth Army was compelled to enjoin economy in the use of gun ammunition ; but, as it recognized that infantry attacks must be adequately prepared and supported, counter-battery fire maintained, and enemy work and movement stopped whenever possible, the order was rather a counsel of perfection. Fortunately on the 17th came news from G.H.Q. that recent deliveries from home had improved the situation, and more ammunition was available for the Fourth Army than General Rawlinson had been led to expect.

On its right the XIII. Corps had yet to secure the ruins Sketch of the sugar refinery, called Waterlot Farm, in the German 12. 2nd Position about half - way between Longueval and Guillemont. Advancing south-eastward at daybreak on the 15th, a company of the 5/Cameron Highlanders (26th Brigade, 9th Division), supported later by two companies of the 4th S. African Regiment, made repeated attempts to carry the farm. Finally the defenders were driven out, but the place was so heavily shelled by the Germans that it could not be occupied and consolidated until the morning of the 17th.

The chief task of the 9th Division was to complete the Sketch capture of Longueval and take Delville Wood, the final 13. objectives laid down for the attack of the 14th. The wood consisted of a thick tangle of trees, chiefly oak and birch, with dense hazel thickets intersected by grassy rides ; covering about 156 acres, it filled the angle formed by the Flers and Ginchy roads, and, as its northern part lay on a reverse slope, the Germans had the advantage of a covered approach from the north-east into the far end of Longueval, which lay in a shallow depression.

Major-General Furse now ordered a fresh attack through the village by the 27th Brigade, and he lent it from his divisional reserve, the 1st S. African Regiment, which had been engaged in Longueval during the night of the 14th/15th. After a bombardment by artillery and Stokes mortars, the 12/Royal Scots went in soon after 8 A.M., bombing up the main street—called North Street—through the shattered buildings. An attempt to advance northward by way of the orchards on the western side made little progress, and all gains were eventually recaptured by the Germans, who had been strongly reinforced. The Royal Scots, well-nigh

15 July. exhausted and now very few in number, made another attempt at 7.30 P.M. with no better result.

The S. African Brigade, ordered to take Delville Wood " at all costs ", moved up before dawn of the 15th, the command of the attack being entrusted to Lieut.-Colonel W. E. C. Tanner (2nd S. African Regiment) who had a little more than half the brigade at his disposal. After a preliminary bombardment, the South Africans advanced at 6.15 A.M. from the 26th Brigade line on the south-western edge of the wood. They cleared the southern half in less than two hours, although progress was very difficult among the shell-holes and the tangle formed of the trunks and branches which heavy bombardments had brought down. Even the rides were not easy to recognize, being partly obliterated by craters and débris. A fresh advance then secured the remainder of the wood, with the exception of the north-western portion whence the Germans, very strongly posted, were to be expelled by a fresh attack. In all, three officers and 135 other ranks, and a machine gun, were captured. The South Africans began to consolidate the ground they had won, although digging among the tangled roots of the undergrowth was difficult and the German shelling never ceased. Hostile machine-gun fire from the north and east swept the edges of the wood, and nearly every man was put into the firing line to repel counter-attacks delivered in succession from the south-east, east and north-east during the early afternoon.[1] The British barrage, put down beyond the wood, in every case proved most effective. Later, the 1st S. African Regiment [2] came up to reinforce, the 9/Seaforth

[1] According to Somme-Nord ii., and other German accounts, the *II./107th Reserve (24th Reserve Division)* attacked from the south-east soon after 11.30 A.M., at five minutes' notice ; it was stopped by artillery and machine-gun fire, and dug in 80 yards from the wood. The assault of the *III./107th Reserve*, which started from the Ginchy—Flers road a little later, met a similar fate, the casualties in the two battalions amounting to 28 officers and 500 other ranks. At 1.30 P.M., the *I./72nd Regiment (8th Division)* advanced against the north-eastern face of the wood, which it could not reach ; nearly all its officers were hit.

[2] In the place of this battalion, the 27th Brigade was given a call upon two battalions of the 35th Division (Major-General R. J. Pinney), of which the infantry had arrived in the XIII. Corps area on 13th July. Its artillery followed on the 15th. The infantry, but not the rest of the division, were " bantams ", i.e., men not less than 5' nor more than 5' 3" in height. The proposal to enlist recruits who were physically fit but less than the minimum height accepted for the Army was sanctioned in March 1915, but there were not enough men of the right type to keep the " bantam " battalions up to establishment during the strain of active service. Consequently, they deteriorated in physique and in morale and, although they passed through

Sketch 13.

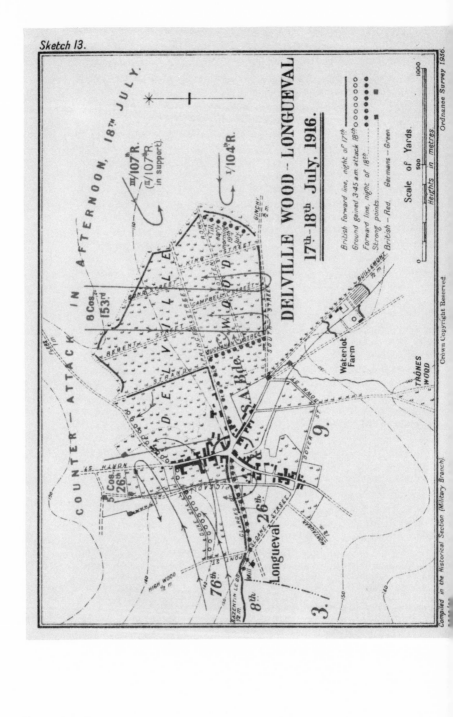

DELVILLE WOOD - LONGUEVAL
17th-18th July, 1916.

Scale of Yards.

Heights in metres.

British forward line, night of 17th
Ground gained 3·45 a.m. attack 18th
Forward line, night of 18th
Strong points
British — Red.   Germans — Green

Compiled in the Historical Section (Military Branch).   Crown Copyright Reserved.   Ordnance Survey 1936.

Highlanders (Pioneers) sent a company to wire the north-eastern edge of the wood, and fresh supplies of ammunition and more tools arrived. As darkness fell, the hostile batteries began a furious bombardment, which preceded an advance of German infantry, and, after this had proved unsuccessful, continued throughout the night.[1]

On the morning of the 16th Major-General Furse **16 July.** ordered a combined assault upon the north-western portion of the wood and the northern part of Longueval. After a bombardment by trench mortars, the 11/Royal Scots (27th Brigade) advanced along the western side of North Street at 10 A.M., and the 1st S. African Regiment attacked from the western end of Prince's Street, which runs eastward into the centre of Delville Wood; but both failed in the face of intense machine-gun fire. The mortars renewed the bombardment and fighting continued without better result, so at 6 P.M. the 9th Division decided to begin afresh. A bombardment of the corps heavy artillery was arranged for 4 A.M. on the 17th in preparation for the assault; but, at 8.40 P.M., the XIII. Corps transmitted an Army order that the objectives must be secured by dawn of the 17th, and the arrangements were amended accordingly. As time was needed to withdraw the foremost infantry posts to a safe distance, the heavy artillery could not open on its nearest targets until after 12.30 A.M.; meanwhile the German bombardment continued, cutting all signal wires, and at 11 P.M. the sorely tried South Africans had to repel another counter-attack.[2]

After about an hour's bombardment by the British **17 July.** batteries, the last two minutes being intense, the infantry assault was launched at 2 A.M. on the 17th. The 27th Brigade attacked astride North Street, whilst the South Africans started northward from Prince's Street and westward from the ride called the Strand; but the concealed

---

the ordeal of the Somme with considerable credit, it was found necessary to reconstitute the infantry of the 35th Division at the end of 1916 with men of normal physique, most of whom came from the Yeomanry.

[1] At 6 P.M. Armin insisted that the *8th Division*, in conjunction with the *12th Reserve Division*, should recapture the wood " at all costs " that night. There was insufficient time for the issue of orders and preparation, but no postponement was permitted. The bombardment began at 9 P.M., and towards midnight an advance was made by the *II./153rd*, *I./153rd* (*8th Division*) and *III./107th Reserve* (under *12th Reserve Division*) from north, north-east and east. The movement was stopped within fifty yards of the wood by artillery, rifle and machine-gun fire. Somme-Nord ii.

[2] " Regt. No. 153 " states that repeated attempts were made to get into the wood during 16th July, but all were stopped by fire with heavy loss.

17 July. machine guns of the enemy had not been destroyed, and, although the mortars were again employed, by noon the operation had definitely failed with heavy loss to both sides.   In the evening Lieut.-Colonel Tanner was wounded and the command passed to Lieut.-Colonel E. F. Thackeray of the 3rd S. African Regiment.   The German batteries, firing high-explosive and gas shell, again concentrated on wood and village at night ; they also bombarded the Montauban area and the artillery positons in Caterpillar Valley.

Lieut.-General Congreve had already resolved that the next attempt should be made by the 3rd Division which was now ordered to complete the capture of the objectives " at all costs " by an attack from the west before dawn of the 18th July.   Major-General Haldane detailed Br.-General R. J. Kentish's 76th Brigade for the task at the very moment when the enemy was making fresh plans to wrest from the British what they had already won.[1]

15 July.   The squadrons of the 20th Deccan Horse and 7th Dragoon Guards which had taken up a position overnight between Longueval and High Wood were withdrawn in the early hours of the 15th.   The movement began at 3.40 A.M., and, being shrouded in the morning mist, was accomplished without loss.[2]   No further attempt was made to get forward in this sector until the 20th July.

Sketch
12.

The XV. Corps, being in possession of part of High Wood,[3] made repeated but unavailing attempts to clear the Germans from the remaining portion during the 15th July. Some 75 acres in extent, High Wood, not so thick as Mametz Wood, was divided by the usual grassy rides ; but there was considerable undergrowth with many young saplings.   Its northern half extended down the reverse slope of the ridge ; its western extremity, on the narrowest

---

[1] The commander of the *8th Division* had arranged to recover the wood on 18th July.   The forward troops were withdrawn on the evening of the 17th to permit of a thorough bombardment which began at 11.45 P.M. Heavy artillery drawn from Armin's and Gossler's corps was employed, and the field artillery of the *8th Division* was supplemented by three batteries of the *12th Reserve Division*.   Somme-Nord ii.

From the details given, it seems that about 116 field and over 70 medium and heavy guns and howitzers came into action.

[2] Casualties had already amounted to 102 British and Indian officers and other ranks ; and 130 horses.

[3] The official battle nomenclature gives separately " Attacks on High " Wood ", 20th-25th July, the previous fighting there being included in the " Battle of Bazentin Ridge " 14th-17th July and the subsequent operations in the later " Battles of the Somme 1916 ".

part of the crest, was invaluable for observation purposes. The Switch Line,[1] which cut through the wood, was admirably sited high up on the reverse slope and almost completely hidden from the British artillery observers ; the wire in front of it was concealed by the long grass.

At 9 A.M. Br.-General J. R. Minshull-Ford's 91st Brigade (7th Division), which on the previous evening had been obliged to reinforce the 2/Queen's and 1/South Staffordshire with the 21/Manchester, began the first of several efforts to advance through High Wood. Little progress, however, could be made in the face of machine-gun fire from that part of the Switch Line within the wood. Then about 2.30 P.M. after putting down a heavy barrage on the southern part, the enemy counter-attacked and gained ground which was only recovered by utilizing the brigade reserve. Major-General Watts arranged for an artillery barrage at 4.45 P.M., and with its assistance another attempt to get forward was made, but met with no better success. Then came fresh counter-attacks, whilst the heavy and persistent German bombardment cut all signal wires, and rendered communication with the rear difficult and dangerous.

Little news had reached XV. Corps headquarters, where the situation of the 91st Brigade was believed to be more precarious than actually was the case. Some confusion, inevitable in wood fighting, prevailed, but the brigade was, at least, holding its own : indeed an officer of the 2/Queen's, occupying the south-eastern part of the wood, described the condition of his battalion as " comfortable ". At 11.25 P.M., with Fourth Army approval, Lieut.-General Horne ordered the complete withdrawal of the 91st Brigade during the night, leaving the wood to be kept under fire by the divisional artillery. By 8 A.M. on the 16th July the **16 July.** 91st Brigade was concentrated behind Bazentin le Grand, having extricated itself with very little fighting. Practically all the wounded were brought in.[2]

Whilst the 7th Division was thus endeavouring to clear High Wood the 33rd Division (Major-General H. J. S. Landon) on its left, made a fruitless attempt to carry the Switch Line covering Martinpuich, in conjunction with an operation of the III. Corps, which attacked Pozières from

---

[1] See page 89.

[2] The Germans, *II./165th (7th Division)* and *III./72nd (8th Division)*, followed up and reoccupied the whole wood. Somme-Nord ii. states that there was " stubborn fighting ", *III./72nd* losing many ; also that the subsequent British bombardment of the wood was heavy and effective.

15 July. the south-east and south.   There was no real co-operation
between the two divisions of the XV. Corps, although it was
understood in the 33rd Division that the 7th was completing the capture of High Wood.   The Switch Line was
said to be " not very formidable ".

On the evening of the 14th July two battalions of
Br.-General A. W. F. Baird's 100th Brigade, 1/9th Highland
L.I. and 1/Queen's, had taken up a position between High
Wood and Bazentin le Petit.[1]   The Highlanders had been
obliged to push three platoons into the western side of the
wood to deal with the enemy there, but they could not get
into touch with the 91st Brigade.   After half an hour's
bombardment, which looked impressive but had little
effect, the Highlanders and Queen's attacked the Switch
Line at 9 A.M. on the 15th.   At the same time, a further
effort was made to clear the western side of the wood.
Although the German machine gunners, firing from the
cover of the trees, took the whole assault in deadly enfilade,
both battalions pressed on very gallantly, some of the
Queen's getting close to the German wire, where Major G.
B. Parnell, the commanding officer, was killed.   Yet success
proved impossible to attain, even after the 16/K.R.R.C. and
2/Worcestershire had been brought forward to reinforce ;
by 4 P.M. the 100th Brigade was back on the line from which
its attack had started.   During the night it was withdrawn
to the vicinity of the mill and cemetery, east of Bazentin le
Petit.

Br.-General F. M. Carleton's 98th Brigade, which had
come up to Bazentin le Petit in the early morning, formed
the left of the 33rd Division attack.   The 1/Middlesex,
advancing on a frontage of 1,000 yards, led the way ;
but as soon as it emerged from the village it came under
enfilade machine-gun fire from both flanks and was also
heavily shelled.   Lieut.-Colonel H. Lloyd was wounded and
the Middlesex casualties mounted rapidly whilst fruitless
attempts were made to get forward.   Between 4 and 5 P.M.
the enterprise was abandoned.[2]

16-17
July.
On the succeeding days preparations for a renewed
assault were much hampered by the bombardment of
Caterpillar Valley with gas and lacrymatory shell.   A few
small changes in the dispositions of the XV. Corps were

---

[1] See page 87.
[2] Parts of the *II./93rd* and *III./93rd* assisted to repel this attack.
In the evening two companies of the *II./93rd* worked forward to a position
500 yards south of the Switch Line.   Somme-Nord ii.

made: on the night of the 17th/18th, the 21st Division, which had repulsed a small counter-attack on the morning of the 15th July, handed over its positions in Bazentin le Petit village to the 33rd Division and withdrew into reserve;[1] and the 7th Division relieved the 3rd Division (XIII. Corps) of 300 yards of front eastward from Bazentin le Grand Wood.

In the III. Corps, the 1st Division (Major-General E. P. Strickland) had relieved troops of the 21st Division along the western edge of Bazentin le Petit Wood on the evening of the 14th July. At 9 A.M. on the 15th the 1/Loyal N. **15 July.** Lancashire (Br.-General A. B. Hubback's 2nd Brigade) attacked north-westward up the trenches of the German 2nd Position and gained about four hundred yards of the front line and two hundred of the support line. Accurate machine-gun fire and the battered state of the trenches prevented further progress, so a fresh attempt was made at 5 P.M. by the 2/Welch (Br.-General H. R. Davies's 3rd Brigade). This was checked at the start by the German machine guns;[2] but after darkness fell the 3rd Brigade linked up with the 34th Division, 600 yards to the north-west, by establishing a line of posts.

The last-named division had attacked Pozières at 9.20 A.M., the 8/East Lancashire of the 112th Brigade (Br.-General P. M. Robinson) starting from the line Contalmaison—Bailiff Wood after an hour's preliminary bombardment. The battalion, which moved off in artillery formation, had to cross some thirteen hundred yards before reaching the first German trench, the forward posts previously established by the brigade having been vacated. When the advance began the barrage raked slowly through Pozières to reach the German 2nd Position north of the windmill at 11 A.M. and there remain; the 112th Trench Mortar Battery and a section of machine guns fired in close support. Fire from hidden machine guns took heavy toll of the attackers, and the advance eventually came to a halt on a line 300–400 yards south of Pozières, although some men went farther. Major-General Ingouville-Williams secured the assistance of the corps artillery for another attempt, and the Reserve Army promised the aid of some

---

[1] From the 13th-17th July, inclusive, the battle casualties of the 21st Division were returned as 142 officers and 3,705 other ranks.

[2] Somme-Nord ii. states that the attacks failed in the face of the rifle and machine-gun fire of the *I./184th* and *II./27th Regiments.*

15 July. of the X. Corps heavy guns for the second half of the hour's bombardment, which was to open at 5 P.M. Nevertheless, when the fresh assault was launched at 6 P.M. it seemed to the East Lancashire that the artillery preparation and support were quite inadequate ; they were not able to get forward quickly enough to anticipate the German machine gunners, who promptly emerged from their undestroyed dug-outs and cellars as soon as the British guns lifted.[1] The advance, however, made some ground, and the position eventually consolidated by the 112th Brigade, with one battalion of the 111th, was half a mile in length, and ran W.S.W. from a point on the Bapaume road 300 yards short of Pozières.

16 July.   On the 16th, at 2 A.M., the 2/Welch (1st Division) made another attempt to bomb up the trenches of the German 2nd Position, but without much result. The mud proved a great handicap to movement, and the fire of the Stokes mortars, although effective, could not be maintained, since it was impossible to carry forward sufficient ammunition. Major-General Strickland, therefore, ordered the 3rd Brigade to make a frontal assault at midnight.

The divisional artillery had spent the whole day wire-cutting, the batteries which fired in direct enfilade from Caterpillar Valley north of Montauban doing very effective work. At 11.50 P.M. the bombardment became intense and ten minutes later fire lifted back from the objective. In darkness and rain the 1/Gloucestershire and 2/R. Munster Fusiliers then attacked north-eastward, keeping close 17 July. behind the barrage, whilst the 2/Welch bombed in from the right. Success was gained at little cost, for the Germans fled in confusion before the bayonet, leaving in their shattered trenches large numbers of dead and wounded. The stormers advanced some three hundred yards beyond their objective, to which they withdrew at dawn; strong posts were established some distance up the communication trenches—now named Welch Alley and Gloster Alley— running north-eastward. On the left, the 1/South Wales Borderers formed a defensive flank in Black Watch Alley, another communication trench running back to the Switch Line. There was no counter-attack on the 17th July, but the forward troops were heavily shelled during the morning.

---

[1] On 16th July a special memorandum was issued by G.H.Q. to the Armies, drawing attention to the importance of attacking infantry advancing close under the field artillery barrage, even at the risk of casualties from British shell.

At 8 P.M. on the 17th the 12/Durham L.I., of the 68th 17 July.
Brigade (Br.-General H. P. Croft) which had relieved the
112th on the front of the 34th Division, delivered an assault
upon the German trench south of Pozières after a bombardment by artillery and trench mortars.   This advance found
the Germans on the alert, and was stopped by machine-gun
fire at an early stage.   As a consequence, an attack upon
Pozières itself, projected for 3.30 A.M. next morning, was
cancelled.

Orders for the 16th July, issued by the Fourth Army at 15 July
11.58 P.M. on the 15th, had directed the XV. Corps to
secure and consolidate the whole of High Wood, and
announced a simultaneous attack by all three corps for the
17th : the XIII. Corps on Guillemont and Ginchy ; the
XV. Corps on the Switch Line between High Wood and
Martinpuich ; and the III. Corps on the German defences
farther to the west, including Pozières.   The French Sixth
Army and the Reserve Army would co-operate on either
flank, whilst the 1st and 3rd Cavalry Divisions and the 2nd
Indian Cavalry Division were to remain in their bivouacs
ready to move at two hours' notice.

At 9.30 A.M. on the 16th,[1] however, the commanders of 16 July.
the III. and XV. Corps, with their chief artillery officers,
attended a conference at Army headquarters, when it was
decided that High Wood should be included in the objectives
of the main operation, now fixed for the 18th July.   There
could, indeed, be little doubt that no important success was
now to be won except by means of another properly
mounted attack upon a broad front.   General Rawlinson
was well aware that the time needed for adequate preparation would be utilized to the full by the Germans in bringing
up reinforcements and in strengthening their line, but he
hoped that, meanwhile, they might be induced to spend
their strength in counter-attacks with which he would be
able to deal.

On this morning a G.H.Q. memorandum [2] outlining Sir Sketch A.
Douglas Haig's future policy reached Army headquarters.
When the Fourth Army had secured the approximate line
Ginchy—Flèrs—Le Sars, the Reserve Army was to attack
northwards from the Ancre valley against the flank of the
Germans facing the Third Army : as soon as heavy artillery

---

[1] On this day there reached the Army Sir Douglas Haig's Special Order
congratulating all ranks on their " very fine feat of arms " on 14th July.
[2] Appendix 11.

16 July. could be released from the Fourth Army it would be added
to the Third for counter-battery work against the German
guns opposing the new advance.

Fourth Army orders for the attack on the 18th were
issued at 4.45 P.M. on the 16th.   Artillery registration was
to begin at once, the German positions being " bombarded
" sufficiently both by day and night to prevent movement
" and work taking place and to destroy strongpoints ".
Many factors, however, contributed to a further delay.
The weather was unfavourable for observation, the British
plans had to be co-ordinated with those of the French, and
the position at Longueval and Delville Wood was unsatisfactory.   Lieut.-General Horne, himself a gunner, whose
XV. Corps was to attack High Wood and the Switch Line,
was very reluctant to resume the offensive before proper
artillery registration had been carried out.

17 July.   On the 17th July, after conferring by telephone with
G.H.Q., and with Lieut.-General Congreve commanding the
XIII. Corps, General Rawlinson met General Foch at Dury
at 12.30 P.M.   Here it was arranged that Ginchy and
Guillemont should be attacked by the British on the 19th,
and the whole German front from Falfemont Farm [1] to the
Somme by the British and French combined on the 20th.
The French agreed to undertake the bombardment of the
farm as well as the counter-battery work on Leuze Wood
and Bouleaux Wood, and on the German batteries south of
them.   It may be noticed that the French were not prepared to attack eastward from Hardecourt across the valley
until General Rawlinson had thrust out his right and
secured the high ground round Guillemont ; thus the Fourth
Army was committed to a preliminary operation before the
Allies carried out a combined advance.   However, there
were to be further alterations in the plan for future operations, and more delays, so that the amended instructions
telephoned to corps commanders and embodied in an Army
order issued at 7 P.M. on the 17th July were cancelled in
their turn.

The Reserve Army, 15th–17th July

Capture of Ovillers

Sketch   On the front of the Reserve Army active trench-warfare
14.   was continued in order to hold the Germans to their

------

[1] In the German 2nd Position nearly a mile south-east of Guillemont.

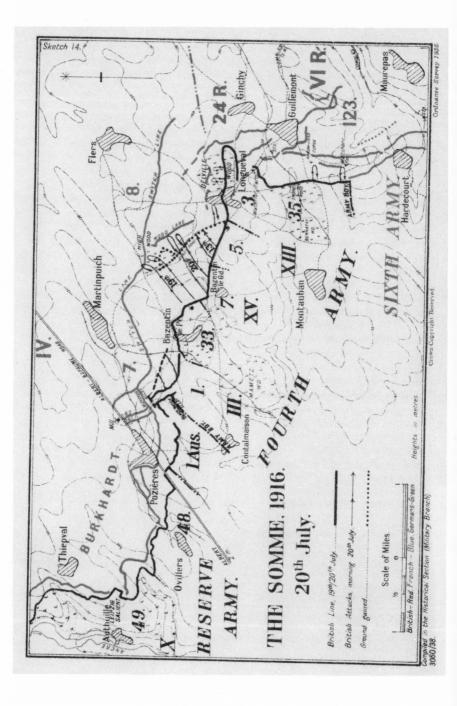

Sketch 14.

THE SOMME, 1916.
20th July.

British Line, 19th/20th July. ————
British Attacks, morning 20th July. ——→
Ground gained. ·········

Scale of Miles.
½   0

British-Red   French-Blue   Germans-Green

Heights in metres.

Compiled in the Historical Section (Military Branch)
3060/38.

Crown Copyright Reserved

Ordnance Survey 1936.

ground and prevent them reinforcing their line farther 15-17
south.   The X. Corps, however, was occupied in completing July.
the capture of Ovillers.   At 2 A.M. on the 15th July the
25th Division attacked from the north-east, east and south,
and the 32nd Division from the south-west, but little
progress was made.   After darkness fell on the 15th the
troops of the 32nd Division were relieved by the 144th
Brigade (Br.-General G. H. Nicholson) of the 48th Division
(Major-General R. Fanshawe),[1] and at 1 A.M. on the 16th
renewed efforts were made to cut off the remnants of the
German garrison.   The 1/5th R. Warwickshire (143rd
Brigade, attached to the 25th Division) closed in from the
north-east and fighting continued during the day, the
74th Brigade (25th Division) and 144th Brigade pressing
in from the east and south.   In the evening two officers and
126 other ranks, all unwounded, of the *II./15th Reserve
Regiment* and *Guard Fusiliers* surrendered, most of them to
the bombers of the 11/Lancashire Fusiliers, who were
attached to the 2/R. Irish Rifles (74th Brigade).[2]   Three
undamaged machine guns were also taken and the village
was reported clear of Germans.   The infantry of the 25th
Division handed over at night to the 145th Brigade (Br.-
General H. R. Done) of the 48th Division, and the relieving
troops at once set about improving the British position.
Next morning the 144th Brigade took 300 yards of the
original German front line on the northern side of the ruins.[3]

The left of the X. Corps, which rested on the Ancre, was
heavily bombarded at intervals with gas and lacrymatory
shells The 49th Division (Major-General E. M. Perceval)
had repelled an attack in the Leipzig salient, east of
Authuille, delivered with the aid of flame-throwers and
bombs on the 15th July.[4]

---

[1] The 48th Division had been relieved by the 38th on the Hébuterne
(VIII. Corps) front during 15th July.
[2] Some of the prisoners were survivors of the *7th* and *8th Companies,
II./15th Reserve Regiment,* who found themselves surrounded.   The senior
company commander said that he had only 30 men left, and that his
repeated requests for relief or reinforcement had been ignored.   The
battalion had been brought down from the Puisieux sector to reinforce
the *Guard Fusiliers,* defending Ovillers.
[3] Somme-Nord ii. states that a withdrawal had to be carried out as
the troops were exhausted and were threatened with envelopment from the
east, whilst few reinforcements were available.   Eighty wounded were left
behind.   According to later reports, " these men were well looked after
" by British doctors ".
[4] The *185th Regiment* (Division Burkhardt) attacked the Leipzig salient
at daybreak with " only partial success ".   There was heavy fighting at the
barricades and many casualties.   Somme-Nord ii.

THE FOURTH ARMY, 18TH–22ND JULY

LONGUEVAL AND DELVILLE WOOD, HIGH WOOD, MALTZ HORN FARM

18 July.　　In view of the stubborn resistance of the enemy opposing the Fourth Army, the Commander-in-Chief now decided to shorten General Rawlinson's front by confiding the attack upon Pozières to General Gough's Reserve Army. Accordingly, at 11 A.M. on the 18th July a conference was held at III. Corps headquarters, when Lieut.-General Sir L. E. Kiggell, the Chief of the General Staff, met General Gough and Lieut.-General Sir W. P. Pulteney, the commander of the III. Corps, with their senior General Staff and artillery officers. Major-General Montgomery, representing General Rawlinson, was accompanied by Major-General C. E. D. Budworth, chief artillery officer of the Fourth Army. It was explained that the I. Anzac Corps (Reserve Army) would relieve the 34th Division (left division of the III. Corps) on the night of the 19th July, but that the Reserve Army's attack upon Pozières could not be launched on the day selected for the next general attack of the Fourth Army, as the available artillery was insufficient to deal with all objectives at the same time.

In the afternoon General Rawlinson conferred with his corps commanders and their senior artillery officers. The shortening of his line, he said, rendered possible certain alteration in the corps frontages, it being particularly important to relieve part of the XIII. Corps which was so heavily involved at Longueval and Delville Wood, and thus allow Lieut.-General Congreve to increase his reserves. The moves ordered were begun without delay ; but the scarcity of good roads available to the Fourth Army, and the difficulties of rearranging routes of supply and evacuation in a restricted area,[1] rendered the readjustment of the

---

[1] From noon on 18th July the French were allotted a larger area behind the battle front north of the Somme, an adjustment which meant the removal of various British headquarters and positions of reserve formations besides some rearrangement of communications. The new boundary line gave Maricourt to the French, passing thence north of the Bronfay Farm— Maricourt road to reach, but not include, the Bray—Fricourt road at a point 1¼ miles north of Bray. The Fourth Army had the right of passage for 150 lorries per day from Maricourt to Bray via Bronfay Farm, and the French were allowed the use of the railway to run by day two supply trains daily into Maricourt. (See Map 1 " 1916 " Vol. I.) This arrangement enabled the French to maintain an extra division north of the Somme.

battlefront, including the relief of exhausted divisions, a 18-19
slower process than General Rawlinson liked. The weather July.
too was bad, heavy rain falling throughout the morning of
the 18th, so that air observation work was hindered and a
further postponement of the general attack could not be
avoided. Having spoken on the telephone with G.H.Q.
and with General Foch, the commander of the Fourth Army
now arranged to assault the line Guillemont—Pozières
(exclusive) on the 22nd July ; the XIII. Corps and the
French XX. Corps would advance on the following day,
their objectives still being the German positions from Falfemont Farm to the Somme. Instructions to this effect were
issued to corps at 7.30 P.M.

Sir Douglas Haig arrived at the headquarters of the
Fourth Army about noon on the 19th July, when, in the
absence of General Rawlinson, then on a visit to the French,
he saw Major-General Montgomery. The Commander-in-
Chief was much concerned about the situation at Longueval
and Delville Wood, mindful that a successful German
counter-attack emerging from Longueval would place in
jeopardy the batteries of all calibres with which Caterpillar
Valley was packed.[1] He gave instructions that the salient
should be widened by pushing out at once to High Wood
and joining up the line Longueval—High Wood—Bazentin
le Petit : Guillemont and Falfemont Farm to be captured
with the least possible delay by operations conducted in
close co-operation with the French, avoiding a series of
disconnected attacks which would invite a concentration of
hostile artillery and all means of resistance : General
Rawlinson to secure Guillemont as a preliminary operation
if he thought it advisable to do so : the Fourth Army to
follow the example of the French, who were pushing forward
small detachments and making good such ground as was
possible without heavy fighting.

Meanwhile, General Rawlinson had visited General
Fayolle, and later in the afternoon General Foch arrived
at Fourth Army headquarters. It was then definitely
arranged that the British XIII. and French XX. Corps
should on the 23rd attack simultaneously the German 2nd
Position from Waterlot Farm to the Somme. The defences
of Falfemont Farm, included in the British objective, were
to be destroyed by the French artillery, which would
also deal with the enemy works at Wedge Wood—on the

---

[1] As a precaution, Montauban had been organized as a " defended
" locality " garrisoned by one battalion.

19 July. north-western slope of the Falfemont Farm spur—prior to the assault.   Then, as a result of Sir Douglas Haig's visit, General Rawlinson issued at 3.30 P.M. on the 19th an order for the XV. Corps to attack High Wood next morning.   He had discussed the situation with Lieut.-General Horne earlier in the day, and the latter had already suggested that this operation might be carried out " to relieve pressure on " the XIII. Corps ".   Lieut.-General Congreve would be making another attempt to clear Longueval and Delville Wood on the morning of the 20th,[1] and had planned a small operation on his right flank to cover the left of the French who intended to launch an attack on both sides of the Somme on this day.[2]   The divisions concerned had been warned accordingly, and the corps' heavy artillery had begun a methodical bombardment of the objectives.

18 July.   The intense German bombardment which had turned Delville Wood into an inferno during the night slackened by 3.45 A.M. on the 18th July when the 3rd Division delivered its attack after an hour's artillery preparation that ended
Sketch with five minutes' intensive fire. The 1/Gordon Highlanders,
13. supported by two companies of the 8/King's Own (both 76th Brigade), moved out from trenches near the windmill, formed to the right, and assaulted Longueval from the west. The orchards north of the village were not carried, but Longueval was occupied as far north as Duke Street, and a line taken up on the north-western edge of Delville Wood in contact with the South Africans, who had advanced from their holding in the eastern half of the wood.   The German batteries, however, increased their fire again, and soon the ruins of Longueval were blazing, whilst dense columns of black smoke arose from the wood : in the words of one officer who was present, " nothing could live outside the " dug-outs ".   Most of the South Africans who were holding positions on the northern edge of the wood were killed or wounded ; in order to save them from annihilation, the troops of the 76th Brigade were withdrawn westward to their assault trenches near the mill.   Heavy rain increased the misery of the combatants.

Soon after 3.30 P.M. German infantry[3] north of the Ginchy road advanced towards Delville Wood in several

---

[1] The continuation of the fighting at Longueval and Delville Wood after 17th July is described below.

[2] See Note I at end of Chapter.

[3] *I./104th Reserve* and *III./107th Reserve*, with *II./107th Reserve*, behind the latter, in support.

waves which melted away when caught by the British barrage, the rifle and machine-gun fire of the South Africans on the south-eastern edge of the wood completing the discomfiture of the enemy.   Other Germans [1] attacked from the north, emerging from the sunken portion of the Flers road, and engaged in a fierce struggle with those South Africans who had survived the bombardment.   The latter, when obliged to fall back, rallied on Colonel Thackeray's position in Prince's Street, but a few remained in the eastern portion of the wood until early next morning.   The Germans reached the southern edge, where they sustained heavy loss from British artillery fire, and also from machine guns in Longueval, when they attempted to break cover.   Meanwhile another enemy attack [2] had been launched from the north and north-west against Longueval, and, after close fighting, the 27th Brigade was forced back to the southern edge of the village.[3]   A critical situation was saved by the Highlanders of the 26th Brigade who advanced at 6 P.M. and, after desperate fighting in which Lieut.-Colonel G. B. Duff, 5/Cameron Highlanders, was severely wounded, regained the line of Clarges Street in the centre of Longueval.

Major-General Furse was determined to attack again without delay, and for this purpose had placed the 19/Durham L.I. (106th Brigade) at the disposal of the 26th Brigade ; but the German bombardment was so heavy and the confusion so great that nothing could be done before darkness fell.

The next attack was made, under corps orders, in the **19 July.** morning by Br.-General H. W. Higginson's 53rd Brigade (18th Division), which had now been lent to the 9th Division.   Brought forward hurriedly, unfed, and with no time for reconnaissance, the 8/Norfolk advanced from the south-western edge of Longueval about 7.15 A.M. on the 19th July, too late to take advantage of the barrage ; but, after a struggle, the battalion cleared the southern portion of Delville Wood, although the Germans had been reinforced. Later the other battalions—10/Essex, 6/R. Berkshire and

---

[1] Eight companies of the *153rd Regiment* (*8th Division*).   They had orders to sweep through the wood and consolidate the line Longueval— Waterlot Farm road.

[2] By five companies of the *26th Regiment* (*7th Division*).

[3] According to Somme-Nord ii. and the various regimental histories, the three attacks were made independently ; companies of storm-troops and many *Flamenwerfer* were engaged besides the troops already mentioned. After darkness fell there was the utmost confusion in the wood and the situation was unknown in rear.   The *153rd Regiment* was reinforced by the *II./52nd* (*5th Division*), other portions of the *52nd* going into Longueval.

19 July. 8/Suffolk—renewed the attack without much result, except to strengthen the positions which had been reached. Fighting continued for the rest of the day, but the German bombardment, which repeatedly cut all signal wires, made it difficult for even brigade headquarters to keep in touch with the situation.[1]

At night the 3rd Division began to relieve the troops of the 9th Division, but not the 53rd Brigade or those South Africans who were still in Delville Wood.[2]

18-20 July.

Sketch 14.

Various reliefs of divisions and adjustments of the Fourth Army were now carried out. In the XIII. Corps, on the night of the 18th July, the 18th Division,[3] next to the French, had been relieved in its positions on the eastern edge of Trônes Wood by the 35th Division, which had one battalion, the 16/Cheshire (105th Brigade) already in occupation of Waterlot Farm. During the day the Cheshire had inflicted heavy loss upon the Germans in repelling three counter-attacks. The 3rd Division, taking over the line held in Delville Wood and Longueval, completed the relief of the 9th Division in the early hours of the 20th. By this time the 3rd Division front from Longueval to the crossroads north-east of Bazentin le Grand had been handed over to the XV. Corps, which had brought in the 5th Division (Major-General R. B. Stephens)[4] on the right of

---

[1] German accounts mention the terrific British artillery fire on 19th July. The whole of the *52nd Regiment* was used in Delville Wood and Longueval, and some of the *12th Grenadiers* were put in. In Longueval, the *26th* asked to be relieved. " All the troops were exhausted, there were " no leaders left, and fresh forces were necessary if the ground gained was " to be held."

[2] The 64th Field Company R.E., which had been attached to the S. African Brigade, was relieved next morning ; it had done excellent work, both in such consolidation as was possible, and as a fighting unit. Since 1st July, the R.E. of the 9th Division had lost 11 officers and over 200 other ranks : more than the equivalent of a field company. Among the wounded was the C.R.E., Lieut.-Colonel E. Barnardiston.

[3] From 14th-21st July the losses of the 18th Division (its 53rd Brigade in Delville Wood—Longueval was not relieved until the 21st) were returned at 129 officers and 2,597 other ranks.

[4] Part of its artillery came in and took up positions in Caterpillar Valley ; the relief of the 7th Division batteries by those of the 5th was completed on the night of the 20th/21st July when the whole of the 7th Division was relieved. As a rule, when the infantry of a division was drawn into reserve its artillery stayed in the line ; but if the division were to be transferred to another Army its gunners were also relieved as soon as possible. It became the practice to take over field-guns *in situ*, so that fire programmes should not be interrupted by the need for fresh registration. Traffic to and from the gun positions was also reduced thereby. The disadvantage lay in the wear-and-tear of the guns in action.

At this stage of the battle a corps with two divisions in the line would

the 7th Division. The III. Corps lent a brigade of the 19th Division to the 33rd Division to hold the left of the XV. Corps line, and had been relieved in the 34th Division sector by the 1st Australian Division (Major-General H. B. Walker) of the Reserve Army.[1] The outgoing troops (68th Brigade) had dug strenuously, under heavy shell-fire, to improve the forward positions, establish a continuous trench line, and provide assembly trenches for the next assault. The relief was accomplished without much difficulty, in spite of a heavy bombardment of gas and lacrymatory shell. _{18-20 July.}

Considerable activity had occurred on the front of the 1st Division, holding the German 2nd Position south-east of Pozières. On the 18th the 2/R. Munster Fusiliers (3rd Brigade) captured, but was unable to hold, the junction of Munster Alley and O.G.2.[2] The division also began to establish a line of battle outposts, supported by strong-points, running north-west from Bazentin le Petit Wood parallel to and half-way between O.G.2 and the Switch Line ; these posts, practically on the crest of the Pozières ridge, were established without much interference from the enemy. In the early hours of the 20th two attempts to secure the Munster Alley junction failed in the face of heavy machine-gun fire.

In the early morning of the 20th July the XIII. Corps made another effort to clear Delville Wood and Longueval, employing for the purpose the two battalions of the 76th Brigade (3rd Division) which had not yet been engaged. An advance from the west [3] was made at 3.35 A.M. by the 2/Suffolk, but there was no sign of the other battalion, the 10/R. Welch Fusiliers, which was to come in from the south. The two leading companies of the Suffolk, with their right flank exposed, pressed on with great resolution and were almost entirely lost.[4] The Fusiliers were ten _{20 July. Sketch 13.}

normally have four divisional artilleries in action. The heavy and medium guns with a corps had not varied much since they were allotted in June, the gun detachments working in reliefs.

[1] For the period 6th-20th July, the 111th and 112th Brigades, under the 34th Division, reported their total losses as 169 officers and 2,818 other ranks. The 68th Brigade, attached to the division 16th-20th July, returned as casualties 13 officers and 240 other ranks.

[2] The old front and support lines were known, respectively, as " O.G.1 " and " O.G.2 ", " O.G." standing for Old German (trench).

[3] From Pont Street, the road running N.N.W. from the windmill. This line was at once taken over and consolidated by the 95th Brigade of the 5th Division (XV. Corps).

[4] " Regt. No. 26 " claims the capture of an officer and 81 other ranks of the Suffolk Regiment.

20 July. minutes late, having been led astray in the dark by a guide, so that they came under British machine-gun fire and lost nearly all their officers before they could form up.   Nevertheless they delivered their attack, and isolated parties of the two battalions carried on the fight, although any chance of success had disappeared.[1]   In the evening the 76th Brigade was able to relieve Colonel Thackeray and his devoted band.   The South Africans had covered themselves with glory at Delville Wood, which is now laid out as a memorial to their dead.   In spite of terrible losses,[2] they had steadfastly endured the ordeal of the German bombardment, which seldom slackened and never ceased, and had faced with great courage and resolution repeated counter-attacks delivered by fresh troops.   Since their first advance into the wood on the morning of the 15th July they had defied all attempts to drive them completely from it.[3]

The fight for Delville Wood reproduced to an even more harrowing degree the conditions which had prevailed at Trônes Wood.   The problem was identical ; for the nature of trench to trench warfare, affording as it did little opportunity to manœuvre, forbade the practice of the pre-war doctrine which aimed at enveloping woods and villages rather than making direct assaults upon them.   Either side, by a concentration of artillery fire, could make the wood practically untenable : with part of it in British possession and part occupied by the Germans, the opposing artilleries ran the risk of killing their own men by bombardment that was never easy to observe.   The best hope of clearing the Germans from Delville Wood and Longueval and of carrying the British line beyond these localities undoubtedly lay in a well co-ordinated attack upon a broad

---

[1] On this day, Major W. la T. Congreve, brigade-major of the 76th Brigade, a most capable and intrepid officer, was killed by a sniper ; he was posthumously awarded the V.C.

A similar honour was won by Corpl. J. Davies and Pte. A. Hill, 10/R. Welch Fusiliers, who killed many Germans with bomb, bayonet and bullet, displaying remarkable courage and initiative.

[2] The South African Brigade went into battle with a strength of 121 officers and 3,032 other ranks, of whom only 29 officers and 751 other ranks were present when the roll was called on 21st July.   The total losses of the 9th Division (1st-20th July) amounted to 314 officers and 7,203 other ranks.

Pte. W. F. Faulds, 1st South African Regiment, was awarded the V.C. for going out under heavy fire on two occasions to bring in a wounded man.

[3] On 20th July the *26th Regiment*, which had been at war establishment on the 13th, and now could only muster 10 officers and 250 other ranks, and the *153rd* were relieved by the *12th Grenadiers*.   This regiment and the *52nd* then held Delville Wood—Longueval under the command of its own (*5th*) division.

front which would prevent the enemy from concentrating 20 July.
his artillery fire upon the wood and village ; but the
operations of the XIII. and XV. Corps on the 20th July
were hardly conceived on such a scale.

The attack of the XV. Corps was made under distinctly
unfavourable conditions. Engaged in consolidating the
line already reached and in carrying out the various reliefs
under a violent and continuous bombardment of high
explosive, shrapnel and gas shell, the infantry were very
tired before zero hour. In many cases, too, the ground
over which the advance was to be made had not been
effectively patrolled. Although no rain fell on the 19th,
visibility was poor, so that accurate registration by the
artillery, largely dependent upon air observation, proved
impossible ; and on the day of the attack mist again
hampered the observers.

On the right (5th and 7th Divisions) the first objective Sketch
was " Black Road "—the track which ran N.N.W. to the 14.
southern corner of High Wood.[1] Br.-General L. O. W.
Jones's 13th Brigade (5th Division) was to advance in
touch with the 7th Division, which had to secure eight
hundred yards of Black Road up to High Wood. The
second objective, some three hundred yards beyond and
parallel to the first, was a track, called " Wood Lane ",
which reached High Wood at its eastern corner. The
capture of High Wood itself was the task of the 33rd
Division, advancing from the south-west.

The British bombardment, which had been maintained
throughout the night, became intense at 2.55 A.M. on the
20th July. Half an hour later, when the barrage lifted off
Black Road and the south-western edge of High Wood, the
8/Devonshire and 2/Gordon Highlanders (20th Brigade of
the 7th Division) advanced. Each battalion deployed
upon a frontage of two companies and the leading lines
began to crawl forward twenty minutes before zero. At
this hour they were close to the first objective and had no
difficulty in reaching it, although subjected to German
shell-fire. On their right, the troops of the 5th Division
came up in line, the German infantry having shown no
disposition to dispute the advance at this stage. Then
Devons and Gordons went on over the crest to Wood Lane,
from which the British barrage lifted at 3.35 A.M. Here,

---

[1] As already mentioned, the 95th Brigade of the 5th Division took over
Pont Street, whence the 3rd Division attack upon Longueval and Delville
Wood started at 3.25 A.M.

20 July. however, the Germans were in force with machine guns
concealed in the standing crops, whilst from High Wood—
not yet cleared by the 33rd Division—came heavy fire,
which took the Gordons in rear.   For over an hour both
battalions attempted to dig in some twenty-five yards
short of Wood Lane, but the position was untenable and
the survivors were obliged to crawl back in small groups to
Black Road, which was consolidated and held.[1]   It was at
first intended to subject Wood Lane to a second bombardment and renew the attack ; but Br.-General C. J. Deverell,
commanding the 20th Brigade, reported that unless High
Wood were captured and the Switch Line beyond Wood
Lane neutralized, such an enterprise could not succeed in
daylight.   After darkness had fallen, the 13th Brigade (5th
Division) relieved the troops of the 7th Division on Black
Road.[2]   A German barrage rendered the movement difficult, killing Lieut.-Colonel B. G. R. Gordon, of the 2/Gordon
Highlanders, and adding considerably to the losses already
sustained.[3]

Meanwhile, the 33rd Division was fighting hard in High
Wood.   At dusk on the 19th the 2/Worcestershire (100th
Brigade) had pushed out a line of posts from Bazentin le
Petit in the direction of the western corner of the wood to
protect the flank of the assault which was to be carried out
by the 5th/6th Scottish Rifles[4] and 1/Cameronians of the
19th Brigade.   Brief verbal orders given to Br.-General
C. R. G. Mayne at 7 P.M. on the 19th July, were followed
by detailed orders at 10 P.M., whilst the battalions were
still in reserve near Mametz.   After a march of over three
miles they formed up near the windmill east of Bazentin le
Petit facing the south-western edge of the wood, some
three-quarters of a mile distant.   Preceded by a line of
scouts, they crept forward and came within assaulting
distance before the barrage lifted from the edge of the wood
at 3.25 A.M.   The Scots then forced their way in,[5] only to

---

[1] Their opponents were the *72nd Regiment* (*8th Division*), which had
held the south-eastern face of High Wood, Wood Lane and the Switch
Line east of High Wood.   Somme-Nord ii.

[2] Pte T. W. H. Veale, 8/Devonshire, was awarded the V.C. for his great
coolness and daring in rescuing a wounded officer who had fallen close to
the German position.

[3] The casualties of the 20th Brigade on this day amounted to nearly
400.   At night, the 33rd Division completed the relief of the 7th Division,
and the latter came out of the battle with total losses (14th-20th July)
returned as 134 officers and 3,279 other ranks.

[4] The 1/5th and 1/6th Scottish Rifles, amalgamated in June 1916.

[5] The south-western edge was held by two companies of the *II./165th
Regiment*, with a company of the *III./72nd* on the south-eastern edge.

come under fire from machine guns in that part of the 20 July. Switch Line which ran through the wood. Fire from a strongpoint at the western corner also wrought much havoc. The 20/Royal Fusiliers, following close behind the right of the advance with the 11th Field Company R.E., now pressed into the fight, and the southern half of the objective was cleared of the enemy. Much confusion ensued, however, for many senior officers were killed or wounded, and about 9 A.M. Br.-General Mayne called upon his remaining unit, the 2/R. Welch Fusiliers.

This battalion was heavily shelled whilst coming forward, but made its attack early in the afternoon. After hard fighting,[1] the Fusiliers reached the northern end of the wood, and the work of reorganization and consolidation began ; but losses had been so heavy and the men were so exhausted that a request was made for the relief of the brigade.[2] The 1/Queen's and 16/K.R.R.C. of the 100th Brigade were accordingly sent up for this purpose. At dusk, however, before these battalions arrived, a German bombardment of gas shell and high-explosive compelled a withdrawal to the southern half of the wood. Hostile infantry followed up and reoccupied the wood in the vicinity of the Switch Line,[3] after which the fighting died down and both sides set to work to reorganize and strengthen their positions. In the darkness the relief of the intermixed units of the 19th Brigade proved a slow and difficult business, but it was accomplished before next morning.[4] The posts put out on the left flank by the 2/Worcestershire were withdrawn.

In the XIII. Corps the 35th Division, on its right flank, had been ordered to carry out an attack at 5 A.M. on the 20th in order to cover the advance of the French left which, as a matter of fact, made no movement : the French judged

---

About thirty prisoners of these companies were secured by the 19th Brigade, and German accounts admit that their losses were very heavy.

[1] The Germans in the wood were reinforced during the day by the whole of the *III./165th* and two companies of the *III./72nd*, with some pioneers and machine guns. Somme-Nord ii.

[2] Two companies of the 18/Middlesex (Pioneers)—recruited from navvies—were set to dig a communication trench back from High Wood. One who saw them observed that " they worked as though they were " opening up Piccadilly, and took as little notice of German shell-fire as " they would have done of the London traffic ".

[3] Somme-Nord ii. states that the Germans fought hard for all they gained. Undoubtedly they encountered scattered parties of Fusiliers and of the other battalions.

[4] The 11th Field Company R.E., which had taken its share of the fighting, lost all its officers and was brought out of action by a corporal.

20 July. it inadvisable to send infantry forward owing to the difficulty of providing artillery support.   The task of the
35th Division was to capture the German trenches between
Maltz Horn Farm and Arrow Head Copse and make good
the area Maltz Horn Farm—Arrow Head Copse—Trônes
Wood as a preliminary to the general attack upon Guillemont and the German 2nd Position.   A preliminary bombardment lasting 30 minutes was carried out, but the
British artillery was not able to observe its effect ; and when
the 15/Sherwood Foresters (105th Brigade) attacked with
one company just south of Arrow Head Copse and one at
the farm, heavy losses were suffered from shell, machine-
gun and rifle fire.   Parties of men who did enter the German
trenches [1] were shelled out again.   After another bombardment, the 23/Manchester (104th Brigade) made an attempt
at 11.35 A.M. with much the same result, losses in the two
battalions amounting to over 450 all ranks.

Preparations for a General Attack

21 July.   Beginning on the 21st July the artillery of the Fourth
Army continued to register the Switch Line and other
future objectives, but although this day and the two
succeeding days were dry and warm, there was considerable
haze and cloud, so that observation from the air often
became impossible.[2]   British machines carrying out this
work suffered little interference from the German aircraft,
which, for the most part, confined themselves to action
against long-distance reconnaissance.[3]

A conference of corps commanders and artillery officers
was held at Fourth Army headquarters in the morning,
when the details of the next general attack were settled :
the XIII. Corps to clear the whole of Delville Wood ; the
XV. Corps to secure the orchards at the northern end of
Longueval, High Wood and the Switch Line on either side
of it ; the III. Corps to take the continuation of the

---

[1] Held by the *133rd Reserve Regiment* (*24th Reserve Division*).
[2] The XV. Corps ordered that when firing protective barrages, in cases
where registration had not been satisfactory and the height of the burst
was doubtful, a third of the barrage was to be high explosive, in order
that the fall of the shell might be more easily observed.
[3] At 1.30 A.M. on 21st July, however, there was a German air-raid upon
Audruicq (11 miles N.W. of St. Omer).   Some ammunition stacked in
wooden boxes in the open was ignited, which started a conflagration.   The
principal loss was 500,000 18-pdr. and 10,000 heavy howitzer (8″ and 9·2″)
shell, but this was compensated for by increased receipts from home.   The
railway centre at Audruicq was not damaged.

Switch Line westward as far as Munster Alley (south-west 21-22 of Martinpuich) and Munster Alley itself, the operations of July. its left flank being carried out in conjunction with the attack of the Reserve Army against Pozières. On the following day the XIII. Corps was to assault the German 2nd Position from Falfemont Farm to Waterlot Farm, including Guillemont, in co-operation with the attack of the French XX. Corps.

The success of the dawn assault on the 14th July encouraged the Fourth Army to persevere with night operations. Zero hour, communicated confidentially later in the day, was fixed at 9.50 P.M. for the main operation and 11.30 P.M. on the 22nd as regards the left flank attack of the III. Corps ; but these times were eventually altered to 12.30 A.M. on the 23rd July for the XV. and III. Corps, in order to synchronize with the Reserve Army attack upon Pozières.[1] The preliminary bombardment was to begin at 7 P.M. on the 22nd, the previous evening, with five minutes' intense fire before the infantry advanced. As will be seen, the decision to carry out several preliminary operations, and the later hour fixed for the XIII. Corps attack, prevented the execution of a general simultaneous assault by the Fourth Army.

On the 22nd July the French, who required more time for preparation after their effort of the 20th,[2] announced that they could not be ready before the 24th, and the task of the right of the XIII. Corps—entrusted to the 30th Division, from reserve—on the 23rd was therefore limited to the capture of Guillemont. Zero hour for this enterprise remained at 3.40 A.M. in order to suit the French, who would assist the advance with artillery fire.[3] The attack of the left of the corps against Delville Wood was to be delivered at the same time.

During the night of the 21st July the XV. Corps relieved the troops of the 33rd Division [4] in and about High Wood

---

[1] Sir Douglas Haig visited both Army commanders on this day and endeavoured to synchronize as closely as possible the times of the various attacks, although he recognized the local difficulties. The moon had entered its last quarter, and set at 3.1 A.M. on 23rd July.

[2] See Note I. at end of Chapter.

[3] Special barrages were to be fired and counter-battery work maintained. General Foch also ordered the XX. Corps to display such activity during the night as to leave the Germans in doubt as to whether an attack was imminent. He also said that the attack of the XX. Corps must not be delayed later than the 24th owing to the risk of exposing the British right. As will be seen, however, the XX. Corps did not participate until 30th July.

[4] The casualties, 15th-22nd July, of the 33rd Division, now withdrawn from the battle, were returned as 263 officers and 4,932 other ranks.

I

21-22 by the 51st Division (Major-General G. M. Harper).   Next
July. day the corps carried out a ten minutes' concentrated
bombardment of the Switch Line.

The left of the 33rd Division front had passed to the III.
Corps, which put in another brigade of the 19th Division ;
but the right of this brigade, between High Wood and
Bazentin le Petit, was not in touch with the newly arrived
brigade of the 51st Division, and the troops had as yet no
knowledge of the ground or of the precise situation of the
enemy.   On the 22nd July a special low-flying air reconnaissance succeeded in verifying a report that there was a
German trench half-way between the forward positions of
the 19th Division and the Switch Line.   This trench, called
" Intermediate Trench ", was observed to be " full of men "
and connected to the Switch Line by a communication
trench just east of the Bazentin le Petit—Martinpuich
road.   It was now named as the first objective of the 19th
Division, the advance to the Switch Line being made one hour
after zero.   On the evening of the 22nd July, therefore, the
XV. Corps arranged, with General Rawlinson's approval, to
put back the hour of its main attack to 1.30 A.M., in order to
preserve co-operation in its advance to the main objective.[1]

The 5th Division (right of the XV. Corps) now proposed
to deal with the Wood Lane line, presumably entrenched
and still held by the enemy, in a preliminary operation
entrusted to the 13th Brigade, which was to attack on the
night of the 22nd, after a special bombardment.

The XIII. Corps made two attempts during the early
hours of the 22nd July to gain ground towards Guillemont,
in order to facilitate the attack against that village.   At
1.30 A.M. a battalion of the 35th Division tried unsuccessfully to carry the German trenches between Maltz Horn
Farm and Arrow Head Copse.   Half an hour later a company of the 3rd Division, which had relieved the left of the
35th as far as the Trônes Wood railway, advanced from
Waterlot Farm on Guillemont railway station, and almost
reached it, but was obliged to fall back under the cross-fire
of machine guns.

By the morning of the 21st, the 1st Australian Division,
which formed the right of the Reserve Army, was established

---

[1] On the afternoon of the 22nd Major-General E. C. Ingouville-Williams,
commanding the 34th Division then in corps reserve, was killed near Mametz
Wood whilst making a reconnaissance.   He was succeeded in the command
on 25th July by Major-General C. L. Nicholson.

in Black Watch Alley and had taken over the portion of 21-22
O.G.1 that lay beyond this trench.   The Australians and July.
the troops of the 1st Division were almost back-to-back at
their point of junction, where there existed a salient both
difficult to defend and unsuitable from which to launch an
attack.[1]

Opposite the VIII. Corps, north of the river Ancre, the Sketch
Germans were observed to be still on the alert and busy 11.
improving their defences as though apprehensive of a
renewed assault.   Englebelmer had been subjected to a
hurricane bombardment on the 18th July, and gas shell was
used freely at times against the British batteries ; otherwise
the German artillery was not very active.   In the X. Corps Sketch
the 144th Brigade of the 48th Division had made some 14.
progress up the German communication trenches on the
spur north of Ovillers during the night of the 18th July ;
but the 145th Brigade, on the right, failed in an attempt to
push forward west of Pozières, where the German positions
were ill-defined and more reconnaissance was necessary.
At 2.45 A.M. on the 21st both brigades attacked again,
but the Germans were ready, and no gain of ground
resulted, although the struggle continued for three hours.
General preparations were pushed on for the attack of the
23rd July, when the 48th Division was to co-operate in the
assault of Pozières by the 1st Australian Division.

General Gough had been ordered to " carry out methodi-
" cal operations against Pozières with a view to capturing
" that important position with as little delay as possible ",
and this he proposed to do by using the 1st Australian
Division, acting directly under his orders, without waiting
for the arrival of the remainder of the I. Anzac Corps.[2]
He was anxious to attack at once, but consented to a
postponement until the early hours of the 23rd, since more
time was needed to complete the necessary assembly
trenches and to perfect the artillery arrangements.

General Gough ordered the attack to be made from the
south-east, not from the south-west.   Although the position
of the right of the 1st Australian Division, in the left half of

[1] See Sketch 17.
[2] The corps (1st, 2nd and 4th Australian Divisions, the last-named
having replaced the New Zealand Division), commanded by Lieut.-General
Sir W. R. Birdwood, had concentrated near Amiens by 14th July.   Its
introduction to warfare on the Western Front had consisted of about three
months in the line near Armentières, under the Second Army.   (For the
expansion and reorganization in Egypt of the Australian Imperial Force,
and the arrival of its divisions in France, see " 1916 " Vol. I., p. 23, f.n. 2,
and pp. 24-5.

21-22
July.
the salient shared with the 1st Division, was cramped and
lacked depth, it was better to launch the assault under
these disadvantages rather than advance from the south-
west—i.e. up the Bapaume road—where the ground was
commanded by the Germans on the Pozières ridge between
the windmill and Mouquet Farm.   Major-General Walker
planned to carry Pozières Trench, that is the German front
line between O.G.1 and the Albert road, at the first bound ;
then to capture the enclosures south of the road ;   and
finally to establish himself in the ruins of the houses along
the near side of the road itself.   On the right, the O.G.
trenches were to be cleared, in corresponding stages, as far
as the windmill.   If all went well, an effort would then be
made to push on farther, through the village.

The right of the 48th Division (X. Corps), whose progress
north of the road towards the head of Mash valley depended,
to a large extent, upon the success of the Australians
attacking the Pozières bastion, was to co-operate by an
attack which would keep in touch with the Australian left.
The 49th Division (left of the X. Corps) would make an
attempt at 2.15 A.M. to extend its hold on the Leipzig salient.

The Australian preparations included the digging of
assembly trenches forward of Black Watch Alley, and this
was done under continuous fire on the nights of the 20th
and 21st July.   An attempt of the 9th (Queensland)
Battalion (3rd Brigade) at 2.30 A.M. on the 22nd to push
forward up O.G.1 and O.G.2 failed in the face of machine-
gun fire and the stout resistance of the German bombers.

NOTE I

THE FRENCH OPERATIONS, 15TH–22ND JULY [1]

Sketches
4, 11.
In the French view the British success on the 14th July permitted
the resumption of combined action north of the Somme.   General
Foch at once reminded General Fayolle that his primary objectives,
whilst the British pushed their advance towards Bapaume, were the
high ground east of Combles and the passage of the Tortille river
near its junction with the Somme.   When, however, the Allied
attack was postponed to the 23rd, General Foch, impatient of delay,
sponsored a preliminary operation, fixed for the 20th, to be undertaken by the Sixth Army north of the Somme.   Moreover, " con-
" trairement aux intentions formelles du généralissime ", he had
approved of General Fayolle's plan to attack on the 18th south of
the river towards Nesle, 12 miles south of Péronne.   For this

[1] F.O.A. iv. (ii.), pp. 256-70.

offensive, which showed such a marked divergence from the general direction of the Allied advance, 11 divisions (including two of the Tenth Army) were to be engaged as against five divisions north of the Somme ; and the heavy artillery to be employed was increased at the expense of the XX. Corps, next to the British.

On the 15th July the Germans counter-attacked and retook part of Biaches, where fighting continued. This reaction of the enemy, combined with the unfavourable weather, caused a postponement of the operations south of the Somme, but a general attack on both sides of the river was delivered on the 20th July. On the north, the French reached the western slopes of the Maurepas ravine, beyond Hardecourt ; the station on the Hardecourt—Maurepas road ; and a line running thence south-eastward some fifteen hundred yards from the German 2nd Position between Maurepas and the Somme. South of the river, the Sixth Army failed between Biaches and Belloy, but made some progress on the northern side of Soyécourt (2 miles south-east of Estrées).[1] The fighting was bitter and the losses heavy on both sides.

Next day General Foch expressed his desire for an attack against the front Cléry—Maurepas on the 23rd, in conjunction with the British effort ; but General Balfourier, commanding the XX. Corps, required more time for preparation and secured 24 hours' respite.

NOTE II

THE GERMANS DURING 15TH-22ND JULY [2]

Although, in the early hours of the 15th July General Sixt von Armin was still doubtful as to how far the British advance had penetrated, he had determined upon a counter-attack by the *8th Division* of his *IV. Corps*. Command of this part of the front was now divided between the *3rd Guard Division* (Longueval—High Wood) and the *7th Division* (thence to Pozières Trench), which had relieved the *183rd* ; but a great admixture of units still prevailed.

Orders for the counter-attack, which was to be supported by the field artilleries of the *8th*, *7th* and *3rd Guard Divisions*, were issued at 2 A.M. on the 15th. The *72nd* and *93rd Regiments* were to move against the line, W.N.W. corner of Longueval—north-west corner of Bazentin le Petit, and each put two battalions in front. The men were tired, after much marching, and the advance was made in the darkness under heavy artillery fire. On the right, the *II./93rd* deployed south of Martinpuich soon after 4 A.M. and got into touch with the troops holding the Switch Line. The *III./93rd* arrived at the Switch Line west of High Wood about the same time. The *III.172nd* had reached a sunken road north-east of High Wood, whilst the *II./72nd* arrived at the Switch Line east of the wood. One company of the latter pushed on and occupied a part of the front line north-west of Longueval. " Owing to the tremendous

---

[1] According to Palat xi., the Tenth Army, farther to the south, attacked towards Soyécourt and Vermandovillers and took the German front line, also repulsing a German advance south of Chaulnes.
[2] G.O.A. x., pp. 366-7, 414-5, Somme-Nord ii, and Gallwitz.

" effect of the British artillery and the activity of the British airmen,
" it was impossible for the attacking battalions to advance by day-
" light. They sought cover in portions of the trenches and shell-holes
" by sections and platoons."

At 5.30 A.M. Armin wanted the troops to make a fresh effort, as
he considered the situation critical, but a further advance was
impossible : the British artillery fire was too formidable, and units
in the battle front were so mixed that difficulties of command were
very great. Moreover, the artillery was not ready.

On the 19th July, by order of O.H.L., command of the German
battle front was reorganized, the troops of the *Second Army* north
of the Somme becoming a new *First Army* under General Fritz von
Below. From the Somme to the Cologne river (W.N.W. of St.
Quentin) the front remained *Second Army*, now under General von
Gallwitz, who also, though junior to Below, was appointed commander
of the " Group " formed by the two Armies. Lossberg remained Chief
of the Staff to Below. Gallwitz, who brought his own Chief of the
Staff, Colonel Bronsart von Schellendorff, came from Verdun where
he had been in command of the operations on the western bank of
the Meuse. He urged offensive action south of the Somme, but
Falkenhayn replied " to hold on is all that matters ". Gallwitz at
once proceeded to reorganize the artillery, which had suffered severely,
and he forbade the expenditure of ammunition on retaliatory or
harassing fire ; it was to be conserved for definite operations.

O.H.L. considered that the extra forces liberated by the cessation
of the offensive at Verdun were not sufficient to justify any departure
from the policy of the strict defensive, it being necessary to reinforce
the Russian front.[1] On the 21st July, Falkenhayn announced that
no more troops could be taken from " quiet " fronts to feed the
Somme battle until they were relieved by " fought out " divisions ;
he required seven such divisions to replace those already brought to
the Somme as reinforcements.

The *8th Bavarian Reserve Division* was required to strengthen the
line opposite the French north of the Somme after the attack of the
20th July. The *117th Division*, coming from the *Fourth Army* in
Flanders, had already been allotted to the *First Army*. The only
other reserve in sight, the *IX. Reserve Corps* (*17th* and *18th Reserve
Divisions*), then en route for the Somme from Rupprecht's *Sixth
Army* on the Arras—Lens front, was allotted by O.H.L. to Gallwitz
for the *First Army*. Another division (*23rd Reserve*, from Champagne) was now under orders for the Somme. In the period 16th-
22nd July Armin's corps was reinforced by 14 batteries of heavy
guns and howitzers ; Gossler's, by 18 batteries. The air force was
augmented by five reconnaissance flights, three artillery flights, three
bombing flights, and two fighter squadrons. Since the opening of
the offensive on the 1st July 13 divisions had been used to reinforce
the German line north of the Somme and three more were about to
enter the battle.

---

[1] Five German divisions were sent from the Western Front to Russia
during July. See Chapter XXI.

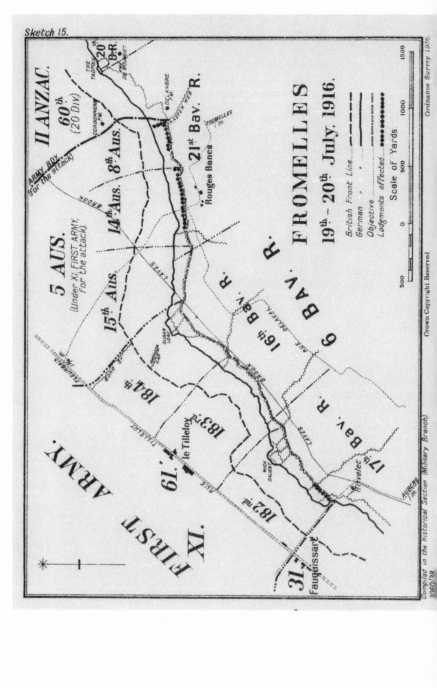

Sketch 15.

FROMELLES
19th – 20th July. 1916.

British Front Line
German
Objective
Lodgements effected

Scale of Yards

II ANZAC.

60th (20 DIV)

5 AUS.
(Under XI, FIRST ARMY, for the attack)

IX. FIRST ARMY.

14th Aus. 8th Aus.

15th Aus.

21st Bav. R.

Rouges Bancs

16th Bav. R.

6 Bav. R.

17th Bav. R.

182nd

183rd

184th

le Tilleloy

Trivelet

Fauquissart

31.

ARMY BDY. (for the attack)

THE TADPOLE

SUGAR LOAF

CHAPTER V

THE SUBSIDIARY ATTACK AT FROMELLES

19TH–20TH JULY 1916

(Sketches 15, B)

On the 5th July G.H.Q. had informed the commanders of the Third, First and Second Armies that the prospects of the Fourth Army were encouraging : " the next few days " may very possibly place us in possession of the enemy's " defences from the Ancre to the Somme " : Generals Monro and Plumer (commanding the First and Second Armies respectively) were each to select a front on which to pierce the enemy line, if all continued to go well with the Fourth Army : the gaps so created were subsequently to be widened, on the assumption that success in the main operation would result in the enemy opposite the First and Second Armies becoming " much weakened and shaken ", and " probably contemplating retreat " : the fronts selected were to be notified as soon as possible.[1]

Next day General Plumer, who was much occupied with preliminary preparations for an offensive against the Messines ridge, informed General Monro that the only locality he considered suitable was his extreme right, and suggested a joint operation at this point should the occasion arise. General Monro agreed in so far that on the 8th July he ordered Lieut.-General Sir R. C. B. Haking,[2] commanding the XI. Corps, to put forward a scheme for an attack by one of his own divisions and one from the Second Army. The **Sketch B.** XI. Corps was holding the front from south-west of Cambrin (south of the La Bassée canal) to E.S.E. of Laventie, the

---

[1] The rôle of General Allenby's Third Army in these circumstances had already been outlined. See " 1916 " Vol. I., p. 266, f.n. 4.

[2] He had commanded the 1st Division at the Battle of Aubers Ridge, May 1915 ; at Loos, in September, his XI. Corps, in reserve at the opening of the battle, was denied the chance to intervene with any prospect of success. See " 1915 " Vol. II.

9-13 junction of the First and Second Armies, and General
July. Haking's plan was to capture Aubers Ridge including the
villages of Aubers and Fromelles. On the 9th, however, he
was informed by General Monro that the capture of Aubers
Ridge was not contemplated.

On the same day General Monro replied to the G.H.Q.
letter of the 5th. He expressed his own preference for an
attack at Hill 70 with the primary object of expanding the
Loos salient and then threatening Douai if the Germans
evacuated Lille : the capture of Aubers Ridge could only be
useful as a preliminary to a " big combined attack of the
" left of the First Army and the right of the Second Army ".
General Plumer informed G.H.Q. on the 10th July that he
could not recommend an attack farther north, but that
General Monro was " prepared to co-operate in an offensive
" against the Aubers Ridge from the neighbourhood of the
" junction of the First and Second Armies " : the Second
Army, which was sending the I. Anzac Corps to the Somme,
could only contribute one division, " with all available
" heavy artillery ", to act under the First Army.

The situation envisaged in the G.H.Q. letter of the 5th
July did not, of course, arise. On the 13th, however,
Major-General R. H. K. Butler, Deputy-Chief of the General
Staff, visited General Monro and informed him that
the Germans had withdrawn troops—estimated at nine
battalions—from the Lille area to reinforce the Somme
front : [1] the Commander-in-Chief, therefore, desired offensive operations to be carried out at the junction of the First
and Second Armies as originally suggested by General
Plumer, who could contribute one complete division, the
artillery of another, some heavy artillery and trench
mortars, and a certain amount of ammunition : at least
two divisions should be employed : the bombardment
might start on the 14th July and culminate in an assault
three days later.

Thus the operation was to be a purely local attack
intended to hold the enemy to his ground and to teach him
that he could not, with impunity, reinforce the main battle
by thinning his line on this front. At 6.30 P.M. on the 13th
General Haking received verbal orders from the First
Army commander, who desired that the preliminary bom-

---

[1] G.H.Q. Intelligence files record considerable railway movement on
the Lille—Douai lines, 9th and 12th July. It was suspected that either
complete formations, or units " milked " from various divisions, were
being sent south. The Intelligence maps (1st-13th July) show no divisions
in the Lille area in reserve to the *Sixth Army*.

bardment should " give the impression of an impending " offensive operation on a large scale ", and limited the infantry objective to the German front-line system.

The Second Army had assigned the 5th Australian Division (Major-General Hon. J. W. McCay), and the artillery of the 4th Australian Division,[1] besides heavy artillery and trench mortars, to the XI. Corps, and preparations were begun at once.   General Haking at first proposed to attack against the front from the Fauquissart—Tri- Sketch velet road to La Boutillerie (1,400 yards north-east of 15. Cordonnerie Farm) using the 5th Australian Division and the 31st and 61st Divisions of his own corps.   Coming to the conclusion, however, that the artillery available was not sufficient, especially as part of it lacked training and experience,[2] he obtained General Monro's approval for the reduction of the attack frontage to some four thousand yards, the left to be directed upon Delangre Farm.

Thus the troops acting under the XI. Corps were committed to a short advance across the flat water-logged Flanders country under the eyes of the enemy on Aubers Ridge whence, during daylight hours, he could watch all the preparations for attack.   As little fighting had taken place in this region for the past fourteen months, the Germans had had ample opportunity to strengthen their breastwork defences, which now included many machine-gun emplacements constructed of concrete, well sited and concealed.   Whilst all depended upon the destructive effect of the British bombardment and the rapid advance of the infantry, success would but bring the British front line under still closer enemy observation.   Consolidation, which meant the construction of sand-bag breastworks, since digging soon reached water-level, was bound to be difficult ; and as no further offensive action was contemplated—or, indeed, feasible with the forces available—the

---

[1] For the formation in Egypt and the arrival in France of the 5th Australian Division see " 1916 " Vol. I. and the Australian Official Account Vol. III.   When the I. Anzac Corps, early in July, began to move from the Second Army to the Somme it exchanged the New Zealand Division for the 4th Australian Division of the II. Anzac Corps, and during 10th-12th July the 5th Australian Division relieved the 4th on the extreme right of the Second Army, " Bond Street " (see Sketch 15), which joined the British front line about 2½ miles E.S.E. of Laventie, being the boundary between the Second and First Armies.   The 4th Australian Division left its artillery behind when it went south.

[2] Both the 4th and 5th Australian Division artillery had had practically no experience of warfare on the Western Front, and they had no trained trench-mortar personnel.   Some of the heavy batteries, too, were newly formed and had never fired in France.

retention of the ground won would present a problem of its own.

Only the Australians and Major-General C. J. Mackenzie's 61st Division [1] were now to be used in the assault. Each division was to have its three brigades in line, and each brigade was to employ two battalions and no more, as the corps commander wished to keep half the infantry in hand, either to take over the captured line or to make a fresh advance if he were permitted to do so. His operation orders were in the hands of the two divisional commanders on the morning of the 14th July, when such batteries as were already in position began to cut the German wire opposite the front and flanks of the XI. Corps. South of the La Bassée canal the I. Corps undertook the relief of the front held by the XI. Corps, whose 39th and 31st Divisions extended northward so that the 61st was able to concentrate upon its attack frontage from the Fauquissart—Trivelet road to Bond Street. In similar fashion the 5th Australian Division closed on its right to occupy the front from Bond Street to Cordonnerie Farm, the New Zealand Division extending its front southward, and the 60th Brigade (20th Division) coming in on the left of the Australians.

The scene of operations partly coincided with that of the Battle of Aubers Ridge fought in May 1915; indeed, the 8th Division had then attacked over the same ground as the 5th Australian Division was about to do, and against the same opponents.[2] The twelve British and Australian battalions which were to carry out the assault represented no greater concentration of infantry than that of May 1915, but there was now a more powerful artillery, with more ammunition, besides trench mortars to help in cutting the German wire.[3] In addition to the batteries contributed by

[1] The 2nd-Line S. Midland Territorial Division which had assembled at Northampton in January 1915. Its training had been delayed owing to lack of arms and equipment, and interrupted by the necessity of supplying drafts to its 1st-Line division; also by its responsibilities as part of the home defence forces. Embarking for France towards the end of May 1916, it took over trenches for the first time on 13th June.

[2] The whole front of attack fell within the sector of the *6th Bavarian Reserve Division*, which extended, as it had in the spring of 1915, from east of Aubers to a point south of Bois Grenier, a distance of about $4\frac{1}{2}$ miles. All four regiments, *17th*, *16th*, *21st* and *20th Bavarian Reserve* from south to north, were in the line, each with one battalion in front, one in support, and one in either local or divisional reserve.

[3] The actual number of guns and howitzers at Aubers Ridge, 1915, was almost the same as at Fromelles, 1916, but no obsolete 4·7″ and 15-pdr. guns or 5″ howitzers fired in the 1916 action. (See " 1915 " Vol. II.)

the Second Army, the artillery on the front of attack was reinforced from the First Army line farther south, to make a total of 296 field guns and howitzers and 78 heavier pieces.[1] As regards heavy artillery, the proportion of guns to frontage of attack was more than that of the Fourth Army for the opening of the Somme offensive on the 1st July.

Whilst wire-cutting continued, the heavy artillery was 16 July. to begin registration and a slow bombardment on the 16th July ; and on the 16th and 17th the German lines immediately north and south of the La Bassée canal were to be bombarded "with a view to inducing the "enemy to move guns opposite that front ". From zero hour on the 17th a special artillery programme was to be carried out until the infantry assaulted seven hours later.[2] During the last three hours of this period there were to be four lifts to barrage lines, at each of which the infantry would show bayonets and dummy figures to induce the enemy to man his parapet in expectation of assault : at the end of each lift, which was to last about five minutes, the artillery would shorten range and continue the bombardment of the German front position, catching the defenders, it was hoped, before they could seek cover again.

At a conference on the 16th July General Haking told

The ammunition allotment for Fromelles was 200,000 rounds for the field guns ; 15,000 for the 4·5″ howitzers ; and a total of 4,350 for the heavy and siege guns and howitzers.

[1] Heavy and siege artillery :
    60-pdrs., 40 ; 6″ hows., 22 ; 9·2″ hows., 8 ; 12″ hows., 5 ; 6″ guns, 2 ; 9·2″ gun, 1. (The Second Army contributed 24 of the 60-pdrs., 16 of the 6″ hows., the eight 9·2″ hows., and 2 of the 12″ hows.)
Field artillery :
    31st Division front (south of attack) : 18-pdrs., 28 ; 4·5″ hows., 16.

    61st Division supported by its own artillery and that of the 8th Division : 18-pdrs., 96 ; 4·5″ hows., 24.

    5th Australian Division supported by its own artillery, that of the 4th Australian Division, and 3 batteries of the 31st Division : 18-pdrs., 108 ; 4·5″ hows., 24.

    The 61st Division had 40 (12 kept in reserve) 2″ trench mortars and two 240-mm. mortars ; the 5th Australian Division twenty 2″ mortars.

[2] 0.00—0.30   Registration by field artillery and trench mortars.
0.30—2.00   Registration and bombardment by 9·2″ hows. and upwards.
2.00—7.00   Wire-cutting by 18-pdrs.
4.00—7.00   Wire-cutting by trench mortars and bombardment by 18-pdrs., and 4·5″ and 6″ hows.
5.00—7.00   Slow bombardment by 9·2″ hows. and upwards.
7.00   Artillery lift to barrage lines.

16 July. his divisional commanders that " the narrow depth of the
" attack should make it possible, with the ammunition
" available, to reduce the defenders to a state of collapse
" before the assault ".   He reminded them, however, that
the leading lines of infantry must deploy as close as possible
to the German wire before the barrage lifted : slowness or
hesitation in the assault would be fatal to success.

The necessary reliefs and concentrations of troops were
still incomplete on the morning of the 16th July, for the
batteries of the 4th Australian Division were not all in
position.   The rather hurried movements, combined with
the work—not yet finished—of getting forward ammunition
and battle stores, were a severe tax upon the energies of all
concerned.   Since its entry into the line, the 61st Division
had carried out eight raids, most of which had involved
sharp fighting, and on the 18th and 19th June had brought
1,500 gas cylinders into the trenches.   Intended to be used
during the course of normal " active trench warfare ", the
gas was released in the Neuve Chapelle and Fauquissart
sectors at 9 P.M. on the 15th July, whilst the reliefs were in
progress ; and although the discharge was stopped after
fifteen minutes, when the wind died away, German artillery
retaliation caused a considerable number of casualties. [1]
On the night of the 15th July a fierce bombardment inflicted considerable loss in the neighbourhood of Cordonnerie
Farm, where the 60th Brigade was about to relieve the
Australians, and a German raiding party got in and captured
a Lewis gun detachment belonging to the 58th Battalion,
which had nearly a hundred officers and men killed and
wounded. [2]

Major-General Butler paid another visit to First Army
headquarters at Chocques on the 16th July and informed
Generals Monro and Plumer, General Haking also being
present, that there was now no urgent need for the XI.
Corps operation : Sir Douglas Haig did not wish the
attack to take place at all unless the commanders on the
spot were satisfied that their resources were, in every way,
adequate.   Both General Haking, who was very confident

----

[1] Between 16th July and daylight 19th July every available man in
the 61st Division not detailed for the assault was employed in removing
gas cylinders from the trenches.   In this period 470 cylinders were taken
out, but the men were by then completely exhausted and no more cylinders
could be moved.

[2] " Bav. Res. Regt. No. 21 " states that the raid was carried out by a
party of 100, which lost 10 killed and 22 wounded, and took 3 prisoners.

of success,[1] and General Monro expressed themselves 16-18
against either postponement or cancellation ; so it was July.
agreed that the operation orders should stand.   After the
conference ended, however, heavy rain fell and Major-
General Butler returned to Chocques to raise the question
of the effect of bad weather on the operations.   General
Monro was absent, but it was impressed upon one of his
staff officers [2] by the Deputy-Chief of the General Staff that
the Army commander had full discretion either to cancel
or postpone the attack for reasons of weather or for any
other cause.

As a matter of fact the 15th July had been hazy and
dull, and even before the rain on the afternoon of the 16th
artillery registration was proceeding too slowly.   Zero
hour, fixed at 3 P.M. on the 16th July for 4 A.M. next
morning, was at 11 P.M. postponed for four hours.   Further
postponements followed, as adverse reports from the
artillery groups reached corps headquarters, and at 8.30 A.M.
on the 17th July—when there was low cloud with drizzling
rain—General Haking informed the Army that he had been
obliged to defer the attack for 24 hours at least : should he
carry it out on the 18th July ?

General Monro would not sanction this.   He was now
anxious to cancel the operation, as, indeed, he could have
done.   Instead, he reported to G.H.Q. at 10 A.M. on the
17th that a postponement had become necessary owing
to bad weather, and that unless conditions improved a
further postponement must be made : he therefore proposed
to cancel the attack, and asked if he were authorized to
inform General Plumer accordingly.   The reply of G.H.Q.[3]
did nothing to relieve the First Army commander of his
responsibility, and with General Monro's approval a corps
order was issued at 7.15 P.M. fixing the 19th July for the
attack, zero hour not to be earlier than 11 A.M.

Two days' respite proved very welcome to all ranks and
all arms, for there had been little time for sleep.   The 18th
July was another cloudy day, but the sky cleared in the

---

[1] He again raised the question of attacking Aubers Ridge, but was
informed that the Commander-in-Chief forbade it.
[2] Lieut.-Colonel S. H. Wilson, G.S.O.1 (Operations).
[3] " The Commander-in-Chief wishes the special operation . . . to be
" carried out as soon as possible, weather permitting, provided always
" that Sir Charles Monro is satisfied that the conditions are favourable
" and that the resources at his disposal, including ammunition, are ad-
" equate both for the preparation and execution of the enterprise."

late afternoon so that with R.F.C. assistance [1] the artillery preparation was able to make good progress. Astride the La Bassée canal the bombardment of the German front was repeated, drawing, as it had done before, a vigorous reply from the hostile batteries. After darkness fell infantry patrols were active, those of the 61st Division reporting no enemy movement and the hostile front line, to all appearances, weakly held. The Australians found it difficult to get near the German parapet opposite their right front, as the enemy had put out covering parties ; in the centre the German wire appeared to be intact ; on the left several gaps were located.

Haze in the early morning of the 19th, preceded a fine day with good visibility. At 7 A.M. the XI. Corps fixed artillery zero hour definitely for 11 A.M., which meant that the infantry would attack in full daylight at 6 P.M. The British bombardment appeared to be dealing faithfully with the German parapet,[2] but it was not, in fact, accomplishing the destruction essential to the success of the infantry assault. On the Sugarloaf salient, opposite the left of the 61st Division, a special concentration of heavy artillery was deemed necessary, and it opened at 2.35 P.M. By this time the Germans, who before noon had begun to bombard the British positions, were shelling heavily the whole front of attack, the communication trenches and Rue Tilleloy, causing some loss.[3] Between 4 and 5 P.M. the field batteries supporting the 61st Division suffered likewise, and, although the damage to the guns was trifling, there were many casualties to personnel and some of the hastily formed ammunition dumps were blown up.[4] The feint " lifts " which repeatedly threatened attack during the afternoon did not induce the enemy to man his parapets.

[1] On 16th July No. 16 Squadron R.F.C. reinforced No. 10 Squadron operating on the front of attack. No. 10 Kite Balloon Section was also available. From 14th July onwards the La Bassée—Lille road from Illies to Beaucamps—some three miles behind the German front—had been kept under constant observation from the air during the hours of daylight.

[2] German accounts agree that considerable destruction was caused and many casualties inflicted. " Bav. Res. Regt. No. 16 " states that its front possessed 75 shelters built into the parapet : these were protected by 22-30 cm. (9″-12″) of concrete, and 60 of them remained intact. Australian reports after the action estimated the German parapet to be 8′ high and from 3′ to 12′ thick ; parados, 7′ high ; dug-outs in strong " island " traverses.

[3] Among the wounded was Lieut.-Colonel F. W. Toll, 31st Australian Battalion, but he continued in command.

[4] Many field batteries were in position within 3,000 yards of the German front line, with their observers in the sand-bagged houses along Rue Tilleloy.

About 5.30 P.M. the infantry began to move out, those 19 July. battalions which had the widest stretches of No Man's Land to cross starting first.[1] In the 61st Division—the average trench strength of battalions was only 550—each attacking company was to issue through an open sally-port at ground level, a method which, at best, did not facilitate a rapid deployment beyond the British wire, and on those parts of the front where the German machine gunners were ready and waiting to open fire each sally-port became a death-trap.[2]

Br.-General A. F. Gordon's 182nd Brigade was on the right, two Stokes mortars being emplaced south of the Trivelet road to deal with any machine guns liable to enfilade the 2/7th R. Warwickshire attack. The two companies of this battalion emerged into No Man's Land and deployed with hardly any loss ; they were only 50 yards away from the German parapet when the guns lifted and they rushed the front line without delay. The wire and the breastwork had been almost completely destroyed, and the Germans who survived were captured before they could resist. For a few minutes the stormers were checked by the wire in front of the support line, losing heavily from enfilade machine-gun fire, but the survivors pressed on and entered their objective. A section of the brigade machine-gun company and a third company of the Warwickshire arrived in the German front trench ; but the enfilade fire from the right was deadly, whilst the captured position was heavily shelled by the German guns.[3] A gallant attempt to bomb northward gained some ground, but the enemy counter-attacked and recovered it. Next on the left, the two companies of the 2/6th Warwickshire had lost more heavily during their deployment ; they pressed on towards the Wick salient until they were checked in front of the German wire, which was almost intact. Machine-gun fire in enfilade at close range now took terrible toll of them. The few men who struggled through towards the German parapet were shot down before they could close. A third

---

[1] On the front of attack the width of No Man's Land varied from 100 to 400 yards.

[2] Timbered underground passages leading out into the " borrow-pit " beyond the parapet had been constructed by the 1/3rd S. Midland Field Company R.E. (attached 183rd Brigade). By some misunderstanding these were not used.

[3] " Bav. Res. Regt. No. 17 " states that about 200 British who got in occupied a switch trench facing Trivelet, but most of them went on and occupied the " second line ", [their objective], killing or capturing the garrison.

19 July. company, which had left the British line to reinforce the assault, was stopped by machine-gun fire whilst still in No Man's Land.

In the centre of the divisional front the companies of the 2/4th and 2/6th Gloucestershire (Br.-General C. G. Stewart's 183rd Brigade) had been shelled as they waited for the signal to advance, the 2/6th Gloucestershire losing over fifty men. Shrapnel caught them as they strove to get out of their sally-ports, so that this method of exit had to be abandoned in favour of an advance over the parapet.[1] In No Man's Land machine-gun fire was so deadly that only a few officers and men succeeded in getting near the German wire, and these were soon killed or wounded.

The 184th Brigade (Br.-General C. H. P. Carter), on the left, had kept its assault companies of the 2/4th R. Berkshire and 2/1st Buckinghamshire ready in the front line since 9 A.M., and casualties from German shell-fire compelled some hurried reorganization barely an hour before the advance was due to begin. The Berkshire, also, were caught by machine-gun fire as they came out of their sally-ports :[2] Lieut.-Colonel J. H. Beer was killed whilst directing the movement from the parapet. Two platoons of the right company managed to struggle forward into No Man's Land, and a few scattered parties reached the German wire, which they found uncut. Being unsupported, they were obliged to fall back again. The Bucks battalion was confronted by the Sugarloaf salient, which was not within effective range of the Stokes mortars. Here, too, the leading troops were checked by machine-gun fire at the sally-ports, so, by the direction of Lieut.-Colonel H. M. Williams, use was made of Rhondda Sap instead ;[3] but the two companies which were thus enabled to deploy did so

[1] Lieut.-Colonel F. A. C. Hamilton of the 2/6th Gloucestershire was wounded about 6 P.M. whilst directing the advance from the front line.

[2] The historian of the *16th Bavarian Reserve Regiment*, whose centre and left confronted the 183rd and 184th Brigades, states that German infantry, machine-gun and shrapnel fire caught the British while they were still trying to " unravel themselves " from their sally-ports. The *III./16th*, in front line, was quite ready for the assault, thanks to the vigilance of its sentries, who did not flinch in the face of the British bombardment.

[3] The 3rd Australian Tunnelling Company had exploded a " pipe-pusher " to extend the sap towards the German line, opening up 220 feet with about six feet of cover. Two other " pipe-pushers " were fired on the 183rd Brigade front ; these were used to provide a covered way for the evacuation of wounded. The Barratt hydraulic forcing jack, known as the " pipe-pusher " pushed forward at a depth of four to five feet underground a pipe filled with ammonal. The fissure which usually resulted from the explosion was calculated to provide a semi-covered way for communication purposes ; it could not quickly be converted into a traversed trench.

in a hail of shrapnel.   The right company was practically destroyed in its efforts to advance ; but on the left a party of the battalion reached the north-eastern face of the salient, and there was sharp fighting on the parapet till all were killed or wounded.   A third company of the battalion, bearing material for consolidation, left the British line at 6.10 P.M. but was stopped by the fire of the German machine guns.

By 7 P.M. Major-General Mackenzie was aware of the success of the 2/7th Warwickshire on the extreme right ; [1] other reports claimed that the 183rd Brigade, in the centre, had made a small lodgment and that a footing had been gained in the Sugarloaf.   In accordance with corps instructions previously received, arrangements were made to reopen the bombardment where the attack had failed, and all three brigades were warned to reorganize for another attempt.   Following a special order, received from General Haking at 7.30 P.M., to extend the hold on the Sugarloaf in order to help the Australians, it became known that the 184th Brigade had no men in the salient ; and eventually the bombardment was continued in preparation for a fresh assault, to be made all along the line at 9 P.M.   At 8.20 P.M., however, the corps commander telephoned instructions to cancel this attack and to withdraw all troops in the captured trenches after darkness fell.

This order reached the 182nd Brigade in time to stop the remaining company of the 2/7th Warwickshire from going forward ; of the other three companies, only a few stragglers and lightly wounded regained the British line, the remainder being overwhelmed.[2]   The four Vickers guns were also lost.   Elsewhere along the front the men still holding on in No Man's Land came back under cover of the bombardment, and as many wounded as possible were brought in.

Major-General Mackenzie held another telephone conversation with the corps commander shortly after 11 P.M. when General Haking determined that the 184th Brigade should " attack the Sugarloaf during the night " after ten minutes' concentrated bombardment ; but at 3 A.M.

---

[1] Thirty prisoners had been passed back, and it was estimated that fifty others had been killed on the way to the British lines by the fire of their friends.

[2] According to " Bav. Res. Regt. No. 17 ", the left of the *III./Bn.*, lying south of the Trivelet road, bombed to its right, whilst two companies of the *I./Bn.* were brought up to attack from the other flank, and from the front.   The total of prisoners, wounded and unwounded, is given as 61.

Br.-General Carter reported that his trenches were being heavily shelled and he could not be ready before daylight. The operation was therefore cancelled, but the corps warned the division to be ready to renew the attack during the morning.

19 July.   The troops of the 5th Australian Division went straight over the parapet and, in consequence, suffered less before deployment than did those of the 61st Division. Battalions were at full strength, and officers and men were eager to come to grips with the Germans.

Attacking next to the 61st Division, the 59th Battalion [1] of Br.-General H. E. Elliott's 15th (Victoria) Brigade had its right directed upon the point where the Layes brook entered the German line. The brook ran diagonally across No Man's Land on the brigade front, but could hardly be considered an obstacle, as its depth was only two feet. The 59th started well, but soon came under deadly machine-gun fire from the Sugarloaf and was checked after covering 300 yards. Next on the left, the 60th Battalion struggled on as far as the German wire, but could do no more. Losses were very heavy, especially in officers, Major G. G. McCrae, commanding the 60th, being killed, and Lieut.-Colonel E. A. Harris, of the 59th, disabled by a shell-burst. The survivors had no thought of retreat and endeavoured to dig in where they lay.

In the Australian centre, the 53rd and 54th Battalions of Colonel H. Pope's 14th (N.S.W.) Brigade suffered less severely in their advance; they stormed the German parapet with hardly a check, and overcame all resistance, capturing a number of Germans and two machine guns. Beyond the front breastworks, however, the Australians emerged into flat fields intersected by watery ditches; there was no sign of a support line.[2] One ditch—in some parts of the front the first or second ditch, in others, the third—was thereupon selected for consolidation, and ten Vickers guns were sent forward for the defence of the new

---

[1] British and Australians did not attack shoulder to shoulder: the flanks of the two divisions were to converge on the objective, and the 59th Battalion concentrated for the assault in the left half of its sector.

[2] According to German accounts, the trenches in rear of the front breastwork on most parts of the front had long been abandoned, and by this time were water-logged: support troops occupied the ruins of farms and similar strongpoints 250–400 yards behind the front line. Thus the British trench maps, which showed an intricate pattern of front and support lines connected by numerous communication trenches, were misleading.

position. Here, too, there were few officers left, Lieut.-
Colonel I. B. Norris, 53rd Battalion, being among the
killed.

The two battalions of the 8th Brigade (Br.-General E.
Tivey) on the left, 31st (Queensland, Victoria) and 32nd
(S. & W. Australia), were met by machine-gun fire from
front and flank ; yet they stormed the German breastwork and pressed on.[1] As in the 14th Brigade, no well
defined support line was visible, but a position for consolidation was selected and the head of a well-sandbagged
communication trench, " Kasten Weg ", was firmly held.

So in the centre and on the left the Australians had
reached their objective,[2] but the new line was neither continuous nor easily defensible. The 14th Brigade sent
forward two companies of the 55th Battalion with stores
and tools, whilst the 14th Field Company, with infantry
to assist, began to dig a communication trench across
No Man's Land. Similar work was started on the left
flank by the 8th Field Company and a party of the 30th
(N.S.W.) Battalion. By this time there was a heavy
German barrage on No Man's Land where, until darkness
fell, every movement provoked bursts of machine-gun fire.

The 15th Brigade had been asked to co-operate in the
renewed attack of the 61st Division fixed for 9 P.M., and,
with Major-General McCay's approval, brought forward its
58th Battalion to make a new attempt east of the Sugarloaf.
By the time that brigade headquarters became aware that
the 61st Division attack had been cancelled it was too late
to stop this advance, which carried some of the 59th forward
with it and then, being quite unsupported, broke down.
The remnants of all three battalions, 58th, 59th and 60th,
drifted back to the Australian lines during the night.

Although the remainder of the 55th Battalion was sent
forward as a reinforcement about 9 P.M., the situation of the
14th Brigade in the German position was becoming desperate. The whole area was under heavy shell-fire, and
bombing encounters had begun on the open right flank
where some of the survivors of the 53rd Battalion, with no
officers left, were isolated. As the night wore on many

---

[1] At 6 P.M. a mine containing 1,200 lbs. of ammonal was exploded in
No Man's Land on the outer flank ; it was hoped that the crater thus
formed would screen the attacking waves from enfilade fire.

[2] They had penetrated the left and centre of the *III./21st Bavarian
Reserve Regiment*, whose right company lay beyond the front of attack.
The Germans formed a defensive flank beyond Kasten Weg, rallying in
front of Delangre Farm.

19 July. men began to find their way back across No Man's Land from this vicinity.[1]

At 8.50 P.M., when dusk was gathering, the 31st and 32nd Battalions (8th Brigade), on the left, asked for support, and the remainder of the 30th was sent to their assistance. Part of the 29th (Victoria) Battalion, from reserve, followed, for ammunition carriers were sorely 20 July. needed ; and about 2 A.M. on the 20th as many more of this unit as could be collected were sent forward from the old Australian front line, reports having been received of German counter-attacks. Consolidation was proceeding under difficulties ; the troops, with few officers left and no experience to guide them, were also handicapped by being obliged to fill their sand-bags with mud, as there was no dry earth. The first attempts to counter-attack were repulsed, but when, at 3.15 A.M. on the 20th, the Germans came on in force from front and left flank, a retirement to the enemy front line became inevitable. Here the 32nd, on the left, was exposed to galling fire from machine guns in Delangre Farm, in De Mouquet Farm, and from the German work known as " The Tadpole " farther to the east.

A withdrawal from the German position was now the only course, and after the 32nd began to fall back across No Man's Land, the 31st followed suit. Many parties fought their way out, others were cut off and captured. The companies of the 29th and 30th, being mixed with the other two battalions, retired with them, and before 5 A.M. all who could had regained the heavily shelled Australian line.[2]

At 5 A.M. on the 20th the divisional commanders met General Haking at Sailly, General Monro also being present, to complete plans for the renewed attack by the 61st Division. Almost immediately, however, Major-General

---

[1] The *III./16th Bavarian Reserve Regiment*, whose right had repulsed the 15th Australian Brigade, reinforced that flank with a company from its *II./Bn.*, in support along Rue Delaval. This company extended to assist the extreme left of the *III./21st Bavarian Reserve Regiment* which had held fast. " Bav. Res. Regt. No. 16 ".

[2] The Bavarian accounts reveal that the counter-attack, ordered by the divisional commander at 8 P.M. on 19th July, was not delivered according to plan owing to the darkness, and to the confusion made worse by the British bombardment. An advance against the 8th Australian Brigade by two companies *I./21st Bavarian Reserve Regiment*, from local reserve, was checked by fire : later two fresh companies, probably *II./Bn.*, attacked up Kasten Weg while the whole of the *I./Bn.*, supported by two companies of the *20th Bavarian Reserve Regiment* came in from the flank. Progress was slow in the darkness, but by 6 A.M. the position was restored.

McCay was informed by telephone of the retirement of his 20 July.
8th Brigade, whereupon General Monro decided to break
off the action, ordering the withdrawal of the 14th Brigade
from its precarious position where Lieut.-Colonel W. E. H.
Cass, of the 54th Battalion, was in command.

A " box barrage " was put round that part of the
German line known to be in possession of the 14th Brigade :
it fell at 5.40 A.M., and at 6.30 A.M. Lieut.-Colonel Cass
received an order, " prepare to retire ". It was 7.50 A.M.
before the definite order to withdraw reached the 54th
Battalion, and some parties never heard of it. The
Germans were well in rear of the right flank, and every
attempt to get back above ground came under heavy fire,
so that the communication trench, now almost completed
by the 14th Field Company, proved invaluable. By 9 A.M.
most of the remnants of the 54th and 55th Battalions, with
those of the 53rd who had hung on to the German position,
had come in. Many of the wounded were rescued, but six
of the Vickers guns, several of them damaged by shell-fire,
had to be abandoned, few of their detachments having
survived.[1]

As the morning wore on the artillery fire on both sides
died down, and British and Germans spent the rest of
the day in repairing their defences. Stretcher bearers
were busy, the Australians arranging a short truce in order
to be able to search for and remove their wounded. The
action, which had cost the assaulting divisions over 7,000
officers and men in killed, wounded and missing,[2] undoubtedly inflicted some loss and damage on the enemy,[3]

---

[1] According to the regimental account, three companies of the *I./16th
Bavarian Reserve Regiment*, in local reserve, were allotted to the counter-
attack on this flank. The leading company began to arrive about 1.15 A.M.
on 20th July, and joined the company of the *II./Bn.* which was already
engaged. Foot by foot the lost front line was regained, but at dawn a
halt was called, as the troops were exhausted, and bombs and ammunition
needed replenishment. On resuming the attack the remainder of the
position was recovered : by 8.10 A.M. the foremost troops had joined hands
with the counter-attack troops of the *21st Bavarian Reserve Regiment*.

[2] The return of casualties showed :

	Officers	Other Ranks
61st Division	79	1,468
5th Australian Div. . . .	178	5,355
Total	257	6,823

The Australian battalions, being up to establishment, had about twice as
many men engaged as those of the 61st Division.

[3] Between 1,600 and 2,000 casualties, if the figures given in the Bavarian
regimental histories may be taken as a basis. German prisoners amounted
to 150, of which the Australians sent back about a hundred.

but there was no reason to suppose that any German reinforcements had been drawn to the front of attack.[1]

The pity of it was that the action need not have been fought, since the First Army had perfect liberty to cancel it. To have delivered battle at all, after hurried preparation, with troops of all arms handicapped by their lack of experience and training in offensive trench-warfare, betrayed a grave under-estimate of the enemy's powers of resistance. The utmost endeavours of the artillery were unable either to subdue the German batteries or to " reduce " the defenders to a state of collapse before the assault ", so the infantry, advancing in broad daylight, paid the price.[2] Even if the German defences had been completely shattered by the British bombardment, and the infantry assault had succeeded, it would probably have proved impossible to hold the objective under the concentrated fire of the enemy's artillery directed by excellent observation. Such a situation had arisen only too often during the minor engagements fought earlier in the year.[3]

NOTE

O.H.L. and Fromelles [4]

Late on the 19th July Falkenhayn telephoned to the *Sixth Army* for news : he believed that the big attack which he anticipated would be made upon the *Sixth Army* had begun. Assured that the situation was in no way critical, he enquired again on the afternoon of the 20th, when Kuhl (Rupprecht's Chief of the Staff) informed him that only a holding attack had been delivered, as was revealed by a captured operation order of the British XI. Corps. Falkenhayn then said he required a fresh corps for the Somme front, and was told that all preparations had been made to send the *IX. Reserve Corps* ; but Kuhl went on to say that although the *56th Division*—it came

[1] German accounts reveal that on 21st July a battalion from the *40th Division* (in the line opposite Ploegsteert) relieved the *III./21st Bavarian Reserve Regiment*, which had suffered very heavily in conflict with the Australians.

[2] The Bavarian Official Account states that the Bavarian batteries " found it difficult to compete with the enemy weight of metal, but " smothered the British trenches with fire ". The artillery of the flank divisions, *50th Reserve* and *54th Reserve*, are said to have lent valuable assistance, and " thus the backbone of the British attack was broken before " it left the trenches at 5.30 P.M."

[3] See " 1916 " Vol. I., p. 191. The Australian official historian (Vol. III., p. 444) observes that " it is difficult to conceive that the operation "as planned was ever likely to succeed " ; and again, " the well-known " difficulties of a narrow-fronted offensive in trench-warfare had been too " lightly faced ".

[4] Rupprecht i., pp. 506–7.

from Verdun—had arrived in the *Sixth Army,* another division was required, as the British might launch similar attacks to that at Fromelles. At 8.30 P.M. *O.H.L.* issued an order that the *183rd Division,* after assembling at Denain (it had been heavily engaged, as we know, in the Contalmaison—Pozières area), was to go to the *Sixth Army* ; but Kuhl was informed by telephone that the *Guard Reserve Corps* must be sent into reserve at Cambrai. Thus the *Sixth Army* was called upon to provide yet another corps for the Somme : its reassurance of *O.H.L.'s* doubts and fears had been only too effective.

CHAPTER VI

THE SOMME

22ND–31ST JULY 1916

(Sketches 11, 16, 17, 18, 19, 20, 21, 22)

THE NIGHT ATTACKS OF THE FOURTH ARMY
22ND/23RD JULY [1]

HIGH WOOD, THE SWITCH LINE AND MUNSTER ALLEY, GUILLEMONT, LONGUEVAL AND DELVILLE WOOD

Sketch 16.

THE bombardment which preceded the series of attacks planned for the night of the 22nd/23rd July opened at 7 P.M. on the 22nd.[2] It undoubtedly put the enemy on his guard, but, there being no moon, the British infantry, advancing in the darkness, was expected to offer few targets to such German machine guns as might contrive to come into action.

22 July.

The first move was made by the 5th Division (XV. Corps), with the purpose of securing Wood Lane [3] as a preliminary to the assault of the Switch Line east of High Wood. Even before the barrage lifted at 10 P.M. the 14/R. Warwickshire and 1/R. West Kent (Br.-General L. O. W. Jones's 13th Brigade) made a considerable advance, being protected by the lie of the ground. When, however, they appeared over the crest and could be seen by the light of the German flares they were taken in enfilade by machine guns firing from the eastern corner of High Wood,

---

[1] See page 113.

[2] Somme-Nord ii. states that aeroplanes flying low over High Wood and the Switch Line directed the British artillery fire " with painful " accuracy ". The troops in and east of the wood suffered so severely that it was intended to relieve them, but the British attacks made it impossible to do so.

[3] Held by one company *I./62nd* nearest High Wood and the *II./72nd Regiment (8th Division)*.

Sketch 16.

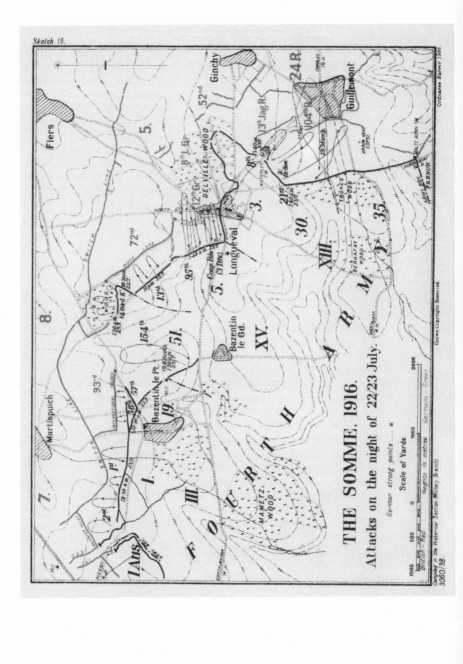

THE SOMME, 1916.

Attacks on the night of 22/23 July.

German strong points ······ ∭

Scale of Yards.

1000   500   0   1000   2000

Heights in metres.   Germans ─ Green

British ─ Red

Compiled in the Historical Section (Military Branch)

3060/38.

Ordnance Survey 1946.

Crown Copyright Reserved.

where a well-wired strongpoint had defied the assaults of a platoon of the 1/4th Gordon Highlanders (154th Brigade). Heavy fire also came from the front, and the check appeared to be complete. After the 2/K.O.S.B. and 15/R. Warwickshire had been sent up, Major-General Stephens ordered the 13th Brigade to make another attempt, if possible carrying forward the advance to the **23 July.** Switch Line at 1.30 A.M. according to the original plan. The German fire was, however, too heavy, and such parties of the West Kent and Warwickshire as were still out in front, endeavouring to dig themselves in, were brought back. On the left some of the West Kent had forced their way into the German trench beyond Wood Lane, and these were among the last to withdraw. As dawn broke the brigade reorganized on its old line, having lost over a thousand officers and men. Lieut.-Colonel D. R. Sladen, K.O.S.B., was among the wounded.

At 1.30 A.M. on the 23rd two battalions of Br.-General C. E. Stewart's 154th Brigade (51st Division, holding the left of the XV. Corps front) advanced to complete the capture of High Wood and to secure 600 yards of the Switch Line adjoining it on the north-west. The attack upon the strongpoint at the eastern corner of the wood and the assault of the 13th Brigade, followed by the attack of the 19th Division presently to be described, had left the Germans very much on the alert, and the 1/4th Gordon Highlanders and 1/9th R. Scots, both of which were new to the ground and had no time for reconnaissance, suffered accordingly. On the right, the Gordons scrambled forward amongst the fallen trees and shell craters of High Wood, losing direction in the darkness, whilst machine-gun fire from positions which could not be located caused them considerable loss. The Royal Scots were shelled as they came up the depression south-west of the wood on their way to attack the Switch Line ; then they encountered, unexpectedly, machine-gun fire at close range from the eastern end of Intermediate Trench, which was well wired and held many Germans who used flares freely. By 3 A.M. both battalions were back in their old positions, having lost nearly 450 of all ranks.[1]

[1] Somme-Nord ii. speaks of bitter hand to hand fighting in High Wood and heavy losses. The *III./165th* (from *7th Division*) and part of the *I./62nd* (from *12th Division*) were reinforced from the Switch Line, and the defence of the northern part of the wood was taken over by the *I./93rd* in the early morning of the 23rd. Intermediate Trench was held by the *II.* and *III./93rd*.

23 July.   The attack of the III. Corps, next on the left, had been delivered at 12.30 A.M.   On the 19th Division front heavy shell-fire greatly hampered the despatch of orders to battalions and the movement of the troops to their assembly positions.   In the 57th Brigade,[1] next to, but not in touch with, the 51st Division (XV. Corps), the 10/R. Warwickshire carried out a last-minute relief of the 10/Worcestershire which had been engaged in several attempts to rush some forward machine-gun posts of the *III./93rd Regiment.* Before the barrage lifted at zero hour, the infantry was to creep forward to within seventy-five yards of its first objective, Intermediate Trench ; but the Warwickshire on the extreme right of the attack were not ready in time to take part.   Next on the left, the 8/Gloucestershire was checked by machine-gun fire from the front and from High Wood; it lost heavily, Lieut.-Colonel A.Carton de Wiart being again wounded.   The 7/South Lancashire and the 7/Loyal N. Lancashire of the 56th Brigade (Br.-General F. G. M. Rowley) could do no better, although the former hung on for some hours in shell-holes outside the German trench.   Between 3 and 4 A.M. therefore a general withdrawal was carried out, and the line reorganized under persistent shell-fire.

In the 1st Division the attacking battalions formed up before zero hour outside the British wire, the Germans sending up lights as they did so and opening fire with machine guns.   Nevertheless, the assault was pressed with great determination.   On the right, the 1/Cameron Highlanders (Br.-General A. J. Reddie's 1st Brigade) and the 10/Gloucestershire, next on the left, were heavily punished by the fire of machine guns concealed in the long grass. Neither battalion could reach the Switch Line, and no better fortune attended the assault of the 2nd Brigade (Br.-General A. B. Hubback), made by the 2/K.R.R.C. and 2/R. Sussex, which had for objective the re-entrant formed by the Switch Line and Munster Alley.   The two battalions were under machine-gun fire from the outset, and the attempt to rush the trenches under cover of the barrage stood no chance of success.   Although some of the Rifles, who lost Lieut.-Colonel H. F. W. Bircham mortally wounded entered the trenches of the *III/27th Regiment,* they were obliged to withdraw again.   Farther to the left, the assault of the 1st Australian Division (Reserve Army) on O.G.1 and O.G.2 made little progress, as will presently be seen.

---

[1] Br.-General G. D. Jeffreys had taken over command a few hours previously.

The German position opposite the junction of the two Armies 23 July.
was a strong one, for the regular rise of the ground north-
westward from Munster Alley to the windmill permitted of
several tiers of machine-gun defence, the light-railway embankment being utilized to great advantage.[1]   At 2.30 A.M.
the 2nd Brigade sent in the 1/Loyal N. Lancashire to
attack Munster Alley, but no progress was possible in the
face of concentrated machine-gun fire.

On the other flank of the Fourth Army the XIII. Corps
attacked at 3.40 A.M., the objectives being Guillemont [2]
for the 30th Division (Major-General J. S. M. Shea) and
Guillemont station, Delville Wood and Longueval for the
3rd Division (Major-General J. A. L. Haldane).

In the 30th Division, the 21st Brigade (Br.-General Hon.
C. J. Sackville-West) set the 19/Manchester, advancing
from the eastern face of Trônes Wood, to assault Guillemont,
whilst the 2/Green Howards struck in south-eastward from
Longueval Alley farther north.   The destructive bombardment appeared to have wrought great havoc ; [3] in addition
the heavy artillery placed a standing barrage upon the
eastern approaches to Guillemont, and also upon the Sketch
southern end of Leuze Wood, the southern face of Ginchy 11.
(two localities which might be expected to harbour German
reserves), Wedge Wood and Falfemont Farm.[4]   When the
infantry advanced, the field artillery, which provided a Sketch
flank barrage south of Arrow Head Copse, was to rake 16.
⁺hrough Guillemont in four lifts, resting on the eastern and
sɔuthern edges of the village at 45 minutes after zero hour.

The 19/Manchester attacked with three companies in
line and suffered few casualties until they reached the
German wire, which they found uncut.   Here they lost
heavily from shell, machine-gun and rifle fire, but forced
their way through the obstacle most gallantly and entered
Guillemont.   The Germans, however, continued to resist,
and those of the battalion who penetrated farthest found
themselves cut off.   Considerable loss was inflicted on the

---

[1] The opponents of the 1st Division were elements of the *27th Regiment*
(*7th Division*), *77th Reserve Regiment* (from *2nd Guard Reserve Division*)
and *I./165th*, all under the *7th Division*.

[2] Officially the " Battle of Guillemont " only covers the fighting 3rd-
6th September on the front Combles ravine—Longueval, which resulted
in the capture of Guillemont, Falfemont Farm and Leuze Wood.

[3] The trenches of the *13th Reserve Jäger*, in front of Ginchy and those
of the *104th Reserve Regiment* at Guillemont were " almost destroyed ".
Somme-Nord ii.

[4] Wedge Wood was in the German 2nd Position about 400 yards north-
west of Falfemont Farm.

23 July. enemy—four machine guns were pushed forward on the right and made good practice against German reinforcements entering Guillemont from the east—but those survivors of the assault who could do so were at length obliged to withdraw. The remnants of the left and centre companies of the Manchester maintained the struggle in the village until they were overwhelmed.[1] To some observers it appeared that Guillemont would have been won had the Manchester received support ; but there was a heavy German barrage on No Man's Land, and news of the situation was slow in arriving at brigade headquarters.

Meanwhile the 2/Green Howards had lost direction in the half-light, being further confused by a smoke screen which was intended to mask this flank of the attack from the Germans in Ginchy.[2] The smoke, drifting on a northerly wind, failed of its purpose ; it obscured Guillemont for a time, and some of the Yorkshiremen who went too far to the right crossed the track of the Manchester advance to be held up by uncut wire on the south-western edge of Guillemont. They eventually fell back to the Trônes Wood trenches. Another party took one trench south of the railway but was then obliged to withdraw to the trenches near Waterlot Farm, disorganizing the advance of the right of the 3rd Division. The latter consisted of two strong bombing parties of the 7/Shropshire L.I., supported by a company of the 8/East Yorkshire (all 8th Brigade), which tried to clear the ground immediately south of the railway. These troops could make little headway and eventually fell back, also on Waterlot Farm where the admixture of troops repelled a counter-attack later in the morning.[3]

The 2/Royal Scots, also of the 8th Brigade (Br.-General E. G. Williams) repeated the attempt to bomb down the trenches from Waterlot Farm on either side of the Guillemont road and railway, and thus capture the station. Some progress was made in spite of machine-gun fire from Ginchy and the north-east, but none of the ground gained could be held.

[1] According to Somme-Nord ii., parties of the Manchester reached the eastern edge of Guillemont, the commander of the *III./104th Reserve Regiment* being " besieged " in his battle-headquarters. A counter-attack was delivered by the regimental storm-troops and part of the *III./Bn.*, but the British held on for many hours, some till 2 P.M. Most of the prisoners had used all their bombs and ammunition, and many were wounded.

[2] The Special Brigade R.E. fired 210 smoke bombs from a position near Waterlot Farm.

[3] Delivered by the right flank of the *104th Reserve Regiment* and said to have been stopped by machine-gun fire. Somme-Nord ii.

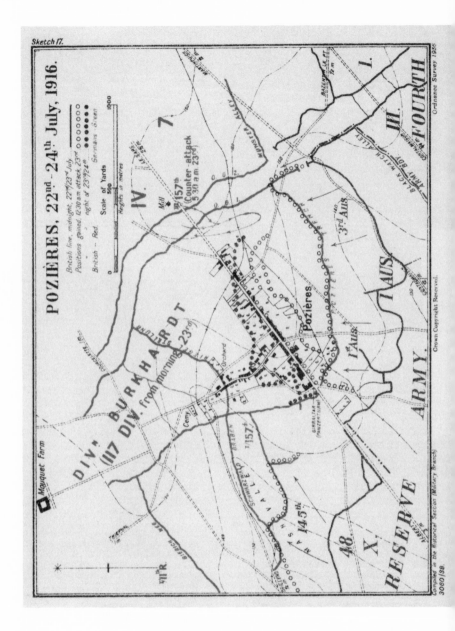

Sketch 17.

POZIÈRES, 22ⁿᵈ – 24ᵗʰ July, 1916.

British line, midnight, 22ⁿᵈ/23ʳᵈ July
Positions gained, 12.30 a.m. attack 23ʳᵈ ○○○○○○
night of 23ʳᵈ/24ᵗʰ ●●●●●●
British – Red.   Germans – Green.

Heights in metres

Scale of Yards
0   500   1000

Compiled in the Historical Section (Military Branch)
3060/38.   Ordnance Survey 1936

The attack of the 3rd Division on Delville Wood and **23 July.**
the northern part of Longueval, made from the west, was
carried out by units of the 9th Brigade [1] (Br.-General H. C.
Potter), which assembled in Pont Street. To clear their
left flank, the 95th Brigade (Br.-General Lord Esme
Gordon-Lennox) of the 5th Division (right of the XV.
Corps) was to deal with the German strongpoints in the
orchards to the north of Longueval. The 3rd Division
battalions—1/Northumberland Fusiliers, 13/King's and
12/West Yorkshire—were new to the ground, and received
their orders very late; and it did not seem to the waiting
troops that the bombardment of their objectives was as
heavy as it might have been. Advancing at 3.40 A.M., the
Northumberland Fusiliers and the other battalions following
closely in rear were assailed by machine-gun fire from the
front and left. After making considerable progress they
were obliged to fall back, rallying on Piccadilly and eventually withdrawing to Pont Street, where they were heavily
shelled. The 1/East Surrey and 1/Duke of Cornwall's L.I.
of the 95th Brigade, met with some success, almost turning
the right flank of the defence. Both crossed the Flers road
and the East Surrey captured a strongpoint, which was
consolidated with the assistance of a party of the 1/2nd
Durham Field Company R.E. The Germans, however,
counter-attacked strongly and, after heavy fighting, both
battalions were forced to withdraw to Pont Street, where
there was now a considerable mixture of units, and much
reorganization was needed. Br.-General Potter, who had
come up to ascertain the situation, was slightly wounded
by a shell-burst; orders issued for a fresh advance were
eventually cancelled; and nothing more was attempted
during the day.[2]

THE RESERVE ARMY, 23RD JULY

POZIÈRES [3]

Delivered at the same time as the attack of the left of **Sketch**
the Fourth Army, the assault of Pozières by the 1st **17.**

[1] Shown as " Comp. Bde." on Sketch 16.
[2] According to the German accounts, the *5th Division* (*12th Grenadiers,
8th Grenadiers* and *52nd Regiment*) was very hard pressed, and the counter-
attacks which had to be made resulted in considerable confusion. Practically all the infantry was engaged ; and as renewed British attacks were
expected, a box barrage was placed round Longueval and Delville Wood.
[3] The " Battle of Pozières Ridge " is the official name for the fighting,
23rd July-3rd September, in the area between Bazentin le Petit—Contal-

23 July. Australian Division resulted in a gratifying success, although it was but the prelude to many weeks of stubborn fighting. The methodical bombardment [1] of the village and the ridge beyond had continued steadily since the 19th July, the volume of fire increasing when darkness fell on the 22nd. Just before zero hour (12.30 A.M. on the 23rd) the heavy artillery provided a five minutes' intense bombardment of the western portion of Pozières between the Bapaume road and the cemetery. In addition to the barrages upon the O.G. trenches and Pozières Trench—the first objective of the Australians—a barrage was put down upon the German line west of the village in order to simulate a preparation for an attack from the south-west.[2]

The assaulting battalions were the 9th (Queensland) and 11th (W. Australian) of the 3rd Brigade (Br.-General E. G. Sinclair-MacLagan) on the right, and the 1st and 2nd Battalions of the 1st (New South Wales) Brigade (Br.-General N. M. Smyth) on the left. Shelled in their assembly positions by the German artillery, they stole forward before zero hour to gain what distance they could before the British barrage lifted. When it did so,[3] the eager Australians rushed forward in the light of the German flares, and, despite a certain amount of rifle and machine-gun fire, secured Pozières Trench without much trouble or loss, few Germans staying to defend it. Only on the extreme right did the assault meet with determined resistance. Repeated

---

maison and the river Ancre, thus including the operations carried out by the left of the Fourth Army. It will be more convenient to trace the course of events, in chronological sequence as far as is possible, upon the whole front held by the Fourth and Reserve Armies.

[1] In addition to the field batteries of the 1st Australian Division and 48th Division (attacking on the left of the Australians), the 25th Division artillery also fired on this front. The bulk of the X. Corps medium and heavy guns were employed, the XLV. Heavy Artillery Group (36th, 55th and 108th Siege Batteries) being at the direct call of the 1st Australian Division from 21st July. This group formed the nucleus of the I. Anzac Corps artillery. The 55th Siege Battery (9.2″ hows.) was an Australian unit ; the 54th Siege Battery (8″ hows.), also Australian, joined the group at the end of July.

[2] During the night 21st/22nd July, the *I./157th Regiment* (*117th Division*) had come in on the north-west side of Pozières, and the Division Burkhardt extended its left flank along Pozières Trench some distance east of the Bapaume road. The commander of the *157th* was now responsible for the defence of the village. On the morning of 23rd July, after the Australian attack, Major-General Kuntz (*117th Division*) took over command of the sector Ancre—Pozières (inclusive) from Major-General Burkhardt. Somme-Nord ii.

[3] An 18-pdr. of the 6th Battery Australian F.A., which had been brought up the Bapaume road to within 200 yards of the front line, opened fire with great effect at zero hour, enfilading the main road through the village.

bombardments had partially destroyed O.G.1 and O.G.2, 23 July. but the advance of the right company of the Queenslanders, made above ground between the two trenches, encountered machine-gun fire, which compelled the stormers to take to the trenches and resort to bombing. No progress had been made when the remainder of the line went forward to the second objective and, although assistance was lent by the 10th (S. Australian) Battalion, the German machine gunners, snipers and bombers continued to take heavy toll of every attempt to advance. When daylight came the only gain was in O.G.1, which had been secured as far as its junction with Pozières Trench.[1]

Meanwhile the attack against Pozières had succeeded. At 1 A.M. the assault of the gardens and enclosures bordering the Bapaume road, delivered by the second wave of the battalions first engaged, encountered little resistance ; by 3 A.M., the 3rd and 4th Battalions on the left, and the 10th and 12th (S. and W. Australia and Tasmania), on the right, had come through and reached the final objective, the near edge of the Bapaume road [2] itself. Here they dug in among the rubble heaps to which successive bombardments had reduced the houses, whilst patrols penetrated the north-western portion of the village. Five field howitzers and a field gun were found and about a hundred prisoners taken.[3] On the right, however, the situation in the O.G. trenches obliged the 3rd Australian Brigade to throw back its flank across the remains of the light railway to face O.G.1, some three hundred yards away.

Consolidation proceeded steadily, although the German shell-fire, which had died down about 2.15 A.M., increased again at 3.30 and continued to be heavy until about 11 A.M. Parties of victorious infantry, on their own initiative, bombed the cellars and hunted among the ruins beyond the Bapaume road. In the village all organized resistance seemed at an end ; although many Australians were shot

---

[1] Two Australians, 2nd-Lieut. A. S. Blackburn (10th Battalion) and Pte. J. Leak (9th Battalion), were awarded the V.C. for their prowess in this struggle.

[2] Albert—Le Sars road on Sketches 17, 18, 19.

[3] Somme-Nord ii. states that the *4th Coy. 157th* and the *10th Coy. 77th Reserve*, holding Pozières Trench just east of the Bapaume road, were almost annihilated. Next on the left, the *6th Coy. 27th* made a " fighting " retreat " north-eastward. A gap was left west of the Bapaume road where the *3rd Coy. 157th* was forced back. The various German headquarters in rear knew little of the situation, and the staff of the *III./62nd*, which came up during the night to dug-outs in the north-eastern part of the village, was captured.

23 July. by German snipers and some were cut off and captured, their enterprise added considerably to the number of prisoners secured by the division.   About 5.30 A.M. a counter-attack, launched by the enemy from the O.G. trenches near the Bapaume road and directed at the gap between the refused right flank of the 3rd Australian Brigade and its posts in O.G.1, had been easily repulsed by rifle and machine-gun fire.[1]

On the left flank touch had not yet been obtained with the 48th Division (X. Corps) which delivered its assault at the same time as the Australians.   Major-General R. Fanshawe had placed his 145th Brigade (Br.-General H. R. Done) on the right, east of the Ovillers—Pozières light railway, and the 144th (Br.-General G. H. Nicholson) on the left.   Ground was to be gained both by advances over the open and by bombing up trenches ;   " flame mortars " [2] were to come into action three minutes before zero hour against the German posts along the railway track.   The infantry was shelled in its assembly positions, and when it advanced the German machine guns—for the most part unharmed by the British bombardment—opened with deadly effect.   In the 144th Brigade, the 1/6th Gloucestershire was literally mown down, only a few bombers succeeding in entering the German line near the railway. These gallant men were soon overwhelmed, and the 1/4th Gloucestershire, which was endeavouring to aid its sister-battalion by bombing forward on the left flank, was ordered to call a halt.   The 1/5th Gloucestershire, the left battalion of the 145th Brigade, fared little better ;   but on its right the 1/4th Oxford & Bucks L.I. captured a considerable length of trench south of the railway after hard fighting in which the 1/4th R. Berkshire also played a part.   As day broke the German bombers retreated eastward up the trenches towards Pozières ;   and a subsequent counter-attack from the direction of the cemetery was checked by

---

[1] It was delivered by three companies of the *III./157th*, brought up from Courcelette as soon as it was reported that the Australians were in Pozières.   The remnants of the *II./27th* joined in and it is claimed by Somme-Nord ii. that some ground was recovered north-west of the Bapaume road where, indeed, there were only roving parties of Australians.

[2] From empty oil drums sunk in the ground, the Special Brigade R.E. discharged smaller drums which burst on impact, when the oil contained in them caught fire ;   their range was 200 yards.   Twenty were dug in along the parados of the front trench.   The moral effect of their discharge is reported to have been considerable.   Major W. H. Livens (see " 1916 " Vol. I.), who did much valuable work with the Special Brigade R.E., was the inventor of this oil projecter.

rifle and Lewis-gun fire, two men of the *157th Regiment* 23 July. being captured.

At 6.30 A.M. the 145th Brigade repeated its left attack with the 1/1st Buckinghamshire. Moving forward close under an excellent barrage, the stormers were in among the surprised Germans as soon as it lifted ; with very little fighting the railway track and the trench east of it on the left front of the brigade were secured, together with 152 prisoners. On the right flank of the brigade, however, the enemy still held the trenches running eastward into the defences of Pozières.[1]

The German bombardment had cut all the signal wires and prevented their repair, so the headquarters of both the 48th and 1st Australian Divisions had to rely for information upon pigeons, runners, and, when morning came, the reports of low-flying aeroplanes. Soon after dawn the pilots located with fair accuracy the positions occupied by the forward troops, the 4th Squadron R.F.C. doing particularly good work and taking great risks in the process.

The day proved to be cool and dull, with much low cloud to render observation difficult, but no rain fell and brighter weather followed. Major-General Walker had prepared an order for a formal attack at 4 P.M. to complete the capture of Pozières ; but both air and artillery observers reported in the course of the morning that the Germans had withdrawn from the village. General Gough [2] thereupon decided that patrols should go forward and the infantry brigades follow up to take possession. It was not until about 5 P.M., however, that the cessation of the British bombardment allowed the Australians to carry out this intention, and even by that time orders had not reached all battalions in the forward line.[3] On the left flank, the 2nd Battalion, of its own initiative, incorporated

[1] Only on the German left, in the sector of the *I./157th Regiment*, was the attack successful. Somme-Nord ii.

[2] At noon the 1st Australian Division came under the I. Anzac Corps again, but General Gough still gave his close attention to the situation at Pozières. It was the only portion of his front (which extended from the O.G. trenches south-east of the Albert—Bapaume road to Hébuterne) where important offensive operations were in progress. An attempt by one battalion of the 49th Division (left division of the X. Corps) to enlarge its hold in the Leipzig salient (see Sketch 29) had been made at 2.15 A.M. on 23rd July, but effected little.

[3] An enemy counter-attack, planned for 5 P.M., to retake Pozières by an advance from the north and north-east never materialized. It was cancelled after the troops encountered the British protective barrage. Somme-Nord ii.

L

23 July. in its line a strongpoint beyond the Bapaume road.[1]   Two companies of the 8th Battalion—from the 2nd (Victoria) Brigade (Br.-General J. K. Forsyth) in divisional reserve—were moved up later and dug in about half-way between the road and the cemetery without encountering any opposition ; but it was nearly midnight before this was done.   Farther east, the left of the 3rd Brigade made some progress and the 12th Battalion, having succeeded in clearing some German dug-outs, entrenched beyond the road with the right of its new line on the railway track. On the extreme right it was the intention to gain ground in the O.G. trenches in co-operation with the British 1st Division ; but, in the face of heavy machine-gun fire, the enterprise was abandoned.

During the day there had been considerable bomb-fighting in the trenches on the front of the 48th Division, where the 143rd Brigade (Br.-General B. C. Dent) relieved the 145th.   On the right, the 1/5th R. Warwickshire did not succeed in its endeavour to join hands with the Australians in Pozières.

Fully alive to the unsatisfactory situation on his right flank, General Gough was determined upon immediate and vigorous action.   At 7 P.M. on the 23rd July he had issued an order for the capture of the O.G. trenches south-east of the Bapaume road by an assault north-eastward after a special bombardment by the Reserve Army artillery, which would be assisted by that of the III. Corps (Fourth Army). The X. Corps was to consolidate the ground it had gained and make a fresh attempt to stretch out its right and join up with the Australian advance.   The III. Corps would attack Munster Alley " either simultaneously with I. Anzac " Corps or later ".[2]   Zero hour was to be " before daybreak " on the 24th July ", but it was obvious that the necessary preparations could not be made in time.   The commander of the Reserve Army was therefore constrained to let the Australians attack as soon as they were ready, and a corps order, issued at 11 P.M., fixed the operation for the night of the 24th/25th, the precise hour to be determined by Major-General Walker.

---

[1] This strongpoint, called " Panzerturm ", was christened " Gibraltar " by the Australians.   According to Somme-Nord ii., firing had been heard from it until 5 A.M.

[2] " Special instructions ", issued at 6.15 P.M. on 23rd July by the Fourth Army, laid down as the immediate task of the III. Corps the capture of the Munster Alley—Switch Line re-entrant, the closest touch being kept with the Australian right flank.

THE SITUATION ON THE 23RD JULY

The reports which had reached General Rawlinson's headquarters during the forenoon left little doubt as to the results of the fighting on the previous night. There had been hopes that the morning of Sunday the 23rd July would see the whole of the Bazentin ridge in British hands : Delville Wood and Longueval secured, High Wood and the Switch Line captured, and patrols pushing forward into Martinpuich. On the right flank, the seizure of Guillemont should have prepared the way for a big Allied attack north of the Somme. Actually no ground whatever had been gained by the Fourth Army, many factors contributing to the failure of the British plan. The existing front, with its many re-entrants and salients, was an unsuitable line from which to launch a general attack, for artillery barrages were difficult to arrange with precision ; cloud and haze had hindered observation, thus diminishing the effects of the preliminary bombardment ; and the decision to assault at night had brought no advantage in the face of an alert enemy warned by previous night and dawn attacks. Moreover, the various alterations of zero hour had resulted in some of the troops receiving their orders very late, whilst many battalions were called upon to advance over ground which they had had little or no opportunity to reconnoitre.

In the infantry a great proportion of the best and most experienced officers and men had become casualties in the previous actions, and the loss of their enterprise and resource was severely felt. The desire of the War Office to cultivate an " Army spirit " at the expense of regimental " esprit de corps " had resulted in the deliberate posting of reinforcement drafts to regiments other than their own. The result was unhappy, since the drafts, containing many wounded men who had recovered, felt a proper pride in their own regiments, and often deeply resented the transfer. A heavy price had to be paid for the consequent, if temporary, deterioration in the fighting efficiency of many battalions.

During the 23rd July Sir Douglas Haig visited the headquarters of the Reserve Army at Toutencourt, those of the III. Corps at Montigny, and also General Rawlinson at Querrieu. He approved of General Gough's plans for the continuation of his attack northward without delay in order to complete the capture of Pozières, and also to make good

23 July. the ridge from the windmill to beyond Mouquet Farm, thereby securing observation over Courcelette and Grandcourt, these forming steps towards the ultimate envelopment of Thiepval ; he emphasized the need of special measures to safeguard and strengthen the junction of the Armies in the neighbourhood of Munster Alley ; and he directed that the three corps of the Fourth Army should each concentrate without delay upon the capture of the German trenches on its front as a preliminary to the next general advance. The fact that the process of breaking through the German defences was taking longer and proving more expensive in men and munitions than had been foreseen did not divert the Commander-in-Chief from his strategic purpose. Whilst the state of " siege-warfare in " the field " persisted, it appeared inevitable that each big attack should be preceded by smaller operations, in order to make good the ground in front of the next enemy position, and, by seizing points of tactical importance, provide a favourable line from which to assault it. There was undoubtedly room for improvement in method, both as regards the employment of the infantry and the concentration of artillery,[1] trench-mortar and machine-gun fire.

The Reserve Army, engaged upon a subsidiary operation which would ultimately be of great importance to the Commander-in-Chief's plan, was already preparing to attack again at Pozières. The Fourth Army issued instructions at 6.15 P.M. on the 23rd July giving in detail the various tasks assigned to each corps as a preliminary to the next general assault. The III. Corps was to secure the Munster Alley—Switch Line re-entrant and Intermediate Trench, joining up the line gained and linking it with the left of the XV. Corps. The latter was to seize the strongpoints at the eastern and western corners of High Wood, connecting them by a trench line, and also to capture the Wood Lane defences and the strongpoints in the orchards north of Longueval. The XIII. Corps was to clear the whole of Longueval and Delville Wood, and, in

---

[1] The arrival of German artillery reinforcements had vastly increased the amount of counter-battery work, and the wear-and-tear of the British guns was a factor to be reckoned with. As an example, between the 1st and 11th July, the XIII. Corps artillery had been augmented with 77 guns and howitzers of various calibres, but by the latter date 292 out of a total of 357 pieces was the average number fit for action at any one time, owing to various defects and the lack of spare parts. A whole brigade of 18-pdrs. had been withdrawn for overhaul. The ammunition supply, except for the 6″ guns, was, on the whole, well maintained ; but complaints of defective ammunition were still rife. See " 1916 " Vol. I., p. 374.

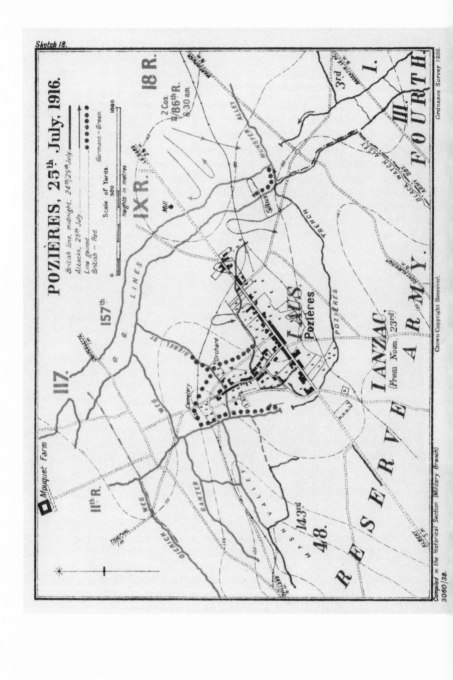

Sketch 18.

POZIÈRES, 25th July, 1916.

British line, midnight, 24th/25th July.
Attacks, 25th July.
Line gained.
British – Red.
German – Green.

Scale of Yards
0   500   1000
Heights in metres

Compiled in the Historical Section (Military Branch)
Crown Copyright Reserved.
Ordnance Survey 1936.
3060/38.

conjunction with the next French attack north of the Somme, to assault the German 2nd Position between Falfemont Farm and Guillemont (both inclusive).

THE RESERVE ARMY, 24TH–31ST JULY
POZIÈRES

The Commander-in-Chief visited General Gough again on the 24th July. This day was devoted by the 1st Australian Division to consolidation and preparation for the new attack, under the very heavy fire of the German batteries, which hampered movement, shattered trenches, and caused considerable casualties.[1]   Major-General Walker had decided upon two separate operations, since the troops detailed to carry by frontal assault the O.G. trenches south-east of the Bapaume road would have to move up over the same ground as those who were to clear the north-eastern part of Pozières.   At 11 A.M. he issued his orders for the capture of the O.G. lines by the 3rd Brigade at 2 A.M. next morning.   Preliminary instructions for the second operation, the clearing of Pozières, which was to take place at 3.30 A.M., were sent out at 4.5 P.M., the formal order following at 8 P.M.   Before dark on the 24th the heavy guns of the Reserve Army opened on O.G.1, whilst those of the III. Corps bombarded O.G.2.[2]

The German bombardment was also heavy on the immediate left of the 1st Australian Division, where the 48th Division had a few bombing encounters during the day, but made no advance.[3]

The hostile batteries which had slackened fire on the Australian positions in Pozières and the approaches thereto soon after 7 P.M., grew very active again between 9 and

Marginal notes: 24 July. Sketch 18.

[1] At 3 A.M. on the 24th another attempt of the Germans to counter-attack had miscarried, owing to the confusion, ignorance of the situation, and the effect of British artillery fire. Somme-Nord ii.

[2] By this time the *117th Division* was about to hand over the Pozières sector to Wellmann's *18th Reserve Division* of the newly-arrived *IX. Reserve Corps*. Wellmann, who was ordered to counter-attack at 4.30 P.M. on 25th July, complained that the German bombardment was too much dispersed ; he was told by the Army that lack of observation facilities, owing to British superiority in the air, forbade better concentration of fire.

[3] At noon the II. Corps staff (Lieut.-General C. W. Jacob) took over command from the X. Corps (Lieut.-General Sir T. L. N. Morland) on the front Bapaume road—river Ancre. Following the policy of thinning the forces on the less active portion of its front, the Reserve Army now had only two divisions (25th and 38th) holding the VIII. Corps line between the Ancre and Hébuterne.

24 July. 10 P.M.   For the assault of the O.G. trenches the 5th and
7th Battalions of the 2nd (Victoria) Brigade were attached
to the 3rd Brigade.   The divisional artillery was to put an
intense barrage upon O.G.1 for two minutes before zero, at
which hour the III. Corps would begin a fifteen minutes'
bombardment of O.G.2 before lifting farther east ; the II.
Corps would bombard the German trenches about the
windmill for an hour, commencing at zero.

The assaulting troops had to file out of Pozières Trench
and turn right in order to form up facing their objective.
Tapes had been laid to guide them, but the two companies
which were to be on the left, with their flank on the Bapaume
road, went astray, and therefore did not take part in the
25 July. attack.   At 2 A.M. on the 25th July, however, the 5th
Battalion, on the right, advanced to the assault and seized
O.G.1.   When the barrage lifted O.G.2 was also entered,
but here the Australians were bombed from both flanks [1]
and eventually had to fall back to O.G.1, where they held on.
After a fierce bombing encounter in this trench the Germans
retained possession of it as far as the railway, the Australian
barricade being about two hundred yards to the south-east.
Meanwhile, on the extreme right of the Australian position,
another bombing fight was in progress, the 10th and 9th
Battalions, assisted later by the other two companies of
the 7th, endeavouring to clear the Germans from the
trench connecting the O.G. lines.   A strongpoint in O.G.1
was captured by the 10th Battalion, but after a bitter
struggle amid the chaos of shell craters the Germans
remained near the junction of O.G.2 and Munster Alley.[2]

At 3.30 A.M. began the movement to secure the remainder
of Pozières and to drive forward up the trenches on the left
in order to cut in behind the enemy opposing the 48th
Division.   The artillery of the 25th Division (II. Corps)
barraged the farther outskirts of the village for fifteen
minutes, commencing at zero, and then lifted to the
German 2nd Position between the windmill and Mouquet
Farm, which the II. Corps heavy artillery was bombarding ;
the Australian field batteries swept in succession the
German trenches, east, north-east and north of the
cemetery.   On the right, the 12th Battalion was exposed
to heavy fire from the unattacked portion of O.G.1 south
of the Bapaume road, and had no chance to link up the two

---

[1] The British 1st Division had not been able to secure Munster Alley.
[2] During this fighting the Germans had been reinforced by two companies of the *II./86th Reserve Regiment* (*18th Reserve Division*).

advances as was intended. Next to the 12th, the 11th 25 July. Battalion reached the light railway beyond the Bapaume road, but was fired into by the 8th, and some confusion resulted. At daylight the 11th was so heavily shelled that it was judged necessary to bring the battalion back to its old line.

The 8th Battalion of the 2nd (Victoria) Brigade, lent to the 1st Brigade for the occasion, went steadily through the village, reached and consolidated a position at the cemetery on the left, and occupied a line of posts following the northern edge of Pozières to and beyond the orchard.[1] The 3rd Battalion was then put in to link up the right of the Victorians with the left of the 3rd Brigade, and the 6th Battalion came up later to consolidate the new forward position where the men dug under a relentless bombardment, and suffered accordingly. Meanwhile, assisted by a barrage put down by the artillery of the 25th Division and by Lewis-gun fire from the right flank, the 4th Battalion had bombed up the trench on the western side of Pozières. Some thirty Germans were killed, and one company, which fled across the open, was caught by machine-gun fire and suffered heavily. Capturing about 700 yards of trench, the battalion got into touch with the 8th at the cemetery, a patrol of Victorians sighting Mouquet Farm. Seventy prisoners and two machine guns had been captured by the 1st Australian Brigade.

At 8.30 A.M. a considerable force of German infantry made its appearance advancing southwards over the crest of the ridge near the windmill. The artillery of the 23rd Division and 1st Australian Division promptly opened upon the unexpected target with devastating effect, great execution also being done by the machine guns of the 3rd Australian Brigade. Some survivors reached the shelter of the O.G. lines, but most of them broke back and disappeared over the crest.[2]

---

[1] Pte. T. Cooke, a Lewis gunner of the 8th Battalion, who was killed on this day, received the posthumous award of the V.C. for his conspicuous gallantry.

[2] According to German accounts, reports from the front line were so misleading that it was believed that the 2nd Position on either side of the Bapaume road was in danger of being lost, and this misapprehension was the cause of the hasty advance of portions of the *86th Reserve Regiment* (*18th Reserve Division*), presumably on the initiative of the battalion commanders concerned. The remainder of the *II./Bn.* moved up to support its forward companies south-east of the road, but came under devastating artillery and machine-gun fire, only small parties reaching the O.G. trenches.

25–26 July.   Throughout the 25th July the Germans maintained a heavy bombardment of the Australian positions by guns of all calibres in preparation for their counter-attack.[1] This terrible ordeal, although steadfastly borne, made it imperative that the exhausted infantry of the 1st Australian Division should be relieved. At night, therefore, the 2nd Australian Division (Major-General J. G. Legge) began to come into the line, the 5th (New South Wales) Brigade (Br.-General W. Holmes) taking over the right from the 3rd Brigade.[2] On the left, the command passed to the 2nd Brigade; but west of Pozières, the 4th Battalion was to remain until patrols of the 48th Division should link up the forward line. In the early hours of the 26th July, the 1/7th R. Warwickshire of the 143rd Brigade at last gained touch with the Australians north-west of the village, after taking some prisoners; but the further advance of the Warwickshire was strongly opposed.

Sketch 19.

At 3 A.M. a company of the newly-arrived 20th Battalion of the 5th Brigade attempted a surprise raid on O.G.1 north of the railway. This enterprise failed with loss after an entry had been gained at one point. Throughout the day the German bombardment continued to be heavy, hindering relief movements and the reorganization of the captured positions. During the afternoon the 17th Battalion and the bombers of the 18th became involved in the Munster Alley fighting. At night the relief of the 1st Australian Division was completed, the 6th (Victoria) Brigade (Br.-General J. Gellibrand) taking over the left sector of the line.[3] Major-General Walker's division had every reason to be proud of its achievement at Pozières, but its losses—due in some measure to inexperience allied with

---

[1] It was never delivered. Knowing the plight of his troops, the commander of the *157th Regiment* reported them not ready, but was threatened by Wellmann with a court-martial if he did not attack. Orders to the *86th Reserve Regiment* are said to have been misunderstood, but these troops, after their experience in the morning, were also spent, and the *Flammenwerfer* and pioneer detachments which were to participate lost heavily from shell-fire whilst coming up from Martinpuich. Eventually Boehn, the commander of the *IX. Reserve Corps*, who blamed all the local commanders, cancelled the operation " on account of the condition of the troops and " the scarcity of gun ammunition ". Somme-Nord ii. and Wellmann.

[2] Landing on the Gallipoli peninsula in August-September 1915, the 2nd Australian Division had taken part in the evacuation. After the campaign it suffered no disintegration through the reorganization and expansion of the A.I.F., but was quite new to offensive warfare.

[3] The artillery of the 2nd Australian Division began to relieve that of the 1st Australian Division on the afternoon of the next day, when two brigades came into action.

Sketch 19.

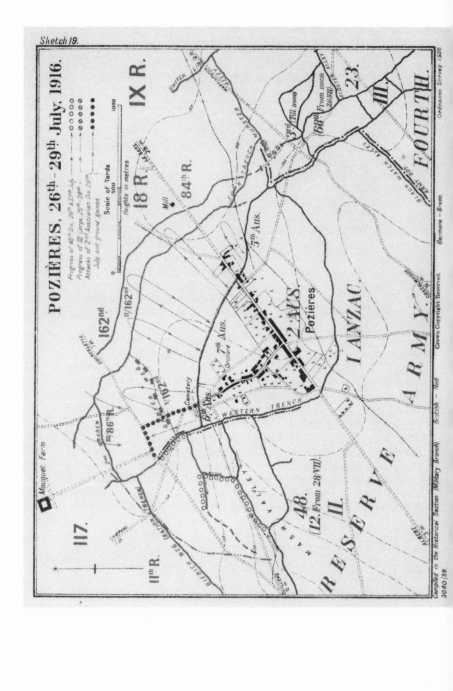

POZIÈRES, 26th–29th July, 1916.

Progress of 48th Div. 26th & 27th July ●○○○○
Progress of III Corps. 26th–28th ●○○○○
Attacks of 2nd Australian Div. 29th ●○○○○
Safe and ground gained ●●●●●

Scale of Yards
0   500   1000

Heights in metres

Compiled in the Historical Section (Military Branch)   British — Red   Germans — Green   Crown Copyright Reserved.   Ordnance Survey 1926.

3060/38.

reckless daring—were grievous, amounting to 178 officers and over 5,100 other ranks.[1]

Early on the morning of the 27th July, the 1/8th Royal 27 July. Warwickshire (143rd Brigade) bombed its way forward to a point just short of the Ovillers—Courcelette track. On the opposite flank the bombers of the newly-arrived Australian battalions were constantly involved in the fighting round Munster Alley, where the 23rd Division had relieved the British 1st Division. The struggle here was fierce and exhausting in the extreme, and continued with little advantage to either side.

On the 27th July the British counter-battery work, particularly successful as regards the German gun positions round Le Sars and Courcelette, somewhat reduced the volume of the German bombardment which had greatly hampered the attack preparations of the 2nd Australian Division. These included the digging of forward trenches and some minor adjustments of the line, which then ran from O.G.2, near the entrance to Munster Alley, to O.G.1, and thence to the light railway junction and along the railway track in front of Pozières to the cemetery.

Although anxious to afford the enemy as short a respite as possible, General Gough judged it advisable to leave the actual day and hour of the assault for the corps commander to determine. Following the Anzac practice, the decision was thus left to the divisional commander, and Major-General Legge selected 12.15 A.M. on the 29th July.[2] On the right flank, O.G.1 between the railway track and the Bapaume road was to be carried by frontal attack ; then, partly by bombing, the whole length of O.G.2 from the road to Munster Alley would be secured. North of the road, the objective was the continuation of the O.G. trenches (German 2nd Position) as far as the Ovillers—Courcelette track, which was to be captured on a frontage of 650 yards

---

[1] Somme-Nord and Wellmann give details of the extensive reorganization and reliefs taking place on the German side. During the morning of 26th July, General von Boehn (*IX. Reserve Corps*) took over from General Sixt von Armin (*IV. Corps*) the Thiepval—Delville Wood front. When the reliefs were completed it was held by the *117th, 18th Reserve, 17th Reserve* and *5th Divisions*. The *I.* and *II./162nd Regiment* (from the *17th Reserve Division*) replaced the *157th* north-west, north and north-east of Pozières, with the *III./84th Reserve* (*18th Reserve Division*) astride the Bapaume road.

[2] General Gough's desire for energetic action was well understood by Lieut.-General Birdwood, who had issued his corps order at 8.30 P.M. on the 26th, the artillery programme having already been framed. A short operation order naming the objectives was issued by the Reserve Army on the morning of the 28th.

28 July. by the left of the assault.   The six Australian field artillery brigades were to place an intensive barrage on the whole extent of O.G.1 north of the Bapaume road for one minute before zero, when fire would lift to O.G.2 for ten minutes, and then lift again to a line 100 yards beyond the objective. The barrage for the left attack upon the Ovillers—Courcelette track was to be provided by the artillery of the 25th Division.

The field guns were already engaged in systematic wire-cutting whilst the heavy artillery of the Reserve Army, II. Corps and Anzac Corps proceeded with a methodical bombardment of the objectives, also of Mouquet Farm and Courcelette.   On the night of the 27th July the 5th Australian Brigade, on the right, endeavoured to improve its forward positions.   Patrols discovered that north of the Bapaume road the wire in front of the O.G. lines, although damaged, was still a considerable obstacle.[1]

At dusk on the 28th July, Major-General Legge began to move up from reserve, through Pozières, the 7th Brigade (Br.-General J. Paton), which was to make the centre attack whilst the 6th (Victoria) Brigade, on the left, assaulted the Ovillers—Courcelette track with one battalion.   South of the Bapaume road, the 5th Brigade, advancing on O.G.1 four minutes after zero hour, would be covered by trench-mortar fire only.[2]

Just before midnight the battalions of the 7th Brigade—28th (W. Australia), 25th (Queensland) and 26th (Queensland & Tasmania)—were assembled along the line of the light railway east of the cemetery, with the 23rd Battalion of the 6th Brigade farther to the left.   At midnight they advanced to make what ground they could towards the German trenches, some six hundred yards away, before the barrage lifted.   German shell-fire soon destroyed all signal wires, and lamp flashes could not be

29 July. distinguished in the dust and smoke, so that the various brigade headquarters were obliged to wait for news of the assault, which was launched punctually at 12.15 A.M.   The 28th Battalion, on the right, had to deal with enemy advanced posts, and, although O.G.1 was overrun, few men

---

[1] Sergt. C. C. Castleton, 5th Machine-Gun Company, who had made many journeys under heavy fire to bring in wounded, was eventually killed whilst doing so.   He was posthumously awarded the V.C.

[2] On the trenches of the *162nd Regiment* numerous aeroplanes and captive balloons had directed the fire of the British artillery during the day.   The bombardment increased at 8.30 P.M. on all positions, levelling the trenches and causing heavy casualties.   Somme-Nord ii.

were able to penetrate the wire in front of O.G.2.   Under 29 July. continuous fire from rifles and machine guns, a withdrawal was made to O.G.1, which proved to be untenable, so that the movement had to be continued back to the starting line. The same experience befell the 25th and 26th Battalions. The 7th Brigade had not failed for lack of gallantry and resolution : it had been set an almost impossible task.[1]

On the left, however, the 23rd Battalion of the 6th Brigade suffered no check in reaching the German trench along the Ovillers—Courcelette track.   Unable to recognize their shell-shattered objective, the two leading waves of Victorians pressed on and suffered heavily from their own barrage before they could be brought back to their proper line.   A thick fog proved of great advantage during the work of consolidation.   The failure on the right obliged the battalion to relinquish part of its gains and to throw back a defensive flank along the track leading to the cemetery.

The right of the II. Corps [2] had made no attack, with the exception of an effort of the 11/Middlesex (36th Brigade) to capture the extension of Western Trench by an advance over the open.   This movement was checked by bombing and rifle fire.   The 23rd Battalion, therefore, held a narrow salient, pointing north-westward, along the Pozières ridge in the direction of Mouquet Farm.[3]

The 5th Brigade attack on the O.G. line south-east of the Bapaume road had been checked by fire at the outset, the trench-mortar bombardment not having subdued the German machine guns.   The failure of the 20th Battalion against the uncaptured part of O.G.1 rendered hopeless the assault of O.G.2 by the 17th Battalion on the extreme right. Heavy losses were suffered before the enterprise was abandoned, but fighting round Munster Alley, where the 23rd Division was heavily engaged with the *I./84th Reserve Regiment*, still continued.

The shattered battalions of the 7th Brigade were with-

---

[1] According to Somme-Nord ii. and Wellmann, three attempts were made to carry the O.G. trenches north of the Bapaume road, and each was repulsed with heavy loss. " The Australians who managed to break in " were dealt with."

[2] On 28th July, the 12th Division (Major-General A. B. Scott) had completed the relief of the 48th Division, which since 16th July had reported as casualties 124 officers and 2,720 other ranks.

[3] Somme-Nord ii. acknowledges the success of the Australians against the *I./162nd Regiment*, which was reinforced by the *III./86th Reserve* arriving to relieve it.   The defenders were forced back to Gierich Weg (called " Ration Trench " by the British) and 2nd Graben.
Wellmann calls the action " a complete victory for my division ".

29–30
July. drawn into reserve, and at 10 A.M. on the 29th July a conference was held at Anzac Corps headquarters. A hasty decision to renew the attack on the night of the 30th July—when the XV. Corps and III. Corps of the Fourth Army would also be engaged—was partly due to Major-General Legge's anxiety to meet the wishes of General Gough, who, it was generally understood, desired to press on with the least possible delay. The 2nd Australian Division had already lost nearly 3,500 officers and men, but its commander judged it to be capable of another effort. Much more time was needed, however, for proper preparations, and the end of July arrived before they were completed.

THE FOURTH A⌐MY, 24TH–31ST JULY

DELVILLE WOOD AND LONGUEVAL, HIGH WOOD, MUNSTER ALLEY, GUILLEMONT, INTERMEDIATE TRENCH

Sketch
16. During the 24th July, another dull and cloudy but dry day, hostile artillery fire was heavy on the fronts of the XIII. and XV. Corps. Air reports spoke of a German concentration of troops in the trenches between Flers and Ginchy, so a British bombardment of these positions was carried out. No counter-attack materialized, and at 8 P.M. when there were signs of a German advance west of High Wood, a heavy British barrage again discouraged any movement of the enemy infantry. At night in the XV. Corps the 51st Division took over the left of the 5th Division line south-east of High Wood with one battalion, and the flank units of the XV. and III. Corps began digging to join up securely between the southern point of High Wood and Bazentin le Petit windmill.

General Rawlinson met General Foch at Dury at 2.30 P.M. and arranged that the Franco-British attack, which had now been tentatively arranged for the 25th, should be postponed for 48 hours so that the artillery could, with more effect, carry on its counter-battery work which was still much hampered by bad visibility. The Germans opposite the French north of the Somme had been kept under terrific bombardment since the 22nd July, when our Allies had opened intense artillery fire as a preliminary to the British attack upon Guillemont delivered upon the following morning.

At 3.45 P.M. on the 24th Sir Douglas Haig arrived at Querrieu and conferred with Generals Foch and Rawlinson.

Sketch 20.

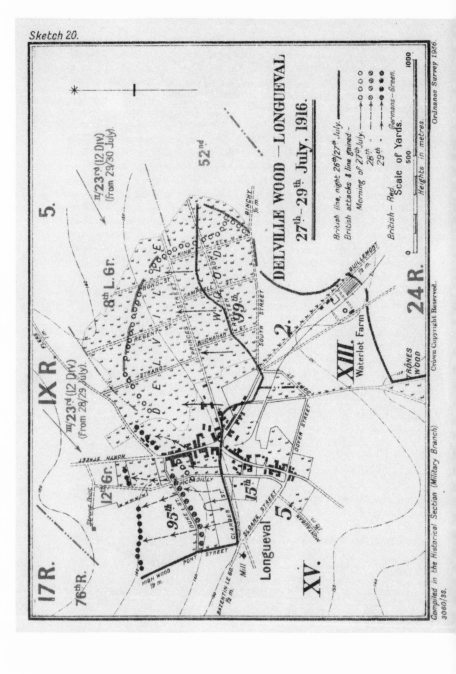

DELVILLE WOOD — LONGUEVAL
27th – 29th July, 1916.

British line, night 26th/27th July.
British attacks & line gained.
Morning of 27th July.
28th.
29th.

British – Red.   Germans – Green.

Scale of Yards.
0   500   1000
Heights in metres.

Ordnance Survey 1926.

Compiled in the Historical Section (Military Branch)   Crown Copyright Reserved.
3060/38.

The Commander-in-Chief insisted on the importance of consolidating in depth the line already reached, and stressed the urgent need of clearing Longueval—Delville Wood as a defensive measure ; he approved of the postponement of the Allied attack, which included Guillemont in its object-ives. Next morning, when General Rawlinson met his corps commanders and their chief artillery officers in conference and put before them his considered appreciation of the situation,[1] he laid particular stress upon the danger of a German counter-attack delivered through Longueval—Delville Wood, and detailed the preparatory measures necessary to counter such a stroke. At the same time, it was decided that the XIII. and XV. Corps should combine to clear Longueval—Delville Wood in one operation, and a plan was drawn up without delay.

For this attack, to be made from the south, it was reckoned that each corps could employ 100 field guns and 100 medium and heavy guns. The preliminary bombard-ment was to last one hour during which the whole of the wood and village north of the zero barrage line could be dealt with thoroughly. In the area Flers—Ginchy—Guillemont the hostile trenches were to be smothered with the assistance of certain batteries of the French XX. Corps and the artillery of the 35th Division ; the 12-inch and 9.2-inch guns of the III. Corps were to fire on the more distant villages. Zero hour was eventually fixed for 7.10 A.M. on the 27th July.

On the night of the 25th began the relief of the 3rd Division [2] in the left sector of the XIII. Corps by the 2nd Division (Major-General W. G. Walker), which had joined the Fourth Army from the Vimy front. The new-comers were to attack the greater part of Delville Wood ; its western portion, with Longueval, formed the objective of the 5th Division (XV. Corps), which was taking over ground to its right. During these preliminaries the Germans kept a heavy barrage on the southern approaches to Longueval ; they had been anticipating a renewal of the British attacks ever since the 23rd July, alarm signals going up from their front line several times a day. From 6.10 A.M. to 7.10 A.M. on the 27th the wood and village were bombarded by as many British guns of all calibres as could be brought to bear. Infantry patrols which went forward to observe the

[24-27 July.]

---

[1] Appendix 12.
[2] Casualties in the 3rd Division, 11th-27th July, were returned as 248 officers and 5,854 other ranks.

effect suffered considerably from enemy shell-fire, but
found a horrible scene of chaos and destruction.

27 July.   The storm of artillery fire [1] which broke over wood and
village at 6.10 A.M. on the 27th July had a very heartening

Sketch   effect upon the waiting infantry.   As soon as the bombard-
20.   ment began about sixty of the *8th Grenadiers* (*Leib Grena-
dier-Regiment*) hurried forward to surrender to the 99th
Brigade (Br.-General R. O. Kellett), about to deliver the
2nd Division attack.   At zero hour the leading companies
of the 1/K.R.R.C. and the 23/Royal Fusiliers, followed by
·trench-mortar and machine-gun sections, advanced through
the chaos of huge shell craters and débris of shattered trees.
In the trench along Prince's Street, which was reached with
little fighting in about ten minutes, were found many
smashed machine guns and a great number of dead and
wounded Germans.   Those of the enemy who survived
either fled or came forward to surrender.   Following the
lifts of the barrage, the advance was continued through the
wood by the rear companies of Rifles and Fusiliers, which
reached the final objective—a line about fifty yards inside
the northern edge—about 9 A.M.   The left of the Fusiliers,
in spite of receiving hostile machine-gun fire from Longueval,
had gone still farther ahead ; but it had to withdraw again
in order to conform to the general line.   So far as could be
seen, no Germans, except the dead and wounded, remained
in the wood.

The 1/R. Berkshire worked forward to " mop up " and
also to protect the flanks, but did not push out to the
eastern edge of the wood.[2]   Consolidation proceeded with
the assistance of part of the 1/1st East Anglian Field
Company R.E.   So far the losses of the attacking
battalions had not been heavy, but from the east the
German artillery now began to enfilade Prince's Street, the
new support position, with considerable effect.

The 15th Brigade (Br.-General M. N. Turner) of the

---

[1] Details of the artillery programme : one hour's preliminary bombardment ; intense fire 7 minutes before zero hour and before each lift ; barrage
to search forward through wood and village in 3 lifts (first at zero, second and
third at intervals of one hour and 30 minutes respectively) and stand on a
final line clear of objectives as long as required ; field batteries to use as
much H.E. as possible on wood and village.   The two corps had concentrated the fire of 369 guns and howitzers, exclusive of counter-batteries.

[2] According to brigade orders, one company was to consolidate the
eastern edge from Rotten Row to Prince's Street, but such a position
invited a concentration of hostile fire.   There was no field of fire or observation to be obtained within the wood, yet to go on clear of it would, in this
case, have left uncovered the right flank of the advance.

5th Division was to advance on the left of the 99th with the 1/Norfolk in front and the 1/Bedfordshire in support. Before zero hour German shell-fire descended so heavily on the front line that nearly the whole of the left company of the Norfolk was buried, and the Bedfordshire were accordingly hurried forward in close support. The Stokes mortars were also put out of action. Nevertheless, the attack started punctually with great dash, and the Norfolk, on the right, pushed well forward inside the western edge of Delville Wood, the Bedfordshire then carrying on the advance which linked up with the 99th Brigade. Longueval itself proved a more difficult proposition, and as all communications were cut, owing to the heavy German barrage south of the village, the extent of the progress made was not known in rear until much later in the day. Several machine guns in the ruins had been untouched by the British bombardment,[1] and there was brisk fighting, although some parties of Germans surrendered at once.[2] The advance of German reinforcements from Flers was checked by the British barrage, but the enemy still held on to the northern portion of Longueval. The line reached by the 15th Brigade, after part of the 16/R. Warwickshire had been absorbed into the fight, ran south-west from the north-western portion of Delville Wood, leaving the orchards near the junction of Duke Street and Piccadilly in enemy hands.

About 9.30 A.M. Germans were seen massing for a counter-attack and, despite the British protective barrage, parties of bombers advanced against the 99th Brigade from the eastern side of Delville Wood and came to grips with the Rifles, who, with assistance from the Berkshire and Fusiliers, managed, at first, to hold their own. The brigade machine guns were handled with boldness, several being emplaced near the front line, and their fire was most effective, although in the end six were put out of action. At length, the persistent efforts of the enemy, who got in behind Prince's Street, caused the right of the line to

[1] The barrage map of the XV. Corps artillery shows the British line at zero hour on the western edge of the village as farther forward than was actually the case ; this explains why these German posts survived the bombardment. At 1.40 P.M. the 15th Brigade asked for howitzer fire on the western portion of Longueval.

[2] In all, 4 officers and 159 other ranks of the *8th Grenadiers* were captured in the wood and village on this day. One German officer said he had endured bombardments at Verdun and on the Russian front, but had never experienced such a shelling as he had just gone through.

27–29 withdraw slightly and face north-eastward.[1] Communi-
July. cations with the rear were repeatedly cut, so that the
situation, even at brigade headquarters, was not clear ; in
contradicting with emphasis an alarmist report of a
successful German counter-attack, the commander of the
99th Brigade had caused it to be assumed at 2nd Division
headquarters that Delville Wood was now entirely cleared
of Germans.   Sniping and bombing continued for the rest
of the day, and at night the 17/Middlesex and 2/South
Staffordshire of the 6th Brigade (Br.-General A. C. Daly)
took over the 99th Brigade front.

Another day of heavy shelling of the Longueval area
followed on the 28th.   The Staffordshire and the Middlesex
had to endure an intensive bombardment which preceded
a counter-attack at 9.30 P.M., but the German bombing
parties which then made desperate efforts against the British
line were driven back.

Meanwhile, preparations had been made to complete the
capture of Longueval.   On the night of the 27th the 15th
Brigade was relieved by the 95th (Br.-General Lord Esme
Gordon-Lennox), and next morning the line of Duke Street
was occupied without opposition.   At 3.30 P.M. on the 29th,
after half an hour's bombardment by the XV. Corps
artillery, another advance was made, the 12/Gloucestershire,
on the left, occupying a line some five hundred yards north
of Duke Street, whilst, on the right, the 1/East Surrey also
made some headway.[2]

The efforts of the XV. Corps being mostly concentrated
upon the Longueval—Delville Wood operation, little more
could be accomplished.   Meanwhile the Germans were
reorganizing their line in the High Wood area   At
Sketch 9.20 P.M. on the 29th July,[3] however, the 51st Division
16. made another attempt to storm the strongpoint at

[1] Sergt. A. Gill, 1/K.R.R.C., who was killed during this fighting, displayed great prowess as a platoon leader, and was posthumously awarded
the V.C.
[2] The three regiments (*12th* and *8th Grenadiers* and *52nd*) of the *5th
Division* had undergone a tremendous ordeal in Delville Wood and
Longueval. " The troops were in a pitiable state : they had had no
" sleep for several nights and no supplies could be got up through the
" British barrage, which also prevented the evacuation of the wounded."
Between 27th and 29th July the equivalent of about three battalions
(mostly from the *12th Division*) appears to have entered the fight as reliefs
or reinforcements.   Somme-Nord ii. and regimental histories.
[3] By the morning of this day the relief of the *IV. Corps* by the *IX.
Reserve Corps* had begun, as we have seen.   The *17th Reserve Division*
replaced the *8th* in High Wood and on either flank of the wood ; the *18th
Reserve Division*, took over from the *7th* the line south of Martinpuich.

the eastern corner of High Wood, a party of the 1/4th Seaforth Highlanders (154th Brigade) going forward after a bombardment by the heavy artillery. The enterprise failed in the face of unsubdued machine guns. Every night the 51st Division dug industriously, though often hampered by shell-fire, in order to link up the left of the XV. Corps with the right flank of the III Corps west of High Wood.

The fighting on the left flank of the III. Corps had 25–29 continued in a series of fresh attempts to secure the Munster July. Alley—Switch Line re-entrant, where the trenches had been shattered out of recognition by repeated bombardments. At 2 A.M. on the 25th July the 3rd Brigade (Br.-General H. R. Davies) of the 1st Division put in the 1/South Wales Borderers to attack Munster Alley ; but, in spite of preparation by the heavy artillery, machine-gun fire from Pozières windmill forced a withdrawal after the bombers had made progress. On the 26th at 3 A.M. the 2/Welch of the 3rd Brigade made an attack. A preliminary bombardment was dispensed with in order to give no warning to the German machine gunners, and the Welch reached what appeared to be the junction of Munster Alley and O.G.2, where they found Australians established.

By noon of the 26th July, the 23rd Division (Major-General J. M. Babington) had carried out the relief of the 1st Division, which left behind two companies of the Welch to deliver another attack at 3 P.M.[1] This made considerable progress up the trench towards the Switch Line, but the Germans counter-attacked with bombs and also over the open ; in spite of the heavy losses inflicted by the fire of their Lewis guns, the Welch were driven back.[2] Another effort, made with Australian assistance, was more successful, but, although the 68th Brigade (23rd Division) took up the task at night, the fight continued to sway to and fro. On the night of the 28th/29th July, however, when the 10/Duke of Wellington's (69th Brigade of the 23rd Division) made a combined attack up the trench and above ground, a notable success was gained after a fierce struggle. Progress

[1] These two companies were relieved in the early hours of the 27th. From 11th-27th July the casualties of the 1st Division amounted to 123 officers and 2,955 other ranks.

[2] Parts of five battalions belonging to the *18th Reserve Division* were engaged in this fighting. According to Somme-Nord ii. and Wellmann, the situation in the O.G. lines south-east of the Bapaume road was a constant anxiety to the divisional commander.

M

29–30 July. in Munster Alley, where the Australians gave valuable help in filling sand bags and passing up bombs and ammunition, was not very great ; but in Gloster Alley,[1] by 5.30 A.M. next morning, a point had been reached beyond the crest of the ridge and only twenty-five yards from the Switch Line. The right flank of the III. Corps (19th Division) had been joined up securely with the left of the XV. by the morning of the 28th July, and the consolidation of this part of the line proceeded under heavy shell-fire.[2]

26–27 July.   At noon on the 26th July General Rawlinson had visited General Fayolle, the commander of the French Sixth Army, to arrange details of the next Franco-British attack. Later in the day, Sir Douglas Haig arrived at Dury to confer with Generals Fayolle and Foch. General Foch said that he intended to attack along the whole front south of the Somme from Lihons to Barleux [3] as soon as he was ready, but he required a three days' bombardment which would begin as soon as the weather had cleared sufficiently : north of the river, he only waited for a clear day which would favour observation during the actual **Sketch 21.** attack. The British Commander-in-Chief told General Foch that he wished Guillemont to be captured as soon as possible—not necessarily as part of a Franco-British attack, although the assault of Falfemont Farm—Maurepas must be one operation. As a result of this interview, General Rawlinson arranged with General Foch next day that on the 30th July an assault should be launched on the whole front : from the Somme to Maurepas, Falfemont Farm and Guillemont; if all went well, the British would be in Guillemont before the French reached their objectives, which were more distant. This decision appeared to satisfy all requirements, for General Fayolle was reluctant to push forward his left until Guillemont was in British hands.

General Rawlinson had promised General Foch that on the day of attack he would further assist by undertaking as

---

[1] 600 yards S.E. of Munster Alley. (See Sketch 19.)
[2] No. 3 Section of the 82nd Field Company R.E., working under the 57th Brigade (19th Division), was engaged under fire in building strong-points in front of Bazentin le Petit village during the night of the 29th/30th July. The infantry assisting the section was withdrawn to prepare for an attack next day, but the sappers volunteered to go on with the work and did so, until nine were killed and nearly all the others wounded. In the village there now stands a brick memorial " To Nine Brave Men ".
[3] See Sketch A. Lihons is 7½ miles south-west of Barleux.

Sketch 21.

THE SOMME, 1916.

Allied attacks, 4·45 a.m., 30th July.

Scale of Yards.

1000   0   1000   2000   3000   4000

Bazentin le Gd.

Longueval

Morval

DELVILLE WOOD

99th

Ginchy

2.

5th

Waterlot Fm.

5.

24 R.

Guillemont

Cemetery

COMBLES

LEUZE WO.

XIII

30.

90th

TRÔNES WO.

BERNAFAY WO.

Orchard

89th

Montauban

Falfemont Fm.

Maltzhorn Fm.

8 BAV. R.

Herdecourt

le Forest

Maurepas

XII R.

Maricourt

SIXTH

XX

102nd R.

Curlu

23 R.

101st R.

CHEM WO.

ARMY

103rd R.

CLÉRY 2¼ m.

Hem

Monacu B Fm.

SOMME

CANAL

Attacks............ ⟶   ⟶
Ground gained. ●●●● ●●●●
British—Red. French—Blue. Germans—Green.

Feuillières

Compiled in the Historical Section (Military Branch)   Crown Copyright Reserved.   Ordnance Survey 1936
3060/38.

many offensive operations as possible along the Fourth Army front. Next day a conference of corps commanders at Fourth Army headquarters arranged the details of these subsidiary attacks. The XV. Corps was to clear the orchards north of Longueval and secure " as much as pos- " sible " of Wood Lane ; but it had also to assist the XIII. Corps with all guns available, undertake the artillery defence of Delville Wood, and fire on Flers, Les Bœufs, and Morval. The III. Corps was to press its attack up Munster Alley, securing also the Switch Line side of the re-entrant, provided that the Australians had previously gained possession of Pozières windmill.

The Franco-British attack was fixed for 4.45 A.M. on the 30th, but Fourth Army instructions, issued at 11 A.M. on the 29th July, gave 6.10 P.M. next day as zero hour for the XV. and III. Corps, which required as much time as possible to make their preparations. There was, however, to be a special bombardment of the objectives of the two corps [1] from 3.45 to 5.15 A.M., in order to assist the early morning Allied attack on the right, and a steady bombardment along the whole front was begun upon the 29th July. The finer weather, which now permitted of valuable photographic work by the Royal Flying Corps, greatly assisted observation.

In the XIII. Corps, the 30th Division, which made special arrangements to patrol the battle front, was to attack through the 35th Division. The 89th Brigade (Br.-General Hon. F. C. Stanley) advancing in touch with the French, had for objective Falfemont Farm and the German 2nd Position north-west of it as far as the southern edge of Guillemont, the objective of the 90th Brigade (Br.-General C. J. Steavenson). Guillemont station and the German trenches north-west of it were to be carried by the 5th Brigade (Br.-General G. M. Bullen-Smith) of the 2nd Division. During the night of the 29th July, when the assaulting troops were moving up to their assembly positions, the German bombardment was very heavy on the Trônes Wood area. In the 89th Brigade, which was to advance from the trenches south of the wood, the 19/King's

28–29 July.

Sketch 16.

Sketch 21.

Sketch 21.

---

[1] It was also arranged that a smoke barrage should be put down on the front of the 23rd Division (III. Corps) at 4.45 A.M. to simulate an attack. The smoke was to be provided by phosphorus bombs, fired from 8 mortars, and smoke candles, under the supervision of a section of No. 4 Coy. 5th Bn. Special Brigade R.E. ; but an unfavourable wind caused this part of the programme to be cancelled.

30 July. was badly shelled with gas and high-explosive, and some of the 90th Brigade underwent a similar ordeal. At dawn a thick fog, which did not clear until after 8 A.M., reduced visibility to less than forty yards.

On the right of the 89th Brigade, Maltz Horn Farm and the trenches running north from it were still in German hands, and at zero hour, 4.45 A.M., the farm was carried by a combined assault, a company of the 2/Bedfordshire attacking from the west, whilst a company of the French 153rd Regiment came in from the south. Over sixty Germans were killed here by the Bedfordshire, and the advance swept on eastward, downhill. The 20/King's, forming the right of the main attack, overran the German front trenches [1] and reached the Hardecourt—Guillemont road. The battalion lost heavily from machine-gun fire as it did so, but began to consolidate the line of the road with the assistance of the 17/King's, which, in small columns, had followed in support. No French troops appeared to be in the vicinity. The 19/King's, next on the left, also sustained many casualties and few men arrived at the road; but farther north a party reached an orchard on the south-eastern outskirts of Guillemont. Major G. Rollo, commanding the battalion, went forward to ascertain the situation, and was severely wounded.

In the 90th Brigade, the 2/R. Scots Fusiliers advanced astride the Trônes Wood—Guillemont track, entered Guillemont from the south-west without much loss, and soon collected 50 prisoners. The leading company waited for the barrage—which was to rake through Guillemont in four lifts—on the line of the church, and then pushed on to the north-eastern edge of the village, where consolidation was begun in touch with a party of the 18/Manchester, on the left. A counter-attack from the direction of the cemetery was repulsed. Two more companies of the Scots Fusiliers then pressed forward and joined the leading company. The 18/Manchester, advancing with its left on the Trônes Wood—Guillemont railway, took many prisoners on reaching the German front trench; [2] but most of the battalion could make little further progress under the cross-fire of machine guns in the quarry and the station. A withdrawal was followed by a fresh advance,

---

[1] Held by the left of the *24th Reserve Division*, whose front extended northward to Guillemont and the trenches west of Ginchy.

[2] Held by troops of the *I./22nd Bavarian Reserve Regiment*, attached to the *24th Reserve Division*. Somme-Nord ii.

in which two companies of the 16/Manchester and two of 30 July. the 17/Manchester shared ; but this effort only resulted in fresh losses.   The left of the brigade attack, two companies of the 16/Manchester, had advanced southward from assembly trenches east of Trônes Wood, forming left on reaching the railway.   These companies were checked by uncut wire south of Guillemont station, whence machine-gun fire caught them in enfilade and compelled a retirement.

Information as to the progress of the attack was not easy to transmit to the rear, and for some time divisional headquarters received no news at all.   German shell-fire had cut most of the wires.[1] Pigeons were employed with success in some cases, but visual signalling was out of the question until about 9 A.M. owing to the fog; and runners crossing the ground between Trônes Wood and Guillemont were exposed to heavy bursts of machine-gun fire.[2]   At 8.55 A.M. Major-General Shea, convinced that some success had been achieved, ordered the line from the western edge of Guillemont to Maltz Horn Farm to be held at all costs.

Early in the afternoon, however, the left of the 19/King's, believing itself isolated, withdrew with difficulty from the orchard near Guillemont ; and the parties of the King's in the road beyond the main German front line fell back later. On the right the prescribed position was entrenched by the 2/Bedfordshire of the 89th Brigade.   In spite of the barrages laid by the heavy artillery on the cross-roads east of the village and round Leuze Wood and Ginchy, the Germans were now coming forward to counter-attack ; but it was difficult for the British batteries to fire on Guillemont, where three companies of the R. Scots Fusiliers still held out. Unfortunately the reserves of both brigades had been expended and defensive considerations were now paramount ; so the Fusiliers, cut off by the German defensive barrage and deprived of all support and assistance, were eventually overwhelmed.   This battalion, which had pressed on with such splendid resolution to its objective, deserved a better fate.   There is ample evidence that it was not easily overcome.[3]

[1] About 3 A.M. a buried cable had been set on fire owing to German shells exploding an ammunition and bomb dump near the brickworks south of Bernafay Wood.

[2] C.S.-M.G. Evans, 18/Manchester, was awarded the V.C. for his gallant service as a runner.   He came back under heavy fire, delivered his message, and then, although wounded, rejoined his company.

[3] About 7.30 A.M. a weak counter-attack against the north-east edge of Guillemont was checked by the fire of the British in the village.   An hour later, when the fog lifted, four companies of the *107th Reserve Regiment*

30 July.   The 2nd Division attack was made by the 2/Oxford & Bucks L.I. and the 24/Royal Fusiliers (5th Brigade) which advanced from the Waterlot Farm area upon Guillemont railway station. Machine-gun fire from Delville Wood protected the left flank of the assault, but the trench mortars had failed to deal with the German bombing posts, and many German machine guns had survived the British bombardment. Some of the Oxford & Bucks L.I. who overran the enemy front positions came close up to the station, and there were killed ; otherwise little progress was made, and the troops were eventually withdrawn to their assembly positions under heavy shell-fire.[1]

In hot sunshine, and under a heavy bombardment, the two brigades of the 30th Division spent the rest of the day in reorganizing the line, the 89th Brigade consolidating the only ground gained : from Arrow Head Copse along the sunken Hardecourt—Guillemont road to Maltz Horn Farm, where the right flank was in touch with the French.[2] The British losses had been very heavy,[3] and at night Lieut.-General Congreve relieved all the forward troops—30th and 35th Divisions—in the right sector of the corps by the newly-arrived 55th Division, commanded by Major-General H. S. Jeudwine.

It is little matter for surprise that the attack made on the 30th July should have taken almost the exact course of the action of the 23rd : the conditions under which it was delivered were practically the same. After the first experience it seemed to the local commanders that an assault against the Guillemont positions from the west—up the exposed shallow trough which marked the termination of Caterpillar Valley—and from the south-west—over a crest and down a slope, both devoid of cover—had little chance of success. This was particularly the case if the right were not supported by an attack in force across the heads of the Maurepas ravine.

---

advanced from Ginchy, but had to be supported by part of the *13th Reserve Jäger*. Eventually other *Jäger* detachments pushed forward, and the British who held out until 2 P.M. were overwhelmed. Three companies of the *104th Reserve Regiment*, advancing from the east, also assisted in restoring the situation. Somme-Nord ii.

[1] The attack had broken in near the point of junction of the *I./22nd Bavarian Reserve* and *107th Reserve Regiments*. According to Somme-Nord, the combined efforts of Saxons and Bavarians had restored the situation by 7.30 A.M.

[2] For the operations of the French see Note I. at end of Chapter.

[3] 89th Brigade, 1,314 ; 90th Brigade, 1,463. The 2/R. Scots Fusiliers lost 17 officers and 633 other ranks.

Sketch 22.

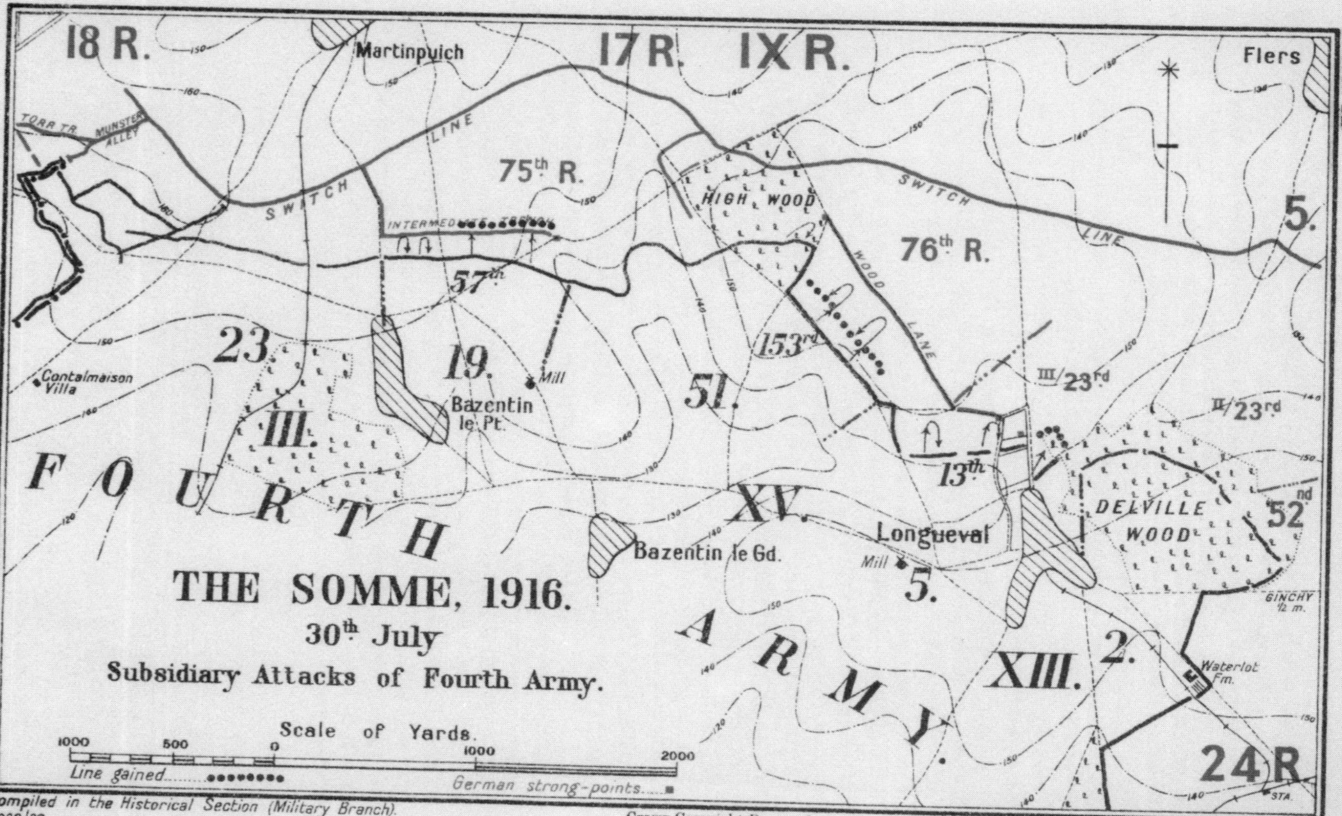

THE SOMME, 1916.
30th July

Subsidiary Attacks of Fourth Army.

Scale of Yards.

Line gained.......
German strong-points.....

Ordnance Survey 1936

Crown Copyright Reserved

Compiled in the Historical Section (Military Branch).
3060/38.

It remains to describe the results of the subsidiary 30 July.
attacks delivered by the Fourth Army on the evening of the
30th July.   At Longueval, the 5th Division advance was
made by the 13th Brigade (Br.-General L. O. W. Jones), Sketch
from the line reached by the division on the previous day, 22.
in order to capture the German strongpoints on the tracks
leading into the village from the north, and also the south-
eastern end of the trench along Wood Lane.   The preliminary bombardment [1] began at 4.45 P.M., increasing in
intensity just before zero hour, but the British artillery
failed to subdue the fire of the German batteries, which was
very heavy on Longueval and Delville Wood, with the usual
barrage south of the village.   For this reason, communications again failed and no messages came back from the
infantry for some time after it advanced at 6.10 P.M.
On the right, the 2/K.O.S.B. was badly shelled on the
north-western edge of Delville Wood.   One company
pushed forward clear of the wood, and, having killed a
number of Germans, dug in.[2]   The 14/R. Warwickshire,
on the left, had crawled forward under the barrage, but
as soon as the assault was delivered heavy rifle and
machine-gun fire checked the whole line, officers and men
going to ground in shell-holes.

The 1/R. West Kent—with a fighting strength of only
175 other ranks—was in support of the Borderers, and was
so heavily shelled that the 1/Bedfordshire (15th Brigade)
was ordered to relieve the right of the line.   This the
battalion eventually did, although it was not provided with
guides and had to find its way forward as best it could.
Meanwhile, the 16/R. Warwickshire (15th Brigade) was sent
forward from reserve, and the day was spent in efforts to
reorganize the line at Longueval, where a great admixture
of troops prevailed and the German bombardment continued without respite.[3]   At night the 14/R. Warwickshire
and most of the other forward troops were relieved, command being transferred to the 15th Brigade.

At 6.10 P.M., also, the 153rd Brigade (Br.-General

---

[1] A gun of U Battery R.H.A. (from the 1st Indian Cavalry Division)
was brought up south of Longueval to enfilade Wood Lane at close range.
[2] It maintained its isolated position for two days, and then withdrew
through the 17th Division which had taken over the front.
[3] The British artillery inflicted severe loss on the Germans, the right
of the *5th Division* having to be reinforced.   The *I./163rd* (*17th Reserve
Division*) was hurried forward in lorries from Ytres (4½ miles east of Le
Transloy) to Beaulencourt, where it was located by British airmen and
heavily shelled.   At night, the *III./23rd* (attached from the *12th Division*)
had to be relieved by the *I./23rd*.   Somme-Nord ii.

30 July. D. Campbell) of the 51st Division (Major-General G. M. Harper) assaulted Wood Lane and the strongpoint at the eastern corner of High Wood.[1]   The 1/5th Gordon High-landers and 1/6th Black Watch advanced close under the barrage against the former objective, but lost heavily from rifle, shell and machine-gun fire.[2]   Some of the Gordons reached the wire—previously unreported—in front of the trench and were there killed ; the survivors of the two battalions, in isolated groups, dug in about two hundred yards in front of their starting line.   The 1/7th Black Watch made their way through the wood towards the strongpoint, upon which a trench-mortar bombardment appeared to have had no effect ; but German shell-fire afterwards compelled a withdrawal.   Lieut.-General Horne, commanding the XV. Corps, wished to have a fresh attack launched at 9.45 P.M., but this proved impracticable and the situation in High Wood remained unaltered.   In reporting the result of the action, Major-General Harper, probably having in mind the rumour of complete success at Delville Wood, suggested that High Wood could only be taken by a special bombardment of heavy guns which would search the whole area and com-pletely demoralize such Germans as should survive.

In the III. Corps, the principal operation was the attack upon Intermediate Trench by the 19th Division. The Switch Line and the north-western corner of High Wood received special attention from the corps heavy artillery, and a smoke cloud screened the right of the advance from the German machine gunners on the western side of the wood.[3]   The 57th Brigade (Br.-General G. D. Jeffreys) had the 7/King's Own (attached from the 56th Brigade), 10/R. Warwickshire, 10/Worcestershire and 8/Gloucestershire in line.   The two first-named battalions, on the right, pressed forward close upon the barrage.   When it lifted they rushed the German defenders, and captured half Intermediate Trench, and the strongpoint at its eastern end, together with over thirty prisoners of the *75th Reserve*

---

[1] The wood was held by the *I./76th Reserve* ; Wood Lane, by the *II./76th Reserve* (*17th Reserve Division*).   Somme-Nord ii. states that these battalions were hard pressed, suffering a great deal from the British bombardment. Reinforcements were called for.

[2] The Germans were reported to have many machine guns in saps run-ning forward from their trench lines.   A captured German instruction on the subject showed that these weapons were also established behind the parados of the trench to fire in enfilade.

[3] Four mortars of the Special Brigade R.E. fired 79 smoke shells.   No machine-gun fire was heard from this direction when the troops went forward.

Regiment.[1] On the left, however, the Worcestershire and **30 July.**
Gloucestershire were later in advancing, and the German
machine guns were able to open with deadly effect.   The
two battalions suffered heavy loss, Major Lord A. G.
Thynne, commanding the Gloucestershire, being among
the severely wounded, and their effort failed.

The captured portion of Intermediate Trench was consolidated with the assistance of the 5/South Wales Borderers
(Pioneers), and the 81st Field Company R.E., a barricade
being erected on the left of the Warwickshire.   A counter-
attack was repulsed,[2] but German shell-fire made work and
movement difficult and communication with the front line
was very precarious.[3]

Farther to the left, the 70th Brigade of the 23rd Division
had co-operated with the 19th Division attack by the fire
of its Stokes mortars, but otherwise was not actively
engaged.   On the left of the III. Corps, the Australians **Sketch**
(Reserve Army) had not yet secured Pozières mill, and no **19.**
further progress was made at Munster Alley.   Aeroplane
photographs, available on the 29th July, showed that O.G.2
was now practically non-existent south of the Bapaume
road, but that the enemy had strengthened his defences by
linking up O.G.1 and Munster Alley by a new fire trench
which the III. Corps heavy artillery had begun to register.
The 23rd Division, on its part, had dug a new line between
Munster Alley and Gloster Alley, forming a salient in the
centre of the Munster Alley—Switch Line re-entrant.

The hostile bombardment was heavy along the whole **31 July.**
Fourth Army front during the 31st July, but fine weather
now allowed counter-battery work to be carried on with **Sketch**
more effect.   Reorganization of the line proceeded, the **22.**
19th Division handing over to the 34th (Major-General C.
L. Nicholson)[4] in the right sector of the III. Corps.   The
5th Division was informed by the XV. Corps that it must
secure its objective of the 30th July without delay ; but

---

[1] A company commander who was captured said that the British
infantry got in so quickly after the barrage lifted that his machine-gunners
had no chance to come into action.

[2] According to Somme-Nord ii. the ceaseless British bombardment
made it very difficult to get a counter-attack delivered.

[3] Pte. J. Miller, 7/King's Own, a runner who struggled on and delivered
his message after being mortally wounded, received the posthumous award
of the V.C.

[4] The artillery relief was completed on 3rd/4th August. The total
casualties of the 19th Division for July were returned as 337 officers and
6,260 other ranks.

31 July. Major-General Stephens reported, with truth, that his brigades were too exhausted for another effort, and urged that the task be given to a fresh division. It was accordingly arranged that the 17th Division (now commanded by Major-General P. R. Robertson) should relieve the 5th on the night of the 1st August.

The results of the 30th July could hardly be viewed with satisfaction ; again very little progress had been made, and that only as the result of heavy casualties and of a great expenditure of ammunition. The Germans, who now held their front lightly, their troops being distributed in depth, continued to resist with great obstinacy. Apart from the blunders committed at Pozières after the loss of the village, their subordinate leading during the last eight days had been extremely capable. As ever, the machine gun played a great part in the defence. On the other hand, there was reason to believe that the Allied pressure might, at any time, cause a definite collapse of resistance on some part of the German front : the enemy losses were known to be very great, and every fresh division he brought to the Somme was at once called upon to relieve exhausted troops in the battle line and to work upon new defensive positions in rear. Unfortunately the time required to complete the carefully concerted preparations, without which no British or French attack of importance could hope to succeed, always provided a valuable respite to the enemy.

From the artillery point of view, too much had been attempted by the British on the 30th July to permit of the thorough preparation of all the attacks delivered. The situation was reviewed from this standpoint at a Fourth Army conference, held at 9.30 A.M. on the 31st July, which was attended by the three corps commanders with their **Sketches** senior artillery officers. General Rawlinson announced **22, 23.** that the capture of Guillemont, to be undertaken only after a thorough preparation, was the most pressing problem; after that step the Ginchy—Leuze Wood position must be secured, the XV. and III. Corps pressing forward meanwhile to obtain possession of the Switch Line. Major-General C. E. D. Budworth, the chief artillery officer of the Army, was of opinion that the XIII. Corps guns could not deal with any other portion of the corps front whilst preparing for the Guillemont attack, and that there was not sufficient artillery available to take Ginchy and Guillemont in one operation. Subsequently an artillery conference arranged that the field guns of the XV. Corps should cover the front

THE SOMME, 1916: 31ˢᵗ July.

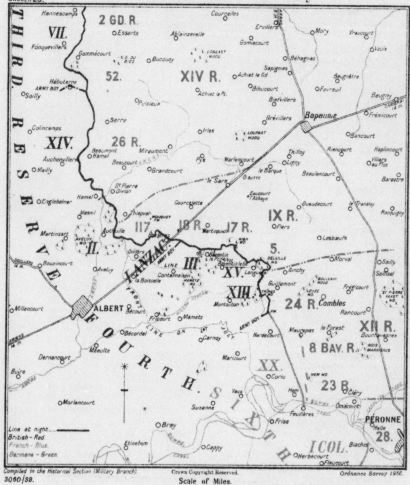

Sketch 23.

THIRD RESERVE

FOURTH SIXTH

VII.
2 GD. R.
52.
XIV R.
XIV.
26 R.
117
18 R.
17 R.
IX R.
II.
LANZAC
III.
5.
XV.
XIII.
24 R.
XII R.
8 BAV. R.
XX.
23 R.
I COL.
28.

Hannescamps
Courcelles
Ervillers
Mory
Vraucourt
Vaux
Fonquevillers
Essarts
Ablainzevelle
Gomiecourt
Behagnies
Sapignies
Beugnâtre
Hébuterne
Achiet le Gd.
ARMY BDY
Bihucourt
Favreuil
Beugny
Sailly
Puisieux
Biefvillers
CAMBRAI 8 m.
Frémicourt
Colincamps
Serre
Irles
Grévillers
Bapaume
Bancourt
Haplincourt
XIV.
Beaumont Hamel
Miraumont
Pys
Warlencourt
le Barque
Beaulencourt
Villers au Flos
Auchonvillers
Beaucourt
Grandcourt
le Sars
Eaucourt l'Abbaye
Guedecourt
le Transloy
Racquigny
Barastre
Mailly
St Pierre Divian
Courcelette
Flers
Lesbœufs
Englebelmer
Hamel
Thiepval
Martinpuich
Mesnil
Martinsart
Authuille
Ovillers
Contalmaison
Longueval
Ginchy
Morval
Sailly
Saillisel
Bouzincourt
Aveluy
la Boisselle
Guillemont
Frégicourt
St Pierre Vaast
Millencourt
ALBERT
Bécourt
Fricourt
Mametz
Montauban
Combles
Rancourt
Bouchavesnes
Dernancourt
Bécordel
Carnoy
Hardecourt
Maurepas
le Forest
8 BAV. R.
Buire
Méaulte
Maricourt
Suzanne
Curlu
Hem
Cléry
Marlancourt
Vaux
Feuillères
Omiécourt
PÉRONNE
Bray
Frise
Biaches
28.
Etinehem
Cappy
Herbécourt
Flaucourt

Line at night._____
British - Red.
French - Blue.
Germans - Green.

Compiled in the Historical Section (Military Branch).
3060/38.
Crown Copyright Reserved.
Ordnance Survey 1956.
Scale of Miles.

as far as an east and west line drawn through the centre of Delville Wood, whilst the zone of its heavy artillery should be bounded by the railway south of Ginchy, the III. Corps heavy artillery extending its zone eastward to include High Wood. Guillemont was to be the special task of the XIII. Corps heavy guns with such assistance as was necessary from the XV. Corps, which had also to concentrate on Ginchy. The counter-battery work was also re-apportioned, the XV. Corps to be ready to deal with the Morval—Lesbœufs area if so required, whilst the III. Corps might be switched on to the Flers—Ginchy sector.

NOTE I

THE FRENCH ATTACK OF 30TH JULY [1]

The French were very disappointed with the achievement of their Sketch Sixth Army north of the Somme on the 30th July, when the objectives 21. included Maurepas and the German defences along the Maurepas—Cléry road down to the river. Considerable success was gained at the start, but much of the ground was recovered by the Germans. Maurepas was not taken. South of the village the German front positions were overrun, progress was made towards Hem Wood, and the enemy was driven from Monacu Farm, east of Hem ; but in many places it seemed that the troops would have to relinquish what they had won in order to permit of a fresh artillery preparation. " L'échec est flagrant." Apart from the fog, which hampered the artillery, failure was attributed to the German method of defence : the enemy front positions were occupied lightly, but with plenty of machine guns ; strong detachments were held close in rear, ready to counter-attack ; snipers, well-hidden, disorganized the French assaulting waves by sudden fire at point-blank range.

General Joffre now postponed the projected attack south of the Somme, where the bombardment on the Lihons—Barleux front had opened on the 29th July, until General Fayolle should be ready to make another effort north of the river. On the 31st July General Foch was summoned to Chantilly, where General Joffre again enunciated the principle of well co-ordinated attacks on broad fronts ; but, as he recognized that the French attacks north and south of the Somme were bound to be divergent, he transferred two of Fayolle's corps (II. and XXXV.) in action south of the river to Micheler's Tenth Army. General Foch then issued fresh instructions to the two Armies : the Tenth, when it should have the means, to destroy the enemy forces which were west of the Somme above Péronne ; the Sixth, in close touch with the British right, to secure the high ground east of Combles (general direction, Bertincourt), and to force the passage of the Tortille river so that its cavalry could advance northward up the left bank.

[1] F.O.A. iv. (ii.), pp. 272-5.

NOTE II

THE GERMAN SITUATION, 22ND-31ST JULY [1]

During the last week of July hardly a day passed without grave news reaching General von Below from some part of the fighting front.   The 23rd brought a crisis at Guillemont, and the defenders at Delville Wood and Longueval were extended to the utmost ; on the 24th, after two attempts to counter-attack at Pozières had miscarried, a break-in west of the village seemed imminent, and next day the Army still had fears for the situation at this point ; on the 27th and 28th, Below, who had no reliable news, considered Delville Wood the danger spot ; and the 30th brought another crisis on the Guillemont—Longueval front.   The flanks of the 1st Position had become corner-stones : between them the battle area had developed and completely altered fighting conditions.   Troops lay in shell-holes more difficult than trenches for the enemy artillery to locate ; but existence in crater defences made enormous demands on the physique and spirit of the men and made it very difficult to exercise command, distribute supplies, and care for the wounded.   Unburied dead infected the air and took away the desire to eat ; warm food could be brought up only at night and seldom reached the front positions, where the fighting troops subsisted on tinned provisions ; there was great lack of water in the summer heat.

The ten battalions of the *24th Reserve Division*, defending the Guillemont sector, lost 5,476 of all ranks between the 14th and 31st July ; the casualties (an incomplete record) of the six regiments in the *7th* and *8th Divisions* (*IV. Corps*) which fought on the front Delville Wood—north of Bazentin le Petit from the 15th July for about twelve days, are shown as 9,498 officers and men ; the infantry of the *5th Division*, not relieved in the Delville Wood sector until the 3rd August, lost 5,000, " rather more than had been sustained " before Verdun in May ".

As has been noted, the *117th Division* and the *17th* and *18th Reserve Divisions* had already been absorbed into the battle opposite the British front.   The *8th Bavarian Reserve Division* had been defending the Maurepas sector since the 21st July ; the *23rd Reserve Division* had taken over the line immediately north of the Somme on the 24th July ; and on the night of the 30th/31st July the *24th Reserve Division* was relieved by the *27th Division* and went into Army reserve.   At noon on the 31st the command of the Gossler " Group " passed to General von Kirchbach, whose XII. Reserve Corps (*23rd* and *24th Reserve Divisions*) had already been so heavily engaged.   The *27th Division*, mentioned above, together with the *26th* (forming the *XIII. Corps*) had been hurried down from the Ypres Salient, the *26th* being destined for the relief of the *5th Division* at Delville Wood—Longueval.

Falkenhayn's anxieties increased as the month drew to a close. Hard pressed for reinforcements to sustain the Somme battle, he had ordered an attack north-east of Souville, on the right bank of the Meuse, in order to retard the transfer of French forces from

[1] G.O.A. x., pp. 369, 371, Somme-Nord ii. and regimental histories.

Verdun to the Somme. The Brusilov offensive had by no means spent itself, for the Russians were continuing their attacks between the Carpathians and the Dniester, and were about to strike again along the river Stochod. " The Austro-Hungarian troops had lost " all confidence in themselves and needed support everywhere " ; [1] Conrad was loth to withdraw divisions from the Italian front, for he feared, with reason, that the Italians would soon take the offensive on the Isonzo. They did so on the 6th August.

At the end of July Falkenhayn summoned Hindenburg and Ludendorff to his headquarters at Pless in Silesia, where the Kaiser had arrived. Brody had fallen to the Russians on the 28th so that Lemberg itself was now threatened and, as a consequence, the Austrians acquiesced in the extension southward of the German command. Thus Hindenburg, German Commander-in-Chief in the East, became responsible for the front from south of Lemberg to the Baltic ; but the task of finding the necessary German reinforcements devolved upon O.H.L.

[1] Ludendorff i., p. 227.

CHAPTER VII

THE SOMME

AUGUST 1916

THE FOURTH ARMY

(Sketches A, 24, 25, 26, 27, 28)

1ST–17TH AUGUST

GUILLEMONT [1]

DURING the second month of the great offensive the Fourth Army continued to play the major part, although increasing importance attached to the operations of the Reserve Army. It was a period of bitter fighting when hardly any ground was gained and the struggle became, more than ever, a grim test of endurance. There was little to encourage or inspire the troops of all arms who fought on the Somme in August : subjected to heavy losses, great hardships, and tremendous physical and moral strain, they had only their own dogged spirit to maintain them.

On the 3rd August an important communication reached the Armies from G.H.Q. setting out the Commander-in-Chief's view of the situation and the methods to be followed in attaining the immediate objective : the whole of the Morval—Thiepval ridge.[2] Sir Douglas Haig was convinced that the German reinforcements in men and guns and the growing strength of the German positions made it impossible to gain any further success without the most careful and methodical preparation : it was also necessary to consolidate against the heavy counter-attacks which were to be expected : the existing phase of the operations should be regarded as a " wearing-out " battle in which the utmost

---

[1] The officially named " Battle of Guillemont " only covers the dates 3rd-6th September.   [2] Appendix 13.

Attack on GUILLEMONT
4·20 a.m., 8th August, 1916.

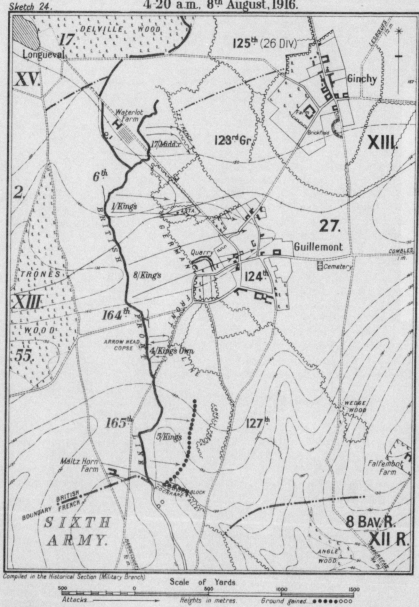

Sketch 24.

DELVILLE WOOD

17

Longueval

XV.

2

6th

1/Kings

TRONES

XIII.

WOOD

55.

164th

ARROW HEAD COPSE

165th

Maltz Horn Farm

BOUNDARY BRITISH FRENCH

SIXTH ARMY.

BRITISH FRONT LINE

GERMAN FRONT LINE

Waterlot Farm

17/Midd'x

8/King's

4/King's Own

5/King's

COCHRANE ALLEY

125th (26 DIV)

Ginchy

Farm

Brickfield

123rd Gr

Quarry

124th

27.

Guillemont

Cemetery

XIII.

COMBLES 1m.

127th

WEDGE WOOD

Falfemont Farm

8 BAV. R.

XII R.

ANGLE WOOD

LESBŒUFS 1½ m.

Compiled in the Historical Section (Military Branch)

Scale of Yards

500   0   500   1000   1500

Attacks ———

Heights in metres.

Ground gained •••••○○○○

Ordnance Survey 1937.

economy of men and material must be practised so as to ensure that the Allies should have at their disposal the " last reserves " when the crisis of the fighting was reached : this could hardly arrive sooner than in the latter half of September : the first necessity was " to help the French " forward " on the right flank by securing, as soon as possible, Guillemont, Falfemont Farm and Ginchy : these operations must be carefully and methodically planned with due regard to economy of means, and no attack launched until " the responsible commanders on the spot are satisfied " that everything possible has been done to ensure success " : on the fronts of the XV. and III. Corps preparations for a renewed attack must, for the time, follow the accepted practice of semi-siege warfare by pushing out saps and digging " parallels " close to the German advanced positions : the immediate objectives of the Reserve Army were the German trenches on the spur south of Mouquet Farm and the old 2nd Position north of the Bapaume road.

General Foch had visited Sir Douglas Haig on the 1st August principally to explain that General Fayolle was in future to concentrate his attention upon the operations north of the Somme, retaining under his command south of the river the front of the I. Colonial Corps only.[1] The French would be ready for a combined effort in six days' time, when their Tenth Army would co-operate by bombarding the German positions south of the Somme. The British Commander-in-Chief received this news with great satisfaction.

General Rawlinson kept in close touch with General Fayolle, and on the morning of the 5th they agreed that on the 7th August the British should attack Guillemont whilst the French improved their position north of Hem ; [2] a combined attack against the line from the Somme to Maurepas and Falfemont Farm would follow on the 11th. At 12.30 P.M. on the 5th General Rawlinson saw General Foch at Dury and explained these plans ; but Lieut.-General Congreve, commanding the XIII. Corps, then telephoned to say that the preparations of the 55th Division were being hampered by the heavy German bombardment and he could not be ready before the 8th August. The question of postponement was referred to

[1] See Note I. Chapter VI. The change came into operation on 5th August, when the boundary between the French Sixth and Tenth Armies ran : wood N.E. of Belloy—Assevillers—Dompierre (all inclusive to the Tenth Army). See Sketch A.

[2] See Sketch 21.

5-7 Aug. Sir Douglas Haig, who arrived at Dury at 3.45 P.M., and the attack was eventually fixed for the 8th, no further delay being permitted. The French, however, proceeded with their plans for the 7th August.[1]

General Rawlinson had readjusted the frontages of his corps with the object of enabling the XIII. Corps to concentrate upon the Guillemont attack.[2] Since taking over the sector opposite Guillemont at the end of July, Major-General H. S. Jeudwine's 55th Division, under cover of a steady bombardment, had been working hard upon advanced trenches in order to bring its line within assaulting distance of the enemy. Farther north, the 2nd Division (Major-General W. G. Walker) did likewise. There were some patrol encounters, and a forward post was established on the Trônes Wood—Guillemont track.

Sketch 24.

The objectives prescribed for the XIII. Corps were limited : the 55th Division was first to secure the spur south of Guillemont, obtaining touch with the French left on the Hardecourt—Guillemont road, and then to capture Guillemont, with the exception of the northern edge and the railway station, which were included in the objectives of the 2nd Division. The latter, in its advance, would carry all the German defences between Waterlot Farm and the village. Into the preliminary bombardment for wire-cutting and general destruction of the German defences there was introduced on the 7th August a series of six " Chinese attacks ".[3] These consisted of sudden and intense barrages of siege and field artillery, lifting forward and back, and lasting about fifteen minutes, as though in preparation for infantry assaults ; apart from the damage and loss inflicted, they were calculated to keep the enemy in doubt as to when and where the real attack would come.

The plans for the assault to be launched on the 8th

---

[1] The French 39th Division, next to the British, did not advance on 7th August, although its artillery was active. Farther south, the attack was launched at 5 P.M. ; it made progress north-west of Hem Wood, where fighting continued, reached the southern edge of the wood, and gained some ground north-east of Monacu, the station being captured. (See Sketch 21.) F.O.A. iv. (ii.), Annexe 2795.

[2] By 3rd August the III. Corps had extended its right to the western edge of High Wood ; on the night of the 4th/5th, the XV. Corps took over Delville Wood from the XIII. Corps. The new boundaries are shown on Sketch 26.

[3] See " 1915 " Vol. II., p. 187. The term, derived from the old Chinese practice of making much noise and show in order to intimidate the enemy, was now used for any demonstration which simulated an attack without involving an infantry advance, smoke often being employed.

August differed little from those of the previous attacks. The heavy artillery of the XIII. Corps was to lift from the German front line fifteen minutes before zero hour (4.20 A.M.) to a line running through the centre of Guillemont. Twenty minutes later it would move to the eastern edge of the village in two lifts at intervals of fifteen and five minutes respectively. The final barrage would be laid on Wedge Wood (German 2nd Position), on the slopes between Ginchy and Guillemont, and in front of Leuze Wood, 1300 yards east of Guillemont.[1]

The divisional artilleries, lifting from the German front line at zero, would rake forward through Guillemont in five stages at ten-minute intervals to a line beyond the village, flank barrages being maintained. As regards the infantry, numerous conferences were held to ensure that everyone, down to section leaders and rank and file, understood what was required of him. Elaborate precautions were taken to ensure that communications should not fail : contact aeroplanes were detailed to watch the progress of the attack ; ground flares, mirrors, lamps and panels were carried by the infantry to show the positions reached ; visual signalling posts and relay posts for runners were organized ; pigeons were taken forward ; and the troops wore bright tin discs on their backs as an additional help to observers. A wireless station was installed in a trench north-east of Favière Wood.

At 4.20 A.M. on the 8th August the infantry went 8 Aug. forward. There was an easterly wind and considerable mist, and the whole field of view was further obscured by dust and smoke, the German artillery having put down a heavy barrage. Visual signalling was out of the question and for a time no runners got back. It was not till after 6 A.M. that headquarters of the 55th Division received any news. On the right, next to the French, the 1/5th King's of the 165th Brigade (Br.-General F. J. Duncan) made some progress across the spur south of Guillemont before being stopped by fire. The bombers of the battalion pushed forward along Cochrane Alley, which ran south-eastward down into the Maurepas ravine and marked the British southern flank ; this trench was eventually blocked by being blown in with guncotton by a party of sappers of the 1/1st West Lancashire Field Company. The line, mostly in

---

[1] Two 12-inch howitzers and eight other heavy howitzer batteries were lent by the XV. Corps, which further assisted by putting down a special barrage on the Ginchy front.

8 Aug. shell-holes, reached by the 1/5th King's was out of touch on both flanks : it represented the sole British gain of the day.[1]   Next to the 1/5th King's, the 1/4th King's Own of the 164th Brigade (Br.-General G. T. G. Edwards) was checked before the wire opposite the south-western edge of Guillemont and, after attempting to dig in beyond bombing distance of the enemy, was forced to withdraw to its assembly trenches.[2]   The 1/8th King's (Liverpool Irish), also 164th Brigade, went forward with great dash, broke through the German front line and, passing north and south of the quarry, fought its way into Guillemont.   Unfortunately a company of the 1/4th Loyal N. Lancashire, which was sent forward to hold the enemy front line, was bombed out of it by a counter-attack from the south. German machine guns were now sweeping No Man's Land, preventing all communication, so the 1/8th King's was left in a hazardous situation.

The 2nd Division attack was made by two battalions of the 6th Brigade (Br.-General A. C. Daly).   Advancing eastward, north of the railway, three companies of the 1/King's swept across the German front line and reached Guillemont station ; but when the fourth company followed in support it found the enemy had reoccupied his front line, and so failed to get in.[3]   The 17/Middlesex issued from the Waterlot Farm position and entered ZZ Trench, but nearly a whole company of the battalion was lost in attempting to bomb southward and join hands with the 1/King's.

The fragmentary and contradictory reports which reached the two divisional headquarters during the morning delayed further action.   Aeroplane observers could distinguish little amid the smoke and dust of battle, and no messages came back from the troops known to be in

[1] The French division next to the British attacked with three companies only.   The left company got down into the ravine south-east of Maltz Horn, where it was stopped by enfilade machine-gun fire from the south ; the other companies made no progress.   Farther south, the French improved their positions north of Hem wood and captured the northern part of the wood itself.   F.O.A. iv. (ii.), Annexe 2820.

[6] 2nd-Lieut. G. G. Coury, who went out with a half-company of 1/4th S. Lancashire (Pioneers) to dig a forward communication trench, rallied some of the retiring troops under heavy fire ; at great personal risk he rescued Major J. L. Swainson, commanding the 1/4th King's Own.   He was awarded the V.C.

[3] The 1/8th King's and 1/King's had lost touch during their advance, and the Germans advanced north-westward through the gap in an attempt to restore their line.   Others had come straight forward from Guillemont, where many of the dug-outs had two or more entrances.

Guillemont. The British trenches forward of Trônes 8 Aug.
Wood were very congested, and suffered a heavy bombardment during the afternoon, so that it proved impossible to
get a fresh attack going in obedience to orders from the
corps " to exploit the success of the 1/8th King's ". Major-
General Jeudwine ordered the 164th Brigade to push
strong parties into Guillemont when darkness fell ; late in
the evening, the XIII. Corps, after referring to Army
headquarters, insisted upon a renewed attack, with the same
objectives, all along the line at 4.20 A.M. next morning.

Nothing was accomplished during the night and not all
the attacking battalions were ready in position at zero hour 9 Aug.
on the 9th August. They had to face heavy machine-gun
fire when they advanced after a hurried bombardment.
Some confusion arose on the left brigade front, where the
166th Brigade (Br.-General L. F. Green Wilkinson) was
replacing the 164th—a very difficult relief—and although
the 1/10th King's (Liverpool Scottish), keeping close behind
the barrage, approached the German wire, it lost very
heavily in two desperate but unavailing efforts to close with
the enemy.[1] Nearly all the officers were hit, including
Lieut.-Colonel J. R. Davidson who was wounded. Next on
the left, the 1/5th Loyal N. Lancashire (also 166th Brigade)
was late through no fault of its own ; starting after the
barrage had lifted, it stood no chance of success. Subsequently, the 1/7th King's attacked from the position won
by its own brigade (the 165th) on the previous day, but
could make no headway.

The 2nd Division put in the 13/Essex (6th Brigade),
which approached the German line south of the railway and
was then driven back, whilst a fresh attempt of the
17/Middlesex to bomb southward from Waterlot Farm met
with failure.

The fate of the 1/8th King's (55th Division) and 1/King's 8 Aug.
(2nd Division), cut off in Guillemont on the 8th August, can
be described in a few words. Whilst the Territorial
battalion, having broken through south of the railway,
enveloped the quarry by north and south, and entered the
village,[2] the Regulars pushed on from the railway station
and reached the northern side of Guillemont.[3] There was
great confusion, mist and smoke hampering British and

---

[1] The V.C. was awarded to the medical officer of the 1/10th King's,
Captain N. C. Chavasse, for his exceptionally gallant work in rescuing
wounded under heavy fire.

[2] The 1/8th King's was engaged with the *III./124th Regiment.*

[3] They drove in the *III./123rd Grenadiers.*

8 Aug. German alike, but eventually the latter counter-attacked with local reserves pending the arrival of a reinforcement of two battalions.[1] When these entered the fight the case of the British became hopeless ; but only after hand to hand struggles were those in Guillemont overwhelmed. Others were forced to surrender at the quarry, but a mixed detachment of both battalions held out at the station until the 9 Aug. evening of the 9th, by which time all were consumed by thirst, many were wounded, and no bombs or ammunition were left.[2]

General Rawlinson had conferred with the XIII. Corps commander and the commanders of the 55th, 2nd and 24th Divisions[3] during the morning of the 9th August, and had given instructions for a renewed attack upon Guillemont which was only to be delivered after the most thorough preparation had been made.

At 11 A.M. Lieut.-General Kiggell, the Chief of the General Staff, arrived at Querrieu to explain the views of Sir Douglas Haig. The Commander-in-Chief considered that the successes of the Russians [4] made it imperative to press on without delay so that no German troops might be spared from France to reinforce the Eastern Front : " at " the same time, we cannot assist our Allies by failing in our " attacks ". He wished to know if sufficient forces had been employed against Guillemont ; suggested that the commander and staff of the XIII. Corps might require a rest ; and raised the question of the use of incendiary shell and of gas and smoke. Finally, he touched upon the failure of communications which had made it impossible to control the fight once the assault had been delivered.

The main problem, however, was how best to deal with the German machine guns hidden in shell-holes and portions of shattered trench and amongst the débris and rubble of what had been Guillemont. These were as difficult to locate as they were to destroy ; and, although the German system of defence laboured under grave disadvantages as

---

[1] *II./124th* and *II./123rd Grenadiers*.

[2] The 1/King's lost 235 of all ranks, including Lieut.-Colonel C. E. Goff killed in Guillemont on 8th August, and could only muster 180 at the close of the action : the casualties of the 1/8th King's amounted to 570.

[3] The 24th Division relieved the 2nd on the night of 9th/10th August. Casualties of the 2nd Division, 24th July–11th August were returned as 196 officers and 4,712 other ranks.

[4] Brusilov's left, still making headway against the Austrian *Seventh Army*, was now approaching the southern passes of the Carpathians. Farther north, the Russian advance was threatening the communications of Bothmer's *Southern Army* in Galicia.

regards control and supply, it was only too effective so long as the machine gunners possessed the spirit and tenacity to hold on under the strain of continuous bombardment.[1]

On the afternoon of the 9th August General Rawlinson settled with General Fayolle the details of the combined advance fixed for the 11th August. The French were to attack south and north of Maurepas, whilst the right of the XIII. Corps secured their left flank by making good the spur south of Guillemont; then Guillemont and Maurepas would be attacked together as soon as the Allies were ready.

Next morning,[2] after the XIII. Corps had reported that **10 Aug.** preparations for the renewed attack upon Guillemont would probably be completed by the 17th August, Lieut.-General W. N. Congreve, who had been struggling against ill-health for some time, was obliged to relinquish his command. His had been a particularly difficult task, for the XIII. Corps was handicapped by its very successes of the 1st and 14th July, which placed it at the right shoulder of the British salient. Confronted by the formidable obstacles of Guillemont and Delville Wood, every attack had to be launched from a cramped position which invited the concentration of hostile artillery fire; moreover, the right of the corps was called upon to co-operate with the French, whose methods were different, and who, also, were obliged to attack over unfavourable ground. Lieut.-General the Earl of Cavan, commanding the XIV. Corps, was summoned to take over the XIII. Corps.[3]

On this day, the 10th August, the bright, hot weather was succeeded by mist and drizzling rain which made aircraft observation impossible and caused the combined attack fixed for the 11th to be postponed until the 12th, which **12 Aug.** proved to be fine and clear. The British part was confined **Sketch** to obtaining possession of the spur south of Guillemont, **24.** the 55th Division being ordered to secure a position running northward for 300 yards from the point where Cochrane Alley met the Guillemont—Hardecourt road. The right flank of the division, so Major-General Jeudwine

---

[1] Several British officers with much battle experience of the Western Front have stated that the Germans never fought better than they did at Guillemont and Ginchy in 1916.

[2] The King visited the Fourth Army area on this day, viewing parts of the battlefield, and inspecting troops in reserve. His Majesty had arrived in France on 7th August, and visited each Army in turn before embarking for England on the 15th.

[3] The staff of the XIV. Corps began to replace that of the XIII., and the right corps of the Fourth Army was styled XIV. from midnight 16th/17th August.

12 Aug. had been assured, would be covered by the advance of the French into the Maurepas ravine. The preliminary bombardment began at 3.30 P.M. and zero hour was fixed for 5.15 P.M., from which time the German positions on the southern edges of Guillemont, as well as the 2nd Position south-east of the village, were kept under intense artillery fire. Two companies of the 1/9th King's (165th Brigade) made the advance, whilst the battalion bombers pushed down Cochrane Alley on the right, and under very heavy rifle and machine-gun fire the appointed line was reached in half an hour. As the French left had failed, however, the companies were withdrawn from their isolated position after nightfall, only a forward block in Cochrane Alley being retained.[1]

Since the end of July General Joffre had become increasingly dissatisfied with the way in which the Somme offensive had developed. Instead of a series of minor actions to which there appeared to be no end, he wanted a reversion to the policy of combined attacks upon a broad front. It was only thus, he considered, that real assistance could be given to the Russians. On the 11th August he wrote to Sir Douglas Haig making definite proposals for the capture of the line Thiepval—High Wood—Ginchy—Combles—Somme by means of three operations beginning on the 22nd ; this much accomplished, an attack against Grandcourt—Courcelette—Martinpuich—Flers—Morval—Rancourt—Bouchavesnes should be delivered about the 1st September. The two Commanders-in-Chief conferred next day at Beauquesne.[2] Sir Douglas Haig proposed, as a first step, a combined attack from the Somme to High Wood, for which he promised the British would be ready on the 18th, and General Joffre assured him that the French would co-operate to the fullest extent.

On the morning of the 13th, General Foch and General Rawlinson settled that, when the British XIV. Corps

Sketch 23.

Sketch 25.

---

[1] The French Sixth Army did make considerable progress on 12th August, carrying most of the German 2nd Position between Maurepas and Cléry on the Somme ; and the south part of Maurepas and the cemetery were taken and held. About mid-way between Maurepas and Cléry the Germans clung to their trenches, and their counter-attacks elsewhere, delivered after darkness had fallen, prevented the French from accomplishing much on the 13th. (See Map 2, " 1916 " Vol. I.)   F.O.A. iv. (ii.), pp. 289-90.

[2] The King and M. Poincaré, the French President, met at Beauquesne on 12th August. Generals Joffre and Haig, who, with General Foch, were present, held their discussion in the afternoon.

attacked Guillemont on the evening of the 18th in con- 13–16
junction with subsidiary attacks by the XV. and III. Aug.
Corps, the French would capture Maurepas, and in addition
would take Angle Wood, on or before the 18th, in order to
cover the British right ; if all went well the XIV. Corps
would attack Wedge Wood and Falfemont Farm at dawn
on the 19th ; and on the 22nd the Allied attack would be
delivered against Le Forest [1]—Bois Douage [2] (immediately
south of Combles) by the French and against Leuze Wood—
Ginchy by the British. In the afternoon, however, Sir
Douglas Haig arrived at Fourth Army headquarters and, as
the result of his understanding with General Joffre, gave
fresh instructions which were based upon a much larger
measure of co-operation from the French.

The Fourth Army attack upon the 18th was now to be
conditional on the French attacking simultaneously along
their whole front north of the Somme ; the XIV. Corps
objectives must be such portion of Guillemont as General
Rawlinson considered it possible to secure, and also Falfemont Farm, provided that Angle Wood had been in British
hands for 48 hours previously ; [3] operations at Delville
Wood must cover the flank of this attack, the other
objectives of the XV. and of the III. Corps depending upon
the artillery and ammunition available after provision had
been made for the main attack ; [4] if success were gained on
the 18th August, preparations would be made for the
Ginchy—Leuze Wood operation on the 22nd, which was to
be carried out simultaneously with a French advance
against the line Le Forest—Cléry. These fresh instructions
had already been conveyed to General Foch.

The British Commander-in-Chief received a visit from
General Foch on the 16th August, after which he replied to
General Joffre's letter of the 11th : he said that certain
local operations were inevitable, and that he had arranged
with General Foch the details of the combined attack on
the 18th, following a preliminary action on the 16th ; [5] the
22nd was already accepted as the date for another combined

---

[1] See Sketch A.

[2] On some French maps " Louage ", which spelling has been adopted
by F.O.A. " Douage " was used for British operation orders and maps.

[3] It had been arranged that the French would hand over Angle Wood
after they had captured it.

[4] The enormous expenditure of ammunition made " economy of means "
a factor of first importance. In the XIII. Corps alone, between 24th June
and 18th August the artillery (all calibres) fired 1,942,132 rounds—about
36,000 tons of shell.

[5] See below.

attack, but he could make no promise regarding the dates of subsequent operations ; he would not have sufficient forces for a large scale attack on the Thiepval front until his right was in a more favourable position.[1]

Following Sir Douglas Haig's visit on the 13th August General Rawlinson arranged with General Fayolle a preliminary operation on the 16th, when the French were to secure Angle Wood and the British the spur south of Guillemont. The British advance was to be made in two stages : first to the Hardecourt—Guillemont road and then to a forward position on the spur in touch with the French at the northern extremity of Angle Wood, thence running north-westward to Arrow Head Copse.

On the night of the 14th/15th August the 3rd Division (now commanded by Major-General C. J. Deverell, Major-General Haldane having taken over the VI. Corps) relieved the 55th Division, which, if it had failed to capture Guillemont, had at least pushed forward the British right to within close assaulting distance.[2]

Zero hour on the 16th was fixed for 5.40 P.M., and the afternoon proved to be bright and hot. Special attention had been devoted to counter-battery work and to communication between aeroplanes and the advancing infantry. The methodical bombardment quickened to three minutes' intense fire before the assault, which was delivered punctually and with great resolution. On the extreme right the 3rd Division put in the 2/Suffolk of the 76th Brigade (Br.-General R. J. Kentish) which cleared Cochrane Alley as far as the Hardecourt—Guillemont road, and, although enfiladed from Lonely Trench, took the trench along the road also.[3] Lonely Trench was too near the British front line to be bombarded and the Stokes mortars had failed to make much impression on it : consequently the 8/King's Own (left battalion of the 76th Brigade) and the 13/King's (right of Br.-General H. C. Potter's 9th Brigade) were received by heavy rifle and machine-gun fire, and could

----

[1] General Joffre deplored the readiness of Generals Foch and Fayolle to co-operate with the British commanders in subsidiary operations ; but the explanation of Fayolle's action was to be found in the difficulties of manœuvre on his front and the vigour of the enemy's reaction there. F.O.A. iv. (ii.), pp. 284-5.

[2] The losses of the 55th Division since the beginning of August were returned as 219 officers and 3,907 other ranks.

[3] There were a few prisoners of the *124th Regiment* which was relieving the *127th* in the southern sector of the *27th Division* front. North of Lonely Trench the British encountered the *123rd Grenadiers*.

make no headway in spite of repeated efforts.   Farther
north, the 4/Royal Fusiliers (9th Brigade) met a similar fate
as it advanced in touch with troops of the 24th Division.

The latter sent forward the 9/East Surrey of the 72nd
Brigade (Br.-General B. R. Mitford) to secure the strongpoints in the German position immediately south of the
Trônes Wood—Guillemont track ; but this effort likewise
failed.   Meanwhile the French 153rd Division which had
advanced into the ravine and almost reached Angle Wood,
had to withdraw again.[1]   After dark it was judged expedient to withdraw the forward line of the Suffolk, the advance
up Cochrane Alley thus representing the sole gain of the
day.   Casualties had been heavy, especially in officers.

In the evening of the 17th August [2] the British front
line was cleared to permit of a bombardment of Lonely
Trench by heavy howitzers.   This ceased at 8 P.M. and two
hours later the 10/R. Welch Fusiliers (76th Brigade) and
the 12/West Yorkshire (9th Brigade) endeavoured to carry
the trench by a surprise assault.   The enterprise miscarried, and another advance against Lonely Trench, made
at 4 A.M. on the 18th by six companies drawn from the
12/West Yorkshire, 2/Suffolk, 8/King's Own, and 10/R.
Welch Fusiliers, was also unsuccessful.

Delville Wood, High Wood, the Switch Line and Munster Alley [3]

The first few days of August were comparatively quiet
so far as the XV. Corps was concerned.   On the night of
the 1st, the 17th Division (Major-General P. R. Robertson)
took the place of the 5th [4] in Longueval and the western
portion of Delville Wood ; this relief proved a very difficult
business, for it was not easy to locate the forward positions,
and the Germans were very close.   The 52nd Brigade

[1] The division made some progress north-west of Maurepas, but lost
ground before a violent counter-attack made at 10.30 P.M. so that the
hope of capturing Angle Wood on the morrow had to be abandoned.
Little was attempted farther south.   F.O.A. iv. (ii.), p. 292.

[2] On this day Lord Cavan was obliged to relinquish his command owing
to illness and Lieut.-General Sir T. L. N. Morland was brought from X.
Corps headquarters (Fourth Army, but in reserve) to succeed him.

[3] The fighting in August at Delville Wood is covered by the official
title " Battle of Delville Wood ", 15th July–3rd September.   The operations west of High Wood fall within the area of the " Battle of Pozières
" Ridge ", 23rd July—3rd September.

[4] The approximate casualties of the 5th Division, 19th July to 2nd
August were 220 officers, 5,400 other ranks.

4–7 Aug. (Br.-General J. L. J. Clarke) was then ordered to attack Orchard Trench, which ran from Wood Lane across North Street and the Flers road into Delville Wood,[1] at 12.40 A.M. on the 4th August, after heavy artillery had carried out a slow bombardment of the trench. There was five minutes' intense fire by the field batteries before zero hour, nevertheless the enemy caught the attacking battalions, 12/Manchester and 9/Northumberland Fusiliers with high-explosive and gas shell, his machine guns joining in. Communications were cut, and it was not till 4.35 A.M. that the division learned of the failure of the attack and of heavy losses incurred.[2]

At night the 17th Division completed the relief of the troops of the XIV. Corps (99th Brigade of the 2nd Division) in Delville Wood. After a methodical bombardment—following special reconnaissance and the taking of aeroplane photographs of the locality—the 51st Brigade (Br.-General G. F. Trotter) attacked at 4.30 P.M. on the 7th to establish a line of posts beyond the wood. The advance of the 7/Border Regiment and 8/South Staffordshire was stopped in the wood by fire ; but at midnight the 10/Sherwood Foresters was able to push forward some posts in front of Longueval. The German trench system now appeared to be more elaborate and better organized, so that the further action of the 17th Division was confined to an endeavour to reach points favourable for observation until its relief by the 14th (Light) Division (Major-General V. A. Couper) on the night of the 12th August.[3]

2–6 Aug.   The 51st Division (Major-General G. M. Harper), holding the left sector of the XV. Corps front, handed over its line as far as the western edge of High Wood to the III. Corps (34th Division) on the night of the 2nd August. In the wood sap heads were pushed out towards the German posts in advance of the Switch Line, and a forward trench was dug closer to the German position along Wood Lane east of the wood. On the night of the 6th August the 51st Division[4] was relieved by the 33rd Division (Major-General H. J. S. Landon), which took in hand the preparations for

---

[1] See Sketch 26.

[2] This operation happened to coincide with the relief of the *Fusilier Bn.*, *12th Grenadiers*, by the *I./121st Regiment*, the *26th (Württemberg) Division* having begun to take over the Delville Wood—Longueval front from the *5th Division*.

[3] The casualties of the 17th Division 1st-13th August were returned as 57 officers and 1,516 other ranks.

[4] The approximate losses of the 51st Division, 22nd July–7th August, were 120 officers and 2,000 other ranks.

the next attack. In High Wood two flame-throwers,[1] and 6–12
a number of burning oil drums and " pipe-pushers " [2] were Aug.
to be used against the German positions, necessitating a
great deal of preliminary engineer work upon emplacements.
There was patrol activity on both sides at High Wood, and
about 1 A.M. on the 12th August the Germans [3] bombed
some of the saps held by the 1/Queen's.

The XV. Corps was proceeding with a methodical
bombardment, paying particular attention to the German
artillery,[4] whilst the enemy was putting in fresh troops all
along the battle-front and strengthening his defensive lines,
most noticeably between Delville Wood and Ginchy.
German observation balloons were now often in evidence.

On the front of the III. Corps the early days of the month 1–11
were more eventful, for the situation at Intermediate Aug.
Trench and that at Munster Alley called for energetic
action. The 16/Royal Scots (Br.-General R. C. Gore's
101st Brigade, 34th Division) tried to extend its hold
of Intermediate Trench [5] on the night of the 1st/2nd
August by bombing westward, but met with no success.
On the 2nd, however, an attack at 11 P.M. resulted in the
gain of a hundred yards. Two companies of the Scots and
two of the 11/Suffolk were ordered to make a frontal
attack at 2.30 A.M. on the 4th, but only one company of the
latter reached the trench. The small footing thus obtained
had soon to be relinquished.

That same evening the 101st Brigade sent in the
15/Royal Scots to bomb westward, which it did without
much success, but on the following night—after the Germans had attacked in their turn—about fifty more yards
of the trench was captured. On the night of the 6th
August the 112th Brigade (Br.-General P. M. Robinson)
took over, but a bombing attack by the 8/East Lancashire,
delivered early next morning did not succeed. The
10/Loyal N. Lancashire made the next attempt, at
2 A.M. on the 11th, advancing both up the trench and
across the open, and in spite of desperate resistance,

[1] Another invention of Major W. H. Livens. Each weighed 2 tons.
The parts had to be brought up in 50 lb. loads and assembled on the spot.
[2] See page 128, f.n. 3.
[3] *134th Regiment* of the *40th Division* which had relieved the *17th
Reserve Division* on the front west of Longueval two days before.
[4] A battery of 60-pdrs. from the Second Army and one of 4·7-inch from
the Third Army, were transferred to the corps to augment the artillery
allotted to counter-battery work.
[5] See Sketches 22 and 27.

12–17
Aug.

another 200 yards was won.[1]   The 11/R. Warwickshire made an unsuccessful frontal attack upon the remainder of Intermediate Trench during the night of the 12th/13th August.   Two days later the 34th Division [2] was relieved by the 1st Division (Major-General E. P. Strickland), and on the evening of the 16th there was a " Chinese " attack.[3]   At 2 A.M. on the 17th three platoons of the 1/Black Watch (Br.-General A. J. Reddie's 1st Brigade) attempted unsuccessfully to clear the Germans from Intermediate Trench by bombing combined with an enveloping movement over the open.   Meanwhile, the 2nd Brigade (Br.-General A. B. Hubback), on the right, had captured the greater portion of a new German trench running westward for about six hundred yards across the Bazentin le Petit road from High Wood.   This assault was made at 10 P.M. on the 16th August, after five minutes' intense bombardment, by three companies of the 2/R. Sussex and two of the 1/Northamptonshire, which barricaded both ends of the trench and pushed out patrols to the north.   At 3.15 A.M. next morning came a German counter-attack from the direction of High Wood, which, after desperate fighting, recovered about ninety yards of the trench.   Some twenty prisoners of the *181st Regiment* were taken in the course of the struggle.[4]

4–6 Aug.

The 23rd Division (Major-General J. M. Babington)—the left of the III. Corps and of the Fourth Army—made a fresh attempt to get forward in Munster Alley on the night of the 4th/5th August, when the Reserve Army was launching an attack.[5]   The 13/Durham L.I. (Br.-General H. P. Croft's 68th Brigade) gained 60 yards of the trench by bombing, but failed in an assault over the open against Torr Trench.   On the afternoon of the 6th August, the 8/Green Howards (Br.-General T. S. Lambert's 69th

---

[1] The *75th Reserve Regiment* (*17th Reserve Division*) was relieved by the *181st* (*40th Division*) on the night of the 10th/11th August.   In its history the *181st* says that the *75th Reserve* lost a trench before the relief was complete and that heavy fighting continued.

[2] Since the beginning of the month, the 34th Division had lost nearly 3,000 of all ranks.

[3] The artillery fired an assault preparation on Intermediate Trench whilst the 1st Brigade did its part by exposing caps and bayonets, blowing whistles, and shouting orders through megaphones.   The demonstration " did not appear to interest the enemy ".

[4] A captured officer said that the British gunnery was extremely good, but that much of the ammunition—especially the 9·2″ shell—was bad.   He bore witness to the dash and resolution of the Sussex and Northamptonshire, who gave his men no time to bring their machine guns into action.

[5] See Chapter VIII.

Brigade) bombed the Germans out of another 150 yards of 6–17
Munster Alley, also securing the eastern part of Torr Aug.
Trench.[1] Fighting continued all night, after the 11/West
Yorkshire (also 69th Brigade) had taken over the attack ;
over twenty prisoners [2] were secured, the Australians
(Reserve Army) on the left lending valuable assistance in
Torr Trench. By the morning of the 8th August the 15th
Division (Major-General F. W. N. McCracken) had relieved
the 23rd.[3]

The Switch Line did not appear to be strongly held, and
at 10.30 P.M. on the 12th August—when the Australians
were also engaged—the 15th Division attacked it. After
a preparatory bombardment followed by fifteen minutes'
normal artillery activity, three battalions strove to secure
the trench from a point 100 yards west of the Martinpuich railway to the junction of the Switch Line and
Munster Alley.[4] On the right the 12/Highland L.I. of the
46th Brigade (Br.-General T. G. Matheson) was checked by
heavy machine-gun fire ; on the left, the 6th/7th Royal
Scots Fusiliers and 6/Cameron Highlanders (Br.-General
W. H. L. Allgood's 45th Brigade) occupied and consolidated
the objective—now much damaged by bombardment—
from Munster Alley to a point 400 yards south-eastward.
The Camerons were in touch with the Australians at the
head of Munster Alley, and " pipe-pushers " were blown to
form communication trenches to the new line.

Attempts to clear still more of the Switch Line by
bombing to the right were continued on the following days.
The 7/Cameron Highlanders of the 44th Brigade (Br.-
General F. J. Marshall), which made a successful frontal
attack on the morning of the 17th August, afterwards lost
heavily under a German bombardment and had to be
reinforced. The pressure of enemy bombing attacks made
westward from " The Elbow "—the name given to the
forward bulge in the Switch Line east of the Contalmaison—
Martinpuich road—was then relieved by a detachment of
the 8/Seaforth Highlanders, which assaulted with the

---

[1] In this fighting Pte. W. Short, a bomber of the 8/Green Howards, was
twice wounded ; but he lay in the trench, with a shattered leg, preparing
bombs for his comrades to throw. He died of his wounds and was posthumously awarded the V.C.

[2] There were representatives of three different regiments, each belonging
to a different division, which had reinforced the troops of the *18th Reserve
Division* here.

[3] The casualties of the 23rd Division, 25th July to 7th August were
returned as 96 officers and 1,547 other ranks.

[4] Sketches 22 and 27.

bayonet and cleared the Elbow.   Meanwhile an advance of
the 10th/11th Highland L.I. (46th Brigade), farther to the
right, extended the British hold on the Switch Line to a
point 120 yards east of the Elbow.[1]

18TH AUGUST : GUILLEMONT ; DELVILLE WOOD, HIGH WOOD, INTERMEDIATE TRENCH

Sketch
25.

The main plan for the attack of the Fourth Army in
conjunction with the French on the 18th August had undergone considerable alteration.   Influenced by the results of
the fighting on the 16th, Generals Rawlinson and Fayolle
arranged next morning that, as the French had yet to secure
Angle Wood, the capture of Guillemont should occupy two
days.   The XIV. Corps objective on the 18th was now to
be a line extending from Angle Wood to the spur south of
Guillemont, and thence through the western side of the
village to the railway station and the German front line
farther north.   The French, instead of attacking along their
whole front north of the Somme, were to secure Angle Wood
on the 18th and carry forward their line south-eastward,
extending their hold on Maurepas ;   they also promised to
make an attack upon a trench junction north-west of
Cléry.[2]   On the 19th the capture of Guillemont was to be
completed by the XIV. Corps in two stages, whilst the
French were to begin to relieve troops in readiness for the
combined attack fixed for the 22nd.

18 Aug.

The day proved to be dull and showery.   Zero hour was
fixed for 2.45 P.M. following a thirty-six hours' methodical
bombardment.   The rate of fire was not to quicken before
the assault, so that the enemy might receive no warning ;
and the advance was to be covered by a " field artillery
" curtain " which the infantry was to follow as closely as

---

[1] The 15th Division was engaged with the *179th Regiment*, holding the
left sector of the *24th Division*, which had relieved the *18th Reserve Division*
on 10th August, and the *181st* in the right sector of the *40th Division*.
" Regt. No. 179 " describes how the British bombardment flattened the
trenches and prevented supplies from reaching the front line, where thirsty
men drank water from the machine-gun jackets.   Other regimental
accounts state that the Scottish bombers out-threw their opponents.

[2] As the combined attacks fixed for the 18th were so dependent upon
the success of the preliminary operation, the check of the 16th modified
considerably the part of the French Sixth Army in the British attack of
the 18th.   F.O.A. iv. (ii.), p. 285.

   In the afternoon of the 17th General Foch instructed General Fayolle
to co-operate on a larger scale, and a more extensive operation was ordered
on the Cléry—Maurepas front.   *Idem*, p. 293.

GUILLEMONT
XIV Corps attack, 18th August, 1916.

Sketch 25.

DELVILLE WOOD

14.
XV.

26.

125th

Ginchy

Waterlot Farm

Farm

Brickfield

XIII.

17th

120th

.157

24.

5.874

BRITISH GERMAN

Quarry

Guillemont

Cemetery

27.

TRONES WOOD

73rd

123rd Gr.

XIV

ARROW HEAD COPSE

FRONT

9th

LINE

76th

WEDGE WOOD

COMBLES ¾ m.

124th

Falfemont Farm

Maltz Horn Farm

COCHRANE ALLEY

BRITISH FRENCH

10 Bav. R.

5 Bav. R.

ANGLE WOOD

OAKHANGER WD.

SIXTH

153.

ARMY.

XX.

1 B.R.

Compiled in the Historical Section (Military Branch).
Crown Copyright Reserved

Ordnance Survey 1937.

3060/38.

Scale of Yards.

500   0   500   1000   1500

Attacks ⟶   Heights in metres.   Ground gained...●●●●●○○○

possible.[1]   To preserve communications during the advance 18 Aug.
chief reliance was placed upon contact aeroplanes to which
the infantry would signal with flares, panels and mirrors ;
but pigeons were taken forward, and in the 3rd Division red
and yellow flags were to be waved from the farthest line
reached.

The XIV. Corps was ordered to gain its final objective
in two stages.   When the German front line had been taken
there was to be a wait of two hours for consolidation and
fresh bombardment before the advance to the general line
Angle Wood—Hardecourt road fork—Guillemont station.
The long pause on the first objective was a new development ; by adopting this more deliberate method of advance
it was hoped that all ground gained would be consolidated
without loss of time, and the infantry preserve a cohesion
which would facilitate mutual support.

On the right, the 76th Brigade (Br.-General R. J.
Kentish) of the 3rd Division attacked with two companies
of the 1/Gordon Highlanders and two of the 10/R. Welch
Fusiliers.   The Highlanders reached their first objective,
near the Hardecourt road ; the Fusiliers swept over the
southern part of Lonely Trench and some of them reached
the road also.   Unfortunately the 1/Northumberland Fusiliers (Br.-General H. C. Potter's 9th Brigade), next on
the left, could make little headway, and the Welshmen,
taken in flank, had to withdraw.   German machine guns
were firing up the slope from the right front of the Gordons,
who, having sent back about twenty prisoners, began to
consolidate their new line ; the French had made some
progress in the Maurepas ravine and were in touch.[2]

The Northumberland Fusiliers made two unsuccessful
attempts to storm the northern part of Lonely Trench and
one unavailing effort to bomb down from the northern end,
whilst the 8/East Yorkshire (attached from the 8th Brigade
and attacking as left battalion of the 9th Brigade) was met
by a heavy cross-fire of machine guns in its assault upon
the German trenches south-east of Arrow Head Copse.
Only a few parties forced their way in, and these were soon

[1] In the XIV. Corps the 18-pdrs. brought their barrage back from the
German front line at zero to No Man's Land, 100 yards in front of the
infantry.   A minute later, when it was reckoned that the latter would be
only fifty yards away, the barrage began to lift forward at the rate of
50 yards per minute.
[2] They increased their hold on Maurepas on this day and advanced
north and south of the village.   Nothing was accomplished farther south.
F.O.A. iv. (ii.), p. 294.

18 Aug. driven out. There was no question of proceeding with the second stage of the attack [1] at the appointed time, for the right of the 24th Division, attacking the western defences of Guillemont, also had made no progress.

In the right sector of the 24th Division, the 73rd Brigade (Br.-General R. G. Jelf) attacked astride the Trônes Wood—Guillemont track. South of the track the 12/Middlesex carried out a good advance on the fringe of the barrage, but was checked at the German front position by the cross-fire of machine guns. Gallant attempts to establish a footing in the trench failed, and the German bombardment was so heavy that a new effort by fresh troops seemed out of the question. Beyond the road a similar experience befell the right of the 7/Northamptonshire ; but the left of the battalion managed to effect a lodgment in the German front line near the quarry, where desperate fighting ensued. This party was later reinforced by a company of the 9/R. Sussex, and at night the position was consolidated with the help of the engineers. On the left, touch had been obtained with the 3/Rifle Brigade, right battalion of the 17th Brigade (Br.-General J. W. V. Carroll), to which fell the chief honours of the day.

The Rifles found it impossible to determine when the barrage started " creeping ", but they advanced with great dash to meet many Germans coming forward to surrender. Not only was the enemy front line taken, but the station and a portion of the Waterlot Farm road, which comprised the second objective, were secured without perceptible pause. Fortunately communication by telephone and by visual signalling, both mirror and shutter, was well maintained, so that the situation was known to the artillery without delay.[2]

Farther north the 8/Buffs, which had been allotted only one objective, made a successful frontal assault upon the northern part of ZZ Trench, where the Germans were taken by surprise.[3] Bombers of the battalion entered the German line on the Waterlot Farm road, and, having joined hands with the 3/Rifle Brigade, bombed their way north-eastward to ZZ Trench. The Buffs collected about one hundred

---

[1] The French were to have captured Angle Wood in the second stage.

[2] The prisoners, about seventy in number, were mostly of the *I./120th Regiment*. Two machine guns were taken.

[3] The *I./125th Regiment* of the *26th Division*, which had extended its left. The regimental history says that since entering the Somme battle the men had become depressed by the evident British superiority in material ; but " the old spirit of the German Army was still intact ".

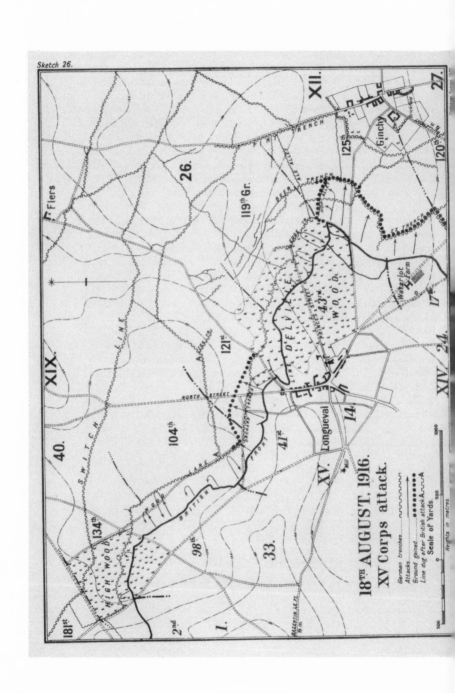

Sketch 26.

18TH AUGUST, 1916.
XV Corps attack.

German trenches
Attacks
Ground gained
Line dug after British attack A⌐⌐⌐A
Scale of Yards

Heights in metres

prisoners, and at the extreme north of ZZ Trench obtained **18-19**
touch with troops of the 14th Division (XV. Corps). **Aug.**

The line of the 76th Brigade, and that of the French on
its right, were heavily shelled by the Germans who, during
the evening, counter-attacked the French and drove them
back to the south-western slopes of the Maurepas ravine.
Some of the Gordons were involved in this withdrawal, and
reports reached 76th Brigade headquarters, whence they
were forwarded to the 3rd Division, that all the captured
ground had been lost. A special reconnaissance, carried
out by a divisional staff officer in the early morning of the
19th, however, established the fact that the enemy in front
of the 76th Brigade had withdrawn to the Falfemont Farm
—Wedge Wood line, and a report from infantry patrols that
Lonely Trench was unoccupied was confirmed by aeroplane
observation.[1] So, on the 19th, the Gordons, Welch Fusiliers, and troops of the 8th Brigade which had been sent up,
were able to proceed with the consolidation of the line
beyond the Hardecourt—Guillemont road, the French, who
came forward again, being in touch on the right.[2] Lonely
Trench was also occupied. During the night of the
19th/20th August the 3rd Division was relieved by the 35th
Division (Major-General R. J. Pinney).[3]

The XV. and III. Corps of the Fourth Army at con- **18 Aug.**
siderable cost also achieved some small successes on the
18th August. In and around Delville Wood Major-General **Sketch**
V. A. Couper's 14th Division (XV. Corps) had two separate **26.**
tasks. On the right, the 43rd Brigade (Br.-General P. R.
Wood)—in touch with the 24th Division of the XIV. Corps
—was to secure the northern part of ZZ Trench, Beer
Trench as far as Ale Alley, Edge Trench,[4] and the German
sap which ran along Prince's Street in the wood. The right

---

[1] The Bavarian Official Account states that the left flank of the *124th
Regiment (27th Division)* was overrun on the 18th and the Army therefore
ordered the withdrawal of the Bavarian right. This was done during the
night, according to " Bav. Res. Regt. No. 10 ", which describes its successful
counter-attack on the evening of the 18th. The counter-attack, and the
German bombardment, obviously covered the general withdrawal. " Regt.
" No. 124 " states that the British drove its centre back to the Wedge Wood
—Falfemont Farm position on the 18th. Its left was overwhelmed.

[2] A reconnaissance showed that Angle Wood had been evacuated by
the enemy.

[3] The 3rd Division, which was much below establishment, especially in
officers, when it came into the line, had lost nearly nineteen hundred of
all ranks.

[4] These German trenches, the position of which had been revealed by
aeroplane photographs, had received simple and convenient names.

18 Aug. battalion, 6/Somerset L.I., advanced close under the barrage at 2.45 P.M., the general zero hour, and reached its objective with little loss, men of the *125th Regiment* [1] surrendering freely. The southern part of Beer Trench was found to have been nearly obliterated by the bombardment. On the left, the 6/D.C.L.I. was not so fortunate; heavily shelled before the start, the companies advanced into a barrage of artillery and machine-gun fire which broke the attack into small groups. Nevertheless, Edge Trench was cleared; but before the resistance along Prince's Street was overcome the Germans had bombed down Edge Trench from the north and recaptured it. [2] Heavy fighting, sometimes hand to hand, continued; but the Somersets, freely using rifle grenades and captured German bombs, made good their hold upon Hop Alley and erected a barricade in Beer Trench. Consolidation of the position proceeded, and during the evening two forward movements of German troops from Pint Trench were checked by infantry fire.

The German line in Delville Wood from Prince's Street to the Flers road was kept under heavy trench-mortar fire, but no infantry attack was launched against it. Two battalions of the 41st Brigade (Br.-General P. C. B. Skinner) assaulted Orchard Trench and the southern end of the Wood Lane line, the left of the advance being in touch with the 33rd Division attack. On the right, the 7/K.R.R.C. got forward close behind, and almost into, the British barrage to find Orchard Trench weakly held. It was captured with ease, and the battalion then dug a new line beyond, with the right flank resting upon the Flers road. The right of the 7/Rifle Brigade advanced in close touch with the 7/K.R.R.C., but its left was enfiladed from that flank, where the attack of the 33rd Division had failed; so only a small portion of Wood Lane was secured. [3]

The main portion of Wood Lane and the German front position in High Wood were attacked by the 98th Brigade (Br.-General J. D. Heriot-Maitland) of the 33rd Division. Wood Lane was to be secured by the 4/King's, in touch with

[1] " Regt. No. 125 " states that its trenches were almost destroyed by the bombardment and that the British infantry, arriving on the heels of the barrage, effected a surprise.

[2] " Gren. Regt. No. 119 " admits that its left flank was in danger of being rolled up during the struggle. Two companies of the *III. Bn.* took part in the counter-attacks, the *I. Bn.*, in the line, having lost very heavily

[3] " Regt. No. 121 " states that the British bombardment had made it almost impossible to defend Orchard Trench ; the *II./121st* had to advance under heavy fire to form a new line and regain touch on the flanks ; this position was taken over by the *I./121st* at night.

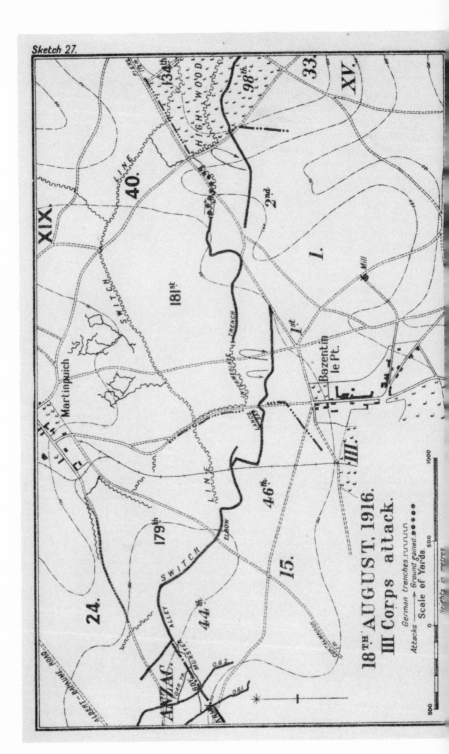

18TH AUGUST, 1916.
III Corps attack.

German trenches
Attacks
Ground gained
Scale of Yards

the 14th Division, and the 1/4th Suffolk. The King's, who 18 Aug. are said to have "walked right into the barrage", came under the fire of Germans in shell-holes and never reached Wood Lane; the Suffolk gained a lodgment therein but had to relinquish it, being bombed from both flanks and enfiladed by machine guns firing from High Wood. Smoke bombs, designed to conceal the advance of the left of the battalion, were fired too late to be of use.

In High Wood it was hoped to derive much assistance from the flame-throwers, thirty burning-oil drums, and the " pipe-pushers " which were to explode their charges underneath the German trenches. The last-named turned out to be ill-adapted for use in soil interlaced with tree-roots; the flame-throwers were buried by British shells, owing to the heavy artillery firing short;[1] whilst the burning oil appeared to have little effect. At zero hour the one " pipe-pusher " which exploded blew a crater in the line of the 2/Argyll & Sutherland Highlanders, which, nevertheless, made persistent but unsuccessful efforts to get forward through the wood.[2] During the evening came urgent calls from the 98th Brigade for reinforcements; but, instead of renewing the assault, the divisional commander judged it prudent to bring up Br.-General C. R. G. Mayne's 19th Brigade and relieve the whole front line before morning.

The attacks carried out by the III. Corps involved, for Sketch the most part, the continuation of the operations already 27. in hand. At zero hour, 2.45 P.M., the 2nd Brigade (1st Division) attacked the German trench on the north-western edge of High Wood with two companies of the 1/Loyal N. Lancashire. The right company pushed out too soon, and was practically annihilated by the British barrage; on the left, the trench was reached without much opposition. Confused fighting followed, but the 1/Northamptonshire,

[1] Complaints of the artillery shooting short were frequent and sometimes justified: the principal reasons for this failing were worn guns, defective ammunition, and inaccurate location of the infantry forward positions. In the XV. Corps it is stated that these complaints sometimes caused the heavy artillery so to lengthen the range as to make its bombardment ineffective. The Germans and the French had the same difficulty, but were not, perhaps, so considerate of their infantry. It should be mentioned that shelling in enfilade by enemy high-velocity guns was liable to—and did on occasion—give the infantry the impression that their own artillery was shooting short.

[2] " Regt. No. 134 " states that the British entered the German line at one point in High Wood; they were ejected by a counter-attack company of the *I./134th*. " Regt. No. 104 ", which pays a tribute to the bravery of the British infantry ("worthy opponents "), says that the situation on this day was critical. Heavy losses are admitted.

18 Aug. bombing eastward from that portion of the trench which had been captured on the previous day, made good progress. Eventually the 2nd Brigade consolidated this trench almost as far as High Wood, a strongpoint being constructed on the extreme right.

The 1st Brigade of the 1st Division had already endeavoured to carry the remaining portion of Intermediate Trench by an early morning attack delivered in thick fog by the 1/Black Watch. Advancing at 4.15 A.M. under an intense field-gun barrage, the Highlanders were disorganized by heavy shell-fire, and some of them lost direction. Small parties, however, burst through the trench, which was mostly defended by bombers, and penetrated seventy yards beyond it, but were afterwards obliged to withdraw. At 2.45 P.M. the 8/R. Berkshire made an attempt, its left being covered by smoke liberated along the whole front of the 15th Division, but the result was the same. British shells, dropping short, stopped a flank attack which was to have emerged from the neighbourhood of Lancs Sap, and the frontal assault of the Berkshire was checked by machine-gun and artillery fire.[1]

The 15th Division, holding the left of the Fourth Army front, made no infantry attack, but the discharge of smoke brought a retaliatory bombardment of some intensity. Whilst consolidation of the captured portion of the Switch Line proceeded, patrols of the 44th Brigade reported that the Germans now appeared to be in occupation of a shell-hole position 600 yards away.

19TH–31ST AUGUST

THE SWITCH LINE, GUILLEMONT; CAPTURE OF INTERMEDIATE TRENCH AND DELVILLE WOOD COMPLETED

On the 17th August a letter from G.H.Q., dated the previous day, had informed General Rawlinson of the arrival of a new offensive weapon—the armoured fighting vehicle known as the " Tank " ;[2] and on the 19th there followed a G.H.Q. memorandum which outlined the plan of a big offensive, tentatively fixed for the middle of September. In this operation it was proposed to exploit the surprise effect of tanks employed in action for the first

Sketch A. time, by " securing the enemy's last line of prepared

---

[1] Lieut.-Colonel J. A. Longridge, G.S.O.1, 1st Division, was killed on 18th August.

[2] See Note, " The Evolution of the Tank " at end of Chapter IX.

" defences between Morval and Le Sars with a view to
" opening the way for cavalry ". Sir Douglas Haig desired
to launch this offensive from the main ridge along the line
Leuze Wood and Bouleaux Wood—Ginchy—High Wood,
thence north-east of Pozières and northward behind
Thiepval to the Ancre beyond Grandcourt. Details of the
plan may be conveniently deferred to a later chapter, for
the immediate tasks of the Fourth and Reserve Armies
were not altered thereby ; but the question of time and
economy of means became of more importance than ever.

Early on the 20th August General Rawlinson conferred
with his corps commanders, explaining that three weeks, at
most, remained in which to secure the prescribed line, and
that only a limited number of new formations was available, as six divisions were to be kept fresh for the September
offensive.[1] Relentless pressure was to be maintained along
the whole Army front, every opportunity being used to gain
ground in small enterprises, especially surprise attacks by
night. It was now settled that on the 21st August the
western side of Guillemont should be secured by the XIV.
Corps, whilst the XV. Corps captured the German front line
in Delville Wood.

Sir Douglas Haig and General Foch had come to a fresh
arrangement on the 19th August, and the plans of the Fourth
Army for subsequent operations were framed accordingly.
On the 24th the XIV. Corps would complete the capture of
Guillemont and advance its line across the spur and the
valley to Angle Wood, whilst the French established themselves in the wood, completed the capture of Maurepas and
advanced to a position within assaulting distance of the
Le Forest—Cléry line. The XV. Corps would approach
within assaulting distance of Ginchy and clear the northern
edge of Delville Wood. On the 26th or 27th the XIV. and
XV. Corps would capture the German 2nd Position from
the slope south-east of Falfemont Farm to Wedge Wood,
the Wedge Wood—Ginchy road and Ginchy itself, the
French keeping pace in the valley north of Maurepas and
securing the Le Forest—Cléry line.

In the XV. Corps [2] the 33rd Division, which had been

---

[1] A G.H.Q. memorandum, dated 15th August, showed a total of 8 new
divisions available, after they had completed their battle training, for the
Fourth Army up to 8th September. These included the Guards, 6th and
20th Divisions (former XIV. Corps of the Reserve Army) already placed at
General Rawlinson's disposal. Six new divisions were similarly shown as
earmarked for the Reserve Army.   [2] See Sketch 26.

holding its front with one brigade, took over the left of the 14th Division up to the Flers—Longueval road on the night of the 19th/20th.   On the following night there were bombing encounters in High Wood, when the 2/R. Welch Fusiliers (19th Brigade) made an abortive attempt to clear the trench on the western edge.   The 1/9th Highland L.I. (100th Brigade) moved on up Wood Lane for 60 yards without opposition.

Meanwhile, there had been indications that the resistance of the Germans in front of the III. Corps was weakening.[1]   West of High Wood patrols of the 1/Northamptonshire (2nd Brigade, 1st Division) had pushed forward in the face of a not very alert enemy on the afternoon of the 19th and entered the Switch Line at a point where it was not occupied.   At night working parties were sent up to dig a battle outpost position almost on the crest of the ridge midway between High Wood and Martinpuich, and about two hundred yards from the northern bulge in the Switch Line.   After dark, too, the 2/K.R.R.C. relieved the 1/Loyal N. Lancashire on the right of the Northamptonshire, and took up an outpost line.   Between 2 and 4 A.M. next morning the Northamptonshire company holding the forward position repulsed a German counter-attack.   A heavier counter-attack developed at 8 A.M. and resulted in the withdrawal—afterwards deemed unnecessary—of the Northamptonshire.   Two companies of the battalion, in a fresh advance, arrived within 80 yards of the ridge, and were then checked by the cross-fire of machine guns.   The enemy had been reinforced, and when, at 2.15 P.M., after a short bombardment, two companies each of the Northamptonshire and 2/R. Sussex made another attempt, they failed with heavy loss.   On the right, the 2/K.R.R.C. was heavily engaged for most of the day, but eventually maintained its forward line.[2]

Farther west, reconnaissances of the 15th Division on the 20th August seemed to show that the Switch Line was empty ; it was occupied as far eastward as the Bazentin le Petit—Martinpuich road, several wounded of the *179th Regiment* being brought in.[3]

---

[1] See Sketch 27.

[2] The *181st Regiment* had at its disposal the *III./104th* (also *40th Division*) and part of the *III./3rd Bavarian Reserve* (from *1st Bavarian Reserve Division*).   According to " Regt. No. 134 ", flanking fire from High Wood was brought to bear on the British.

[3] " Regt. No. 179 " admits that there was a gap towards the left of its line (junction of *24th* and *40th Divisions*), but states that the danger of the

In the XIV. Corps,[1] the 35th Division, when relieving the 21 Aug. 3rd, had also taken over the right of the 24th Division as far as the Trônes Wood—Guillemont track. About 5 A.M. on the morning of the 21st the division made an unsuccessful attempt to seize a German strongpoint opposite Arrow Head Copse. During the previous night, on the right flank of the division, the French had occupied Angle Wood, and touch was now obtained with them along the slope of the ravine. The 24th Division was under a heavy bombardment, but on the morning of the 21st parties of the 3/Rifle Brigade and 8/Buffs occupied without fighting most of that portion of ZZ Trench which led into Guillemont.

The attacks delivered at 4.30 P.M. on the 21st achieved no success. The task of the 35th Division was eventually limited to discharging smoke in order to cover the right flank of the 24th Division, which set the 8/Queen's (72nd Brigade) to attack the quarry, and one company each of the 1/Royal Fusiliers and 3/Rifle Brigade (17th Brigade) to advance south-eastward from the vicinity of Guillemont station. The Queen's had to withdraw after heavy bomb fighting ; the other troops encountered many Württembergers of the *120th Regiment,* and had good shooting at close range, but suffered such loss that they could not hold the ground they gained.

In the XV. Corps [2] the 8/K.R.R.C. (41st Brigade of the 14th Division) advanced to establish posts in the German front line in Delville Wood, smoke being discharged to cover the flanks of the movement ; but the battalion was stopped by rifle and machine-gun fire with the loss of nearly two hundred officers and men. At midnight a somewhat hurriedly prepared attack was made by the 100th Brigade (33rd Division) against the German trench running from Wood Lane eastward towards the Flers road : [3] on the right, the 2/Worcestershire was not ready, so the 1/9th Highland L.I. went forward alone, to be checked by heavy rifle and machine-gun fire when near the objective.

Fourth Army instructions for the attack on the 24th,

British breaking through at this point and reaching Martinpuich seemed past on this day, as the *3rd Bavarian Reserve Regiment* had arrived.

[1] See Sketch 25.

[2] See Sketch 26.

[3] It was occupied by the *104th Regiment (40th Division),* whose left flank now rested on North Street, and by the *121st Regiment (26th Division).* The trench had been dug to cover the gap caused by the capture of Orchard Trench by the 14th Division on 18th August. See page 194.

22-23   issued at 6 P.M. on the 22nd August, considerably modified
Aug.   the objectives of the XIV. Corps. The French, so it was
stated, would advance along their whole front north of the
Somme, and the right of the 35th Division, which took over
Angle Wood on the night of the 22nd/23rd, was to progress
with them, but not to attack the German 2nd Position.
The 20th Division (Major-General W. Douglas Smith),
having completed the relief of the 24th Division [1] by the
morning of the 22nd, had as objectives the northern
outskirts of Guillemont and the German trenches on the
south-western edge of Ginchy. The XV. Corps was to
push forward its whole line clear of Delville Wood, and
a small operation was to be undertaken by the III.
Corps.

At 9.15 P.M. on the 23rd August a heavy German bombardment opened on the trenches of the 20th Division
and, in spite of the vigorous reply of the British artillery,
at 10.30 P.M., enemy infantry attacked the 11/K.R.R.C.
(59th Brigade) south of the railway.[2] The movement
was checked, chiefly by machine-gun fire; but there
was considerable confusion in the trenches, congested as
they were by pioneer and R.E. working parties, and at
12.30 A.M. on the 24th the German bombardment opened
again, stopping all work for the night. At 11 A.M. the part
assigned to the 20th Division in the evening operation
was cancelled, since it had not been possible to complete
the necessary preparations. The 35th Division had also
suffered heavily from shell-fire, and its infantry was
reported to be in no condition to assault.[3] General
Rawlinson therefore cancelled the whole XIV. Corps
operation, except the movement of the right of the 35th
Division in combination with the French advance.

24 Aug.   At 5.45 P.M. on the 24th, the general zero hour, the left
of the French I. Corps attacked and entered the old German
2nd Position south-east of Falfemont Farm.[4] Enfilade
fire from the farm caused the flank of the advance to be

---

[1] The casualties of the 24th Division for August were reported as 190
officers and 3,347 other ranks.

[2] Only patrol encounters are mentioned by the German regimental
histories, and, in these, it is stated that the British were the aggressors.
The *XIII. Corps* (*27th* and *26th Divisions*) was at this time in process of
being relieved by " Group Kirchbach " (*111th* and *56th Divisions*) on the
front Angle Wood—Longueval.

[3] The division had supplied very heavy working parties before coming
into the line, and it was now very tired indeed, so that arrangements had
to be made for its early relief.

[4] See Sketch 25.

thrown back, touch being obtained with posts of the 35th 24 Aug.
Division below the Falfemont Farm spur.[1]

The XV. Corps was faced with the task of clearing
Delville Wood and establishing a forward line from the
junction of Beer Trench and Hop Alley to Wood Lane.[2]
The 14th Division attacked with the 8/K.R.R.C. (41st
Brigade) and the 9/K.R.R.C., 5/Shropshire L.I. and 5/Oxford
& Bucks L.I. (all 42nd Brigade) in line. On the right, the
8/K.R.R.C. was checked with heavy loss in front of Ale
Alley. Assisted by a barrage which " crept " in lifts of
25 yards, the other battalions made good progress through
the wood until the exposure of their right flank brought
them to a halt, thereby preventing the occupation of most
of Beer Trench. Eventually the Oxford & Bucks L.I., on
the left, consolidated their objective, their flank being on
the Flers road in touch with the 33rd Division. From the
right flank of the battalion the new line ran due south to
the wood, thence south-eastward along its edge to Prince's
Street, the position being signalled by flares and thus easily
located by the contact aeroplanes. Over two hundred
prisoners of the *119th Grenadiers* and *121st Regiment* and
more than a dozen machine guns were taken.[3] Early on
the 25th August the 9/Rifle Brigade (42nd Brigade) cleared
Edge Trench nearly as far as its junction with Ale Alley.

The 33rd Division objective was the new German front
trench between Wood Lane and the Flers road, including
Tea Trench which linked up the line with the road itself.
The three assaulting battalions of the 100th Brigade—
2/Worcestershire, 16/K.R.R.C. and 1/Queen's, from right
to left—were heavily shelled in their assembly positions, but
a smoke screen covered the left flank from enfilade fire
when the advance began. In spite of considerable losses—
Lieut.-Colonel M. L. Crofts of the Queen's was wounded—
the troops went forward in splendid style, and success was
gained all along the line, their supporting artillery having

[1] The French I. Corps completed the capture of Maurepas on this day,
its line extending in a salient beyond the village half-way to Le Forest.
Farther south, the VII. Corps failed except for a small advance in front of
Cléry. General Fayolle had insisted upon the most careful artillery preparation, but the German batteries were unsubdued and the German
machine guns caused great havoc. F.O.A. iv. (ii.), pp. 295-6.

[2] See Sketches 26 and 28.

[3] " Regt. No. 121 " says that the *88th Regiment (56th Division)* was
beginning to take over when the attack started. " Gren. Regt. No. 119 "
admits a critical situation ; practically the whole regiment was in action.
The *125th Regiment* was relieved by the *35th Fusiliers (56th Division)* after
the fighting had died down. " The days on the Somme were the worst in
" the War."

24 Aug. served the stormers well. On the left, bombers of the
1/Queen's pressed forward up Wood Lane and secured the
trench junction,[1] but the German bombardment which
followed somewhat delayed the consolidation of the new
position.

In the III. Corps [2] another attempt was made to complete the capture of Intermediate Trench, each end being
attacked by a company of the 2/R. Munster Fusiliers (3rd
Brigade). The movement was defeated by heavy rifle and
machine-gun fire, the preparatory trench-mortar bombardment, which extended over two hours, having done little
damage to the defenders.[3] At the same time, the 6/Cameron
Highlanders (45th Brigade of the 15th Division) made an
unsuccessful attempt to bomb down the trench along the
Bazentin le Petit—Martinpuich road from the Switch Line,
which was now in British hands as far to the eastward as
the road.[4]

25 Aug.   Conferring with his corps commanders on the morning
of the 25th August, General Rawlinson read a G.H.Q. letter,
received the previous evening, which emphasized the
extreme importance of securing Ginchy, Guillemont and
Falfemont Farm without delay. The Commander-in-Chief
considered the task well within the power of the troops and
artillery available, provided that the higher commanders,
bearing in mind the standard of training which existed
among the troops and subordinate leaders, gave their
personal attention to the details of preparation.

The Army commander decided to bring the 5th Division
into the XIV. Corps for the attack south of Guillemont ; to
confide the capture of Ginchy to the 7th Division ; and to
allot the High Wood and Wood Lane objectives to the 1st
Division. The commander of the XIV. Corps reported that
the 20th Division would be ready by the 29th, and that the
5th Division, which had not yet come into the line, could
hardly complete its preparations before that date. It was

[1] The *II./181st Regiment* had been put in to hold the front line, one
company being annihilated during the fighting. The histories of the
German regiments concerned bear witness to the efficiency of the British
artillery fire, which smashed an attempted counter-attack by the *II./181st*
and portions of the *104th.*
[2] See Sketch 27.
[3] The 1st Division line was under very heavy shell-fire, and the troops
holding it suffered severely.
[4] According to " Regt. No. 179 ", the *24th Division* had taken over the
right sector of the *40th* a few days previously, and troops of the *133rd
Regiment* seem to have been holding Intermediate Trench at the time.

then settled that the XIV. Corps should take Guillemont 25-29
and the old German 2nd Position as far as Falfemont Farm Aug.
(inclusive) ; the XV. Corps, Ginchy, completing also the
capture of the Beer Trench line ; [1] and the III. Corps the
northern part of Wood Lane and the German front trench
in High Wood, in addition to joining up the captured
portion of the Switch Line with the forward trenches west
of the wood.   The employment of cloud gas was considered
impracticable having regard to the state of the forward
trenches and the long " carry " necessary to get the
cylinders into position.   All the gas shell available for the
60-pdrs.[2] would be required for counter-battery work, but
lacrymatory shell could be used against cellars and dug-outs,
shrapnel being fired when their occupants should be driven
into the open.

The Commander-in-Chief arrived at Fourth Army headquarters about noon, and was made acquainted with the
new dispositions and plans ; at 8 P.M. instructions were
issued by the Army for the renewal of the attack on the
29th, when the French would co-operate along their whole
front north of the Somme.   By the next afternoon, however, Sir Douglas Haig had prevailed upon the French to
agree to a postponement until the 30th.   There had been
rain on the afternoon of the 25th and the weather grew
worse and worse, turning the chalky ground to clinging
treacherous mud in which the digging of assembly trenches,
the opening up of fresh approaches to the front line, and the
movement of ammunition and battle stores proceeded
slowly and with infinite labour.   The bad visibility seriously
hampered the gunners when the preparatory bombardment
opened at 8 A.M. on the 29th, and at noon G.H.Q., on the
initiative of the French, announced a postponement until
the 1st September.   In the afternoon of the 29th there was
a violent thunderstorm, and next day General Foch notified

---

[1] The XV. Corps decided against attacking on a broader front, Lieut.-
General Horne considering that he had not sufficient artillery to do so.

[2] On 16th May Sir Douglas Haig had asked for the following supplies of
lethal gas shell to be provided by 15th June : 4.5″ how., 20,000 ; 4.7″ gun,
4,000 ; 60-pdr. gun, 16,000 : thereafter, he would require 5,000, 1,000 and
4,000 rounds, respectively, per week.   Nothing approaching these quantities was at this time available.   On 17th July Sir Douglas asked for all
gas shell " for any nature of gun or howitzer " which could be sent, as he
was dependent for gas bombardment upon the French batteries lent to
him.   On 31st July he fixed his requirements at 30,000 rounds per week in
the proportion, 6 : 4 : 1 for 4.5″ how., 60-pdr. and 4.7″ gun, respectively.
Production, which had to wait upon research, still lagged, however, and
by the end of 1916 only 160,000 shell had been filled with lethal or partly
lethal mixtures.

Sir Douglas Haig that the French could not now be ready before the 3rd September.[1] Thereupon the date of the British attacks was again altered to conform.[2]

26-28 Aug.   From the 26th August onward the German artillery maintained a heavy fire upon the British forward positions and the approaches thereto. In the III. Corps, the 1st Division continued its operations against Intermediate Trench,[3] the 1/S. Wales Borderers (3rd Brigade) bombing westward on the evening of the 26th as far as the Martinpuich road. The battalion made further progress next day, with some assistance from the Munsters, prisoners of the *23rd Bavarian Regiment* being secured. In the early morning of the 28th the 15th Division took over the front of the 3rd Brigade, and, by the 30th, posts established on either flank and in rear had completely cut off the Germans still holding out in Intermediate Trench. Their surrender was accepted in the afternoon.[4]

In the meantime, on the night of the 27th/28th, the 1st Division had taken over the High Wood positions and the greater part of the line facing Wood Lane from the 33rd Division (XV. Corps), which made a little progress up Wood Lane on the 29th.

On the other flank of the XV. Corps, Br.-General J. McC. Steele's 22nd Brigade of the 7th Division (Major-General H. E. Watts) relieved the right brigade of the 14th Division on the night of the 26th/27th August. On the following afternoon a surprise attack of the 10/Durham L.I. (43rd Brigade of the 14th Division) drove the Germans from their holding in Edge Trench and allowed of a barricade being placed in Ale Alley.[5] At last Delville Wood was completely in British hands.[6] Another enterprise, carried out on the evening of the 28th by the Durham L.I. in

---

[1] General Joffre had suggested this further postponement. F.O.A. iv. (ii.), p. 297.
[2] Sir Douglas Haig had now determined that, at the same time, the Reserve Army should deliver an attack astride the Ancre. See Chapter VIII.
[3] Sketch 27.
[4] Four officers and 123 other ranks of the *17th* and *23rd Bavarians* (*3rd Bavarian Division*) were taken. This division had relieved the *24th* on the front between High Wood and the Albert—Bapaume road, 27th/28th August, and " Bav. Regt. No. 17 " states that the " dangerous salient " (Intermediate Trench) held by *No. 8 Coy.* was about to be evacuated, but the order was given too late.
[5] Sketch 28.
[6] In this affair 60 prisoners of the *118th Regiment* (*56th Division*) were captured.

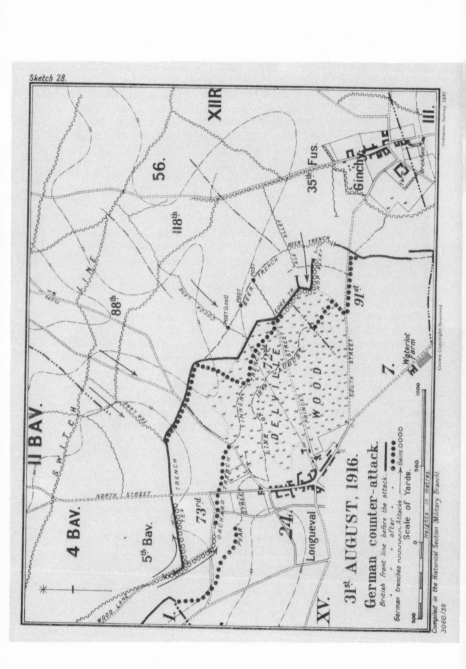

Sketch 28.

31st AUGUST, 1916.
German counter-attack.

British front line before the attack. ——
„   „   „   after   „   „ ——
German trenches ∿∿∿∿ German Attacks ——→ Gains ○○○○
Scale of Yards
Heights in metres.

Compiled in the Historical Section (Military Branch)
3060/38

Ordnance Survey 1937.
Crown Copyright Reserved.

concert with the 1/R. Welch Fusiliers (22nd Brigade), aimed **28-31** at clearing Ale Alley as far east as Beer Trench, but was not **Aug.** successful.

It was decided, since the postponement of the general attack permitted, to complete the relief of the 14th and 33rd Divisions,[1] whose troops were very tired, by Major-General J. E. Capper's 24th Division. This operation was concluded by the morning of the 31st August, after the 9/Rifle Brigade (42nd Brigade) had established posts along the remains of Beer Trench south-east of Cocoa Lane, and pushed out a sap from the end of Prince's Street.

THE GERMAN COUNTER-ATTACK AT DELVILLE WOOD, 31ST AUGUST

Evidence of the arrival of German reinforcements [2] and **Sketch** the abnormal activity of the enemy batteries had already **28.** led the XV. Corps to expect a counter-attack. It came on the 31st August, the first fine day for nearly a week.

The troops of the 24th Division had arrived in the front line during the previous night soaked to the skin and under heavy shell-fire, which increased after dawn broke. German aeroplanes, flying low, then reconnoitred the front positions— an unusual experience for our troops at this period. Then an intense bombardment, which the utmost efforts of the British artillery failed to subdue, heralded the infantry assault delivered about 1 P.M.

The 21/Manchester (91st Brigade of the 7th Division), holding the extreme right of the corps front opposite Ginchy, was not involved; but the storm troops of the *35th Fusiliers* attacked the next battalion, the 1/South Staffordshire, bombing along Ale Alley and down towards Hop Alley. The first assault was repulsed by rapid fire, and a second, delivered about 2 P.M., was also dealt with after heavy fighting in the trenches immediately east of Delville Wood. After another visit from the German aeroplanes, the bombardment increased in fury about 4.30 P.M., and a third assault, at 7 P.M., compelled the survivors of the South Staffordshire to withdraw into the wood. Here, on the left, a stand was made in Edge Trench in touch

---

[1] Casualties returned for August : 14th Division : 156 officers, 3,459 other ranks ; 33rd Division : 149 officers, 3,697 other ranks. Employed for ten days on clearing and consolidation work in Delville Wood, the 89th Field Company R.E. (14th Division) lost 50 per cent of its personnel, and nearly all its officers.

[2] See Note at end of Chapter VIII.

31 Aug. with the refused right flank of the 1/North Staffordshire, the neighbouring battalion. On the right, the Longueval—Ginchy road was held, and in the wood a platoon of the 2/Queen's came up, after darkness fell, to reinforce the defenders.[1]

The 1/North Staffordshire (right battalion of Br.-General B. R. Mitford's 72nd Brigade) had started to dig rifle pits in advance of its front line, so as to escape the German bombardment. It had no frontal attack to contend with, and only relinquished a portion of Edge Trench on its right. Next to the North Staffordshire, the 8/R. West Kent was obliged to withdraw its right to Inner Trench owing to the severity of the bombardment ; a strongpoint established in Cocoa Lane was seized by the enemy. The left portion of the West Kent front and the line beyond the Longueval—Flers road, held by the 9/R. Sussex of the 73rd Brigade (Br.-General R. G. Jelf), was assaulted by the *88th Regiment* at 1 P.M., but the attackers were held off by rifle, machine-gun and artillery fire.[2] Farther west, the left battalion of the 73rd Brigade, the 13/Middlesex, had suffered severely under the bombardment, its total losses amounting to nearly four hundred. The enemy advanced from his barricade in Wood Lane and, in the course of heavy fighting, pressed back the Middlesex and bombed his way along Tea Trench, the British front line, nearly as far as North Street. Another detachment pushed south-eastward into Orchard Trench, and was there held, mainly by the efforts of the 2/Leinster which was hurried up by companies from brigade support. Fire from the right flank of the 1st Division (III. Corps) also assisted to check the German advance.[3]

---

[1] " Fus. Regt. No. 35 " says that six of its flame-throwers were covered in mud, and could not be used. The first two assaults failed owing to inadequate artillery preparation, but the evening effort was " a wonderful victory ".

[2] " Regt. No. 88 " states that the assault was delivered by three companies, with storm-troops attached, advancing on both sides of the trench known to the British as Tea Lane. Many casualties were suffered from the start and progress was from shell-hole to shell-hole. Eventually, with nearly all the officers gone, the troops were pinned down between the British and German lines by British artillery fire. The survivors crawled back after darkness fell, and could only be reassembled in the Flers defences.

[3] According to " Bav. Regt. No. 5 ", the assaulting troops consisted of three columns formed from the *I./Bn.* with flame-throwers and bombers, and one company of the *3rd Jäger Bn.*, which had been especially trained as a " storm-battalion ". Bombing eastward along Tea Trench, Orchard Trench and the British third trench, the attack was intended to join hands with that of the *56th Division.*

The German bombardment had wrought such havoc to **31 Aug.** the XV. Corps communications that it was late at night before the extent of the German success was known in rear. When, however, reports indicated that the enemy effort had spent itself, plans were made to recover the lost ground early next morning.

CHAPTER VIII

THE SOMME

AUGUST 1916 (*concluded*)

THE RESERVE ARMY

(Sketches A, 29, 30)

THE FIGHTING ON POZIÈRES RIDGE AND THE ATTACKS TOWARDS THIEPVAL [1]

Sketch A. As part of the operations of which the ultimate aim was the capture of the Pozières—Grandcourt ridge, the Commander-in-Chief had in mind an attack north of the Ancre to prevent the Germans from sending reinforcements southward from the Hébuterne—Ancre front and, at the same time, to close in on Thiepval from the north. Accordingly on the 30th July, G.H.Q. had directed the Reserve Army to prepare plans for an attack from its front north of the river. Sir Douglas Haig's instructions of the 2nd August,[2] however, clearly defined General Gough's immediate task : by a methodical progression, to capture the old Sketch German 2nd Position from Munster Alley to Mouquet Farm 29. and also the trenches on the spur south of the farm, employing no larger forces than were necessary. For the present, therefore, General Gough was attacking with one division of the I. Anzac Corps and one of the II. Corps, from Munster Alley—the right boundary of the Army—to a point in the German trenches opposite the Nab, a frontage of rather more than three thousand yards from east to west.

The I. Anzac Corps and the extreme right of the II. Corps suffered much the same handicaps as the XIII.

---

[1] These operations are all covered officially by the title : " The Battle " of Pozières Ridge ", 23rd July—3rd September, " The Fighting for Mou- " quet Farm " appearing as a tactical incident therein.

[2] Appendix 13.

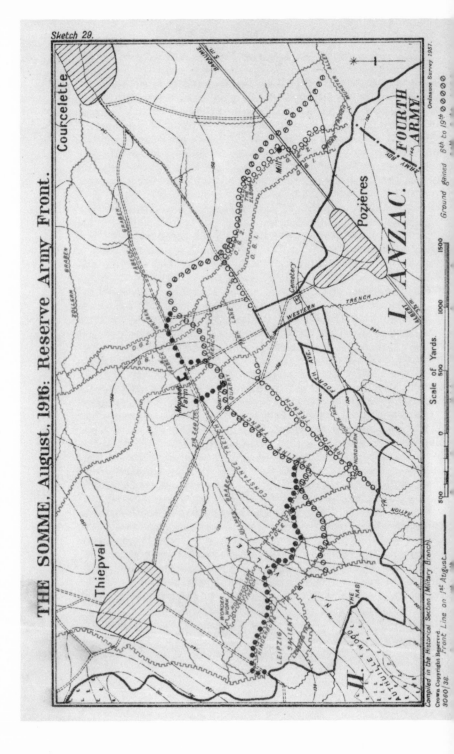

Sketch 29.

THE SOMME, August, 1916: Reserve Army Front.

Courcelette

Pozières

Thiepval

I. ANZAC.

FOURTH ARMY.

II.

Mouquet Farm

Cemetery

WESTERN TRENCH

THE NAB

LEIPZIG SALIENT

Compiled in the Historical Section (Military Branch).

Crown Copyright Reserved.
3060/36.

Ordnance Survey 1937.

Scale of Yards.
500   0   500   1000   1500

Front Line on 1st August. ●●●●●●●

Ground gained 5th to 19th ⊕⊕⊕⊕⊕

Corps on the right flank of the Fourth Army : obliged to advance from the tip of a salient, their cramped positions and the approaches thereto made difficult the assembly and the relief of troops, whilst inviting the concentrated fire of the German artillery.   The Australian front took in flank the German 2nd Position, of which Mouquet Farm formed a strong outwork ; the right of the II. Corps was confronted by the communication trenches—now converted into fire trenches and containing many deep dug-outs—that ran back from the original German front line south of Thiepval.

The artillery preparation for the renewed attack of the **3-4 Aug.** 2nd Australian Division (Major-General J. G. Legge) upon the O.G. lines began on the evening of the 31st July, but Major-General A. B. Scott's 12th Division was the first to make progress.   At 11.15 P.M. on the 3rd August the 8/Royal Fusiliers of the 36th Brigade (Br.-General L. B. Boyd-Moss) charged forward under an artillery barrage and captured the south-western portion of Fourth Avenue ; at the same time the 6/Buffs of the 37th Brigade (Br.-General A. B. E. Cator), assisted by a smoke screen which covered the left flank, took a strongpoint at the lower end of the trench.   Bombers of the two battalions then gained a footing in the centre portion of Ration Trench (the German " Gierich Weg "), two officers and 90 other ranks—mostly of the *11th Reserve Regiment*—being taken.   Next morning the advance of British patrols north-eastward was checked by machine-gun fire and the appearance of some three hundred Germans from the direction of Mouquet Farm.[1]

The 2nd Australian Division had devoted all its energies to digging assembly trenches some two to three hundred yards from the German line, and improving its communications through Pozières.   Ten batteries of heavy howitzers (Anzac and II. Corps) were carrying out four destructive bombardments, each of an hour's duration, per day.   The field-guns fired a special series of hurricane barrages which simulated preparation for an immediate assault, and, with the help of the 2-inch mortars, they also cut the German wire.   German retaliation was fierce and effective, despite the British counter-battery work, so that the Australian

---

[1] According to Wellmann and " Res. Jäger Bn. No. 9 " (the *Jäger* had relieved part of the *86th Reserve* in position astride the Thiepval road on the night of 3rd/4th August), touch had been lost with the *11th Reserve* (*117th Division*) by dawn of the 4th, and the *Jäger* feared that the British would get in behind them.   They claim to have delivered a successful counter-attack at noon.

pioneers, infantry and engineers sustained heavy losses whilst digging at night.[1]   Hopes had been entertained that preparations would be completed by the 2nd August ; but, despite the utmost effort by all concerned, the assault trenches were far from ready by that day.   Although anxious to give the enemy as little respite as possible, General Gough, on corps representation, agreed to a postponement until the 4th August ; zero hour, decided by the divisional commander, was to be 9.15 P.M., so that the troops might reach their objectives before darkness fell. Meanwhile the bombardment continued.

The field artillery was to open an intense barrage upon O.G.1 at zero hour, lift to O.G.2 three minutes later, and then lift three times, 50 yards at a time, at intervals of ten, two and two minutes.   Smoke bombs, discharged from mortars, were to cover the flanks of the assault at Munster Alley on the right, and beyond the Courcelette track on the left.[2]   In order to simulate attack preparations on the rest of the Reserve Army front, the 49th Division (left division of the II. Corps, immediately south of the Ancre) was to bombard certain points in the German line and put down smoke barrages in Nab valley and the Ancre valley at 9 P.M., whilst the XIV. Corps, farther north beyond the river, would discharge gas and smoke and carry out special bombardments at the same time.[3]

4 Aug.   The assembly of the assaulting troops on the evening of the 4th was not accomplished without considerable confusion and loss, for the German artillery fire was heavy on communication trenches and " jumping-off " positions. All difficulties, however, were overcome by the determination and energy of subordinate leaders ; and, for the most part, the leading waves moved forward punctually at 9.15 P.M. in order to get close to the barrage before it lifted.

South-east of the Bapaume road Br.-General W. Holmes's 5th (N.S.W.) Brigade attacked with the 20th Battalion on the right and the 18th on the left.   Here

---

[1] The Germans often appeared to have mistaken the movement of working parties for infantry advancing to the assault.   Wellmann records repeated attacks made upon various parts of the German front opposite the Australians by night or early morning from 1st-4th August.   All these " attacks " were, of course, repulsed.

[2] By No. 2 Coy., 5th Bn., Special Brigade R.E.   The smoke barrage on the right flank was to be fired from 9.17 to 9.37 P.M.

[3] The wind being unfavourable, no gas or smoke was discharged by the II. and XIV. Corps ; but the bombardments were duly carried out.

O.G.1 was captured easily, but hand to hand fighting 4 Aug. occurred before O.G.2 fell to the third and fourth waves of the assault. This trench was so badly damaged by the British bombardment that it was not easily recognized, and some of the more ardent spirits ran into the British barrage as they pushed forward beyond. Consolidation began promptly, Lewis-gun posts being established along the site of O.G.2. On the right, the 20th blocked the entrance to Torr Trench and formed a defensive flank, for the attack of the 68th Brigade (left of the Fourth Army) on Torr Trench had failed.[1]

Between the Bapaume road and the track leading to Courcelette, the 7th Brigade (Br.-General J. Paton) employed three battalions : from right to left, the 27th (South Australia), 25th (Queensland) and 26th (Queensland & Tasmania), the 22nd Battalion of the 6th (Victoria) Brigade forming the extreme left of the frontal attack. Here, as elsewhere, the foremost infantry reached O.G.1 on the heels of the barrage, finding the German wire no obstacle ; but the third and fourth waves were caught in the hostile protective barrage, and suffered considerable loss. There was some loss of direction in the advance, so that the O.G. lines between the Bapaume road and " The Elbow " were assaulted by only three companies of the 27th Battalion, the other battalions crowding to the left. Nevertheless, O.G.1 was everywhere occupied without much trouble, and the attack swept on to O.G.2. Near the road on the right this trench had been obliterated and was not occupied by the 27th Battalion ; neither was the site of the windmill, also included in the objective of the 7th Brigade. Farther to the left, the Australians caught the German machine gunners before they could open fire, many of the defenders being bombed in their dug-outs, and after some sharp fighting most of O.G.2 fell into Australian hands. German dead, grim testimony to the effective fire of the British artillery, lay in hundreds about and beyond the captured trenches.

The main task of the infantry had been accomplished in less than an hour. On the left flank, however, the prevailing wind was unfavourable for smoke, and a detachment of the 23rd Battalion (6th Brigade), which was to link up with the O.G. lines along the Courcelette track, was checked by the fire of a machine gun from the north. It was not until late on the 5th August, after this machine

---

[1] See page 188.

5 Aug. gun had been captured, that the left flank was made
secure.[1]

Patrols had pushed forward in the darkness, the British
barrage ceasing at midnight for a time to facilitate reconnaissance. Consolidation began under a fierce hostile
bombardment. The intention was to hold the captured
position by Vickers and Lewis-gun posts and a small infantry garrison ; but the inevitable German counter-attack
developed before the preparations were completed. About
4 A.M. on the 5th the 7th Brigade saw lines of Germans
advancing up the slopes from Courcelette ; the fire of the
machine guns took heavy toll of them, and some came forward
to surrender. Those who sought cover in shell-holes were
bombed by Stokes mortars. The 27th Battalion, assisted
by the 28th (W. Australia) then pushed forward and dug in
round the windmill and on the O.G.2 position near the
Bapaume road. On the right flank of the 26th Battalion,
north of the Elbow, about one hundred Germans tried to
bomb their way in shortly before 5 A.M. They were driven
off by Lewis-gun fire, leaving ten prisoners behind—the
Australians had now captured more than five hundred
Germans—and soon afterwards spasmodic bombing attempts upon the left of the Australian line were defeated
with the help of the 24th Battalion from reserve.[2]

4 Aug. Meanwhile, the 12th Division had not been idle. At
10 A.M. on the 4th August Major-General Scott had decided
to complete the capture of Ration Trench and secure its
junction with Western Trench, the hour of assault to
synchronize with that of the Australians. Accordingly,
after the heavy artillery had fired upon suspected enemy
strongpoints and upon his rear communications, the
infantry advanced under a field artillery barrage at 9.15 P.M.
On the right, the 7/R. Sussex and 9/Royal Fusiliers attacked
frontally, whilst the 8/Royal Fusiliers (all 36th Brigade)
bombed up from the left. After a sharp struggle which
lasted most of the night, Ration Trench was cleared and

---

[1] Wellmann states that at 5 A.M. on 5th August the situation, as
reported to the *18th Reserve Division*, was that " the British were in com-
" plete possession of the windmill heights " ; between the *31st Reserve* (in
Torr Trench) and *9th Reserve Jäger* (in Park Lane) the *II./84th Reserve*
and *I./162nd* had lost their trenches, and local counter-attacks had
collapsed owing to the hostile protective barrage which had been put
down.

[2] Wellmann says that a counter-attack was delivered by two companies
of the *I./162nd* (from Army Group reserve at Warlencourt) and two of the
II./162nd. Some of these troops got into the lost position, but could not
stay there.

occupied, a lodgment being gained beyond the Thiepval 4-5 Aug.
road, where for a time the fight surged to and fro. The
junction with Western Trench was not reached, for two
platoons of the Royal Sussex which advanced northwards
astride Western Trench were checked by rifle and machine-
gun fire. Farther to the left, the 6/R. West Kent, with
some assistance from the 6/Queen's (both 37th Brigade) had
seized, by means of bombing attacks, the uncaptured
portion of Ration Trench in their sector. After dawn broke
on the 5th August, a number of Germans were discovered
lying out in shell-holes between Fourth Avenue and Ration
Trench ; finding themselves cut off, these parties gradually
surrendered to the number of three officers and 112 other
ranks.[1]

The success of the Australians, which brought con-
gratulations from Sir Douglas Haig and from the commanders of the Army and the corps, had wrested from the
Germans the crest of the Pozières ridge, so that on the
5th August the troops of the Commonwealth looked down
the north-eastward slope towards Courcelette. Although
several German batteries, which soon changed their positions, were in full view, few hostile troops or trenches could
be seen in this direction ; but, as the Reserve Army was
now to push north-westward astride the ridge, the situation south of Mouquet Farm, opposite the junction of the
I. Anzac and II. Corps, was of paramount importance. In
this quarter patrols soon discovered that the enemy was
holding his trenches strongly, and spasmodic firing and
bombing continued.

General Gough was very anxious to start his next
attack without delay. It would be launched from the
Courcelette track, as far as the I. Anzac Corps was concerned, the II. Corps keeping pace on the left ; but for a
fresh operation fresh troops were needed. The O.G. lines,
which now constituted a long defensive flank, were subjected
to a terrific bombardment throughout the 5th August,
German batteries in the area Thiepval—Grandcourt being
able to enfilade the position to the ever-increasing loss and
disorganization of the battalions holding it. From the
R.F.C. came reports of increased railway traffic at Bapaume,
and several German balloons were seen in the air, additional
signs of an impending counter-attack which the weary 2nd

---

[1] Belonging to the *9th Reserve Jäger* (*18th Reserve Division*) and *11th
Reserve* (*117th Division*). The German accounts state that *No. 2 Coy.* of
the *Jäger* was cut off.

5-7 Aug. Australian Division, now very weak in numbers, could hardly be expected to resist.

Already it had been decided to relieve the 5th Brigade south-east of the Bapaume road, and this was accomplished, with infinite difficulty owing to the German bombardment, soon after midnight, 5th/6th August by the 45th (N.S.W.) Battalion of Br.-General D. J. Glasfurd's 12th Brigade, 4th Australian Division.[1] North-west of the road, under the same trying conditions, the 48th (S. & W. Australia) Battalion of the same brigade succeeded in relieving the 7th Brigade as far as the Elbow by dawn of the 6th. No sooner was this completed than an attempted German counter-attack upon the O.G. lines from the direction of Courcelette had to be dispersed by small-arms fire.[2]

At night the German bombardment was more furious than ever, destroying many of the Australian posts and causing heavy loss. Soon after 4.15 A.M. on the 7th August—when the 14th (Victoria) Battalion (Br.-General C. H. Brand's 4th Brigade) had taken over the line from the Elbow northward, and the 15th (Queensland & Tasmania) Battalion, the left flank of the position—a German counter-attack burst through the posts of the 14th and 48th in the vicinity of the Elbow. The British barrage dispersed the enemy supporting troops, and, although some Australians were captured, the confused fighting at close quarters on the near slope of the ridge eventually ended in the complete rout of the Germans who had advanced so far. This result was primarily due to Lieut. A. Jacka, of the 14th Battalion, who issued from a dug-out in O.G.1 with a small party and attacked the enemy in the rear.[3]

[1] The division had been formed in Egypt in February 1916. For details of the expansion of the A.I.F. after the Gallipoli campaign see the Australian Official Account, Volume III. The 4th Division had arrived in France during June, and its only experience on the Western Front amounted to a short term of normal trench warfare. It was commanded by Major-General Sir H. V. Cox, who had led the Indian Brigade at Gallipoli.

[2] The Australians hardly realized that a counter-attack had been intended. Wellmann states that General von Boehn visited his head-quarters during the 5th, when it was planned that the *II.* and *III./163rd* and one battalion of the *157th* should attack upon the right, and the *I./63rd* and *I./163rd*, on the left [the *63rd* was from the *12th Division*, in reserve, and the *163rd* from the *17th Reserve Division*]. Artillery ammunition had first to be replenished. The troops advanced about 4.30 A.M. on 6th August, and Wellmann, at Warlencourt, received very inaccurate reports. He thought at first that a success had been gained.

[3] The Australian Official Account describes Lieut. Jacka's deed as " the most dramatic and effective act of individual audacity in the history " of the A.I.F." As a private in Gallipoli he had won the V.C., the first Anzac to do so.

Meanwhile the 45th Battalion, which had assisted the 69th
Brigade (left of the Fourth Army) during the night in its
progress up Munster Alley, easily repulsed a feeble advance.[1]
At 10.30 A.M. on the 7th August Major-General Cox
assumed command of the Anzac front, which was now
occupied entirely by troops of his 4th Australian Division.[2]

The right of the 12th Division in Ration Trench— 6-8 Aug.
opposite the junction of the *117th Division* and *18th Reserve
Division*—had been subjected to repeated attacks. At
4 A.M. on the 6th August the enemy advanced from the
north-east with *Flammenwerfer* and bombs, forcing back
the 9/Royal Fusiliers (36th Brigade). This battalion then
extended in the open on either side of Ration Trench and
eventually kept the Germans in check by rifle and Lewis-
gun fire.[3] On the morning of the 8th, the 35th Brigade
(Br.-General A. Solly-Flood), which had relieved the 36th,
was attacked in Ration Trench from both flanks. The left
attacks, delivered at 3 A.M. and 7.30 A.M., made little
impression ; but on the right the 5/R. Berkshire was forced
to retire some distance after fierce fighting in which both
sides sustained heavy loss.[4]

The next British attack, in preparation for which the
heavy artillery had already opened on the German front
line—called Park Lane by the Australians—beyond the
Courcelette track, was a combined effort by British and
Australians, made at 9.20 P.M. on the 8th August. The
15th (Queensland & Tasmania) Battalion drove the Germans [5] from the greater part of Park Lane, taking nearly
fifty prisoners, and entered the O.G. trenches on the right ;
the 7/Suffolk (35th Brigade) was checked by uncut wire in
its assault up Ration Trench, and unsubdued machine guns
brought its advance up Western Trench to a standstill.
Thus the trench junction, in reality a strongpoint, was not
captured, and the Australians were eventually withdrawn

---

[1] From German accounts it appears that the counter-attack troops
south-east of the Bapaume road made little effort to close. By the
evening Wellmann admits that his *18th Reserve Division* was almost at
its last gasp.
[2] The 2nd Australian Division returned its casualties as 222 officers
and 6,624 other ranks for the period 25th July—7th August.
[3] This appears to have been the right of the counter-attack delivered
mainly against the Australians. See page 214.
[4] " Regt. No. 157 " states that one company of *III./157th* took by
bombing a British sap and barricade. The attacks on the right were
delivered by part of the *86th Reserve*.
[5] *9th Reserve Jäger.*

9-11 Aug. from that portion of Park Lane west of the track leading to Mouquet Farm. At midnight of the 9th/10th August, after a special bombardment, the trench junction was seized, together with three machine guns, a *Flammenwerfer*, and some thirty Germans, by the 16th (S. & W. Australia) Battalion.[1] The whole of Park Lane was then occupied by the Australians, and on the evening of the 10th August the 4th Australian Brigade took over the front line of the 12th Division as far as the Pozières—Thiepval road. A light rain had begun to fall, but there was as yet little mud to impede movement.

In his order for the next operation, issued on the 10th August, General Gough gave as the Anzac objective the German front positions now running across the O.G. lines, and thence south of a small quarry to the Pozières—Thiepval road; the 12th Division was to capture Skyline Trench, and the German front trenches running westward to the original German line opposite the Nab, where the 49th Division (left sector of the II. Corps) would attack. Eventually the II. Corps task was modified; west of Skyline Trench " holding attacks " only were to be delivered. Zero hour was fixed for 10.30 P.M. on the 12th August, and the usual destructive bombardment was begun without delay.

With the approval of the corps and the Army, Major-General Cox determined to make what progress he could in the meantime. At 1 A.M. on the 11th August, after a preparatory bombardment, the 13th (N.S.W.) and the 16th (S. & W. Australia) Battalions pushed forward from Park Lane under a barrage. In the O.G. lines the 13th established a forward post south-east of Mouquet Farm, and repelled with loss an attack made upon it by German bombers at dawn; farther to the left, the 16th Battalion arrived on the lip of a depression, facing the quarry upon the opposite slope. The advanced positions of the Australians were heavily shelled during the morning of the 11th August; but a German counter-attack delivered from Mouquet Farm in the afternoon was repulsed by rifle and Lewis-gun fire, the

---

[1] Before this success the *117th Division* (south of Thiepval to the O.G. lines) had been relieved by the *16th Division*. At the same time the *XIX.* (*Saxon*) *Corps* (" Group Laffert ") was taking over from Boehn's *IX. Reserve Corps*, the *24th Division* relieving Wellmann's *18th Reserve Division*, and the *40th* the *17th Reserve Division*. Thus the Australian attack had encountered the *69th Regiment*, whilst the *133rd* (*24th Division*) confronted the flank position in the O.G. lines, the *139th Regiment* of the same division being on its left.

artillery completing the discomfiture of the enemy.[1] The German bombardment had reduced the Australian forward line to a series of small posts, and hindered the preparations for another advance that night, which eventually took the form of a reconnaissance. In the early hours of the 12th, 12 Aug. German bombers, supported by a strong detachment, attacked the post of the 13th Battalion in the O.G. lines, but were driven off by fire. Later in the day, it was judged expedient to relieve the weary 16th Battalion on the left, so the 50th (S. Australia) Battalion from the 13th Brigade (Br.-General T. W. Glasgow) was sent forward to replace it.[2]

At 10.30 P.M. on the 12th August the assault as planned was delivered from the O.G. lines north of the Courcelette track to the German front trench opposite the Nab. As the result of its previous advance the 13th Battalion, on the right, had little to do ; it was, however, obliged to refuse its left in order to keep touch with the 50th. The field-artillery barrage was satisfactory, but some platoons of the 50th had not received their orders, so the assault, which started from Park Lane and Ration Trench, did not go well. On the left, at the Thiepval road the objective was reached in touch with the right of the 12th Division, but the centre swung right-handed. One party reached the remains of Mouquet Farm but could not maintain itself there, and eventually the South Australians occupied a line of posts some hundred yards short of their objective except on the left at the Thiepval road.

South-west of this point the 7/Norfolk and 9/Essex (35th Brigade) had formed up on tapes laid in No Man's Land, and moved to the assault of Skyline Trench—so named because it ran along the crest of the spur—close behind an excellent barrage. Encountering little opposition, they occupied their objective and collected about twenty prisoners of the *29th Regiment*. Patrols which pushed on down the slope towards the Nab valley, however, met with considerable resistance, so each battalion established two strongpoints in the captured trench, and withdrew all troops not required to man them. The " holding attacks " carried out by the 37th Brigade

[1] From the prisoners captured, it appeared that this was a combined effort of parts of the *69th (16th Division)* and *133rd (24th Division)*.

[2] For over three days and nights Pte. M. O'Meara, 16th Bn., had shown particular enterprise and courage in getting up supplies and evacuating wounded through the incessant German bombardment. He was awarded the V.C.

12-14
Aug. (7/East Surrey and 6/R. West Kent), farther west, resulted in heavy fighting and considerable loss, but 15 prisoners, also of the *29th Regiment*, were sent back.   The 1/8th West Yorkshire (146th Brigade, 49th Division), which assaulted the German barricade in the original enemy front line opposite the Nab, managed to progress a short distance.

On the 13th August General Gough received a visit from the Commander-in-Chief, who warned him to be prepared for counter-attacks, as the Germans seemed to have been reinforced on his front.   In the evening, an Army order was issued for the resumption of the attack on the night of the 14th, the Australian objective to be that portion of " Fabeck Graben " which lay beyond the Mouquet Farm— Courcelette track, and also the farm itself ; the II. Corps was to push forward from Skyline Trench and join up with the Australian left flank at the junction of the Thiepval road with the Mouquet Farm track.

The 48th Division (Major-General R. Fanshawe) had relieved the 12th [1] during the day, and in the evening the 4th Australian Division replaced its 4th Brigade by its 13th, putting the 51st (W. Australia) Battalion on the right in the O.G. trenches, but retaining the 13th Battalion in the line.

A terrific enemy bombardment continued to fall on Skyline Trench [2] which, as it ran down the crest of the spur and thus afforded observation over Nab valley, was a serious loss to the Germans.   Whilst a strong garrison invited heavy loss from shell-fire, a weak one was liable to be overwhelmed by counter-attack, especially as there were Germans in the trench near its left flank.   Such, indeed, was the fate of two companies of the 1/4th Oxford & Bucks L.I. (Br.-General H. R. Done's 145th Brigade) when, about midnight, 13th/14th August, the enemy, at the second attempt, regained possession of the trench except at a point near the Thiepval road.   Here a party of the defenders held on in touch with the Australians.[3]   A German advance against Ration Trench was driven back with loss by rifle and machine-gun fire, but attempts by bombing parties to re-capture Skyline Trench failed against superior numbers.

---

[1] The 12th Division reported as casualties, 123 officers and 2,594 other ranks during the period 27th July—13th August.

[2] The infantry afterwards reported that British heavy howitzers were shooting short on Ration Trench and Skyline Trench, but there was no means of getting this rectified as all communications had been cut.

[3] The counter-attack was delivered by the *II./68th Regiment* and other troops of the *16th Division*.

At 5.15 A.M. on the 14th, an attack by the 1/4th R. Berk-
shire (also 145th Brigade), delivered across the open from
Ration Trench, was beaten back by fire. So Skyline
Trench remained in German hands ; and as its loss exposed
the left flank of the forward Australian position, the
Australian objective was modified. This was now to be
Fabeck Graben as far as O.G.1, thence a line south-west-
ward, including the quarry, to the junction of Skyline
Trench and the Thiepval road. At the same time, the II.
Corps would recapture Skyline Trench.

During the evening of the 14th the Australian front
positions and communications were heavily shelled, causing
such confusion and loss that a properly co-ordinated advance became out of the question. The effort was made at
10 P.M. under a full moon. On the right, the 51st Battalion
met with deadly machine-gun fire, fell into disorder, and
was eventually rallied on its starting line ; but on this
flank the 49th (Queensland) Battalion of the 13th Brigade
made the situation secure by occupying ground well to the
eastward of the O.G. lines. The 13th Battalion, in the
centre, pressed forward and, swerving to the right,
established bombing posts in Fabeck Graben between
O.G.1 and O.G.2. These could not be held without
support, so their garrisons made a fighting withdrawal
before dawn of the 15th. On the left, the 50th Battalion
was smashed by the German barrage and, although endeavours were made by small groups of men to dig in
beyond the quarry, a withdrawal soon became imperative.

Starting at 10 P.M., bombing parties of the 1/1st Buckinghamshire (145th Brigade) worked up the communication
trenches from Ration Trench and, after some stubborn
fighting, cleared most of Skyline Trench by 5 A.M. on the
15th August. At the same time, the 1/6th Gloucestershire
(Br.-General G. H. Nicholson's 144th Brigade) was fighting
gamely for possession of the German trenches on the slope
at the south-western end of Skyline Trench, but met with
no success. The recaptured position had been very much
damaged by repeated bombardments and the German guns
soon opened on it again ; so many casualties were suffered
that by 3 P.M. the Bucks battalion had to confine itself to
holding the heads of the communication trenches. In the
evening the battalion pushed out posts 100 yards in front
of Skyline Trench, withdrawing these to the site of the
trench when the German bombardment died down. The
attack against the trenches at the south-western end of

15 Aug. Skyline Trench was renewed after dark by the 145th Brigade (1/5th Gloucestershire, assisted by 1/1st Buckinghamshire) and 144th Brigade (1/4th Gloucestershire), but no lasting success was obtained.

The 4th Australian Division—very weary, for those battalions which had not been used for the night assaults or for holding the line had toiled hard carrying up water, ammunition and battle stores [1]—was now relieved by the 1st Australian Division, Major-General Walker assuming command of the Anzac front at 5 P.M. on the 16th August.

On the 15th August the Commander-in-Chief had instructed the Reserve Army to make its next attacks coincide with those of the Fourth Army fixed for the 18th and the 22nd : the projected operations north of the Ancre were to remain in abeyance for the present, but the Reserve Army might undertake minor operations north and south of the river, if such were advisable in connection with the occupation of the Thiepval ridge : no more troops were available, and it might be necessary to hold the line north of the Ancre with only two divisions.[2] Two days later the Commander-in-Chief visited General Gough, who now proposed to attack astride the Ancre on the 30th using two divisions, "with a view to completing the capture of Thiepval "ridge"; but this operation would depend upon the satisfactory progress of his right wing.   In common with General Rawlinson, he had been informed of the big offensive contemplated for mid-September, but these plans made no difference to the immediate task of the Reserve Army.

Sketch 29. Zero hour for the operations of the 1st Australian Division projected for the 18th August did not coincide with that of the main attack of the Fourth Army.   The capture of the new German front trenches south of the Bapaume road was to be undertaken by the 2nd Australian Brigade (Br.-General J. K. Forsyth), whilst the 1st Australian Brigade (Br.-General N. M. Smyth) gained a line west of the O.G. trenches parallel to the Mouquet Farm—

---

[1] From 29th July to 16th August the 4th Australian Division reported as casualties, 109 officers and 4,652 other ranks.

[2] The command of the left sector of the Reserve Army (Ancre—Hébuterne) passed from the XIV. to the V. Corps (Lieut.-General E. A. Fanshawe) at noon on 16th August.   Although the line was held at this time by the 20th, Guards and 6th Divisions (north-south), the relief of the 20th by the Guards was actually in progress, the 20th Division being under orders to join the Fourth Army.

Courcelette track, and some two hundred yards from it.
The right brigade of the 48th Division, holding Skyline
Trench, was not to attack, but the II. Corps now intended
the left brigade to push forward along the eastern slopes of
the Nab valley.

On the night of the 16th the preparations of the 1st **16-17**
Australian Brigade were hindered by spasmodic counter- **Aug.**
attacks delivered from Fabeck Graben. These were caught
by the protective barrage, and some parties which attempted
to close were dispersed by Australian rifle and machine-gun
fire. The 1/4th Oxford & Bucks L.I. (145th Brigade),
holding Skyline Trench, discovered enemy movement on its
front during the following night and, about 10.15 P.M.,
called for a pre-arranged barrage which came down
promptly on the front and left flank, crushing an intended
counter-attack before it started.

The first of the Reserve Army attacks on the 18th
August was delivered by the II. Corps at 5 P.M., when the
left brigade of 48th Division achieved a very heartening
success. The heavy and field artillery had isolated the
objective by continuous and well-directed bombardments ;
smoke, discharged by the 49th Division from opposite
Thiepval, drifted south and interfered somewhat with
artillery observation, but may have deceived the enemy as
to the scope of the infantry attack. To render further
assistance machine guns of the same division, near the
Ancre, opened overhead fire upon the German communications. The infantry pushed forward quickly under a
" surprise barrage ", and although the 1/6th and 1/5th R.
Warwickshire, with bombing parties of the 1/7th R. Warwickshire (all of Br.-General B. C. Dent's 143rd Brigade),
on the extreme left, encountered stubborn resistance in
places, after a time the Germans began to surrender freely.[1]
On the right, round the slopes of the Skyline Trench spur,
the 1/4th Berkshire (145th Brigade) lent effective support,
and attacks made at dawn on the 19th August gained still
more ground. The front line of the left brigade, 48th
Division, then ran almost due west from Skyline Trench to
the original German front line north-east of the Nab.

The Australians advanced at 9 P.M. on the 18th. South-
east of the Bapaume road, the 2nd Australian Brigade, always
under heavy shell-fire, had developed the T-heads of several
saps beyond O.G.2 into more or less adequate " jumping-off "

---

[1] Nine officers and 416 other ranks of the *29th, 68th* and *69th Regiments*
(all *16th Division*) were taken.

18 Aug. trenches, thereby halving the distance to be traversed in the assault. On the right, the German line lay beyond the crest of the ridge, and here the 8th Battalion, which had not received the barrage time-table but moved forward at the first lift, made three gallant attempts to enter the German trenches. All failed in the face of deadly machine-gun fire. Beyond the light-railway track, the 7th Battalion could do no better, fire from a German strongpoint at the junction of the Bapaume road with a track running northward to Courcelette taking heavy toll of the whole line. A few Victorians who entered this strongpoint were killed, and before dawn of the 19th the battalion was back in its " jumping-off " trenches. North-west of the Bapaume road, the 6th Battalion, which had orders to dig a trench from the strongpoint to the Elbow, now joined up the Elbow with the left post of the 7th Battalion on the road.[1]

The preparations of the 1st Brigade had suffered from uncertainty as to the precise location of the Australian line, the supporting artillery firing short and causing some loss. In consequence, the objective on the right was changed to a new German trench in front of Fabeck Graben. The advance was made mostly by strong bombing parties which followed close behind the barrage, but the 3rd Battalion —east of the O.G. lines—had to wait until the artillery had lengthened its range, and no progress was achieved. Farther west, however, the 4th Battalion managed to establish posts in Quarry Trench near the track leading to Mouquet Farm, several counter-attacks on them being repelled in the course of the night. On the left a line was consolidated level with the quarry.

19 Aug. During the 19th August Major-General Walker relieved his 1st Australian Brigade by the 3rd (Br.-General E. G. Sinclair-MacLagan), and at night the 144th Brigade replaced the 145th preparatory to taking over next day the whole of the 48th Division line. In the left sector, of the II. Corps, between the Ancre and the Nab, the 25th Division (Major-General E. G. T. Bainbridge) relieved the 49th. For many weeks the 49th Division had assisted, in some measure, the advance of the right wing of the Reserve Army by means of special bombardments and discharges of smoke, besides maintaining active trench-warfare and pushing forward parallels in order to approach within assaulting distance of

[1] The brigade had been engaged with the Saxons of the *139th Regiment*, holding the centre sector, and the left of the *133rd*, holding the right sector of the *24th Division*.

Thiepval on the west.[1] Lieut.-General Jacob now planned
an advance of the left of his right division (48th) northward
up the Nab valley, whilst the 25th Division made a converging attack from the Leipzig salient. The II. Anzac
Corps was still concerned to carry its north-westward thrust
up to and beyond Mouquet Farm.

On the front of the II. Corps some progress by bombing **20-21**
was made on the 20th August in the trenches north-east **Aug.**
of the Nab by the 1/6th Gloucestershire (144th Brigade)
and fighting, without definite result, continued in this
quarter during the 21st.

On the 21st General Gough gave his corps commanders
an outline of future operations for the capture of Thiepval, which he hoped to accomplish by the 1st September. An attack would ultimately be developed north of
the village ; as a preliminary step he reckoned on the I.
Anzac Corps reaching a line, facing north-west, 500 yards
beyond Mouquet Farm, and on the II. Corps securing Pole
Trench, and its continuation north-westward to the German
front line, including the Wonder Work. All this was to be
accomplished by the 25th August.

Both the I. Anzac and the II. Corps attacked at
6 P.M. on the 21st August, the principal objective of the
3rd Australian Brigade being Fabeck Graben east of the
O.G. lines. German aircraft were very active during
the day and discovered the preparations, which were then
hindered by a heavy bombardment ; nevertheless the
advance started well under an effective barrage. The 10th
(S. Australia) Battalion, on the right, forced its way into
Fabeck Graben, but could not stay there unsupported,
enfiladed as it was by machine-gun fire from the right.
Eventually it established a line south of the Mouquet Farm
—Courcelette track. On the left, the 12th (S. & W.
Australia and Tasmania) Battalion met with little opposition and made some ground, one party again reaching the
ruins of Mouquet Farm where dug-outs were bombed
before the pressure of superior numbers compelled a withdrawal. Bombers of the 12th accounted for a German
strongpoint at the junction of the Courcelette track and
O.G.1, and the specially detailed " raiding parties " of the
11th, which were very late in starting, eventually linked up
the forward positions of the flank battalions. During the

---

[1] The division had been X. Corps reserve on the opening day of the
Somme offensive (see " 1916 " Vol. I.), and it had taken over its front
south of the Ancre on 8th July. Its total casualties, 1st July—19th August
were returned as 204 officers and 4,971 other ranks.

night and the following day renewed efforts to push on were made by bombing parties, despite a heavy German bombardment. When the 6th Brigade of the 2nd Australian Division took over the front on the night of the 22nd the centre was established on the Courcelette track from O.G.1 to the south-eastern corner of Mouquet Farm.

21-23 Aug. At 6 P.M. on the 21st the 1/4th Gloucestershire started from the Nab trenches, and advanced over the open to attack the south-eastern face of the Leipzig salient, moving close behind an excellent barrage. The position had been well pounded by the heavy artillery and the front trench was entered before the Germans were prepared for resistance, so that most of them surrendered. Consolidation proceeded, the 1/4th Gloucestershire being now in touch with its sister battalion, the 1/6th, at the entrance to Hindenburg Trench. On the other flank, the 1/Wiltshire (7th Brigade, 25th Division), equally well served by the artillery, increased its hold of the Leipzig salient by seizing Lemberg Trench, a " pipe-pusher " being used to demolish a German barricade. Nearly two hundred prisoners—of the *28th Regiment* (*16th Division*)—were gathered in during these operations.[1]

In the early morning of the 22nd August, through thick mist, the Germans counter-attacked the forward posts of the 1/6th Gloucestershire east of Hindenburg Trench with some success, but were driven back after a Stokes mortar bombardment. In the evening the enemy tried again, both by bombing and by attacking over the open, but failed with heavy loss. From 10 P.M. onwards three attacks on the 1/4th Gloucestershire were repelled by bombing and by Lewis-gun fire, and 15 prisoners of the *15th Reserve Regiment* were taken.[2] On the afternoon of the 23rd two companies of the Bucks battalion suffered heavily in an attempt to advance along the eastern slope of the Nab valley.

From now onward the operations of the two corps are best described independently. The I. Anzac Corps still strove to push forward north-westward along the Pozières ridge, and the II. Corps continued to attack towards Thiepval, almost due north, up the Nab valley and the slopes on either side of it, each commander initiating a series of local actions.

---

[1] " Regt. No. 28 " relates a pitiful tale of blown-in dug-outs and buried men. The *III./28th* is said to have been " partly annihilated ", and losses in officers were very heavy.

[2] Of the *2nd Guard Reserve Division*, but used to reinforce the *16th Division*.

Dealing first with the II. Corps, at 4.10 P.M. on the 24th August,[1] after a special bombardment by the heavy artillery in which the trench mortars joined, the 3/Worcestershire and 1/Wiltshire (Br.-General C. E. Heathcote's 7th Brigade, 25th Division) attacked and captured in fine style Hindenburg Trench, the chord of the Leipzig salient. A smoke screen served to hide the movement from German observers in Thiepval, and the advance over the open followed the barrage so closely that the Germans, caught unprepared, were overcome by bomb and bayonet after a brief resistance.[2] On the extreme left, however, beyond the road leading to Thiepval, the bombers of the Wiltshire were held up some distance from their objective. Consolidation proceeded under a German bombardment which became intense just before 6 P.M. on the 25th August, when the enemy trenches were observed to be crowded with men. A British barrage was called for and came down promptly with great effect, preventing the threatened counter-attack. At 7 P.M. on the 26th an unsuccessful attempt was made by the 8/Loyal N. Lancashire (7th Brigade) to clear the western flank of Hindenburg Trench.

The 48th Division attacked again at 7 P.M. on the 27th August, when the 1/8th R. Warwickshire (143rd Brigade) assaulting a portion of Constance Trench on either side of Pole Trench ran into its own barrage, and swerved to the flanks. Some parties got in on the right and captured a number of Germans, but, being counter-attacked from Pole Trench and down Constance Trench, they were forced to withdraw when the survivors became too few to hold what had been won. Farther to the left, the 1/4th R. Berkshire and the 1/5th Gloucestershire (145th Brigade), advancing over the open with bombers on their western flank, carried the loop of trenches south-west of Pole Trench and sent back 50 prisoners.[3]

---

[1] On 22nd and 23rd August began the relief of the *16th*, *24th* and *40th Divisions* by the *Guard Reserve* and *II. Bavarian Corps*, four divisions replacing three.

[2] Two officers and 140 other ranks were captured. They belonged to the *I.* and *II. Bns.* of the *93rd Reserve* (*4th Guard Division*) which had just relieved the *28th Regiment*. " The time spent near Thiepval was one of " the worst the division experienced ", says the divisional historian.

[3] These belonged to the *5th Guard Grenadiers* (*4th Guard Division*), whose history states that the British attacked " in dense masses " and almost annihilated one company in hand to hand fighting. A counter-attack was more or less successful, but trenches were lost. The *Fusilier Bn.* on the evening of the 28th took over " Ullmer Graben and bits of " Constanzer Graben [Constance Trench] ", finding a terrible scene of destruction caused by the British bombardment.

28-31 Next morning, in mud and rain, the 25th Division
Aug. began to relieve the 48th, which was to be transferred to the
V. Corps north of the Ancre.[1] The only fresh operation
undertaken on the front of the II. Corps before the end of
August was another attempt to clear the left flank of
Hindenburg Trench. Made by the 8/South Lancashire
(75th Brigade, 25th Division) at 4 P.M. on the 28th, it was
defeated by machine-gun fire which caused considerable loss.

23-26 Command of the Anzac front passed from the 1st [2] to
Aug. the 2nd Australian Division at 9 A.M. on the 23rd, Major-
General Legge having his 5th Brigade on the right, and
his 6th Brigade facing the Mouquet Farm position on
the left where a furious German bombardment had still
to be endured. Patrols of the 6th Brigade found Fabeck
Graben strongly garrisoned, but the situation about
Mouquet Farm was not cleared up.

The next attack was intended to capture Zig Zag Trench
on the left, whilst bombing detachments, advancing east of
the farm, secured a footing in Fabeck Graben. A surprise
bombardment of the objectives by 26 heavy and medium
howitzers had barely concluded when, at 4.45 A.M. on the
26th, the Australians went forward behind a field artillery
barrage. On the right, the bombers of the 24th Battalion
could do little in the face of machine-gun fire and showers
of bombs from Fabeck Graben. The 21st Battalion swept
over Constance Trench and the Courcelette track, and
reached Zig Zag Trench without seeing many Germans.
Unfortunately most of the stormers, who could recognize
no land-marks, swerved to the right, continued on, and
eventually occupied a trench running northward with the
farm on their right front. They had taken with them a
company of the 22nd Battalion which had orders to form a
defensive flank on the left ; but they were now outnumbered
by the enemy and assailed on all sides, the survivors being
obliged to surrender after a stout resistance. On the
extreme left a German strongpoint at the junction of the
Thiepval road and Mouquet Farm track was won and lost
again, but a post was maintained in the centre of Zig Zag
Trench. A counter-attack upon it, delivered at 7.20 A.M.,
was repulsed.[3]

---

[1] From 13th August onward, the casualties in the 13 battalions of the
48th Division were returned as 87 officers and 2,418 other ranks.

[2] During its second tour in the Somme battle, the 1st Australian Division
reported as casualties, 92 officers and 2,562 other ranks.

[3] The history of the *2nd Guard Reserve Regiment*, holding part of
Constance Trench, Mouquet Farm and Fabeck Graben states that the right

The 6th Brigade was relieved on the night of the 26th 26-30 by the 4th Brigade from the 4th Australian Division, and **Aug.** at midnight, 27th/28th August, the 14th (Victoria) Battalion endeavoured to seize two German strongpoints, one at the junction of the Thiepval road and Mouquet Farm track, and another at the end of Zig Zag Trench near the farm. This accomplished, a line was to be established linking them with the post already held in Zig Zag Trench. The preliminary bombardment did not appear to be very effective, but bombing detachments got into both strongpoints. After heavy fighting they were driven out by superior numbers, bringing back one prisoner. It was now obvious that the cellars of Mouquet Farm formed an elaborate underground stronghold with many exits and entrances hard to discover among the shell-craters and piles of débris ; and that the Germans were able to emerge after the Australians had passed and assail them from the rear.

Command was handed from the 2nd to the 4th Australian Division at noon on the 28th August,[1] and Major-General Cox made an attempt to secure Fabeck Graben, Mouquet Farm and Zig Zag Trench in one operation on the night of the 29th, employing the 13th (N.S.W.) and 16th (S. & W. Australia) Battalions of the 4th Brigade. A terrific bombardment, to which the enemy replied vigorously, was directed upon the objectives during the 28th and 29th August. On these days rain fell in torrents, converting the ground into a sea of chalky slime. At 11 P.M. on the 29th the 13th Battalion, on the right, struggled manfully forward towards Fabeck Graben, to find the enemy on the alert. Lewis guns and rifles were choked with glutinous mud, but groups of Australians forced their way forward into the trench and occupied about one hundred and fifty yards from O.G.1 eastward. Although its left flank failed, the right of the 16th Battalion entered Fabeck Graben at a point behind the farm. A fierce confused struggle continued around the farm and in Fabeck Graben, until the Australians, who were outnumbered, withdrew.[2]

---

sector was overrun and the company holding the farm was in a critical situation. An officer and 30 other Australians are said to have been captured after a counter-attack by the *II./Bn.* The history of the *4th Guard Division* says : " If a break-through at Mouquet Farm occurs the com-" munications and battery positions of the division are in jeopardy ".

[1] The 2nd Australian Division, which was not completely relieved until 29th August, had lost 36 officers and 1,231 other ranks.

[2] " Guard Res. Regt. No. 1 " states that " a few British " who broke through its right were dealt with. " Guard Res. Regt. No. 2 " states that

Preparations for a fresh attack were put in hand without delay, the 12th relieving the 4th Brigade ; but on the 31st August, the 1st Canadian Brigade (1st Canadian Division) took over the right sector of the Anzac front, heralding the arrival of the whole corps which was about to replace the I. Anzac Corps.

The commander of the Reserve Army had issued an order on the 24th August which revealed his plan of developing the attack upon Thiepval. An assault would be made astride the Ancre, one division on either side of the river,[1] where the 49th Division again took over the Thiepval sector on the 26th. The part to be played by the right of the II. Corps and the I. Anzac Corps was defined in a new order dated the 29th : II. Corps to capture the Wonder Work and the trench line east and west of it ; I. Anzac Corps to secure Fabeck Graben and Mouquet Farm. By order of the Commander-in-Chief the whole operation was to synchronize with the combined offensive of the Fourth Army and the French, and General Gough thus had to conform to the repeated postponements— chiefly on account of the unfavourable weather—agreed upon between Sir Douglas Haig and the French. Originally fixed for the 30th August, the Reserve Army operations were thus delayed until the 3rd September.

NOTE

The German Situation in August and the Change in the High Command [2]

During August the German troops and commanders were subjected to an ever-increasing strain. Regimental histories repeatedly refer to heavy losses, company strengths in some battalions dwindling

---

[1] the British penetrated the left flank (Fabeck Graben) as far as the " big " dug-out " at the farm. They were driven out by counter-attack after a platoon of the defenders had been annihilated. Bombs and bayonets were used and overhead fire from carefully sited machine guns is said to have been very effective. Touch with the *5th Guard Grenadiers*, on the west, was restored after the action.

[1] The V. Corps (Ancre—Hébuterne) had waged active trench-warfare during the latter half of August. The 6th, 20th and Guards Divisions left to join the Fourth Army, and the 48th (from II. Corps), 2nd and 39th, arrived. The 39th was to attack north of the Ancre and preparations were well in hand.

[2] G.O.A. x., pp. 373-4, 381-2, 385-9, 420-3, 634-45, 662-76, Gallwitz, Rupprecht, Schwarte, Wendt and Falkenhayn.

THE SOMME, 1916: 31st August.

THIRD. RESERVE. FOURTH. SIXTH.

VII. V.

26 D.R. XIV R. 52. 26 R. 4 GD. 16 R. 6 D.R.

II BAV. 3 BAV. 4 BAV. 56. XII R. XV. XIV. III. 2 GD. I BAV. R. I GD. VII. XXXIII. 28.

Hannescamps, Essarts, Courcelles, Erviliers, Mory, Vraucourt, Fonquevillers, Gommécourt, Ablainzevelle, Gomiecourt, Yaulx, Hébuterne, ARMY BDY., Bucquoy, LOREAST WD., Behagnies, Sapignies, Baugnâtre, Sailly, Achiet le Gd., Bihucourt, Favreuil, Beugny, Colincamps, Puisieux, Achiet le Pt., Biefvillers, CAMBRAI 16 m., Serre, Irles, Grévillers, Bapaume, Frémicourt, Miraumont, Pys, LOUPART WD., Thilloy, Ligny, Bancourt, Beaucamp Hamel, 26 R., Grandcourt, Warlencourt, le Barque, Haplincourt, Beaucourt, le Sars, SUTTE, Beaulencourt, Villers au Flos, Mailly, St. Pierre Divion, Eaucourt l'Abbeye, Barastre, Hamel, Courcelette, II BAV., Englebelmer, Thiepval WD., Martinpuich, HIGH WD., Flers, Gueudecourt, le Transloy, Rocquigny, Mesnil, Authuille, Contalmaison, Bazentin le Gd., DELVILLE WD., Lesboeufs, Martinsart, AVELUY, Villers, BERNAFAY WD., Longueval, Morval, Sailly, Saillisel, Bouzincourt, Aveluy, la Boisselle, Montauban, Guillemont, BOULEAUX WOOD, XII R., Millencourt, ALBERT, Bécourt, Fricourt, Mametz, ARMY BDY., LEUZE WD., Combles, Frégicourt, ST. PIERRE VAAST WD., Rancourt, Bécordel, Maricourt, Hardecourt, Maurepas, le Forest, Bouchavesnes, Dernancourt, Méaulte, Carnoy, I., 2 GD., I BAV. R., Buire, Curlu, I GD., Morlancourt, Vaux, Ham, Cléry, Omiécourt, Suzanne, Feuillères, PÉRONNE, Bray, Frise, SOMME, Halle, 28., Etinehem, Cappy, Herbécourt, Biaches, Flaucourt

Line at night ——— British—Red. French—Blue. Germans—Green.

Scale of Miles

Ordnance Survey 1937.

to eighty and even less before relief which was often asked for in vain. The *IX. Reserve Corps* was shattered by making repeated counter-attacks at Pozières ; Wellmann gives the losses of his *18th Reserve Division*, 24th July–9th August, as 178 officers and 8,110 other ranks (infantry, 142 and 7,115), but thinks they were heavier still.

The various German reliefs opposite the British battle-front have already been noticed. Of the ten divisions which entered the struggle during August, the *26th* came from the *Fourth Army* in Flanders ; the *16th*, the *4th Guard* and *1st Guard Reserve* (*Guard Reserve Corps*) came from the *Second Army* (Gallwitz) opposite the French ; the *24th* and *40th* (*XIX. Corps*), *3rd Bavarian* and *4th Bavarian* (*II. Bavarian Corps*) and *56th* and *111th* all came from the *Sixth Army* (Rupprecht). At the end of the month the German Sketch 30. front from Thiepval to Angle Wood (opposite the junction of the British and French) was held by six divisions instead of five.

Few divisions came out of the battle with less than 4,500 casualties, and many suffered to a considerably greater extent. The policy of a rigid unyielding defensive still persisted, but in consequence of the heavy losses sustained higher commanders began to recommend that the front line should be held more lightly. As, however, there was so little protection against artillery fire for supports and local reserves, the strength of formations continued to dwindle at an alarming rate.

Troops coming in were surprised and depressed by the Allied superiority in material. Movement behind the front was rendered so precarious by continuous shell-fire that regiments usually brought in, on the man, sufficient rations and water—mineral water, for no filtered was obtainable—for their four or five days' tour. Engineer and labour troops had a heavy task in constructing rear lines ; there was a great shortage of props for dug-outs and wire for obstacles. The railways were overstrained in transporting reinforcements and tired divisions, supply trains were held up, and difficulties were increased by the artillery bombardment of stations and the Allied air attacks upon stations and important junctions. The light railway system was insufficient, most of the material and personnel required having still to be transferred from Verdun ; the main burden of transportation and supply fell upon horsed and motor lorries, supplemented by country-carts, working over roads adequate in themselves, but difficult to keep in repair with the personnel available.

The batteries suffered great loss. Wellmann states that the gun-parks could not replace damages ; defective ammunition caused many burst barrels, whilst numerous defects developed in the overworked guns ; material for gun-pits was scarce and almost impossible to bring forward over the heavily shelled roads. Gallwitz reveals that from the 26th June to 28th August, 1,068 field guns of the 1,208 in his two Armies were captured, destroyed or had become unserviceable ; likewise 371 of his 820 heavy guns. Allied superiority in the air was still very marked, although German reinforcements were arriving regularly after the middle of July.[1] The reinforcement of the heavy artillery, although asked for in good time, took place too late; and it was not until Gallwitz's scheme of centralized control got into working order that the counter-battery work and barrages improved, and co-operation between artillery and aeroplane became

---

[1] See " The War in the Air," Vol. II., p. 236.

an accomplished fact. Gallwitz had again considered his plan for a counter-stroke (" relief attack "), but there were not sufficient troops and artillery ammunition to carry it out. On the 15th, O.H.L. asked the *Second Army* to do without any fresh troops for the time being ; it will have been observed that Gallwitz had to reinforce Below from his own resources.

Having been obliged to send troops from France and Germany [1] to strengthen the Russian front, Falkenhayn was much embarrassed by the shortage of trained reserves. Rupprecht records that at the beginning of August the *II. Bavarian Corps* received drafts of *Land-sturm*—men over 38 years of age who had never served before—and these had to be sent back, " as they are merely a danger ".

At Verdun the German attack north-east of Souville on the 1st August had met with little success, and was immediately followed by French attacks in the same region at Fleury and Thiaumont. Falkenhayn directed the Crown Prince to use such means as were still at his disposal to keep alive the impression that the German offensive would be systematically pursued. Fighting continued, but the initiative had passed to the French who, during the month, made some progress in their efforts to reduce the German salient west of Fort Vaux.

Before leaving for Pless, on the Eastern Front, where he arrived on the 16th, Falkenhayn told his Army commanders that the strict defensive must be maintained in order to keep fluid for emergencies as large a force as possible. On the 25th August—the change appears to have been effected on the 28th—he appointed Rupprecht commander of a new Group of Armies formed of the *Sixth*, *First* and *Second*, Gallwitz reverting to the command of the *Second* alone, and General von Falkenhausen taking command of the *Sixth*. As regards the Western Front, this was the last order issued by Falkenhayn from O.H.L.

Falkenhayn's anxieties and responsibilities were increasing in the other European theatres of war. The Russians had driven back the Austrian Second Army on the Sereth, in front of Lemberg, 8th-10th August, and, farther south, still made progress towards the Carpathians ; to the north, heavy fighting was renewed on the Stochod on the 21st August. The Italian offensive on the Isonzo, which began on the 6th, resulted in the capture of Gorizia three days later. On the 27th, Rumania declared war upon Austria-Hungary, and, next day, Germany declared war upon Rumania, and Italy upon Germany.

The entry of Rumania into the War dealt the final blow to Falkenhayn's fast waning prestige. He had few friends at German G.H.Q. Earlier in the month the Chancellor, Bethmann-Hollweg, had advised the Emperor that the retirement of Hindenburg, whose relations with O.H.L. were becoming more and more strained, " would have the most serious political consequences ". On the 28th August the Emperor was prevailed upon to make the change, and next day Hindenburg, with Ludendorff as First Quartermaster-General, succeeded Falkenhayn as Chief of the General Staff.

Falkenhayn had succeeded Moltke in September 1914, and re-

[1] By the end of August 10 complete divisions had been despatched to the Eastern front, one of these being intended for the campaign against Rumania.

established the confidence of the German Armies after their failure at the Marne ; in 1915 he drove the Russians from Poland, Galicia and Courland, then proceeding to compass the defeat of Serbia. These preoccupations had prevented him from continuing the offensive in the West, where he saw the only hope of victory. Undoubtedly he underrated the British powers of resistance at Ypres in 1914 and 1915, and likewise those of the French at Verdun in 1916, when he over-estimated the effects of " defeatist " propaganda in France. It is, however, remarkable that he should have accomplished so much, for he was always the object of political and military intrigue, had never enjoyed the confidence of his Army commanders, and possessed, in Conrad von Hötzendorf, a most intractable ally. He must be accounted one of the ablest of the German leaders.

German official criticism of Falkenhayn's strategy starts with the observation that he should have completed the overthrow of the Russians in 1915, remaining upon the strict defensive in the West where, if necessary, ground could have been yielded. In 1916, feeling more or less secure in the East, he aimed at the defeat of Britain " the arch-enemy ", by military action in the West combined with unrestricted submarine warfare, after the offensive at Verdun had dealt effectively with France ; but he should not have so underestimated his enemies. Russia proved herself a still dangerous antagonist in 1916 ; far from being broken by the Austro-Hungarian attacks, Italy launched a counter-offensive ; Verdun became a German failure. It is conceded, however, that a better solution of Falkenhayn's problems in 1915–16 is difficult to suggest, and he is praised for his undoubted achievements during nearly two years of command.

CHAPTER IX

PLANS FOR A MID-SEPTEMBER OFFENSIVE

(Sketches A, 31)

Aug. ON the 1st August, when there was still hope of further results from Brusilov's offensive, the Commander-in-Chief, in a special report to the Chief of the Imperial General Staff, for the information of the War Committee, expressed his satisfaction at the results so far achieved upon the Somme. The crisis at Verdun had passed, but there could be no slackening of effort on the part of the British Armies " without prejudicing, probably fatally, the offen-" sive of our Allies and their hopes of victory ". By maintaining a relentless pressure, " giving the enemy no " rest and no respite from anxiety " until well into the autumn, Sir Douglas Haig said that he expected to inflict such losses as would amply compensate for those sustained. " It would not be justifiable to calculate on the enemy's " resistance being completely broken by these means with-" out another campaign next year. But, even if another " campaign prove to be necessary, the enemy will certainly " enter on the coming winter with little hope left of being " able to continue his resistance successfully through next " spring and summer, and I am confident that it will prove " beyond his power to do so provided the Allies maintain " their determination to fight on together, vigorously, to a " successful conclusion."

The Commander-in-Chief had been kept fully informed of the progress made in the construction of the tanks,[1]

[1] The Note at end of Chapter, " The Evolution of the Tank ", might be read at this stage. Whilst G.O.C. First Army Sir Douglas Haig had remained in ignorance of the idea and construction of tanks ; he first heard of them late in December 1915 from Mr. Winston Churchill, then a serving officer in France, who came to G.H.Q. As a result Major H. J. Elles, R.E. (at that time G.S.O.2 in the Operations Branch at G.H.Q., later to become

and was eager to employ them as soon as a sufficient July. number were ready. He appreciated that this " climbing " armoured vehicle—proof against small-arms fire, shell splinters, and shrapnel, armed with two 6-pdr. guns and several machine guns, and capable of crashing its way over trenches and through wire-entanglements, hedges and walls —would, in the rôle of machine-gun destroyer, prove a valuable auxiliary to the infantry assault ; and that the moral effect upon the enemy infantry and machine gunners, unaware that such a machine existed and at a loss to know how to defend themselves against it, might well be decisive. Sir Douglas Haig would have used the tanks on the 1st July had any been available, and, although G.H.Q. tentatively suggested later in that month that production should be suspended until twenty fully equipped machines had been seen in a definite tactical scheme, he continued to press for their earliest possible delivery.

Among those responsible for the inception and production of the tanks there was, at this time, a fear that if they were used in " small driblets " the valuable element of surprise would be sacrificed to very little purpose. It was urged that whereas 150 tanks might be ready in September, 350 more could take the field in January 1917, and that the initial employment of the larger number would do more to ensure final success on a large scale than would the use of small detachments at a much earlier date. Another point raised was the importance of allowing more time for training the commanders and crews. The engineer experts who had evolved the design and were supervising the manufacture of the tank contended that the machines had to run so many miles in the course of trials, the training of crews, and demonstrations that the limited number available by mid-September would be practically worn out and therefore unfit for service in the field.

All these considerations were brought to Sir Douglas Haig's notice by Sir William Robertson at the request of Mr. Lloyd George, Secretary of State for War. Replying on the 29th July, the Commander-in-Chief said that he was fully alive to the disadvantages of using the tanks before the full number on order was available ; but he pointed out that the general offensive then being prosecuted by all the

---

G.O.C. Tank Corps), was sent home without delay to report upon developments. Thereafter, at tank trials and conferences in England, Major-General R. H. K. Butler, Deputy-Chief of the General Staff, represented G.H.Q.

July-
Aug. Allies could only be maintained for a limited period, and
that, " if the enemy is not forced from his entrenched
" positions—as there is good hope he will be—before the
" autumn, it is unlikely to prove possible to arrange for
" another simultaneous effort on a large scale before next
" spring ".   So he would have no hesitation in using even
a few tanks if valuable results could be gained thereby ;
but he added, " it is not my intention to employ tanks in
" small numbers unless and until I am convinced that the
" advantages to be gained by doing so are great enough to
" outweigh the disadvantages of making known to the
" enemy the existence of these new engines of war ".

The Commander-in-Chief was disappointed to hear on
the 11th August that no tanks could arrive before the 1st
September, and at once urged that their despatch should be
expedited : four days later he was informed that the first
six machines were on their way.   On the 16th, he sent to
the Fourth and Reserve Armies the first notice of his projected mid-September offensive in which the tanks were to
play their part.[1]

The introduction of the tank was not, however, the only
or even the chief factor in the Commander-in-Chief's
decision to revert to his original objective, a break-through.
It will be recalled that on the 2nd August he had informed
his Army commanders that the " wearing-out battle " must
be continued until the crisis of the struggle was reached,
which might not be before the latter half of September.[2]
Since the beginning of August the examination of prisoners
and of captured documents and letters tended to show that,
coincident with the rapidly mounting German losses, a
steady deterioration of morale had set in.[3]   If the enemy
were given no respite it seemed reasonable to suppose that
by the middle of September he would be near breaking
point.   Writing to Sir William Robertson on the 22nd
August, Sir Douglas Haig said that he was counting on 50

[1] See page 196.
[2] Appendix 13.
[3] British Intelligence reckoned that by 25th August the German
casualties on the Somme amounted to over 200,000, and that 43 divisions
had been used on the battle-front, four of them twice, including 27 engaged
opposite the British.   G.O.A. x. shows 49 divisions employed upon the
Somme (25 against the British) up to the end of August.   Five of the 49
had been used twice, and the casualties, given division by division, total
243,129.   The losses of corps, Army and other troops are not mentioned,
nor are the lightly wounded included.

According to the A.G.'s returns, the British casualties up to the end of
August (Fourth and Reserve Armies only) amounted to 196,277.   The
French official figure is 70,351.

tanks, at least, for the big attack. " Even if I do not get so Aug.
" many as I hope, I shall use what I have got, as I cannot
" wait any longer for them, and it would be folly not to use
" every means at my disposal in what is likely to be our
" crowning effort for this year."

In the minds of some in Government circles there was
at this time a growing doubt as to whether the heavy
casualties sustained on the Somme were being justified by
results.[1] It is true that by the end of August the resources
of the Empire immediately available were unable fully to
make good the losses of the Armies in France, and it remained to be seen what additional numbers of men would
be supplied by the Second Military Service Act, which had
come into operation on the 8th June. The maintenance of
the forces in Egypt, Mesopotamia, Salonika, India and
East Africa was an additional drain on man-power. At
home, apart from mounted troops and cyclists, there were
eleven divisions, of which the only one (3rd Australian
Division) intended for France was not yet trained and
equipped. Of the other ten,[2] one was in Ireland ;[3] five
were composed of men fit for home service only who were
drafted overseas as they became fit for general service ; and
the other four were definitely allotted to home defence and
not to be liberated until the War Committee could be
persuaded that all risk of invasion was past. Thus there
was no immediate prospect of adding any divisions to the
56 [4] already in France.

On the other hand, in Macedonia the Bulgarian attacks
against the flanks of the Allies had been stayed, and
General Sarrail was preparing a counter-offensive in the

[1] On 5th August the War Committee had expressed their complete
confidence in Sir Douglas Haig. The Prime Minister, Mr. Asquith, visited
G.H.Q. in France, 6th/7th September, and showed his personal approval
of the Commander-in-Chief's policy.

[2] All nominally 2nd-Line Territorial divisions, but voluntary enlistment
in the Territorial Force had been stopped by the First Military Service
Act, which became law on 27th January 1916.

[3] The Easter rebellion in Ireland had caused the despatch of the 59th
(2nd N. Midland) Division, of which one brigade had sharp fighting in
Dublin. The division remained in Ireland to reinforce the garrison, which
consisted mainly of Irish troops : Special Reserve units of Irish regiments
and newly raised reserve battalions which supplied drafts to their Service
battalions.

[4] 47 British and 9 Dominion. There were also 5 cavalry divisions. In
addition to the divisions mentioned in " 1916 " Vol. I. (p. 24), as having
arrived in France during the period January-July 1916, the 4th Canadian
Division landed early in August. It brought no artillery, and the Lahore
Division batteries, which had been with the 3rd Canadian Division (see
" 1916 " Vol. I., p. 20, f.n. 1), were therefore attached to it.

Aug. direction of Monastir ; the Italians were planning to resume their attacks on the Isonzo ; Rumanian forces were invading Transylvania ; and Brusilov had not yet relaxed his efforts. At the end of August, therefore, a redoubled effort in the West appeared to be due, for the purpose of sustaining and encouraging the Allied operations launched, or about to be launched elsewhere, and of preventing the despatch of further German reinforcements from France to other theatres of war. Such action could only take the form of renewed pressure on the Somme, to which offensive the British resources in France had been fully committed ; [1] it was impossible to break off the struggle and try elsewhere, apart from the fact that such a confession of failure would have done incalculable moral damage to the cause.

Sir William Robertson has observed that, " while certain " Ministers thought Haig was doing too much fighting, the " French military authorities complained that he was doing " too little ".[2] On the 25th August, General Joffre had pressed for the 5th September as the date of the big Allied offensive already agreed upon between the two Commanders-in-Chief.[3] In Sir Douglas Haig's view, however, the capture of the Falfemont Farm—Guillemont—Ginchy position by the Fourth Army—in co-operation with a further advance by the French Sixth Army north of the Somme—was an essential preliminary to the big attack ; and this operation was postponed, later, as we have seen, on account of unfavourable weather, until the 3rd September. On the 27th August he replied to General Joffre, explaining that, after the above objectives had been secured, it would be necessary to relieve nearly all his divisions and to redistribute his heavy artillery ; he therefore estimated that the big attack could not be launched before the middle of September " at the earliest " ; and he expressed the hope that the French would then co-operate to the fullest possible extent. Next day brought General Joffre's reluctant acquiescence in this arrangement [4] and his assurance that, when the British did attack, the French would give the utmost support to their right wing.

Sketch 31.
G.H.Q. assumed that during the early part of September the right of the Fourth Army would reach the line Leuze

---

[1] See " 1916 " Vol. I., p. 265.
[2] " Soldiers and Statesmen," i., p. 271.   [3] See page 182.
[4] F.O.A. iv. (ii.), pp. 286-7.

Sketch 31.

THE SOMME, 1916:
Plan of
mid-September Offensive
(Battle of Flers-Courcelette).

Scale of Miles.

½ 0 1 2 3 4

Heights in metres.

REFERENCE.

Principal German Defences.	
British Front Line	
French "	
1st Objective (Green Line)	
2nd " (Brown ")	
3rd " (Blue ")	
4th " (Red ")	
Extent of projected break-through.	X o o o o X
Direction of French Attacks.	→

Ordnance Survey 1937.

Compiled in the Historical Section (Military Branch).

3060/38.

CAMBRAI 16 m.

ARRAS 11 m.

Achiet le Gd.

Achiet le Pt.

Bapaume

Grévillers

Warlencourt

Grandcourt

Pusieux au M.

Serre

Mirauimont

Beaucourt

Beaumont Hamel

St. Pierre Divion

Thiepval

Ovillers

la Boiselle

Pozières

Contalmaison

Bazentin

Martinpuich

Courcelette

le Sars

Pys

Irles

Finlay

Ligny

Beaulencourt

Ie.Transloy

Lesboeufs

Morval

Sailly Saillisel

PERONNE 5 m.

Frégicourt

Rancourt

Combles

Guillemont

Ginchy

Longueval

Delville Wd.

Flers

Gueudecourt

Fricourt

Mametz

Montauban

ALBERT

ANCRE

RESERVE V.

II.

CDN.

III.

FOURTH

XV.

XIV.

SIXTH

Wood—Ginchy. General Rawlinson would then be con- Aug.
fronted by the Combles defences which, continuing towards
Flers, linked up with the oft-mentioned Switch Line. The
latter, branching forward from the German 3rd Position
about half a mile south-east of Flers, was still uncaptured
as far west as the Bazentin le Petit—Martinpuich road,
where it joined the defences of Martinpuich. Farther back
lay the German 3rd Position. Under construction when
the offensive opened on the 1st July, this line had been
worked upon assiduously and was now of considerable
strength : from the head of the Combles ravine it ran across
the easternmost spur of the main ridge and thence north-
westward along the lower ground to the Ancre, incorporating—opposite the Fourth Army front—the defences
of Morval, Flers, Eaucourt l'Abbaye and Le Sars. From
the ridge west of Morval there branched away a back line
which covered the villages of Lesbœufs and Gueudecourt
before turning westward beyond the Bapaume road to link
up with the 3rd Position again. In rear of this position the
enemy was known to be digging a further series of defences,
but the intention was to deal him such a blow as to render
him incapable of maintaining a solid front on the newly
entrenched line.

Instructions, dated the 16th August, from G.H.Q. to the
Fourth and Reserve Armies [1] announced that it was hoped
to make use of fifty or sixty tanks (" Heavy Section "
armoured cars), which were expected to arrive from England
" during the next few weeks ", in offensive operations on a
large scale about the middle of September. The objective
of the Fourth Army might be the German 3rd Position
from Morval to Le Sars (both inclusive), " and possibly
" the gun positions beyond " ; that of the Reserve Army
the continuation of this line from Le Sars to Pys, and the
formation of a defensive flank along the Ancre. A list of
the fresh troops available showed eight divisions for the
Fourth Army and six for the Reserve Army, the allotment
of tanks being tentatively fixed at 36-42 and 18-24,
respectively. The scope of this operation was more clearly
defined by G.H.Q. in its communication of the 19th,[2] which
stated that the main attack would be pressed south-east of
the Albert—Bapaume road " with the object of securing
the " enemy's last line of prepared defences between Morval
" and Le Sars with a view to opening the way for the
" cavalry ". A flank guard of all arms would then be

[1] Appendix 15.   [2] Appendix 16.

Aug. established on the line Morval—Le Transloy—Bapaume, whilst an attack north-westward was pressed in co-operation with the frontal offensive. Fifty tanks were now to be allotted to the Fourth Army; if more than that number had arrived in France, one or more sections [1] would probably be available for the Reserve Army. Generals Rawlinson and Gough were required to submit their plans of attack by the 28th August, showing how they proposed to employ the tanks.

As early as the 3rd December 1915 Mr. Churchill had submitted to the War Committee his " Memoranda on " Variants of the Offensive " [2] in which the capabilities of " caterpillars ", as the machines were called, were brought to notice, and suggestions for their employment offered. The section concerning them began : " The cutting of the " enemy's wire and the general domination of his firing line " can be effected by engines of this character. About " seventy are now nearing completion in England and " should be inspected. None should be used until all can " be used at once. They should be disposed secretly along " the whole attacking front two or three hundred yards " apart ". The section closed with the words : " Above all " *surprise* ".[3]

This paper was shown, before it was printed, to Field-Marshal Sir John French, but not to Sir Douglas Haig. In February 1916, however, Lieut.-Colonel (now Major-General Sir E. D.) Swinton, then Assistant-Secretary of the War Committee, drew up a paper [4] which described the construction, armament, capabilities, and limitations of the tank ; it also included very comprehensive suggestions for its employment. This paper was printed for circulation to the War Committee in February 1916,[5] and the tactical principles set forth in it won the approval of Sir Douglas Haig. They are of considerable significance and may be summarized as follows :

The chance of success of the new arm lies in its ability to effect a complete surprise, and therefore the machines should

---

[1] There were six tanks in a section.
[2] Printed as a Committee of Imperial Defence paper, dated 7th January 1916.
[3] Appendix 17 which reproduces Mr. Churchill's paragraphs on " caterpillars ".
[4] Appendix 18.
[5] After its receipt at G.H.Q. in April, a copy was sent to General Rawlinson, but not, it would appear, to General Gough.

not be used " in driblets " ; the fact of their existence should be
kept secret until " the whole are ready to be launched together
" with the infantry assault in one great combined operation ".
Tanks to attack in line at least 100 yards apart which, reckoning
on 90 machines, gives a frontage of, approximately, five miles.

The initial assembly positions, well camouflaged, to be about
two miles behind the British line whence the routes forward
must be carefully reconnoitred. The next move, carried out by
night, to bring the machines to a position of readiness immediately in rear of the front trenches ; the attack to be delivered
just before dawn, when there is sufficient visibility to move but
too little to present a target to the enemy artillery.

Gas and smoke might profitably be employed in the attack.
The tanks to precede the infantry and draw the rifle and
machine-gun fire of the German first system, the infantry
following in time to reach the front trench at the moment when
the machines have climbed the parapet and are beginning to
enfilade the line. As soon as the infantry have the situation in
hand the tanks to resume the advance, preferably along the
communication trenches to the next objective. Large forces of
infantry to be sent forward at the outset in order to keep the
momentum of the attack going through the successive enemy
positions. Strong bodies of bombers would be required to
attend the tanks and deal with deep dug-outs and cellars.

The whole mass of the tank-infantry attack should be able
to move quickly enough to keep ahead of the German barrage
when it first falls, and to continue to do so as the enemy shortens
his range during the progress of the advance. Thus the best
results would be obtained by an attempted " break-through ",
rather than by a step-by-step progression with special artillery
preparation at each stage. A tank will carry enough petrol for
a 60 miles' run,[1] and an advance of 12 miles is therefore well
within its capabilities over any but very unfavourable ground.
Thus our troops might expect to get right through the German
defensive zone in one operation, and preparations to send
forward guns, reinforcements, ammunition and supplies should
be made accordingly.

It would not be possible to dispense with the usual wire-
cutting by artillery and trench-mortars before the assault, if the
free passage of the infantry were to be assured : a tank could
only crush its own width of entanglement. An elaborate
bombardment of the lines in rear, rarely effective, as has been
proved, should not be needed ; but, as the tanks are highly
vulnerable to shell-fire, counter-battery work becomes of
paramount importance and probably involves a special concentration of heavy artillery, with improved air reconnaissance

---

[1] This aspiration was not fulfilled. The " estimated mileage without
" refilling " of the Mark I. tank was 23.

and observation. Every possible means should, indeed, be taken to neutralize or destroy the German batteries, including the employment of lethal gas shell in large quantities and of bombing aeroplanes.

Finally, the tanks should be under infantry command, as their rôle is that of auxiliary to the infantry arm.

Aug.   With the instructions of the 16th August, however, G.H.Q. had sent to the Fourth and Reserve Armies its own description of the tanks and their organization and equipment, with special " preliminary notes on tactical employ-" ment of tanks ".[1]   The vulnerability of the machine to shell-fire was emphasized.   " Its safety lies in surprise, in " rapid movement, and in getting to close quarters.   It " must emerge from cover (either material cover or the cover " of smoke or darkness), and it must return to cover or " find other concealment or safety when its task is done. " Also it must have the infantry with it."

It was therefore directed by G.H.Q. that the tanks should be used against the villages, woods, strongpoints, and hidden machine-gun positions which experience had shown were the chief obstacles to the success of an infantry assault.   " Such objectives could generally be identified " previously ",[2] and against each of these would move an allotted number of tanks closely supported by infantry : every tank-infantry attack to be a definite, limited operation, under one commander.   " Whenever tanks are " employed special attention must be paid to counter-" battery work, and the tank should move under cover of a " close barrage which should not lift from the objective " until the tanks are close to it."   Individual tanks might also be used for various purposes behind the battle-line, and it was suggested that their 6-pdr. guns might prove of great value in close support of the infantry during the final stages of an assault ; but the attack in groups or pairs against selected objectives would be their principal rôle.

Thus the small number of tanks available had assisted to modify the original conception of their tactical employment.   In effect, the method advocated by G.H.Q. was, perhaps, better adapted to a step-by-step advance than to a single operation which partook of the nature of a " break-" through ".   So, at least, thought General Rawlinson whose Army was to deliver the main blow.   In any case, he wished to run no risks of leaving a number of tanks stranded

---

[1] Appendix 15.
[2] The experience of the fighting troops was very much to the contrary.

behind the German lines, and thus exposing to the enemy Aug. the secrets of their construction.

Influenced by the fact that there would be a full moon on the 11th September, General Rawlinson proposed to effect a break-through by operations extending over three successive nights. His three corps would each have two of the fresh divisions in line and two others in reserve. On the first night the tanks would be used by moonlight to " put the infantry into " the first objective, Combles— Sketch Bouleaux Wood—Flers—High Wood—Martinpuich, the 31. machines withdrawing to cover behind the old British front line by dawn, when artillery could be moved forward. Thus the centre corps would gain a footing in the German 3rd Position at Flers. On the following night the tanks would assist in effecting a lodgment in the back line near Lesboeufs, and two sections (12 machines) might move along the 3rd Position from Flers to Le Sars. Infantry would occupy the position as it was cleared by the tanks, the latter returning before daylight down the Bapaume road ; but the capture of Courcelette by the Reserve Army would be necessary in order to safeguard the left flank. On the third night the capture of the back line from Lesboeufs to the Bapaume road would be effected by the method employed on the first night.

The plan did not commend itself to Sir Douglas Haig, who doubted whether it would be possible for the tanks to move forward and back through three successive nights ; moreover, he required bolder measures at the first onset. On the last day of the month he issued further instructions,[1] emphasizing that the attack must be planned as a decisive operation : the commander of the Fourth Army was to secure as quickly as possible Morval, Lesboeufs, Flers and Gueudecourt, thus penetrating the last defensive system at its nearest point and creating a gap for the passage of the cavalry. A strong force of all arms was then to establish a flank position on the line Morval—Le Transloy— Bapaume and also assist in the rolling up of the enemy defences to the north-west, whilst these were being heavily attacked from the front. Great boldness and determination were required of all ranks, for it was of great importance to reach without delay the enemy's artillery positions and so capture his guns.

The Commander-in-Chief's views had already been conveyed verbally to General Rawlinson by Lieut.-General

[1] Appendix 19.

R

Aug. Kiggell, and after a Fourth Army conference, at which the corps commanders and their chief general staff and artillery officers were present, a new plan was submitted on the 31st August. General Rawlinson now proposed to make a weightier thrust on a narrower front whilst attacking strongly along his whole line. Morval, Lesboeufs, Flers and Gueudecourt would all be captured on the first day, the left flank of this advance being protected by taking up a line running from the south of Martinpuich to a point in the German 3rd Position north-west of Flers. On the right a defensive flank would be formed from Falfemont Farm to Morval, eventually joining hands with the French at Sailly-Saillisel and thus " pinching out " Combles. Each corps would use three divisions in line,[1] and most of the tanks would be allotted to the XIV. and XV. Corps, which were to deliver the main attack. The machines were to advance in small groups, moving a little ahead of the infantry, to reduce strongpoints and trench junctions, and going forward to the next trench line when one system was secured.

As regards the cavalry, General Rawlinson advocated that the five divisions be disposed one behind the other, with the head of the force west of Montauban. Lieut.-General C. T. McM. Kavanagh, who was to command the Cavalry Corps,[2] should decide when, where and in what force to advance, acting on reports which he was to receive direct from the XIV. and XV. Corps.

The corps commanders of the Fourth Army had been warned of the supreme importance of " forcing the battle " to a decision at the earliest possible moment " ; but General Rawlinson, who had also gone into the question of moving forward the artillery, considered that his most difficult problem might be the maintenance of communications which would involve " the rapid reconstruction of " roads . . . to enable this large force to be supplied with " food and ammunition when they have gained the more " distant line of villages. We shall require all the labour " battalions we can muster in order to carry out this work " expeditiously, and on the success or failure of their

---

[1] The total frontage of this projected attack was about 10,000 yards, of which the XIV. and XV. Corps were each allotted some 3,000 yards. The extreme left of the III. Corps, holding a rather wider front, would only have to advance about 300 yards, and its extreme right about 2,000 yards, whereas the tasks of the other corps involved an advance of from 3,500 to nearly 4,000 yards.

[2] He relinquished the command of the I. Corps to do so, and a cavalry corps staff was assembled.

" endeavours will depend whether we can maintain our-
" selves on this high waterless and roadless plateau after
" we have captured it." [1]

Sir Douglas now had little criticism to offer, but wanted
tanks and infantry to " start and advance level to the first
" objective ", the tanks making for the strongpoints whilst
the infantry, covered by the usual field artillery barrage,
stormed the intermediate lengths of trench. He thought,
however, that the tanks might have to anticipate the
arrival of the infantry in the support or reserve trenches of
the front system in order to quench the fire from these
positions.

General Gough's plan contained no detailed proposals
for the employment of the tanks : he preferred to wait till
he " knew more of their capabilities ". Primarily he was
concerned with the capture of Courcelette. If he had
already carried Thiepval his advance would be north-
eastward with his right on the Bapaume road, his left
securing the German trenches along the spur between
Courcelette and the German 2nd Position north of Mouquet
Farm. If Thiepval had not yet fallen, he would have to
clear the 2nd Position as far as Zollern Graben as a preliminary operation. Subsequently, he would push forward
down the spurs towards Pys, occupying the high ground
above Miraumont.

In conveying his approval on the 1st September, the Sept.
Commander-in-Chief informed General Gough that Martinpuich would be assaulted by the Fourth Army simultaneously with the attack on Courcelette. Later in the day,
however, Lieut.-General Kiggell saw each Army commander separately and found that, whilst General Gough
regarded the capture of Martinpuich as essential to his plan,
General Rawlinson was not disposed to attempt it during
the first advance, as he considered that his III. Corps was
not strong enough for this additional task. He wished to
deal with the village by envelopment at a later stage, and
spoke personally on the telephone to Sir Douglas Haig, who
agreed to this course.

Thus by the 1st September the general plan for the

---

[1] The commander of the Fourth Army personally regarded the offensive
as a legitimate gamble. " We shall have no reserves in hand, except tired
" troops, but success at this time would have a great effect throughout the
" world and might bring the Boche to terms. If we fail, we shall have all
" the winter in which to recuperate, and there will be no counter-attack
" left in the enemy. It is worth the risk." " Life of General Lord
" Rawlinson " by Major-General Sir F. Maurice, p. 170.

Sept. break-through, fixed on that day for the 15th of the month, was settled, and the rôle of the tanks defined. The time for preparation was short when it is considered that many of the machines could only arrive in time to go straight into action ; that commanders and staffs were for the most part quite unfamiliar with the tanks ; that the preliminary training of infantry and tanks together was essential to success ; that the programme of artillery bombardment and support had to be adapted to the special conditions created by the introduction of the new weapon ; and that problems of supply were complicated by the assembly of the large force of cavalry.

Sir Douglas Haig had definite plans for the participation of the other British Armies in the event of a break-through. On the 6th September he warned the Third Army to be prepared to attack in the vicinity of Gommecourt about the 20th, with the object of penetrating the hostile defences on Sketch A. a wide front between Bucquoy and Monchy : the heavy artillery should assist the counter-battery work of the Reserve Army which, it was hoped, would then be advancing northward towards Achiet le Grand and Achiet le Petit. In this case, the Third Army would also engage the enemy along its whole front south of the Scarpe. At the same time, the First Army, which was also promised tank assistance, was told to prepare for the assault of Vimy Ridge on the 30th September in co-operation with the further advance of the Third, Reserve and Fourth Armies.

On the 7th September the Commander-in-Chief instructed the Second Army to start an aggressive policy of raids and bombardments about the middle of the month. So far as his resources permitted, General Plumer was also to press on with his preparations for the capture of Mount Sorrel and of the Messines—Wytschaete ridge.

In co-operation with Vice-Admiral R. H. S. Bacon, commanding the Dover Patrol, and with the Home authorities, Sir Douglas Haig also arranged a demonstration to persuade the Germans that a landing was intended on the Belgian coast. On the 11th September a brigade of the 4th Division, with one brigade of field artillery, marched through Dunkirk to the docks and embarked infantry in lighters and guns in a monitor. The troops returned in the evening, and repeated the whole movement next day.[1]

---

[1] " Trutzig und Treu ", by Admiral Jacobsen commanding the *1st Marine Division*, states that agents and reconnoitring aeroplanes reported

On the 9th September, the day that Ginchy was taken,[1] Sept.
General Joffre again urged Sir Douglas Haig to hasten the
date of the big British attack.   In his letter he expressed
his conviction that the German forces and defences opposite
the junction of the Allied Armies were in a weakened condition, and his disbelief in the preliminary operations
judged necessary by his confrère.   The British Commander-in-Chief could only regret his inability to comply ;
but he hoped that General Foch would find it possible
to capture Frégicourt, and so cover General Rawlinson's Sketch
right, before the British advance began.   On the 12th, 31.
General Joffre promised that Frégicourt should be attacked
as soon as his Sixth Army had taken its first objectives and
changed the direction of its advance northward ; [2] and he
suggested the advisability of capturing in the first advance
both Martinpuich and Courcelette on the left of the main
attack.   This suggestion was not without influence on the
British plans.[3]

NOTE

The Evolution of the Tank [4]

In pre-War days several inventors had evolved designs for
machines calculated, more or less, to fulfil the functions of what
was afterwards known as the " Tank ".   One such design was submitted in 1911 to the Austro-Hungarian Government ; which took
no action.   Mr. L. E. de Mole, an Australian engineer, forwarded
to the War Office in 1912 plans and specifications for a machine

---

naval preparations at Sheerness and Dover and landing exercises at Dunkirk ; there were fears of a British landing, and the Belgian coast defences
were strengthened and reinforced.

On 18th September, Sir Douglas Haig discussed plans for an actual
landing with Vice-Admiral Bacon.   The project had been examined in
1915 and again in early 1916 (See " 1916 " Vol. I.).   It was to be revived
in 1917.

[1] See Chapter X.

[2] The French had begun their big offensive north of the Somme on 3rd
September ; fighting died down on the 6th and operations on a large scale
were resumed on the 12th.   See Note at end of Chapter X.

[3] See Chapter XI.

[4] The Minutes of the Proceedings (October 1919) and the Findings
(November 1919) of the Royal Commission on Awards to Inventors (Claims
in Respect of the Invention of Tanks) have been consulted and are frequently quoted herein.   There are many books to which reference may be
made for further details, notably Major-General Sir Ernest Swinton's
" Eyewitness " ; Sir Albert Stern's " Tanks 1914–18 : The Log-Book of a
" Pioneer " ; Rear-Admiral Sir Murray Sueter's " The Evolution of the
" Tank " ; and Mr. Winston Churchill's " The World Crisis " (abridged
and revised edition).

" which anticipated and in some respects surpassed that actually " put into use in the year 1916 ". This invention was " put aside " because the occasion for its use had not then arisen ", and no further attention was ever given to it. In Berlin a German inventor gave a not very successful demonstration of his " land-cruiser " in 1913.

Caterpillar tractors for the road transport of heavy guns were, however, being used by the British Army in 1908 and Major (now Major-General Sir) E. D. Swinton, R.E., heard of the Holt tractor, which did cross-country work, in July 1914. Very early in the War he concerned himself with the problem of finding an effective answer to the German machine-gun defence, which in 1915 took such heavy toll of the British infantry. His first conception of a " machine-gun " destroyer ", able to negotiate wire and trenches, dates from October 1914, when, after discussing it at G.H.Q. with Major-General G. H. Fowke, the Engineer-in-Chief, he communicated it to Lieut.-Colonel (now Sir Maurice) Hankey, Secretary of the War Council.

Although still serving in France as " Eye-witness ",[1] Major Swinton made many unsuccessful attempts between October 1914 and May 1915, both at G.H.Q. and in London, to get his project taken up.

On the 4th January 1915, being on leave from France, he called upon the Director of Fortifications and Works [2] (Major-General G. K. Scott-Moncrieff), who promised to have the matter investigated. After speaking to the Director of Artillery (Major-General H. G. Smith) and the Assistant Director of Transport (Colonel H. C. L. Holden), as guns and mechanical transport were involved, General Scott-Moncrieff wrote next day to the Master-General of the Ordnance (Major-General Sir Stanley von Donop). The next step was the formation of an " informal committee " which witnessed early in February 1915 the trial of a Holt tractor dragging a truck of 5,000 lbs. weight over a course of trenches, barbed wire, and other obstacles at Shoeburyness. On the 13th February the A.D.T. reported in a letter to the M.G.O. that the result was unsatisfactory ; and on the 1st March Major-General Scott-Moncrieff asked the A.D.T. if he could suggest the name of any firm competent to design a suitable " land " cruiser ". Colonel Holden replied on the same day, " I am afraid I " cannot ", and no further action was taken.

Colonel Hankey had embodied the Swinton proposals in a " Memorandum on Methods of Attack ", dated 28th December 1914 and circulated to the members of the War Council at the beginning of January 1915. Mr. Winston Churchill, First Lord of the Admiralty, welcomed this paper as likely to forward a project which he already had at heart. Major Swinton's activities were quite unknown to him, but as early as October 1914 he had asked Rear-Admiral Bacon (as he then was), the general manager of the Coventry Ordnance Works, to adapt for the crossing of trenches a caterpillar tractor designed for the haulage of 15-inch howitzer equipment. Mr. Churchill wrote privately to Mr. Asquith, the Prime Minister, on the 5th January 1915 urging the necessity of experimenting with an armoured caterpillar tractor which would crush wire-entangle-

---

[1] See " 1916 " Vol. I., p. 145.
[2] The chief Royal Engineer appointment in the Army since the abolition of that of Inspector-General of Fortifications by the Esher Committee, 1905.

ments and cross trenches. His letter was handed by the Prime Minister to Lord Kitchener, who passed it, with instructions for the necessary research to be carried out, to the M.G.O. Eventually, but not until the 9th June 1915, a War Office committee held a trial of the Bacon tractor—it possessed 8-feet driving wheels and portable bridging gear—over the Shoeburyness course. This machine proved incapable of crossing a double line of trenches five feet across, and nothing more was done.

Thus failed two efforts to procure for the Army an armoured fighting vehicle intended to increase the power of the offensive in trench warfare. The evolution of the tank was due to research and experiment conducted, under Mr. Churchill's patronage, independently in an entirely different quarter. The Armoured Car Division of the R.N.A.S., commanded by Commander (now Captain R.N.) F. L. M. Boothby, had been occupied since September 1914 with plans for the development of the armoured car into a cross-country fighting vehicle. On the 19th January 1915 Mr. Churchill, who was not content to rely upon the outcome of his letter to the Prime Minister, instructed Commodore F. M. (now Rear-Admiral Sir Murray) Sueter, Director of the Air Department at the Admiralty, to experiment with steam-rollers as a trench-smashing agency. In February, however, Major (now Group Captain) T. G. Hetherington, R.N.A.S., laid before the First Lord of the Admiralty designs for a " land battleship ", and before the end of the month Mr. Churchill had sanctioned the formation of a " Landship Committee " to organize and control the work of evolving an armoured fighting vehicle which could negotiate trenches and wire. To provide for the necessary expenditure he made, upon his own responsibility, an allotment from Admiralty funds. Mr. (now Sir) Eustace H. W. Tennyson-d'Eyncourt, Director of Naval Construction, was appointed chairman of the committee, and the services of Colonel R. E. Crompton [1] and Mr. L. A. Le Gros were secured as consultants. Under this direction valuable work in the way of design and experiment was carried out in the strictest secrecy by the Armoured Car Division of the R.N.A.S. ; but ignorance of the Army's exact requirements proved a great handicap. A deputation of three officers, unsponsored by the War Office and Admiralty, which visited G.H.Q. to obtain information was obliged to return without it.

In the Army in France there was no lack of ideas for providing a way out of the " siege-warfare in the field " *impasse*. For instance, in June 1915, Major (now Colonel) A. I. R. Glasfurd, a brigade-major in the 9th Division, submitted a scheme for negotiating wire and trenches by means of a " ped-rail " machine : an armoured motor vehicle fitted with machine guns, a lethal spray and a grapnel. Suggestions for its tactical employment were included, but no action appeared to have been taken by G.H.Q., although the General Staff had an " Experimental Branch ".[2]

Early in June 1915 the attention of Sir John French was at last directed to Lieut.-Colonel Swinton's detailed proposals for the con-

[1] A retired officer who had served with R.E. in South Africa, and naval " veteran " of the Crimean War, he had a great reputation as an expert on road traction problems ; he was also an engineer of remarkably comprehensive knowledge and experience.

[2] Subsequently handed over to the R.E.

struction and use of " caterpillar machine-gun destroyers ", and later in the month the Swinton memoranda were forwarded by G.H.Q. to the War Office. At the end of June the War Office got into touch with the Admiralty committee, which were then given full details of what the Army required the machine to do. By this time Mr. Churchill had left the Admiralty, but as a member of the War Committee he used all his influence to facilitate the work of research, experiment and construction. " It was primarily due to the recep- " tivity, courage and driving force of Mr. Winston Churchill that the " general idea of the user of such an instrument of warfare as the " ' Tank ' was converted into a practical shape." [1]

At the end of August Colonel Swinton, then acting Secretary of the Dardanelles Committee,[2] was the prime mover, with the backing of the Prime Minister, in effecting proper co-ordination of effort : experiment and design under the Admiralty working to War Office requirements ; manufacture, the responsibility of the Ministry of Munitions. The Admiralty committee, later called the " Tank " Supply Committee " in the interests of secrecy,[3] came directly under the Ministry in February 1916. Lieutenant (now Lieut.-Colonel Sir Albert) A. G. Stern, R.N.A.S., who had done splendid service as secretary since the original formation, became chairman, and among the members were Colonel Swinton and Mr. d'Eyncourt.

The machine eventually evolved by Mr. (now Sir) William A. Tritton, of Messrs. William Foster & Company, Ltd., Lincoln, and Lieutenant (now Major) W. G. Wilson, R.N.A.S., was given a secret trial at Hatfield on the 2nd February 1916 before a distinguished company, which included Lord Kitchener, Sir William Robertson, Mr. Balfour (First Lord of the Admiralty) and Mr. Lloyd George (Minister of Munitions), with representatives of the War Office and of G.H.Q. France. The results were deemed so satisfactory that an order for 100 of this model, known as " Mother " and the prototype of the Mark I. tank, was given later in the month.

The personnel necessary for the experimental ground work carried out under the Landships Committee and Tank Supply Committee was provided throughout by the officers and ratings of No. 20 Squadron, R.N. Armoured Car Division. In March 1916 Colonel Swinton was appointed to raise and command the new unit which was to man the tanks. This unit, christened " Heavy Branch " Machine-Gun Corps " [4] in May, took in from the motor machine-gun batteries which were being disbanded about 700 partly-trained men. Many of these proved unsuitable for the new arm of the service, and the same must be said of the drivers transferred from the Army Service Corps (Mechanical Transport). The junior officers, of whom only a few possessed engineering experience, were partly

[1] Minutes of the Proceedings of the Royal Commission on Awards to Inventors.

[2] In the absence of Colonel Hankey at the Dardanelles. The War Council had been renamed the " Dardanelles Committee " in May 1915 (see " 1914 " Vol. II., pp. 10-11).

[3] The box-like body of the machine suggested that some such name as " reservoir " or " cistern " be employed, in order to conceal its real purpose. " Tank " was adopted on 24th December 1915. In September 1916 the tanks were referred to in some G.H.Q. and Fourth Army messages as " armadillos ".

[4] It became the Tank Corps in June 1917.

selected from cadet units [1] ; most of the seniors were Regulars.   The first " establishment " provided for 6 companies each of 25 tanks with a personnel of 28 officers and 255 other ranks.[2]   Preliminary instruction was carried out at a camp near Bisley.   In June, as soon as some tanks were available, intensive training began at Elveden (near Thetford), Suffolk.   The way in which the secret of the new weapon was kept throughout the whole period of research, manufacture and training was " one of the most remarkable exhibitions " of patriotic restraint in the whole course of the War ".[3]

Two types of the Mark I. tank were used in the Somme battles ; the following are particulars of the more heavily armed, or " male ", machine :

Length (with tail) . . .	32' 6"
,, (without tail) . .	26' 5"
Width	13' 9"
Height to top of tracks . .	7' 4½"
Weight, fully equipped . .	28 tons
Engine	6-cyl. 105 h.p. Daimler
Maximum speed . . .	3.7 m.p.h.
Petrol capacity . . .	46 gallons
Estimated mileage without refilling	23
Maximum width of trench that could be crossed . . .	10' 0"
Armament	two 6-pdrs. and 4 Hotchkiss machine guns
Ammunition carried . . .	324 rounds of 6-pdr. 6,272 S.A.A.
Crew	1 officer, 7 other ranks.

The " tail ", two heavy wheels at the rear, was an additional aid to steering, but its primary object was to help the tank over rough ground and to minimize the shock when the machine, so to speak, " took a fence ".   As its wheels were continually getting out of order and its connections liable to break, the tail was abandoned in later types of tank.

The " female ", designed particularly to deal with a rush from close quarters, had an armament of machine guns only, 5 Vickers and 1 Hotchkiss, and carried a much greater supply of S.A.A. ; its weight was 27 tons.   In other respects it was identical with the " male ".

---

[1] On 14th February 1916 the Army Council decided that all candidates for temporary commissions, other than those with previous military experience as officers, should pass through a cadet unit.   These were formed at home as follows : Cavalry cadet squadrons attached to reserve cavalry regiments; R.A. cadet schools attached to certain artillery training brigades; R.E. cadet schools at training centres ; Infantry cadet battalions.

[2] See Appendix 15 for details.

[3] " Eyewitness ", p. 247.

CHAPTER X

THE CAPTURE OF GUILLEMONT, FALFEMONT FARM AND
LEUZE WOOD [1]

1 Sept. EARLY on the 1st September the XV. Corps took measures
to regain the positions lost on the previous evening.[2]   In
the 24th Division the 2/Leinster (73rd Brigade) attempted
a bombing attack soon after daybreak along Orchard
Trench, but the opposition proved too strong.   Another
effort, made with bombers from the right of the Pear Street
line at 9.50 A.M., also failed.   In the afternoon, however,
the 3/Rifle Brigade (17th Brigade) was brought up, and at
6.30 P.M. the battalion cleared the Germans from Orchard
Trench by frontal assault, also securing Wood Lane as far
as a point just short of the enemy barricade at the Tea
Trench junction.   Casualties were so heavy that the attack
could not be carried forward against Tea Trench, which was
strongly held and appeared to have suffered little from the
British bombardment.

The 91st Brigade (7th Division), on the eastern side of
Delville Wood, had put in two platoons of the 2/Queen's at
5 A.M. to bomb along the edge as far as Hop Alley, but the
attack failed under machine-gun and rifle fire.   At 3 P.M.
the 1/North Staffordshire—right battalion of the 24th
Division—bombed forward for some twenty yards down
Edge Trench.   The trenches in this quarter had been

---

[1] The official name " Battle of Guillemont ", 3rd-6th September, covers
the front Combles ravine—Longueval, thus including the XV. Corps
attacks on Ginchy 3rd-6th September, and the operations (also XV. Corps)
at the eastern end of Delville Wood.   [2] See page 207 and Sketch 28.

Sketch 32.

XII R.

COMBLES

BOIS DOUAGE

FRENCH

XV.

Giuchy

Ginchy

LEUZE WOOD

The Quadrilateral

THE QUADRILATERAL

Quarry

Faffemont Fm.

48

WEDGE WOOD

ANGLE WOOD

Guillemont

Brickfield

Fort

20.

5.

Waltz Horn Fm.

ARROW HEAD COPSE

Waterlot Fm.

LONGUEVAL ¾ m.

TRÔNES WOOD

XIV.

BERNAFAY WOOD

MONTAUBAN ¾ m.

HARDECOURT

MADAME WOOD

3RD–6TH SEPTEMBER, 1916.
XIV Corps Operations.

British assembly trenches ⌐⌐⌐⌐   German trenches ⌐⌐⌐⌐
Line reached 3rd Sept ○○○○   Line reached 5th Sept. ●●●●
            4th ●●●●   6th ●●●●

Scale of Yards.
500   0   500   1000

Heights in metres.

Ordnance Survey 1937.

Crown Copyright Reserved.

Compiled in the Historical Section (Military Branch).
3060/38

nearly obliterated by repeated bombardment, and at noon 1-2 Sept. next day, when the Queen's tried again, little ground was gained among the shell craters in the face of snipers and bombers. The failure to dislodge the Germans from the eastern corner of the wood and the trenches near by was fraught with most unfortunate consequences, as will be seen in due course.

Preparations for the attack of the Fourth Army in co-operation with the French were pushed on apace : no rain had fallen since the 30th August, and conditions promised to continue favourable for the 3rd September. At 8 A.M. on the 2nd the preliminary bombardment opened on the fronts of the XIV. and XV. Corps, and also on that of the 1st Division (III. Corps) which was to attack Wood Lane and the German front line at High Wood. The hostile artillery had been generally active during the previous night, but now retaliated chiefly upon the XV. Corps, the forward trenches dug by the 7th Division for the assault on Ginchy being shelled for the first time.

Except in the XIV. Corps there was to be no quickening of the rate of heavy artillery fire previous to the assault. At intervals during the preparatory bombardment field batteries searched with shrapnel the ground between the German main positions in order to deal with the many machine-gun posts established there. The rolling or creeping barrage which was to cover the advance of the infantry was now an established practice and the troops were becoming accustomed to keeping as close as possible to it.[1]

In order to reach a more favourable position from which Sketch to launch the mid-September offensive, the final objective 32. of the XIV. Corps was now to be a line facing north-eastward through the farther edge of Leuze Wood, thus securing the spur above Combles. The right of the corps, on the slope of the ravine, was expected to gain touch with the French advance on Savernake Wood.[2] It had been

---

[1] The 5th Division (attacking on the right next to the French) ordered the infantry to keep about 25 yards behind the barrage, which was to move at the rate of 50 yards per minute.

[2] In the Fourth Army instruction of 25th August, and in the XIV. Corps operation order of the 28th, the Combles ravine was named, quite properly, as inclusive to the French. Subsequent instructions issued by the corps gave the point of junction with the French, after the capture of the final objective, as the light railway in the ravine, a disposition which was tactically unsound, as the ravine thus became a divided responsibility. The 5th Division operation order, issued on 1st September, named the railway as the boundary from the outset.

arranged with the French Sixth Army that Falfemont Farm should be stormed, as a preliminary operation, at 9 A.M. on the 3rd when the French left (I. Corps), which had reached the edge of Oakhanger Wood, would also advance. The main attack along the whole Allied front would be delivered at noon.

3 Sept.   Major-General Stephens's 5th Division (right division of the corps) had its 13th Brigade (Br.-General L. O. W. Jones) in assembly trenches on the slope of the Leuze Wood spur, some four hundred yards from Falfemont Farm [1] in the German 2nd Position. The attack on this objective was made by the 2/K.O.S.B., which started forward in perfect order at 8.50 A.M., its right directed upon Point 48 and its left upon the north-western corner of the farm enclosure. Unfortunately the French 127th Regiment, in the ravine, was prevented from moving by the fire of German machine guns ; worse still, the barrage of French 75's intended to cover the advance of the Borderers did not open.[2] Smitten by rifle and machine-gun fire in front and flank, the battalion lost nearly three hundred of all ranks in a very gallant attempt to carry out its impossible task. Some observers reported that the assault had succeeded : there was certainly no withdrawal of the leading lines for all lay killed or wounded. As soon as the truth became known at brigade headquarters preparations were made for another attempt. Meanwhile the enemy began to shell the assembly trenches of the brigade.

Punctually at noon the 95th Brigade (Br.-General Lord Esme Gordon-Lennox) of the 5th Division advanced to the assault of the German front trenches on the spur south of Guillemont, the 12/Gloucestershire being on the right and the 1/Cornwall L.I. on the left. The two battalions carried, with some loss, the German front line which had suffered much in the bombardment ; several dug-outs and a machine-gun post on the near slope of the depression opposite Wedge Wood were then seized without much trouble. At 12.50 P.M. the advance was continued by the same battalions, which captured the German 2nd Position from Wedge Wood (exclusive) to the south-eastern edge of Guillemont. On the whole, the enemy resistance was easily overcome, the marksmanship of the 1/Cornwall L.I.

---

[1] Held by the *164th Regiment* (*111th Division*), the *4th Guard Grenadiers* (*2nd Guard Division*) being in the trenches to the south-east.

[2] Without notice being given to the British, the French guns had been called upon to deal with a German counter-attack farther south.

accounting for many German machine-gunners ; [1] but the 3 Sept.
Gloucestershire were taken in enfilade by fire from Falfemont Farm and suffered accordingly. At the same time
the 13th Brigade made another effort, the 15th and 14/R.
Warwickshire renewing the attack upon the K.O.S.B.
objective, also advancing against the German 2nd Position
as far as the northern corner of Wedge Wood. Although
the French had begun to move forward at noon they had
made no attempt to clear the enemy from the slopes of the
Combles ravine,[2] and enfilade fire from the right again
checked the advance on Falfemont Farm. The only gain
was on the left, where the 14/R. Warwickshire managed
first to occupy an old battery position and then to get a
footing in the near loop of the trench immediately south of
Wedge Wood, taking 17 prisoners and two machine guns.
Both battalions reported that the artillery support—provided this time by British batteries, but at very short
notice—had been " feeble ", also that the creeping barrage
had come down behind the 14/R. Warwickshire.

At 2.50 P.M. the 95th Brigade, which was admirably
served by the artillery throughout the action, advanced to
its third objective, the Wedge Wood—Ginchy road on the
slope north of Wedge Wood, and this was secured with
little trouble. The Gloucestershire and Cornwall L.I. then
began to consolidate, in touch on the left with the 20th
Division which had carried Guillemont, as will presently be
described. About a hundred and fifty prisoners were sent
back, chiefly of the *73rd Fusiliers* and *164th Regiment*.[3]
The support battalions of the brigade had been moved
forward as the advance progressed, whilst the arrival of the
troops on their successive objectives had been signalled
by flares which were promptly reported by both air and
ground observers.

Major-General Stephens had been obliged to replace

---

[1] This is significant, for the British infantryman was becoming more
and more disposed to rely upon the bomb rather than the bullet : he is
hardly to be blamed, for at home musketry was not given its due importance in the training of new drafts and the mud of the Somme put many a
rifle out of action.   Later in the year a newly appointed battalion commander said that his men might as well have been armed with pikes for all
their musketry was worth.

[2] The left of the French attack was made up the spur north-east of
Maurepas and entered Bois Douage. For the operations of the French,
1st-14th September, see Note at end of Chapter.

[3] " Fus. Regt. No. 73 " states that at the beginning of the action there
was a gap between the regiment and the *164th* in the German 2nd Position
(Falfemont Farm—Wedge Wood). It is said that *I./73rd*, holding the
front trenches south of Guillemont, was surprised and almost annihilated.

3 Sept. the 13th Brigade by the 15th (Br.-General M. N. Turner) before he could renew the attack upon the Falfemont Farm line, so that, although a fresh bombardment opened at 2.45 P.M., it was 6.30 P.M. before the infantry advanced. On the right the 1/Cheshire, supported by part of the 16/R. Warwickshire, failed, as might have been expected, since the German machine guns were still active on the right flank. The 1/Bedfordshire, however, took Wedge Wood, part of the battalion reaching the Ginchy road in the area of the 95th Brigade.

No Germans could be seen in front of the 95th Brigade, but an advance to its final objective, the near edge of Leuze Wood, was not sanctioned : such a movement might have turned the Falfemont Farm position, but promised to create an awkward salient unless the 20th Division co-operated on the left. The latter, which had captured Guillemont and had also reached the Wedge Wood— Ginchy road, was in no condition to do more : its own left had been thrown on the defensive by the failure of the XV. Corps at Ginchy. At 7.35 P.M. the 5th Division forbade further attacks that night, but the commander of the 15th Brigade, who had taken over the right sector, was warned that he would be required to secure the Falfemont Farm line on the afternoon of the following day.[1]

The capture of Guillemont was the task of Major-General W. Douglas Smith's 20th Division. Thanks to previous efforts, the British front line was very close to the village on the west and south-west, whilst the assembly trenches which had been dug near the station now facilitated a frontal attack from the north-west also.[2] Br.-General C. D. Shute's 59th Brigade, which had the southern part of Guillemont as its objective, was so weak in numbers— it mustered 1,650 rifles—that the 6/Oxford & Bucks L.I. (60th Brigade) and 7/Somerset L.I. (61st Brigade) reinforced it for the assault. The 47th Brigade (Br.-General G. E. Pereira) was brought up from the 16th (Irish) Division in corps reserve to replace the 60th Brigade [3] for the attack upon the northern part of the village.

---

[1] In the 5th Division the average strength of battalions before the assault was 700 ; losses amounted to 40 per cent, mostly wounded.

[2] Guillemont had been almost obliterated by bombardment ; an aeroplane photograph, taken on 29th August, of the southern part of the village revealed nothing but a sea of craters. Many deep dug-outs were still intact, however, and there were subterranean galleries which connected all the wells in the place.

[3] The 60th Brigade was so reduced by casualties and sickness that its relief had been regarded as imperative.

Guillemont was to be cleared, and the advance carried 3 Sept. to the Wedge Wood—Ginchy road, in three stages.[1]   The field artillery barrages were calculated accordingly, each infantry bound being covered by a barrage which became intense before beginning to creep—the rate through the village was 100 yards in four minutes—thus providing a signal for the stormers to get forward as close as possible. The assembly and communication trenches received little German fire during the morning, although a " Chinese attack "—bursts of rapid fire as though to pave the way for an assault—by the British artillery took place at 8.15 A.M., and a special bombardment, lasting half an hour, of the area north-east of Guillemont began at 8.33 A.M.

On the extreme left of the 59th Brigade, the 10/K.R.R.C. pressed forward before zero hour and, although casualties from the British barrage were suffered, the battalion was thus enabled to take the enemy by surprise.   Not to be out-done, the 6/Connaught Rangers of the 47th Brigade followed suit on the northern side of Mount Street.[2]   At noon the rest of the line advanced, and in twenty minutes the 59th Brigade—11th and 10/Rifle Brigade and 10/K.R.R.C. from right to left—had reached the first objective, the line of the Hardecourt road and thence northward to Mount Street.[3] The 10/K.R.R.C. was obliged to " mop up " in the area of the 6/Connaught Rangers (47th Brigade) on its left, for the impetuous Irishmen had swept on without quelling all resistance in the vicinity of the quarry.[4]   On the left flank of the division the dashing assault delivered south-east-ward by the 7/Leinster (47th Brigade) from the trenches beyond Guillemont station had carried all before it.[5]   By 12.30 P.M. divisional headquarters knew from aeroplane

---

[1] In order to maintain the impetus of the assault the 59th Brigade planned to reach the first objective in two bounds, and the second in two more, fresh troops passing through for each bound, after the first advance.

[2] Pte. T. Hughes, 6/Connaught Rangers, was wounded but returned to the fray and, single-handed, disposed of a German machine-gun detachment ; although again wounded, he brought in several prisoners. He was awarded the V.C. for his prowess.

[3] A " push-pipe " mine and flame-thrower had failed to deal with a German strongpoint opposite Arrow Head Copse, but this centre of resistance was overcome by the Rifle Brigade in the first rush, many Germans being killed.

[4] One company was detached for this purpose ; a platoon of the 11/K.R.R.C., which assisted, was led by a F.O.O. of the CVIII. Brigade R.F.A.

[5] Lieut. J. V. Holland, at the head of the battalion bombers, rushed forward through the British barrage and bombed the surprised Germans in their dug-outs with great effect.   He was awarded the V.C.

3 Sept. reports that the first objective was taken along the whole front.

The advance to the second objective at 12.50 P.M. met with considerable artillery and machine-gun fire, but suffered no check. In the 59th Brigade the leading battalions were reinforced by the 6/Oxford & Bucks L.I. and 7/Somerset L.I. ; the 8/R. Munster Fusiliers, of the 47th Brigade, passed through the Rangers. By 1.15 P.M. the troops were consolidating in the vicinity of North Street and South Street, avoiding the actual traces of the roads. Then, at 2.50 P.M., began the advance to the line of the Wedge Wood—Ginchy road, opposition having, for the most part, completely broken down. First to reach the road was the 59th Brigade, whose commander wired back to the division suggesting that fresh troops be pushed through, as there seemed to be " nothing in front ".[1] In the 47th Brigade, the 6/Royal Irish, which had taken up the attack to the strains of the battalion pipers, was followed by some of the Munsters whose ardour could not be restrained. These troops, having gathered in many prisoners, were soon prolonging to the north the line of the 59th Brigade just beyond the road.

Reorganization was well in hand before 3.30 P.M., the 59th Brigade ordering forward the 7/Cornwall L.I. (detached from the 61st Brigade) into Guillemont, where a company of the 11/Durham L.I. (Pioneers), engaged upon consolidation, had been joined already by the 83rd Field Company R.E. The flow of supporting troops and carrying parties was well maintained, and touch with the 95th Brigade of the 5th Division on the right was established later. It was known at divisional headquarters that the 7th Division (XV. Corps) had entered Ginchy.

At 5.15 P.M., however, Major-General Smith received a report from the 47th Brigade that the 7th Division had been forced out of Ginchy, whereupon he asked for a barrage to protect his left flank. At the same time, he forbade a general advance to the Leuze Wood line, but ordered strong patrols to be pushed forward in that direction. Measures taken to secure the flank of the corps by getting troops in position astride the Guillemont—Ginchy road owed much to the initiative of a company commander of the 12/King's (61st Brigade), whose battalion had been sent up to rein-

---

[1] Communications had held fairly well : runners were doing good service, and a certain amount of visual signalling was possible. The F.O.O.'s did excellent work.

force the 47th Brigade. At 5.30 and 6.30 P.M. German attempts to counter-attack in this quarter were checked by rifle and Lewis-gun fire.[1]

After darkness fell rain added to the trials of the troops and promised to make movement difficult on the morrow, but a line was gradually linked up in touch with the 7th Division on the south-western outskirts of Ginchy, extending thence south-eastward to the Wedge Wood—Ginchy road. This line was held by the 47th Brigade and attached troops, with a party of the 7th Division (XV. Corps) on the extreme left, the 59th Brigade becoming responsible for the front facing eastward along the Ginchy—Wedge Wood road.[2] Before daylight faded German aeroplanes flew over the captured area, and the hostile artillery then opened a heavy and accurate bombardment. Shortly after 8 P.M. patrols of the 7/Somerset L.I. were sent out towards Leuze Wood but encountered no Germans.[3]

The penetration of the German 2nd Position by the 5th Division and the capture of Guillemont by the 20th Division represented the only gains of Sunday the 3rd September.[4] At 11 P.M. General Rawlinson ordered a general resumption of the attack next day at 3.10 P.M., the preliminary bombardment to open as soon as daylight came.

The 4th September proved to be a windy day with 4 Sept. heavy showers and bright intervals, conditions which persisted on the morrow. By order of the corps, the 5th Division was to carry the German 2nd Position from Point

---

[1] Sergt. D. Jones, 12/King's, commanded a platoon which held a covering position well forward on the southern edge of Ginchy until relieved on 5th September, repelling several counter-attacks by fire. He was awarded the V.C.

[2] The 59th Brigade and its three attached battalions had a casualty list of nearly fourteen hundred ; among the wounded were Lieut.-Colonels C. A. Blacklock, 10/K.R.R.C., W. V. L. Prescott-Westcar, 10/Rifle Brigade, and C. J. Troyte-Bullock, 7/Somerset L.I. The 47th Brigade lost over a thousand of all ranks, including Lieut.-Colonel J. S. M. Lenox-Conyngham, 6/Connaught Rangers, killed.

[3] According to its history, the *76th Regiment* (right sector of the *111th Division*) was distributed in great depth, *II./76th* and a machine-gun company holding Guillemont with no other troops nearer than the *III./76th* in the Quadrilateral—Leuze Wood line. The *II./76th* suffered severely from the preliminary bombardment and was mostly overwhelmed, a few wounded struggling back about 2.30 P.M. with the message " Guillemont is " English ! " The British barrage prevented the *III./76th* from delivering a counter-attack. There was a gap on the left and the situation in Ginchy was obscure, so little could be done.

[4] Over seven hundred wounded and unwounded Germans were taken, and the enemy dead lay thick on the captured ground.

4 Sept. 48 as far as Wedge Wood and also Valley Trench in the depression to the north of Wedge Wood ; at a time subsequently fixed at 6.30 P.M. the advance was to be continued to the Leuze Wood line, which was also named as the objective of the 20th Division. Both divisions were told that, if such a step were essential to success, they could use the battalions of the 16th Division which had been allotted to them.[1]

The 15th Brigade (5th Division) accordingly prepared for another frontal attack on Falfemont Farm, the 1/Norfolk being now in actual touch with French troops. The latter, however, did not advance at 3.5 P.M., when the Norfolk left their trenches only to be checked by machine-gun fire from the Combles ravine. On the left, a party which entered the south-west corner of the farm was bombed out again ; but a company of the 1/Cheshire worked round under the shelter of the spur, whilst the 1/Bedfordshire, starting from Wedge Wood, began to bomb south-eastward along the German trench. The Bedfordshire gathered in over 130 prisoners, mostly *164th Regiment*, together with several machine guns, and by 4 P.M. the northern and western corners of the farm enclosure were taken. Reinforced by the 16/R. Warwickshire, the Norfolk, who had been working forward from shell-hole to shell-hole, made another unsuccessful attempt to storm the farm at 5.30 P.M., so it was then decided that the 16/R. Warwickshire should sap forward towards the objective during the night. Patrols of the Bedfordshire and Cheshire on the crest of the Leuze Wood spur had assisted to prevent the approach of German reinforcements, which were also caught by British artillery fire as they advanced from the direction of Combles.

Meanwhile in the 95th Brigade, two companies of the 1/East Surrey had advanced from the Ginchy road and occupied Valley Trench without trouble, the battalion reporting that " our own shrapnel caused the only casualty ". Two companies of the 1/Devonshire passed through later and reached the edge of Leuze Wood about 7.30 P.M. Here the British barrage prevented further progress ; but, after a message had been sent back to the artillery by a F.O.O., the Devonshire were able to enter the wood and begin to

---

[1] 7th and 8/R. Irish Fusiliers (49th Brigade) to 5th Division ; 48th Brigade to 20th Division. At 2 P.M. Sir Douglas Haig came to Army headquarters and emphasized that the capture of the high ground Leuze Wood—N.E. of Ginchy was of the first importance, but that the fresh divisions must be economized as much as possible.

consolidate a line inside it. Very few Germans had been seen.[1]

In the 20th Division the situation was governed by the uncertainty as to what was happening in Ginchy. So far as was known, the 7th Division had parties established in the village, so Major-General Smith hesitated to ask a second time for a protective barrage on his left flank. Yet the enemy seemed to be in considerable strength between Ginchy and the loop of trenches known as " The Quadrilateral ". Before daylight on the 4th, the forward troops of the 47th Brigade had been relieved by battalions of the 60th Brigade ; but the troops of the 59th Brigade, although very tired, remained in the line. The afternoon advance resolved itself into the forward movement of patrols under the British barrage, and even these were late in starting. On the right, the 7/Somerset L.I. succeeded in establishing posts from the western corner of Leuze Wood northwestward to the Guillemont road ; on the left vigorous sniping from Ginchy hindered the attempt to make ground along the track of the light railway. The day closed in heavy rain, which made the relief of the 59th Brigade by two battalions of the 49th Brigade (16th Division) a slow and difficult process.[2]

In spite of the weather, the forward troops of the 5th Division were not idle during the night. The German resistance was obviously weakening, and by 3 A.M. on the 5th September Falfemont Farm was in the possession of the Norfolk, who pushed patrols towards Point 48. By 7.30 A.M. the whole objective was cleared.[3] An hour later, the 15th Brigade sent out two companies of the 16/R. Warwickshire, which established a line down the slope of the ravine, linking up the 95th Brigade in Leuze Wood with the French left, now on the railway in Savernake Wood. The desultory fire of the German artillery did little to hinder this movement ; it was the British protective barrage which discouraged further advance. General Rawlinson was at XIV. Corps headquarters when, at 11.45 A.M., two reports, forwarded from the 5th Division, arrived from the officers

5 Sept.

---

[1] Both the *III.* and *II./73rd Fusiliers* appear to have been in Leuze Wood. A counter-attack in the early morning had been checked by the British barrage. " Fus. Regt. No. 73."

[2] " Regt. No. 76 " states the *III.* and *I. Bns.* were holding the Quadrilateral—Leuze Wood trench with some troops out in front. Touch on the left with the *73rd Fusiliers* was not secured until night, when a company of the *III./107th Reserve (24th Reserve Division)* came in to fill the gap.

[3] Some of the prisoners belonged to the *4th Guard Grenadiers*.

5 Sept. commanding the Bedfordshire and the Norfolk : each urged that fresh troops should push through and take up the advance, as the Germans were obviously disorganized and inclined to retreat.   The Army commander at once instructed the corps to push out boldly to seize Leuze Wood and the high ground between the wood and Ginchy.

The 15th Brigade therefore called upon the 7/R. Irish Fusiliers (49th Brigade) to relieve the Warwickshire and attack Combles Trench[1] at 4 p.m., at which hour the barrage was to lift 100 yards beyond the objective.   When the Irishmen advanced, however, they came upon wire amongst the standing corn and tall weeds, and, in the face of accurate machine-gun fire, could not get forward.   Another attempt was made at 7.30 p.m., and likewise failed.   On the other flank of the division, the Devonshire of the 95th Brigade had advanced at 4 p.m. and occupied the German trench in Leuze Wood, meeting with little opposition.

In the 20th Division, the 49th Brigade (Br.-General P. Leveson-Gower) had relieved the 59th, and command passed to the 16th Division (Major-General W. B. Hickie) at 9.20 a.m. on the 5th September.[2] Posts had already been established along the Guillemont—Leuze Wood road, and these were converted into a continuous trench during the day.   In the evening, the 7/R. Inniskilling Fusiliers linked up along the road with the 5th Division at the northern end of Leuze Wood.   On the left, the relief of the 60th Brigade by the 48th (Br.-General F. W. Ramsay) had been delayed owing to the guides going astray and only began at dusk on the 5th September.   At 8.15 p.m. the corps ordered an attempt to be made to secure the German trench between Leuze Wood and the Quadrilateral, but the incoming battalions were not ready to do so.

6 Sept.   South of Leuze Wood, the Kensingtons (168th Brigade, 56th Division)[3] had relieved the 7/R. Irish Fusiliers (attached 15th Brigade) by 3 a.m. on the 6th September, which proved to be a fine autumn day.   The staff of the 15th Brigade suggested that it might be best to attack down Combles Trench from Leuze Wood instead of making a frontal

---

[1] The front line of the *164th Regiment* since the capture of Falfemont Farm.

[2] The 20th Division casualty returns (all units) show 129 officers and 2,830 other ranks, over the period 22nd August–8th September.

[3] Reports of French progress (patrols were said to have reached the outskirts of Combles) had caused the XIV. Corps at 5.18 p.m. to warn the 56th and Guards Divisions to be ready to move.   These divisions were to be in the front line for the big offensive.

attack as the Fusiliers had done ; but the Kensingtons, who 6 Sept.
were new to the ground, preferred to wait until darkness
fell before making this movement.[1]   Their entry into
Leuze Wood was then disorganized by a German counter-
attack,[2] and nothing was accomplished.

During the night of the 5th/6th September, the 8/R.
Irish Fusiliers (49th Brigade) relieved the Devonshire on
the 95th Brigade front, and next morning advanced across
the Combles—Ginchy road.   On the right Bouleaux Wood
was entered, but the battalion was out of touch on its
flanks, and all day long a heavy German barrage was
maintained across the spur south-west of Leuze Wood.
At night Br.-General G. G. Loch's 168th Brigade (56th
Division) began to take over the whole of the 5th Division
front ; and at 7.30 P.M., when the London Scottish were
about to relieve the Irish Fusiliers, there were reports of
a German counter-attack, the front line of the Fusiliers
withdrawing across the road.   The main trench in Leuze
Wood was, however, held, and by 10.30 P.M. the Scottish
had repulsed the Germans, and taken twenty prisoners.[3]
At 1.35 A.M. on the 7th September command passed to the
56th Division (Major-General C. P. A. Hull).[4]

Patrols from the left of the 16th Division which had
tried to advance along the light-railway track in the early
morning of the 6th lost many men by fire from the Quadrilateral when they reached the higher ground, and could
not go far.   Fighting continued in Ginchy on this day, and
the left brigade (48th) was under continuous shell-fire.
About 3 P.M. General Hickie ordered the brigades to advance
their inner flanks across the spur south-east of the railway,
and the 49th Brigade did so by swinging forward its left
from the Guillemont—Leuze Wood road to face north-east.
The 8/Inniskilling Fusiliers, digging in on this line, was
interrupted by the German barrage which preceded the
German counter-attack at Leuze Wood ; but work was
afterwards resumed, and continued throughout the night.
The 48th Brigade could do little owing to fire from the

---

[1] They had French troops on their right near the bottom of the ravine
(Savernake Wood) and they saw a French attack towards Combles fail at
3 P.M.

[2] See below.

[3] " Res. Regt. No. 107 " states that the regiment relieved with two
battalions the front line of the *73rd Fusiliers* and *76th Regiment* on the
night of the 5th/6th, but makes no mention of this counter-attack.

[4] For the period 26th August—7th September the casualty returns of
the 5th Division (all units) showed a wastage of 133 officers and 4,100 other
ranks.

south-eastern edge of Ginchy, and from the vicinity of the
Quadrilateral.

The Fight for Ginchy : Operations, Delville Wood—High Wood

3 Sept.   In the XV. Corps the 7th Division (Major-General
H. E. Watts), which was to capture Ginchy on the 3rd
September, had been given as a final objective the high
Sketch ground east of the village on a line approximately north and
33.   south through Ginchy Telegraph,[1] the right to be established in touch with the XIV. Corps.   During the night of
the 2nd/3rd September, the 22nd Brigade (Br.-General
J. McC. Steele) relieved the 91st in the forward trenches
south of and on the Longueval—Ginchy road.[2]

The Germans at the eastern point of Delville Wood and
in Ale Alley and Hop Alley commanded the ground between
Waterlot Farm and Ginchy over which the 22nd Brigade
was to move to the assault.   It was therefore arranged that
the bombing company [3] of the 91st Brigade, assisted by
bombers of the 2/Queen's, should clear the left flank by
attacking five minutes before zero hour in co-operation
with the 9/East Surrey, right battalion of the 24th Division.

At 10.25 a.m. the British bombardment quickened and
at 11.20 a.m. became intense.   The field-gun barrage was
due to fall on the German front line at noon, the general
zero hour, and five minutes later, having given time for the
assaulting infantry to get close—the distance between
the British and German lines was about four hundred
yards—it would creep through the village in three principal
lifts, paying particular attention to the eastern end of Ale
Alley and to Waterlot Farm.[4]

[1] Ginchy Telegraph—site of an old semaphore station, relic of the
Revolutionary wars, on the highest point east of the village—no longer
existed, although shown on maps and mentioned in operation orders.

[2] On 1st and 2nd September the *4th Bavarian Division* extended its
left as far as the Longueval—Flers road ; the *56th Division*, at the same
time, withdrew into reserve the *88th Regiment*, which was thus available
to reinforce the *35th Fusiliers* in Ginchy.

[3] At this time the organization of bombers varied in different divisions.
Some, like the 7th Division, maintained brigade grenade (bombing) companies ; others kept all trained bombers in the ranks of their battalions
except when they were required for a special task.

[4] Called henceforward " The Farm " to distinguish it from the buildings
on the Longueval—Guillemont road.   These were really a sugar refinery,
as already explained.   The real farm was in the south-west quarter of
Ginchy.

Sketch 33.

II BAV.

XII R.

Ginchy

III.

XV.

XIV.

Longueval

High Wood

DELVILLE WOOD

Waterlot Fm

7.

24.

3RD – 8TH SEPTEMBER, 1916.
XV Corps Operations.

British Front line, 3rd September.
Ground gained by 8th
German trenches

Scale of Yards.
0   500   1000

500   500

Heights in metres

Compiled in the Historical Section (Military Branch)
3060/38.

Ordnance Survey 1837

Crown Copyright. Reserved.

The 91st Brigade bombers began their attack up the 3 Sept. south-eastern edge of Delville Wood towards Hop Alley at 11.55 A.M., but the smoke of their " fumite " grenades only served to advertise their approach to the German machine gunners and snipers. The East Surrey detachment, which did its best to get forward from the sap north of Ale Alley, had received orders and counter-orders, so the ill co-ordinated effort achieved nothing in spite of supporting trench-mortar fire.

At noon the two battalions of the 22nd Brigade advanced from their assembly trenches. When the barrage lifted the 20/Manchester, on the right, swept forward into the southern portion of the village without perceptible check, and was lost to view. On the left, the 1/R. Welch Fusiliers, encountering enfilade fire from the German machine guns in Ale Alley, was not successful. An attempt to take Hop Alley and Beer Trench—both strongly held—by an advance over the open was for the most part checked with con-siderable loss. Nevertheless parties established themselves in shell-holes about forty yards south of Hop Alley, and the southern portion of Beer Trench was occupied. The right company got into the northern part of Ginchy and seemed to make good progress, but " nothing was ever heard of " them ". The company which followed in support, under increasing machine-gun fire from front and flank, managed to pass a few men forward as far as the edge of the orchards north-west of the village, and here they were joined by parties of the 2/R. Warwickshire. This battalion was to have occupied Ale Alley, when it should be captured, as a defensive flank, besides reinforcing the Ginchy attack as required.

Meanwhile, as was reported to 22nd Brigade head-quarters at 3.50 P.M., the 20/Manchester had reached the enclosures on the farther side of Ginchy and began to consolidate a position along their eastern and south-eastern edges.[1] The work proceeded under machine-gun fire, whilst the Germans, who remained in the northern part of the village, began to work round the left flank. Finally, a determined counter-attack from the north forced back most of the survivors, who drifted westwards towards Porter Trench. The greater portion of two supporting companies of the Warwickshire was involved in this retirement, but

[1] " Fus. Regt. No. 35 " states that the line on the western side of Ginchy, held by its *I./Bn.*, had been stiffened by parts of the *I./88th*. " Ginchy was lost by the noon attack of the British."

3 Sept. one party held on near the sunken portion of the Guillemont road south-west of Ginchy, where it was in touch with the refused left flank of the XIV. Corps.   It beat back, chiefly by Lewis-gun fire, a determined counter-attack delivered later in the afternoon.[1]

At 2.15 p.m. Br.-General Steele had detailed a company of his reserve battalion, the 2/Royal Irish, with a detachment of bombers, for a fresh attempt to clear the left flank. Two hours later a F.O.O. reported that the Manchester were retiring through Ginchy, and the Royal Irish were then ordered to re-occupy the village in conjunction with their left attack which was to be delivered at 5 p.m.   Starting at that hour from Pilsen Lane, two attempts were made to reach Hop Alley over the open, whilst the bombers attacked along the edge of the wood ; nothing was gained, although some men joined those of the Welch Fusiliers in the forward position confronting Hop Alley.   The other companies of the Royal Irish were somewhat disorganized by German shelling on their way up to the front, and lost heavily from machine-gun fire before reaching Stout and Porter Trenches, where they found mixed parties of Warwickshire and Manchester.   This was the limit of their advance.

The German bombardment, which had begun about twenty minutes after zero hour, continued to be very heavy and accurate on the British trenches.   No messages came back from Ginchy, and the lack of information diminished the prospect of repairing the fortunes of the day.   During the afternoon contact aeroplanes had reported flares seen at various points in the village, but later there was no response when these were called for by signals from the air. At 6.50 p.m. the 7th Division telephoned to the corps asking for a fresh bombardment by the heavy artillery, after which Major-General Watts proposed to put in the 20th Brigade (Br.-General H. C. R. Green) for the next attempt.   Lieut.-General Horne decided to refer to the Army the question of employing a fresh brigade, since the 7th Division had been selected for the mid-September offensive and its strength should have been conserved accordingly.

----

[1] A counter-attack by two companies *I./88th* with some of the *I./35th Fusiliers*, was launched from Pint Trench about 3.30 p.m.   Another company of the *I./88th* and one of the *III./35th Fusiliers* found it difficult to get forward from the east through the southern part of Ginchy, and " after " a severe struggle " could do no more than hold the south-eastern part of the village.   German artillery fire is said to have stopped a British advance from the direction of Guillemont ; meanwhile, the northern counter-attack had succeeded.   German regimental histories.

The 22nd Brigade, now very weak in numbers, with few officers left and its units disorganized, subsequently received orders to make another effort, the 20th Brigade being brought forward to hold the existing line. When, however, about 8.30 P.M., it was established by a patrol that the Germans had re-occupied the village in some force,[1] and corps and divisional headquarters realized the state to which the 22nd Brigade was reduced, its immediate relief was sanctioned. The 21/Manchester (detached from the 91st Brigade) was to secure the left flank in Delville Wood, whilst the 20th Brigade, brought up in lorries to Mametz from its billets about Buire, would take over Stout and Porter Trenches and attack Ginchy.[2] A corps order, issued at 11.45 P.M., directed the 7th Division, if already occupying part of Ginchy, to take immediate steps to complete the capture of the village ; otherwise the attack was to form part of the renewed offensive ordered by the Fourth Army for the afternoon of the next day.

The attack of the 20th Brigade was eventually made by 4 Sept. the 9/Devonshire about 8 A.M. on the 4th September. It started well, but, after entering Ginchy, encountered a hail of shrapnel and machine-gun bullets, and the battalion, having lost many officers, was obliged to withdraw to Stout, Porter and ZZ Trenches soon after 9 A.M.[3] Major-General Watts visited corps headquarters later in the morning and obtained permission to postpone a fresh effort until just before dawn of the 5th. He considered that a surprise attack in the dark stood the best chance of success,[4] and intended to make it with the 2/Gordon Highlanders and 8/Devonshire.

The 21/Manchester, in Delville Wood, attacked eastward, using two companies, at 2 P.M., but could not close with the Germans who were in strength between Ale Alley and Hop Alley. Another company, attacking northward

[1] " Regt. No. 88 " describes a frontal attack to regain Ginchy at 6 P.M., when two companies of its *III. Bn.* cleared the village assisted by a company of the *I./Bn.* and one of the *III./35th Fusiliers*, after fierce fighting with spades and axes. [This may mean that isolated parties of the 22nd Brigade were holding out in the village up to that hour.] No touch was obtained on the left, the *76th Regiment* having been driven from Guillemont.

[2] Its leading battalion, the 9/Devonshire, did not arrive at Mametz until 9.15 P.M., and the night was spent in issuing bombs and battle-stores, and moving up to the front line.

[3] " Regt. No. 88 " says that this attack was beaten off by infantry fire, as the German batteries did not reply to signals from the front-line.

[4] A fresh bombardment of Ginchy was ruled out owing to the possibility of parties of the 22nd Brigade being still there.

from Pilsen Lane against Hop Alley, likewise failed, and the troops lay out in shell-holes under fire until it was possible to withdraw them at dusk.[1] During the night part of the 2/Border Regiment (20th Brigade) relieved the troops on the extreme left flank of the 20th Division in the area of the XV. Corps.

5 Sept. At 2.20 A.M. on the 5th the 20th Brigade reported to the 7th Division that the 2/Gordon Highlanders could not be in position to attack for another three hours, and that even then, owing to the bad state of the ground, nothing more than reorganization of the front positions would be possible. Major-General Watts consented to this course, and subsequently agreed that the attack should be postponed until 3.30 A.M. next morning. Officers of the 22nd Brigade who had withdrawn their isolated parties from the edge of Ginchy and the area south of Hop Alley during the previous night reported that the village was held principally by machine gunners, and that a night attack seemed to offer every prospect of success. As a preliminary operation, at 5.30 P.M., the 2/Queen's—brought up from the 91st Brigade—attempted to secure the eastern point of Delville Wood, putting in two companies after trench mortars had fired a two-hours' bombardment. Unfortunately the fire of the mortars was difficult to observe and did little damage ; when the Queen's advanced they were met by machine-gun fire, but they gained and held the edge of the wood as far as a point north of the head of Hop Alley. Consolidation, assisted on the right by the 8/Devonshire, then proceeded under heavy fire from the German artillery.

6 Sept. The Gordons were badly shelled during the night, losing many officers, and when their advance began on the early morning of the 6th September, the leading companies lost their way in the darkness. A fresh start was made about 5.30 A.M., with the 9/Devonshire now in support. The Highlanders, much hindered by slippery mud, gradually approached the western side of Ginchy, but they could not reach it in the face of the German machine guns hidden in the débris of the village and firing at short range. Meanwhile, the 8/Devonshire, which was to form a defensive flank on the left, had extended eastward from Pilsen Lane and was digging in ; and, although a German flanking movement from the north of Ginchy drove in the more

---

[1] " Fus. Regt. No. 35 " states that the hardest fighting on this day was at Delville Wood, where its *I./Bn.* sustained heavy loss.

advanced parties of the battalion, the general line was held.

Major-General Watts now arranged for another bombardment of the Farm and the area north of it.   At 2 P.M. the Gordons advanced again, two companies of the 9/Devonshire coming in on the right from the direction of the Guillemont—Ginchy road.   This fresh effort, made behind a field-gun barrage, was at first successful, although some of the British shells fell short and caused the Gordons loss. Parties of both battalions got into the village and sent back prisoners of the *35th Fusiliers*, but the German barrage made it impossible to reinforce them.   About 4.30 P.M. a counter-attack [1] compelled a withdrawal to the British front line which then came under violent hostile shell-fire. Major-General Watts was obliged to report that his division could do no more.

The 7th September was a comparatively quiet day.   At **7 Sept.** 4 P.M. the 2/Queen's made an unsuccessful attempt to storm the eastern corner of Delville Wood behind a barrage of rifle grenades ; and in the evening the relief of the 7th Division [2] was begun by troops of the 55th and 16th Divisions, the latter thus extending the XIV. Corps front to the left. [3]

North-west of Longueval on the 3rd September the left **3 Sept.** attack of the XV. Corps was carried out in conjunction with the III. Corps operation which aimed at securing Wood Lane and the German front line in High Wood.   At noon a company of the 8/Buffs (17th Brigade, 24th Division) **Sketch** advanced from the extremity of the III. Corps line to carry **33.** the southern portion of Wood Lane by frontal attack, whilst bombers of the battalion worked forward on the right from Sap A.   Both movements were checked, chiefly by fire from the strongpoint at the junction of Wood Lane

---

[1] Delivered principally by two companies of the *III./88th* and one of the *I./104th Reserve (24th Reserve Division)* put in as an additional reinforcement.

[2] Since 23rd August the casualty returns of the 7th Division showed a total loss of 174 officers and 3,626 other ranks.

[3] On the night of 7th September the *5th Bavarian Division* from Lens began to relieve the *56th Division* (Longueval—Flers road to Ginchy inclusive).   The *19th Bavarians* took over the defence of Ginchy ; there was much confusion and at first the newcomers did not know if the British had already taken the village which, after repeated bombardments, had " completely disappeared from the surface.   Only remains of walls and " angles of hedges show what had formerly been a settlement of human " beings."   Regimental history.

3-8 Sept. and Tea Trench, and a fresh attempt made at 4 P.M. likewise failed.   At night, however, the 7/Northamptonshire (lent by the 73rd Brigade to the 17th) occupied, with little opposition, the near end of Tea Lane.[1]

On the following night, 4th/5th September, the 165th Brigade (Br.-General F. J. Duncan) of Major-General H. S. Jeudwine's 55th Division relieved the 17th Brigade in the left sector of the 24th Division front.   At 7 P.M. on the 6th the 1/6th King's made bombing attacks on Wood Lane without much success ;   the 1/7th King's, however, encountered little resistance in bombing westwards along Tea Trench.   The incoming division had ordered the line north-east of Delville Wood to be advanced to within assaulting distance of Tea Support, and on this night the 1/7th King's started work on forward posts between Tea Lane and the Flers road.   Twenty four hours later, after the front troops had been relieved, patrols of the 1/5th King's encountered no opposition in Wood Lane, the eastern end of which was occupied to a point well beyond the Tea Trench junction.   At 1.20 A.M. on the 8th a party of the enemy attempted to advance in this quarter and was dispersed by Lewis-gun fire.   Meanwhile the 1/5th and 1/9th King's joined hands in Tea Trench without hindrance, and found it so knocked about by shell-fire that most of it had to be dug afresh.   Patrols went several hundred yards up North Street and the Flers road without encountering any Germans.   Next day consolidation, proceeded under considerable sniping and shell-fire.

The right brigade, 72nd, of the 24th Division, between the Flers road and the left of the 7th Division just north of Ale Alley, had been relieved by the 166th Brigade (Br.-General L. F. Green-Wilkinson) on the night of the 5th September.[2]   Here the enemy shelling fell principally upon Delville Wood and Longueval, the front line almost escaping attention.   Coming up from reserve on the nights of the 7th and 8th, the 1/5th South Lancashire and 1/10th King's (Liverpool Scottish) dug and occupied a new forward line, which prolonged that established by the 165th Brigade.   The German infantry made no attempt to interfere.   On the night of the 7th, when the 164th Brigade

---

[1] On the evening of 2nd September the *9th Bavarians (4th Bavarian Division)* had taken over the front of the *88th Regiment* as far as the Flers—Longueval road.   " Bav. Regt. No. 9 " states that British attacks were repulsed on 3rd September.

[2] Since coming into the line at the end of August the 24th Division had lost nearly two thousand officers and men.

(Br.-General G. T. G. Edwards) relieved the left of the 7th Division, Major-General Jeudwine assumed command of the whole XV. Corps front, which he held with his three brigades.

In the III. Corps at noon, the general zero hour, on the 3rd September the 1/Cameron Highlanders (1st Brigade, 1st Division) attacked Wood Lane, with all four companies in line and a detachment of the 8/Berkshire on their right. On the extreme right, next to the Buffs of the 24th Division, no progress was made, but in the centre and on the left the Camerons took the trench after some hand-to-hand fighting and gained another hundred yards before beginning to consolidate as best they could, a carrying party with tools and material having gone astray.[1] The 1/Black Watch (also 1st Brigade) attacking the German front line in High Wood, had the help of blazing oil drums, " pipe-pushers ", and flame-throwers, the objective being too close for artillery bombardment ; in addition, a mine was exploded [2] under the German strongpoint at the eastern corner of High Wood 30 seconds before zero hour. The mine crater was seized by the right company of the Black Watch, consolidation began with the assistance of a section of the 23rd Field Company R.E., and bombers worked some distance westward along the German front trench. Unfortunately the " pipe-pushers " in the wood had blown back, and a Stokes mortar, firing short, had ignited the oil drums prematurely, so that considerable confusion prevailed when the other companies of the Black Watch began to advance. They were held up by machine-gun and rifle fire.

Towards 3 P.M. the Germans counter-attacked from the Switch Line north-east of High Wood, pressing on regardless of the British barrage and machine-gun and rifle fire, which took heavy toll of them. They captured the mine-crater and were then able to enfilade the left of the Camerons, which was obliged to retire about 3.30 P.M. ; an hour later, the right of the battalion, now in a precarious position, was ordered to do likewise. The only consolation was the ample evidence of the loss inflicted on the Germans : wounded and unwounded prisoners—mostly of the *5th Bavarian Regiment*—totalled eighty.

3 Sept.

Sketch 33.

---

[1] Prisoners of the *II./5th Bavarians* spoke highly of the dash displayed by the Camerons, advancing close behind the British barrage.

[2] The 178th Tunnelling Company R.E. used a charge of 3,000 lbs. of ammonal.

4-8 Sept.   Not much was demanded of the III. Corps on the 4th
September. Its artillery joined in the general bombardment, and at 3.10 P.M. there was a "Chinese" attack on
High Wood with gas bombs and smoke bombs. The
infantry did not participate.

By Army instructions an attempt was made to secure
the western half of High Wood[1] at 6 P.M. on the 8th September, when the 2/Welch (3rd Brigade, 1st Division) advanced
with its right about the centre of the wood. The right
company got its objective without much trouble ; the left
company was checked by fire. Farther to the left, the
1/Gloucestershire (also 3rd Brigade) attacked the south-
western face of the wood. The battalion, very weak in
numbers, had to deal with Germans ensconced in wired
shell craters, and some bayonet work was needed before the
objective was reached. Losses were heavy, and Lieut.-
Colonel A. W. Pagan, who led the advance in person, was
wounded. Meanwhile, two companies of the 9/Black
Watch (44th Brigade of the 15th Division) had come in
from the left and carried a German trench beyond the
western corner of the wood, repulsing by Lewis-gun fire a
German counter-attack which was delivered soon afterwards. Unfortunately the Gloucestershire were not supported in their forward position, the German artillery and
machine-gun barrage delaying the advance of reinforcements. After a counter-attack had been repulsed at 8 P.M.,
a withdrawal was ordered, and carried out before midnight.
This movement left the right flank of the Black Watch
uncovered, and they too had to withdraw ; in the wood the
isolated company of the Welch hung on until after 4 A.M.
next morning and then came back. Many Germans were
killed in this affair, and nearly fifty prisoners, mostly of the
18th Bavarian Regiment, were taken.[2]

THE FIGHTING ROUND LEUZE WOOD : CAPTURE OF GINCHY[3] : CAPTURE OF WOOD LANE

Sketch   General Rawlinson had told the XIV. Corps on the
34.   morning of the 5th September to secure Combles " as soon
"as possible". Had Ginchy been taken by the morning of

---

[1] See Sketch 27.

[2] The *18th Bavarians* (left of the *3rd Bavarian Division*) had part of its
III./Bn. in High Wood.

[3] Officially the "Battle of Ginchy" embraces only operations on the
front Combles ravine—Longueval on 9th September.

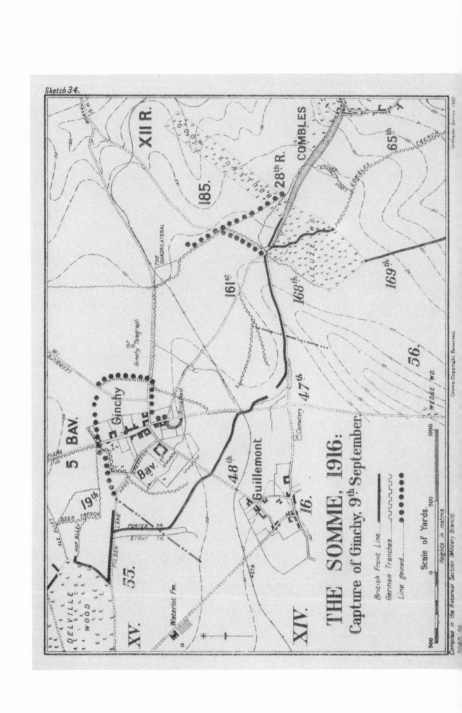

Sketch 34.

THE SOMME, 1916:
Capture of Ginchy, 9th September.

Scale of Yards.

British Front Line
German Trenches
Line gained

Heights in metres.

Compiled in the Historical Section (Military Branch)

Crown Copyright Reserved.

Ordnance Survey 1937.

the 6th he would have thrust forward his right flank without 6–8 Sept.
delay and was prepared to send up the cavalry at the first
sign of a German debâcle.   Unfortunately, the attempt to
conserve the strength of the fresh divisions, and the
necessity of preparing for the big offensive in the midst
of active operations, considerably hampered the efforts
of the Fourth Army ; and in the up-shot the available
reserves were sensibly depleted before the great attack
began.

At 11.50 P.M. on the 6th an Army operation order was
issued for the resumption of the attack on the 9th : [1] the
XIV. Corps to secure the line of the Combles—Leuze Wood
road, the Quadrilateral,[2] and Ginchy ; the XV. Corps to
take Beer Trench and Ale Alley ; the III. Corps to capture
Wood Lane and the eastern corner of High Wood.[3]   The
bombardment was timed for 7 A.M. with no quickening of
fire before zero hour, fixed for 4.45 P.M., the heavy artillery
of the XV. Corps assisting that of the XIV.

By the morning of the 8th September the 56th Division
had relieved the right of the 168th Brigade by the 169th
(Br.-General E. S. D'E. Coke), the London Rifle Brigade
occupying the southern part of Leuze Wood, in touch with
the French in Combles ravine.   The 168th Brigade took
over ground to the left along the Leuze Wood—Guillemont
road, thus relieving part of the 49th Brigade (16th Division),
which was drawn into reserve.   The 16th Division, having
abandoned the forward trench dug by the 8/Inniskilling
Fusiliers,[4] then held its front with the 47th Brigade (Br.-
General G. E. Pereira) and 48th Brigade.[5]

At 11.30 A.M. on the 8th the 169th Brigade attempted
to push south-eastward towards Combles, the L.R.B.
bombing down Combles Trench from Leuze Wood.   Some
progress was made, but at 5.15 A.M. next morning a heavy

[1] The French Sixth Army was also to attack again on the 9th, but
General Foch met Sir Douglas Haig at Fourth Army headquarters on 8th
September and expressed his regret that more time was needed for preparation.   The French attacks were resumed on the 12th (see Note at end of
Chapter).
[2] In front of this trench loop there was dead ground, over sixty
yards wide, containing wire hidden in long grass.   Aeroplane photographs merely revealed an outer belt of wire efficiently cut by the British
artillery.
[3] It will be noticed that Ginchy was now the responsibility of the XIV.
Corps.
[4] See page 261.
[5] On the German side, the *185th Division* (now comprising the *65th*,
161st and *28th Reserve*) began the relief of the *111th Division* on 7th/8th
September.

counter-attack, made chiefly by bombers, compelled a withdrawal.

9 Sept. In the main attack, the 169th Brigade had the task of establishing a defensive flank along the slopes of the Combles ravine,[1] and at zero hour, 4.45 p.m. on the 9th September, the L.R.B. advanced from the south-eastern edge of Leuze Wood against Loop Trench, but was obliged to retire in the face of fire from artillery and machine guns.[2] The battalion was reinforced by part of the 1/2nd London, and, acting on a false report that the Germans had penetrated Leuze Wood, Br.-General Coke afterwards sent up the 1/16th (Q.W.R.), with orders to restore the situation and capture Loop Trench. The Queen's Westminster, moving forward in the misty darkness and having to negotiate the German barrage, did not arrive before 11 p.m., when it was judged advisable to wait for daylight. Meanwhile by 6.15 p.m., the 1/9th London had captured the German main line in Bouleaux Wood and north-westward as far as the Morval road. The battalion was heavily shelled whilst digging in.[3]

Advancing at zero hour from assembly trenches south of the Leuze Wood—Guillemont road, the 168th Brigade had to move north-eastward, pivoting on its right, to attack the Leuze Wood—Quadrilateral line. On the right, the 1/4th London (Royal Fusiliers), keeping close under the barrage, easily reached its first objective, which lay about three hundred yards ahead. The companies of the 1/12th London (Rangers), on the left, were exposed to the rapid fire of rifle and machine guns from front and flank ; only the right company reached its first objective, the Leuze Wood—Ginchy road, and then too late to follow the barrage when it lifted at 5.25 p.m. The Fusiliers went on again at that hour and reached their final objective, the German trench south-east of the Quadrilateral. Losses were heavy during the advance, but consolidation was begun, and touch obtained with the 1/9th London near the Morval road, whilst patrols pushed forward down the slope

[1] The French, who did not attack on 9th September, had done the same on the opposite side. It had been agreed to " pinch out " Combles as the Allied advance progressed.

[2] This " hard struggle " absorbed part of the *II./28th Reserve*, which reinforced the *III./Bn.* holding the regimental sector. The *I./65th*, next on the left (Combles sector), also assisted. " Res. Regt. No. 28."

[3] Groups of the *11th Company* in Leuze Wood and Bouleaux Wood were overrun. Part of *I./28th Reserve* reinforced the line, and it is claimed that some lost ground was recaptured. Touch with the *161st* was lost, and established by patrols later. " Res. Regt. No. 28."

towards Morval. Detached parties of Germans which approached as darkness fell were dispersed by Lewis-gun fire ; later, a German working party was located and suffered the same fate.[1]

The left of the Rangers was definitely held up by fire from the enemy trenches south-east of Ginchy, as were the Irish troops of the 16th Division next on the left. The right of the Rangers, whose objective was the Quadrilateral, made another advance, but losing direction, came up behind the centre of the Fusiliers. A heavy German barrage rendered communication with the front line difficult, and the thick autumn mist which arose as the sun set prevented observation from the air, so that brigade and divisional headquarters received little information. The Kensingtons, brought forward to hold the assembly trenches, had been used piecemeal to safeguard the left of the brigade, and after darkness fell the London Scottish were called upon to link up between the Quadrilateral and the Irish troops reported to be in Ginchy. Believing that the Quadrilateral had been captured, the Scottish advanced in **10 Sept.** six waves about 12.15 A.M. on the 10th, but darkness and mist again caused a loss of direction. There was confused fighting, one party of Germans which attacked the Scottish from the rear being routed with the bayonet, and when dawn broke some of the battalion found themselves amongst the Fusiliers and Rangers in and about the trench south-east of the Quadrilateral.

Fighting continued on the extreme right of the XIV. Corps during the 10th September. At 7 A.M., in heavy mist, the Queen's Westminster (1/16th London), attacked south-eastwards from Leuze Wood ; but the covering barrage was feeble, owing to a telephone breakdown, and no ground could be gained whilst machine guns in Loop Trench and along the sunken Combles road were still in action. Another effort at 3 P.M., made with the assistance of a company of the 1/2nd London after a Stokes mortar bombardment, progressed a hundred yards, and was then driven back by shell-fire. As attempts to bomb up to the Quadrilateral failed, nothing was accomplished on the front of the 56th Division on this day. At night the 169th Brigade was replaced by a composite brigade from the 5th

---

[1] This attack appears to have demolished the left flank of the *161st*, prisoners admitting heavy losses. " Regt. No. 65 " states that it despatched two companies to fill a gap in the line here, and that these took up a position along the railway north-west of Bouleaux Wood.

T

Division, the 168th being relieved by Br.-General G. H. B. Freeth's 167th Brigade.

9 Sept.   The left attack of the XIV. Corps on the 9th September was delivered by the 16th Division.   During the previous six days most of Major-General Hickie's troops had been engaged in the operations conducted by the 5th and 20th Divisions : now the three brigades were under his own command, but all weak in numbers and very tired.   Br.-General Ramsey, whose 48th Brigade was to capture Ginchy, reported that his men would require to be relieved as soon as they had taken the village, and he was assured that this would be done.

On the left of the 56th Division the 6/Royal Irish and 8/R. Munster Fusiliers of the 47th Brigade, with a detachment of the 6/Connaught Rangers in support, received belated orders to wait two minutes after zero hour in order to allow of a final intense bombardment.   The 48th Brigade, however, advanced punctually at 4.45 P.M., its movement bringing down the German counter-barrage. The leading lines of the 47th Brigade then pressed forward, only to be stopped by machine-gun fire at close range, the German second trench having received most of the British bombardment.   Renewed attempts also ended in failure, although the 7/R. Inniskilling Fusiliers (attached from the 49th Brigade) was brought up as reinforcement.

This check involved the 1/R. Munster Fusiliers, which formed the right of the 48th Brigade assault, but a wheel to the flank routed the nearest Germans, and the Munsters pressed on.   Irishmen were already streaming into Ginchy ; [1] beyond the Guillemont road, the 7/R. Irish rifles, closely followed by the 7/R. Irish Fusiliers (attached from the 49th Brigade), had met with slight opposition, and before 5 P.M. they reached the first objective which followed the line of the road called Hans Crescent and thence ran south-eastward through Ginchy.   At 5.25 P.M. the 8/R. Dublin Fusiliers, which had followed the 1/R. Munster Fusiliers, carried on the attack through the village, the 8/R. Inniskilling Fusiliers (from the 49th Brigade) coming in on their right.   Meanwhile, the 9/R. Dublin Fusiliers, with men of the 7/R. Irish Rifles who had made no pause on the first objective, and some of the 7/R. Irish Fusiliers, were clearing

---

[1] Held by the *I./19th Bavarians*, who were also in the trenches east of Delville Wood.   The *II./19th* was in close support, but east of Ginchy touch with the *161st* (*185th Division*) was only maintained by patrols.

the western part of Ginchy. A number of Germans sur- 9–10
rendered, others fled towards Flers and Lesboeufs, and the Sept.
eager Irishmen, following in pursuit, had to be brought back
before consolidation could begin on a line through the
orchards on the northern side of the ruins. A section of
the 156th Field Company R.E. proceeded to construct a
strongpoint at the corps boundary on the Delville Wood
road, a similar work being put in hand on the Lesboeufs
road to strengthen the other flank.

Thus the honour of capturing Ginchy fell to the 48th
Brigade with two battalions of the 49th. Two hundred
prisoners were collected, but the losses of the six battalions
were very heavy, especially in officers,[1] and the new
position formed an awkward salient which invited counter-
attack. The Germans did, indeed, make several attempts
to re-enter Ginchy during the evening, and in repulsing
them a distinguished part was played by the engineers. On
the left flank of the brigade, the XV. Corps had made
no progress, for, although the Germans had relinquished
their hold on the eastern point of Delville Wood, the 164th
Brigade (55th Division) was unable to secure Hop Alley
and Ale Alley. A frontal attack from Pilsen Lane at the
general zero hour had resulted in some troops entering Hop
Alley only to be forced out by artillery and machine-gun
fire.[2]

The 3rd Guards Brigade (Br.-General C. E. Corkran)
had already moved to relieve the 16th Division. During
the night of the 9th/10th September the 1/Welsh Guards
took over Ginchy from the 48th Brigade, a very difficult
operation and not accomplished without some fighting,
for parties of Germans were still to be encountered. The
4/Grenadier Guards came up a little later to relieve the 47th
Brigade in the angle formed by the Wedge Wood—Ginchy
road and the Leuze Wood—Guillemont road, but the new-
comers found themselves out of touch with the Welsh

---

[1] Lieut.-Colonel H. P. Dalzell-Walton, 8/R. Inniskilling Fusiliers, and
Captain W. J. Murphy, commanding 9/R. Dublin Fusiliers, were killed.
Lieut.-Colonel FitzR. E. P. Curzon, 6/Royal Irish (47th Brigade) was killed
by a shell on the night of 9th/10th September.

[2] The left company of the *I./19th Bavarians* south-east of Ginchy had
held its own, although its fate was for a time unknown. Opposite Delville
Wood the line had also been maintained. One company in Ginchy had
been rolled up from the left (" we had reached the bitter end "), and here
the Irish advance carried away part of the *II./19th* in rear. Attempts to
counter-attack from north of the village made by *II./19th* at 6.20 P.M. and
9 P.M. (when the troops lost their way in the darkness) did not succeed.
" Bav. Regt. No. 19."

Guards.   Major-General G. P. T. Feilding, commanding the
Guards Division, took over the sector at 10 A.M. on the
10th September, but some parties of Irish troops were not
relieved until the evening of that day.[1]   Meanwhile, the
Welsh Guards had been heavily attacked from the north-
east through the early morning mist, the Germans getting
into Ginchy again for a time.   Other attacks were beaten
off about 11 A.M., and again in the afternoon, after a fierce
struggle and heavy loss on both sides.   In this fighting a
part was borne by the 1/Grenadiers which had been sent up
to fill the gap between the Welsh Guards and the 4/Grenadier
Guards.[2]

9 Sept.   At the junction of the XV. Corps and III. Corps the
attack of the 9th September consisted of another attempt
to carry Wood Lane, the 1st Division (III. Corps) also
endeavouring to clear High Wood.   For the assault on
Wood Lane[3] the 1st Division employed the 2/K.R.R.C. and
2/R. Sussex (2nd Brigade), which captured their objectives
in splendid style, although with considerable loss.   On
their right, the Rifles obtained touch with the 165th
Brigade (55th Division, XV. Corps), the 1/5th and 1/6th
King's having secured the lower end of Wood Lane at the
second attempt by bombing forward from Orchard Trench ;
but the Sussex, on the left, had to dig a defensive flank
to connect with the line in High Wood where the attack
had failed.

The 1/Northamptonshire (also 2nd Brigade) had occupied a new crater formed by a mine exploded at the eastern
corner of the wood 30 seconds before zero hour,[4] but lost
it, after a bitter fight with bombs, about ninety minutes
later.   In the wood the Northamptonshire and 2/R. Munster

---

[1] The losses of the 16th Division (infantry, R.E. and pioneers), 1st–10th
September, were returned as 240 officers and 4,090 other ranks out of 435
and 10,410.   The division departed to join the Second Army.

[2] A company of the *II./14th Bavarians* had been used to strengthen
the German line.   At 7.25 A.M. on 10th September a counter-attack was
launched by the *III./19th* advancing astride the Ginchy—Lesboeufs road.
Owing to the " terrible bombardment ", no reports were received from the
leading companies until after nightfall, and then battalion headquarters
was informed that the attempt had failed.   " The confusion had become
" even more pronounced ".   The *III./14th* was then put in, but suffered
heavily from murderous machine-gun and artillery fire : few who got into
Ginchy were able to retire again.   Regimental histories.

[3] See Sketch 33.

[4] A charge of 3,000 lbs. of ammonal was used, and the explosion cut
into the crater formed on 3rd September, inflicting considerable loss upon
the Germans occupying it.

Fusiliers (3rd Brigade), on their left, could make no headway, the Munsters even being attacked in their turn ; and the 10/Gloucestershire (from the 1st Brigade), advancing against the western face, entered the wood only to be forced out again by bombing attacks and enfilade machine-gun fire. In all, 55 unwounded prisoners, mostly of the *5th Bavarian Regiment*, were brought back and a few machine guns were captured.[1]

Fighting continued on the front of the XIV. Corps, 11–13 which was chiefly concerned in pushing forward its centre Sept. so as to include the Quadrilateral and Ginchy Telegraph in its line before the big offensive should be launched.[2] On the night of the 11th/12th September the sector of the 3rd Guards Brigade was taken over by the 1/Grenadiers and 2/Scots Guards with orders to round up the Germans still occupying the re-entrant in the brigade front. The line was advanced, and by daybreak next morning two officers and 114 other ranks of the *III./14th Bavarians* had been sent back as prisoners. At 6 A.M. on the 12th the 1/Grenadiers made a little ground towards Ginchy Telegraph, whilst the 1/8th Middlesex (167th Brigade), which had repulsed a German counter-attack 24 hours earlier, did likewise southeast of the Quadrilateral : as a converging movement, however, the operation was a failure. Before the 2nd and 1st Guards Brigades took over the line on the following night the Grenadiers pushed eastward from Ginchy for some distance, astride the Morval road.[3]

By this time the 6th Division (Major-General C. Ross) had taken over the centre of the XIV. Corps front from the Leuze Wood—Morval road to the outskirts of Ginchy, relieving the left of the 56th Division and the right of the Guards. Patrols had discovered no live Germans in the trenches immediately south-east of Ginchy and at 6 A.M. on the 13th September the 71st Brigade (Br.-General FitzJ. M. Edwards) attacked the Quadrilateral from the southwest. Although the line of the Leuze Wood—Ginchy road

---

[1] The *II./5th Bavarians* (*4th Bavarian Division*) had been holding Wood Lane, with one company in shell-holes near its southern end. The regimental history regrets "the loss of many good, irreplaceable men".

[2] See Sketch 34.

[3] On the night 11th/12th September the *5th Bavarian Division* relieved the *19th Bavarians* north and north-east of Ginchy by the *7th Bavarians* ; on the following night the division began to relieve the *161st Regiment* (*185th Division*) in and about the Quadrilateral, putting in the *21st Bavarians*.

11–13 was gained and held, further advance was stopped by the
Sept. fire of the German machine guns ; and a fresh effort, made
at 6 P.M. likewise came to nothing.   The two battalions
concerned, 9/Suffolk and 2/Sherwood Foresters, reported a
total loss of 21 officers and 500 other ranks in these gallant
but unfortunate affairs.   After darkness fell a company of
the 2/Irish Guards (2nd Guards Brigade) suffered heavy loss
in an attempt to deal with some German machine-gun posts
near the Ginchy—Morval road ; but on the northern edge
of Ginchy the 2/Grenadiers (1st Guards Brigade) advanced
and straightened the line.

Lord Cavan had previously decided that if the evening
operation against the Quadrilateral should fail the " situa-
" tion must be accepted ", and the general attack of the
15th September launched from the existing line.[1]   At an
Army conference on the 11th it had been suggested that the
56th Division should carry Loop Trench next day when the
French were to attack,[2] but Major-General Hull pointed
out that he already possessed good observation over
Combles, and that his right flank was adequately protected
by his present line along the south-eastern edge of Leuze
Wood : he would much prefer to save his men for the big
operation.   General Rawlinson agreed to this course,
observing that Loop Trench could then be secured " with
" the aid of tanks ".

On the 12th September, at a XV. Corps conference,
Lieut.-General Horne announced that when the general
attack was launched he proposed to clear up the situation
east of Delville Wood where the awkward re-entrant in
the British line was liable to hamper both his own right
and Lord Cavan's left.   He would use two tanks for this
purpose.

THE RESERVE ARMY [3]

THE ATTACK ASTRIDE THE ANCRE

3 Sept.   General Gough's preparations for his postponed attacks
which were to continue the envelopment of Thiepval had
been pressed forward energetically in spite of the bad
weather, and it was hoped to make substantial progress on

---

[1] Lord Cavan resumed command of the XIV. Corps on 10th September.
[2] See Note at end of Chapter.
[3] The official name " Battle of Pozières Ridge " covers the fighting east
and south-east of the Ancre up to the 3rd September inclusive, but not
the attack north-west of the river on that day.

Sketch 35.

THE SOMME, 1916:
Ancre Operations, 3rd Sept.

British Front Line ———
German trenches ∿∿∿∿
Objective –·–·–·–

Scale of Yards
0   500   1000
Heights in metres

Thiepval

SCHWABEN REDOUBT

XIV. R.

26 R.

St Pierre Divion

III/66th

STRASBURG LINE

I/180th

APES NOSE

146th

II.

147th

4.9.

121st R.

119th R.

116th

Hamel

117th

39.

V.

MARY REDAN

BEAUMONT HAMEL

14.4th (4.8.)

Mill

ANCRE

Compiled in the Historical Section (Military Branch).
3060/38.

Ordnance Survey 1937
Crown Copyright Reserved

the 3rd September. Although the Anzac Corps and the
right of the II. Corps were allotted very limited objectives,
the attack astride the Ancre was more ambitious. South-east
of the river, the left of the II. Corps (49th Division) was to
carry two lines of German trenches on a frontage of 1,000
yards ; on the following day it was to secure both St. Pierre
Divion and the Strasburg Line, which linked that village
and Schwaben Redoubt, with a view to further progress
east and south-east against the redoubt and towards
Thiepval. The 39th Division (V. Corps), beyond the Ancre,
was expected to capture three lines of hostile trenches on
the spur south of Beaumont Hamel and, by an advance up
the river valley, cover the flank of the 49th Division during
its first advance. Plans were made, in the event of success,
for the II. Corps to push in towards Thiepval from the
south and south-east on the succeeding days.

The infantry of the 49th Division (Major-General E. M.
Perceval) assaulted at 5.13 A.M. from its assembly trenches
along the Hamel—Thiepval road. It advanced under an
excellent field-gun barrage whilst the heavy artillery shelled
the German positions to the south-east of the objective, the
near face of the Schwaben Redoubt and the Strasburg Line,
Thiepval being subjected to a hail of gas bombs and
ammonal bombs discharged by the Special Brigade R.E.
The greater part of No Man's Land was crossed with few
casualties, and on the right the 1/4th and 1/5th Duke of
Wellington's of Br.-General E. F. Brereton's 147th Brigade
occupied most of the German front line and penetrated
as far as the support trench. Unfortunately some loss of
direction occurred during the advance, so that the 1/5th
Duke of Wellington's, which had suffered rather heavily
in negotiating the German wire, failed to capture the salient
called Pope's Nose, and other parties of Germans were left
in possession of their front line. Galling machine-gun fire
opened from Schwaben Redoubt and also from the Strasburg
Line, whence a counter-attack by bombing parties was soon
delivered. On the left, the 146th Brigade (Br.-General
M. D. Goring-Jones) did not do so well: most of the 1/6th
West Yorkshire, being enfiladed by machine-gun fire from
Pope's Nose, failed to force an entry into the German front
trench, and few men of the 1/8th West Yorkshire, next to
the river, reached the enemy support line.

Mist prevented visual signalling, and so many runners
failed to negotiate the German barrage that for some time the
situation remained unknown in rear. Then unmistakable

3 Sept. signs of failure were seen : the West Yorkshire began to drift back and by 7.30 A.M. all of the 146th Brigade who could had regained the British trenches. The groups of the 147th Brigade in the German trenches maintained the fight stoutly until bombs ran short, and then, with most of their officers killed or wounded, the survivors began to make their way back, suffering further loss as they did so. By 10 A.M. the withdrawal upon this part of the front was complete.[1]

Br.-General Goring-Jones had been anxious to make another attempt with fresh battalions, but the retirement of the 147th Brigade resulted in new orders for a general resumption of the attack in the evening. These were cancelled later, for the division was in no condition to deliver it.[2]

There was little fault to find with the artillery preparation and support ; [3] but a frontal attack, with no attempt at surprise, upon this portion of the original German defences, commanded as it was by Schwaben Redoubt, seems to have offered little chance of success. Moreover, the troops were very tired, and in the attacking battalions were many partially trained reinforcements posted from many different regiments. These men displayed a certain apathy and lack of determination, in sharp contrast to the devotion of the platoon leaders who died with their usual gallantry, and to the splendid resolution of the older soldiers. It is but fair to add that so inexperienced were some of the new arrivals that when they were called upon to follow the British barrage they thought they were asked to walk into a German one.

Beyond the river the 39th Division (Major-General G. J. Cuthbert) also attacked on a frontage of 1,000 yards. It had Br.-General M. L. Hornby's 116th Brigade (11/R. Sussex and 14/Hampshire) on the right and Br.-General R. D. F. Oldman's 117th Brigade (16/Rifle Brigade and

---

[1] The relief of the *III./180th* (*26th Reserve Division*) in the St. Pierre Divion sector had just been completed by the *III./66th* (detached from the *52nd Division* facing Hébuterne) when the attack was launched. The German regimental histories state that the British who got in were turned out by bombing counter-attacks, the *III./180th* taking part.

[2] The four battalions engaged had sustained over twelve hundred casualties.

[3] A battery of the CCXLVI. Brigade R.F.A. (49th Division) in action south-west of Hamel, was shelled and had many casualties. Captain W. B. Allen, R.A.M.C., dressed all the wounded under heavy fire, completing his task although he received four shell wounds. He was awarded the V.C.

17/Sherwood Foresters) on the left; the 4th/5th Black Watch **3 Sept.** (118th Brigade) was detailed to work up the Ancre valley and keep the advance in touch with that of the 49th Division. All battalions were much under establishment.[1] The artillery preparation appeared to be satisfactory and wire well cut,[2] and the advance at 5.10 A.M., when an intense barrage opened on the German front line, started well.

In the 116th Brigade both battalions secured the German front trench, which was badly damaged, without much opposition, the Germans who stood up to fire at the stormers becoming targets for the brigade machine guns firing overhead. The Hampshire, who had lost more heavily, made little advance beyond the enemy front line ; the Sussex drove the Germans from parts of the support trench, some men reaching the final objective. In the Ancre valley the Highlanders suffered from machine-gun fire and could do little more than support the right of the Sussex : in any case, their progress depended upon the success of the attack along the higher ground. The 16/Rifle Brigade, right battalion of the 117th Brigade, had lost direction, and few entered the German position, whilst, on the extreme left, the Sherwood Foresters were held up by machine guns firing from inside the British flank barrage. Mist and the smoke of the bombardment prevented observation ; No Man's Land was swept by fire of all kinds,[3] so that it was difficult for runners to get back with reports of the situation.

The troops who had secured a footing in the German trenches fought gamely but with little chance of success. The repulse of the 49th Division enabled the enemy to enfilade his lost trenches from the vicinity of St. Pierre Divion ; German guns of heavy calibre shelled the captured front line ; and parties of hostile bombers, each from twenty to forty strong, soon attacked from either flank. Withdrawal, however, only began when the supply of British bombs became exhausted, and some parties of the

---

[1] 116th Brigade, 1,879 rifles ; its two assaulting units numbered about 1,300. 117th Brigade, 2,714 rifles.

[2] It was now the growing practice of the Germans to throw out loose wire through which it was very difficult for the British artillery to cut passages. The ordinary entanglement consisting of wire stretched taut between pickets was much easier to deal with.

[3] Tunnels had been driven forward from the British trenches by the 174th Tunnelling Company R.E., and the ends were opened up in No Man's Land prior to zero hour ; but it was found impossible for the pioneers, working in the open under heavy fire, to dig forward to the German front-line.

3 Sept. Sussex and Black Watch did not come in till nightfall.[1] Once the failure of the 49th Division became known, the corps commander judged it undesirable to use the meagre reserves of the 39th Division in another attempt to secure an objective which would only have created an awkward salient in the British line.[2]

OPERATIONS SOUTH OF THIEPVAL : THE FIGHTING ON POZIÈRES RIDGE

At the same hour on the 3rd September the II. Corps attacked from Hindenburg Trench against the German front line south of the Wonder Work—the capture of which was deferred—whilst on the left an attempt was made by advancing eastwards to capture the original German front line on a frontage of 500 yards northward from the Thiepval road.[3]   These operations were conducted by Major-General E. G. T. Bainbridge's 25th Division, the 75th Brigade (Br.-General E. St. G. Pratt) using two companies of the 3/Worcestershire (attached from the 7th Brigade) and two companies of the 2/South Lancashire for the right attack. The left attack was confided to the 1/Wiltshire, also from the 7th Brigade.   In each case, the troops advanced with great resolution and, in spite of heavy losses, entered the German line, where they were subjected to such deadly artillery and machine-gun fire that consolidation proved impossible and withdrawal inevitable.[4]   Among the casualties were Lieut.-Colonels W. B. Gibbs, 3/Worcestershire, and H. T. Cotton, 2/South Lancashire, killed ; and Major S. S. Ogilvie, 1/Wiltshire, wounded.

The I. Anzac Corps made another attempt to capture Fabeck Graben, from the Courcelette track westward, and Mouquet Farm, and, although not wholly successful, the operations resulted in the only gain of the day.

The 13th Australian Brigade (Br.-General T. W. Glasgow) employed for this operation the 49th (Queens-

---

[1] The five battalions of the 39th Division which took part in the assault lost nearly 1,850 of all ranks.   Captain F. T. Skinner, commanding the 14/Hampshire, was killed.

[2] The sector, including the Ancre valley, attacked by the 39th Division was held by the *119th Reserve Regiment*.   It is admitted that the British reached the third line.   Nearly the whole of the regiment appears to have been engaged, and two companies of the *I./121st Reserve* came up through Beaumont Hamel to assist the counter-attacks.

[3] See Sketch 29.

[4] The trenches attacked were held by the *5th Foot Guard Regiment* in the left sector of the *4th Guard Division*.

land), 52nd (S. & W. Australia and Tasmania) and 51st
(W. Australia) Battalions, whose leading waves advanced
close under the barrage at 5.10 A.M.   On the right, the 49th
carried Fabeck Graben, where the Germans fought stoutly,
few surviving the struggle ; in the centre, the 52nd engaged
in a bitter fight with bomb, bayonet and rifle butt, but
could not altogether clear their part of the trench ; and on
the left, the 51st reached the farm before the defenders
could emerge from their dug-outs, some of the Australians going beyond their objective.   Two officers and
100 men, mostly of the *1st Guard Reserve Regiment*, were
captured, but the three Australian battalions were not in
touch on the captured line, and there were many officer
casualties.

A heavy German barrage came down, and soon the
enemy attacked in his turn.   Repulsed by the fire of the
49th, he drove back the 52nd and enveloped two companies
of the 51st in a trench beyond the farm.   After a very
gallant resistance, the survivors of this detachment were
captured ;   meanwhile the farm was lost, the Germans
entering it from the north-east by tunnels not located by
the Australians.   The 50th (S. Australia), remaining battalion of the brigade, was absorbed into the fight, and the
chief necessity was now to safeguard the left of the 49th,
which still held on to about three hundred yards of Fabeck
Graben.   In the afternoon, part of the 13th Canadians
(Royal Highlanders) arrived, followed next day by more
Canadian troops.   The Germans were then bombed back
and a barricade was erected on the right ; the left of the
captured portion of Fabeck Graben was linked up with the
Australian position astride the O.G. trenches.[1]

The Canadian Corps (Lieut.-General Hon. Sir J. H. G.
Byng) was now replacing the I. Anzac Corps in the line.
Command passed at 3 P.M. on the 3rd, and at noon Major-
General Cox (4th Australian Division)[2] handed over to
Major-General A. W. Currie, commanding the 1st Canadian
Division.   The relief of the 13th Australian Brigade was
completed by the 3rd Canadian Brigade (Br.-General G. S.

[1] Portions of all three regiments of the *1st Guard Reserve Division* took
part in this fighting ; reinforcements came from the *4th Guard Division*,
on the west, and from the *133rd Reserve (24th Reserve Division)*.   On 5th
September the *45th Reserve Division* began to relieve the *1st Guard
Reserve Division*.

[2] The casualties of the 4th Australian Division 27th August–4th
September were returned as 64 officers and 2,423 other ranks.

5-12
Sept.
Tuxford) under very heavy shell-fire by 8.30 A.M. on the 5th September,[1] the last of the Australians to leave being the 49th Battalion after it had repulsed four rather half-hearted counter-attacks during the day and night of the 4th.

Enough has been said to show that Australia has every reason to be proud of the devotion and gallantry of her troops in the fiery ordeal of the Somme battle. Little opportunity for spectacular achievement had been vouch-safed them ; but the men had proved themselves skilful and self-reliant—if at times over-reckless—fighters, and their leaders were quick to benefit by their first experience of offensive warfare on the Western Front.

Sir Douglas Haig wished the Canadian Corps to have a chance to settle in before undertaking any offensive operations ; but there was little respite on the Mouquet Farm front. During a battalion relief in the early morning of the 8th September, the Germans, after several attempts, regained their lost portion of Fabeck Graben.[2] In the evening two other attacks near the farm were repulsed, and similar attempts of the enemy to regain ground during the four following days were likewise defeated. At 4.45 P.M. on the 9th—zero hour also for the French and for the Fourth Army—the 2nd Canadian Battalion (1st Brigade of the 1st Canadian Division) attacked the German front trench astride the railway track leading to Martinpuich. After hand to hand fighting the objective was secured on a frontage of 500 yards, and more than sixty prisoners of the *211th Reserve Regiment* were sent back. Touch was maintained with the 15th Division (III. Corps, Fourth Army), but the new line was mercilessly shelled by the enemy, who delivered several counter-attacks all of which were repulsed.[3]

On the night of the 11th/12th September, the 2nd Canadian Division (Major-General R. E. W. Turner) took over the right sector of the corps front, and twenty-four hours later the 3rd Canadian Division (Major-General L. J.

---

[1] The 1st Canadian Brigade had taken over the right sector of the Anzac front at the end of August.

[2] According to German accounts, by detachments of the *1st Guard Reserve Division* and some volunteers of the *211th Reserve* (*45th Reserve Division*). After this affair command passed to the latter division.

[3] Corpl. L. Clarke, 2nd Canadian Bn., won the V.C. on 9th September. He attacked, almost single-handed, a party of about twenty Germans and routed them, capturing one after he had received a bayonet thrust in the leg.

Lipsett) came in on the Mouquet Farm front, the 1st Canadian Division being withdrawn into corps reserve. The German bombardment rarely slackened, and by the 13th September the corps had lost a total of 97 officers and 2,724 other ranks.

The 25th Division was relieved in the right sector of the 7-14 II. Corps by the 11th Division (Lieut.-General Sir C. L. **Sept.** Woollcombe) on the 7th September.[1] In the early morning of that day the 49th Division front east of the Ancre was heavily bombarded for two hours with lacrymatory and gas shell mixed with high explosive. About a hundred men were affected by the gas. It appeared that the enemy, being apprehensive of a fresh attack, had hoped to catch the troops in their assembly positions.[2]

Although the Reserve Army had now been ordered to husband its resources—only the Canadian Corps had an active part to play in the first stages of the big offensive—corps commanders were left at liberty to initiate minor attacks which promised to be profitable. General Gough would not permit more than two battalions to be employed simultaneously, and Lieut.-General Jacob decided that under these conditions the 11th Division might gain ground on the Thiepval spur. Advancing from Hindenburg Trench behind an excellent barrage at 6.30 P.M. on the 14th September, two companies of the 8/Duke of Wellington's and two of the 9/West Yorkshire (Br.-General T. H. F. Price's 32nd Brigade) carried without a pause the German front line and then the Wonder Work, together with 250 yards of Hohenzollern Trench on the right ; also the trench on the left as far as the Thiepval road.[3] Beyond the road a detachment of the 6/Green Howards made an appreciable advance and secured the left flank. All this was accomplished at slight cost, but the enemy shelled his

[1] The 11th Division, which had fought in Gallipoli, arrived in France from Egypt at the beginning of July 1916 ; its brigades had spent a few weeks in the trenches near Arras.

[2] On 4th September the V. Corps had discharged gas S.W. of Hébuterne and S.W. of Beaumont Hamel, using 986 cylinders in all on a frontage of 1,600 yards. The statements of prisoners subsequently captured indicated that the German troops suffered severely.

From 10th September the whole corps front—Ancre to Hébuterne—was held by two divisions only, 39th and 2nd, each with three brigades in line : it was not the intention of Sir Douglas Haig to attempt any important operation beyond the Ancre, but very active trench warfare had to be carried on unceasingly in order to hold the Germans to their ground.

[3] See Sketch 29.

lost positions very heavily, the total British casualties amounting to over 700 officers and men.[1]

NOTE

The French Operations, 3rd-14th September [2]

Sketches A, 40. Map 1 ("1916" Vol. I.). The French Sixth Army attacked along its whole line north of the Somme at noon on the 3rd September and achieved a considerable success. The greater part of Cléry, most of the German defences along the Cléry—Le Forest road, and the village of Le Forest were captured ; but on the extreme left the I. Corps afforded no assistance to the British right, although the high ground south of Combles was occupied and Bois Douage was entered. Next day the I. Corps was obliged to defend the edge of the Combles ravine, south-west of the village, against strong German counter-attacks, and could make little progress north-eastward from Le Forest towards Rancourt ; farther south, the VII. Corps advanced its left flank and improved its positions round Cléry. On the 5th September the capture of Falfemont Farm by the British enabled the French left to get in touch across the Combles ravine ; patrols pushed forward outside the south-eastern edge of Combles and Ferme de l'Hôpital ($\frac{1}{4}$ a mile east of Le Forest) was captured. The VII. Corps cleared Cléry and obtained touch with the XXXIII. Corps (right of the Sixth Army), which had occupied Ommiécourt on the south bank of the Somme. Next day an attempt of the I. Corps to advance south-east of Combles did not succeed.

On the 4th September the Tenth Army had attacked south of the Somme from Chilly to Barleux (both inclusive), but the results of three days of heavy fighting were unsatisfactory ; although Soyécourt was captured and Chilly enveloped, Barleux, Derniécourt and Vermandovillers remained in German hands.

The bad weather and the state of the ground now combined with the necessity of carrying out extensive reliefs to impose a halt in the operations. It was not until the 12th September that General Fayolle attacked again, the XXXIII. Corps being directed on Mont St. Quentin, the VII. on Bouchavesnes, and the I. Corps, which masked Combles by occupying the Maurepas—Frégicourt road, upon Rancourt. Good progress was made on this day. The I. Corps carried Bois d'Anderlu, and, on the right, broke through the German defences north-west of Marrières Wood ; the VII. Corps captured Bouchavesnes, which was but feebly defended, and formed a defensive flank facing south-east, less progress having been made farther south between Cléry and Feuillaucourt.

The direction of the I. Corps advance was now northward, its right directed on Rancourt and Sailly-Saillisel. It attacked again on the 13th, gaining some ground towards Rancourt and making good progress up the German trenches as far as Le Priez Farm. The VII.

[1] The *89th Reserve Brigade* had relieved the *4th Guard Division* between Mouquet Farm and Thiepval. Prisoners of the *209th Reserve Regiment* were taken at the Wonder Work, and men of the *213th Reserve* farther west.

[2] F.O.A. iv. (iii.), pp. 84-137.

Corps repulsed violent counter-attacks at Bouchavesnes ; nearer the Somme deep mud and heavy German fire prevented any advance. Nothing of importance was achieved by the XXXIII. and the VII. Corps on the 14th September, but the I. Corps, attacking later than the others, pushed its line a little nearer Rancourt and captured Le Priez Farm. At this stage an interval for reorganization and the carrying out of reliefs was greatly to be desired, but it was recognized that the big British offensive which was to open on the 15th September must be supported. Frégicourt, which Sir Douglas Haig had hoped to see in French hands before that date, was not yet captured.

The needs of the Tenth Army as regards ammunition and reserves were subordinate to those of the Sixth, but General Foch wished the offensive south of the Somme to be maintained so far as the available means permitted. The Tenth Army, however, undertook no enterprise of importance after the 6th September ; from the 9th until the 12th the Germans made frequent counter-attacks in the region of Berny, and recovered some ground.

CHAPTER XI

THE BATTLE OF FLERS—COURCELETTE

TACTICAL PLANS AND PREPARATIONS

(Map 1 ; Sketches A, 31)

Sept. THE Fourth Army plans for the new offensive were the subject of many Army and corps conferences throughout the first fortnight in September. When, on the 11th, formal orders and instructions were issued [1] corps commanders were well advanced with their preliminary measures, and the particular problems of each had been discussed and, so far as might be, settled.

Preparations proceeded whilst heavy fighting continued on the whole front of the XIV. Corps, and whilst the XV. and III. Corps were still engaged round Delville Wood and High Wood, so that an extra strain was thrown upon all concerned, especially the engineer services and the pioneer, labour, and transport units. The repair of damage wrought by German shell-fire to pipe-lines, water-points, shelters and roads often caused the diversion of effort which was urgently needed for work on new installations, tracks and hutments. Accommodation for the reinforcing divisions had to be provided ; communications to the front line required to be improved and duplicated, battery positions and battle headquarters constructed, new dumps formed, water supplies organized ; and arrangements had to be made for the carrying forward of essential services in the wake of the new advance.[2]

[1] Appendix 20.

[2] For work on forward roads and tracks, under Major-General R. U. H. Buckland, Chief Engineer, labour and material were concentrated at the expense of the Fourth Army back areas, which, however, benefited by the pushing forward of railheads to Albert and Fricourt. A broad-gauge line was opened as far as Maricourt before 10th September, and a metre-gauge track was nearly through to Montauban by that date.

The first phase of the offensive, as planned, involved a Sept.
series of the usual trench-to-trench assaults, with limited
objectives, carried out methodically according to a pre-
arranged time-table.

As his first objective (named the " Green Line ") Map 1.
General Rawlinson selected the Switch Line, together with Sketch
its connecting defences which covered Martinpuich, his 31.
right flank to secure possession of the forward slopes of the
high ground north-west of Combles. This represented an
advance of 1,000 yards or more on the front between the
Quadrilateral and Delville Wood, and of about six hundred
yards elsewhere.

The second objective (called the " Brown Line ")
included the German 3rd Position in front of Flers (XV.
Corps) and a series of subsidiary defences between Flers and
Martinpuich (III. Corps), involving a further advance of
500-800 yards on the main front of attack.

The third objective (" Blue Line "), 900–1,200 yards
beyond the second, comprised the German 3rd Position and
back position covering Morval and Lesboeufs (XIV. Corps),
and the village of Flers (XV. Corps) ; it extended so far
westward that an advance of some 350 yards by the III.
Corps would begin to envelop Martinpuich and threaten the
German gun positions south of Le Sars.[1]

The fourth objective (" Red Line "), 1,400–1,900 yards
beyond the Blue Line, included Morval and Lesboeufs
(XIV. Corps), together with Gueudecourt and its defences
(XV. Corps) ; the XV. Corps was to form a flank facing
north-westward between Gueudecourt and the German 3rd
Position beyond Flers. When these two corps arrived on
the Red Line they would have broken through the principal
enemy defences on a frontage of nearly $3\frac{1}{2}$ miles.[2]

As the attack progressed, the defensive flank above
Combles was to be extended by the right of the XIV. Corps
to the slopes south-east of Morval, the advance of the French

[1] It did not include that portion of the back position covering Gueudecourt, owing to the fact that, as the main advance was north-eastward, the
XV. Corps artillery would have to push forward to effective range before
it could provide the necessary support for such an assault.
[2] On 6th September Sir Douglas Haig reminded General Rawlinson that
the enemy might be preparing defences on the Bapaume—Beaulencourt—
Le Transloy line. Air reconnaissance during the first fortnight in September revealed a trench line covering Sailly-Saillisel and Le Transloy,
and, some 2,500 yards farther back, entrenchments E. and S.E. of
Bapaume extending in front of Riencourt, Villers au Flos, Rocquigny
($1\frac{1}{2}$ miles east of Le Transloy), thence behind Le Mesnil to the south. See
Sketch A.

U

Sept. Sixth Army, on the other side of the valley towards Frégi-court and Sailly-Saillisel,[1] combining to isolate Combles with its deep cellars and catacombs.[2] The left of the Fourth Army (III. Corps), west of Martinpuich, would link up with General Gough's right.

The Reserve Army was to play a subsidiary part in the opening stages of the offensive. On the 4th September, however, Lieut.-General Kiggell, Chief of the General Staff, visited General Gough to acquaint him with Sir Douglas Haig's intentions in the event of the Fourth Army failing to make such headway : the centre of the attack might then be shifted to the front of the Reserve Army, which, reinforced by troops and artillery from General Rawlinson's command, would be called upon to overwhelm the Thiepval position and establish itself there for the winter.

Reserve Army operation order, issued on the 12th September, directed the right of the Canadian Corps to attack in conjunction with the III. Corps of the Fourth Army, its object being to secure as many points of observa-tion as possible over the hostile Flers—Le Sars—Pys position. The II. Corps was to seize any opportunity to gain ground, particularly south of Thiepval into which gas cylinders would be projected, whilst the 49th Division dis-charged smoke as though to screen an advance. Beyond the Ancre the V. Corps was to provide smoke-screens at selected points and to carry out two raids.

The main attack of the Canadian Corps was to be made by the 2nd Canadian Division on a frontage of about one mile between its junction with the 15th Division (III. Corps) and the Ovillers—Courcelette track. On the right, where the objective was the outlying defences of Cource-

---

[1] General Fayolle's orders to the French Sixth Army were for the I. Corps to attack Rancourt and Frégicourt (" direction Sailly-Saillisel "), forming a defensive flank towards Combles, whilst the V. Corps—now introduced into the line as the French advance was expanding N., N.E., E. and S.E.—gained a footing on the southern edge of St. Pierre Vaast Wood. The VII. Corps and XXXIII. Corps were to undertake operations east of Bouchavesnes and Cléry, respectively. F.O.A. iv. (iii.), p. 137. (See Sketch A.)

[2] " The Combles catacombs are large subterranean caves, improved " into dug-outs near the church, and with their covering of about 30 " metres of earth and rock afford exceptional protection. These caves " are provided with three or four exits in all directions and offer the support " companies in and close to Combles excellent shelter when shelling is " heavy. There is also a first aid post here and accommodation for the " slightly wounded and sick. Naturally, the air is insufferably bad and " has to be continually improved with oxygen." Extracted from the history of the *65th Regiment*, which was holding the Combles sector.

lette including the sugar factory, this movement represented
an advance of 1,000 yards, the distance dropping to less
than 400 yards on the extreme left where the 3rd Canadian
Division would cover the flank. After the preliminary
bombardment the infantry was to go straight through to
its final objective, really a continuation of the Fourth
Army's first objective, the Green Line.

Zero hour being fixed for 6.20 A.M. (British " summer "
time) on the 15th September, General Rawlinson reckoned
on reaching the fourth objective (Red Line) before noon,
which would leave eight hours of daylight for the exploitation of his success. Two cavalry divisions were to be
passed through the Morval—Gueudecourt gap with the least
possible delay, and when a force of all arms had made
secure the eastern flank (Sailly-Saillisel—Bapaume) the bulk
of the Fourth Army would be free to advance northward,
rolling up the German defences which lay in its path. No
homogeneous force under a selected commander was to be
held in readiness for this occasion ; [1] but the Cavalry
Corps was given as its first objective [2] the high ground
between Rocquigny (1½ miles east of Le Transloy) and
Bapaume, also the enemy batteries in the area Le Sars—
Warlencourt—Thilloy, the XIV. and XV. Corps being
ordered to support the cavalry on the Rocquigny—
Bapaume line " as early as possible ". The railways by
which German reinforcements might arrive [3] were to be
" interfered with as much as possible " by the cavalry,
which would also raid corps and divisional headquarters.

A special Fourth Army instruction laid down the
principles to be observed in a general advance of all arms : [4]
in the first stage, precedence to be given to the guns moving
forward to support the later phases of the infantry attack ;
once the Red Line was reached and the artillery was in
action in its forward positions the rapid advance of the
cavalry became all-important ; when its leading divisions
had passed through the gap, light wagons with reserves of
food and ammunition for the infantry must have right of
way.[5] It was recognized that the passage of the cavalry
required careful regulation—" any attempt to push too

[1] See General Gough's rôle in 1st July offensive, " 1916 " Vol. I., pp.
267, 297, 305, 308.
[2] See Appendix 21.
[3] Achiet le Grand, Bapaume, and certain stations between Bapaume
and Cambrai were mentioned.
[4] Appendix 22.
[5] The infantry was to carry two days' rations on the man.

Sept. " much cavalry through at one time will only lead to con-
" fusion and delay "—and that its advance must be continuous and methodical. The construction of the necessary
roads and tracks for wheeled and horse traffic through the
shell-cratered area was to begin as soon as the attack
started, special parties being detailed for the purpose.[1]

Since the opening of the struggle on the 1st July the
G.H.Q. memorandum, " Training of Divisions for Offen-
" sive Action ", issued on the 8th May,[2] had been supplemented by others, but no new tactical ideas had been
introduced. Emphasis had, however, been laid upon certain
important points which tended to be forgotten or neglected
in the stress of battle : formation of infantry in the assault,
waves followed by small columns ; thorough " mopping
up " of captured trenches ; the bomb not to be allowed to
supplant the bullet ; proper consolidation of captured
positions ; machine-gun fire, direct and indirect, from the
rear ; Lewis guns on flanks and in forward positions ;
Stokes mortars as close-support weapons.

An important consideration was the time allowed the
fighting troops to prepare for an attack : it had been
estimated that at least six hours were required for the
passage of orders from corps to company commanders, so
great importance was now attached to the early issue of
preliminary instructions, which allowed opportunity for
reconnaissance and other essential preparations before
executive orders were received. This was a matter which
concerned artillery as much as infantry orders.

As regards battle communications, cases had occurred
of corps headquarters—usually well served by contact
aeroplanes—knowing more of the tactical situation than the
brigades in front, so that measures for the prompt forward
transmission of information were necessary. Signal arrangements now provided for the use of contact aeroplanes
on an increased scale, and sites for signal stations within
the hostile lines were to be selected beforehand, the utmost
use being made of German material. In the event of a
general advance it would be impossible to get out cable

---

[1] Divisions in the line were allotted routes on which they were to
start work at zero : thus, the 41st Division pioneers were to make a horse-
track, Montauban—Longueval—Flers, thence an up-and-down track to
Gueudecourt ; later, the C.E. XV. Corps would take these over and make
them fit for mechanical transport, using the personnel of the Labour
companies.
[2] See " 1916 " Vol. I., Appendix 17.

lines quickly enough, and it was reckoned that the establish- Sept. ment of a single telegraph line from brigade to division and thence to corps was as much as could be expected : this to be supplemented by relays of runners, cyclists, horsemen and motor-cyclists. Pigeons were to be kept for emergencies. Wireless stations were to be attached to the headquarters of many infantry brigades, but this method had the disadvantage that messages could be tapped by the enemy ; in any case, transmission would be slow and uncertain, as one station was liable to interfere with others.

The artillery of the Fourth Army was reinforced by five 60-pdr. batteries, one 6-inch howitzer battery and two 9.2-inch howitzer batteries, in addition to the field brigades of the newly-arrived divisions.[1] General Rawlinson was anxious to push forward before the opening of the battle as many batteries as possible in order to minimise artillery movement during the earlier stages of the fight, and the XV. Corps was able to accomplish a great deal in this Sketch A. direction.[2] Batteries selected to move forward during the

[1] At the opening of the battle there were in action :
XIV. Corps (G.O.C. R.A., Br.-General A. E. Wardrop) : Field artillery (Guards, 6th, 16th, 24th, 56th Divisions and one brigade 20th Division) : 18-pdrs., 244 ; 4.5″ hows., 64.
    Heavy and Siege artillery (4 groups). Howitzers : one 15″ ; two 12″ ; twenty 9.2″ ; eight 8″ ; forty 6″. Guns : two 9.2″ ; twenty-eight 60-pdrs. ; four, 4.7″.
XV. Corps (G.O.C. R.A., Br.-General E. W. Alexander) : Field artillery (5th, 7th, 14th, 21st, 41st and N.Z. Divisions) : 18-pdrs., 248 ; 4.5″ hows., 72.
    Heavy and Siege artillery (5 groups). Howitzers : two 12″ ; sixteen 9.2″ ; twenty-four 8″ ; twenty-four 6″. Guns : four 6″ ; thirty-four 60-pdrs. ; eight 4.7″.
III. Corps (G.O.C. R.A., Br.-General T. A. Tancred): Field artillery (15th, 23rd, 47th, 50th and 55th Divisions) : 18-pdrs., 228 ; 4.5″ hows., 64.
    Heavy and Siege artillery (5 groups). Howitzers : one 15″ ; four 12″ ; twelve 9.2″ ; sixteen 8″ ; twenty-eight 6″. Guns : one 12″ ; one 9.2″ ; ten 6″ ; forty 60-pdrs. ; eight 4.7″.
At a rough computation, there was one field gun (or howitzer) to every 10 yards of front, and one heavy gun (or howitzer) to every 29 yards. The figures on 1st July were respectively 21 and 57 ; at the Battle of Messines, June 1917, 10 and 21.
[2] Between 11th and 14th September most of the XV. Corps 60-pdrs. were brought farther up Caterpillar Valley from north of Mametz to the vicinity of Montauban ; the 6″, 8″ and 9.2″ howitzers from the Carnoy—Mametz valley to the Montauban—Bernafay Wood area ; and the two 12″ howitzers on railway mountings from the Loop (midway between Bray and Fricourt) to Maricourt. The bulk of the field artillery was pushed forward close behind Longueval and about Bazentin le Grand village and wood.
    In the XIV. Corps two field brigades came into action at Maltz Horn plateau early in the month, and before the battle opened nine more had found positions behind Wedge Wood—Guillemont—Waterlot Farm. It

Sept. early stages of the attack were equipped with portable bridges for the negotiation of trenches.

The Reserve Army had allotted to the Canadian Corps (G.O.C. R.A., Br.-General H. E. Burstall) three groups of heavy artillery,[1] and the 2nd Canadian Division, which was to make the main attack, had the support of nine field artillery brigades.[2] The 3rd Canadian Division, providing the defensive flank, had the assistance of six field artillery brigades,[3] and two more were kept in corps artillery reserve until the action should develop.

The first appearance of the tanks involved certain modifications in the artillery programmes.[4] On this account, the efforts made to increase the effectiveness of the British counter-battery work were all to the general good ; not only were they calculated to minimize the risk of tanks being destroyed by German shell-fire, but they also increased the prospect of pushing forward without undue loss large bodies of supporting and reserve troops. Of very doubtful expediency, however, was the order to leave lanes about 100 yards wide in both stationary and creeping barrages up to and including the first objective.[5] Through these lanes the tanks were to move in advance of the infantry upon their first objectives, certain strongpoints and trench junctions which had received special attention from the heavy artillery during the preliminary bombardment. Batteries firing from a flank, however, found it impossible to leave so narrow and well-defined a gap in their barrage lines. Some group commanders, anxious to reduce the risk of tanks being hit by British shells, provided for much wider lanes ; in any case prompt artillery action would be

---

was not possible to move the heavies forward, as no suitable positions were to be found.

The III. Corps, likewise, was unable to move its heavy artillery which was concentrated in Sausage Valley (E. and S.E. of La Boisselle) and in the Fricourt vicinity. The field batteries remained round Mametz Wood and in Caterpillar Valley and Sausage Valley, the last-named area being crowded with guns of all calibres. Several of the reinforcing field brigades took up positions in the open, relying upon net camouflage, in some cases obtained in haste by local purchase as far afield as Calais and Boulogne.

[1] Howitzers : sixteen 9.2″ ; twelve 8″ ; twenty 6″. Guns : sixteen 60-pdrs. One 12″ howitzer was out of action through wear.

[2] Artillery of 1st Canadian and 18th Divisions, with one brigade of the Lahore Division : total, 18-pdrs., 114 ; 4.5″ hows., 28.

[3] Artillery of 2nd Canadian Division and two brigades of 48th Division : total, 18-pdrs., 72 ; 4.5″ hows., 20.

[4] General Rawlinson was disposed to make as little alteration as possible in the accepted method of bombardment and attack, for he did not expect too much of the tanks.

[5] See XV. Corps Artillery Operation Order No. 47 (Appendix 25).

necessary to fill the gaps in the barrage in the event of the Sept. failure of the machines.

The general plan of advance as far as the fourth objective (Red Line) on the main front of attack, Morval-Gueudecourt (both inclusive) was worked out as follows : [1]

The tanks advance before zero hour in time to effect a tactical surprise by arriving on the Green Line 5 minutes before the infantry.

Zero hour (6.20 A.M.). The infantry leaves its trenches and approaches the creeping barrage [2] some 100 yards ahead, following it to the assault of the Green Line at 6.26 A.M., when it begins to move forward at the rate of 50 yards per minute.

6.40 to 6.50 A.M. The creeping barrage lifts from the Green Line to enable the infantry to occupy this objective.

7.20 A.M. Infantry and tanks advance together to the assault of the Brown Line, following the creeping barrage which moves at the rate of 100 yards in 3 minutes.

7.45–7.50 A.M. The creeping barrage lifts from the Brown Line to enable tanks and infantry to occupy this objective.

8.5–8.10 A.M. The creeping barrage, now become a covering barrage, lifts to enable the tanks to advance to their objectives on or about the Blue Line.

8.20 A.M. The infantry advances to the assault of the Blue Line.

10.35–10.40 A.M. The covering barrage lifts to enable the tanks to advance from the Blue Line.

10.50 A.M. The infantry advances to the assault of the Red Line (XV. Corps barrage lifts from the Gird trenches, in 3 stages, beginning from the right, at 10.50, 11.15 and 11.20 A.M.).

11.50 A.M. The bombardment of Gueudecourt ceases and the XV. Corps tanks and infantry complete the capture of the Red Line on that front.

It was not considered that the artillery could effectively cut the German wire in positions beyond the second objective (Brown Line) ; but the tanks, going on in advance, might here be of great service in making passages for the infantry.

---

[1] See also " Time Table of Attack ", following XV. Corps Operation Order No. 51 (Appendix 24) and XV. Corps Artillery Operation Order No. 47 (Appendix 25). Certain times and distances varied slightly to suit local conditions. On the XV. Corps front the Gueudecourt defences (Gird Trench and Gird Support) lay well beyond the Blue Line and the barrages were arranged accordingly. In the XIV. Corps, only the extreme left had a Brown Line objective.

[2] The XIV. Corps employed half its field artillery in the creeping barrage and half in the stationary barrage ; the XV. Corps used 25 per cent and 75 per cent respectively.

In the Reserve Army, the tanks, working in two groups each of three machines, were to advance at the same time as the infantry against the limited objective of the 2nd Canadian Division.

The first detachment of tanks had left Thetford for France on the 13th August, and by the 6th September both C and D Companies Heavy Branch Machine Gun Corps were assembled at Yvrench (9 miles north-east of Abbeville). Here a training centre on a small scale had been organized by Lieut.-Colonel J. Brough who then returned to England, leaving Lieut.-Colonel R. W. Bradley in command of all tank units in France. On the 3rd September Sir Douglas Haig had brought General Joffre to inspect the machines, whilst staff officers and others came daily in their hundreds to make acquaintance with the new arm. In spite of the limited facilities, some gun practice and exercises in handling and management were carried out, but there was practically no opportunity for tanks and infantry to train together.[1] On the 6th September began the forward movement, made by rail, to " The Loop "—midway between Bray and Fricourt—where trials over ground with confluent shell-holes, representing the worst conditions likely to be encountered, showed a speed of about 15 yards per minute, or rather greater than half a mile an hour. Detachments of infantry from some of the assaulting divisions attended such demonstrations as could be arranged whilst the overhaul and tuning-up of the machines proceeded.[2] Here, again, staff and regimental officers, eager for a first sight of the machines, visited the camp in embarrassing numbers.

Forty-nine tanks were expected to be available,[3] and all but seven of them were allotted to the Fourth Army,[4] which had issued general instructions for their employment.[5] Two nights before the assault the tanks would move to

[1] Detachments from all three brigades of the 56th Division carried out some attack practice with tanks at St. Riquier, near Yvrench, at the end of August.

[2] From 10th-14th September inclusive, the fitters of No. 711 Coy. A.S.C. (M.T.) worked day and night on these tasks.

[3] C Company (Major Holford Walker) and D Company (Major F. Summers). Ten machines remained in reserve, but not all of these were fit for action on 15th September.

[4] Actually, the numbers to be employed were : XIV. Corps, 16 ; XV. Corps, 18 ; III. Corps, 8. The Canadian Corps (Reserve Army) planned to use 6.

[5] Appendix 20.

corps assembly positions situated from one to two miles Sept.
behind the British front line, and on the subsequent night
to their points of departure in the vicinity of the front
trenches : the noise of these movements would be covered
by the engines of aeroplanes detailed to fly low over the
German forward positions during the hours of moonlight.[1]
In the attack the infantry was never to wait for tanks
which might, for any reason, be delayed ; and tanks were
expected to do everything possible to help infantry in
difficulties. Simple flag and lamp codes were arranged
from tanks to infantry and aircraft in order to signal " out
" of action " and " am on objective ". A proportion of the
tanks were to carry pigeons.

Corps were responsible for reconnoitring and taping
the routes of their tanks when the preliminary movements
from the Loop began, every assistance being given to the
tank commanders. Actually tanks came under the command of the divisions in whose sectors they were to operate,
and were assisted by divisional staff officers.[2] Many
divisions detailed small parties of infantry to accompany
the machines and remove wounded from their path, and
these escorts were also to provide protection from close
assaults.[3]

At 6 A.M. on the 12th September, half an hour after the
dawn of a fine but cloudy day, the preliminary bombardment opened.[4] It continued unceasingly until zero hour
on the 15th, when fire was to become intense without
previous warning. The whole German defensive system
was shelled systematically, results being checked at intervals by air photography ; in addition, the heavy guns

[1] The moon was full on 11th September ; its light was indispensable
to the tanks, which could not move in darkness with any certainty.

[2] Information as to his route was supplied by a divisional staff officer
to each tank commander, aerial and panorama serial photographs being
consulted. The course laid down was marked on a map, special features
pointed out, and compass bearings given. Then, with the aid of the corps
time-table, the tank commander was to prepare his own map showing the
distinctive features of his route, his compass bearing from point to point,
and the time at which he must arrive at each. It is to be feared that in
many cases young and inexperienced tank commanders found themselves
overburdened with directions and instructions, which, in many cases, had
to be memorized, as there were not enough copies to go round. A further
difficulty was that old trench lines which were perfectly visible from the
air and easy to photograph were often indistinguishable by ground
observation.

[3] See 41st Division Operation Order No. 42 (Appendix 26) and " Orders
" Regarding Tanks Issued by the 41st Division " (Appendix 27).

[4] See XV. Corps Artillery Operation Order No. 46 (Appendix 23).

Sept.

Sketch A.

Map 1.

and howitzers fired on Bapaume and all villages as far back as Le Mesnil, Rocquigny (1½ miles east of Le Transloy), Barastre, Bancourt and Grévillers. During daylight, the field batteries were chiefly employed in wire-cutting, assisted by ground and air observation, but took every opportunity of inflicting loss and preventing hostile movement. At night harassing fire was directed upon roads, trench junctions and approaches to villages; battery positions were shelled with gas.[1] Thus the preliminary bombardment differed little in character from previous artillery preparations, but the fire was more intense [2] and, perhaps, better controlled, whilst indirect machine-gun fire at night was employed to a greater extent.

The 13th September brought low cloud and frequent showers which rendered air-observation almost impossible,[3] but the following day was fine ; and as the bombardment proceeded the German artillery fire diminished, even upon the front of the XIV. Corps, where the fighting in the Leuze Wood—Ginchy area had not died down.

Meanwhile, the divisions of the Fourth Army which were to deliver the assault completed their movements into the battle-line, extensive reliefs being carried out.[4] The relief of the 55th Division (Major-General H. S. Jeudwine), holding the XV. Corps front, began on the night of the 10th/11th September, when the New Zealand Division (Major-General Sir A. H. Russell) took over the left brigade sector, together with the right of the III. Corps held by a

---

[1] The XV. Corps expended 9,000 rounds of 4·5″ gas shell (chlorine compound) during the nights 13th/14th and 14th/15th September on certain trench junctions and works in front of Flers and on dug-outs located in the village.

[2] The daily returns of ammunition expended by the Fourth Army, made up from noon to noon, were : 11th/12th September, 95,584 rounds ; 12th/13th, 98,878 ; 13th/14th, 120,693 ; 14th/15th (zero hour 6.20 A.M. on 15th), 288,787.

[3] The assistance of the R.F.C. was not, of course, confined to air-observation and photography ; since the beginning of the battle there had been frequent bombing raids upon railways, dumps and villages behind the German lines. On 6th September Achiet le Grand railway station was bombed effectively and on the 14th a large dump at Irles suffered likewise. Although additional air reinforcements had reached the Germans at the beginning of September the British airmen still maintained with success their offensive against the hostile machines and aerodromes. An intense bombing of aerodromes opposite the whole front of the British Armies was carried out on 7th September. See " The War in the Air " Vol. II.

[4] The taking over the centre and left of the XIV. Corps by the 6th and Guards Divisions has already been noticed ; likewise the arrival of the 2nd and 3rd Canadian Divisions in the Canadian sector of the Reserve Army front. See Chapter X.

brigade of the 1st Division.   At the same time, the 41st Sept. Division (Major-General S. T. B. Lawford) relieved the centre brigade of the 55th Division, and by the morning of the 13th September, the 14th Division (Major-General V. A. Couper) [1] had relieved the right brigade of the 55th Division.   In addition to occupying and digging a forward line beyond Delville Wood, the 55th Division had earned the thanks of the incoming troops for the admirable work it had done on communication trenches and other battle preparations.

Lieut.-General Horne was now desirous of clearing the Germans from the " pocket " east of Delville Wood before the general attack was launched, and the 14th Division was therefore ordered to cut off the enemy in that area by digging eastward north of Ale Alley, whilst the Guards co-operated from the Ginchy side.   This enterprise failed, and General Rawlinson then gave his consent to a preliminary operation, starting at 5.30 A.M. on the 15th September. Two tanks of the XV. Corps and one of the XIV. Corps were to be employed in it, after a special bombardment by heavy artillery.

In the left sector of the III. Corps, the right brigade of the 15th Division was relieved by the 50th Division (Major-General P. S. Wilkinson) on the 9th and 10th September.[2] Next on the right, in the High Wood sector, the 47th Division (Major-General Sir C. St. L. Barter) completed the relief of the 1st Division by the evening of the 11th September.[3]

Whilst confident that considerable successes would be won at the outset of the battle, the Commander-in-Chief

[1] Selected in place of the 7th Division, which, after its efforts to capture Ginchy, was in no condition for offensive action.   The 14th Division had been relieved in the Delville Wood sector at the end of August, and Lieut.-General Horne considered that it needed more time to recuperate, but it was adjudged the fittest of the divisions available.

[2] It is worthy of note that having been in the line continuously since 8th August, the 15th Division attacked with remarkable success on 15th September, and was not relieved until four days later.

[3] When all the reliefs were accomplished, General Rawlinson had the following divisions in reserve :

20th Division moving up from Corbie to Happy Valley—Citadel (N. of Bray), thence, before zero hour, to Talus Boisé—Billon Farm, about 4 miles behind XIV. Corps front.

21st Division (arrived from Arras front 13th September) in Buire—Dernancourt area about 9 miles behind III. Corps front.

55th Division in Ribemont area immediately S.W. of 21st Division.

5th Division in Treux—Maricourt area, opposite Buire—Ribemont.

Sept. was not yet satisfied that commanders and troops were in the temper to abandon the methods of attack to which they were so well accustomed when the time should come for the adoption of less deliberate measures. On the 13th September, therefore, G.H.Q. addressed to the Fourth and Reserve Armies a further call for bold and vigorous action, depicting the situation as follows :

On the front of attack, besides a superiority of at least four to one in infantry, we have a more numerous artillery, practical supremacy in the air, and a large mass of cavalry immediately available to exploit to the full a successful assault by the other arms.

In addition we have a new weapon of war which may well produce great moral and material effects.

The enemy in our front is not only numerically very inferior but he has suffered repeated defeats in the last $2\frac{1}{2}$ months, during which he has been driven from one strong position after another. He has undergone and is still being subjected to great loss and hardship, and there is convincing evidence that his morale has deteriorated in consequence to such an extent that many of his men are only held to their tasks by the severity of German discipline. Several times already we have seen great confusion and disorganization in the enemy's ranks as a result of our successful assaults, and it is only the great depth of his defences and the consequent difficulties of a rapid advance by our troops that have enabled him to recover in time to oppose our further attacks.

The result of all that has already been accomplished is that he has now comparatively little depth or strength in the defences behind him, and his reserves are weak and composed entirely of units which have already suffered defeat.

Under such conditions risks may be taken with advantage which would be unwise if the circumstances were less favourable to us.

The assault must be pushed home with the greatest vigour, boldness, and resolution, and success must be followed up without hesitation or delay to the utmost limits of the power of endurance of the troops.

It must be made clear to all ranks that the enemy is to be given no time to recover from a successful assault on his defences and that by acting on this principle a success sufficient to repay

---

23rd Division in Millencourt—Bresle—Baisieux area, some $9\frac{1}{2}$ miles behind junction of Fourth and Reserve Armies.

1st Division in Franvillers—Montigny area, immediately S.W. of 23rd Division.

The 20th, 21st and 23rd Divisions were in reserve to the XIV., XV. and III. Corps respectively ; the others were in Army reserve.

all the great efforts made during the last 2½ months is now Sept. within reach.

Then followed definite instructions for the action to be Sketch A. taken as soon as the break-through was accomplished : the Fourth Army to operate against Bapaume—Butte de Warlencourt — Le Sars — Eaucourt l'Abbaye, capturing Martinpuich by a turning movement ; the Reserve Army to secure Courcelette as a preliminary to acting against the Pys—Grandcourt—Thiepval ridge.

In consequence of this communication, which he circulated to corps and divisions, General Rawlinson wrote to General Gough next day explaining that, when the XIV. and XV. Corps had broken through, the III. Corps would advance northward on Eaucourt l'Abbaye and Le Sars, outflanking Martinpuich ; but he was careful to add that this movement would probably take place on the second day, the 16th. Still regarding the III. Corps front as his defensive flank, he had no intention of carrying Martinpuich by direct assault, which he feared might prove a costly operation, nor did he wish to commit General Pulteney's reserves until the success of the XIV. and XV. Corps had been placed beyond all doubt. On receipt of General Rawlinson's message, General Gough conferred with his corps commanders. He anticipated that the III. Corps Map 1. (Fourth Army) would probably stand fast on the outskirts of Martinpuich until the morning of Saturday the 16th, when the Canadian Corps would advance in touch with the 50th Division ; [1] but he instructed the Canadians to occupy Courcelette at any time if it should be possible to do so without assistance. The II. Corps was warned to be prepared to take over the Mouquet Farm front if the advance went well, but a projected attack upon the farm was cancelled.

Once again, however, the Commander-in-Chief intervened to ensure the adoption of a bolder course. Visiting General Rawlinson on the afternoon of the 14th September, he pointed out the importance of enabling the Reserve Army to come into action with full effect at the earliest possible moment, which could not arrive before Martinpuich was secured. This must be done as soon as Flers had been captured and not left until the following day. Sir Douglas Haig then went to Toutencourt and, in the

[1] A converging movement which would " shut out " the 15th Division (left division of the III. Corps).

Sept. absence of General Gough, left a message that all preparations must be made for capturing Courcelette on the afternoon of the 15th ; and that directly Courcelette and Martinpuich were in British hands both Armies should begin a combined advance northward.

General Gough had, in effect, anticipated the eleventh-hour instructions of the Commander-in-Chief. At 7 P.M. on the 14th September General Rawlinson, for his part, sent the III. Corps instructions to take further action on the morrow if its attack proved successful : the 47th Division to advance over the spur towards Eaucourt l'Abbaye ; the 50th Division to occupy the area north-east of Martinpuich ; the 15th Division to complete the capture of Martinpuich with the aid of tanks. The III. Corps, in its turn, issued a special order at 11.30 P.M. which directed that if all objectives were carried next day a further advance would be made " three hours after zero " : the 15th Division was to push patrols through Martinpuich, whilst the 50th secured Prue Trench, further down the slope east of the village, and threw forward its left to join the right of the Canadian Corps (Reserve Army) at the mill beyond the Eaucourt l'Abbaye road. The four tanks working with these divisions were to be prepared to assist in the capture of Martinpuich.

The other corps commanders had also given fresh orders for tank action after the capture of the fourth objective. At 11.30 A.M. on the 14th, the XV. Corps directed that instead of withdrawing to a rendezvous south of Longueval, the machines were to concentrate at Seven Dials (west of Gueudecourt), " in readiness to assist a further advance ". They would come back to refill at Flers when night fell. The XIV. Corps, which had selected a rendezvous for re-assembly west of Guillemont, announced at 2.45 P.M. that the tanks would concentrate in the ravine north of Bouleaux Wood, to be at the disposal of the cavalry, " if the latter " were operating east of Morval ". Also two troops of corps cavalry [1] were ordered to be in readiness to advance at 7.30 A.M. on the 15th.

On the night of the 13th September the tanks moved

---

[1] Since April 1916 each corps had possessed one cavalry (generally a Yeomanry) regiment as corps troops. These regiments were formed of the squadrons withdrawn from the divisions which, henceforward, had no mounted troops. At the same time corps cyclist battalions had been formed of the divisional cyclist companies.

up from the Loop to their assembly places,[1] where supplies Sept. of petrol, oil, water, rations and ammunition had been collected. The distances covered, in moonlight, following specially taped tracks, averaged over four miles, and the few tanks which developed minor mechanical troubles on their way were successfully replaced by machines from reserve before dawn. After daybreak the tank commanders reconnoitred their routes to the front line.

The divisions of the Cavalry Corps arrived in their Sketch A. forward positions during the 14th September, riding across country so as to add nothing to the volume of battle traffic on the roads and other routes. The 1st Cavalry Division halted on the northern side of Carnoy, the 2nd Indian Cavalry Division south of Mametz ; further back, the 2nd Cavalry Division assembled north of Bray, one brigade remaining south of Dernancourt with the 1st Indian Cavalry Division. In rear, the 3rd Cavalry Division was west of the Ancre between Bonnay and La Neuville, nine miles south-west of Albert.

At dusk on the whole front of attack the assaulting battalions left their bivouacs and marched forward to occupy their assembly trenches. This movement was carried out with little loss or confusion, and most of the troops arrived in time for a few hours' sleep. All were fed, and in some cases a rum ration was issued. Throughout the chill autumn night the British bombardment continued, whilst the German batteries were comparatively quiet, shelling fitfully such localities as Ginchy and Delville Wood. The tanks, whose crews had had little rest during the previous forty-eight hours, were again in motion, for they had to reach their points of departure, in or near the front line, before dawn. Their journeys varied in length from one mile to two, and, although the routes were taped and guides provided, progress in the misty moonlight over the shell-shattered ground, with deep mud in places, proved difficult, hazardous and slow. Some tanks had engine, or other mechanical, trouble and could not even start upon

[1] Fourth Army :
    XIV. Corps : W. edge of Wedge Wood (56th Division) ; valley 600 yards S.E. of Bernafay Wood (6th Division) ; S.W. edge of Trônes Wood (Guards Division).
    XV. Corps : " Green Dump ", by roadside mid-way between Longueval and Bazentin le Grand.
    III. Corps : Behind Bazentin le Petit Wood (47th and 50th Divisions) ; S. edge of Contalmaison (15th Division).
  Reserve Army :
    Canadian Corps : Albert (2nd Canadian Division).

Sept. this last stage to the battle front ; others attempted to pass over disused dug-outs which caved in and ditched the machines. Reports of the deployment were anxiously awaited at corps headquarters, and eventually it transpired that out of 42 tanks which were to be employed upon the Fourth Army front, 30 had arrived.[1] The six attached to the Canadian Corps (Reserve Army) all reached their departure points without serious trouble.

Air reconnaissance far behind the German lines had revealed no abnormal activity upon the roads and railways in the area Lens—Douai—Orchies—Valenciennes —Le Quesnoy—Cambrai, so the arrival of important reinforcements on the threatened front seemed unlikely ; troop movements which had been detected in the forward areas were accounted for by the reliefs known to be in progress. From the opening of the Somme offensive British Intelligence had been able to follow with tolerable accuracy every change in the German order of battle, and it was now computed that of 32 enemy divisions engaged since the 1st July 19 had departed to other fronts

Map 1. and six were resting and refitting in reserve.[2] Seven German divisions were known to be in position between Combles and the Ancre, but confronting the ten divisions of the British Fourth and Reserve Armies which were to make the initial attack there were rather less than five ; and two of these had already been heavily engaged about Leuze Wood and Ginchy. Examination of prisoners taken in the last few days seemed to show that the enemy morale was definitely on the decline.

Zero hour was awaited by commanders and troops in hopeful expectancy.[3] Officers and men of the fresh divisions—Guardsmen, New Zealanders, Canadians, Londoners, North Countrymen of the 50th, and the representatives of a dozen English counties in the 6th and 41st—were determined to prove themselves in this, the sternest test of modern war. The battle-tried troops who had spent themselves in so many small and hurried attacks were at least exhilarated by the sights and sounds of offensive

[1] In the XIV. Corps, 9 out of 16 ; 14 (one arriving later) out of 18 in the XV. Corps ; 7 out of 8 in the III. Corps.

[2] Actually, up to 14th September, there had been engaged against the British 30 divisions, one of which had entered the battle for the second time. The reinforcements which arrived during the Battle of Flers—Courcelette amounted to the equivalent of 6 divisions.

[3] It was not until the small hours of the 15th that some battalions were informed of the actual time, 6.20 A.M., fixed for the infantry assault.

preparations on the grand scale. Comparatively few had Sept. seen the tanks or knew much of them ; but on their way forward all had been heartened and impressed by the spectacle of the massed artillery in action, and many had observed the long columns of horsemen, whose presence in such numbers seemed to express a confident anticipation of victory.

CHAPTER XII

THE BATTLE OF FLERS—COURCELETTE

15TH–22ND SEPTEMBER 1916

(Map 1 ; Sketches 36, 37)

MIST in the early morning of the 15th September heralded a fine autumn day with some cloud ; but, as the ground had not yet recovered from the recent rains, mud still proved a handicap to movement in trenches and low-lying places. The preliminary bombardment, which had now continued for three days and nights, gave to the enemy no indication of the hour of attack, the most powerful and the most extensive launched by the British since the 1st July, nor had he any foreknowledge of the new engine of warfare he was about to face.[1] From the air when the barrage opened there could be seen dark lanes, " drawn as it might " be by a child's stubby finger in dirty snow ",[2] across the familiar expanse of smoking shell-bursts which enveloped the whole front. It was along these lanes in the barrage that the tanks were about to advance.

THE FOURTH ARMY ON 15TH SEPTEMBER
XIV. CORPS

Map 1. Sketch 37.   In Lord Cavan's XIV. Corps, which formed the right of the British attack, the 56th Division (Major-General C. P. A. Hull) was to establish a defensive flank along the north-western slopes of the Combles ravine during the first stage

---

[1] Kite balloons had reported " armoured cars " behind the British line, but even this discovery was not known to most of the German troops, although vague rumours of a British armoured fighting vehicle were prevalent in some quarters.

[2] " Sagittarius Rising " by Cecil Lewis, p. 142.

of the advance. The 6th Division (Major-General C. Ross) **15 Sept.** was still confronted by the Quadrilateral, half a mile north of Leuze Wood, which barred the way to its first objective. If, however, the 56th Division were able to make steady progress through and north of Bouleaux Wood, threatening thereby to envelop the Quadrilateral, the first task of the 6th Division would be rendered much easier ; and the subsequent advance of that division and of the Guards Division (Major-General G. P. T. Feilding) north-eastward over the highest part of the ridge to Morval and Lesboeufs, respectively, would stand a good chance of success. An unknown factor was the moral and material effect of tank action : no less than three tanks were to make the Quadrilateral their first objective, whilst the advance, previous to zero hour, of three other columns, each of three machines, was expected to prove of material assistance to the Guards.

The 56th Division set the 169th Brigade (Br.-General E. S. D'E. Coke) the task of advancing across the slopes of Combles ravine to secure Loop Trench, whilst maintaining touch with the French on the railway track at the bottom of the ravine. During the night of the 14th/15th September, the 1/2nd London had dug assembly trenches south of Leuze Wood parallel to Combles Trench, and before dawn a tank was ready at the corner of the wood. The machine moved out to the attack just before 6 A.M., and twenty minutes later, when the creeping barrage came down, the two leading companies of infantry advanced with their right directed upon the junction of Combles Trench and Loop Trench. The German barrage was late and, in spite of some uncut wire, Combles Trench was entered and occupied without much trouble ; the tank which, in the words of the infantry " thoroughly frightened the foe ", lent great assistance. The intention was now to pivot on the right and take Loop Trench and the Loop by frontal assault, but this could not be done in the face of the unsubdued cross-fire of machine guns.

Bombing attacks were then made up Loop Trench and down Combles Trench, where the fight continued all day, absorbing the whole of the 1/2nd London and also the bombers of the London Rifle Brigade who were sent up in the afternoon. The tank was hit by a shell when in the vicinity of the Loop, and was unable to move again ; but its machine guns kept the German bombers at bay for five hours and did great execution. Eventually it was destroyed

15 Sept. by fire and the crew abandoned it. When darkness fell the Londoners had constructed a barricade down the slope in Combles Trench well forward of the trench junction ; but in the Loop they were still 80 yards from the sunken road, on which a last attack was made at 11 P.M. without success. The 169th Brigade, however, was not far short of its sole objective for the day.[1]

The 167th Brigade (Br.-General G. H. B. Freeth) had first to prolong the defensive flank northward through the higher part of Bouleaux Wood, thus commanding Combles from the north-west. In the general advance from the first to the third objective the brigade was to clear the remainder of the wood and link up with the 6th Division in the valley beyond. There the 168th Brigade (Br.-General G. G. Loch) would pass through and secure the British right flank during the capture of Morval, eventually linking up with the French advance in the vicinity of the cross-roads beyond the village. The 1/1st London of the 167th Brigade was to carry the advance as far as the first objective, capturing on its way the German front trench in Bouleaux Wood and northward to Middle Copse. On the right, it was to bomb down towards Combles and join hands with the 169th Brigade at the junction of the Loop and the sunken road leading down into the village.

Of the two tanks which were to assist the 1/1st London, one split a track on its way forward, but the other had reached the point of departure near the western corner of Bouleaux Wood. This machine moved slowly towards Middle Copse, drawing considerable fire as it did so, some twenty minutes before the infantry attacked at 6.20 A.M. There were early reports of complete success, but in the wood the 1/1st London, who reported the creeping barrage as " ineffectual ", were stopped at once by uncut wire and the accurate fire of machine guns : the German trench, too near the British front line to be effectively bombarded, and hidden from observation by the undergrowth, appeared to be little damaged and fully manned. It was not possible to launch the bombing attack south-eastward from the wood, but on the left the Londoners entered the German trench and penetrated almost as far as Middle Copse. In the meantime the tank had proceeded to the extremity of

----

[1] Its opponents belonged to the *28th Reserve Regiment* (right sector of the *185th Division*), whose history records fierce fighting and a British partial success.

Bouleaux Wood, and cruised about until it became ditched 15 Sept. near the enemy front line. It was then boldly attacked by German bombers,[1] and was eventually abandoned after every one of the crew had been hit.

The 6th Division (Major-General C. Ross), next on the left, delivered its assault under particularly unfavourable conditions. Repeated bombardments, even with aeroplane observation, had had little effect upon the Quadrilateral. As has been mentioned, this centre of resistance situated close behind the crest of the high ground east of Ginchy, was protected by wire which lay in a depression, concealed by grass and weeds. Reports from artillery and infantry officers convinced Br.-Generals W. L. Osborn and FitzJ. M. Edwards—commanding respectively the 16th and 71st Brigades, which were to attack—that the artillery preparation had been generally ineffective, and Major-General Ross held the same opinion.

On the right, the 16th Brigade reckoned to carry the Quadrilateral by an attack of the 8/Bedfordshire over the open from the south-west, whilst one company bombed forward up the trench on the right. The 1/Buffs was to follow in support, passing through the Bedfordshire on the first objective and advancing without further pause to the third. The final objective, Morval and a line beyond, was allotted to the 2/York & Lancaster, supported by the 1/King's Shropshire L.I. On the left, the 71st Brigade proposed to use the 9/Norfolk and 1/Leicestershire to capture Straight Trench as far as the boundary with the Guards Division ; these two battalions would then push on to the final objective supported by the 9/Suffolk and 1/Sherwood Foresters.

The three tanks allotted to the division were all intended to make the Quadrilateral their first objective. Unfortunately only one reached the rendezvous, the cross-roads east of Guillemont ; of the others, one broke its tail and one developed engine trouble on the way up. As soon as these failures were reported to Major-General Ross, he asked that the tank " lane " in the creeping barrage should be filled up. The Corps, which had foreseen such a contingency, caused the necessary orders to be issued by

[1] At 11 A.M. a pigeon message to this effect was received from the tank commander by the 56th Division, which ordered the 167th Brigade to lend assistance. " Res. Regt. No. 28 " mentions the appearance of a tank (" *Panzerautoähnlicher Tank* ") on both the right and left front of the regiment. The machine on the N.W. side of Bouleaux Wood is said to have been " destroyed " by bomb throwing.

the commander of the corps artillery, Br.-General A. E. Wardrop. These orders were received but, through pure mischance, were not acted upon by the commander of the divisional artillery.

The first movement on the 6th Division front was the advance of the single tank following the railway track along its north-western side towards the Quadrilateral. The machine passed through the right of the Norfolk about 5.50 A.M. and, by mistake, opened fire on the waiting troops. This was stopped by the gallant action of Captain A. J. G. Crosse, 9/Norfolk, who approached the tank under heavy fire and pointed out its true direction. The machine was afterwards seen to turn northward and move parallel to Straight Trench, firing as it did so.

The frontal attack of the Bedfordshire (16th Brigade), delivered at 6.20 A.M. north-eastward upon the Quadrilateral, was met by deadly machine-gun fire and had no chance of success ; nor could the 1/Buffs, which advanced at 6.35 A.M. from trenches at the head of the valley near the Leuze Wood—Ginchy road, impart fresh impetus to the movement. On the right the Bedfordshire bombing party was held up in the trench south-east of the Quadrilateral. The Norfolk and Leicestershire (71st Brigade), advancing in fine style against Straight Trench, passed through the Suffolk and the Foresters, which held the brigade front, and thence out of sight over the crest. The Leicestershire, on the left, overran with ease a forward shell-hole position, but both battalions were then confronted with wire that was almost undamaged and were smitten by streams of machine-gun bullets from front and right flank. The survivors took cover in shell-holes and stayed there. The tank, with German bullets through its sponsons and petrol running low, had already returned.[1]

In the Guards Division the assaulting brigades were obliged to form up amid a mass of shell craters in order to be clear of the ruins of Ginchy—always a target for the German gunners. On the right, the 2nd Guards Brigade (Br.-General J. Ponsonby), which had the 3/Grenadiers and 1/Coldstream in front and the 1/Scots Guards and 2/Irish Guards in second line, assembled south-east of the frequently barraged Ginchy—Lesboeufs road. So cramped was the position that there was only ten yards' distance between

---

[1] The Germans, in several cases, fired at the tanks the armour-piercing bullets provided for use in trench warfare against snipers' steel loop-hole plates.

each of the nine " waves ", the brigade having four platoons per battalion in line on a frontage of about four hundred yards.   It was intended that the whole brigade should pass right through to the final objective.   The 1st Guards Brigade (Br.-General C. E. Pereira), on the left, occupied a frontage of similar extent, but with the flanks bent back, the left being well inside the corps boundary. The 2nd and 3rd Battalions of the Coldstream were in the van, with the 1/Irish Guards in second line, and 2/Grenadiers in rear.   The Coldstream were to carry the advance as far as the third objective, after which the Irish Guards would go through to the final objective, the Grenadiers being employed to protect the left flank and lend general support in the later stages of the attack.

Of the ten tanks allotted to the Guards, the right group of three arrived without mishap at its rendezvous east of the Ginchy—Lesboeufs road.   These machines were to be directed first upon the southern point of the German position, known as " The Triangle ", which marked the right boundary of the division.   Of the centre group, which had the north-western point of the Triangle as its first objective, none appeared, for one was detained at Trônes Wood with mechanical trouble, and the other two, on their way forward, came to grief among the shell craters round Ginchy.   The left group, which was to start from the western side of Ginchy and advance up Pint Trench and Lager Lane on the left flank of the division, was represented by two tanks, the third remaining at Trônes Wood owing to mechanical trouble.   The tenth tank, which was detailed to co-operate with the XV. Corps in clearing the " pocket " east of Delville Wood before zero hour, arrived at Ginchy, reported trouble with its tracks, and took no part in the action.

This preliminary operation, carried out by troops and one tank of the 14th Division at 5.15 A.M.,[1] encountered some opposition, but, so far as concerned the 1st Guards Brigade—waiting in packed ranks for the general bombardment to become intense and the creeping barrage to fall— appeared to be entirely successful.

On the front of the Guards, the tank advance previous to zero hour produced little effect.   One of the machines on the right flank broke its tail and could not start ; the others lost direction and veered eastwards towards Straight Trench on the front of the 6th Division, eventually returning

[1] See page 318.

15 Sept. without having made much impression on the German defence.[1] On the left flank, the two tanks started late, soon lost direction, and steered right-handed towards the German trenches. One was " ditched " and the other was forced to return with very little petrol left.[2] Thereafter no tanks operated upon the front of the Guards Division.

At 6.20 A.M., when the creeping barrage fell, the Guards moved forward steadily some thirty yards in rear of it. As the right of the 2nd Guards Brigade topped the crest of the high ground, moving north-eastward, it came under terrific fire from Straight Trench and the Quadrilateral, opposite the front of the 6th Division. In spite of heavy loss—Lieut.-Colonel B. N. Sergison-Brooke, 3/Grenadiers, was among the wounded—Grenadiers and Coldstream pressed on, although tending to drift to the left of their proper course. The rear battalions came close upon their heels. Some distance beyond the crest Germans were found occupying an advanced position in shell-holes, and nearly all the defenders were shot or bayoneted ; then, without further check, the advance continued, all four battalions mixed together, until it swept into the northern part of the Triangle and part of Serpentine Trench, farther to the left. The three belts of wire in front of this position had been well cut by the British artillery which had also wrought havoc in the trenches, and the onset of the Guards soon overcame all resistance, a number of prisoners being taken.[3] By 7.15 A.M. the 2nd Guards Brigade, woefully

---

[1] One machine had engine trouble ; the other reported that it had been ordered by an infantry officer to return. These two tanks, and the solitary tank which advanced on the 6th Division front, are undoubtedly those referred to in " Bav. Regt. No. 21 ". It is said that they bore blue-and-red crosses on their sides and at first were thought to be " stretcher-"lorries" ; but they were soon recognized as the new tanks of which rumour had already spoken. About 6 A.M., in the face of a heavy fire, they approached the Bavarian line, raked the trench with their machine guns for several minutes, and then turned back.

[2] Both machines reported that they had knocked out machine guns and taken prisoners. Although there is mention of the noise the tanks made coming forward during the previous night, no war diary or report of the Guards Division makes any reference to tanks in action on this day. The history of the *7th Bavarians*, which held the front astride the Ginchy—Lesboeufs road, states that two tanks advanced *behind* the British infantry.

[3] " Bav. Regt. No. 7 " (the regiment held the centre sector of the *5th Bavarian Division*) states that 20–30 British aeroplanes machine-gunned the defenders as the Guards advanced. With little artillery support, there was no hope of making an effective resistance. The remnants of the two front battalions rallied on the *III./Bn.*, ready to defend the " Gallwitz Riegel " (British third objective in front of Lesboeufs) ; but the attack then appeared to have spent itself.

reduced in numbers, and with few officers left, had reached 15 Sept. a part, at least, of its first objective.[1]

The 1st Guards Brigade advanced with equal precision at zero hour, the left of the 3/Coldstream having to wheel up into its proper alignment. Almost at once, however, both Coldstream battalions were met by machine-gun fire from the junction of Pint Trench with the sunken portion of the Flers road, and officers and men fell fast. For a moment there was a check, and then the Coldstream rushed forward and overwhelmed the Germans, killing some and capturing others together with four machine guns and a trench mortar. Men of the 1/Irish Guards, eager to get into the fight, were already mixed with the two Coldstream battalions, as also was a portion of the 1/Coldstream (left of the 2nd Guards Brigade). The 1st Guards Brigade, deflected northward by this encounter instead of continuing north-eastward, pressed on. It overran an enemy shell-hole position and reached and stormed the first objective at about the same time as did the 2nd Guards Brigade. But this admixture of the three Coldstream battalions and 1/Irish Guards, with a few of the 3/Grenadiers who had strayed from the extreme right of the divisional front, were occupying a portion of the trench beyond the corps boundary. To the right the Germans still held Serpentine Trench on both sides of its junction with Calf Alley.

An attempt was now made to sort out the different battalions, who were all crowded together with few officers left, and, whilst the men of the 1/Coldstream were being moved to the right, their commanding officer, Lieut.-Colonel Hon. G. V. Baring, was killed. The other three battalion commanders[2] held a short conference, and decided that they had reached the third objective—in reality, still 1,300 yards ahead. A pigeon message to that effect was sent back.[3] The mistake is understandable, for no part of the objectives had been visible from the forming-up positions of the brigade, and few landmarks could be distinguished in the shell-shattered landscape. Moreover, that part of the second objective assigned to the brigade

[1] In this fighting, Lance-Sergt. F. McNess, 1/Scots Guards, won the V.C. He led a bombing party with great courage and determination, continuing to do so after he had been severely wounded.

[2] Lieut.-Colonels R. B. J. Crawfurd, 2/Coldstream ; J. V. Campbell, 3/Coldstream ; and R. C. A. McCalmont, 1/Irish Guards.

[3] An artillery F.O.O., who was in the captured trench, identified it as the first objective, but no message from him appears to have come through.

15 Sept. faced almost due east, and did not coincide with any German trench.

It was known at XIV. Corps headquarters that the initial attack had been launched to time along the whole front, but the morning mist and the heavy smoke of the bombardment had prevented the contact aeroplanes from following the progress of the three divisions. From the Combles ravine to Ginchy the German barrage was sufficiently heavy to delay, if not to prevent, communication with the front line by telephone or runner. Only the extreme left (1st Guards Brigade) of the corps was concerned with the capture of the second objective, but as the morning wore on reports received by the corps seemed to show that the Guards had advanced to attack the third objective at about the appointed hour, 8.20 A.M. It was evident that the 6th Division had received a check, but the 56th Division was reported to have reached the first objective. How many tanks remained in action was uncertain.

On the extreme right, as we know, the 169th Brigade of the 56th Division was fighting in the trenches east of Leuze Wood.[1] Although not yet aware whether its leading battalion, the 1/1st London, had succeeded, the 167th Brigade sent forward two companies of the 1/7th Middlesex at 8.20 A.M. to pass through and gain the third objective, beyond Bouleaux Wood. The Middlesex stood no chance of success so long as the German riflemen and machine-gunners in the wood remained active ; although a second effort was made with the two remaining companies, they could do no more than reinforce the 1/1st London in the captured line on the left.

At 8.20 A.M. the 6th Division also made another effort, the Suffolk and Foresters of the 71st Brigade advancing in the tracks of the Norfolk and Leicestershire who lay scattered in shell-holes before the western side of the Quadrilateral and Straight Trench. The movement, most gallantly carried out, only resulted in fresh sacrifice of life, for the German machine-gun fire remained unsubdued despite a fresh bombardment of the Quadrilateral. Part of the 1/7th Middlesex, forming the left of the 56th Division, was now in the trench running south-east from the Quadri-

---

[1] Part of the *III./28th Reserve* was here reinforced during the day by companies of the *I. Bn.*, which were machine-gunned by British aeroplanes whilst coming forward. Some help was also received from the *65th Regiment* in Combles. Regimental history.

lateral where there were also men of the 16th Brigade : Buffs, Bedfordshire, and some of the 2/York & Lancaster, which had been brought forward in readiness for the last stage of the advance.

At 9 A.M. Major-General Ross asked the 56th Division to co-operate with his 16th Brigade, and Major-General Hull agreed.   The new plan of the 6th Division was for the 16th and 71st Brigades to converge upon the Quadrilateral from the north, west and south at 1.30 P.M., whilst the 18th Brigade (Br.-General R. J. Bridgford), brought up from reserve, moved through the area of the Guards Division and advanced upon Morval.   The latter movement was decided upon owing to erroneous reports of the great progress made by the Guards—at one time they were even said to be in Lesboeufs—and the whole operation was calculated to carry out the intention of the corps order, received by the 6th Division about noon, to pass the reserve brigade through the Guards area whilst the 56th Division " cleared up the "situation" on the other flank.   A corps message to Major-General Hull stated that his part would be to clear Bouleaux Wood, and that the attack would not be launched without thorough artillery preparation.

Almost immediately, however, air reports gave the corps commander a more accurate idea of the situation upon the right front of the Guards, where, as will presently be seen, very few troops had penetrated beyond the first objective.   Lord Cavan, therefore, cancelled the 1.30 P.M. attack, and just before 2 P.M. informed the 6th Division that Straight Trench must be attacked from the north at 7.30 P.M. after an hour's bombardment by the heavy artillery.   The troops of the 6th Division which had been ordered to deliver the afternoon attack were stopped in time ; but the 167th Brigade, on the immediate right of that division, was unable to get orders to the 1/8th Middlesex.   This battalion, which had great difficulty in moving forward to Leuze Wood over a heavily shelled area, endeavoured to attack at 1.40 P.M. through the 1/1st London and 1/7th Middlesex, but lost heavily to no purpose, and was eventually withdrawn to Leuze Wood.[1] By the evening, however, the 1/1st London and 1/7th

---

[1] " Res. Regt. No. 28 " says that this attack was checked by the help of the machine guns of the *21st Bavarians* (left of the *5th Bavarian Division*) and that a critical situation arose north of Bouleaux Wood owing to heavy losses and the paucity of reserves.   At night the survivors of the *I.* and *III. Bns.* were relieved by the *II.* in the regimental sector.

15 Sept. Middlesex had pushed northward and occupied Middle Copse.

The Guards Division was involved in heavy fighting after it had obtained part of its first objective. On the right, the 2nd Guards Brigade had to form a defensive flank, and bombing parties composed of men from all battalions in the brigade carried on a stern fight to clear the trenches of the Triangle. This was accomplished about noon. A further advance, with so few men available and no co-operation from the 6th Division, seemed out of the question ; nevertheless, a mixed party numbering about one hundred—Scots, Irish and Grenadiers—pushed forward nearly half a mile and reached a point in front of the third objective south of the sunken road leading into Lesboeufs from Ginchy. Meanwhile, the 2/Grenadier Guards (1st Guards Brigade) had emerged from the ruins of Ginchy about 7.30 A.M., its mission being to support the attack of its brigade on the final objective. The battalion pressed on north-eastward maintaining its true direction by the Ginchy—Lesboeufs road and, whilst still in artillery formation, came under heavy fire from the uncaptured portion of Serpentine Trench. The Grenadiers deployed, and by a bayonet charge secured a footing in this line, which they eventually cleared by bombing outwards until they found themselves in touch on the right with some of their own 3rd Battalion (2nd Guards Brigade), and had almost joined up with the Coldstream, of the 1st Guards Brigade, on the left. Thus the first objective on the whole front of the Guards Division was secured.

The troops of the 1st Guards Brigade in the first objective farther to the north-west had reorganized, and Lieut.-Colonel Campbell, the senior officer, now realized that the third objective still lay ahead. He therefore decided upon a fresh advance. As they started, the men of the 2nd and 3/Coldstream ran into a heavy German barrage ; but they pressed on to the sound of their leader's hunting horn,[1] and by 11.15 A.M. had captured a portion of the second objective outside the corps boundary.[2] Some of the 1/Irish Guards on the extreme left joined up with troops of the 14th Division which formed the right of the XV. Corps. Once more the captured position was mistaken

---

[1] For his gallant leadership on this day Lieut.-Colonel J. V. Campbell was awarded the V.C.

[2] In the second objective two battalion staffs of the *14th Bavarians* (right sector of the *5th Bavarian Division*) were taken.

for a portion of the third objective, and messages to that effect were sent back during the afternoon. Reports from contact aeroplanes, however, made it quite clear to corps headquarters that on no part of the corps front had the third objective been reached.

Major-General Feilding had been told by Lord Cavan before 10 A.M. that he must help the 6th Division " by "cutting in behind the Boche", but when the true situation was ascertained this project was dropped. A suggestion from Br.-General Ponsonby that the 3rd Guards Brigade (Br.-General C. E. Corkran) should come through to take Lesboeufs, could not be accepted by the divisional commander, whose chief concern now was to consolidate the ground which had been won. At 3.20 P.M. he allotted one battalion of the 3rd Guards Brigade to the 2nd, and one to the 1st Guards Brigade. Shortly afterwards he was informed by the corps that a brigade of the 20th Division, from corps reserve, was at his disposal.

The 4/Grenadiers moved up on the right about 5 P.M. and one company—no more than one was, in fact, needed— assisted to strengthen the exposed flank of the 2nd Guards Brigade around the Triangle, where bombing attacks and counter-attacks continued. By this time the advanced party of the 2nd Guards Brigade had been forced by a German counter-attack to withdraw,[1] but a further enemy movement against the right of the 2nd Guards Brigade was repulsed by rifle and Lewis-gun fire. Sent forward about 5.30 P.M. to reinforce the 1st Guards Brigade, the 2/Scots Guards advanced through a German barrage, Lieut.-Colonel R. S. Tempest being wounded. The battalion joined Lieut.-Colonel Campbell, but the trenches were so crowded that all the companies but one were kept in support behind the left.

Having received orders from the Fourth Army that the general attack was not to be resumed until the morrow, Lord Cavan had telephoned to the 56th Division at 4 P.M. ordering it to consolidate its position. He informed Major-General Feilding that the Guards Division would attack the third objective next day, after a fresh bombardment. It remained to be seen what success would attend the evening attempt of the 6th Division to retrieve its fortunes.

---

[1] Delivered by the remnants of the *7th Bavarians*, which, it is claimed, drove back the British entrenching beyond their first objective, and then dug in on the ground. Regimental history.

15 Sept.   Straight Trench and the Quadrilateral were being subjected to another fierce bombardment by the corps heavy
artillery, but most of the shells cleared the crest and burst
harmlessly behind the Quadrilateral.   Two companies of
the 11/Essex (18th Brigade) assembled for the attack north-
west of Leuze Wood; the 2/Durham L.I. (also 18th
Brigade) moved two companies up to the Triangle, now
held by the Guards, in readiness to bomb down Straight
Trench.   Both battalions were new to the ground, and the
troops arrived in their positions with no time to spare;
the Essex were even in ignorance as to the precise situation
of the Quadrilateral.   Br.-General Bridgford, commanding
the brigade, was dubious of success, as he considered, with
reason, that the bombardment had not been effective.
When the assault was delivered, at 7.30 P.M. the Essex, who
were supported by the 2/York & Lancaster (16th Brigade),
came under fire from the Germans occupying Bouleaux
Wood in their right rear, and were obliged to withdraw;
the Durham L.I. entered Straight Trench and bombed
southward for about a hundred yards, but could do no
more.

XV. Corps : Capture of Flers

The three divisions of Lieut.-General Horne's XV.
Corps, forming the left of the main attack, were rather better
placed than the XIV. Corps, although the right flank had
to be cleared as a preliminary operation.   Fourteen tanks—
out of eighteen allotted to the XV. Corps—had gained their
points of departure, the majority of these machines being
intended to deal with Flers and the strongpoints and sunken
roads in the vicinity of that village, before pushing on to
the Gueudecourt defences.

To expel the Germans from the " pocket " east of
Delville Wood, and thereby straighten the front before the
general zero hour, the 14th Division (Major-General V. A.
Couper) detailed two companies of the 6/K.O.Y.L.I. from
the 43rd Brigade (Br.-General P. R. Wood) in reserve.
These companies were to support, by bombing, the advance
of three tanks.   As it happened, only one machine was
available, seeing that the Guards' tank broke down at the
start, and the tank which was to work south-eastward from
a point in front of Delville Wood was ditched on its way to
Sketch the departure point.   At about 5.15 A.M. the remaining
36.   tank (D1) started forward from Pilsen Lane, followed about
a quarter of an hour later by the K.O.Y.L.I. bombers.

THE TANKS AT FLERS
15th Sept., 1916.

Sketch 36.

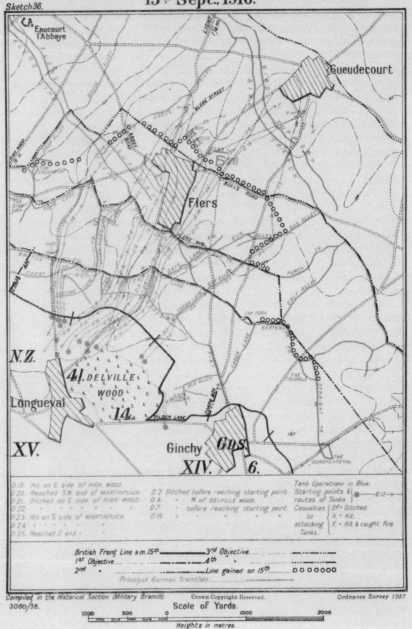

D 13. Hit on E. side of HIGH WOOD.
D 20. Reached S.W. end of MARTINPUICH.
D 21. Ditched on E. side of HIGH WOOD.
D 22. "   "
D 23. Hit on S. side of MARTINPUICH.
D 24. "   "
D 25. Reached E. end "

D 2. Ditched before reaching starting point.
D 4. " W of DELVILLE WOOD.
D 7. " before reaching starting point.
D 19. "   "

Tank Operations in Blue.
Starting points & routes of Tanks.
Casualties to attacking Tanks.
D². = Ditched.
H. = Hit.
F. = Hit & caught fire.

British Front Line a.m. 15th   3rd Objective.
1st Objective.   4th   "
2nd   "   Line gained on 15th.
Principal German Trenches.

Compiled in the Historical Section (Military Branch).   Crown Copyright Reserved.   Ordnance Survey 1957.
3060/36.

Scale of Yards.
1000   500   0   1000   2000

Heights in metres.

The enemy had already abandoned the head of Ale Alley, 15 Sept. and now began to withdraw from Hop Alley, so that little resistance was encountered at the start. The tank, which crossed Hop Alley, accounted for a few Germans, but soon afterwards was hit by a shell which destroyed its steering gear.[1] Near Ale Alley the K.O.Y.L.I. came under the fire, at short range, of machine guns in rear of their right flank, and lost all their officers. The Yorkshiremen promptly turned back, quelled this opposition with bomb and bayonet, and then reorganized under their N.C.O.'s in order to take part in the main advance with the leading troops of their division.

The nearer objectives of the 14th Division lay on the Map 1. slopes of the ridge south-east of Flers ; the third objective Sketch lay along the Flers—Lesboeufs road (called " Bulls Road "), 37. which ran across the lower ground beyond; the final objective included Gueudecourt. Br.-General P. C. B. Skinner's 41st Brigade was in front with orders to take the first and second objectives ; the 42nd Brigade (Br.-General F. A. Dudgeon) would pass through and secure the third and fourth. The advance started at zero hour, 6.20 A.M., in splendid style, one tank (D3) moving a little in advance Sketch of the infantry on the left, making for Cocoa Lane. Of the 36. other two machines in this group, one had become ditched in Delville Wood on its way up, and the other (D5), arriving late, afterwards made a spectacular advance, unsupported, on Gueudecourt, as will presently be described.

The 8/Rifle Brigade and 8/K.R.R.C., which led the 41st Map 1. Brigade, suffered considerable loss from machine guns in Sketch Pint Trench, but there was no check, although many 37. Bavarians had to be routed out of shell-hole positions before Tea Support was reached. The men were so eager that they ran into the British barrage, and suffered accordingly,[2] but Tea Support and Pint Trench were taken without delay. Dead Bavarians were many and those of the defenders who survived soon surrendered. At Tea Support the tank (D3) was damaged beyond repair by fragments of a shell, but the two battalions went on to the Switch Line (the first objective), which was captured about 7 A.M. Dug-outs were bombed, two machine guns seized, and many prisoners collected, whilst skirmishers went out to deal with

---

[1] It was brought in by A.S.C. mechanics later in the day.

[2] Many 18-pdrs. were having trouble with their buffer-springs and their rate of fire was reduced thereby ; for this reason the barrage was not so heavy and well-defined as it should have been.

15 Sept. snipers firing from shell-holes. On the right were found men of the K.O.Y.L.I. who had kept pace with the advance and linked it up with the Guards, but the 8/K.R.R.C. was not in touch with the 41st Division on the left, and so formed a defensive flank to watch the low ground south of Flers. Consolidation proceeded under difficulties, for the Switch Line, already knocked about by the British bombardment, was now heavily shelled by the enemy. Here Lieut.-Colonel W. R. Stewart, 8/Rifle Brigade, was wounded.

A German barrage was on the northern edges of Delville Wood when, at 6.30 A.M., the rear battalions of the brigade appeared, the 7/K.R.R.C. emerging from the wood, and the 7/Rifle Brigade moving over the open ground to the east of it. Both units encountered isolated opposition which caused some disorganization, cost many officers and men, and delayed the advance to the Switch Line, now crowded with the front battalions and many dead and wounded, both British and German. The attack upon the second objective —a continuation of the Flers defences named Gap Trench— was consequently not launched until 8 A.M., 40 minutes behind time, the 7/Rifle Brigade going on " in small parties " to occupy the trench without much trouble, for the enemy was disposed to surrender.[1] On the left, the 7/K.R.R.C. had a similar experience, but it was not in touch with the 41st Division, which appeared to be involved in confused fighting at the southern approaches to Flers. Later in the morning, the Rifle Brigade established touch with the Guards, who, as already related, had encroached upon the 14th Division front.

Meanwhile, the 42nd Brigade had moved forward at zero hour from its assembly position on the rear slopes of Caterpillar Valley some three thousand yards behind the British front.[2] Marching on a compass bearing, the battalions on the right (9/Rifle Brigade, followed by the 9/K.R.R.C.) passed east of Delville Wood, and the others (5/K.S.L.I., with the 5/Oxford & Bucks L.I. in rear) through the wood. Deploying some four hundred yards before they reached the Switch Line, the leading battalions

---

[1] The 14th Division was opposed by the right of the *14th Bavarians*, which held the right sector of the *5th Bavarian Division*. The regimental history states that the British bombardment had cut all telephone wires and, as the light signals of the infantry were obscured by the smoke, the German batteries were very late in opening fire. Attacks by low-flying aeroplanes are mentioned.

[2] The brigade diary notes : " Barrage seems magnificent [6.25 A.M.] ; " Boche red lights all over the place [6.50 A.M.] ; Reports from artillery, " all going well [7.20 A.M.] ".

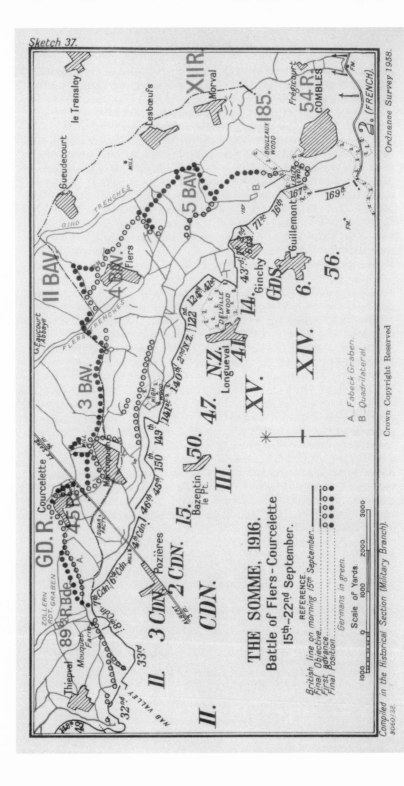

Sketch 37.

le Transloy

Gueudecourt

Lesboeufs

Morval

XIIR.

185.

Frégicourt

54 R.

COMBLES

2. (FRENCH).

Ordnance Survey 1938.

GIRD

MILL

TRENCHES

5 BAV.

BOULEAUX WOOD

B

167th

169th

II BAV.

4 BAV.

Flers

FLERS TRENCHES

71st

16th

Guillemont

G.Eaucourt
l'Abbaye

3 BAV.

122nd

12th 41st

2nd N.Z.

140th

141st

DELVILLE WOOD

43rd

14.

Ginchy

GDS.

6.

56.

XV.

41.

N.Z.

47.

Longueval

149th

150th

46th

Bazentin
le Pt.

50.

III.

XIV.

GD. R.

Courcelette

45 R.

45th Cdn.

A.

Pozières

2 CDN.

15.

3 Cdn.

SUGAR
FACT.

4th Cdn.

6th Cdn.

1st Cdn.

CDN.

ZOLLERN
RDT. GRABEN

89 R.Bde.

Mouquet
Farm

ALBERT

MILL

5 Bde.

8 Bde.

II.

33rd

II.

Thiepval

32nd

NAB VALLEY

246th

49.

THE SOMME, 1916.
Battle of Flers-Courcelette
15th–22nd September.

REFERENCE.

British line on morning 15th September. ————
Final Objective. ·········
First advance. ooooooo
Final Position. ●●●●●●●

Germans in green.

Scale of Yards.

1000   0   1000   2000   3000

A...Fabeck Graben.
B...Quadrilateral.

Crown Copyright Reserved

Compiled in the Historical Section (Military Branch)
3060/38.

of the brigade then moved on, and just before 9 A.M. (about 15 Sept. 30 minutes behind the time-table) passed over Gap Trench to attack the third objective.[1]

The 9/Rifle Brigade lost heavily by enfilade machine-gun fire from the right as it approached Bulls Road, and came to a halt in shell-holes some distance short of the objective. Lieut.-Colonel T. H. P. Morris had been mortally wounded, and every other officer hit except one very junior subaltern. On the left the K.S.L.I. became somewhat dispersed in passing through the foremost troops of the 41st Brigade, and German machine guns enfiladed the battalion from the left before it had passed Gap Trench. Like the Rifle Brigade, it was brought to a halt before it reached the road, and began to dig in. Following the Rifle Brigade came the 9/K.R.R.C., which lost Lieut.-Colonel E. W. Benson, killed, in the early stages of the advance, and eventually overtook the leading battalion.[2] On the left, the Oxford & Bucks L.I., which had overtaken the Shropshire, linked up with the 9/K.R.R.C. at the Ginchy—Gueudecourt road. Although exposed to effective shell-fire all the way, the brigade had carried the advance of the 14th Division beyond the divisions on its flanks, and now every movement drew machine-gun fire from right and left.

The 41st Division[3] (Major-General S. T. B. Lawford), Map 1. in the centre of the corps front, was to capture Flers in the Sketch course of its advance to the third objective. It was on this 37. portion of the front that the biggest concentration of tanks was to operate, four starting up the Longueval—Flers road, and six assembling at the northern end of Longueval to move against the centre and western side of Flers. Other machines from the New Zealand front were to cross and lead the way to the fourth objective. Of the original ten, seven arrived at their points of departure, but few, if any, made ground before the infantry advanced.

The division attacked with two brigades. In the 124th Brigade (Br.-General W. F. Clemson), on the right, the 10/Queen's and 21/K.R.R.C. led, with the 32nd and 26/Royal Fusiliers furnishing the second line. In this

[1] In accordance with the time table (see Appendix 24) this advance should have been preceded by the tanks, but none was now available.

[2] North of Gun Alley a party of the 9/K.R.R.C. under a sergeant rushed two field guns in a sunken road down which the German artillery-men were chased. Seven of the fugitives were killed, and the party actually reached Gird Trench before retiring. Three field guns were captured in this advance of the two battalions.

[3] This division had arrived in France in May, had occupied a quiet sector of the line near Ploegsteert, and then spent three weeks in training.

15 Sept. formation the four battalions were to go right through to the fourth objective, a position beyond Gueudecourt facing north-east, with the right clear of the village and the left resting upon the Gird trenches. The front waves formed up in No Man's Land before zero hour, and the attack started well, some of the men pressing on so eagerly that they were killed or wounded by the creeping barrage. At first there was little resistance, Tea Support having been so shattered by the bombardment that those of its defenders who remained alive had little heart for fighting. The Switch Line (first objective) was captured by 7 A.M., and the consolidation of the position was put in hand. The rear battalions had now overtaken and were mingled with the others, but soon after the appointed time, 7.20 A.M., the advance to the second objective (Flers Trench, south-east of the village) began. This was taken half an hour later after some fighting, and parties of the brigade then pushed on towards the third objective.

Next on the left, the 122nd Brigade (Br.-General F. W. Towsey) attacked with the 15/Hampshire and the 18/K.R.R.C. leading, followed by the 11/R. West Kent and the 12/East Surrey, which were to carry on the advance after the third objective had been taken.[1] The final objective was the defensive flank to be established facing north-west, astride the Gird trenches on the right, and in touch on the left with the New Zealanders at the Flers—Ligny road. Several tanks advanced with the brigade at zero hour, and the barrage was reported as " excellent ; " just what the men had been trained to expect ". German machine guns and rifles took toll of the stormers as they swept over Tea Support, but in twenty minutes the first objective was taken.[2] Here smoke bombs were used to clear those dug-outs which had been left intact by the British bombardment. The second objective (Flers Trench) was secured with even less trouble, many Germans running back without their arms and equipment. The machine guns of the tanks accounted for a number of these fugitives, and there was a considerable haul of prisoners[3] One machine

---

[1] See Appendices 28 and 29 for the brigade operation order and that of the 18/K.R.R.C.

[2] At the very start of the advance Lieut.-Colonel C. P. Marten, 18/K.R.R.C., his adjutant, signalling officer, and trench-mortar officer were all killed by one shell.

[3] The 41st Division was opposed by the *9th Bavarians* holding the left sector of the *4th* Bavarian Division. The regimental history says that most of the *I.* and *III. Bns.* were captured during the morning.

(D15) had been hit by a shell in front of the Switch Line, 15 Sept. and the whole crew were killed or wounded by shrapnel after they had left it ; one (D14) was ditched south of Sketch Flers ;[1] and one (D18) which got as far as Flers Trench 36. was also hit, but managed to withdraw later.

The 122nd Brigade now had to storm Flers, and establish itself upon the third objective beyond. There were still four tanks in action, and one (D16) went forward into the village just before 8.20 A.M., the infantry pressing on when the barrage lifted. The scene in Flers was without precedent in war. Firing as it went, the tank lurched up the main street followed by parties of cheering infantry.[2] Three other tanks (D6, D9, D17) had begun to move along the eastern edge of the village, smashing into strongpoints and houses which contained machine guns, and spreading panic among the defenders who survived. Most of the Bavarians, however, had fled towards Gueudecourt, and although a few parties of desperate men held out for a time, all resistance was at an end by 10 A.M.

The pressing need was to occupy the third objective along the farther edge of Flers and reorganize for the final advance ; but few regimental officers were left in the 122nd Brigade, and many of the men seemed under the impression that with the capture of the village their task was done.[3] Map 1. During the reaction following the stress and excitement of Sketch their successful assault, the enemy bombardment, which 37. now grew heavy and was assisted by direct observation, had the worst effect upon inexperienced troops, for the most part leaderless although still in good heart. The tendency was to drift back in small parties to the shelter of the captured trenches south of the village, although these positions also were now under considerable shell-fire.[4] Some isolated groups, however, pushed on and reached the third objective.

The New Zealand Division (Major-General Sir A. H. Russell), the left division of the corps, had to advance over

---

[1] This tank is reported to have advanced from Flers next morning, and was eventually found, " absolutely blown to bits ", near the roadfork south of Gueudecourt ; there was no sign of its crew or commander.

[2] An air report, timed 8.45 A.M. and passed on from the III. to the XV. Corps, ran, " Tank seen in main street Flers going on with large number " of troops following it ". The newspaper correspondents exploited this message to the full.

[3] Orders had been received late by the battalions, and the rank and file were not fully acquainted with them.

[4] Whilst endeavouring to rally and reorganize the troops on this line, Lieut.-Colonel A. F. Townshend, 11/R. West Kent, was mortally wounded.

15 Sept. the crest on the eastern side of High Wood and carry the Switch Line (first objective) on the reverse slope. Then, after clearing the outlying trenches (second objective) of the Flers defences, the third objective, north-west of the village was to be secured. The final objective of the New Zealanders was a continuation of the defensive flank to be formed by the left of the 41st Division ; it extended south-westward to Flers Support Trench, and to reach it involved a wheel north-westward, pivoting on the left. Two battalions, the 2/Auckland and 2/Otago of the 2nd N.Z. Brigade (Br.-General W. G. Braithwaite) were to take the Switch Line, after which the 3rd N.Z. (Rifle) Brigade (Br.-General H. T. Fulton) would come through, the 4th Battalion carrying the second, and the 2nd and 3rd Battalions, the third objective. Finally, the 1st Battalion would establish the defensive flank. Four tanks were to be employed : three to account for intervening strong-points and then skirt the north-western edge of Flers before turning into the 41st Division area beyond the Blue Line ; one to operate upon the left flank. All arrived safely at their departure point on the road about six hundred yards north of Longueval, but none succeeded in getting forward before the infantry advanced.

So keen was the Otago Battalion that its leading lines started forward 30 seconds before zero hour.[1] Many casualties were caused, first by the British barrage, then by enfilade machine-gun fire from High Wood. Nevertheless, the first wave swept over Crest Trench without a check, and the Otago pursued the fleeing enemy down the farther slope to the Switch Line. The 2/Auckland, to which Coffee Lane proved no great obstacle, kept pace on the right, where the Germans seemed to be more numerous, and the first objective was in New Zealand hands by 6.50 A.M., the defenders having been allowed no time to get their machine guns into action. As soon as all resistance was at an end, a new trench was started sixty yards in front of the Switch Line. A quarter of an hour later the first waves of the 4th Rifles, " in high spirits, some of them singing ", passed through along the whole New Zealand front and lay down as close as possible to the barrage. Although no tanks had as yet come forward so far, the battalion advanced without difficulty at the time appointed, 7.20 A.M., and captured the second objective half an hour later.

---

[1] Following the example, it is said, of the 1/7th London (47th Division, III. Corps), next on the left, which advanced at 6.19 A.M.

The 2nd Rifles and 3rd Rifles, following closely, pressed 15 Sept.
on to the attack of the third objective at 8.20 A.M., the
barrage having already lifted in anticipation of the advance
of the tanks.   On the right, the 2nd Rifles took 85 prisoners
in Flers Trench and found Flers Support empty, but
machine-gun fire from the north-western corner of the
village made further progress a costly effort.   Abbey
Road, to which there was a drop of nearly twenty feet from
ground level, possessed many dug-outs which were still
intact, and here stubborn fighting took place.   Before
11 A.M., however, these intervening obstacles had been
overcome, and the survivors of the 2nd Rifles were digging
in on the third objective, their right in the 41st Division
area just north of Flers.   The 3rd Rifles, on their left, had
been held up by uncut wire before Flers Trench, and could
do little until the tanks came on the scene.   One of the four Sketch
machines (D10) had been hit by a shell and put out of 36.
action at Fat Trench, where it became a target for the
enemy gunners ; but about 10.30 A.M. two tanks (D11 and
D12) arrived, crushed the wire, dealt with the machine
guns, and assisted in the capture of about a hundred
Bavarians.[1]   The 3rd Rifles now had little trouble in Map 1.
getting forward to join its sister battalion in the third Sketch
objective ; no touch was obtained on the left in Flers 37.
Support Trench, with the 47th Division (III. Corps), and
this flank was therefore refused.   The check at Flers
Trench had delayed the advance of the 1st Rifles, which
was intended to establish the defensive flank, and part of
this battalion had become involved in the fighting on the
right at Abbey Road.   It was therefore not until 11.30 A.M.
that the 1st was reorganized and ready to go on.

By reports from contact aeroplanes, which had no
difficulty in distinguishing the red flares lit by the foremost
troops, and messages received from forward observing
officers—and even some by pigeon from various battalions
—corps headquarters had been able to follow the progress
of infantry and tanks as far as the second objective.   Soon
after 10 A.M. it seemed evident that the advance to the
third objective had begun along the whole corps front.
Lieut.-General Horne received over the telephone about

[1] The New Zealanders encountered the *5th Bavarians*, right of the *4th
Bavarian Division*, and part of the *18th Bavarians*, belonging to the adjoining *3rd Bavarian Division*.   The Bavarian regimental histories mention
the arrival of the tanks and state that their men were quite powerless
against them.

15 Sept. 10.45 A.M. the assurance of the 14th Division that the forward flow of troops was being maintained, so that the 42nd Brigade should be ready to advance upon Gueudecourt at 10.50 A.M., according to time-table. An air report received at 11 A.M. said that there were few Germans in the Gird trenches in front of the village. Twenty minutes later the corps commander had a telephone conversation with Major-General Lawford—as yet without knowledge of the conditions on his own front—who said his troops (41st Division) were north of Flers, but that he was uncertain of the position of the New Zealanders, and feared his left flank might be exposed if his advance continued. Was he to consolidate or push on ? Major-General Lawford was informed of the check to the New Zealanders' left at Flers Trench—already overcome—and told that the advance could not stop ; he must protect his own flank as he made headway. The corps then ordered the 64th Brigade (Br.-General H. R. Headlam) of the 21st Division, the only division in corps reserve, to move up to Pommiers Redoubt, mid-way between Mametz and Montauban, and more than four miles south-west of Flers.

At the appointed time, 10.50 A.M., the corps barrage began to lift from the Gird trenches, but the 14th and 41st Divisions were in no condition to follow up the success they had won. On the right of the 14th Division, the 9/Rifle Brigade, supported by the 9/K.R.R.C., endeavoured to advance across Bulls Road at 11.20 A.M. in order to attack the Gird trenches, but the movement was stopped by machine-gun fire from Gird Trench near the right boundary of the corps. Reduced to about 350 rifles in all, the two battalions then improved a shell-hole position running south-eastward to Gas Alley, where some men of the 1st Guards Brigade assisted to prolong the defensive flank. The left was in touch with the Oxford & Bucks L.I. on the third objective at the Ginchy—Gueudecourt road, for by this time the Oxfordshire and K.S.L.I. had reached Bulls Road on the left portion of the divisional front.[1]

Few Germans could be seen in the Gird trenches, which appeared to have little wire in front of them, so that a further advance appeared feasible. Appeals for reinforcements had been made, and Major-General Couper's reserve, the 43rd Brigade, began to arrive at Montauban

[1] Lieut.-Colonel W. F. R. Webb, 5/Oxford & Bucks L.I., was wounded for the second time about noon, and had to leave his battalion.

soon after 11.30 A.M.; but its leading battalion was still 15 Sept.
some $3\frac{1}{2}$ miles behind Bulls Road.[1] Artillery assistance
was not easy to provide, since many field batteries were on
the move to forward positions, coming under heavy shell-
fire as they did so and suffering much delay through the
heavy state of the ground. The only tank (D5) still in
action on the divisional front—the machine which had Sketch
arrived too late to play its part in the preliminary operation 36.
east of Delville Wood — did, indeed, reach Gueudecourt
before noon and engage a German battery, forcing the
gunners to take shelter in a dug-out. After cruising about
whilst waiting for the infantry to advance, the machine
withdrew, but was then shelled by the battery and set on
fire.

In the 41st Division, the troops of the 124th Brigade Map 1.
had made little progress beyond Flers Trench, for the Sketch
battalion commanders were doubtful of the situation on 37.
their left in Flers. Disquieting reports having reached
Br.-General W. F. Clemson, he went up in person to set the
attack going again. He arrived at 2.30 P.M. to find that
considerable confusion prevailed, and it was not until
3.20 P.M. that about two hundred men of the 124th Brigade
—mostly 10/Queen's and 21/K.R.R.C., led by the commanders of these battalions, Lieut.-Colonels R. Oakley
and the Earl of Faversham—made a fresh advance on
the third objective. Br.-General Clemson, as soon as
they arrived, also pushed forward two companies of the
23/Middlesex (from Br.-General C. S. Davidson's 123rd
Brigade, in reserve), which had been sent up to reinforce
him, and the remainder of the battalion followed later.
This movement of the Queen's and K.R.R.C. reached the
western end of Bulls Road, where Lord Faversham was
killed,[2] and established touch with parties of the 122nd
Brigade on the left; but attempts to advance against the
Gird trenches were driven back by machine-gun fire.[3]

Between 11.30 A.M. and 1 P.M. there was little action on

[1] According to the Bavarian regimental histories, the remnants of the
I. and *II./14th Bavarians* which had been engaged by the 14th Division
and the left of the Guards Division rallied in the Gird trenches, where the
III./14th Bavarians arrived from Le Transloy about 11.30 A.M., having
come forward over the open in small columns.

[2] Lieut.-Colonel Oakley, 10/Queen's, was wounded later in the
afternoon.

[3] The *I./10th Bavarians* (*6th Bavarian Division*) reached the Gird
Trenches about noon, and found all the dug-outs blown in by the British
bombardment. It repulsed British attacks at 1 P.M. and 4 P.M. "Bav.
Regt. No. 10".

15 Sept. the front of the 122nd Brigade, which, as we know, had some parties in the vicinity of the third objective. Then Br.-General Towsey, who had received reports of a withdrawal from Flers, sent forward his brigade-major, Major Gwyn Thomas, to take control of the situation. Arrived in Flers Trench, this officer sent Lieutenant E. T. G. Carter, 228th Field Company R.E., whose sappers were working on a strongpoint, to advance round the eastern edge of Flers with all the men he could collect. Major Gwyn Thomas did the same on the western side of the village, where he got into touch with the New Zealanders ; he reached the third objective before 3 P.M. and joined forces with Lieutenant Carter just as the advanced parties of the brigade, believing themselves isolated, were about to withdraw. Not only was the line established, but, beyond it, Box and Cox and Hog's Head [1] were occupied. Two companies of the 23/Middlesex, whose commander, Lieut.-Colonel W. C. C. Ash, was hit, assisted to hold the line, which was further strengthened by five Vickers guns of the 122nd Brigade.

Sketch 36.
Of the four tanks which had assisted in the capture of Flers, one (D6) had gone on as far as the outskirts of Gueudecourt, where, during the morning, it engaged a German battery with its 6-pdr. gun. One of the enemy pieces was put out of action, but a German shell hit the machine, which burst into flames. Another tank (D9) reached Box and Cox, and, after working up Glebe Street at the request of the New Zealanders, was hit several times by shells. It was abandoned, burning furiously, nearly all the crew being killed or injured. The third (D16) reached the third objective, and then returned without mishap, whilst the fourth (D17), having been hit twice by shells, was abandoned on the eastern side of Flers and removed later.

Map 1.
Sketch 37.
In the New Zealand Division, two companies of the 1st Rifles had attacked Grove Alley (north-west of Flers) at 11.30 A.M. in order to establish the defensive flank beyond. They were covered by the Vickers guns attached to the 2nd Rifles, but were met by fire from the ridge overlooking their objective. The exposed right flank, which had to swing half-left as it advanced, suffered severely ; and although a footing was obtained in the centre of Grove Alley, the position was obviously untenable in view of the fact that

[1] Trenches constructed by the Germans for bombing practice had been so named.

Germans were now seen advancing in considerable force 15 Sept. from the direction of Ligny.[1] Before withdrawing to the third objective between 2 and 2.30 P.M., one of the two field guns found in the trench was rendered unserviceable.

Three of the tanks attached to the New Zealand Division Sketch had reached the vicinity of Flers. One (D12) had its tail 36. damaged by a shell, became ditched on the western side of the village, was hit again whilst being dug out, and had to be abandoned; one (D8), deputed to work up the left boundary of the corps, reached Abbey Road and returned again, but could do little owing to its prisms being shattered by fire and the commander and driver blinded by the glass splinters; the third (D11), at the request of the New Zealanders, took up a position on the Ligny road near Box and Cox, and remained there all night in readiness for further action.[2]

At 2.40 P.M. Lieut.-General Horne telephoned to the Map 1. 14th and 41st Divisions to say that the corps artillery was Sketch beginning a fresh bombardment of the Gird trenches and 37. Gueudecourt, and that he would give two to three hours' notice if a fresh advance were to be made. He then informed the Fourth Army that he proposed to attack at 5 P.M., and asked if the reserve brigades should be so used even if the Guards made no further effort to get Lesboeufs : he only had one division in reserve. Soon after 3 P.M. General Rawlinson, who by this time had been informed of the general situation on the Army front, cancelled all further attacks for the day—it was understood that the advance was to be resumed on the morrow—and at 3.45 P.M. divisions were instructed that the third objective was to be linked up securely and consolidated, under cover of a field artillery barrage.

During the afternoon parties of Germans trickled steadily forward into the Gird trenches, many advancing in open order, from the direction of Le Transloy, less than two

[1] According to the Bavarian accounts, parts of the *5th Bavarians* and *5th Bavarian Reserve (4th Bavarian Division)* came into position astride the Flers—Ligny road about 11.30 A.M. Divisional orders were to hold "Gallwitz Riegel" (Gird trenches) at all costs. It is stated that these troops counter-attacked at 1.30 P.M.

[2] By the afternoon, Grove Alley (astride the Ligny road) was occupied by the equivalent of 2½ battalions, including the *I./9th Bavarians* and half the *II./10th Bavarians (6th Bavarian Division)*. " Bav. Regt. No. 5."

15 Sept. miles east of Gueudecourt. A section of an enemy
field battery galloped out from behind Le Transloy, and
was able to come into action with impunity south-east of
Gueudecourt, whilst a movement on Flers from the north
was also observed. Along the whole front of the XV. Corps
the German artillery fire increased as the day wore on, and
at 6.45 P.M., in the fading light, a half-hearted counter-
attack down the Gueudecourt—Ginchy road was repulsed
by the fire of the advanced troops of the 14th Division.
Soon afterwards another enemy attempt, coming this time
from the north-east, drove in some posts of the Irish Guards
(1st Guards Brigade), which had by this time been
established beyond the second objective, and thereby
caused the 14th Division to strengthen its defensive flank
in Gas Alley. After darkness fell, the 43rd Brigade, from
reserve, began the relief of the 42nd Brigade in readiness
for the resumption of the attack next morning.

Between 5 and 6 P.M. the weak 124th Brigade detachment on the third objective repulsed by rapid fire two
counter-attacks delivered in splendid order but without a
covering barrage.[1]

Acting under corps instructions, Major-General Lawford
had already taken measures for the consolidation of Flers.
He sent up the remainder of the 123rd Brigade for this purpose, the 10/R. West Kent occupying the Switch Line,
where Lieut.-Colonel A. W. Martyn was wounded, and the
20/Durham L.I. going into the trenches round the village.
The 233rd Field Company R.E. worked all night on the
Flers defences. The movements of the battalions were not
completed without some confusion and delay, but after
darkness fell the 11/Queen's, assisted by part of the
23/Middlesex, began to take over the whole front of the
41st Division, which was on the third objective but also
included Hog's Head and Box and Cox.[2] Patrols main-

---

[1] It was hoped to recapture Flers and the Flers Line, and troops of the
6th Bavarian Division, now arriving, were used. The *II./10th Bavarians*
is said to have relieved part of the *14th Bavarians (5th Bavarian Division)*
in the Gird trenches and to have launched a counter-attack upon Flers in
the afternoon. This was checked by the British barrage. At 5.10 P.M.,
the *III./10th Bavarians* and the *III./5th Bavarians (4th Bavarian Division)*
attacked, but could only gain 250 yards. Another account describes an
advance at 5.30 P.M. which gained 500 yards, a shell-hole position astride
Gas Alley [that is in front of the refused right flank of the 14th Division]
being occupied for the night. Before darkness fell, the *I./10th Bavarians*
and two battalions of the *11th Bavarians* were in the Gird trenches from
Gueudecourt south-eastward. Regimental histories.

[2] Before the relief, Lieut.-Colonel H. J. Walmisley-Dresser, 12/E.
Surrey, was mortally wounded by a shell.

tained touch with the 14th Division and the New Zealand 15 Sept.
Division on the flanks.

III. Corps : Capture of High Wood and Martinpuich

Although the objectives of Lieut.-General Pulteney's Map 1.
III. Corps (47th, 50th and 15th Divisions, from right to Sketch
left) were limited, its rôle was of considerable importance. 37.
Not only had the corps to protect the flank of the Fourth
Army's main attack, but upon its success also depended, to a
great degree, the progress of the right of the Reserve Army.
In front of the 47th and 50th Divisions the second and third
objectives ran from east to west along the reverse slope of
the ridge, these trenches linking the Flers defences with
Martinpuich. Possession of even the first objective would
bring under observation the low-lying country extending
north-eastward to Bapaume. The 15th Division, on the
left, was to halt on the near edge of Martinpuich in the first
instance ; but, if all went well, the village would be secured
so that the converging flanks of the 50th Division and the
2nd Canadian Division (Reserve Army) could meet north
of the village as the advance pressed on.

The 47th Division (Major-General Sir C. St. L. Barter),
having received strict injunctions to cover the New Zealand
left, attacked with two brigades. On the right, the 140th
Brigade (Br.-General Viscount Hampden) placed the 1/7th
and 1/15th London in the van ; after they had taken the
first objective—traced to include the Switch Line and the
northern point of High Wood—the 1/8th London was to
come through and secure the second, the final objective
being allotted to the 1/6th London. In the first stage of
the advance the 1/15th London had to clear the enemy from
High Wood in conjunction on its left with the 1/17th
London of the 141st Brigade (Br.-General R. McDouall)
which allotted the first objective to this battalion and the
1/18th London. The 1/20th and 1/19th London were then
to go straight through.

The corps had been allotted eight tanks, of which four
were to pass through High Wood [1] and four were to be

---

[1] The opposing lines in High Wood were too close to permit of artillery
bombardment, so the corps hoped that the tanks would prove their value
here. Since the tank officers were doubtful if their machines could
negotiate the tree stumps the divisional commander would have preferred
the tanks to advance along the edges of the wood.

15 Sept. employed against Martinpuich. Only one of the machines failed to reach its rendezvous before zero hour.

The infantry advanced at the appointed time with great steadiness and resolution. On the extreme right, east of High Wood, the 1/7th London, with one company of the 1/15th London, reached the Switch Line on the reverse slope of the ridge without encountering much resistance. They dug in a little way beyond, linking up with the New Zealanders. High Wood, however, was not to be cleared without paying a heavy price. The four tanks started at the same time as the infantry, but were of little assistance. Two machines which went forward from the southern point of the wood found the going so difficult that they turned eastward into more open ground, one losing direction entirely and becoming ditched in the British front line after firing by mistake on our own men, whilst the other came to grief in a shell-hole.[1] The third succeeded in crossing the German front trench in the wood and enfiladed the support line until struck by a shell and set on fire ;[2] the fourth, on the left, was ditched before reaching the enemy trenches, its crew then fighting with the infantry.[3]

The infantry assault in the wood was checked by machine-gun fire almost at the outset, and no progress could be made in spite of the reckless bravery of officers and men. Whilst a confused struggle continued and losses grew heavy, part of the 1/8th London (140th Brigade) and the 1/20th and 1/19th London (141st Brigade), advancing to attack the second objective at 7.20 A.M., began to crowd forward into the wood and join in the fight. After Lieut.-Colonel A. P. Hamilton, 1/19th London, had been mortally wounded in directing a fresh assault, Br.-General McDouall decided to ask for a special bombardment of the wood. Strenuous efforts were made to reorganize the press of troops in readiness for another effort.

Meanwhile, on the extreme right of the 140th Brigade, part of the 1/8th London—less than two companies—had advanced and entered Flag Lane, the second objective. Then at 8.20 A.M. came the 1/6th London to pass through and capture the Flers trenches north-east of the knot of trenches named " The Cough-Drop ". This battalion

[1] The crew remained under shell-fire for 14 hours digging out the machine.
[2] It was reported that a German infantryman had crept up to the tank, opened a loop-hole and shot one of the crew in the leg.
[3] This tank remained in the wood until destroyed by shell-fire on 21st September.

suffered very heavily from shell and machine-gun fire during its advance, and, although a few men reached the Flers trenches they could not stay there. The Cough Drop, however, was taken and held, and an effort was made to link up with the New Zealanders by digging eastward.

Owing to the conformation of the British line, the troops of the 50th Division (Major-General P. S. Wilkinson), in the centre of the corps front, started their attack well forward of those upon their flanks. It was hoped that a swift advance would help the progress of the flank divisions, but nothing, it seemed, could compensate for the delay in driving the Germans from High Wood.

The 149th Brigade (Br.-General R. M. Ovens),[1] next to the 47th Division, sent forward the 1/4th and 1/7th Northumberland Fusiliers to go right through to the third objective, the other two battalions following in support and reserve. Hook Trench (the first objective) was entered by both of the leading units about 7 A.M., few Germans, except dead and wounded, being encountered, and touch was preserved with the 1/4th East Yorkshire (150th Brigade), on the left. The advance to the next object- ive (Starfish Line—The Bow), which started up to time, proved more difficult, for the leading waves were enfiladed from High Wood, and some confusion ensued. At 8.10 A.M. the 1/4th Northumberland Fusiliers was ordered to help the 47th Division by bombing towards the wood, from which parties of Germans emerged to counter-attack. The 1/6th and the 1/5th Northumberland Fusiliers were pushed forward to support the advance and soon after 10 A.M. the 1/7th Northumberland Fusiliers was reported to have reached the sunken road south of the Bow. Losses were known to be very heavy, and confused fighting con- tinued on the right, north-west of High Wood, where the 1/6th Northumberland Fusiliers provided a defensive flank. Later in the morning parties of the brigade gained a footing in the Starfish Line at several points.

On the left of the 149th, the two tanks with the 150th Brigade (Br.-General B. G. Price) went forward in advance of the infantry and were of considerable assistance. One machine reached the first objective and enfiladed the trench, inflicting much loss until hit by two shells in quick succession ; the crew then salved the guns and joined the infantry. The other passed over the trench, and, with the

---

[1] He had succeeded Br.-General H. F. H. Clifford, killed by a shell on 11th September, and had only been in command for a few hours.

15 Sept. hostile infantry fleeing before it, reached the vicinity of the third objective after accounting for three German machine guns on the eastern outskirts of Martinpuich. Shelled continually but never hit, this tank eventually returned, with a bullet through its oil cylinder, to replenish its petrol.[1]

The 150th Brigade had the 1/4th East Yorkshire and 1/4th and 1/5th Green Howards in line, the three battalions to go through to the final objective supported by the 1/5th Durham L.I. The first objective was taken without difficulty before 7 A.M., many prisoners running into the British lines without an escort,[2] and the advance continued without serious check. Before 10 A.M. the third objective was reported to have been gained, but the success was not quite so complete. On the right, the 1/4th East Yorkshire, its flank in the air, was obliged to withdraw to Martin Trench ; farther to the left, the Starfish Line was held near its junction with Martin Alley. At 9.5 A.M. the 1/8th Durham L.I. (from Br.-General N. J. G. Cameron's 151st Brigade, in reserve) had been placed at the disposal of the 150th Brigade.

The 15th Division (Major-General F. W. N. McCracken) had the assistance of two tanks which were to approach Martinpuich from the south-west, but one machine was hit by a shell before it reached its departure point. In the first instance the division had only to capture two lines of trenches and establish itself on a line through the south-western end of the village. On the right, the 45th Brigade (Br.-General W. H. L. Allgood) had the 11/Argyll & Sutherland Highlanders and 13/Royal Scots in front, with the 6/Cameron Highlanders in support and the 8/York & Lancaster (attached from the 23rd Division) and the 6th/7th R. Scots Fusiliers in reserve. The attack met with no great opposition, for the British bombardment had done its work well : the surviving Germans were, for the most part, disposed to surrender, although the Argyll were obliged to bomb Tangle South and encountered some resistance in the sunken (Longueval—Martinpuich) road beyond.

The 46th Brigade (Br.-General T. G. Matheson), on the left, with the 10/Scottish Rifles, 7th/8th K.O.S.B. and

---

[1] " Bav. Regt. No. 17 " says that the tanks were a surprise. They negotiated shell-holes and trenches with ease, and opened a way for the infantry by attacking with their fire every centre of resistance.

[2] Prisoners were of the *I.* and *II./17th Bavarians*, whose dead and wounded were very plentiful.

10th/11th Highland L.I. leading, the 12/Highland L.I. in support, and the 9/York & Lancaster (attached from the 23rd Division) in reserve, was equally successful. The necessary change of front on the extreme left in order to deal by frontal attack with the sunken road running south-westward out of Martinpuich was executed with great precision. Factory Lane, the objective, was reached soon after 7 A.M., and here the 10th/11th H.L.I. joined hands with the Canadians of the Reserve Army. Although the British barrage was still on the northern part of Martinpuich, the K.O.S.B. sent patrols forward along the western side of the village.

The solitary tank started behind the infantry, finding progress difficult over the bad ground, but its appearance had hastened the flight of the enemy from Bottom Trench over the crest to Tangle Trench. It silenced several machine guns and crushed in some dug-outs on the south-western outskirts of Martinpuich before returning for more petrol. It was under fire all day and sustained damage to its tail.[1]

At 9.20 A.M., according to the programme, the artillery lifted from Martinpuich and both brigades sent in strong patrols. Shortly after 10 A.M. the 10/Scottish Rifles (46th Brigade) began to entrench in the village along the line of the objective. The 45th Brigade brought in more prisoners, including a battalion commander and his adjutant.

The check at High Wood, where so many battalions had been absorbed into the struggle, caused the corps, with Army approval, to name the Starfish Line as the main position to be consolidated, thus implying that when the second objective had been secured little further progress would be expected. This message was issued to divisions at 10.30 A.M.

At 11.40 A.M., after the 140th Trench Mortar Battery had fired 750 Stokes mortar shells into High Wood —a hurricane bombardment which only occupied 15 minutes—the Germans began to surrender to bombing parties of the Londoners which worked forward round the flanks. Several hundred prisoners were collected,[2] and six machine guns and two 10·5-cm. howitzers were captured

---

[1] Later in the day the G.O.C. 46th Brigade used this tank to take forward supplies of S.A.A.

[2] They were mostly of the *23rd Bavarians* (centre of the *3rd Bavarian Division*).

15 Sept. when resistance came to an end. The survivors of the 141st Brigade, scattered in trenches and shell-holes, were then reorganized as a composite battalion to hold the first objective. So High Wood, which had defied every British effort since the 14th July, fell at last to the 47th Division ; but it was now nearly 1 P.M. and the capture of the Starfish Line, 700 yards ahead, had yet to be accomplished. The German batteries were shelling the captured ground with great fury, placing barrages on all approaches to the new forward positions.

About 3.30 P.M. the 1/21st and 1/24th London, belonging to Br.-General F. G. Lewis's 142nd Brigade, in reserve, received orders direct from the division to carry on the attack. These battalions, which had no time for reconnaissance, advanced to High Wood about an hour later, but were not able to make a simultaneous assault. Passing east of the wood, the 1/21st London and one company of the 1/24th went forward about 5.30 P.M. with splendid resolution through artillery fire which inflicted heavy loss ; brought to a halt in front of the Starfish Line by the fire of machine guns which the British barrage had not been able to subdue, many of the survivors remained out in shell-holes rather than withdraw. As the light began to fade the other three companies of the 1/24th London, which had experienced great difficulty in getting clear of the western side of the wood and forming up for the attack, made an equally gallant and hopeless effort to reach the objective.[1] Thus, when darkness fell, the 47th Division held no organized positions forward of the first objective, except on the extreme right, where the 1/6th London occupied the Cough Drop and was now in touch with the New Zealanders.

At 12.50 P.M. Major-General Wilkinson, commanding the 50th Division, allotted the 1/9 Durham L.I. (from the 151st Brigade, in reserve) to the 149th Brigade, in order to ensure the complete occupation of the Starfish Line on his front. During the afternoon, however, the German shell-fire so increased in volume that the 149th Brigade found it more and more difficult to maintain its forward positions,

---

[1] " Res. Regt. No. 229 " (the regiment belonged to the *50th Reserve Division*, which was due to begin the relief of the *3rd Bavarian Division* on the night of the 15th/16th) states that the *I./229th Reserve* had been hurried forward from the vicinity of Bapaume, and by the afternoon was occupying the Flers line in front of Eaucourt l'Abbaye. These trenches were crowded with the *I./231st Reserve* (*50th Reserve Division*) and the *II./133rd Reserve* (*24th Reserve Division*) ; all three battalions counter-attacked to retake " Foureaux Riegel " (the Switch Line) at 4 P.M.

and suffered severely in its attempt to do so. By 3.30 P.M.
men of all four Northumberland Fusilier battalions were
back in Hook Trench and about a hundred of the 1/7th
were in the sunken road south of the Bow. The 1/9th
Durham L.I. had not yet been engaged. At 1.50 P.M. the
150th Brigade, on the left, had been ordered to push patrols
into the northern end of Martinpuich, so as to link up with
the 15th Division ; but it was reported to 50th Division
headquarters at 4 P.M. that the brigade had been shelled
out of the Starfish Line and was holding on to Martin Alley
and Martin Trench. Major-General Wilkinson, however,
still hoped to secure the whole of his final objective. At
5.45 P.M. he ordered the 151st Brigade to assault Prue
Trench between the right boundary of the division and
Crescent Alley at 7.30 P.M., the 150th Brigade to occupy the
continuation of Prue Trench, joining up with the 15th
Division in Martinpuich.

The 15th Division was already in possession of Martinpuich. At 3 P.M. the 6/Cameron Highlanders (45th Brigade)
had advanced, and, after some bombing encounters, drove
the Germans from the north-eastern end of the village,
taking many more prisoners.[1] The remainder of the ruins
was occupied by the forward troops of the 46th Brigade, who
encountered few Germans, and established a chain of posts
facing north-west towards Courcelette. At night the
brigade put the 9/York & Lancaster and 12/Highland L.I.
into the front line, where they were in touch with the
Canadians in Gunpit Trench. On the right flank, the
Camerons, finding that none of the 50th Division had
reached Prue Trench, linked up with the 1/5th Green
Howards at the junction of Martin Alley with the Starfish
Line.

It remains to describe the effort of the 50th Division to
reach Prue Trench east of Crescent Alley. The 1/5th
Border Regiment and 1/6th and 1/9th Durham L.I. (151st
Brigade) began to assemble in Hook Trench during the late
afternoon, and, after three postponements, the assault was
launched at 9.40 P.M. following a special bombardment.

---

[1] In Martinpuich the 15th Division captured officers and men of the
17th Bavarians (right sector, *3rd Bavarian Division*) ; the *133rd Reserve*
(*24th Reserve Division*), which had sent up one battalion as reinforcements ;
and the *211th Reserve* and *40th Field Artillery Reserve* (both *45th Reserve
Division* confronting the Canadians). A field-gun battery and a 5·9″
howitzer were taken.

" Bav. Regt. No. 17 " states that the remnants of the regiment were
withdrawn to the " Below Stellung " (Flers line) at night.

Z

15 Sept. The 1/5th Border Regiment, on the right, was not in position—its guides had been at a loss—but the leading companies of the Durham battalions went forward gamely in the face of accurate machine-gun fire which caused them heavy casualties. Small parties of both units entered Prue Trench, but were all killed or wounded; others who had established themselves in the Starfish Line were driven out by bombing and rifle fire at close range. Eventually, the Durham L.I. dug in behind the Northumberland Fusiliers who were holding the sunken road south of the Bow. At 11 P.M. the Border Regiment on the right made its belated effort, but was only able to make a little ground before digging in.

The Reserve Army on 15th September
Canadian Corps : Capture of Courcelette

Map 1.
Sketch
37.

The 2nd Canadian Division (Major-General R. E. W. Turner), forming the right of the corps, next to the III. Corps of the Fourth Army, had two brigades in line. On the right the 4th Brigade (Br.-General R. Rennie) set the 18th (W. Ontario), 20th (Central Ontario) and 21st (E. Ontario) Battalions to advance straight through to the objective; on the left, in the 6th Brigade (Br.-General H. D. B. Ketchen), the 27th (City of Winnipeg) and 28th (North-West) Battalions were to do likewise, the 31st (Alberta) following in support as " moppers-up " and carriers. All were warned that success was to be exploited to the utmost. A group of tanks was to move up the Bapaume road—one machine on the road itself and one on either side—as far as the sugar factory, which one tank was to attack, whilst the others turned down Factory Lane towards the right boundary of the corps. On the left flank of the division three tanks were to make for Sugar Trench and move along it to attack the factory—known to be strongly organized for defence—from the north. Infantry and tanks were to start together at zero hour, but the former was not to wait for the machines if they should lag behind.

The noise of the tanks arriving at their forward positions was undoubtedly heard by the enemy, but the slow barrage he put down upon communication trenches and back areas proved to be part of a previously planned attack upon the 4th Canadian Brigade. Parties of German bombers advanced at 3.10 and 4.30 A.M., and only by prompt and energetic action of the 18th, 19th (Central Ontario) and 15 Sept. 20th Battalions was the situation restored in time for the assault preparations to be completed before 6.20 A.M.

The creeping barrage came down about fifty yards from the German front line, and the Canadian advance, assisted by the covering fire of machine guns, went well from the start, although considerable resistance was encountered. In less than fifteen minutes the Germans were driven from their front trenches, and Factory Lane, which contained many dead and wounded, was reached by the 4th Brigade about 7 A.M. Groups of snipers and machine-gunners who refused to surrender were either shot or bayoneted. The 21st Battalion, with some assistance from the 20th, cleared the sugar factory, taking 125 prisoners ; under the buildings was a deep dug-out, which yielded six officers, including a battalion commander, and fifteen others.[1] The progress of the 6th Brigade was not quite so rapid, but the two battalions reached their objective soon after 7.30 A.M. The 28th Battalion, on the left, had to subdue a strongpoint where the line of the objective cut the Ovillers—Courcelette track ; when this had been done an advance up the track cleared a number of the enemy from McDonnell Trench,[2] and secured a forward position from which machine-gun fire could be brought to bear eastward across the new Canadian front.[3] All the assaulting battalions had suffered considerable loss from shell and machine-gun fire, but consolidation proceeded, and patrols were pushed out to keep contact with the retiring enemy. On the right, Lewis-gun posts were soon established in the sunken (Martinpuich—Courcelette) road beyond Gunpit Trench. Three patrols of the 28th Battalion, on the left flank, got into Courcelette and out again before the British barrage lifted, as had been arranged, at 7.33 A.M.

The tanks had been unable to keep pace, but their very appearance had a good effect, giving to the troops, it was said, " a feeling of superiority and security ". One machine of the right group was ditched before crossing the Canadian front line, owing to a shell damaging the steering gear, and

---

[1] The trenches south of Courcelette were held by the *211th Reserve* (the left of the *45th Reserve Division*), the *III. Bn.* being west and the *II. Bn.* east of the Albert—Bapaume road.

[2] It was so spelt on some of the operation maps in use at the time.

[3] The Germans encountered belonged to the *210th Reserve*, whose history states that the left flank of its *I./Bn.* had lost touch with the *211th Reserve*.

15 Sept. the crew tried in vain to dig it out under fire. The two others reached the sugar factory, to find the Canadians in possession and then returned, but one of these machines had not only found some targets for its Hotchkiss guns but on its way forward laid 400 yards of telephone cable which it carried in a drum on its tail. One tank in the left group developed track trouble, and could not advance from the departure point, but two machines eventually crossed the line of the objective and were ditched beyond remedy in McDonnell Trench after doing considerable execution.[1] Their crews, also, dug away for hours under shell-fire before giving up their attempts to get the machines clear.

Meanwhile, on the front of the 3rd Canadian Division (Major-General L. J. Lipsett), the 5th Canadian Mounted Rifles [2] had, as arranged, secured its portion of the objective in order to protect the left of the main attack.[3] Without suffering much loss the C.M.R. killed many Germans, bringing fire to bear upon those who fled back over the open. In order to protect their own left flank they established a bombing block in the trench leading to Fabeck Graben. Farther west, the 1st C.M.R. attempted to raid the old German 2nd Position, but was prevented by shell-fire from entering the trench ; farther west still, a party of the same battalion, covered by a smoke barrage, put down by the 5th Battalion of the Special Brigade R.E., raided Mouquet Farm and accounted for about fifty Germans.[4]

At 8.25 A.M. Major-General Turner, having been informed that the attack had succeeded, issued orders that when the barrage lifted at 9.20 A.M.—the hour at which the 15th Division was sending patrols into Martinpuich—posts were to be pushed forward to the sunken road beyond Gunpit Trench and also established along the southern edge of Courcelette.[5] South-east of the Bapaume road this measure

[1] Officer prisoners were reticent upon the subject, but one of the captured rank and file said in English that the use of tanks was " not war " but bloody butchery ".

[2] The 8th Brigade of this division was formed of six Canadian Mounted Rifle regiments, permanently dismounted and organized as four infantry battalions.

[3] The 8th Canadian Brigade occupied the whole front of the 3rd Canadian Division. The 7th Canadian Brigade, shown as holding the right sector in Map 1 was in reserve at the opening of the battle.

[4] The farm was held by the *II./212th Reserve Regiment*.

[5] The 2nd Canadian Division, in a message to the corps, urged that its 5th Canadian Brigade, from reserve, should advance and capture Courcelette without delay.

involved no more than the reinforcement of the posts 15 Sept.
already established, and this was done, touch being obtained
with the 15th Division (III. Corps, Fourth Army) on the
right. It proved more difficult to obtain a footing on the
southern edge of Courcelette, and during the afternoon
attempts of the enemy to counter-attack from the ruins of
the village were repulsed by the fire of the Colt machine
guns.[1]

During the morning General Gough had conferred with
Lieut.-General the Hon. Sir J. H. G. Byng, commanding the
Canadian Corps. It was understood that the left of the
Fourth Army would occupy Martinpuich in the afternoon,
and at 11.10 A.M. the Canadian Corps issued orders for an
attack upon Courcelette and Fabeck Graben, which ran
down the eastern slope of the Pozières ridge into the village.
Courcelette was to be assaulted by the 5th Brigade
(Br.-General A. H. Macdonell), whilst the 3rd Canadian
Division would carry Fabeck Graben and dig in along
the crest of the slope beyond. Orders were explained
verbally to battalion commanders of the 5th Brigade about
1 P.M. The main attack was to cross an east and west line
on a level with the northern end of the sugar factory at
6 P.M., the left of the brigade resting on Taffy Trench,
which would mark the right of Br.-General A. C. Macdonell's
7th Brigade (3rd Canadian Division). All units concerned
sent scouts forward during the afternoon to reconnoitre the
ground. At 5.30 P.M., whilst these fresh battalions were
moving up from Pozières through two heavy German
barrages, news was received by the corps of the occupation
of Martinpuich.

The 22nd (Canadien Français) Battalion and 25th
Battalion (Nova Scotia Rifles) of the 5th Brigade reached
their position to time, and waited until 6.15 P.M. when
the creeping barrage lifted. Courcelette was then taken
without much difficulty, and its dug-outs methodically
cleared. The 26th (New Brunswick) Battalion had followed to " mop up ", and many prisoners were collected.[2]
The line reached included the cemetery and the quarry on
the eastern edge of the village, whence fire was opened

---

[1] German accounts record the arrival of the *I./212th Reserve Regiment*,
brought forward from Pys, about mid-day. This battalion occupied Sugar
Trench, north-east of the factory, where it suffered terribly in the afternoon
from the British fire.

[2] A few minutes after 7 P.M. a contact aeroplane dropped at divisional
headquarters a map showing Canadian flares along the eastern and northern
edges of the village.

15 Sept. on the fleeing Germans. In the 7th Brigade, which had to start from Sugar Trench, Princess Patricia's Canadian L.I., on the right, found it hard to distinguish any landmarks in the shell-shattered landscape, and met machine-gun resistance among the craters farther forward, where it had to correct its direction. Heavy loss was sustained, but the P.P.C.L.I., who took over seventy prisoners from the shelters and dug-outs along McDonnell Trench, secured the eastern portion of Fabeck Graben, joining hands with the 5th Brigade. At the junction of Zollern Graben and Fabeck Graben, however, there was a gap, some two hundred yards wide, which remained in German hands. Two P.P.C.L.I. platoons farther to the left linked up with the 42nd Battalion (Royal Highlanders of Canada), which had secured its portion of Fabeck Graben without much difficulty, and taken a score of Germans belonging to the *210th Reserve Regiment*.

At 6.30 P.M. the 4th C.M.R. (8th Brigade) had joined in the advance on the extreme left, and, although heavily punished by the German barrage, extended westward the Canadian hold on Fabeck Graben and formed a bombing block facing that flank. Here also about twenty prisoners were collected, and two machine guns were taken.[1]

By 8.15 P.M., through the smoke and gathering darkness, the 49th (Edmonton) Battalion was advancing with orders to pass through the front of the 7th Brigade and occupy a forward line within assaulting distance of Zollern Graben. This the battalion failed to accomplish, being handicapped by the difficulties of the ground and exposed to accurate machine-gun fire ; but two companies took and held the chalk pit in advance of Fabeck Graben, to which a communication trench was dug. Otherwise, the line already held was thickened, but the aforementioned gap remained. There was no further change in the forward positions of the Canadian Corps ; Germans who remained in the maze of trenches east of Courcelette cemetery and of the quarry farther north, counter-attacked several times, but were held in check.[2] The pioneers had done excellent work on forward communication trenches, although exposed to heavy shell-fire ; the

---

[1] " Res. Regt. No. 210 " states that its *II. Bn.*, reinforced by its *III. Bn.* from Zollern Graben and by ration carriers and working parties, was engaged in Fabeck Graben.

[2] *I./212th Reserve* is described as being involved in heavy fighting on the eastern edge of Courcelette in the evening before its remnants were withdrawn. Regimental history.

engineers had made good progress with tracks and strong- 15 Sept. points, the sugar factory being converted into a strong defended locality by the 5th Field Company C.E. The company also developed the water supply at the factory, where there was a well.

The General Situation : Preparations to Renew the Attack

On the Fourth Army front the results of the day fell far short of the desired achievement. It is true that the enemy had been dealt a severe blow—his 3rd Position captured on a front of 4,500 yards, High Wood and the villages of Flers, Martinpuich and Courcelette taken, heavy casualties inflicted upon him—but the XIV. and XV. Corps were still confronted by that part of the German 3rd Position which covered Morval and by the back line defending Lesboeufs and Gueudecourt. Until these three localities were occupied there could be no question of a break-through, and the check had gained for the disorganized enemy a valuable respite. On the right of the Fourth Army, the French had made no progress. At 11.30 a.m. G.H.Q. received a message that General Fayolle would assault at 3 p.m., after a heavy bombardment extending also south of the Somme. Then, at 4.45 p.m. came the news that the attack upon Frégicourt and Rancourt had failed, but would be renewed after further artillery preparation.[1]

Once the morning mist had cleared, Fourth Army headquarters received abundant situation reports from the contact aeroplanes which located with ease the red flares shown freely—perhaps too freely [2]—by the advancing infantry, and could also follow the movements of the tanks. General Rawlinson had been kept informed of the troubles of the 6th Division from 8 a.m. onwards, and also of the true state of affairs on the front of the 56th Division. Even so, the sum total of information received from all sources by the Army proved conflicting in character, and a report arriving from the XIV. Corps as late as 1.55 p.m. quoted the report of a F.O.O. that the Guards were in Lesboeufs. It was not until 3.33 p.m. that the corps was able to report

---

[1] For the operations of the French see Note at end of Chapter.
[2] Flares were sometimes lit by small groups of men in precarious or isolated forward positions which they were compelled to vacate soon afterwards.

15 Sept. the approximate situation of the Guards. At this hour, too, the third objective on the Morval—Lesboeufs front was said to be strongly held by the enemy. The occupation of Martinpuich was not definitely reported to the Army until 9.25 P.M., the hour at which a message from the Reserve Army announced the capture of Courcelette.

By 3 P.M., however, General Rawlinson realized that the initial impetus of the attack was spent, and that, owing to the heavy losses of the forward troops on the greater portion of the Army front, he would have to draw upon his reserve divisions if the effort were to be renewed upon an adequate scale.[1] This he was not disposed to do without fresh artillery preparation, and so, with Sir Douglas Haig's approval,[2] appropriate orders were issued to the corps : there would be no further advance that day, but all divisions must link up and consolidate their forward positions covered by their field artillery, of which many batteries had already moved forward.[3] The evening attack of the 6th Division (XIV. Corps) and the renewed attacks of the right and centre of the III. Corps (47th and 50th Divisions) against the third objective were allowed to proceed. Orders for the resumption of the operations next morning at 9.25 A.M. were telephoned to corps at 5.50 P.M., written instructions following at 8 P.M. The intention was still " to enable the Cavalry Corps to push through to its " objectives and complete the enemy's defeat " ; therefore all attacks were to be pushed home with the utmost energy and the enemy given no time to recover.

The XIV. Corps was to carry the third objective in front of Lesboeufs and then the village itself ; but the attack upon the remainder of the corps objectives (Morval and a line beyond) was only to be launched if Lesboeufs should be

---

[1] The majority of the infantry battalions engaged had lost 300–400 of all ranks, and officer casualties were very heavy, including many battalion commanders. In the 122nd Brigade (41st Division) units went into battle with an average strength of more than 600, and lost 50 per cent. About three officers per battalion were left.

[2] The Commander-in-Chief visited General Rawlinson in the afternoon.

[3] The Guards Division (XIV. Corps) had moved forward 10 batteries to positions on the western edge of Guillemont, behind Ginchy, and near the S.E. corner of Delville Wood. In the XV. Corps, the movement began soon after 8 A.M., batteries following each other at half-hourly intervals; by dawn of the 16th, 32 batteries were in action forward of Delville Wood. The III. Corps had some twenty batteries in action behind High Wood and north of Bazentin le Petit village and wood by daylight on the 16th. All these movements were carried out over deeply cratered ground, and called for terrific exertions, the gunners being assisted by sappers and pioneers who prepared rough tracks. The work was done under heavy and persistent shell-fire, which caused many casualties.

secured and the evening attack of the 6th Division prove 15 Sept. successful.

The XV. Corps had as objectives the Gird trenches and Gueudecourt ; when these were taken, the advance would continue, driving forward on the left, north of the Gueude-court—Eaucourt l'Abbaye road, to join up with the III. Corps.

The first task of the III. Corps was to capture the third objective along its whole front ; then to push forward its right, and, in two stages, reach Eaucourt l'Abbaye and the spur south-west of it.

Each corps could utilize those of its tanks which were still in working order, but the crews which had been in action all day were to be replaced ; night firing by the artillery would be vigorous, wire-cutting and bombardment of the German positions beginning as soon as the light permitted ; the cavalry was to be ready to move at short notice after 9 A.M.

At 9.40 P.M. G.H.Q. was informed that the French had been unable to renew their attack, but would do so on the morrow in co-operation with the Fourth Army, which was informed accordingly. The only other action of G.H.Q., apart from warning the First Army to release the 30th Division, and the Second Army the 4th Division, was to point out that the Albert—Bapaume road (inclusive to the Fourth Army) should now be the boundary between the Fourth and the Reserve Armies. Before midnight, the Fourth Army was informed direct that the French would assist with artillery fire only unless the XIV. Corps attacked Morval ; in that case, the French infantry would again attack Frégicourt and Rancourt.

Lord Cavan's orders, issued at 8.55 P.M., for the XIV. Corps concerned only the Guards Division, which was to take the third objective on its front and then Lesboeufs, forming a defensive flank towards Morval and linking up on the left with the XV. Corps. The Guards were to use the 61st Brigade (from the 20th Division in corps reserve) and the 3rd Guards Brigade, whose commander (Br.-General C. E. Corkran) reported to Major-General Feilding, at mid-night, that conditions were very unfavourable for attack : the front line was packed with men of many units, there was " nowhere to form up ", and he predicted failure.[1]

---

[1] Of the 3rd Guards Brigade, the 1/Grenadiers had been used during the 15th for carrying parties ; the 4/Grenadiers had supported the right attack, becoming involved in the fight ; and the 2/Scots Guards, had suffered in supporting the left, losing its commander and second-in-command. The

15 Sept.   The orders of the XV. Corps, issued at 8.25 P.M., required the capture of the previous day's objectives to be completed. On the right, the 14th Division would use its 43rd Brigade, from reserve, which did not complete the relief of the front line until 6 A.M. on the 16th. Major-General Lawford telephoned at 8.30 P.M. to say that he had only one battalion in the 41st Division available for attack, so Lieut.-General Horne reluctantly placed at his disposal the 64th Brigade (Br.-General H. R. Headlam) of the 21st Division.[1] At 11.20 P.M. additional objectives were given to the 41st Division, which was now to push out its left along the Gird trenches as far as their junction with Goose Alley (about a thousand yards east of Eaucourt l'Abbaye) and to the New Zealanders, who were to take Goose Alley, between the Gird trenches and Flers Support.

The III. Corps [2] ordered the 47th Division to seize the spur south-west of Eaucourt l'Abbaye, whilst the 50th Division, on its left, was to secure Prue Trench and extend north of Martinpuich. As all the London battalions were now very weak in numbers, the commander of the 142nd Brigade was promised, with corps approval, the assistance of a battalion from the 23rd Division in attacking the Cough Drop, assumed to be held by the Germans but in reality in possession of the 1/6th London.

Map 1. Sketch 37.   The right of the Reserve Army had accomplished all that the Commander-in-Chief expected in the first instance ; but, in spite of the capture of Martinpuich and Courcelette, the " combined advance northward " on this part of the front was not yet feasible owing to the situation farther east. Nevertheless, General Gough was still prepared to act vigorously on his right, with a view to a movement on Pys.[3] In the course of the day, three field artillery brigades

---

only unit of the brigade which was comparatively fresh was the Welsh Guards.

[1] These battalions received their orders at 1 A.M. on the 16th and marched at 2.10 A.M., having six miles to cover in rain and darkness, over trenches, shell-craters and other obstacles.

[2] Preliminary instructions were issued at 7 P.M., and the operation order at 11.45 P.M.

[3] During the day Pys had been bombarded by the 6″ guns of the V. Corps—north of the Ancre—with thermite shell. Raids had been carried out by the corps both in the early morning and at night.

In the II. Corps, which had carried out much counter-battery work and enfiladed with effect the area in front of the Canadians, the 11th Division lost a bombing block at the N.W. approach to the Wonder Work about 10 P.M., but recaptured it before the 49th Division took over the Wonder Work sector on the night of the 15th/16th.

had moved forward to positions immediately south-east of 15 Sept.
Pozières ;   by   the   evening,   the   Canadian   Corps   cavalry
regiment had patrolled as far as Courcelette and had set
parties to work upon a forward track in the direction of the
village.

General Gough, who called upon the Commander-in-
Chief at Beauquesne at 9 P.M., issued his operation order an
hour later : the Canadian Corps was to occupy Mouquet
Farm that night, and, on the morrow, to extend its gains
" by pushing out in all directions possible " ; the II. Corps
to " bomb forward at once and secure Constance Trench ",[1]
discharge gas cylinders into Thiepval, and, " as soon as
" possible,   make   ground   towards   Thiepval   from   the
" Wonder Work ".   The rôle of the V. Corps beyond the
Ancre would be confined to raiding activity.   At 10.45 P.M.,
however, General Gough visited Canadian Corps headquarters to define the objective of the Canadians as Zollern
Graben, and also Zollern Redoubt in the German 2nd
Position about a mile east of Thiepval.

On this day the R.F.C. flew more hours and had more
fighting than on any day since the War began.[2]   Counter-
battery operations on the Fourth Army front revealed the
location of 150 batteries, 70 of these being engaged.   There
were numerous air combats,[3] and British pilots, with reckless daring, flew very low over the trenches in order to
ascertain the progress made by the infantry and to engage
the German defenders with machine-gun fire.   German
battery positions were attacked in the same fashion.
During the morning a bombing raid was made upon the
station at Vélu (5 miles east of Bapaume), attacking
four trains, three of which appeared to be hit.   Reconnaissance of the enemy back areas disclosed no abnormal
movement except westward from Cambrai, where the
troops seen were estimated at about one division.[4]

---

[1] During the night of the 15th/16th the 11th Division began to drive
the Germans from Constance Trench, which, with Danube Trench, is shown
on Map 1 and Sketch 37 as captured on 15th September. See Chapter
XIII.

[2] " The War in the Air " Vol. II., p. 272.

[3] On the whole front of the attack the R.F.C. reported 12 hostile
machines driven down and crashed ; 7 others driven down, believed out of
control ; and 2 kite balloons destroyed.

[4] The arrival on the battle-front of parts of the *6th Bavarian* and *50th
Reserve Divisions* has been noticed in the narrative.

NOTE

THE FRENCH ON 15TH SEPTEMBER [1]

After its exertions of the previous days, the French Sixth Army required time to prepare for a fresh attack, but the obligation to co-operate with the British was paramount. The artillery of the I. Corps opened at daybreak to support the attack of the British XIV. Corps ; its infantry advanced at 3 P.M. The French left, around Combles, " où la mission était nettement défensive ", had a bombing encounter in Bois Douage. A little progress was made north of Priez Farm, but the movement on Rancourt was checked by artillery and machine-gun fire. Farther east, the V. Corps, in action for the first time, failed to secure the southern edge of St. Pierre Vaast Wood ; the VII. Corps, attacking eastward from Bouchavesnes, did no better. Near the Somme the XXXIII. Corps achieved a small " rectification " of its front.

---

[1] F.O.A. iv. (iii.), pp. 137-9, Annexe 420.

CHAPTER XIII

THE SOMME

THE BATTLE OF FLERS—COURCELETTE
15TH–22ND SEPTEMBER, 1916 (*concluded*)

16TH–22ND SEPTEMBER

(Map 1 ; Sketches A, 36, 37)

THE showers of rain which fell on the evening of the 15th September made the muddy, shell-shattered ground still more difficult to negotiate ; nevertheless, the movement of batteries, the relief of forward battalions, the conveyance of food, water and battle stores, and the work of the engineers and pioneers who were striving to improve communications to the new front, went on throughout the night. In bringing down the wounded, stretcher-bearers laboured to the point of exhaustion, despite the assistance they received from the combatant troops and from parties of prisoners.

The 16th September proved fine, although considerable 16 Sept. cloud prevailed. Part of the Cavalry Corps was kept at hand and the heavy artillery continued its bombardment of the objectives which were not yet taken ; but from now onward the operations developed into local attacks—ever costly in men and munitions and making heavy demands upon the spirit and endurance of the troops—designed to prepare the way for the resumption of the offensive on a large scale.

THE FOURTH ARMY

In the XIV. Corps on the 16th September control rested Map 1. largely in the hands of Major-General Feilding, commanding Sketch 37. the Guards Division, since the right and centre of the corps (56th and 6th Divisions) had merely to protect the right flank of the attack with artillery fire.[1] Br.-General W. E.

---

[1] The 56th Division was involved in some bombing encounters during the day. The commander of the 2/York & Lancaster (16th Brigade, 6th

16 Sept. Banbury's 61st Brigade—attached to the Guards from the 20th Division—had left Trônes Wood at midnight and the leading battalions, 7/D.C.L.I. and 7/Somerset L.I., were assembled at 5 A.M. in shell-holes about two hundred yards in front of the first objective of the 15th, held by the 2nd Guards Brigade. They suffered from heavy trench-mortar fire before zero hour, 9.25 A.M., when they went forward to approach the creeping barrage before it lifted. After a steady advance the original third objective from the right boundary of the Guards Division to a point just south of the Ginchy—Lesboeufs road, was captured without much difficulty, and a considerable number of prisoners taken.[1] The 7/K.O.Y.L.I. was brought up to safeguard the right, where Stokes mortars and Vickers guns were emplaced, and the 12/King's reinforced the left. German bombing attacks on this flank persisted until well into the afternoon. The whole brigade, only 1,200 strong at the beginning of the action, suffered severely from German shell-fire but maintained its position.

On its left the 3rd Guards Brigade (Br.-General C. E. Corkran) had started late and made little headway : the collection and reorganization of the Guards battalions had, indeed, proved so difficult a task that the attack would probably never have been delivered but for the grim determination of all ranks to push forward. It was nearly 1.30 P.M. when, without artillery support, the 1/Grenadiers and Welsh Guards made their effort in the face of accurate machine-gun fire. They persevered until they were about 250 yards from their objective, where they dug-in facing north rather than north-east—it is said that the Welsh Guards mistook Gueudecourt for Lesboeufs—their left being in Punch Trench. At night, in pouring rain, the 20th Division (Major-General W. Douglas Smith) took over the whole front of the Guards Division [2] with the 60th Brigade (Br.-General Hon. L. J. P. Butler) and 59th Brigade (Br.-General C. D. Shute). The latter had considerable difficulty in relieving the 3rd Guards Brigade, whose position was not accurately known.

Division) made proposals for an attack upon the Quadrilateral, but the corps was in favour of a fresh operation prepared by methodical bombardment.

[1] Some belonged to the *238th Reserve (52nd Reserve Division)*. The *XXVI. Reserve Corps (51st* and *52nd Reserve Divisions)* was arriving from Ypres to relieve the *185th* and the *5th Bavarian Divisions* on the Combles—Lesboeufs front. This relief was completed by 18th September.

[2] For the period 10th-17th September the Guards Division reported over 4,900 casualties.

The XV. Corps attacked all along the line at 9.25 A.M. 16 Sept. Before that hour aeroplane reconnaissance had reported no enemy in the communication trenches leading back to the Gird trenches, which, so far as could be seen from the air, did not appear to be held. During the morning several messages reached the Fourth Army that the Gird trenches and Gueudecourt had been captured, and not until late in the afternoon was it ascertained that no such success had been achieved. Communications were much hampered by the heavy German barrages, which cut telephone wires and prevented or delayed the progress of runners ; aeroplanes began to look in vain for the infantry flares, which, being wet, often failed to ignite.

On the front of the 14th Division (Major-General V. A. Couper) the creeping barrage was weak, and started too far in front of the infantry ; the bombardment by the heavy artillery seems to have been ineffective. The 6/Somerset L.I. (Br.-General P. R. Wood's 43rd Brigade), which formed the right of the attack, was exposed to fire from the Germans in Gas Alley, and could make little progress. Part of the battalion, however, occupied a half-dug trench which was presumed to be Gird Trench, and the capture of the latter was reported. West of the Ginchy—Gueudecourt road the 10/Durham L.I. of the same brigade was smitten by streams of bullets from front and right flank as soon as its advance began. Open country, which still contained some crops, and, with many folds in the ground, sloped down to Gueude-court, was ideal for machine-gun defence. The foremost survivors took cover in shell-holes, and the attempts of the 6/K.O.Y.L.I. and 6/Cornwall L.I. to reinforce the front battalions only increased the toll of casualties. An order to renew the attack at 6.55 P.M. was faithfully carried out, but had no hope of success, so that the line at night showed little advance on that of the morning.

Br.-General H. R. Headlam's 64th Brigade (21st Division), which made the 41st Division attack, had experienced considerable difficulty in getting forward in rain and darkness over the shell-shattered area round Flers. The whereabouts of the forward line was not known, and the brigade—15/Durham L.I. and 9/K.O.Y.L.I. in front, with the 10/K.O.Y.L.I. and 1/East Yorkshire in close support—eventually advanced from the south-eastern side of Flers, quite 1,300 yards behind the barrage line. Late in starting, and exposed from the outset to shrapnel and machine-gun fire, the leading battalions suffered heavily

16 Sept. before they passed through the forward positions of the 41st Division. The movement continued, however, and a few prisoners were taken from shell-holes ; but, although a few of the foremost troops approached to within a hundred yards of Gird Trench, the attack could not be pressed home. A tank (D14), coming up from Flers, overtook the K.O.Y.L.I. whilst they were still advancing and went on towards Gueudecourt, but was struck by a shell and became a total wreck.[1] The 64th Brigade rallied on Bulls Road ; owing to the destruction by shell-fire of brigade signal head-quarters in Flers, corps orders for a renewed effort in the evening arrived too late to be obeyed.

The New Zealand Division, left of the corps, had brought up the 1st N.Z. Brigade (Br.-General F. E. Johnston). After enduring heavy shell-fire and repulsing an enemy attempt to advance down the Ligny road about 9 A.M., the 1st Wellington attacked at zero hour and secured their portion of Grove Alley. In consequence of the misfortunes of the 64th Brigade, further operations were cancelled, and the New Zealand right, which rested at a point just short of the Ligny road, was made secure by the 1st Canterbury, a trench being dug back to Box and Cox.

The tank (D11) which had remained in readiness on the Ligny road all night had done great execution when the Germans attacked the New Zealanders. It also took part in the subsequent advance, covering about three hundred yards before a shell burst underneath it and destroyed the gear box.

Little was accomplished on the front of the III. Corps. In the 47th Division the 1/23rd London (Br.-General F. G. Lewis's 142nd Brigade) advanced from Crest Trench thirty minutes before zero hour, its left directed upon the Cough Drop 1,300 yards away : arrived here, the line was to pivot on its left, pressing forward to consolidate the spur behind Prue Trench, west of the Cough Drop, whilst patrols pushed into Eaucourt l'Abbaye. Beyond the Switch Line the companies were heavily shelled and machine-gunned, became scattered, and could do little more than occupy the knot of trenches called " The Starfish ". One company, however, reinforced the remnants of the 1/6th London in the Cough Drop.[2]

---

[1] See page 323, f.n. 1 and Sketch 36.

[2] " Bav. Regt. No. 18 " (the regiment was opposite the right of the 47th Division) states that a big counter-attack was planned but, as the English continued their advance, this could not be launched. The history

The 151st Brigade (Br.-General N. J. G. Cameron) of 16 Sept. the 50th Division attacked Prue Trench east of Crescent Alley, but, although small parties of the 1/5th Border Regiment and 1/9th Durham L.I. reached the objective, they were overwhelmed or driven out : not even the Starfish Line was secured.   West of Crescent Alley the 150th Brigade (Br.-General B. G. Price) set the 1/5th Durham L.I. to attack Prue Trench, but the battalion swerved too far to the left.   Attempts were made, later in the day, to bomb along Prue Trench from Martin Alley, but little ground was gained.

The 15th Division had to repel a counter-attack in the early morning, and Martinpuich and its vicinity were heavily shelled all day.[1]   To the north-west of the village posts were established nearer Twenty-Sixth Avenue, and the front up to and inclusive of the Albert—Bapaume road was taken over from the Canadians of the Reserve Army.

Although hindered in reconnaissance by low cloud, the R.F.C. did not relax its efforts, infantry, transport and even batteries being attacked by machine-gun fire, whilst bombs were dropped on troops, villages, and on Vélu aerodrome, five miles east of Bapaume.   There were many combats in the air.   Counter-battery operations resulted in 142 enemy batteries being located, and 45 engaged, yet German barrage fire continued to be heavy and embarrassing.

On this day G.H.Q. instructed the First and Second Armies to arrange the release of fresh divisions for the Somme offensive which, it was stated, would continue to be pressed.   At 10 p.m., with G.H.Q. approval, the Fourth Army issued verbal orders to the Cavalry Corps to move back three divisions.   The 1st Indian and 2nd Cavalry Divisions remained in their forward positions, south of Dernancourt and in the Bray—Dernancourt area respectively.

On the morning of the 17th Fourth Army orders were Map 1. issued for an attack next day to complete the capture of the Sketches 36, 37.

---

of the *229th Reserve* (*50th Reserve Division*, relieving *3rd Bavarian Division*) states that there was a gap at " Sachsen Weg " (Drop Alley), where the *II. Bn.* suffered severely.

[1] A number of prisoners of the *12th* and *23rd Bavarians* (*3rd Bavarian Division*) and the *229th Reserve* (*50th Reserve Division*) were taken. " Res. Regt. No. 229 " states that *I./229th Reserve* advanced about 4.30 A.M. from the Flers Line astride the Eaucourt l'Abbaye—Martinpuich road.   Troops of the *231st Reserve* (also *50th Reserve Division*) were on the right, and some of *133rd Reserve* (*24th Reserve Division*) on the left. The object was to close a gap in the line and reach Martinpuich.

2 A

17 Sept. original objectives ; but, after General Rawlinson had discussed the situation with the Commander-in-Chief, he held a conference at Army headquarters at noon. He then announced that the main operations were postponed until the 21st, partly in order to synchronise with the next attack by the French who could not be ready before that date.[1] In preparation for this next attempt, the 18th would be devoted to straightening and improving the Army line : the XIV. Corps to secure the Quadrilateral and the remainder of its original third objective ; the XV. Corps to bomb down Gas Alley, and also to establish good " jumping-" off " positions for the attack upon the Gird trenches; the III. Corps, still the defensive flank of the Army, to capture the original third objective and—if the Canadians were still advancing—to seize Martinpuich mill and the trenches north-east of it. Zero hour would be 5.50 A.M.[2]

At the conference General Rawlinson had revealed a threatened shortage of 18-pdr. ammunition, of which over 600,000 rounds had been expended since the 12th September the stock in France having been reduced by over two-thirds in the last week. The situation as regards the supply of howitzer ammunition of all calibres was satisfactory, but the Army commander said that expenditure in general must be " eased down " and devoted to the objectives of the 18th. The bombardment for the big attack would begin at 7 A.M. on the 20th September. Another matter brought up by General Rawlinson was the tendency " to use troops up too quickly ", and he warned corps commanders that he saw no prospect of further reinforcement before the 21st.[3]

Mist and cloud hindered artillery and air operations

---

[1] General Foch visited Sir Douglas Haig on the afternoon of 17th September and promised that on the next occasion Frégicourt should be attacked by a fresh division. It was arranged that the French would make a strenuous effort to get Sailly-Saillisel (1¾ miles east of Morval) when the British delivered their next attack upon Morval, Lesboeufs and Gueudecourt.

[2] In the afternoon Army operation orders were also issued for 21st September : XIV. Corps to carry Morval and Lesboeufs, and form a defensive flank extending N.E. from Bouleaux Wood ; XV. Corps to capture Gueudecourt and establish itself on the under-feature N. of the Gueudecourt—Eaucourt l'Abbaye road ; III. Corps likewise to establish itself upon the forward slopes N.E. of Martinpuich.

[3] The situation disclosed was :
XIV. Corps had relieved Guards by 20th Division, but would require Guards for next big attack.
XV. Corps had relieved 14th by 21st Division, and was about to relieve 41st by 55th Division.

on this day ; the infantry was mainly concerned in reorganizing and consolidating its positions. The 60th Brigade, in the right sector of the 20th Division south of the Ginchy—Lesboeufs road, was attacked from 1.30 P.M. onwards, the enemy frontal advance being repulsed by Lewis-gun and rifle fire, whilst his bombing parties, which made some progress on either flank, were eventually driven out by the 12/K.R.R.C. and 12/Rifle Brigade. In the evening, when heavy rain began to fall, Br.-General C. D. Shute, whose 59th Brigade had taken over a very unfavourable position from the 3rd Guards Brigade, was called upon to capture the original third objective opposite the left sector of the division. This attack started at 6.30 P.M., three weak battalions—11/Rifle Brigade, 10/Rifle Brigade and 11/K.R.R.C.—advancing with inadequate artillery support and no co-operation on their flanks ; they were checked by machine-gun fire and no ground was gained. A little later in the evening the Germans bombed forward down Gas Alley, and, for a time, the junction of the XIV. and XV. Corps was threatened. In consequence, the XIV. Corps gave up its intention of completing the capture of the original third objective on the morrow. On the front of the XV. Corps, the relief of the 14th Division by the 21st (Major-General D. G. M. Campbell) finished at 9 A.M., and in the evening the 55th Division (Major-General H. S. Jeudwine) began to take over the centre sector from the 41st Division.[1] The III. Corps, heavily shelled all day long made strenuous efforts to establish a continuous front, the weary troops digging hard.[2]

Following a wet night, rain fell nearly all day on the 18th September. It was now difficult, often impossible, for wheels to move across country ; there was not enough labour and material for work upon tracks and roads which, in places, were dissolving into deep slime. Forward

18 Sept.

III. Corps was about to relieve 15th by 23rd Division, and would have to relieve 47th by 1st Division as soon as possible.

The only remaining division in the Army was the 5th, of which one brigade had been attached to the 20th Division.

[1] The 41st Division, which came into the line again on 25th September, reported 3,798 casualties for the whole month. In the 14th Division, for the period 13th-20th September, the casualty return showed 4,098.

[2] On the 15th Division front two artillery officers of the 23rd Division reconnoitred as far as Martinpuich mill and found it deserted. Just south of the mill three abandoned 77-mm. guns were discovered. Six Germans of the *230th Reserve* (*50th Reserve Division*) were found in the battery dugouts and brought in.

18 Sept. batteries had to depend more and more upon pack transport for their supply of ammunition. As September wore to a close, the troops of all arms began to regard the mud as their chief enemy.

Upon the extreme right of the Army the 56th Division attacked at 5.50 A.M. The Queen's Westminster (169th Brigade) were checked by machine-gun fire in their attempt to carry the sunken Combles road, running south-eastward to the Loop, and the German trench beyond it ; the London Rifle Brigade, on their right, made some progress by bombing. The 167th Brigade, was to secure the south-eastern face of Bouleaux Wood as far as the first objective of the 15th September, by attacking with its left on Middle Copse ; but, as the troops[1] could not reach their assembly positions owing to the mud and the water-logged shell-holes they had to negotiate, the assault was never delivered.

The attack of the 6th Division on the Quadrilateral and Straight Trench resulted in a complete success, and the establishment, as ordered, of a new line 500 yards beyond, overlooking the valley in front of Morval. After the Quadrilateral had been shelled with gratifying accuracy,[2] the 1/K.S.L.I. (Br.-General W. L. Osborn's 16th Brigade) advanced north-eastward from the Ginchy—Combles road at 5.50 A.M. with its left on the railway track, and, keeping close behind the barrage, swept into the Quadrilateral. There was a short, sharp fight in which the 14/Durham L.I. (Br.-General R. J. Bridgford's 18th Brigade) bore a part, coming in on the left and then proceeding to clear the dug-outs in the sunken road beyond. Meanwhile, the 2/York & Lancaster (16th Brigade), closely supported by effective Stokes mortar fire, had bombed in from the south-east, and then assisted to carry forward the right, the battalion linking up with the 56th Division at Middle Copse and even pushing a patrol down the slope as far as the north-east corner of Bouleaux Wood. Straight Trench at first defied a frontal attack by the 1/West Yorkshire (18th Brigade), but the bombers of the battalion fought their way down from the north to meet those of the 14/Durham L.I., whilst a detachment passed over the trench near the left boundary of the division and took the Germans in rear. The action yielded about 140 unwounded prisoners[3] and seven machine

---

[1] London Scottish and 1/4th London attached from the 168th Brigade.

[2] The 18th Brigade had dug a special trench, well forward, from which a F.O.O. could watch the fall of the shell.

[3] Mostly *21st Bavarians* (*5th Bavarian Division*) now due for relief. The regimental history records " wild and determined hand to hand

guns, German dead and wounded lying thick in the captured 18 Sept. positions.

The right of the 20th Division sent forward a fighting patrol, which inflicted further loss and brought in twenty prisoners and a machine gun. During the day the enemy appeared to be concentrating on the higher ground near Morval, but he was dispersed by artillery fire.[1]

In the XV. Corps, where the 55th Division had completed the relief of the 41st by 3.30 A.M., fighting was confined to the left flank, bombers of the 1st Otago (1st N.Z. Brigade) forcing the Germans back up Flers Support almost to its junction with Goose Alley.

At the general zero hour the 47th Division (right of the III. Corps) set parties of the 140th Brigade (Br.-General Viscount Hampden) to bomb up Flers Trench and Drop Alley towards the junction of these two trenches, and considerable ground was gained. Meanwhile detachments of the 1/23rd and 1/24th London (142nd Brigade) attacked the Starfish Line, but in the face of machine-gun fire could do little more than reinforce that portion of the trench already held. Later in the day German bombers drove the Londoners eastward towards the Starfish, but were driven back in their turn at night.

Next on the left, the 50th Division found it impossible to assault until the afternoon, owing to the bad state of the ground and an effective German bombardment. About 4.30 P.M. the 150th Brigade (1/5th Durham L.I. assisted by bombers of the 1/4th and 1/5th Green Howards) bombed eastward along the Starfish Line and Prue Trench, and almost reached Crescent Alley. On the other hand the 1/8th Durham L.I. (151st Brigade) failed in its attempt to bomb up this trench from the south. The 15th Division, also heavily shelled, consolidated its forward posts, denying Martinpuich mill to the enemy.

In the XIV. Corps the 5th Division (Major-General R. B. Stephens) began the relief of the 6th Division [2] before darkness fell, and, under cover of night, the 20th Division

---

" fighting ", the *III./Bn.* losing 175 in killed alone. Justifiable pride is displayed in the stubborn defence of the Quadrilateral, which, it is explained, was not a " *Feste* ".

[1] Three tanks were to be ready at zero hour at the head of the shallow valley west of Leuze Wood : they were not required. At 1.50 P.M. a squadron (Hants. Carabiniers) from the Cavalry Corps reached 16th Brigade headquarters near Wedge Wood, only to be sent back again.

[2] The casualties of the 6th Division, up to 15th September, were reported to be 3,463.

18 Sept. started a trench from the captured portion of the third objective north-westward to the right of the XV. Corps. The 47th and 50th Divisions (III. Corps) began a trench to link up the Starfish with the Bow, and the 23rd Division (Major-General J. M. Babington) completed the relief of the 15th, on the left wing of the Army.[1]

General Rawlinson had been informed by G.H.Q. in the afternoon of the 18th that four fresh divisions would be available as soon as they could be relieved by battle-worn Fourth Army formations ; but that, if all went well on the 21st, the 4th and 30th Divisions could, in any case, be used " to exploit the success ".

19-20 Sept. At a conference held at noon on the 19th September, a very wet day, General Rawlinson, who had seen General Fayolle, explained to his corps commanders that the French Sixth Army could not be ready to attack on the 21st owing to the bad weather : a definite postponement of 24 hours— to be lengthened, if necessary, to 48 hours—had therefore been agreed upon. The delay was not altogether a disadvantage, for the conveyance of ammunition and battle stores through the mud was proving a tiring and tedious business, whilst the XIV. Corps still required time to bring its artillery into advanced positions. Corps commanders were warned that, in the meantime, they must continue to husband ammunition. In the afternoon a postponement of 24 hours was formally announced by the Army.

A further postponement of 24 hours—bringing the date of the offensive to the 23rd—was made at 1 P.M. on the 20th September, a day of rainstorms and no sun. On the same afternoon Sir Douglas Haig visited the Fourth Army commander, whose plans met with his general approval ; but the Commander-in-Chief had decided that the Reserve Army must be prepared to secure Thiepval and the Thiepval ridge at an early date. He therefore required General Rawlinson to hand over as many tanks as he could spare to General Gough, who would be attacking on the 23rd if the weather permitted. The two cavalry divisions were to remain in their advanced positions for the next offensive, but if not then required they would rejoin the Cavalry Corps, which was to be kept in being to train in the area west of St. Pol.

---

[1] The casualties of the 15th Division were returned in monthly totals. For August—September, the division having been in the line for six weeks without relief during this period, the figures are 6,732.

At 4 P.M. on the 21st September, General Foch called 21 Sept.
on the British Commander-in-Chief, and explained that,
as so much ammunition had been expended by the French
Sixth Army in repelling counter-attacks on the previous
day,[1] time was required for replenishment. It was therefore agreed that General Fayolle and General Rawlinson
should attack together on the 25th September, zero hour
to be " not before noon " in order to give the French good
observation for the first stage of the preparatory bombardment.

From the 19th until the 22nd September the Fourth 19-22
Army was engaged in local encounters, mostly carried on Sept.
in deep mud and waterlogged trenches and shell-holes ;
but the III. Corps eventually secured without fighting the Map 1.
remainder of its original objectives. Hostile artillery fire Sketch
was still violent, and, as a result of German reinforcement 37.
in the air, enemy observation balloons appeared in considerable numbers.

On the right of the XIV. Corps the 56th Division dug
assembly trenches north-east of Middle Copse, and sapped
forward south of the copse towards Bouleaux Wood, which
the Germans still held.[2] By the morning of the 21st the
Guards had relieved the 20th Division ;[3] and at night the
6th Division took over the captured portion of the third
objective from the 1st Guards Brigade, thus converting the
corps front into four divisional sectors.[4] The Guards took
over ground from the XV. Corps, including Gas Alley.
Bombing attacks down this trench towards the Gird trenches
by the 1/Lincolnshire (62nd Brigade, 21st Division) on the
20th, and by the 4/Grenadiers (3rd Guards Brigade) on the
22nd, made a little progress.

The junction of the XV. and III. Corps at the Flers
Line was the scene of some fierce fighting. At dusk on the
19th September the 2nd Auckland (2nd New Zealand
Brigade) bombed up Flers Support towards its junction
with Goose Alley on the crest of the ridge, whilst the
1/15th London (140th Brigade) advanced up Drop Alley to
get into Flers Trench. The New Zealanders made good

---

[1] See Note at end of Chapter.
[2] Prisoners of the *II./235th Reserve* and *I./236th Reserve* (both *51st Reserve Division*) were secured on the divisional front.
[3] The 20th Division, which had entered the battle very weak in numbers, lost 1,291 officers and other ranks, 10th-23rd September.
[4] Each covered by 5 brigades of field artillery, except that on the right (the Combles flank), to which 3 were allotted. The forward batteries were deployed on the low ground in the Wedge Wood vicinity.

19-22 Sept. progress, but the tired Londoners were driven back to the Cough Drop. Early on the morning of the 20th, the 1st Division (Major-General E. P. Strickland) relieved the 47th,[1] and the 1/Black Watch (Br.-General A. J. Reddie's 1st Brigade) co-operated with another New Zealand attack at 8.30 P.M. There was no bombardment, and the Germans, taken by surprise, were driven back by the 2nd Canterbury to a point beyond Goose Alley, a company of the Highlanders advancing up Drop Alley to join hands. A German counter-attack,[2] made partly over the open, threatened to cut off the foremost New Zealanders, but a fresh effort of the 2nd Canterbury drove the enemy back after a struggle. Drop Alley, as far as its junction with Flers Trench, was then occupied by the Black Watch.

The 23rd Division (Major-General J. M. Babington), which began to relieve the 15th in the left sector of the III. Corps on the night of the 18th September, took over, also, from the 150th Brigade (50th Division), Starfish and Prue trenches west of Crescent Alley. Twenty-four hours later the 69th Brigade (Br.-General T. S. Lambert) was heavily attacked from the alley, but, although driven back, soon regained what it had lost. The 21st September was dull, but no rain fell, and at night patrols of the 1st, 50th and 23rd Divisions discovered that the enemy had abandoned Starfish and Prue trenches, which were gradually occupied. The consolidation of these positions began on the 22nd, which proved to be a fine autumn day. Further reconnaissance on the front of the III. Corps failed to locate any Germans south-west of Eaucourt l'Abbaye, whilst the 23rd Division reported that Twenty-Sixth Avenue (a communication trench running back from Courcelette to the Le Sars defences) appeared to be empty.

THE RESERVE ARMY

16 Sept. On the 16th September and succeeding days General Gough, with the big operation against Thiepval in mind, continued his efforts to make progress on the high ground east of the village. More would have been attempted **May 1.** if the weather had not been so unfavourable, and the **Sketch** **37.** Fourth Army offensive in consequence postponed; but the

---

[1] Casualties reported by the 47th Division 10th-22nd September amounted to 4,554 all ranks.
[2] The *13th Bavarians* (*6th Bavarian Division*) were the opponents of the New Zealanders.

Canadian and the II. Corps continued to press the enemy, 16-19
the former meeting with particularly fierce opposition. Sept.

Before daylight on the 16th the 1st C.M.R. (Br.-
General J. H. Elmsley's 8th Brigade) had established
a line of posts from the left boundary of the Canadian
Corps up the Courcelette track as far as Mouquet
Farm. The attempt of the 3rd Canadian Division (Major-
General L. J. Lipsett) to secure Zollern Graben and
Zollern Redoubt began at 5 P.M., when the Royal Canadian
Regiment and 32nd Battalion (Br.-General A. C. MacDonnell's 7th Brigade) attacked northward from Fabeck
Graben. Unfortunately the destructive bombardment
had fallen beyond the objective, and the two battalions
were checked by machine-gun fire, so that the 9th
Brigade (Br.-General F. W. Hill), which had been hurried
forward with orders to form up between Fabeck Graben
and Zollern Graben and attack Zollern Redoubt from
the east at 6.30 P.M., had to be held back. The German
bombardment was very heavy, and darkness fell before
the troops could be reorganized and preparations made for
a fresh assault. During the night Br.-General Hill's brigade, which had already suffered considerable loss, relieved
the 7th Brigade.

Meanwhile the 49th (Edmonton) Battalion and the
P.P.C.L.I. of the 7th Brigade had bombed inwards and
closed the gap in Fabeck Graben, taking over sixty
prisoners.[1] At 7.30 P.M. the 2/C.M.R., had bombed some
of the dug-outs at Mouquet Farm.

On the 17th September at 5 P.M. Br.-General
A. H. MacDonnell's 5th Brigade (2nd Canadian Division,
Major-General R. E. W. Turner), advanced to clear the
Germans from the maze of trenches immediately east of
Courcelette, but the enemy was very strong, and, after a
fierce bombing struggle, remained in possession : indeed, at
one period during the night, the situation here seemed
critical. By the morning of the 18th the 1st Canadian
Division (Major-General A. W. Currie) had taken over the
sector, and the policy of pushing out posts well to
the north was continued. On the night of the 19th,
however, a German counter-attack upon the 4th Battalion forced an entry at the north-eastern corner of

[1] Pte. J. C. Kerr, 49th Battalion, although wounded, ran along the top
of the trench and opened fire with his rifle at point-blank range upon the
Germans below him, killing several. For this bold action, which brought
a speedy end to the enemy resistance, he was awarded the V.C.

20-22
Sept.
Courcelette, and the situation was only restored after a two hours' struggle. At 4 A.M. on the 20th the same battalion, by Lewis-gun, rifle and bomb, repulsed a further onslaught. An hour later the 3rd Canadian Division made another attack on Zollern Graben, the 58th Battalion (9th Brigade) starting to bomb westward, whilst a company of the 43rd (Cameron Highlanders of Canada) captured a considerable length of trench by a surprise frontal attack from the south. A stern struggle persisted throughout the morning, both in trenches and shell-holes, until the enemy, aided by a smoke screen and a plentiful use of rifle grenades, recaptured at the fifth attempt practically all he had lost.[1]

After darkness had fallen upon the 22nd September the 1st Canadian Division found little difficulty in occupying some of the trenches on the eastern side of Courcelette. West of the village the main Canadian front then ran along Fabeck Graben and the Mouquet Farm track ; but a line of strong forward posts was held in front of Fabeck Graben and a footing had been retained in Zollern Graben immediately west of the junction of the two trenches.

16-22
Sept.
The right of the II. Corps (11th Division, Lieut.-General Sir C. L. Woollcombe) made progress between Mouquet Farm and the Leipzig salient, south-west of Thiepval. Before dawn of the 16th bombers of the 6/Lincolnshire (Br.-General J. F. Erskine's 33rd Brigade) had gained a footing in Constance Trench, south-west of Mouquet Farm, and that same night secured the whole of it up to the Thiepval—Pozières road, whilst the 6/Border Regiment occupied the western half of Danube Trench. Little opposition was encountered, although German shell-fire subsequently grew heavy. German attempts to recover Constance Trench were foiled by the 9/Sherwood Foresters. The boundary between the II. and Canadian Corps was thrice adjusted, leaving the right of the 11th Division east of Mouquet Farm, which was still in German possession.[2]

The 49th Division, holding the left sector of the II. Corps which extended as far as the Ancre, carried out several raids with varying success. Some progress was made towards Thiepval up the old German front line by the

---

[1] The Canadians were engaged with part of the fresh *26th Regiment* (*7th Division*), which had taken over the line here.

[2] The history of the *165th Regiment* (*7th Division*) states that, after relieving the *213th Reserve* (*89th Reserve Brigade*) on the night of 20th/21st September it had one company in the farm.

1/7th Duke of Wellington's, of Br.-General C. G. Lewes's 147th Brigade.[1]

North of the Ancre the V. Corps persevered with infantry raids, while its artillery cut the German wire and continued counter-battery work. By the morning of the 20th the 39th Division had taken over the whole corps front from the Ancre to Hébuterne, thus releasing the 2nd Division.

The primary object of a visit paid by the Commander-in-Chief to Reserve Army headquarters on the 20th was to review the plans for the capture of Thiepval and the Thiepval ridge : but, when these had been secured, he considered that an attack eastward, north of the Ancre, would be feasible, and he told General Gough to begin the necessary preparations. Next day the date of the Thiepval attack—a much bigger operation than any yet undertaken by the Reserve Army—was fixed for the 26th September.

RESULTS OF THE BATTLE : THE TANK IN ACTION

By the afternoon of the 15th September there remained little hope that the great autumn offensive would attain its ultimate objectives. The failure to secure the Quadrilateral, clear the enemy from the approaches to Ginchy, and occupy the northern end of High Wood before the main attack was launched exerted, perhaps, a deciding influence upon the fortunes of the day ; but at many other points the infantry suffered heavy casualties and lost cohesion and impetus during the early stages of the assault. The Germans fought bravely and well, machine gunners and bombing detachments proving the backbone of the infantry defence.[2] Some surrenders, it is true, were induced by the great havoc wrought by the British bombardment, and local panics were caused by individual tanks ; but there was no sign of widespread demoralization. In spite of the assiduous counter-battery work of the British, hostile artillery barrages came down with great effect soon after the first shock of the assault, hampering the forward flow of reserves,

[1] Prisoners of the *209th Reserve Regiment* (*89th Reserve Brigade*) were taken near the old German front line on 17th September ; and on the 20th and 22nd men of the *III./93rd Regiment* (*8th Division*) surrendered near Mouquet Farm.

[2] Some machine-gun crews lay " doggo " in shell-holes, allowing the first waves of the assault to pass on and often eluding the " moppers-up " who followed ; later, short-range fire was opened upon support battalions which were moving forward under the impression that the ground in front of them had been cleared.

interfering with communications so as to make control of
the battle difficult in the extreme, and hindering the consolidation of the captured trenches.[1]   It was under these
conditions, so often experienced by the British, that vain
efforts were made to renew the pressure along the main
front of attack after the advance had fallen far behind the
time-table.

Of the 36 tanks which reached their points of departure
along the fronts of the Fourth and Reserve Armies before
zero hour on the 15th, less than a dozen played a part in
the capture of strongpoints and trenches, although in
certain localities the moral effect of the new engine of
warfare was considerable.[2]   It is not surprising that the
two solitary machines which, unsupported, eventually
reached the forward slopes in front of Gueudecourt should
have met disaster at the hands of the German gunners.

Unfortunately the Fourth Army plan of attack, in
principle methodical as usual, actually " gambled " to a
considerable extent upon the success of the tanks.   For
instance, three were to reach the unsubdued Quadrilateral
before the infantry, and four were to quell the resistance in
High Wood, but at both these points the task proved too
much for the machines.   In the first case, failure is to be
attributed mainly to mechanical breakdown, and, in a
smaller degree, to the fact that the crew of the one tank
which came into action lacked experience and training ; in
the second, the decision of the corps to send the tanks into
the wood was a tactical blunder which the local infantry
and tank commanders tried in vain to avert.   Furthermore,
in the advance to the third objective tanks were substituted
for the familiar creeping barrage, a rôle which they were
unable to fulfil effectively owing to the fact that so few
then remained in action.

It is no matter for surprise that the tanks which went
into action on the 15th September should have proved
unequal to their heavy responsibilities.   The co-ordinated
action of artillery, tanks and infantry had received too little
study.   Tank tactics were something altogether new to

Map 1.
Sketch
37.

---

[1] The German artillery concentrated chiefly upon the opposing infantry
and forward areas.   Except when brought up to forward positions, British
batteries suffered comparatively little from enemy fire during the Battles
of the Somme 1916.

[2] The examination of prisoners and captured documents showed that
the surprise was complete.   In one case some Germans thought that the
smoke from a tank's exhaust was a discharge of gas and strove to adjust
their gas masks as they ran away.

corps, divisional and brigade commanders—secrecy was very much a two-edged weapon—and the decision to use the machines in small " packets " along the whole front of the main attack unfortunately prevented the tank company commanders from exercising any tactical control over their units. It has already been noticed that the tank commanders and crews were hastily trained and generally inexperienced ; many individuals could not distinguish between a British and a German barrage. As for the machines themselves, they had not been constructed to negotiate such heavily cratered ground as the Somme battlefield. Some of them had run so many miles in the course of trial and demonstration that they were nearly worn out before going into battle ; and there was a general lack of spare parts, tools and workshop facilities. Supply officers were slow to realize that the large requisitions made by the tank companies for petrol and oils were really needed, and, as the tanks had no transport for the purpose, forward dumps of these essentials had, as a rule, to be formed by infantry parties, sometimes supplied with considerable reluctance.

If the afternoon of the 15th September had seen British and Indian cavalry crossing the Péronne road between Rocquigny and Bapaume, the wisdom of employing tanks on this day could hardly have been questioned. The course of events, however, appeared to show that those— and they are a very distinguished company—who had protested against what they termed the premature disclosure of the new weapon had cause for their apprehension. They felt that the real mission of the tanks was to recapture, perhaps with decisive effect, the priceless element of surprise, and that this could only be done by waiting until sufficient numbers were available for a specially mounted attack upon a broad front over favourable ground. Had not this opportunity been frittered away ?

On the other hand, it may be said that in perfecting and exploiting a new weapon it is wise to proceed by a process of trial and error both on the testing ground and in the field : one can rarely expect to arrive at sound tactical methods by theory alone. An officer who subsequently commanded tanks in action under very different circumstances stated that the Battle of Flers—Courcelette was " a " very valuable try-out ". He regarded as too appalling to contemplate the prospect of attacking with 300 or 400 Mark I. tanks absolutely untested in battle. It is not

denied that from the performance of the Mark I. tank on
the Somme certain lessons in construction and design were
learnt,[1] although, to some extent, continued experiment
behind the line might have served the same purpose.
There remains the question of secrecy and surprise. If,
instead of employing a limited number of tanks in the
autumn of 1916, several hundreds of them had arrived in
France to train with infantry during the winter the secret
could hardly have been kept until the spring. To what
extent the nature and capabilities of the tank would have
become known to the enemy in the meantime, and what
anti-tank measures he would have taken, it is, of course,
impossible to say.

The very limited success achieved by the tanks on their
first appearance,[2] and for over a year afterwards, may have
misled the German High Command as to their potentialities.
In any case, the enemy was so slow to adopt counter-
measures that, at Cambrai in November 1917, the successful
surprise attack employing 362 tanks of improved design
encountered no opposition in the form of special anti-tank
defences,[3] whilst in March 1918 the progress of the German
offensive owed nothing to tank assistance. Official German
investigation has reached the conclusion that the Army did
not realize at first the importance of tanks, and that
industry subsequently failed to overcome the very real
difficulties in the way of their speedy production.[4] Thus,
if the employment of the tanks on the Somme in September
1916 is to be regarded as a parallel case to that of the

---

[1] One result was that Sir William Tritton began work upon the design
for a faster, lighter tank : " the Whippet ".

[2] " The cross-country armoured motor vehicle or ' tank ' appeared
" unexpectedly on the Somme. . . . At its first appearance it might
" have achieved important success. However the German troops soon
" learnt to know its vulnerable parts and attack it accordingly. The low
" speed, small numbers, and large target surface of the tank of this period
" made it a comparatively easy prey for the artillery who, after a very
" short time, detailed special guns to engage it." G.O.A. xi., p. 133.

[3] It is now affirmed that the *54th Division*, which held part of the front
attacked, had been specially trained to deal with tanks. See " Wissen
" und Wehr," May, 1937.

[4] " It may well be said that the importance of tanks was not at first
" estimated by our Army commands as highly as was found necessary by
" later experience. When the construction of tanks was begun the work
" was not organized efficiently enough, or pressed on fast enough for the
" tanks to have been ready in large numbers in 1918. Our industries were
" capable of producing them. On the other hand, the great difficulties
" with regard to the provision of material and labour must not be under-
" estimated ". " Die Ursachen des Deutschen Zusammenbruchs im Jahre
" 1918 " (Proceedings of the German Official Investigation of the Causes
of Collapse in 1918), Vol. III., p. 86.

premature use of gas by the Germans at Ypres in 1915,[1] the British, at any rate, escaped the penalty which the Germans eventually paid.[2]

The small number of tanks fit for action after the first day of the battle, and the fact that the infantry was still committed to the trench-to-trench assault with artillery protection following the usual artillery preparation, offered little encouragement for the development of tank tactics.[3]

At the beginning of October detailed reports on the performance of the machines were received by G.H.Q. from the corps and Armies as well as from the Heavy Section, Machine Gun Corps.[4]   General Rawlinson considered that the tank was not at present sufficiently reliable to justify any departure from " normal tactical methods " in order to make use of it : in dealing with strongpoints and villages when the infantry was held up it had an undoubted value : it required greater engine-power so as to attain a greater speed, stronger armour to resist field-gun projectiles, and a smaller handier weapon in place of the 6-pdr. gun : the personnel needed more technical and tactical training : a bigger establishment of tank workshops and artificers was absolutely necessary.   General Gough, whose Army had used very few tanks, was of opinion that they would prove of great assistance in trench warfare if their mechanical weaknesses could be overcome.

On the 5th October a memorandum appeared over the signature of the Chief of the General Staff announcing that " in the present stage of their development " tanks were to be regarded as entirely accessory to the ordinary method of attack, and their employment must not interfere with the combined action of infantry and artillery, either by depriving the former of their protective barrage or by bringing down prematurely an enemy barrage.   In the attack the ideal to aim at was the arrival of the tanks on the enemy trenches just — say 50 yards — ahead of the infantry.

---

[1] See " 1915 " Vol. II., p. vi.

[2] See " Gas : The Story of the Special Brigade R.E." by Major-General C. H. Foulkes, for the full story of British progress and achievement in chemical warfare 1915–18.

[3] On 17th September Sir Douglas Haig received Colonel Swinton and told him that, although the tanks had not achieved all that had been hoped for, they had saved many lives and fully justified themselves.   He wanted as many as possible, and at the same time suggested improved armour and a heavier machine.   Two days later, Major-General R. H. K. Butler, Deputy C.G.S., was sent home to attend a conference at the War Office, and convey the Commander-in-Chief's request for 1,000 tanks.

[4] The views of battalions, brigades and divisions naturally varied according to their experiences of the tank in action.

Careful arrangements for bringing the tanks up to their starting points and the most thorough reconnaissance of the area of operations were essential.

Thus, in the concluding stages of the Somme offensive the tank could never do more than act, on occasion, as a " valuable accessory " to the accepted methods of attack ; and during the great part of 1917 it had no better chance to prove its value. When, in the Battle of Cambrai, the action of artillery, infantry and tanks was properly co-ordinated, the tactics employed derived in considerable measure from the theory put forward in the Swinton memorandum dated February 1916.[1] At Cambrai, how-ever, surprise was secured by what is now called the " predicted fire " of a mass of artillery concentrated in secret : the preliminary work of the 3rd Field Survey Battalion R.E. enabled the guns to open suddenly upon the enemy batteries, and to put down a protective barrage well ahead of the tanks, without advertising their intention by previous registration. As regards the actual co-operation of infantry and tanks in the attack, modern doctrine differs little in its essentials from the practice of September 1916. To-day, however, the infantry, with an armament adapted for the purpose, has the additional responsibility of dealing with the hostile anti-tank weapons.[2]

NOTE

THE FRENCH OPERATIONS, 16TH-22ND SEPTEMBER [3]

At 10 P.M. on the 15th September General Fayolle called upon the Sixth Army to resume its operations next day " avec la plus " grande activité " ; but this general order was not " à proprement " parler un ordre d'attaque ". It was imperative to relieve the troops in the line, so whilst the counter-battery artillery of the I., V. and VII. Corps was active on the 16th, the infantry merely remained in readiness to advance should the British attack compel an extensive German withdrawal. This day and the following days were devoted to reliefs—the V. Corps extended its right and the VI. relieved the remainder of the VII. Corps front—and to the preparation for the combined French and British attack fixed for the 21st, but eventually postponed until the 25th September. On the evening of the 18th, however, two surprise attacks of the I. Corps

---

[1] Appendix 18.
[2] See F.S.R. II. (1935), Section 60 (6) ii.
[3] F.O.A. iv. (iii.), pp. 139-150.

gained a little ground south and south-east of Combles.[1] In spite of the bad weather, the German artillery was very active, and counter-attacks were repulsed east of Cléry on the night of the 19th/20th September. Next morning the Germans counter-attacked unsuccessfully between Priez Farm and Rancourt, and made a desperate attempt to retake Bouchavesnes ; they got into the village and were only driven out again after desperate fighting. South of Bouchavesnes the VI. Corps also repulsed a counter-attack.

The Tenth Army, south of the Somme, attacked on the 15th and again on the 17th September, when Berny, Deniécourt and Vermandovillers[2] were captured in spite of desperate resistance and frequent counter-attacks. Having no reserves in hand, General Micheler could not follow up his success.

Map 1.
Sketch A.

---

[1] An officer of the 1/16th London, the nearest British battalion, observes : " These operations were carried out just like a set-piece practice, " by successive advances : very pleasant to see ".

[2] On the Santerre plateau.   Berny is a mile south of Belloy (see Sketch A) and Vermandovillers 3 miles S.W. of Berny, with Deniécourt in between.

CHAPTER XIV

THE BATTLE OF MORVAL

25TH–28TH SEPTEMBER 1916

(Map 2 ; Sketches A, 38)

PREPARATION

Map 2. THE final objectives of the Fourth Army's renewed offensive,
Sketch in co-operation with the French on its right, were those
38. which had not been secured during the Battle of Flers—
Courcelette ; that is, on the main front of attack, the
villages of Morval and Lesboeufs for the XIV. Corps, and
Gueudecourt for the XV. Corps.   This involved an advance
of from 1,200–1,500 yards which was to be accomplished
methodically in three principal stages : the first, to the
third objective of the 15th September and the Gird trenches
south of Gueudecourt ; the second, to the sunken Combles
—Gueudecourt road west of Morval and Lesboeufs, with the
line prolonged over the spur south-east of Gueudecourt and
through the centre of that village ; and the last, to the far
side of Morval, Lesboeufs and Gueudecourt.   The advances
from the first and second objectives were to begin respectively
one and two hours after the initial assault ; as, to suit
the French, zero hour had been fixed for 12.35 P.M.,[1] the
infantry was expected to arrive on the final objectives
before 3 P.M.

The XIV. Corps now had four divisions in line, Lord
Cavan being of opinion that a narrower frontage would give
each division greater penetrative power by facilitating the
forward flow of supports and reserves.   The advance of the

---

[1] The French were never in favour of the dawn attack.   They preferred
to assault later in the day, taking advantage of the good morning light to
direct the final stage of the destructive bombardment.

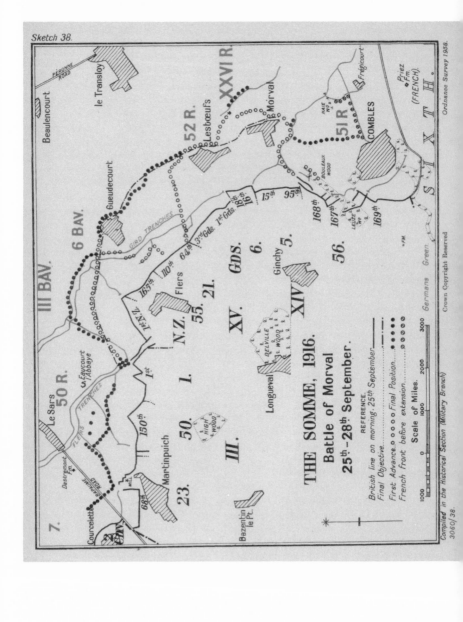

Sketch 38.

THE SOMME, 1916.
Battle of Morval
25th-28th September.

REFERENCE.
British line on morning 25th September _____
Final Objective _____
First Advance ○○○○○ Final Position ●●●●●
French Front before extension ○○○○○

Scale of Miles.
1000   0   1000   2000   3000

Compiled in the Historical Section (Military Branch)   Ordnance Survey 1938.   Crown Copyright Reserved

3060/38.

right brigade of the 5th Division (Major-General R. B. Sept. Stephens) from the second objective to capture the southern and more extensive portion of Morval was to be made, under the usual creeping barrage, in four bounds with halts of 30 minutes in between. The 6th Division (Major-General C. Ross) was actually in possession of some 700 yards of the old third objective, and, as the Germans on its flanks were too close to permit of artillery bombardment, the division was to supply that deficiency with concentrated machine-gun and Stokes-mortar fire, beginning at zero hour.

To safeguard the right flank of the Army, the 56th Division (Major-General C. P. A. Hull) was ordered to secure fire positions near the northern corner of Bouleaux Wood in order to command the valley north-east of Combles. Special artillery, Stokes-mortar and machine-gun barrages were to be maintained upon the wood, which was to have been " neutralized " by a smoke barrage if the wind had proved favourable. The 56th Division was also to keep under fire the northern and north-eastern exits of Combles. Major-General Hull was empowered to arrange direct with the commander of the French 2nd Division, on his right, for a combined effort to capture the village. This operation, in which two tanks supported by infantry were to advance down the road from Bouleaux Wood whilst the French attacked from the south, was fixed for the 26th September should the continued resistance of the enemy make it necessary.

The rôle of the few tanks available [1] had been carefully discussed at the conference on the 19th September.[2] General Rawlinson had pointed out the difficulty of con-cealing the machines in advanced positions from dawn to zero hour, and decided that they must be kept hidden in reserve ready to move up for the attack upon the villages—the final objectives—if tank assistance should then be required. On the 20th Sir Douglas Haig expressed his dis-approval of the use of tanks at Gueudecourt where the approaches were over very open ground easily swept by German artillery fire.

---

[1] On 24th September Lieut.-Colonel Elles, R.E., was appointed to com-mand the Heavy Section Machine Gun Corps in France. He was respon-sible for the advanced training and tactical employment of the tanks under G.H.Q. Tank H.Q. in England undertook the preliminary training of new tank units and was responsible for the supply and maintenance of the tank forces in the field. Colonel Elles, who had been a G.S.O. 2 (Operations) at G.H.Q., took over his new duties before the end of September.

[2] See page 358.

Two brigades of the 1st Indian Cavalry Division (Major-General H. P. Leader) were to assemble at Mametz, the whole division to be in readiness to advance as soon as Lesboeufs and Gueudecourt had been captured : [1] the squadrons were then to move by a route east of Flers and Gueudecourt on Thilloy and Ligny Thilloy, supported by the III. Corps. The employment of the cavalry in any force was not considered practicable unless it could pass the Lesboeufs—Gueudecourt line by 6.30 P.M.,[2] which would be about $1\frac{1}{2}$ hours before dark ; but small detachments for reconnaissance and the destruction of batteries might be pushed forward as long as the light lasted. On the morning of the 24th, when General Rawlinson visited his corps commanders, he told them that if all went well and there was opportunity for cavalry action the XV. Corps must push forward along the Gird trenches whilst the III. Corps captured Eaucourt l'Abbaye.

Although the weather had changed for the better, bad visibility hampered the artillery preparation. The 23rd September was fine but not very clear. The preliminary bombardment opened at 7 A.M. next morning in a heavy autumn mist which curtailed counter-battery work, and a haze persisted throughout the day. Bombs were dropped by the R.F.C. on Le Sars, Warlencourt, Thilloy, Sailly and several battery positions ; and a vigorous air offensive was maintained against the railways in the Lille—Douai area for the purpose of hampering the despatch of hostile reinforcements to the Somme front from the north.[3]

At 5.50 A.M. on the 24th, the 56th Division made an effort to bomb down Combles Trench in order to join hands with the French 73rd Regiment attacking from the south-east ; but, although the 1/9th London (169th Brigade) made some progress, the Germans were speedily reinforced and regained all that they had lost. A German attack made in the mist at 6 A.M. on the 6th Division was repulsed principally by the rifle and Lewis-gun fire of the 1/Buffs (16th Brigade). At 8 A.M. an attack, also in thick mist, by the 12/Durham L.I. (68th Brigade, 23rd Division, the left of the III. Corps) against Twenty-Sixth Avenue east of the

Marginal notes: Sketch A.　23-24 Sept.　Map 2. Sketch 38.

---

[1] The XIV. and XV. Corps each had a squadron allotted to it for immediate action should the opportunity arise.

[2] The distance from Mametz to the Lesboeufs—Gueudecourt line was $6\frac{1}{2}$ miles as the crow flies.

[3] See " The War in the Air " Vol. II., pp. 328-9 for an account of the particularly successful raid carried out by the I. Brigade R.F.C. on 25th September.

Bapaume road, was repulsed by machine-gun fire ; on the other flank of the III. Corps the 1/Black Watch (1st Brigade, 1st Division) started at 8.30 P.M. to bomb up the Flers trenches, but made no progress.

Apart from these encounters, no infantry fighting took place during the two days which preceded the attack, but German shell-fire on such localities as the Quadrilateral, Ginchy and Flers grew very heavy at times.   The repeated postponements had enabled all divisions, by strenuous work at night, to dig better " jumping-off " trenches, which in many cases represented some gain of ground ; but frequent and harassing reliefs had been necessary in order that the assaulting troops should arrive in their battle positions comparatively fresh.   Even so, the long wait from daylight to 12.35 P.M.—over 6½ hours during which little or no movement was possible—could not be otherwise than tedious and tiring to officers and men.

25TH SEPTEMBER : CAPTURE OF MORVAL AND LESBOEUFS

Monday the 25th September, first anniversary of the Battle of Loos, was fine and sunny, with some haze.[1]   The **25 Sept.** German batteries had fired a good deal during the previous night, but there was little shelling of the packed assembly trenches during the morning.   Then at 12.35 P.M. the creeping barrage crashed down 200 yards beyond the British line and the infantry advanced to the assault.   The battalions of the XIV. Corps, admirably served by their artillery, advanced steadily and methodically, with no delay and few serious checks, to their final objective.   For the most part the Germans who had survived the bombardment were caught before they were prepared for resistance ; some even fled unarmed.   The enemy defensive barrage generally fell too late, and British casualties, except in a few units, were by no means heavy.   It was a heartening experience, a success well deserved by four divisions which, since the beginning of the month, had given repeated proof of their gallantry and endurance, too often with little reward.

Before reaching the first objective the 1/East Surrey (95th Brigade, Lord Esme Gordon-Lennox), the right

---

[1] The R.F.C. continued to bomb villages, troops and trenches and engaged the German machines which were becoming more enterprising. Counter-battery work was well maintained on the Army front ; **124 active** batteries were located on this day, 47 engaged and 24 silenced.

25 Sept. battalion of the 5th Division, suffered heavy loss from the fire of the Germans holding an embankment north of the Combles railway track. On its left flank a strongpoint at the Ginchy—Morval road held out until the 1/Devonshire (also 95th Brigade), which had swung left to avoid uncut wire, worked down the trench from the north. The 1/Norfolk (Br.-General M. N. Turner's 15th Brigade) was led by Lieut.-Colonel P. V. P. Stone in person,[1] and took the first objective in one rush, killing many Germans and capturing over a hundred. The left of the battalion, which thus linked up with the 6th Division, received splendid assistance from the Stokes-mortar fire of the 16th Brigade and the bombers of the 1/Buffs.

On the other flank of the 6th Division, the right of the 2/Grenadiers (Br.-General C. E. Pereira's 1st Guards Brigade) was held up by three belts of uncut wire, and officers and men began to fall fast. But it was seldom that heavy losses stopped the Guards. They cut the wire by hand, covered by their own marksmen and bombers, then rushed in and captured the trench. Next on the left, the 1/Irish Guards of the same brigade, and the 2/Scots Guards (Br.-General C. E. Corkran's 3rd Guards Brigade) found few Germans ready to withstand them, but the 4/Grenadiers, forming the extreme left of the corps attack, unexpectedly came under fire from a trench in front of Gird Trench. This they stormed with the bayonet, slaying over a hundred of the enemy, and eventually arrived, a little late, on the first objective. The junction of Gas Alley and Gird Trench remained in German hands ; but in the main, to use the words of a very senior Guards officer, " the whole show was " going like clockwork ".

On the right flank of the corps the 56th Division, attacking only from the 168th Brigade trenches, had waited for seven minutes after zero hour in order to assault in line with the 5th Division. Then the 1/4th London and the London Scottish advanced under cover of " an effective " enfilade artillery fire ", the first-named battalion clearing the northern end of Bouleaux Wood after killing a number of Germans occupying shell-holes in front of it. The London Scottish soon carried the first trench running from

[1] Lieut.-Colonel Stone had obtained permission to lead the attack on the score that his battalion had recently received three large drafts composed of men of three other regiments, and that the new-comers had not settled down. He is said to have " treated the attack as a pheasant shoot, " with his servant as loader ", and to have accounted for quite a number of the enemy.

the wood to the light-railway track, but then came under 25 Sept. fire from the embankment beyond the track. This position was stormed by some of the East Surrey, of the 5th Division, who advanced across the open, whilst the left of the London Scottish arrived in time to assist in clearing the dug-outs. By 1.30 P.M. all resistance ended; 80 prisoners, with four machine guns, had been taken.[1] Going on beyond their objective, the London Scottish then stormed a second trench—unknown to exist until photographed from the air on the previous day—which gave an excellent view over the Combles—Morval valley. There was no sign of the French advance, which was to move upon Frégicourt from the south and eventually gain touch with the British at the cross-roads east of Morval. The activities of patrols were circumscribed by the protective barrage.

Punctually at 1.35 P.M. the main advance was resumed by the 5th, 6th and Guards Divisions. The East Surrey, forming the right of the 5th Division, had no farther to go ; the Devonshire and the 1/Bedfordshire (15th Brigade)—the latter, which passed through the Norfolk, afterwards complained that the creeping barrage was too slow—captured their portion of the sunken road in ten minutes, killing or capturing all the Germans they encountered. In the 6th Division, the Buffs (Br.-General W. L. Osborn's 16th Brigade) and the 2/Durham L.I. and 11/Essex of the 18th Brigade (Br.-General R. J. Bridgford) did likewise, sustaining few casualties and meeting with little resistance : the Buffs record that " the dressing was very accurately " maintained during the advance ". The 2/Grenadiers and 1/Irish Guards bombed many crowded dug-outs in the sunken road, and the Scots Guards of the 3rd Guards Brigade kept pace with them ; but the 4/Grenadiers now found its outer flank exposed, owing to the failure of the XV. Corps to secure the Gird trenches. Part of the Grenadiers therefore faced north, but some of the battalion went on to the second objective with the Scots Guards.

An hour later began the final advance upon the two villages. The 95th Brigade of the 5th Division put in the 12/Gloucestershire and 2/K.O.S.B.[2] to storm the southern

---

[1] " Res. Regt. No. 235 " states that part of the *236th Reserve* (right sector of the *51st Reserve Division*) appeared to be totally destroyed here. *235th Reserve* was in the line west of Combles, the village being held by the *234th Reserve* (left sector of the *51st Reserve Division*).

[2] Attached from the 13th Brigade in place of the 1/D.C.L.I., which had been much reduced by sickness. All battalions of the 95th Brigade were weak in numbers and sorely needed rest.

25 Sept. half of Morval, which, although set to be accomplished in four deliberate " bounds ", occupied less than an hour and a half. To the Borderers the enemy " seemed demoralized " and not inclined to show much fight ", and " nearly every " man in the battalion secured a trophy ". The 1/Cheshire (15th Brigade) which had passed through the Bedfordshire, were in possession of the northern part of Morval soon after 3 P.M.[1] On the front of the 6th Division, the 2/York & Lancaster, supported closely by the 1/K.S.L.I. (both 16th Brigade), had come through the Buffs, their " parade-like, " steady advance " taking them east of the Morval— Lesboeufs road ; and on their left the 1/West Yorkshire (18th Brigade) had gone on to clear the southern part of Lesboeufs, finding few Germans in its way.[2] This battalion was in touch on the left with the 2/Grenadiers, which, with the 1/Irish Guards, had easily secured the remainder of the village ;[3] behind them the two Coldstream battalions of the 1st Guards Brigade were coming forward in support.[4]

The 3rd Guards Brigade had sent the 1/Grenadiers through to take the final objective, and this battalion, passing north of Lesboeufs, did so by 3.30 P.M. One company, however, faced north astride the sunken road leading to Gueudecourt in order to prolong the defensive flank of the corps held by the 4/Grenadiers and by the Welsh Guards which had been sent up for the purpose. Forward of the Gird trenches, this line ran inside the prescribed boundary of the corps.

The XIV. Corps had overrun the last of the German main defences on a frontage of nearly two thousand yards ; batteries were seen in the act of withdrawal, and most of the hostile infantry was retiring out of contact.[5] Whilst consolidation proceeded all along the new line the Germans began a heavy bombardment of Morval and Lesboeufs, but, once the ruins of these villages had been thoroughly

---

[1] According to " Res. Regt. No. 239 " (*52nd Reserve Division*) the British bombed the headquarters dug-out of the *III./239th Reserve* in Morval at 3 P.M. It appears that the battalion was practically annihilated.

[2] The 6th Division overwhelmed two companies of the *239th Reserve* on the southern edge of the village.

[3] Held by the *240th Reserve*, centre of the *52nd Reserve Division*.

[4] Captain H. W. Verelst, commanding the 2/Coldstream, and his adjutant, were killed by a shell.

[5] Pte. T. A. (" Todger ") Jones, 1/Cheshire, went forward alone to engage a sniper, whom he killed, and he then accounted for two more Germans. Reaching a German trench, he induced the occupants of several dug-outs to surrender, and marched back over 100 prisoners, including several officers, through the British protective barrage. For this audacious enterprise he was awarded the V.C.

explored, they were kept clear of all but small bodies of troops. The 5th and 6th Divisions completed their day's task by occupying the spurs projecting east and north-east of Morval. At 6 P.M. the 16/R. Warwickshire (15th Brigade) went forward and dug in more than two hundred yards beyond the eastern edge of the village ; a little later the 2/York & Lancaster (16th Brigade) established posts which ran from Morval mill north-westward to Lesboeufs.[1]

The approximate situation of the forward positions was reported by contact areoplane to Army headquarters about 5.30 P.M. Half an hour earlier a message from the French Sixth Army had announced the capture of Frégicourt ; but at 6 P.M. Lord Cavan telephoned to say that the village was still holding out.[2] When, during the afternoon and early evening, battalion commanders sent back word that there was little opposition in front and that cavalry might now be of use, Lord Cavan decided to take no action, having regard to the uncertain situation on his flanks.[3]

The two tanks attached to the 56th Division remained at their place of assembly in the depression west of Leuze Wood. The 5th Division had three machines concentrated north-east of Guillemont ready to assist in the capture of Morval, and all followed up the advance. Two soon became ditched, and the third, which arrived at Morval about dusk, was sent back again. The Guards Division had three tanks in reserve near Ginchy but did not use them.

The 21st Division (Major-General D. G. M. Campbell), forming the right of the XV. Corps, was to capture Gueude-

---

[1] Lieut.-Colonel A. St. J. Blunt, 2/York & Lancaster, was wounded whilst returning at night from an inspection of the forward line.

[2] The left of the French I. Corps had been held up by machine guns firing from the S.E. edge of Combles, and gained very little ground ; in the centre, the Maurepas—Frégicourt road was reached ; on the right, progress was made east of Frégicourt, but the village was not taken. Rancourt (see Sketch A) was captured early in the afternoon by the XXXII. Corps (which had taken over the right sector of the I.), but the right of the corps was stopped by machine-gun fire. For the same reason, little was accomplished by the V. Corps east of Bouchavesnes, and the VI. Corps S.E. of that village, whilst the XXXIII. Corps, astride the Somme, found its progress towards Feuillaucourt (where the Péronne—Bapaume road crosses the canal) sternly disputed. F.O.A. iv. (iii.), pp. 171-3.

[3] The *III./235th Reserve* (*51st Reserve Division*) and parts of the *239th Reserve* and *240th Reserve* (*52nd Reserve Division*) were ordered to recapture Morval, but only made a short advance, which covered the withdrawal of the artillery. At night the front was along the Le Transloy road about 1,000 yards E. of Morval, with a gap on the left. The Sailly defences (S. of Le Transloy), were held as a second position. German regimental histories.

25 Sept. court,[1] taking the Gird trenches in its first assault and then advancing to the farther side of the village in two stages. The right of the division would then link up with the Guards (XIV. Corps) at the fork on the Gueudecourt—Le Transloy road.

On the right, the 10/K.O.Y.L.I. and 1/East Yorkshire (Br.-General H. R. Headlam's 64th Brigade) attacked the Gird trenches, but both battalions were held up by uncut wire, and, whilst they were trying to force their way through, came under machine-gun fire from the trench beyond. Most of the survivors remained out in shell-holes until night came, when they were ordered to withdraw. The 1/Lincolnshire (attached from the 62nd Brigade) was so heavily shelled as it came forward on its way to secure the second objective that it was halted in the British front line. One company of the Lincolnshire, on the extreme right, combined with the 4/Grenadiers in an attack upon the junction of Gas Alley, the boundary between the XIV. and XV. Corps, with Gird Trench. Although this point was not carried, touch with the XIV. Corps was preserved.

The 9th and 8/Leicestershire (Br.-General W. F. Hessey's 110th Brigade) were next on the left. They ran into a German barrage early in their advance, but Goat Trench, half-way to Gird Trench, was taken by the two leading companies of each battalion without serious opposition. When the barrage lifted the advance was resumed, but, although the entanglement had been well cut, enfilade machine-gun fire from the right took heavy toll of the attackers and prevented the capture of Gird Trench. Lieut.-Colonel C. H. Haig,[2] 9/Leicestershire, came along Pilgrim's Way—a track leading from Flers to Gueudecourt —from Goat Trench and reorganized the forward troops ; he had sent back a runner to hurry forward the reserve companies, but as the man was wounded before he reached them, no help arrived. Eventually a defensive flank was formed by the 9/Leicestershire along Watling Street (a sunken portion of the Ginchy—Gueudecourt road) on the right, and on the left a party of the 8/Leicestershire main-tained a footing they had won in Gird Trench, where, during the afternoon, touch was obtained with the 55th Division.

---

[1] The Bavarian Official Account states that in the Gueudecourt sector (*6th Bavarian Division*) the British bombardment had caused the with-drawal of all machine guns from the trenches into safer intermediate positions.

[2] He was wounded, but did not leave his battalion until next day.

Some men of the 8/Leicestershire are said to have pushed 25 Sept.
on into Gueudecourt; if this be true they were not seen
again.[1] The great disorganization on the divisional front,
and the many casualties to runners, prevented the true
situation from becoming known in rear until much later.
Reports from observers that our men were in Gueudecourt
led divisional headquarters to believe for a time that the
village had been taken.

The 55th Division (Major-General H. S. Jeudwine), next
on the left, had two objectives : first, the Gird Trenches as
far to the north as the sunken Gueudecourt—Factory
Corner road, and the road as far as, but not including,
Factory Corner, 1,200 yards north of Flers; secondly, the
road between Gueudecourt and the Gird trenches, to be
reached by a forward wheel of the right, at 2.41 P.M.
Major-General Jeudwine used his fittest brigade, the 165th
(Br.-General F. J. Duncan) and the 1/7th, 1/6th and 1/9th
King's went forward in splendid style, keeping close to the
barrage. The three battalions secured their first objective
soon after 1 P.M., many Germans being killed or captured,
and the 1/6th King's blocked the Gird trenches north of
the road.[2] On the left, the 1/9th King's found many
German dead, killed by the bombardment, in Grove Alley,
which they cleared with bomb and bayonet. At 2.40 P.M.
the 1/7th and part of the 1/6th King's continued the advance
and gave the brigade a footing in the sunken road between
the Gird trenches and Gueudecourt. Touch with the New
Zealanders on the left was obtained later in the day, whilst
the right flank linked up with the men of the 110th Brigade
in the Gird trenches, the 1/5th King's being brought forward
from reserve to reinforce the whole line.[3]

The New Zealand Division (Major-General Sir A. H.
Russell) had been ordered to form a defensive flank facing
N.N.W. astride Goose Alley, the communication trench
running back to the Gird trenches. Br.-General F. E.
Johnston's 1st N.Z. Brigade was timed to carry out this

---

[1] The opponents of the 21st Division were the *238th Reserve* (right of
the *52nd Reserve Division*) in the Gird trenches S.E. of Watling Street,
and the *I./6th Bavarians* (left of the *6th Bavarian Division*) in front of
Gueudecourt. German regimental histories.

[2] A section of the 1/1st West Lancashire Field Company R.E., especially
sent up for the purpose, blew in Gird Trench. The division adopted the
sound principle of keeping its sappers in hand until consolidation was due
to begin ; sections then went forward to their appointed tasks.

[3] The 165th Brigade had driven in the *II./6th Bavarians*, some of whom
were forced to their left on to the *I./Bn.* The regimental history states
that the headquarters of the *II. Bn.* was captured.

25 Sept. operation in 25 minutes, with two pauses of the creeping barrage. After assembling in the captured part of Grove Alley, the 1/Canterbury, 1/Auckland and 1/Otago were heavily shelled for two hours during the morning, whilst the batteries in front of Delville Wood suffered likewise, and Flers was bombarded as usual. Starting at the general zero hour, the advance kept close to the creeping barrage and was supported by machine-gun fire, which lifted later to the Gird trenches. Little resistance was encountered, and a battalion staff of the *13th Bavarians* [1] surrendered to the Canterbury battalion at Factory Corner.[2] After a pause, the Otago rushed the south-western part of Goose Alley, taking 30 Bavarians and three machine guns. Exactly to time, the New Zealanders were established upon their final objective, in touch with the 1st Division (III. Corps) in Flers Support, and, later, with the 55th Division beyond Factory Corner. In the evening Flers Support was taken over from the 1st Division according to previous arrangement.

At 2.50 P.M. Lieut.-General Horne had warned the New Zealand and 55th Divisions to be prepared to go on and capture the Gird trenches astride the Factory Corner— Ligny road ; but the check at Gueudecourt caused this operation to be postponed. At 5 P.M., when corps headquarters were informed of the state of affairs on the 21st Division front, Major-General Campbell was ordered to make another effort, using a tank [3] against the Gird trenches and the village. The divisional commander, however, wished to postpone the operation until next morning, and, after conferring with Lieut.-General Horne by telephone, he obtained the corps commander's consent to this course.[4]

The III. Corps was not so heavily engaged.[5] In the 1st Division (Major-General E. P. Strickland), the 1/Black Watch, of Br.-General A. J. Reddie's 1st Brigade started

---

[1] The Bavarian Official Account states that the *11th Bavarians* had taken over from the *13th* here, but the regimental histories show that the relief was not complete. The capture of *II./13th Bavarians* headquarters is admitted.

[2] There was a copious supply of well water here, and a valuable dump of engineer stores.

[3] The two tanks allotted to the XV. Corps had been brought up to the N.E. exit of Flers under the orders of the 21st Division, and were intended for such an eventuality. One machine had been damaged by shell-fire.

[4] In the evening the German situation was grave : there were not sufficient troops in hand to counter-attack west of Gueudecourt and also at Lesboeufs. Bavarian Official Account.

[5] Its opponents belonged to the *50th Reserve Division*, the *230th Reserve* and *229th Reserve Regiments* being in line from east to west.

to bomb up the Flers trenches at zero hour, and about 25 Sept. 300 yards were gained after a sharp fight. Flers Support, as has been stated, was afterwards taken over by the New Zealanders. In the centre of the corps front the 150th Brigade (Br.-General B. G. Price) of Major-General Wilkinson's 50th Division had established posts along the line of its objective during the previous night. On the night of the 25th an advanced post was established beyond the turn of Crescent Alley. The 23rd Division (Major-General J. M. Babington), on the left, was called upon to take the western portion of Twenty-Sixth Avenue with the help of two tanks starting from Gunpit Road, west of Martinpuich. One of the machines became ditched and could take no part; the advance of the other over the crest between the opposing lines drew down a German barrage upon the assaulting companies of the 10/Northumberland Fusiliers (Br.-General G. N. Colville's 68th Brigade), which also encountered accurate machine-gun fire. No headway could be made, and an attempt to bomb forward from the trench west of Martinpuich mill likewise failed.

At 10 P.M. on the 25th September, General Foch, who was extremely disappointed at the slow progress of the French left, paid a visit to Sir Douglas Haig, and explained that General Fayolle's advance northward upon Sailly- Sketch A. Saillisel was cramped by St. Pierre Vaast Wood, which blocked the approach to the near edge of Saillisel. Might he be permitted to pass troops through Morval in order to attack Sailly-Saillisel from the west? The British Commander-in-Chief at once offered to hand over to the French both Morval and Lesboeufs, and also the Dernancourt—Maricourt metre-gauge railway which was now being extended north-eastward towards Guillemont. General Foch expressed his surprise and gratification,[1] and it was thereupon decided that arrangements for the extension of the French left should be settled in detail by conference at Fourth Army headquarters next day.

Seeing that an attack upon the Le Transloy line would have to be made across the low ridges which were commanded by the higher ground at Sailly-Saillisel, Sir Douglas Haig decided that the XIV. Corps, after assisting to clear the enemy from Combles, must wait upon the French; and he rightly judged that on the remainder of its front the

[1] A personal letter of thanks arrived from General Joffre on 27th September.

25 Sept. Fourth Army would be able to do little more than complete the capture of its objectives. The Reserve Army offensive was now of chief importance, for the capture of Thiepval might be expected to open up new possibilities.

Map 1. At 11 P.M. the Fourth Army issued telegraphic in-
Sketch structions for the morrow : the XIV. Corps to surround
38. Combles in co-operation with the French ; the XV. Corps, to capture the Gird trenches and Gueudecourt. These were the main tasks, but the XV. Corps and III. Corps were ordered to gain as much ground as possible by pushing forward patrols west of the Factory Corner—Ligny road, preparatory to carrying their advance northward on both sides of Eaucourt l'Abbaye " at an early date ".

26TH SEPTEMBER : CAPTURE OF COMBLES AND GUEUDECOURT.

A German officer captured by the 5th Division about 10 P.M. on the 25th had stated that the enemy intended to evacuate Combles during the night ; a similar report had reached the XIV. Corps from the French.

The 56th Division took action accordingly. At 10.40 P.M a detachment of the London Scottish (168th Brigade) began to push southward along the light railway track and
26 Sept. before dawn of the 26th was within 500 yards of Combles ; meanwhile patrols of the 1/4th London had worked through the northern half of Bouleaux Wood, finding no Germans, whilst the 1/1st London (167th Brigade) did likewise through the southern half. At 2.10 A.M. a shower of red rockets, followed by a single green one, went up from the German trenches west and north-west of the village. This appeared to be the signal for the retirement of the enemy rear parties ; by 3 A.M. the 1/1st London patrols had penetrated un-opposed as far as the Orchard, and one had already entered Combles and met the French.[1] Farther south, the London Rifle Brigade (169th Brigade) was working steadily forward down Combles Trench, and at 4.15 A.M. had joined hands with the French at the light-railway track, handing over to them 200 Germans who had surrendered The 1/1st London, pushing into the village by the Ginchy road, captured prisoners of the *234th Reserve* and *235th Reserve Regiments*. At 7 A.M. the London Scottish were greeting

---

[1] " Res. Regt. No. 235 " states that a withdrawal was made without hindrance to the " Gallwitz Riegel " (German 3rd Position S.E. of Morval) : a difficult movement, admirably executed.

French patrols on the railway at the north-eastern exit of 26 Sept.
Combles.[1]   A captured order showed that the headquarters
of the *I./234th Reserve Regiment* had departed at 10 P.M. on
the previous night : probably eastward by the communication trench which crossed the valley to join the German 3rd
Position north of Frégicourt.[2]   Some parties making northward towards Morval had been shot down by the London
Scottish.

Whilst the searching and clearing of Combles proceeded,[3]
the 56th Division pushed forward troops to dig in facing
eastward between Combles and Morval, the right in touch
with the French, who had at last entered Frégicourt.[4]   The
French were to advance on Haie Wood in the afternoon,
and the 168th Brigade was therefore ordered to preserve
touch by pressing forward down that part of the German
3rd Position between Frégicourt and Morval which had
been named Mutton Trench.[5]   As an air reconnaissance
revealed that the enemy was still in occupation of Mutton
Trench, the 1/12th London (168th Brigade) was ordered
to attack in the afternoon behind two tanks ; but the
machines became ditched near Morval on their way forward
and the operation was therefore postponed and eventually
abandoned.

On the greater part of the XIV. Corps front the 26th
September, another fine autumn day, was devoted to consolidation and to regaining touch with the enemy.   A corps

[1] French patrols were sent into Combles during the night.   There was
some fighting, but at dawn the 110th Regiment cleared the S.E. portion
of the village and made 200 prisoners.   The 73rd Regiment entered from
the S.W. and French and British joined hands.   Between Combles and
Frégicourt a large number of Germans were routed and brought under
effective machine-gun fire as they fled back to Haie Wood.   F.O.A. iv.
(iii.), Annexe 663.

[2] " Res. Regt. No. 235 " observes " that Combles was not encircled
" earlier may be accounted for by the village marking the boundary
" between French and British ".

[3] Most of the booty was gathered in by the French.   According to
Palat the principal items were 1,500 rifles, 2 million rounds of S.A.A.,
15,000 rounds of gun ammunition, and a big store of grenades.   Prisoners
amounted to 500, " the remains of two battalions ".

[4] According to F.O.A. iv. (iii.), Annexe 663, Frégicourt was occupied
" dans la deuxième partie de la nuit " (25th/26th September).

[5] General Fayolle was anxious to have Mutton Trench, on his left
flank, cleared prior to his attack on the Haie Wood—St. Pierre Vaast
Wood line.   This attack was delivered at 4 P.M., and at night the Fourth
Army was informed that it had been successful on the flanks, but was
stopped by machine-gun fire in the centre.

The I. Corps had made some progress east of the Frégicourt—Le
Transloy road, but its advance up the trench north of Frégicourt had stopped
short of the wood.   F.O.A. iv. (iii.), p. 176.

26 Sept. order, issued at 10 A.M., dealt chiefly with the necessity of establishing a strong defensive position and reflected the Commander-in-Chief's decision to defer the attack upon the Le Transloy line.   The 5th Division, which had made a little progress down Mutton Trench, also managed to seize a portion of Thunder Trench—a German position some eight hundred yards east of Morval—but could not complete its capture owing to machine-gun fire from the direction of Sailly-Saillisel.   The division was relieved at night by the 20th Division, and by the 6th, which extended its front southward.[1]   In front of Lesboeufs patrols of the Guards [2] had encountered during the day fire from snipers and isolated machine guns sufficient to render impracticable the employment of cavalry.   Just before noon a hostile counter-attack was observed by the left of the Guards ;   it was delivered south-westward towards the eastern edge of Gueudecourt, but the Germans were caught by the fire of more than sixty field guns, hundreds of the survivors fleeing unarmed towards Le Transloy.   On the left flank of the corps the 3rd Guards Brigade had been able to advance in consequence of the success, now to be related, of the right of the XV. Corps.

The tank from Flers which was to assist in the capture of Gird Trench came up Pilgrim's Way about 6.30 A.M. and passed along the trench, firing as it did so.   Bombers of the 7/Leicestershire (110th Brigade) followed, with two companies of that battalion in support.   The Germans were driven steadily south-eastward towards the Guards Division, those who took refuge in dug-outs being bombed and those who fled back across the open coming under Lewis-gun fire. There was no escape.   A British aeroplane had called down an accurate bombardment upon the trench, and, after signalling for the shelling to cease, it flew low and raked the surviving Germans with machine-gun bullets.   Eight officers and 362 other ranks surrendered,[3] the number of dead and wounded being very great.   The British loss amounted to five.

[1] For the period 19th-26th September the 5th Division returned a casualty list of 1,749 officers and men.

[2] The Guards Division had asked for the protective standing barrage to be placed well forward so that patrols could move about freely : they were to take their chance if an S.O.S. barrage had to be put down.

[3] Mostly of the *238th Reserve* (*52nd Reserve Division*), including the battalion commander.   The Bavarian accounts say that the tank attack annihilated the remains of the *I./6th Bavarians* in front of Gueudecourt, battalion headquarters being captured.

The Gird trenches were then occupied by the 15/Durham 26 Sept.
L.I. which advanced from the 64th Brigade front, the
victorious tank turning towards the south-eastern edge of
Gueudecourt before withdrawing. The XV. Corps ordered
infantry patrols to push into the village, and at 11 A.M.
called upon a squadron of the Cavalry Corps to reconnoitre
the higher ground to the north-west and north-east, in
conjunction with patrols of the XV. Corps cavalry regiment,
the South Irish Horse.[1]

About noon a squadron of the 19th Lancers (Sialkot
Cavalry Brigade, 1st Indian Cavalry Division) left Mametz,
and, proceeding mostly at a trot, came up by a track east of
Flers and turned towards Gueudecourt [2] under artillery and
machine-gun fire from its right front. A mounted patrol
then moved eastward round the village, but was heavily
shelled on turning north and had to withdraw ; the remainder of the squadron dismounted and entered Gueudecourt from the south-west about 2.15 P.M. A troop of the
South Irish Horse, also on foot, reached the north-west
corner about the same time, and fire was opened with
Hotchkiss guns and rifles upon Germans seen to the north
and north-east. Meanwhile, the 110th Brigade had felt its
way forward cautiously, the 6/Leicestershire following its
patrols into Gueudecourt about 4.30 P.M. Half an hour
later about three battalions of the enemy advanced from the
direction of Thilloy and took cover in the grass and standing
crops a mile to the north of Gueudecourt. This ground was
searched by the field artillery and no further movement was
seen.[3] The cavalry withdrew about 6 P.M., and an hour later
the Leicestershire began to dig in on the far edge of the village.

The advance of the 64th Brigade had been resumed
by the 15/Durham L.I., with the 10th and part of the
9/K.O.Y.L.I.[4] Before 5.30 P.M. a position was taken up

---

[1] The Welsh Guards (extreme left of the XIV. Corps) had reported
that it was possible to walk about in the open with impunity, and that the
few Germans encountered had surrendered.

[2] The squadron crossed without trouble two trenches filled with British
infantry.

[3] " Res. Regt. No. 230 " states that the *I./72nd* (from the *8th Division*
opposite the front of the Reserve Army) was ordered to " occupy " Gueudecourt. Probably the movement observed was only the reinforcement of
the German line in the neighbourhood of Luisenhof Farm (on the Ligny
road 1,500 yards north of Factory Corner).

[4] Captain J. Brindley of the 1/E. Yorkshire, who was wounded, with a
party of his own men and some of the 10/K.O.Y.L.I., appears to have led
this advance, and to have sent back several prisoners. This officer and
those with him had refused to withdraw after the abortive attack of the
previous day.

2 c

26 Sept. some distance short of the final objective, the Gueude-court—Le Transloy road, and the 12/Northumberland Fusiliers (Br.-General C. G. Rawling's 62nd Brigade) then came forward to take over the front. This battalion advanced a little farther so as to dig in along the road, its right resting on the junction with the Lesboeufs road, where touch with the Guards was obtained. At 10 P.M. the 10/Green Howards (also 62nd Brigade) relieved the Fusiliers in the left portion of the line.

Under Fourth Army instructions, the XV. Corps had already informed the 55th and New Zealand Divisions that a new attack would be made in order to secure that part of the Gird trenches between the Gueudecourt—Factory Corner road and Goose Alley, and also the remainder of Goose Alley. The corps order for this operation was telegraphed to divisions at 9.15 P.M. and zero hour was fixed for 2.15 P.M. next day.

The III. Corps had little to do on the 26th, orders for the 23rd Division to occupy Twenty-Sixth Avenue being cancelled because it was understood that the right of the Canadian Corps (Reserve Army) was not advancing.[1] At 11 P.M., however, the 1st and 50th Divisions made a surprise attack upon a new German trench, called Flers Switch, joining Flers Trench to Crescent Alley. On the right, the 1st Division was checked by enfilade machine-gun fire, but the Northumbrians secured a footing at the western end and bombed up Crescent Alley as far as Spence Trench, which was really a continuation of Flers Switch. Bombing attacks by the 1st Division gained but little ground in Flers Trench.

In the afternoon of the 26th September a conference was held at Fourth Army headquarters in order to arrange the extension of the French line.[2] The French left was to rest

Sketch A. upon the south-eastern edge of Lesboeufs, and the boundary was traced north-eastward (leaving Le Transloy as an objective of the British) to the Péronne—Bapaume road, thence N.N.E. embracing the western edge of Haplincourt, one mile north of Barastre. An order for the necessary reliefs and for certain adjustments of corps boundaries was

---

[1] See Chapter XV.
[2] The main points were settled by Generals Rawlinson and Fayolle. Lieut.-General Kiggell (C.G.S.) and Br.-General J. H. Davidson from G.H.Q. attended, and General Weygand (General Foch's C.G.S.) arrived later.

issued by the Fourth Army on the afternoon of the 27th, 27 Sept. following a conference of corps staffs.[1]

27TH–28TH SEPTEMBER : EXTENSION OF THE FRENCH FRONT

A fine morning turned to cloud and rain when, in the afternoon, creeping barrages were put down along the whole front of the Army in order to assist the XV. Corps attack by threatening a general advance. The XIV. Corps line was heavily shelled, counter-battery measures securing only a temporary respite from the German fire. Towards evening the 20th Division made a little progress down Mutton Trench, but could not clear it entirely.[2]

The XV. Corps attack upon the Gird trenches and Goose Alley was launched at 2.15 P.M. On the 55th Division front the 1/8th King's (Liverpool Irish) of the 164th Brigade (Br.-General C. I. Stockwell) took its objective in splendid style with little loss : the enemy appeared to be demoralized, and his dead were numerous. The 1st N.Z. Brigade had a bigger task, but the 1/Canterbury, on the right, made a successful advance and linked up with the Liverpool Irish on the Ligny road. In the centre, the 1/Auckland, which had to negotiate uncut wire, likewise succeeded ; but three companies of the left battalion, 1/Otago, were almost annihilated by shell-fire and streams of machine-gun bullets after reaching the forward slope beyond the Factory Corner—Eaucourt l'Abbaye road. The remaining Otago company, on the left, succeeded in bombing forward up Goose Alley which, beyond Abbey Road, was mostly found to have been blown in by repeated bombardments. Posts were established in this part of the trench, but the New Zealanders were still opposed by Germans holding the junctions of Goose Alley with the Gird trenches.[3]

---

[1] Rearward the boundary passed roughly S.W. through the centre of Guillemont and then along the Guillemont—Maricourt road, which was common to British and French. The metre-gauge railway to Maricourt was to come under control of the French, who were also to take over the work of extending it to Guillemont, the British XIV. Corps being allowed the use of the line for the purposes of supply. Necessary gun positions in the French zone—in the valleys S.W. of Morval, N. of Combles and S. of Ginchy and Guillemont—were retained by the British.

[2] The French made no attack of importance after 26th September. See Note at end of Chapter.

[3] According to the German accounts, parts of the *10th, 11th* and *13th Bavarians* (*6th Bavarian Division*) were being relieved by the *66th Reserve* (*7th Reserve Division*). Prisoners of all these regiments were captured.

27 Sept.   In the III. Corps during the afternoon and evening of this day the 1st Division secured most of its portion of Flers Switch by frontal attack and bombing, but all efforts to bomb eastward into Flers Trench were steadily opposed. At night the 47th Division [1] began to take over from the 1st.[2] The 50th Division had pushed patrols along Crescent Alley towards Eaucourt l'Abbaye ; on the left, Twenty-Sixth Avenue was entered by way of Spence Trench and some progress made towards the Flers trenches. Between Crescent Alley and Twenty-Sixth Avenue posts were established within two hundred yards of the Flers trenches [3] and then a halt was called, for the division was well in advance of its neighbours. The 23rd Division, which owed much to the enterprise of its artillery F.O.O's, occupied without fighting the whole of Twenty-Sixth Avenue south-west of Spence Trench, and swung forward its left in touch with the Canadians at the Bapaume road. In the evening, however, a patrol which endeavoured to approach Destremont Farm was received with heavy rifle and machine-gun fire.

28 Sept.   The 28th September was cloudy with fine intervals and some showers. Little infantry action took place, but the artillery, favoured by the excellent facilities for observation which had now been won along the whole line, was able to fire with effect at hostile working-parties and keep communication trenches, tracks and roads under a harassing bombardment. The German batteries were also active, shelling principally the ruins of Morval, Lesboeufs and Gueudecourt, and certain forward routes to the new front.

During the night of the 27th/28th September the XIV. Corps had begun to hand over its right front to the French, a complicated operation which concerned the 56th and 20th Divisions, which were withdrawn,[4] as well as the 6th Division. It was completed with admirable accord, and comparatively little interference on the part of German

[1] Now commanded by Br.-General W. H. Greenly, who had just replaced Major-General Barter.
[2] The 1st Division had reported over 1,400 casualties since 20th September.
[3] The *50th Reserve Division* was falling back to Eaucourt l'Abbaye—Le Sars line, being relieved by the *6th Bavarian Reserve Division* from Flanders as it did so.
[4] The casualties returned by the 56th Division for the whole month of September amounted to 5,538 of all ranks.

artillery, by the morning of the 29th.   Before leaving the line, the 20th Division had occupied another 300 yards of Mutton Trench, but the posts in it were not taken over by the French.   Patrols of the Guards Division had found the enemy active 400 yards ahead.

In the XV. Corps an early morning attack upon the **28 Sept.** junctions of Goose Alley with the Gird trenches was cancelled, owing to the non-arrival of a tank and the heavy shelling of the 1/Wellington (1st N.Z. Brigade) whilst it was moving up.   Later, a reconnaissance disclosed that the trench junctions lay in a saucer-like depression and were clearly untenable unless the Gird trenches on the higher ground beyond were also cleared of Germans.   On the night of the 28th/29th a brigade (attached to the 21st Division) of the 41st Division took over the front of the 55th,[1] which had reported the Germans to be digging half a mile away.

The III. Corps consolidated its forward positions, the left of the 23rd Division pushing on in combination with the Canadians.   A company of the 70th Brigade advanced against Destremont Farm, but could not force an entrance, being met with machine-gun fire at close range and showers of bombs.

So the battle of Morval died down.   The advance on the 25th September was the most successful operation of the Fourth Army since the dawn attack of the 14th July ; but against the capture of Morval and Lesboeufs had to be set the slow progress of the French, which hampered the British right.   Thus the left of the main attack, striking north-eastward through Gueudecourt, was invested with particular importance, and here success was not gained until the second day.   Badly shaken, unable for the moment to present a continuous front, obliged to extemporize new field defences, the Germans had yet contrived to withdraw their artillery intact ;[2] and after the first 24 hours of battle, the Fourth Army, with no fresh divisions available and the troops in the line all very tired, could do little more than regain contact with the enemy.

---

[1] Casualties of the 55th Division, 17th-29th September, were returned as 1,555 all ranks.

[2] Only two field guns were captured by the Fourth Army, and these fell to the III. Corps, conducting operations of secondary importance.

NOTE

French Co-operation in the Battle of Morval [1]

Special preparations were made by the French for the combined attack, " une véritable offensive d'ensemble analogue à celle du 1ᵉʳ " juillet ". Since the divergent advances of the Sixth Army, eastward and north-eastward, would be accentuated by the movement due north in touch with the British right, General Fayolle required considerable reinforcement of guns and troops. General Foch, therefore, gave him more artillery by drawing upon the Tenth Army, south of the Somme, and G.Q.G. consented to the transfer of some batteries from Verdun.[2] One air squadron was taken from the Verdun front to supplement the ten squadrons with the Sixth Army. General Fayolle put in the XXXII. Corps to take over the right of the I. Corps.

Sketch A. The ultimate objective of the Sixth Army was a line within assaulting distance of the German defensive system Moislains (1¾ miles east of Bouchavesnes)—Le Transloy, no important advance being required of the VI. Corps, south-east of Bouchavesnes or of the XXXIII. east of Cléry. After the meagre results of the 25th September, General Foch intervened to ensure that the weight of the I. and XXXII. Corps attack should be directed due north on Sailly-Saillisel, the V. Corps covering the right of the movement. The general attack delivered at 4 P.M. on the 26th achieved very little, and at 3.30 P.M. next day another effort brought a similar result : the enemy resistance had stiffened and his artillery fire was very heavy. General Fayolle then decided that nothing more could be done without thorough artillery preparation.

[1] F.O.A. iv. (iii.), pp. 154–80. The movements of the French on the immediate right of the Fourth Army are described in the footnotes to this chapter.
[2] In exchange for 155-mm. howitzers, G.A.N. was able to lend G.A.C. for the Verdun front some heavy siege guns and trench mortars.

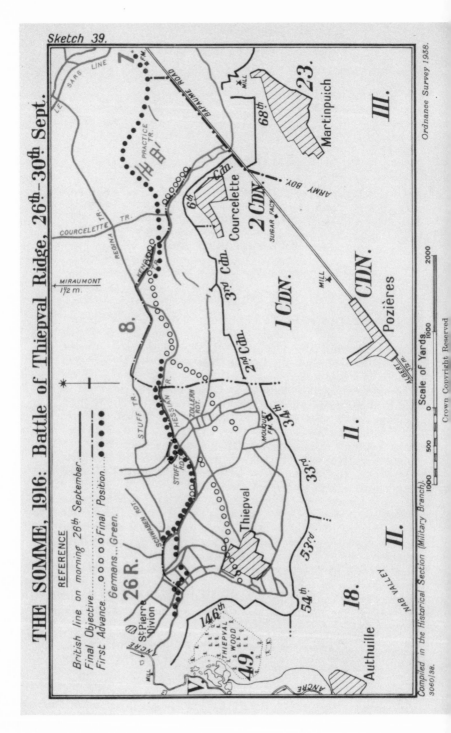

Sketch 39.

THE SOMME, 1916: Battle of Thiepval Ridge, 26th.–30th. Sept.

REFERENCE

British line on morning 26th September......
Final Objective......
First Advance......ooooo Final Position.....
Germans......Green.

MIRAUMONT
1½ m.

Scale of Yards

Compiled in the Historical Section (Military Branch).
3060/38.

Ordnance Survey 1938.

Crown Copyright Reserved

CHAPTER XV

THE BATTLE OF THIEPVAL RIDGE

26TH–30TH SEPTEMBER 1916 [1]

(Map 3 ; Sketches A, 39)

THE PLAN AND PREPARATIONS

ALTHOUGH the Battle of Flers—Courcelette had not accomplished all that had been hoped, Sir Douglas Haig was convinced that the German reserves were now almost exhausted, and that the time was approaching for General Gough to strike hard : indeed, the slow progress of General Rawlinson's right, dependent as it was upon the advance of the French, made vigorous action on the left of the British fighting front all the more desirable if the Allied pressure were to be maintained.   As soon as the Thiepval ridge had Sketch A. been secured the Commander-in-Chief contemplated an eastward advance, with tank assistance, on Serre from the Hébuterne sector, combined with an attack north-eastward from the Beaumont Hamel valley.

Subsequent operations depended upon weather conditions and also, to a considerable extent, upon the British resources available after it had been determined what could be employed with profit on the right in co-operation with the French.   The general idea was disclosed by the Commander-in-Chief to General Gough, and to General Allenby commanding the Third Army, on the 24th September : when the Reserve Army attacked eastward towards Achiet le Grand, the Third Army was to be prepared to take

---

[1] The official title for the battle (Reserve Army front from the Albert—Bapaume road to Serre) covers only 26th-28th September ; but fighting continued for many days afterwards, so it appears best to follow this stage of the offensive up to the end of the month.

Sept. Gommecourt and the spur south-east of that village for the purpose of covering General Gough's left.[1] With this scheme in mind, Sir Douglas Haig was able to send a reassuring reply to General Joffre, who, in a letter dated the 23rd September, had emphasized the importance of a combined effort delivered with maximum forces in order to reach the line Bertincourt—Bapaume—Achiet le Grand at the earliest possible date.

Map 3. For the capture of the Thiepval ridge, " the ridge which Sketch " runs from Courcelette to Schwaben Redoubt ", the 39. Reserve Army operation order was issued at 10.30 A.M. on the 22nd September. Corps commanders had already been informed verbally that the date of the attack would be the 26th September, and zero hour was subsequently fixed as 12.35 P.M.

The attack frontage, which extended from the eastern edge of Courcelette to the original German front line south of Thiepval, about 6,000 yards was divided equally between the Canadian Corps (Lieut.-General Hon. Sir J. H. G. Byng) and the II. Corps (Lieut.-General C. W. Jacob). Each corps had two divisions in the line. The main attack was to be delivered in three stages, a halt of ten minutes being allowed on the first objective and one of an hour on the second.

The Canadians, who were to cover the extreme right flank of the Army by a small advance, had as their main objective the German trenches on the spur north-west of Courcelette. The right of the II. Corps was faced with the task of carrying Zollern Redoubt [2] in the second stage of the advance, and Stuff Redoubt [3] in the third stage, both these works being situated in the old German 2nd Position, the latter upon the crest of the ridge. The left of the corps had to assault Thiepval, completing the capture of the village in the second stage, and finally to secure Schwaben Redoubt, which stood practically on a level with Stuff Redoubt and overlooked the descent towards the Ancre at St. Pierre Divion. It was distinctly laid down that the Germans must be driven from the whole crest-line, so that

---

[1] Sir Douglas Haig reckoned that the Third Army could employ 3–4 divisions and a proportion of tanks. The main operation he saw as a surprise attack delivered without artillery bombardment by 50–60 tanks in line.

[2] Called Goat Redoubt, originally, by the British, but the German name (" Feste Zollern ") had now become Anglicised.

[3] On 1st July the Ulstermen of the 36th Division had penetrated almost as far when they broke through from the west along the slopes north of Thiepval. See " 1916 " Vol. I., p. 416.

the region southwards, towards Albert, might be shut from Sept. enemy view and complete observation obtained over the valley of the upper Ancre.[1]   The original German front line west of Thiepval would have to be cleared systematically as the advance progressed.

Thiepval, situated almost at the top of the tongue-like spur projecting southward from the main ridge, had long been reduced to ruins by bombardment, but the majority of its deep cellars and dug-outs were judged to be still intact ; likewise, the three redoubts and the original German front line might be expected to contain plenty of underground shelter which the heaviest shell-fire had not destroyed.   It was in these localities that the hardest fighting was to be anticipated,[2] so of the eight tanks available six were allotted to the II. Corps.[3]

Some 230 heavy guns, howitzers and mortars and 570 field guns and howitzers,[4] the bulk of the Reserve Army artillery, were employed, the batteries of the V. Corps north of the Ancre, being able to bombard the river crossings and take the German defences and communications in rear. The action of the machine guns in the Canadian Corps and II. Corps was carefully co-ordinated, overhead barrages being arranged to fall between the artillery barrage lines.   The preliminary bombardment opened on the

---

[1] At 11.25 P.M. on 25th September General Gough announced that " in " the event of great success " both corps were to push on.   " It is quite " possible that the resistance of the enemy might break altogether." The Canadian Corps was given the low spur south of Pys as a further objective ;   the II. Corps was to advance upon Grandcourt.   (See Sketch A.)

[2] Reserve Army Intelligence had not entirely succeeded in elucidating the German order of battle.   Opposite the Canadians was the *7th Division* (*393rd, 72nd* and *26th Regiments* from east to west) ;   next came the *8th Division* (*93rd, 165th* and *153rd Regiments*), holding from Zollern Redoubt (inclusive) to the eastern edge of Thiepval ;   and then the *26th Reserve Division*, which had been in this region since the autumn of 1914, and now held Thiepval with the *77th Reserve* (attached from the *2nd Guards Reserve Division* holding the Gommecourt sector) and the *180th Regiment.* Next to the latter, between Thiepval and St. Pierre Divion was the *66th Regiment* (*52nd Division*).   [On Map 3 for " 11th R " read " 77th R."]

[3] At this time there were 20 tanks fit for service, and of these General Rawlinson had retained 12 for use in the Battle of Morval.

[4] Counting the batteries in action north of the Ancre this represents an average of one field gun (or howitzer) to every 10.5 yards of front attacked and one heavy gun (or howitzer) to every 26 yards, about the same artillery support as the Fourth Army had at Flers—Courcelette. The artilleries of the 1st, 2nd and 4th Canadian Divisions and the 18th Division supported the Canadian Corps ;   those of the 11th, 25th, 48th and 49th Divisions, with some batteries of the 2nd Division attached, supported the II. Corps.   Under the V. Corps, north of the Ancre, were the artilleries of the 39th and 2nd Divisions.

23rd September in weather unfavourable for observation, and, although visibility improved during the succeeding days, from now onward a thick mist always prevailed in the mornings and evenings. On the afternoon of the 24th September, 500 lacrymatory shells were fired into Thiepval from the west by No. 2 Special Company R.E., with the result that the German trench mortars, which had been very active, were silenced altogether by 5 P.M.[1]

As a preliminary operation, the Army had ordered the capture of Mouquet Farm, which hitherto had defied all the assaults of British, Australian and Canadian troops. On the evening of the 24th a company of the 6/York & Lancaster (32nd Brigade, 11th Division) secured the north-western corner of the expanse of rubble which was all that was to be seen of the farm above ground. Then, however, after a heavy German barrage had come down upon the British front line, a strong bombing attack, covered by accurate machine-gun fire, compelled withdrawal.

Infantry reliefs were carried out so as to bring the assaulting troops into the line as fresh as possible before dawn on the day of assault. On the night of the 22nd/23rd September the 1st Canadian Division (Major-General A. W. Currie) had taken over the left sector of the corps from the 3rd Canadian Division (Major-General L. J. Lipsett), and forty-eight hours later was relieved in the right sector by the 2nd Canadian Division (Major-General R. E. W. Turner). In the II. Corps, the 18th Division (Major-General F. I. Maxse), which had received three weeks' battle training on its way back to the Somme from Flanders and was in fine fettle, relieved the 49th Division (Major-General E. M. Perceval), south of Thiepval, on the night of the 24th/25th. The 146th Brigade (Br.-General M. D. Goring-Jones), which continued to hold the front facing eastward from Thiepval to the Ancre, came under Major-General Maxse's command. Alert and expecting a fresh attack,[2] although in ignorance as to when it would fall, the Germans had harassed by intermittent bombardment the work of digging assembly trenches and forming dumps of battle stores. Nevertheless, the assaulting troops filed into their places before dawn of the 26th without serious mishap, and, remaining immobile throughout the fine autumn morn-

---

[1] 4-inch mortars were used. Prisoners afterwards testified to the effect of the bombardment which temporarily incapacitated large numbers of men.

[2] German accounts state that the *First Army* issued a warning order on 22nd September ; also that the *180th Regiment*, in Thiepval, had seen the British digging their assembly trenches.

ing which had followed a somewhat rainy night, drew little 26 Sept.
fire from the enemy.

26TH SEPTEMBER : CANADIAN CORPS

The 2nd Canadian Division, on the right, had Br.- Map 3.
General H. D. B. Ketchen's 6th Brigade in the line.   It was Sketch
given only one objective : the German front position east 39.
and north-east of Courcelette ; but, when this was taken,
posts were to be pushed forward in order to command by
fire all approaches to the new position from the north-east
and north.   At zero hour two tanks were to arrive on the
extreme right flank near the Bapaume road and then,
turning northward, to make a wide movement round Courcelette, coming back by a route west of the village.[1]   The
28th (North-West) Battalion, which had its right on the
Bapaume road, was to gain as much ground as possible
under cover of the tank advance; but the main attack was
confided to the 29th (Vancouver) and 31st (Alberta)
Battalions, in the line north of Courcelette.

At 12.35 P.M. the shrapnel barrage came down some
fifty yards in front of the German line, and massed machine
guns contributed overhead fire in further support of the
assault : almost immediately the enemy began a vigorous
bombardment of the Canadian front and the ruins of
Courcelette.   On the right flank of the 6th Brigade the
tanks failed.   One had become ditched on the way forward,
and the other, after crossing the Canadian front line, was
hit by a shell which exploded all its ammunition and reduced
it to a total wreck.   The 28th Battalion, under heavy shell-
fire, therefore remained in its trenches.   The 29th Battalion, however, advanced at zero hour and in ten minutes
captured its objective, the German front line, where little
resistance was offered.   Most of the defenders fled, and one
machine gun was captured.[2]   The 31st Battalion did not
fare so well : smitten by machine-gun and rifle fire from
front and left flank as soon as it went forward, it could not
reach the German line except on the extreme right next to
the 29th, where one platoon and a Lewis-gun detachment
secured a footing.[3]

[1] The machines were to start from a concealed position in the ruins
of Courcelette which they reached before daybreak.
[2] The blow had fallen upon the left of the *393rd Regiment* (*7th Division*),
holding the left of the divisional sector, its flank resting on the Bapaume road.
[3] It had encountered the front battalion of the *72nd Regiment* in the
centre of the *7th Division* front.   The regiment held on stoutly, in spite

26 Sept. The smoke of the bombardment obscured the view of observers, and the German barrage cut all telephone wires, so that it was not until after 2 P.M. that Major-General Turner heard of the success of the 29th Battalion. A few minutes later he learnt of the check to the 31st, now, with hardly an officer left, lying in shell-holes in front of its objective. At 5.40 P.M. the 6th Brigade was informed by the division that a fresh bombardment had been arranged, and that the assault must be renewed at an hour to be selected by Br.-General Ketchen. Accordingly, at 10.50 P.M., the 31st, with the assistance of a company of the 27th (City of Winnipeg) Battalion, tried again, and was successful in occupying the German front line as far as the East Miraumont road, about one hundred yards east of the junction with Courcelette Trench which ran northward over the crest. Two small counter-attacks were repulsed during the night.

A modification had been made by Lieut.-General Byng in the orders given to the 1st Canadian Division. Regina Trench,[1] the third and final objective, lay high on the reverse slope of the spur north-west of Courcelette, and farther west, at its southern bend, extended across the head of the valley leading down to Miraumont on the Ancre. Owing to the difficulty of observation some uncertainty remained as to whether the wire in front of the trench had been effectually cut, so the infantry was instructed to halt on the second objective.[2] Patrols were then to go forward, behind a protective barrage, to ascertain if the capture of Regina Trench appeared to be feasible. Major-General Currie was then to use his own discretion as regards a fresh advance, but, in any case, the enemy must be driven over the crest of the ridge.

Br.-General G. S. Tuxford's 3rd Brigade on the right of the division attacked with the 14th Battalion (R. Montreal Regiment) and the 15th Battalion (48th High-landers of Canada). The hostile batteries had opened with

---

of heavy losses, reinforcing the front line with part of its reserve battalion. Thus it maintained its position, although the troops on either flank were driven back. " Regt. No. 72 ".

[1] The German name for the trench which linked Schwaben Redoubt and the Le Sars line (2,000 yards N.E. of Courcelette) was " Staufen Riegel ". The Canadian name for it was Regina Trench ; it was known as Stuff Trench on the front of the II. Corps.

[2] On this line the 1st Canadian Division would be level with the final objective of the 11th Division (II. Corps). Both divisions were warned that no gap must be allowed to develop between the two corps as the advance progressed.

vigour a full minute earlier but failed to catch the leading 26 Sept. waves of the assault.   Rifle and machine-gun fire soon took toll of the Montreal men, who, in spite of losses, covered the 400 yards to Sudbury Trench, their first objective,[1] and captured it.   There was little close fighting and, 40 prisoners having been secured, the advance was resumed soon after 1 P.M.   By 2.40 P.M. brigade headquarters learned that the 14th Battalion had gained and was consolidating its final objective, the eastern half of Kenora Trench, which, from the top of the spur, ran back to Regina Trench.   Next on the right, as we have seen, the 31st Battalion was checked, whilst on the left the Highlanders had been unable to keep pace.   German bombers soon attacked against both flanks of the 14th Battalion ; but they were repulsed, and attempts to counter-attack from the front were likewise defeated, the Montrealers holding on grimly under a heavy bombardment.   They were reinforced later by a company of the 16th Battalion (Canadian Scottish).

The 15th Battalion, having formed up in the open beyond its assembly trenches as soon as the creeping barrage fell, met with unexpected resistance at the outset from a forward position on the right.   Here the Germans were only quelled by sheer hard fighting which cost many officers and men.   Undeterred, the Highlanders went on and secured their first objective, pushing forward again, after a short pause, and dealing in their progress with German machine gunners and snipers ensconced in shell-holes and short lengths of trench.   By the middle of the afternoon the battalion was digging in practically on the line of the second objective, which lay just short of the crest and did not coincide with any German trench.   Later, the right flank got in touch with the 14th Battalion, and the left linked up with the 2nd Brigade.   In the evening another company of the 16th Battalion came forward to stiffen the line.[2]

The 2nd Brigade (Br.-General F. O. W. Loomis) attacked with its left on the Pozières—Grandcourt road, of which the farther side marked the corps boundary.   The line of advance lay across the eastern end of the highest part of the ridge, to the head of the valley leading northward to Miraumont ; flanking the objectives were the commanding

---

[1] It was so named in the operation orders of the battalion, although a corps map shows this trench as beyond the first objective.

[2] About 8.30 P.M. the headquarters of the 13th Battalion (R. High-landers of Canada), in brigade reserve in Courcelette, was struck by a shell, which also exploded a store of petrol.   Lieut.-Colonel V. C. Buchanan was killed, and the whole of the headquarters personnel killed or injured.

26 Sept. Zollern and Stuff Redoubts, so that the early capture of these strongholds by the 11th Division of the II. Corps was of the greatest importance to the Canadians.

The 5th (Western Cavalry) Battalion and 8th Battalion (90th Rifles), each with a company of the 10th Battalion attached, went forward in splendid style, although the rear waves of the assault were caught by the German barrage before they were clear of the front line. Almost at once, the 8th suffered from enfilade machine-gun fire from the left. The Germans in Zollern Trench, leading to Zollern Redoubt, seemed, however, to be taken by surprise, and this, the first objective, was soon secured except on the left flank, where the assistance of the 10th Battalion was required. About one hundred prisoners were taken, and before 1 P.M. the battalions were forming up beyond Zollern Trench in readiness for a further advance. The 5th Battalion now found the creeping barrage too slow, but the second objective, Hessian Trench—a continuation of the line of the final objective allotted to the 11th Division —was captured without much difficulty all along the line.[1]

On the right, the 5th Battalion was in touch with the 3rd Brigade, but the other flank remained exposed to such accurate bursts of machine-gun fire from the II. Corps area, that two platoons of the 10th Battalion, going forward to reinforce Zollern Trench, were almost annihilated. There was no sign of the 11th Division in either Zollern or Hessian Trenches, and eventually a party of the 10th Battalion bombed along Zollern Trench and established a barricade.[2] Conflicting reports were received from patrols as to the state of the wire in front of Regina Trench and the strength of the defenders. Meanwhile, machine-gun fire from the west had made untenable the left portion of Hessian Trench, so that the 8th Battalion, much reduced in numbers, was now holding only the right half of its second objective. About 4 P.M. Br.-General Loomis ordered a defensive flank to be dug from Hessian Trench back to Zollern Trench, and for this purpose succeeded in obtaining sappers and pioneers from the 3rd Canadian Division, in corps reserve. The bulk

---

[1] German regimental accounts admit that the attack of the 3rd and 2nd Canadian Brigades destroyed the front battalion of the *26th Regiment* (right of the *7th Division*) and most of the support battalion. The survivors, with two companies of the reserve battalion, then manned Regina Trench, being responsible for a frontage of 1,700 yards.

[2] On this flank the 2nd Canadian Brigade was engaged with the *93rd Regiment* (left of the *8th Division*), whose left rested some distance east of Zollern Redoubt.

of the work, however, was done by the 7th Battalion 26 Sept.
(1st British Columbia), which took over the left flank at
10.30 P.M. Twenty minutes later, the division informed
the brigade that troops of the 11th Division were in
Hessian Trench east of Stuff Redoubt—as a matter of
fact, the situation in this area was not nearly so favourable
—and that the remainder of the trench must be occupied
at daybreak next morning in order to link up the line.

The results of the day were not considered unsatisfactory by the Canadian Corps, for the main attack,
delivered by the 1st Canadian Division, had almost reached
the crest of the ridge.[1] At 6 P.M. Lieut.-General Byng
informed General Gough by telephone that, " on the whole ",
the situation was good, and that, although both attacking
brigades of the 1st Canadian Division had lost heavily,
there were plenty of troops available. The Canadian left
flank was, perhaps, the chief anxiety, but the II. Corps
promised later that the situation here should be restored by
the 11th Division, which would employ fresh troops to do so.

26TH SEPTEMBER : II. CORPS

On the right, the 11th Division (Lieut.-General Sir C. L.
Woollcombe) had for its final objective Hessian Trench,
situated on the highest part of the ridge, and also Stuff
Redoubt ; but strong patrols were eventually to go forward
and occupy, " if possible ", Stuff Trench—the continuation
of Regina Trench. Next to the Canadians, the 34th
Brigade (Br.-General J. Hill) had first to carry Mouquet
Farm ; then to fight its way up the old German 2nd
Position and capture Zollern Redoubt ; and, finally, to
secure Stuff Redoubt. Two tanks were to assist in the
reduction of these centres of resistance,[2] but, as will be
seen, neither entered the fight.

The brigade attacked with the 8/Northumberland
Fusiliers and 9/Lancashire Fusiliers, a bombing party of the
last-named battalion seizing the known exits from the
cellars of Mouquet Farm thirty seconds before zero hour.

---

[1] According to German regimental accounts, the enemy had hoped to
counter-attack, but Captain Vethacke, commanding the battle sector of
the *26th Regiment*, reported that only a big operation with adequate forces
would be of any use. The requisite troops were not available, and at
8 P.M. Army headquarters ordered Regina Trench and the Le Sars line to
be held, withdrawals to this position to begin at 2 A.M. next morning.

[2] From their positions west of Pozières the machines were to move on
Mouquet Farm, where they were timed to arrive at zero hour. Their route
was then northward into the German 2nd Position.

26 Sept. Both battalions reached and occupied the first objective—a line astride the old German 2nd Position south of Zollern Redoubt—without many casualties. The rear waves barely escaped the German barrage which came down promptly upon the British front line and caused considerable loss, including all four company commanders, to the columns of the 5/Dorset moving forward in support. After the prescribed halt of ten minutes—too short a time, according to the Lancashire Fusiliers, in which to clear the trench and dispose of prisoners—the advance was resumed in the teeth of accurate machine-gun and rifle fire from Zollern Redoubt, Hessian Trench and Stuff Redoubt.

Pressing on most gallantly, although officers and men fell fast, the Northumberland Fusiliers became engaged in a desperate struggle around the deep dug-outs of the old German 2nd Position, including the southern half of Zollern Redoubt. Cohesion was lost, the " moppers up " were killed and wounded almost to a man, and the sole remaining officer could do no more than collect some fifty men and dig in on the right facing Zollern Trench. This remnant had made itself tolerably secure by nightfall, by which time a few of the other survivors were ensconced in shell-holes to the west of the old German 2nd Position. Only five men survived of the platoon which moved up the sunken Pozières—Grandcourt road with orders to keep in touch with the Canadian left, and these eventually mingled with the Dominion troops. The right of the Lancashire Fusiliers had been almost annihilated by fire from Zollern Redoubt, and heavy fighting ensued in Midway Line—the trench which connected Mouquet Farm with Schwaben Redoubt—where the Germans had emplaced six trench mortars. Few men and only one officer reached the battalion's second objective, Zollern Trench,[1] where they secured a footing but were out of touch on either flank. The leading companies of the 5/Dorset had reached High Trench, the German front line, and parties pushed on to mingle with what was left of the two battalions of Fusiliers.[2]

[1] The western portion of Zollern Trench linked up the redoubt of that name with Thiepval.

[2] " Regt. No. 93 " states that its companies in Zollern Redoubt, and in Zollern Trench farther east, held on, a defensive artillery barrage supplementing their rifle and machine-gun fire, until the advance of the Canadian left made the position precarious ; the survivors eventually retired " as " best they could " to Stuff Trench, which was named by the divisional commander as the new line of defence, but advanced positions were not to be given up. The evacuation of Zollern Redoubt appears to have been carried out during the night.

Here also it was impossible to follow the progress of 26 Sept. the advance owing to the smoke of the German bombardment, and also to the fact that the infantry had found movement over the open to be almost impossible on account of the hostile fire.   Before 1.30 P.M. it was reported that the second objective had been gained, and an hour later, following the receipt of other over-optimistic messages, Br.-General Hill ordered a section of Vickers guns and one section of the 86th Field Company R.E. to the northern side of Zollern Redoubt in order to consolidate it.   Soon afterwards the commanding officers of the two Fusilier battalions, having received no news of their companies, started forward to ascertain the situation.   They discovered some scattered parties in what has been described as " an empty " battlefield " ;   hostile machine guns in Zollern Redoubt were active and there were bursts of machine-gun fire from the Germans in Mouquet Farm.

At the farm, amongst the rubble heaps and at the cellar entrances, confused fighting persisted, a party from the 11/Manchester, in brigade reserve, having relieved that of the Lancashire Fusiliers.   Both tanks had become ditched before reaching the farm, but the crew of one arrived to take part in the struggle, using their machine guns with some effect ;   men of the 5/Dorset also assisted and a detachment of the 6/East Yorkshire (Pioneers) arrived to join them.   At length, about 5.30 P.M., smoke bombs were thrown into the cellars whereupon the survivors of the garrison, an officer and 55 other ranks, surrendered.[1]

Darkness fell upon a scene of great confusion.   Little authentic information had reached brigade and divisional headquarters, where, for a time, it was believed that the final objective had been reached in the afternoon.   Whilst awaiting a clearer report of the situation, the Dorsetshire were ordered to make good Zollern Redoubt and establish touch with the Canadians.   Lieut.-Colonel C. C. Hannay, commanding the battalion, who reached a point south of the redoubt a little before midnight, then set about the difficult task of collecting his companies.   By this time the 11/Manchester had three companies in and just beyond the German front line.

Next on the left, the 33rd Brigade (Br.-General J. F. Erskine) had the easier task of attacking up the head of the Nab valley.   The frontage of 1,000 yards diminished to

---

[1] *No. 6 Coy* of the *165th Regiment,* holding the centre of the *8th Division.*

26 Sept. 500 on the final objective, and, in consequence, fewer troops were employed, arrangements being made to reinforce them at need.　When the 9/Sherwood Foresters and 6/Border Regiment had taken the first objective—Schwaben Trench, which ran from Mouquet Farm to Thiepval—the Border Regiment was to consolidate it.　Three companies of the Foresters were to go on and secure Zollern Trench—between Midway Line and Thiepval—and two companies would then advance to the final objective.

All went well at the start, although the Foresters pressed on too quickly, and suffered casualties from the creeping barrage.　Joseph Trench, the German front line, was taken without difficulty, and at 12.45 P.M. the two battalions entered the first objective, from which two machine guns fired until the last moment.　Here all resistance was soon overcome, the Border Regiment then proceeding to consolidate the whole line.　Over a hundred prisoners were sent back,[1] and about 1 P.M. the Foresters resumed the advance, being lost to view over the sky-line.　On the right, the dug-outs in Midway Line, full of Germans who refused to come out, were bombed effectively, and in little more than half an hour Zollern Trench was taken, with nearly two hundred prisoners and three machine guns. The reserve company of the Foresters came forward to reinforce, and an hour later the advance on the final objective began.

Communication by runners, contact aeroplane, even by visual signalling, had been well maintained, and soon after 4 P.M. Br.-General Erskine learned that Hessian Trench, the final objective, was taken and 40 more Germans made prisoner.　Machine-gun fire from Zollern Redoubt had, however, prevented the occupation of 250 yards of Hessian Trench on the right flank, and, although parts of all four companies of the Foresters were now in the final objective, reinforcements were still required.　The battalion was in touch on the left with the 53rd Brigade (18th Division) in Zollern Trench, but not in Hessian Trench.　The 7/South Staffordshire, was employed in clearing communications to the new front, but also subdued some parties of the enemy who had continued to hold out in Midway Line.　Four platoons of the battalion were sent forward in the early evening to Hessian Trench, where they assisted to repel a bombing attack from the right.　For the 33rd Brigade, the

---

[1] By 2 P.M., 6 officers and 95 other ranks, belonging to the *153rd, 165th* and *93rd Regiments*, had passed brigade headquarters.

day may be said to have gone well : casualties, mostly wounded, amounted to less than 600—of these, more than half were sustained by the Foresters—and the reserve battalion, 6/Lincolnshire, was still in hand, although it had supplied many men for carrying parties.[1]

The 53rd Brigade (Br.-General H. W. Higginson), which formed the right of the 18th Division attack, had also to advance from the Nab valley, but its objectives included the eastern portion of Thiepval, so that the left battalion had to move up the spur where the ruins of the village stood. Beyond Thiepval the highest portion of the ridge jutted forward into the centre of the line of advance, the final objective—that portion of Midway Line connecting Hessian Trench with Schwaben Redoubt—lying just beyond the brow.

At zero hour, the 8/Suffolk and 10/Essex, each with platoons of the 8/Norfolk attached as " moppers up ", pushed forward quickly, and were clear of their assembly trenches before the barrage lifted. They thus escaped the German barrage, which, as anticipated, fell upon the British front line a few minutes later.[2] The Suffolk, who are reported to have " moved and fought with great pre-" cision ", swept over the German front line with ease, many of the enemy running forward unarmed to surrender. Within twelve minutes of the start, the first objective, Schwaben Trench, was occupied, the enemy resistance being easily overcome. On the left the Essex kept pace in similar style, and found in the sunken road running through Thiepval [3] numbers of Germans who appeared to be waiting to surrender.[4] The appearance of a tank undoubtedly contributed to this frame of mind, but the machine became ditched soon afterwards in Schwaben Trench.[5]

---

[1] The success of the 33rd Brigade had been obtained against the left of the *153rd Regiment* and the right of the *165th*. German regimental accounts state that 1½ battalions of the *153rd Regiment* (holding the right of the *8th Division*, with its flank on the eastern edge of Thiepval) were destroyed. The 53rd Brigade of the 18th Division shared in this success.

[2] By Br.-General Higginson's orders, the reserve battalion, 6/R. Berkshire, was kept back instead of automatically occupying the vacated assembly trenches, and likewise escaped the enemy fire.

[3] The Pozières—St. Pierre Divion road. As the Essex entered Thiepval the Germans released two pigeons : but it was nearly 30 minutes before the enemy artillery opened on the ruins of the village.

[4] The 53rd Brigade was engaged with the right of the *153rd Regiment*, and also with part of the *77th Reserve Regiment* (left of the *26th Reserve Division*), both of which suffered very heavy loss.

[5] From their places of concealment farther down the Nab valley, two tanks were to move on the eastern end of Thiepval, afterwards making for

26 Sept.　　After halting for the prescribed ten minutes on the first objective, the two battalions, still in excellent shape, advanced to the line of Zollern Trench and occupied it without much trouble by 1.15 P.M., the Suffolk linking up with the Foresters of the 33rd Brigade, and the Essex soon discovering troops of the 54th Brigade on the north-eastern side of Thiepval.　The creeping barrage was excellent, and the destructive bombardment appeared to have crushed the hostile snipers and machine gunners, so that losses at this stage were comparatively slight.

The advance up the hill to the final objective proved a sterner ordeal.　The Suffolk covered about two hundred and fifty yards, and were then checked by rifle and machine-gun fire from front and flanks.　Attempts were made to dig in among the shell-holes, but movement was practically impossible until dusk, when a withdrawal to Zollern Trench was carried out.　The Essex could do no better, for they were enfiladed from the north-western corner of Thiepval, which still defied the efforts of the 54th Brigade, and they also came under heavy fire from Bulgar Trench and Martin Trench.[1]　An effort to bomb up these trenches was made in the evening, but accomplished little.　The 8/Norfolk had been collected in Schwaben Trench, and Major-General Maxse had warned the brigade that it might be required to renew the attack that night.　At 6.20 P.M., however, Br.-General Higginson was able to inform his battalions that further operations were postponed until the morrow.

To the 54th Brigade (Br.-General T. H. Shoubridge) fell one of the most difficult tasks of the day : the capture of the western half of Thiepval and the original German front system.　The final objective was Schwaben Redoubt,[2] which crowned the top of the ridge nearly half a mile Sketch A. beyond the village.　In the valley north of Mesnil, the batteries of the 49th Division fired their barrage in enfilade to the line of the infantry advance ; the ridge between Mesnil and Hamel offered excellent, if rather distant, observation, as it had done on the 1st July.[3]

The 12/Middlesex, attacking on the major portion of the

Schwaben Redoubt.　One machine became ditched before it could get into action.

[1] Communication trenches running back from Thiepval to Midway Line and Schwaben Redoubt, respectively.

[2] Taken and held all day by the 36th (Ulster) Division on 1st July. See " 1916 " Vol. I., p. 403.

[3] See " 1916 " Vol. I., p. 399.

26 Sept.

Map 3.
Sketch
39.

narrow frontage allotted to the brigade, was to go through Thiepval, whilst one company of the 11/Royal Fusiliers advanced up the German front system. The Fusiliers also provided a company to follow the Middlesex and clear all dug-outs and cellars as far forward as the second objective, a line beyond the village. In the final stages of the advance another Fusilier company would take up this task, the remaining company of the battalion being available to reinforce wherever needed. The 6/Northamptonshire, in close support, could be used if necessary to effect the capture of the final objective ; the 7/Bedfordshire was kept in reserve. Two tanks, concealed in Caterpillar Copse—south of Thiepval Wood—were to move eastward in time to arrive with the infantry at the remains of Thiepval château, situated at the south-western end of the village. After lending assistance at this point, the machines were to move on Schwaben Redoubt, in co-operation with the two from Nab Valley, on the right flank of the brigade.

The assault started well, for here, as elsewhere, the leading waves anticipated zero hour by getting clear of their assembly trenches before the German barrage came down. First to gain contact with the enemy were the Fusiliers in the original German front line, where a stern struggle was waged with rifle, bayonet, bomb, Lewis gun and machine gun, amid the chaos of shattered trenches and unsuspected dug-outs still intact. The Middlesex went on unchecked until they approached the edge of Thiepval ; machine-gun fire from the ruins of the château then held up the advance until a tank arrived and crushed all resistance.[1]

The right of the Middlesex now forged ahead steadily, but the left made slower progress, the tank soon becoming ditched in Thiepval. Fighting in detached parties in the German front line, the Fusiliers found it impossible to keep pace with the barrage. The leading company had been reinforced by another and the reserve " mopping up " company was pushed in to fill a gap on the frontage of the Middlesex, whose right had swerved eastward.[2] At 1.30 P.M. the German barrage was still heavy upon the assembly trenches, through which the Northamptonshire were moving.

---

[1] German accounts confirm the prompt effect of tank action here. The other machine had become ditched and took no part.

[2] Lieut.-Colonel C. C. Carr, commanding the 11/Royal Fusiliers, and his adjutant, were both wounded about 1 P.M.

26 Sept. The leading parties of the Fusiliers on the left [1] eventually reached the first objective, a line passing through the centre of Thiepval. At 2.30 P.M. Lieut.-Colonel F. A. Maxwell, commanding the Middlesex, who had established his headquarters at the château, reported to the brigade that his right was on the second objective—that is beyond the village—but that his left was held up. The precise situation was not easily determined, since the two battalions, much mixed together, were still fighting for isolated points in the German defences.[2] Another message from the Middlesex, received by pigeon at 3.20 P.M., stated that the two battalions were " practically expended ", and raised the question of putting in fresh troops. This information was at once transmitted by the brigade to Major-General Maxse, with the suggestion that a new bombardment was necessary before attempting to carry on the advance. Meanwhile a defensive barrage was put down on an east and west line through the cemetery, 150 yards beyond the northern edge of Thiepval.

The 6/Northamptonshire was now beginning to arrive in the vicinity of the château, but German shell-fire had already caused the battalion heavy loss, Colonel G. E. Ripley being mortally wounded. As fast as the companies appeared they were sent forward to reinforce both Middlesex and Fusiliers, their advance from the château coming under heavy fire from machine guns and snipers. When darkness fell all available men of the three battalions, under Lieut.-Colonel Maxwell, the only surviving battalion commander, were reorganized to hold and consolidate a continuous line which, on the right, was just clear of the village. The northwestern corner of Thiepval and the German front trenches facing west beyond the first objective still remained in enemy hands, and bombing encounters persisted at various points until a late hour.[3]

---

[1] A notable capture in the old German front line was an elaborate telephone headquarters, described as " palatial ".

[2] A certain amount of information was received by brigade headquarters from special O.P.'s of the 146th Brigade in the British front line facing east. Eventually, the 7/Bedfordshire in Thiepval Wood established regular communication with Lieut.-Colonel Maxwell by runner post.

[3] Gerster states that the commander of the *I./180th Regiment* was last seen near the church in the centre of Thiepval, where he and the men with him, refusing to surrender, were overwhelmed. According to German regimental accounts, the whole of Thiepval was evacuated, the new line of defence being some distance from the northern edge of the village, and extending on the left by way of Bulgar Trench to the British final objective.

Just before 6 P.M. divisional headquarters announced that it was not proposed to attempt a further advance that night.   Half an hour later a message ordered a renewal of the attack next morning by the 54th Brigade, to which would be attached one battalion of the 146th Brigade [1] and one of the 55th Brigade. About midnight, however, Br.-General Shoubridge was informed that the attack upon the Schwaben Redoubt would not be undertaken before the afternoon of the 27th, and would probably be deferred until the 28th.

The 54th Brigade had done all that could be expected in a fight where the prowess of the individual soldier largely decided the issue.   For the most part, the enemy fought to the death ;   he was only to be overcome by desperate courage, skill-at-arms, and the enterprise of small groups of men, often led by privates after officers and N.C.O.'s had been killed or wounded.   At one point, Private F. J. Edwards of the Middlesex rushed forward alone and bombed a machine gun whose fire was holding up the advance and threatened to compel a withdrawal.   At another critical moment, Private R. Ryder, of the same battalion, brought his Lewis gun into action under a hail of bullets and cleared a German trench.[2]   These were not isolated acts : they typify the fighting spirit of the three battalions which on this day sustained 840 casualties out of a total strength of 2,290 officers and men.

As on so many previous occasions, the day's operations had resulted in a partial success.   Both the Canadians and the II. Corps had made a notable advance at some points ; but, although the enemy's losses were heavy, the most commanding positions on the Thiepval ridge remained in his hands, and he still appeared to be capable of a vigorous resistance.   At 8.45 P.M. the Reserve Army announced by telegram that " all objectives given in to-day's operations " hold good for to-morrow ".   Furthermore, General Gough, who was still uncertain whether the 11th Division had carried Stuff Redoubt, called upon the II. Corps " to clear " up the situation all along the front and get into touch with " the Canadian Corps during the night ".

[1] Patrols of this brigade were out in No Man's Land in observation of the Germans still occupying their front line west of Thiepval.
[2] Both men received the V.C., the award to Pte. Ryder being also in recognition of his gallant conduct in the subsequent fighting.

27TH–30TH SEPTEMBER : CANADIAN CORPS

Map 3.
Sketch 39.

27 Sept.

Lieut.-General Byng, who still had no precise information as to the situation of his forward troops, was first
concerned to link up his line with the right of the II. Corps,
and to complete the capture of the first objective opposite
the 2nd Canadian Division. In a message despatched to
divisions about midnight of the 26th/27th September these
operations were stated to be preparatory to the assault of
Regina Trench, which Major-General Currie, commanding
the 1st Canadian Division, was to carry out when he was
ready. Soon after 7 A.M. on the 27th September corps
headquarters were informed of the result of the 6th Brigade
(2nd Canadian Division) attack, made at 10.50 P.M. on the
26th.[1] Later Major-General Turner proposed a fresh attack
north-eastward to complete the capture of his 6th Brigade's
objective ; but the situation was unexpectedly eased by
the withdrawal of the Germans near Courcelette.

A heavy hostile bombardment had persisted all night
and continued throughout the morning which was fine.
Early in the afternoon, by which time rain had set in, the
28th (North-West) Battalion, right of the 6th Brigade,
discovered that the enemy was retiring, and began to push
forward patrols. At 6 P.M. the 29th (Vancouver) Battalion,
in occupation of the German front line beyond Courcelette,
reported a similar movement and acted likewise. The
28th Battalion maintained touch with the left of the
III. Corps (Fourth Army) on the right ; on the left it
joined hands with posts of the 29th Battalion established
in North and South Practice trenches, two training grounds
which lay 400 yards north-east of the captured German front
line. Flares were seen in the Le Sars line, and some successful encounters with enemy patrols ensued. The 31st
(Alberta) Battalion was now able to occupy, without
fighting, the remainder of the previous day's objective,
and patrols began to work northward, prisoners of the
72nd and *165th Regiments* being sent back.[2] Later in the

[1] See page 396.
[2] " Below Stellung " (the Le Sars line) and " Staufen Riegel " (Regina
Trench) now formed the German line of resistance. By 7.30 A.M. the *72nd
Regiment* is said to have completed its dispositions in the eastern end of
Regina Trench, troops in forward positions having been withdrawn.
Heavy losses had been sustained and the *1./93rd Regiment* (from Group
reserve in Warlencourt) reinforced the *III./72nd* in Regina Trench in the
afternoon. The *III./165th* (from the *8th Division*) had also been put in.

evening, when very few German guns were firing, the 27th 27 Sept. (City of Winnipeg) Battalion, which had reinforced the 31st, was instructed to carry out a more extended reconnaissance in order to ascertain if Regina Trench were still occupied. A troop of the corps cavalry regiment [1] was ordered forward to the right flank, with instructions to patrol towards Destremont Farm, beyond the Army boundary, at dawn of the 28th.

The 1st Canadian Division had a less satisfactory day. By 3 A.M. on the 27th the parties of the 14th Battalion (R. Montreal Regt.) holding Kenora Trench had lost two-thirds of their numbers, and, with so few men available, had been unable to maintain touch with the 15th Battalion (48th Highlanders) on their left. Being thus isolated, the only remaining officer decided to withdraw to a support trench which had been dug some one hundred and fifty yards in rear. This was done without difficulty, all the wounded being brought back. During the morning, however, two platoons of the 16th Battalion (Canadian Scottish) arrived, and Kenora Trench was then reoccupied without opposition. In the afternoon a heavy hostile bombardment began, and, about 6 P.M., a bombing counter-attack from the left was only repulsed with difficulty. About two hundred Germans were then seen massing on the right under cover of machine-gun fire which enfiladed the position, and another withdrawal to the support trench was therefore made.

Lieut.-General Byng, however, required Kenora and Regina Trenches to be in Canadian hands before the contemplated relief of the 3rd Brigade by the 5th Brigade of the 2nd Canadian Division. Accordingly, when Major-General Currie was informed of the second withdrawal, about 7.45 P.M., he said that Kenora Trench must be reoccupied " even if it required the last man in the brigade to " do it ". As a consequence, the brigade, at 8 P.M., ordered the 14th Battalion, although very weak in numbers and hardly capable of further effort, to make a fresh advance. Lieut.-Colonel R. P. Clark, the commanding officer, believed that the troops on his left were to co-operate in the new attack. This, however, was not the case ; for the 15th Battalion, which had been lying all day close under the crest of the spur where it escaped most of the hostile shell-fire, began to hand over to the 24th Battalion (Victoria

[1] A composite unit formed from the 19th Alberta Dragoons and 1st Canadian Hussars.

27-28 Rifles) of the 5th Brigade soon after dark. It was not until
Sept. 2 A.M. next morning, 28th September, that Lieut.-Colonel
Clark, with such force as he could assemble, delivered his
attack upon Kenora Trench. About seventy-five men went
forward through rain and mud against an alert enemy who
put down an artillery and machine-gun barrage which made
success impossible.[1]

In the early hours of the 27th September patrols of the
7th Battalion (1st British Columbia) of the 2nd Brigade
had pushed westward along Hessian Trench into the II.
Corps area and encountered neither British nor German
troops; but by the time a whole company of the
Canadians arrived to take possession, the enemy had
reoccupied the trench. He was promptly attacked and
driven westward towards Stuff Redoubt and northward
to Stuff Trench, but later in the morning returned in
considerable force. Fighting continued until a Canadian
barricade was firmly established at the corps boundary in
Hessian Trench. Meanwhile touch had been gained with
the 11th Division in Zollern Trench, but machine-gun fire
from Stuff Redoubt swept the area between Zollern and
Hessian trenches all day. At 11 P.M. the 8th Brigade
(Br.-General J. H. Elmsley) of the 3rd Canadian Division,
began to take over the line from the 2nd Brigade.[2]

During the night of the 27th/28th September, it was
reported that infantry patrols had been checked by a heavy
German barrage placed east of the Practice trenches; other
messages indicated that Regina Trench in the neighbourhood of Courcelette Trench had been abandoned by the
Germans. At dawn on the 28th a cavalry patrol rode out
through the right of the 28th Battalion, which was establishing itself in the German front line north of the Bapaume
road, but at once drew machine-gun fire from Destremont
Farm.

After a rainy night the sun was only seen at intervals
during the day. The sodden ground and the heavy

---

[1] " Regt. No. 26 " states that the situation was obscure on the evening
of the 27th ; there had been heavy losses and the troops were much intermixed. " Reinforcements arrived in numbers sufficient to prevent the
" English advancing farther." That part of Regina Trench faced by the
1st Canadian Division was eventually held by some of all three battalions
of the *26th Regiment* and of *I./153rd*, with various pioneer detachments.
The sector was transferred to the *8th Division* during the afternoon.

[2] " Regt. No. 93 " states that Hessian Trench east of Stuff Redoubt
was held all day, several attacks being repulsed.

shelling of the Canadian forward area delayed the move- ment of troops and hampered communication with the front line.[1] Br.-General Ketchen had been informed by his divisional commander at 12.15 A.M. that the 19th (Central Ontario) and 21st (E. Ontario) Battalions (4th Brigade) and the 26th (New Brunswick) Battalion (5th Brigade) would be sent up to press the advance.

On the extreme right the 19th moved forward east of Courcelette about 7 A.M., and found its progress towards Destremont Farm checked by a hostile protective barrage ; but a line was eventually established, facing north-east, beyond the Practice trenches. The 26th Battalion, which reached Courcelette at 5.30 A.M. and, after passing through the 31st Battalion, advanced astride Courcelette Trench about 7 A.M., was checked by galling machine-gun fire from Regina Trench. A fresh bombardment was asked for, but another attempt to advance, made at 3 P.M., fared no better. Again at 8.30 P.M. the attack was renewed, but all to no purpose, and the 26th Battalion, which had lost 200 of all ranks, then relieved the 31st on the line of the first objective.[2]

The right of the 26th Battalion, which rested on the East Miraumont road, about one hundred yards east of Courcelette Trench, became the right of the 5th Canadian Brigade, for after the abortive attack made by the remnants of the 14th Battalion at 2 A.M. on the 28th, no time had been lost in completing the relief of the 3rd Brigade—and of the 1st Canadian Division—the 25th Battalion (Nova Scotia Rifles) replacing Lieut.-Colonel Clark's unit.[3] The 2nd Canadian Division, having thus extended its front westward, now had two brigades in the line. Command of its right sector passed to the 4th Brigade (Br.-General R. Rennie), the troops of the 6th Brigade being gradually withdrawn after the 19th Battalion had carried forward the advance. The 21st Battalion, which had come in to link up the advance

---

[1] German regimental accounts say that the morning mist hampered the advance of the Canadian right, little movement being observed until after aeroplane reconnaissance became possible.

[2] " Regt. No. 26 " mentions two attacks in the evening, both repulsed by fire. It is said that the storm-battalion of the *8th Division* was allotted to this front for the purpose of counter-attacking next morning. After midnight there arrived two companies of the *1st Marine Regiment* from Miraumont to reinforce the line.

[3] The latter had lost 10 officers and 360 other ranks ; casualties in the 3rd Brigade amounted to over eleven hundred. During the month of September the 1st Canadian Division reported the loss of 6,254 of all ranks.

28 Sept. of the 19th and 26th, relieved the 29th Battalion in the centre of the brigade front during the afternoon.

Optimistic and misleading reports of the progress made by the 26th Battalion had meanwhile resulted in the 25th and 24th Battalions—centre and left of the 5th Brigade—being ordered to push patrols into Regina Trench, which was to be occupied " if possible ". The 24th tried to bomb in from the west whilst two companies attempted a frontal attack, but the enterprise was defeated by uncut wire and a heavy barrage.

West of the Grandcourt road, which ran north-westward from Courcelette and crossed Regina Trench at its southern angle, responsibility for the front of the 8th Brigade—held by the 1st and 2nd C.M.R.—had passed to Major-General L. J. Lipsett, commanding the 3rd Canadian Division. Arrangements were made to co-operate with an attack by the 11th Division on Hessian Trench at 6 P.M., but this operation was postponed until noon next day.

At 1 P.M. on the 28th September, the Reserve Army had issued an order which gave a series of objectives to be attained by certain dates in combination with the future attacks of the Fourth Army.[1] By the 1st October, the Canadian Corps was required to be on a line running north of the Practice trenches continuing westward to include Kenora Trench, but not Regina Trench. This position represented a very small advance from the front already held ; but no opportunity of gaining ground was to be lost, as Lieut.-General Byng impressed upon his divisional commanders when he conferred with them on the morning 29 Sept. of the 29th September.

Much rain fell on this day, but there were bright intervals. The hostile bombardment persisted, whilst the 4th Brigade, on the right, with the 19th and 21st Battalions in front, continued to consolidate its position, the 19th in touch with the left of the Fourth Army, which captured Destremont Farm about 6 A.M.[1]

The Canadian line now extended westward from the farm, to turn almost north-westward across the Dyke Road gully (running from Courcelette north-eastward between North and South Practice trenches) and thence back, almost at right angles, beyond North Practice trenches where the 21st Battalion had pushed well forward to avoid a German standing barrage. Br.-General Macdonnell, commanding

[1] See Chapter XVI.

the 5th Brigade, had received verbal instructions from
Major-General Turner to capture 1,500 yards of Regina
Trench opposite the centre of the Canadian front ; but the
brigadier urged that, before committing his infantry to the
assault, aeroplane photographs should be taken in order
to make sure that the bombardment had been effective.
Eventually, at 6 P.M., patrols were sent forward with orders
to fall back if they encountered serious resistance ; and, as
they were met by heavy fire, nothing more was attempted.[1]
At night the 22nd (Canadien Français) Battalion, attached
from the 4th Brigade, took over from the 26th, which was
judged to be in need of relief.

The 8th Brigade launched its attack at noon in combination with the advance of the 11th Division (II. Corps)
on its left.   Covered by the fire of two Stokes mortars, the
2nd C.M.R. by frontal assault secured a footing in Hessian
Trench beyond the corps boundary, and also wrested the
head of a communication trench from the enemy.   During
the afternoon the battalion was heavily shelled, and two
German counter-attacks recovered some ground which
was captured again by an effort of the Canadian bombers.[2]

The 30th September, a dull day without rain, saw no 30 Sept.
change on the front of the 4th Brigade on the right.   No
German infantry was seen in advance of the Le Sars
defences but hostile artillery fire hampered the activities
of patrols and made communication difficult.

Major-General Turner's proposals for an attack on
Regina Trench by the 5th Brigade drew fresh protests from
Br.-General Macdonnell and his battalion commanders :
these officers were unanimously of opinion that their men
were too exhausted to carry out a further operation,
pointing out that the fighting strength of the brigade was
now only 1,134.   Moreover, there were so many complaints
of the artillery " shooting short " and causing loss to the
infantry, that a fresh bombardment of the objective was interrupted in order to check the fall of the shell.   Eventually

---

[1] " Regt. No. 26 " describes an assault delivered about this time ; it
was " badly led and annihilated by barrage fire ".   A counter-attack
delivered by the *8th Division* storm-battalion in the early morning is stated
to have been " scattered by artillery fire ", probably the Canadian protective barrage.

[2] In this fighting, the C.M.R. and the 32nd Brigade (11th Division)
took between them 64 prisoners belonging to the *165th* and *93rd Regiments*
and the *119th Reserve Regiment*.   Two companies of the last-named (*26th
Reserve Division*) had reinforced the line here.

30 Sept. a divisional order postponed the new assault until the 1st October. At night, however, the 22nd Battalion succeeded in digging and occupying a forward line astride Courcelette Trench.[1]

The 8th Brigade (3rd Canadian Division) in Hessian Trench was still under a heavy bombardment. Nevertheless, bombers of the 2nd C.M.R. participated in an 11th Division attack which completed the capture of this trench beyond the Canadian left; and there was also fighting at a forward bombing post on the Courcelette—Grandcourt road, which the 1st C.M.R. lost and regained. So severe was the hostile bombardment at night that the relief of the front-line troops could not be undertaken.

27TH–30TH SEPTEMBER : II. CORPS

An 11th Division order, issued at 2.15 A.M. on the 27th **27 Sept.** September, fixed 10 A.M. as the hour for the renewal of the attack. Br.-General Hill had already sent forward officers' patrols to ascertain the precise location of his forward units, **Map 1.** but it was not till after daybreak that the situation on the **Sketch** front of the 34th Brigade became at all clear to him. At **39.** 6.30 A.M. it was known that the Germans had withdrawn from Zollern Redoubt, and here the remnants of the 8/Northumberland Fusiliers were gradually collected, and later, withdrawn from the fight.[2] West of the redoubt the 9/Lancashire Fusiliers, reinforced by part of the Dorset, was able to occupy Zollern Trench as far as Midway Line. The 11/Manchester, which was now in Zollern Trench east of the redoubt and had gained touch with the Canadians, was ordered to push on at zero hour and occupy Stuff Redoubt, reported clear of the enemy, and Hessian Trench, the final objective.

From daylight onward, all movement was carried out under heavy bombardment. When the Manchester advanced at 10 A.M. they were soon stopped by accurate machine-gun fire from Stuff Redoubt and Hessian Trench, which were obviously held in strength.[3]

---

[1] " Regt. No. 26 " mentions an unsuccessful attack at 8.45 P.M. upon Regina Trench in this vicinity. The regiment, which gives its losses from 17th-30th September as 25 officers and 1,556 other ranks, was relieved at night by the *1st Marine Regiment.*

[2] Lieut.-Colonel C. E. Fishbourne, 8/N.F., was wounded by a shell on the morning of the 28th.

[3] " Regt. No. 93 " states that Hessian Trench, now the front line, was held in this sector by three of its own companies, two of *I./165th* and two of *III./153rd.*

At noon Lieut.-General Woollcombe conferred with his three brigadiers and gave verbal orders for a general attack at 3 P.M. to complete the capture of the allotted objectives. As the 34th Brigade was far spent, it was decided that two battalions of the 32nd Brigade, in reserve, should assault Stuff Redoubt and Hessian Trench, " clearing up on the " way ".   Accordingly, the 9/West Yorkshire and 6/Green Howards, which were already moving forward, prepared to attack from the line of Zollern Trench ; but a postponement of the attack was then ordered with the object of giving all concerned more time for preparation.

No word of this postponement reached the West Yorkshire.   The battalion arrived at Zollern Trench, east of the redoubt, some minutes after 3 P.M.   Although there was no sign of the Green Howards on its left, it went forward to the assault with great resolution, the barrage lifting directly the movement was seen.   New to the ground—a chaotic mass of muddy shell-holes and trenches, smashed dug-outs and broken wire—the troops swerved to the left and then, although received with fire, won a footing in the southern part of Stuff Redoubt.   The attack of the Green Howards materialized an hour later. It started without an artillery barrage,[1] and, perhaps for this reason, took the Germans in Hessian Trench west of Stuff Redoubt by surprise.   Eighty prisoners and two machine guns were taken with very little loss to the battalion, which occupied the trench in touch on the left with the 33rd Brigade, and on the right with Stuff Redoubt, where some parties mingled with the West Yorkshire.

In this fighting, parties of the 11/Manchester and 5/Dorset rendered invaluable service by carrying forward bombs which were urgently needed ; and at 9 P.M. the 11/Manchester bombed forward some distance from Zollern Redoubt along the trench leading north-eastward to the left of the Canadian Corps.   An hour later the command of the sector passed to Br.-General T. H. F. Price of the 32nd Brigade.

The 33rd Brigade which, as we have seen, held part at least of all its objectives, was principally concerned with joining up its flanks.   At 12.40 A.M. an appeal for reinforcements had arrived from the Sherwood Foresters and South Staffordshire in Zollern and Hessian trenches, so at 6 A.M.

---

[1] A barrage was put down by the LVIII. Brigade R.F.A. when it was seen that the advance had begun.

27 Sept. a company of the Border Regiment was sent forward, another following later. During the morning a bombing attack from the left flank was repulsed, and before noon the Staffordshire bombers, pushing eastward along Zollern Trench, had linked up with the 34th Brigade. The 3 P.M. attack took the form of a frontal assault by one company of the Border Regiment on the uncaptured portion of Hessian Trench which was secured, together with 64 prisoners and two machine guns. Later, the right linked up with the Green Howards of the 32nd Brigade,[1] and the Border Regiment then took over the whole of the brigade front. Heavy hostile shelling of Hessian Trench interrupted its consolidation. After darkness fell, however, patrols reached the crest of the ridge without seeing any Germans.

Next on the left, the 53rd Brigade of the 18th Division had got well forward with the work of consolidation by 6 A.M. on the 27th, when Br.-General Higginson visited the front line. Later in the morning a strong bombing party of the 10/Essex, covered by the fire of Stokes mortars, attempted to drive the Germans back up Bulgar Trench. Some fifty yards were gained, in spite of the fact that the assault was impeded by the fire of British heavy artillery.

The 54th Brigade had arranged for the 7/Bedfordshire to take over the front now held by the other three battalions, Middlesex, Royal Fusiliers and Northamptonshire. This was to be completed by 7 A.M. on the 27th, and the Bedfordshire, supported by the 1/5th West Yorkshire (146th Brigade), were to attack the final objective at a later hour. When the exact situation of the forward troops became known, however, the relieving battalion was allotted the less arduous task of clearing, as soon as possible, the north-western corner of Thiepval. The relief, carried out with complete success, was described by Major-General Maxse as " the finest example of discipline in battle and " efficiency in a crisis yet displayed by the division " : in spite of the alteration in orders, the heavy shelling, the

---

[1] " Regt. No. 153 " states that portions of the *93rd, 153rd* and *165th Regiments* were in Stuff Redoubt, and the regimental commander was informed that it had been taken by the afternoon assault. Two fresh companies of the *153rd* were ordered up at night to recapture the redoubt, but their commander found, to his great relief, that there were still Germans in the work. His reinforcement was badly needed. Two companies of the *II./119th Reserve* (*26th Reserve Division*) are also said to have been moved forward to retake the redoubt.

darkness, and the difficult and unknown ground, two com- 27 Sept. panies of the Bedfordshire were in Thiepval, ready to assault, at 5.45 A.M.

At that hour they pressed forward with bomb and bayonet, since a sudden attack dispensing with artillery support seemed to offer the best chance of success. Rapid progress was made on the left, but the right was held up by machine-gun fire until 2/Lieut. T. E. Adlam, a formidable bomb-thrower, led a rush across the open. This onslaught, in which the officer received a wound in the leg,[1] was successful, and by 11 A.M. the Bedfordshire, who secured 70 prisoners, were consolidating a position beyond the edge of the village, in touch on the right with the 53rd Brigade.[2]

It was not until the attack had succeeded that the bulk of the other battalions, Royal Fusiliers, Middlesex and Northamptonshire, were withdrawn from the Thiepval area, a company of the 1/5th West Yorkshire then coming forward to the southern edge of the ruins in support of the Bedfordshire. These movements, carried out deliberately in broad daylight, resulted in surprisingly few casualties.

Major-General Maxse rightly judged that the assault of the final objective, including Schwaben Redoubt, stood little chance of success whilst Stuff Redoubt remained in German hands ; therefore, with corps and Army approval,[3] he postponed this enterprise until the morrow. He decided to use the battalions of the 55th Brigade as reinforcements, and now allotted the capture of Schwaben Redoubt to the 53rd Brigade, which had suffered less than Br.-General Shoubridge's command.

During the night, the 74th Brigade, from the 25th Division (Major-General E. G. T. Bainbridge) in corps reserve, relieved the 146th Brigade in the line east of the Ancre.

The 32nd Brigade, having taken over the right sector of 28 Sept. the 11th Division, was expected to complete the capture of

---

[1] 2/Lieut. Adlam, who remained in action until 28th September, when he was wounded again, received the V.C.

[2] " Regt. No. 180 " admits the loss of ground in this attack. At night Schwaben Redoubt and the approaches thereto were held from right to left by companies, all very weak in numbers and much intermixed, of the *77th Reserve, 180th* and *66th*.

[3] Both Lieut.-General Jacob and General Gough visited him on 27th September.

28 Sept. Stuff Redoubt on the 28th September, and also to link up with the Canadian left by securing Hessian Trench. Br.-General Price intended to use the 8/Duke of Wellington's, which had put two companies into Zollern Trench during the night, for the assault of Hessian Trench; at the same time, the mixed detachment of West Yorkshire and Green Howards holding on in Stuff Redoubt was to complete the capture of that work.

Zero hour was fixed for 6 P.M., but the Duke of Wellington's, hampered by heavy shell-fire and congestion in the trenches, was not ready, and the hour passed with nothing attempted. Later in the evening, however, the Yorkshiremen in Stuff Redoubt, most ably commanded by Captain A. C. T. White[1] of the Green Howards, bombed their way forward from the right and took most of the northern face of the redoubt. Unfortunately they could not hold what they had won, owing to lack of men and of bombs with which to meet the German counter-attacks.

The 33rd Brigade, heavily shelled all day, confined itself to active patrolling towards Stuff Trench, which was seen to be held in strength by the enemy.[2]

The operations of the 18th Division on the 28th are best described as a whole. Preparations for the attack of the 53rd Brigade upon Schwaben Redoubt, fixed for 1 P.M., were successfully completed under fire, forming-up places being taped on a line astride Zollern Trench, facing north-west, parallel to Bulgar Trench. On the right, the Suffolk were to take the remainder of Midway Line, whilst the 7/Queen's (attached from the 55th Brigade) stormed the redoubt. " Moppers up " were provided by the 8/Norfolk. In the 54th Brigade, the two fresh companies of the 7/Bedfordshire, were ready to attack between the redoubt and the German front system.

All started well at the appointed hour; Bulgar Trench was taken without much trouble, and, although the enemy fought stoutly in Midway Line, the Suffolk were approaching the eastern end of Schwaben Redoubt by 2.30 P.M., having secured 21 prisoners. The battalion was in touch on its right with the 11th Division. Being quite new to the ground, the Queen's were inclined to lose their bearings, and swerved too far to the left; they had some fighting

---

[1] This officer was awarded the V.C.

[2] German regimental accounts record repeated attacks against Stuff Redoubt, Hessian Trench and Stuff Trench. " Regt. No. 153 " says that " portions of our garrisons still holding on in front were gradually pressed " back to Stuff Trench ".

in Martin Trench, which led northward from Thiepval to 28 Sept.
Schwaben Redoubt, and came under galling fire from the
redoubt itself. The Bedfordshire, following the barrage
closely, came up level with the northern edge of the
cemetery, although fire from Schwaben Redoubt had taken
grievous toll of their right moving over the open.

The Queen's were now pushing the Bedfordshire towards
the left. The latter, reinforced first by their supporting
companies and then by the 1/5th West Yorkshire, waged
a grim struggle for possession of several strongpoints in
the original German front line. Progress was slow and
costly, and Br.-General Shoubridge therefore urged that
efforts should be concentrated upon the redoubt, which
commanded the slope to the west. Meanwhile the Queen's
had gained a footing in the southern face of the redoubt
and captured about fifty Germans. They also secured the
south-western corner, whence they endeavoured to advance
northward, but were obliged to establish a barricade.
West of Schwaben the front was readjusted, the Queen's
handing over their positions to parties of the Bedfordshire
and West Yorkshire.

At 3 P.M. the brigade commanders took counsel together
and agreed that the best chance now lay in pushing forward
up the western face of the redoubt. Fighting, difficult to
control in the maze of trenches and shell-holes, still continued, and by 5 P.M. the Queen's were in possession of the
whole of the southern face, in touch on the right with
the Suffolk occupying Midway Line, and on the left with
the intermingled troops of the 54th Brigade. Br.-General
Higginson now ordered consolidation, for he felt that his
troops could accomplish no more ; but farther to the left
the struggle was not yet over.

Here the Bedfordshire and W. Yorkshire began to break
down the German resistance. They not only cleared the
western face of the redoubt, but also won a trench which
faced north-west across the slope beyond. This was
accomplished by 8 P.M., at which hour fighting patrols of
the 11/Lancashire Fusiliers (74th Brigade), having crossed
No Man's Land, secured a lodgment in the German front
system. Working eastward, the Fusiliers linked up with
the left of the 54th Brigade, and sent back 30 prisoners.[1]

---

[1] " Regt. No. 66 " says that the English pressed forward on both sides
of Schwaben Redoubt, but were driven back by a counter-attack of its
I./Bn., which was almost destroyed in the subsequent fighting. The
British entered Schwaben Redoubt. During the day the sector was

28 Sept. There were spasmodic bombing encounters during the night, during which the 7/R. West Kent (from the 55th Brigade) was moving forward to take over the front of the 54th Brigade.

29 Sept.   Reference has already been made to the Reserve Army order, issued on the 28th September, regarding future objectives.   It directed that Stuff Redoubt and Schwaben Redoubt should be captured by the 29th September and Stuff Trench by the 1st October, so that neither the 11th nor the 18th Divisions could afford to relax its efforts.

In the 11th Division a fresh attempt of the 32nd Brigade to clear the enemy from Stuff Redoubt, and from Hessian Trench to the east of it, was made at noon on the 29th, when the left of the Canadians assisted.[1]   A special Stokes-mortar bombardment supplemented the creeping barrage which covered the frontal assault of three companies of the 6/York & Lancaster upon Hessian Trench.   Most of the trench was captured and the York & Lancaster joined hands with the Canadians, who gave valuable help, just inside the corps boundary ; but the Germans remained in possession of about two hundred yards of the trench immediately east of Stuff Redoubt.   Meanwhile, the in-domitable Yorkshiremen in the redoubt had made another onslaught upon its northern face and almost cleared it, but again had to withdraw when their supply of bombs ran out. In the evening this detachment repulsed a strong counter-attack upon the southern face.[2]   As the 32nd Brigade had no fresh troops at its disposal, the 33rd Brigade was now ordered to supply one battalion as reinforcement and the 7/South Staffordshire was warned accordingly.

On the front of the 18th Division, the 8/Suffolk, occupy-ing the right of the 53rd Brigade—the upper portion of Midway Line—was relieved by the 6/R. Berkshire in the early morning.   Br.-General Higginson decided that the 7/Queen's, in the southern face of Schwaben was in no condition to attack ; few of the battalion had had any sleep since the battle began, and most of the officers and N.C.O.'s were casualties.   The day was therefore devoted

---

reinforced by companies of the *91st Reserve* (*2nd Guard Reserve Division*) and *119th Reserve* (*26th Reserve Division*).

[1] See page 413.

[2] " Regt. No. 153 " states that the British attacks on this day made it impossible to withdraw the troops of the *8th Division*.   This was not accomplished until 30th September.

to reorganization and consolidation of the position, the 8/East Surrey (also of the 55th Brigade) relieving the Queen's at night.

The narrow 54th Brigade front was the scene of a continuous struggle.[1] At 6.30 A.M. the 7/R. West Kent (55th Brigade) began to take over the whole line from the western face of Schwaben Redoubt to the German front system. There was fierce fighting during the relief, and by 7.30 A.M. a hostile bombing attack had recaptured a trench junction north-west of the redoubt.[2] On the western face of Schwaben the combat continued all day, with heavy losses on both sides. German bombing attacks, each preceded by a bombardment, failed to make much impression on the West Kent, who attacked in their turn at 10 P.M., but the ground they gained could not be held, as the supply of bombs ran short. The battalion was called upon to relieve the 74th Brigade in the German front system as far west as the German front line, and this operation was completed by 3 A.M. on the morning of the 30th September.

Br.-General Sir T. Jackson (55th Brigade) had now assumed command of the whole divisional front, held by the 6/R. Berkshire (53rd Brigade) and his own 8/E. Surrey and 7/R. West Kent.

The II. Corps renewed its efforts at 4 P.M. on the 30th September. To drive the Germans from the " pocket " in Hessian Trench, three convergent bombing attacks were launched by the 11th Division after a preliminary bombardment. A party of the 6/York & Lancaster (32nd Brigade) pressed along Hessian Trench from the east ; the 7/South Staffordshire (lent by the 33rd Brigade) advanced from Zollern Trench up the old support line of the German 2nd Position ; and Captain White started his Yorkshiremen in an attack from the southern face of Stuff Redoubt. After hard fighting the enemy resistance was overcome, and before dark the 11th Division was in possession of all its objectives with the exception of the northern half of the redoubt.

At night, the 25th Division (Major-General E. G. T.

30 Sept.

---

[1] " Res. Regt. No. 119 " says that the *26th Reserve Division* ordered a counter-attack at 6 A.M. to clear the British from Schwaben. Portions of the *II./180th* and *119th Reserve* were to make it, but the morning mist and heavy shell-fire so delayed movement that it came to nothing.

[2] Nearly a whole battalion of the *180th* and two companies of the *119th Reserve* were engaged here, according to German regimental accounts.

30 Sept. Bainbridge) began the relief of the 32nd Brigade, having completed that of the 33rd Brigade by 8 P.M.[1]

The 18th Division was again heavily engaged, for at dawn a German counter-attack caught the East Surrey before they had time to settle down and drove them from the southern face of Schwaben. The position was promptly restored with the bayonet, but meanwhile the West Kent had been forced back down the western face, which remained in German hands. At 4 P.M., under cover of a heavy barrage, the East Surrey attacked the northern face, advancing astride the trenches on the right and across the open on the left. The assault was successful, the whole of the northern face being occupied, but farther to the left, two platoons of the 7/Buffs,[2] supported by the West Kent, could make no progress up the western face.[3] The inevitable counter-attack came at 9 P.M., when the very tired East Surrey in the north face were assailed from the west. They fought gamely, but were obliged to give ground as far as the entrance to Stuff Trench, where they held on.[4]

Thus at the end of September the task of the Reserve Army was not yet completed. The troops had fought with skill, courage and perseverance, but the Thiepval ridge was a position of great strength and not to be taken quickly or at light cost, provided its defenders were prepared to pay the price of a dogged and desperate resistance. British and Germans alike often maintained the struggle to the point of physical exhaustion in trenches deep in mud. The attack was not conducted as an operation of semi-siege warfare, so all depended upon infantry *élan* allied with the usual destructive bombardment and creeping barrage ; yet, on the slopes of the ridge in the confused fighting along trenches and around shell-craters and dug-outs, it was often impossible for the artillery to provide close support to the assaulting troops. In the later attacks, a greater degree of co-ordination along the whole front might have increased the prospects of success.

---

[1] The casualties of the 11th Division, 26th-30th September, were returned as 143 officers and 3,472 other ranks, about 70 per cent of these being wounded.

[2] Also 55th Brigade. The battalion was about to relieve the E. Surrey.

[3] " Regt. No. 180 " records that two companies of its *II./Bn.* repulsed this attack, inflicting and receiving heavy losses.

[4] " Res. Regt. No. 119 " describes an " encounter battle " at Schwaben Redoubt. Of two companies of the regiment, "only a very few escaped", all machine guns being put out of action.

NOTE

THE GERMAN SIDE IN SEPTEMBER [1]

At the beginning of the month Crown Prince Rupprecht viewed the shortage of men and ammunition with grave concern ; the frequent relief of the troops engaged with the British could not be avoided. Two fresh divisions—the *185th* from the *Third Army* and the *5th Bavarian* from the *Sixth*—took over the Leuze Wood— Ginchy front during the first fortnight in September ; between Martinpuich and Thiepval the *Guard Reserve Corps* was relieved by the *89th Reserve Brigade* (equivalent to a division), and the *45th Reserve Division*, both from the *Fourth Army*. By " milking " existing divisions, troops had also to be found for the Eastern theatre. Counter-attacks were contemplated to recover Delville Wood, the Pozières ridge near Mouquet Farm, and—after the 9th September —Ginchy, but there were not sufficient means for any of these enter- prises : indeed, Rupprecht became doubtful if he could withstand the Allied pressure much longer.

The new O.H.L.—Hindenburg as virtual Commander-in-Chief with Ludendorff fulfilling the functions of the Chief of the Staff— had assumed control on the 29th August to face, as it is said, " the " most serious crisis of the War ". On the 2nd September O.H.L. ordered the strict defensive at Verdun, the German Crown Prince being called upon to provide troops for the Rumanian campaign and reinforcements for the Somme. Next day, Rupprecht was informed that he would receive important reinforcements of infantry, artillery and aircraft, and also a larger allotment of ammunition. On the 5th the higher commanders on the Western Front were adjured to make proposals for the construction of rear positions with a view to shorten- ing the line and thus economizing troops.

Hindenburg and Ludendorff now paid their first visit to the Western Front. Crown Prince Rupprecht, the German Crown Prince, the Duke of Württemberg, Generals Gallwitz and Below, the Chiefs of the Staff of the Groups of Armies and Armies, Admiral Schröder, commander of the Flemish coastal area, and other officers assembled at Cambrai to meet them on the 8th September. Hinden- burg, who remarked that he had " succeeded to an evil inheritance ", said that there were no reserves for a return to the offensive except against Rumania. Kuhl, Rupprecht's Chief of the Staff, revealed the gravity of the situation on the Somme : at the end of 14 days a division's defensive value was exhausted. Yet he did not advocate a voluntary withdrawal in order to shorten the front, for such a movement, whilst the battle was in progress, was " difficult and " dangerous ".

Certain tactical questions were discussed, and Lossberg, Chief of the Staff of Below's First Army, expressed his disagreement when Luden- dorff advocated an "elastic " defence. Ludendorff considered that the infantry was in the habit of clinging to ground of no tactical value

[1] G.O.A. xi., pp. 1, 9-12, 17, 18, 30-41, 55-70, 73-9 ; Rupprecht, Luden- dorff, Gallwitz, Kuhl and Schwarte.

and lost heavily thereby ; that deep dug-outs and cellars were often " man-traps " ; that, in the infantry, hand-grenades had supplanted the rifle of which the use was " almost forgotten ". He counselled that the front line should be thinly held.

General Gallwitz, commanding the *Second Army* south of the Somme, continued to be very anxious for the safety of his line, but Rupprecht most feared a rupture at the junction of the *First* and *Second Armies*, whilst the British seemed bent on smashing the centre (Flers—Courcelette) of Below's *First Army*. He felt obliged to denude Gallwitz of reserves in order to sustain Below.

The Battle of Flers—Courcelette was a great blow to the *First Army*. On the first day, the 15th September, " a very heavy day " even according to Somme standards ", the German defence in the Flers—Gueudecourt region was " as good as completely broken " by the tanks ; but the British infantry did not follow up quickly enough and the crisis was overcome by the arrival of reinforcements. Nevertheless, the first British tank attack had severely shaken the morale of the troops who encountered it. Losses were very great.[1] During the battle all six German divisions in the line between Combles and Thiepval had to be relieved, the new arrivals, from east to west, being the *51st Reserve* and *52nd Reserve* from the *Fourth Army* ; the *6th Bavarian* from the *Fifth Army* ; and the *50th Reserve*, *7th* and *8th* from the *Sixth Army*. Gallwitz, who had prepared twenty crossings over the Somme canal and removed his heavy guns to the eastern side as a precaution against a further French advance, appealed in vain for reinforcements. The needs of the *First Army* were considered to be paramount.

On the 18th Rupprecht reported to O.H.L. that the loss of fresh portions of the front must be regarded as inevitable ; he wished to arrange a wholesale relief of the divisions engaged, but doubted if this could be completed before the middle of October : he had the organization of rear positions in mind, but work upon them was largely prevented by hostile shell-fire. Ludendorff had urged a counter-attack at Bouchavesnes to hold off the French from Mont St. Quentin, and the failure of this on the 20th September was a great disappointment. Schwarte says that it might have been better planned.

A Hindenburg " memorandum ", issued on the 21st, said that in the West the Somme front was all-important and must have first call on every available division : the German Crown Prince's Group of Armies must supply reinforcements in exchange for exhausted divisions. Next day, when Rupprecht asked for eight or ten divisions to complete his scheme of relief, the Verdun front could only promise six for exchange.

The losses suffered on the 25th and 26th (Battle of Morval) were reported to be the heaviest since the 1st July : a break-through between Bouchavesnes and Gueudecourt was threatened, so O.H.L. allotted five more divisions and a number of heavy batteries to

---

[1] The *210th Reserve Regiment* (*45th Reserve Division*), engaged against the Canadians 5th-19th September, lost two-thirds of its strength and 13 of its 18 machine guns, which consisted of 9 German, 3 French, 3 Belgian and 3 Russian weapons. The *6th Bavarian Division*, engaged with part of the British XV. Corps in the Battle of Flers—Courcelette, lost 50 per cent of its infantry, and one regiment had only 3 officers left.

" the apparently insatiable Somme front ". Ludendorff announced that the relief of divisions after 14 days in the line could only be carried out at the points where the fighting was heaviest.

More reinforcements were indeed urgently needed, for between the opening of the Battle of Morval and the end of the month Rupprecht had been obliged to put into the line all his available troops. The *7th Reserve Division* from the *Fifth Army*, and the *6th Bavarian Reserve* and *18th Reserve Divisions*, both from the *Sixth Army*, replaced the *6th Bavarian*, *50th Reserve* and *52nd Reserve*, opposite the British Fourth Army ; during the Battle of Thiepval Ridge, units of the *24th Reserve Division*, in *First Army* reserve, and of the *2nd Guard Reserve Division*, holding the Gommecourt sector, were used in the defence, other troops being brought down from the Hébuterne sector. Thus in September the Germans were obliged to put in opposite the British no less than 13 new divisions, and to use such other forces as were available.

After the fall of Thiepval, O.H.L. " without ascribing any blame ", called for a careful investigation of the cause of recent defeats. Rupprecht notes that by this time both the troops and their commanders were losing heart, and there were constant complaints of the helplessness of the infantry against the British tanks. During the month, the most costly of all in casualties, 213 train-loads of field artillery ammunition (26,880 rounds per load) and 217 train-loads of heavy artillery ammunition (6,000 rounds per load) had been expended on the Somme.

On the 6th September O.H.L., which was not wedded to " the " old mistaken policy of not yielding a foot of ground until obliged " to do so ", had announced that reconnaissance was being made for a shorter line in order to economize troops. On the 15th, when O.H.L. issued a formal order for a strict defensive on all fronts and the employment of all available forces against Rumania, Rupprecht was instructed to prepare a rear line. The position chosen ran south-eastward from Arras by St. Quentin and Laon to the Aisne ; it was calculated to shorten the front of Rupprecht's Group of Armies by some fifty kilometres, or nearly thirty-two miles, and to take about three months to complete. About the 23rd September orders were given for work to begin, and thus there gradually took shape a strong defensive system of great depth, containing a large number of concrete machine-gun emplacements and dug-outs, and planned with due regard to the experience gained in the Somme offensive. It was called the " Siegfried Stellung ", but to the British will always be known as the Hindenburg Line.

Hindenburg and Ludendorff had lost no time in taking measures for the expansion of the Army and for an increased output of munitions, both urgent needs.

Before his departure Falkenhayn had ordered the formation of seven new divisions ; during September O.H.L. arranged for the raising of 15 more, four on the Eastern Front and 11 on the Western Front. The infantry was found partly by incorporating in the field armies men " fit for garrison duty " who replaced the trained soldiers withdrawn to form the nuclei of the new divisions. The artillery was raised in Germany. In this way the total number of divisions was increased from 175 to 197.

On the 31st August O.H.L. put forward the " Hindenburg "Programme ", designed to double the ammunition output and treble that of guns and machine guns. It also proposed to organize for war the whole population of Germany, those who were not taken for service in the armed forces to be incorporated as workers on a military basis, the age limits for the Army to be extended from 19-39 to 16-60. The military training of youth and the employment of women were comprehensively provided for in this scheme. There were many administrative problems to overcome before the munitions industry could be organized upon the proposed lines, and it was not until November that a special department (*Kriegsamt*) was constituted " on the model of the British Ministry of Munitions ", under General Gröner, hitherto chief of the Field Railways. The new body assumed control of all raw materials—coal, iron and steel were included—in addition to all munitions production. There was great political opposition to O.H.L.'s proposed war organization of the whole population since the proletariat was already becoming restive under hardships and restrictions. A bill for " National Auxiliary " Service " was certainly introduced into the *Reichstag* but, as passed into law on the 5th December, it simply made all men between the ages of 17 and 60 who were not serving in the armed forces liable for war-work.

Sketch 40.

THE SOMME, 1916: 30th September.

Line at night _____
British - Red
French - Blue.
Germans - Green.

Compiled in the Historical Section (Military Branch)
3060/38.

Crown Copyright Reserved.

Scale of Miles

Ordnance Survey 1937.

CHAPTER XVI

THE SOMME 1916

(Map 4 ; Sketches A, 40, 41, 42, 43)

THE PLANS FOR OCTOBER

WITH the capture of the Thiepval ridge almost completed Sketches, and the villages of Morval, Lesboeufs and Gueudecourt A, 40. secured, Sir Douglas Haig considered it advisable to combine the action of the Reserve and Third Armies with that of the Fourth Army.[1] In a G.H.Q. letter, dated the 29th September, the Armies were instructed to begin preparations for the next big attack, which was to have the following objectives :

Fourth Army : Le Transloy, Beaulencourt, ridge beyond the Thilloy—Warlencourt valley, Loupart Wood (1 mile E. of Irles) ;

Reserve Army (attacking northward from the Thiepval ridge) : Loupart Wood (exclusive) through Irles to Miraumont ;

Reserve Army (attacking eastward from the Beaumont Hamel—Hébuterne front) : direction Puisieux, the right to meet southern advance at Miraumont, cutting off any German forces still holding out in the valley of the upper Ancre ;

Third Army : to cover the left of Reserve Army by securing spur south-east of Gommecourt.

Every effort was to be made to launch this attack by the 12th October. Meanwhile the Fourth Army was to push on north-eastward to gain possession of the spur covering Le Transloy and Beaulencourt,[2] and northward to the near side of the Thilloy—Warlencourt valley. The

---

[1] See page 391.
[2] The French did not expect to assault Sailly-Saillisel until 7th or 8th October, and it was agreed that if they were able to advance on Rocquigny before the 12th, their left should be covered by the British right.

Sept. Reserve Army was to link up the left of the above line with its position on the Thiepval ridge : Sir Douglas Haig saw no object in pushing forward at once down the ridge to the Ancre, but he pointed out that General Gough might consider the advisability of occupying the spur west of Pys. In any event, both Armies were to exert continuous pressure on the enemy, gaining ground wherever opportunity offered.

The Commander-in-Chief considered that, in normal autumn weather, the above tasks were well within the capacity of the Armies ; [1] but, as the month wore on, rain and mist and mud proved too great a handicap. The frequent failure of attacks, and the inevitable postponements and curtailments of the operations already ordered, compelled a drastic revision of the British plans.

THE FOURTH ARMY

THE BATTLE OF THE TRANSLOY RIDGES, 1ST–20TH OCTOBER [2]

Sketch 41.

The measures already taken by General Rawlinson for an advance north-eastward and northward by definite stages conformed to the immediate intentions of the Commander-in-Chief. A Fourth Army operation order, dated the 28th September, aimed at straightening the left of the front on the 1st October by the capture of Eaucourt l'Abbaye [3] and also of the Flers line [4] as far as Le Sars. This involved an attack along the whole front of the III. Corps. The New Zealand Division (XV. Corps) [5] was to

[1] Certain economies in artillery ammunition had to be ordered at the end of September, and on the 30th the Commander-in-Chief asked for R.F.C. reinforcements. At this time, the monthly wastage in fighting and long-distance reconnaissance aircraft was reckoned at 75 per cent ; moreover, the Germans were now employing faster and handier machines which threatened British supremacy in the air. See " The War in the Air " ii., pp. 296-7.

[2] The official name includes the operations of the Fourth Army 1st-18th October, but the fighting on the front of the III. Corps may be reckoned as continuous up to the 20th. Sketch 41 is provided for the initial operations at the beginning of October.

[3] Eaucourt l'Abbaye consisted of two large farms, in the same enclosure, built on the site of an Augustine abbey. Several of the ancient cellars were in good condition.

[4] This part of the German 3rd Position from Flers to beyond Le Sars was generally called so, although sometimes referred to as the Le Sars line.

[5] At the beginning of October Lieut.-General Horne assumed command of the First Army, replacing Sir C. C. Monro, who had been appointed Commander-in-Chief in India. Lieut.-General J. P. Du Cane, who

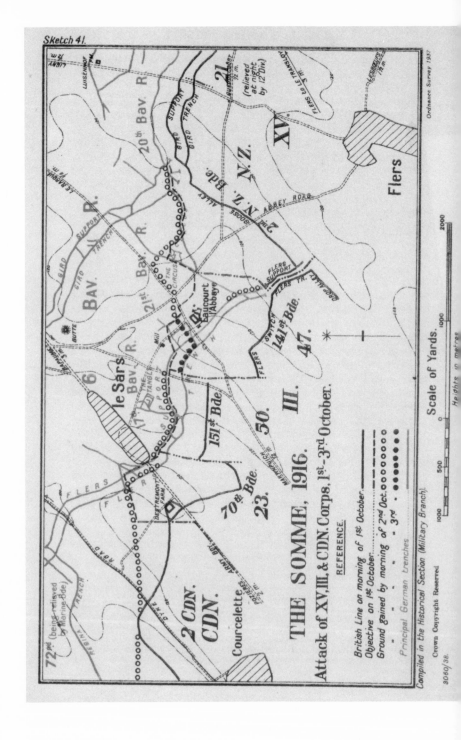

Sketch 41.

THE SOMME, 1916.

Attack of XV, III. & CDN. Corps, 1st - 3rd October.

REFERENCE.

British Line on morning of 1st October. ——————
Objective on 1st October. ————————
Ground gained by morning of 2nd Oct. ooooooooooo
" " " " 3rd • •••••••••

Principal German trenches

Scale of Yards.

Compiled in the Historical Section (Military Branch).

Crown Copyright Reserved

Ordnance Survey 1937

3060/38.

prolong the new position eastward by swinging forward its left which would pivot upon the Gird trenches 1,500 yards east of Eaucourt l'Abbaye.

On the 29th September, which brought rain with brief intervals of sunshine, the 6th Division and the Guards (XIV. Corps), occupied unopposed some trenches beyond Lesboeufs.[1] In the III. Corps, at 5.30 A.M., a company of the 8/York & Lancaster (70th Brigade, 23rd Division) stormed Destremont Farm, gaining touch with the Canadians on the left later in the day. The 1/18th London (141st Brigade, 47th Division) began to bomb up Flers Trench in the evening. On the 30th September, which was dull but fine, the battalion drove the Germans back to a point beyond Flers Switch, whilst the 2nd Rifles (N.Z. Rifle Brigade attached to the 2nd N.Z. Brigade) kept level in Flers Support.

At 7 A.M. on the 1st October,[2] a fine autumn day, a deliberate bombardment opened along the whole Army line and continued without increase in the rate of fire until zero hour, 3.15 P.M. In the captured part of the Gird lines behind the right of the attack the Special Brigade R.E. had installed 36 oil projectors, which were discharged one minute before the infantry went over. Thirty oil-drums burst satisfactorily and enveloped the greater part of the New Zealand objective in red flame and heavy black smoke.[3]

Nevertheless, the advance of the 2nd New Zealand Brigade—2/Canterbury and 2/Otago, mustering less than 850 rifles in all—was promptly greeted with machine-gun fire which caused considerable loss before the enemy position was overrun. The Canterbury, however, was soon in possession of the Gird lines at their junction with Goose Alley, also of the eastern portion of Circus Trench, which

1 Oct.

---

succeeded to the command of the XV. Corps, had been B.G.G.S. III. Corps, Artillery Adviser at G.H.Q., and, since November 1915, at the Ministry of Munitions. He had never held a command in war.

[1] On the night of 29th/30th September, the 20th Division (XIV. Corps) relieved part of the 21st Division (XV. Corps), thus extending the left boundary of the XIV. Corps to the south-eastern edge of Gueudecourt. On the following night the 56th Division relieved both the 6th Division and the Guards. Casualties returned by the 6th Division (14th-30th September) were 5,000, and by the Guards (18th-30th September), 2,340.

[2] " Summer " time ended at midnight 30th September/1st October for both the Allies and the Germans.

[3] Some prisoners complained bitterly of this method of warfare. " Bav. Res. Regt. No. 21 " states that the " *Brandbomben* " caused great havoc.

1 Oct. ran south-westward down the slope to link up with the Flers system. The Otago, attacking from Goose Alley with their left on Abbey Road, passed well beyond their shattered objective and the abandoned German strongpoint called " The Circus ".[1] The companies were rallied on the Le Barque road, and, reinforced by part of the 2/Wellington, established a line in touch near Abbey Road with the 1/19th London, of the 47th Division. The excellence of the field artillery barrage, combined with the dash of the infantry, had achieved a quick success, and the New Zealanders were not seriously disturbed in their new positions. Their losses were heavy, but they captured about two hundred and fifty prisoners.[2]

In the III. Corps, the 47th Division (Br.-General W. H. Greenly) employed the 141st Brigade, which attacked with three battalions and two tanks.[3] The 1/19th London, on the right, was checked by machine-gun fire when fifty yards from the German trenches, and waited in shell-holes for the tanks. Losses had been heavy, but it was easy to get forward after the two machines had passed along the Flers lines from right to left ; so, whilst the rear waves of the battalion began to consolidate Flers Support, the leading troops pushed on past Eaucourt l'Abbaye to join the New Zealanders on the Le Barque road. The 1/20th London, in the centre, had Eaucourt l'Abbaye as its objective. After the tanks had passed its front, the battalion crossed the Flers trenches, swept on through the buildings without clearing them of the enemy, and prolonged the forward line of the 1/19th London. Having assisted the advance of two battalions, both tanks became ditched in the Flers lines west of Eaucourt l'Abbaye. The 1/17th London, left battalion of the brigade, had been checked by uncut wire and unsubdued machine guns, so when the Germans [4] counter-attacked south-eastward down the trenches, the tanks, being immovable and unsupported, were set on fire and the crews withdrawn.

---

[1] Sergt. D. F. Brown, 2nd Otago, who had displayed similar prowess on 15th September at the battle of Flers—Courcelette, rushed, single-handed, a machine gun which was holding up the advance ; but he was killed soon afterwards. He received the posthumous award of the V.C.

[2] The history of the *21st Bavarian Reserve* (*6th Bavarian Reserve Division*) records the capture of the staffs of its *II.* and *III.* Bns., and states that attempts to counter-attack did not succeed.

[3] The tanks assembled at the Starfish and made for the right of the divisional front, about 1,500 yards ahead. They had orders to pass up the Flers trenches to Eaucourt l'Abbaye.

[4] Part of the *II./17th Bavarian Reserve*, according to Bavarian accounts.

From the centre of the corps front, the 151st Brigade 1 Oct. (Major-General P. S. Wilkinson's 50th Division) attacked with the 1/6th Durham L.I., a composite battalion formed of the 1/5th Border Regiment and the 1/8th Durham L.I.,[1] and the 1/5th Northumberland Fusiliers, attached from the 149th Brigade. The 1/6th Durham L.I., its flank exposed by the failure of the Londoners' left, lost heavily from the fire of the German machine guns, and could do no more than gain a precarious footing in Flers Trench. The commander of the battalion, Major G. E. Wilkinson, having been wounded before zero hour, Lieut.-Colonel R. B. Bradford, whose 1/9th Durham L.I. was in support, came forward under heavy fire to rally the foremost troops.[2] As the result of his efforts, a renewed assault by parts of both battalions secured Flers Trench by about 9.30 P.M. The composite battalion and the Northumberland Fusiliers had captured the Flers lines in the centre and on the left without much trouble, the Germans being allowed no time to organize an effective resistance.[3]

In the 23rd Division (Major-General J. M. Babington), the left of the corps, the 11/Sherwood Foresters and 8/K.O.Y.L.I. of the 70th Brigade had formed up outside their assembly trenches, which ran S.S.E. from Destremont Farm. The Foresters took Flers Trench and most of Flers Support, where they linked up with the 151st Brigade, but there was stubborn resistance to be overcome beyond the Bapaume road before the Germans could be bombed back up Flers Trench by the 8/K.O.Y.L.I., which joined hands with the Canadians. The 9/York & Lancaster provided much needed reinforcement, but patrols which tried to enter Le Sars were checked by fire from the houses.

It was not until early next morning that the situation 2 Oct. became at all clear at divisional and corps headquarters;[4] but the 47th Division knew of the failure of the 1/17th London, and sent forward the 1/23rd London (attached from the 142nd Brigade) during the night to renew the attack over the same ground. Advancing at 6.45 A.M. on

---

[1] The 1/5th Border Regiment was too weak in numbers to attack as a battalion.

[2] For his gallant conduct and capable handling of the situation, Lieut.-Colonel Bradford was awarded the V.C.

[3] A report from the 3rd Squadron R.F.C. described the British barrage, seen from the air, as a rigid wall of fire ; and the troops of the 50th Division, in particular, were said to have advanced in splendid order within fifty yards of it.

[4] Bavarian accounts show that Eaucourt l'Abbaye was " regarded as " lost " on the afternoon of the 1st.

2-4 Oct. the 2nd October, this battalion, tired and very weak in numbers, had little chance of success ; it was withdrawn after sustaining some 170 casualties, chiefly from machine-gun fire.[1]

The 50th Division had completed its task before dawn of the 2nd, thanks to the energetic action of Lieut.-Colonel Bradford, who, with the 1/6th and 1/9th Durham L.I., had driven the Germans from Flers Support. He barricaded his right flank, where the 47th Division had failed to get forward, against the persistent assaults of the enemy who was kept at bay by bombing and by Stokes-mortar fire.[2]

Rain set in about 11 A.M. on the 2nd October and con-tinued to fall with little intermission throughout the two following days. At noon on the 3rd patrols of the 1/18th London, which had relieved the 1/17th, reported that there were few Germans in the Flers trenches covering Eaucourt l'Abbaye. The battalion moved forward later, practically unopposed, to occupy a position north-west of the buildings, in touch on the right with the 1/20th London, and on the left, in Flers Trench, with the 68th Brigade (23rd Division) which had relieved the 151st Brigade.[3] In front of Le Sars, the 69th Brigade, which had taken over the front of the 70th, made an unsuccessful attempt before dawn of the 4th to bomb up Flers Support beyond the Bapaume road.[4]

1 Oct.   In the XIV. Corps and the right sector of the XV. Corps slight gains of ground had been made under cover of an hour's intensive bombardment, which started at 3.15 P.M., on the 1st October. South-east of Morval the French had attacked without much success on that day, the German machine guns in Haie Wood proving the chief obstacle.[5]

[1] On 2nd October Major-General G. F. Gorringe, coming direct from Mesopotamia, took over command of the 47th Division from Br.-General Greenly.
[2] The III./17th Bavarian Reserve rallied along the Eaucourt l'Abbaye —Le Sars road, where it was reinforced by the III./16th Bavarian Reserve. Detachments of the 362nd Regiment (4th Ersatz Division) took over the defence of the village. Regimental histories.
[3] This completed the relief of the 50th Division, which, from 10th September to 3rd October, showed a casualty list of 4,072 all ranks.
[4] By 3rd October the 4th Ersatz Division, from Flanders, had relieved the 7th Division west of the Bapaume road, extending its left to take over the Bavarian right, including Le Sars. Up to this date the losses of the 17th Bavarian Reserve Regiment are given as 22 officers and 1,624 other ranks. Regimental histories.
[5] The French were striving to enlarge their hold upon the trench run-ning S.E. from Haie Wood to Rancourt. North of the wood the I. Corps obtained a footing in Mutton Trench [See Map 2]. F.O.A. iv. (iii.), pp. 186-7.

Various reliefs were carried out by the XV. Corps,[1] and 2-5 Oct. general preparations were in train for the next stage in the advance of the Fourth Army which had been fixed for the 5th October. On the right, General Rawlinson Sketch A. aimed at securing a low ridge which ran north-westward towards Thilloy and afforded good observation over Le Transloy and Beaulencourt ; in the centre, the line was to be advanced to a position overlooking the ravine west of Ligny ; and on the left it would be prolonged beyond Le Sars to include the Butte de Warlencourt.[2] General Fayolle had agreed to send forward his left to cover the British right, although he intended to make his main effort a day later.

The heavy rain now compelled a postponement of the operations, if only to allow time to bring forward sufficient artillery ammunition.[3] On the morning of the 4th October [4] General Rawlinson informed his corps commanders that the attack was deferred until the 7th, and that the general bombardment would begin at 3.15 P.M. on the 6th. The French were glad to conform by postponing their own attack for a day, so the synchronization of the Allied efforts was really brought about by the bad weather.

In the III. Corps, the 47th Division completed its Sketch occupation of Flers Support without opposition on the 4th 41. October, and after dark on the 5th pushed forward its line to include the ruined mill north-west of Eaucourt l'Abbaye. The 23rd Division had made an unsuccessful attempt to secure Flers Support north of the Bapaume road at 6 P.M.

---

[1] On the night 1st/2nd October the 12th Division (Major-General A. B. Scott) relieved the 21st in the right sector, and 48 hours later the N.Z. Division handed over to the 41st (Major-General S. T. B. Lawford). The losses of the 21st Division (16th September-1st October) were returned as 4,152 ; the New Zealanders had been in action since the opening of the Battle of Flers—Courcelette on 15th September, and their total losses amounted to nearly 7,000.

[2] A chalk mound some sixty feet high, on the slope of the spur overlooking the Bapaume road where the Gird lines crossed it. The Butte afforded excellent observation of the low ground to the south-west and also in the opposite direction towards Bapaume in which area were many battery positions ; its importance was fully appreciated by both British and Germans.

[3] Despite the state of the ground, some field batteries moved up to advanced positions : between Ginchy and Morval and S.E. of Gueudecourt in the XIV. Corps ; around Flers in the XV. Corps ; near High Wood and in Martinpuich in the III. Corps. The heavy artillery was now deployed on the general line : Guillemont—valley, Delville Wood to Bazentin le Petit—north of Mametz Wood.

[4] By attacks on the 3rd and 4th the French (XXXII. and I. Corps) had established themselves facing north-east upon the line Rancourt— Morval. F.O.A. iv. (iii.), pp. 187-8.

2 F

4-6 Oct. on the 4th.[1] On the 6th the trenches called " The Tangle ",
on the eastern side of Le Sars, were occupied by a company
of the 11/Northumberland Fusiliers (68th Brigade) which
came under heavy fire and was later withdrawn.

From the 4th October onward the weather improved,
there being high winds and little rain, but low cloud hindered
observation from the air.   On the front of the XIV. Corps,
in particular, the enemy forward positions—he was known
to be holding various trenches and gun-pits in advance of
the Le Transloy defences—were difficult to determine, and
the position of the British front was only approximately
known at corps and Army headquarters.   The Germans
seemed to have more guns in action than ever, judging by
their persistent shelling which increased in volume along
the whole front of the Army after the preliminary bombardment opened on the 6th October.   Nevertheless,
preparations for the attack were not unduly hampered
thereby and the troops suffered little loss as they waited in
their assembly positions throughout the morning of the
7th, which was fine.   The assault was to be delivered at
1.45 P.M.

7 Oct.   The first objective of the XIV. Corps was a more or less
continuous line of trenches from 100 to 500 yards distant.
On the right, next to the French, the 56th Division (Major-
General C. P. A. Hull) attacked with the London Scottish,
Map 4, 1/4th London and 1/12th London (168th Brigade), and
Sketch the 1/1st London and 1/7th Middlesex (167th Brigade).
42. From the start the London Scottish found difficulty in
keeping touch with their Allies, whose advance was eastward rather than north-eastward ; but the battalion
captured the southern group of gun-pits and also the
southern end of Hazy Trench, 200 yards beyond.   As
it had not so far to go, the 1/4th London started two
minutes later, and was held up by machine-gun fire
from the northern gun-pits, which it then tried to
outflank from the right.   Advancing four minutes after
zero hour, the 1/12th London failed before Dewdrop
Trench, north-east of Lesboeufs, which had been shelled by
Stokes mortars as it was too close for artillery bombardment.   The 1/1st London met with no success against

---

[1] The wire had to be cut by hand and the small party of 10/Duke of
Wellington's (69th Brigade) which entered the trench held on until bombs
and ammunition were exhausted. 2nd-Lieut. H. Kelly, who carried back
his wounded sergeant-major, was awarded the V.C. for his gallant leadership.

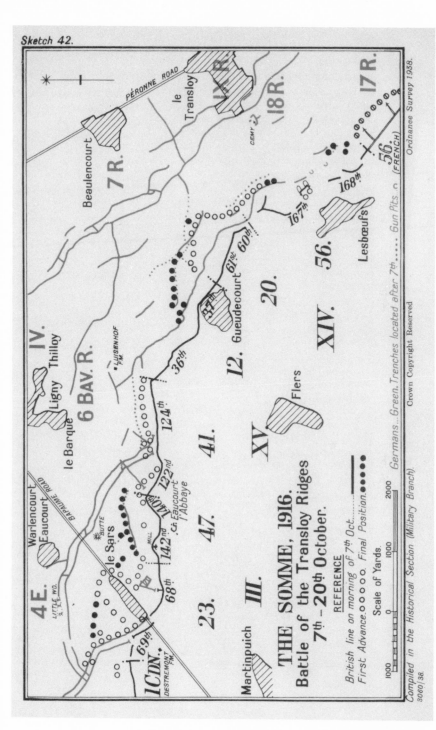

Sketch 42.

PÉRONNE ROAD

le Transloy

Beaulencourt

7 R.

19 R.

18 R.

CEMY

17 R.

56.
(FRENCH)

168th

167th

61st 60th

57th

36th

Gueudecourt

20.

12.

XIV.

Lesbœufs

56.

IV.

Ligny Thilloy

6 BAV. R.

LUISENHOF FM

124th

41.

XV.

Flers

le Barque

Warlencourt
Eaucourt

BAPAUME ROAD

BUTTE

MILL

70th

122nd

142nd

Gd Eaucourt
l'Abbaye

47.

III.

68th

23.

4 E.

LITTLE WD

le Sars

DESTREMONT FM

69th

I CDN.

Martinpuich

Ordnance Survey 1958.

Crown Copyright Reserved

Germans...Green.Trenches located after 7th.......Gun Pits.□

THE SOMME, 1916.
Battle of the Transloy Ridges
7th – 20th October.

REFERENCE

British line on morning of 7th Oct. ......
First Advance.○○○○○ Final Position.●●●●

Scale of Yards

1000   0   1000   2000

Compiled in the Historical Section (Military Branch).
3060/38.

Spectrum Trench,[1] except on the left, where bombers joined 7 Oct.
hands with the 1/7th Middlesex. The latter had carried
the southern portion of its continuation, Rainbow Trench,
near the divisional boundary, after close fighting and heavy
loss.[2] A counter-attack was repulsed by the London
Scottish and 1/4th London, but after darkness had fallen
renewed enemy pressure compelled a withdrawal.[3] The
extreme left of the French did likewise, but they had made
an appreciable advance farther to the east.[4]

In the 20th Division, the 6/Oxford & Bucks L.I. and
12/Rifle Brigade (60th Brigade) carried Rainbow Trench
with slight loss, for the Germans showed little inclination
to resist, and provided " good shooting " as they fled.
The advance continued to the line of Misty Trench, 150
yards ahead, where touch was obtained on the right with
the 1/7th Middlesex and on the left with the 61st Brigade.
The latter had also succeeded, for due east of Gueudecourt
the 7/K.O.Y.L.I. and 12/King's had met a line of Germans
coming forward from Rainbow Trench to surrender.
Having occupied Rainbow Trench, the two battalions
advanced another 300 yards and secured the south-eastern
portion of Cloudy Trench which they found in bad condition. As the 12th Division (XV. Corps) had not come up,
the King's had to refuse their left ; the new line, which
was consolidated from Cloudy Trench westward towards
the Beaulencourt road, was named " Shine " Trench ".
About 350 yards of Rainbow Trench south-east of the road
remained in enemy possession. Soon after 5 P.M. a
German counter-attack from Beaulencourt was broken up,
principally by rifle and machine-gun fire, the enemy
streaming back in disorder.[5]

The first objective of the XV. Corps (12th and 41st

[1] The ingenuity of staffs, commanders and others was constantly
exercised in finding names for new German trenches.

[2] This battalion took 70 prisoners of the *84th Reserve Regiment*, holding
the right sector of the *18th Reserve Division* which had relieved the *52nd
Reserve Division* at the end of September.

[3] Their opponents belonged to the *86th Reserve Regiment*, left sector of
the *18th Reserve Division*.

[4] The French I. Corps broke through some of the German defences
west of Sailly [Sketch A]. The left flank made a small advance but had
to withdraw slightly at night to maintain touch with the British. East
of the Péronne—Bapaume road the XXXII. Corps made progress towards
Saillisel and St. Pierre Vaast Wood. F.O.A. iv. (iii.), p. 193.

[5] Prisoners taken by the 20th Division belonged to the *72nd Reserve
Regiment* (centre of *7th Reserve Division*) astride the Gueudecourt—
Beaulencourt road), and the *66th Reserve*, next on the left. " Res. Regt.
"No. 72 " says that its position south of the road was overrun and losses
were heavy.

7 Oct. Divisions) was the German front line consisting of the north-western continuation of Rainbow (later named Hilt) Trench and Bayonet Trench (newly located as regards its western half beyond the Flers—Thilloy road) as far as the Gird lines, the advance involved averaging about three hundred yards.

A few minutes before zero hour the enemy placed a machine-gun barrage on the front trenches of the 12th Division and shelled the whole forward area ; in particular, a fierce bombardment of the Gueudecourt ruins hampered the advance of the 37th Brigade, on the right. The 6/Buffs, in touch with the 20th Division, entered Rainbow Trench but suffered such heavy loss in doing so that the position could not be held.[1] The 6/R. West Kent, next on the left, failed before machine-gun fire, and the 36th Brigade could do no better for the same reason, the 9/Royal Fusiliers and 8/Royal Fusiliers losing very heavily. A few men of the latter battalion who got into Bayonet Trench were overwhelmed.

On the front of the 41st Division beyond the Thilloy road the fire of unsubdued machine guns held up the 32nd and 26/Royal Fusiliers (124th Brigade) in the same fashion when they were half-way to Bayonet Trench ; but the survivors were able to establish themselves in this forward position. Here they were reinforced by the 21/K.R.R.C. and 10/Queen's, the whole brigade, at night, mustering less than the establishment of a battalion. The 122nd Brigade, on the left, which had reinforced the 15/Hampshire and 11/R. West Kent by the 18/K.R.R.C. and 12/East Surrey, was in a similar state. At the Gird lines a discharge of burning oil had failed, but the bombers of the West Kent made a little progress up both trenches. Farther west, the brigade had made a slight advance, and was in touch with the III. Corps.

The III. Corps (47th and 23rd Divisions) had first to make an advance of about five hundred yards which involved the capture of half of Le Sars ; the remainder of the village was to be secured when the attack was resumed against the Butte de Warlencourt and the Gird lines [2] as far west as the junction of the Gird with the Flers system.

The 140th Brigade, holding the whole front of the 47th

[1] There were some prisoners of the *36th Reserve* and *72nd Reserve* (both *7th Reserve Division*).

[2] Here generally known as the Warlencourt line, running as it did in front of the village of Warlencourt Eaucourt situated on the slope beyond.

Division,[1] had first to capture a German trench called 7 Oct. " Snag Trench "[2] dug across the eastern slope of the depression leading north to Warlencourt; the centre of this objective lay 500 yards ahead, half-way between the British front line and the Butte.   The 1/8th London was checked by terrific machine-gun fire, and the 1/15th London and 1/7th London, which were to pass through and continue the advance, suffered a similar fate.   All that could be done was to establish a few posts near the Le Barque road in touch with the 41st Division.[3]

It was the 23rd Division (Major-General J. M. Babington) which achieved the striking success of the day.   At zero hour the 68th Brigade, on the right, sent forward the 12/Durham L.I., supported by a tank which reached the British front line a minute after the infantry had advanced. The machine did excellent service in assisting to clear the Germans from the Tangle, but, after turning left at the sunken Eaucourt l'Abbaye—Le Sars road beyond, it was hit by a shell and destroyed.   The 12/Durham L.I. found the road enfiladed by machine-gun fire from Le Sars, and was held up for a time.   Meanwhile the 9/Green Howards (69th Brigade) had advanced into the south-western part of Le Sars towards its objective, the cross-roads in the village.   Between these two battalions, the 13/Durham L.I. (68th Brigade), whose mission it was, in the second stage of the advance, to push through and complete the capture of Le Sars, was thrust into the fight about 2.30 P.M. and joined hands with the Green Howards at the cross-roads. After stubborn fighting the German resistance collapsed and the village was cleared.   The 12/Durham L.I. had consolidated the sunken road in front of the Tangle and established forward posts to protect the right flank of the division.   The 13/Durham L.I. and Green Howards now proceeded to put out posts round Le Sars, and Lieut.-Colonel M. E. Lindsey, 13/Durham L.I., asked for two fresh companies and a tank in order to attack the Butte from the west.   These reinforcements were not available.

Twenty minutes after zero hour the 11/West Yorkshire (69th Brigade) had made a frontal assault against Flers

[1] The 142nd Brigade, shown in the left sector on Map 4 and Sketch 42, was at this time in reserve.

[2] This name was used later; to the 47th Division it was known as Diagonal Trench.

[3] Snag Trench was held by the *III./16th Bavarian Reserve* and other elements of *6th Bavarian Reserve Division*.   Bavarian accounts describe the British bombardment as " frightful " and losses as very heavy.

7 Oct. Support beyond Le Sars, only to be checked by the enemy's barrage and by machine-gun and rifle fire from the exposed left flank. A renewed attack, assisted by bombers who advanced up the trench from Le Sars, was, however, successful, the fleeing Germans coming under effective fire from the British in the village and from the divisional artillery. The 10/Duke of Wellington's arrived to play a part in the later stages of the fighting on this flank, and at night the 69th Brigade was in occupation of the two Flers trenches to a point some three hundred yards inside the Army boundary.[1]

In the rain which began to fall at night and persisted throughout the next day the collection and evacuation of the wounded, the reorganization and relief of units and the consolidation of such ground as had been gained proceeded along the whole Army front. The 23rd Division renewed 8 Oct. the attack at 4.50 A.M. on the 8th October, at which hour the Reserve Army was due to move. Two companies of the 8/York & Lancaster (70th Brigade) cleared the Flers system as far as the Army boundary, and a post was established commanding the quarry on the Pys road, 750 yards north-west of Le Sars, which had been abandoned by the enemy.[2] At night the 47th Division made another attempt upon Snag Trench, the 1/21st and 1/22nd London (142nd Brigade) crawling forward and attempting to rush the position as the barrage lifted. The trench was entered on the left, but enfilade fire from the right, where the Germans held on, prevented its occupation. The 1/22nd London established forward posts on the Eaucourt l'Abbaye —Warlencourt road, and, farther west, in touch with the 23rd Division.

On the right flank of the Army, the 56th Division (XIV. Corps) attacked at 3.30 P.M. on the 8th October. Rainy Trench, north-east of Lesboeufs, and most of the captured portion of Spectrum, farther north, had been evacuated so that Dewdrop and Spectrum trenches could be bombarded without risk to the infantry. The London Rifle Brigade (169th Brigade), which reached Hazy Trench, had much the same experience as the London Scottish on the previous

---

[1] The Canadian Corps (right of the Reserve Army) did not attack on this day.

[2] On 7th and 8th October the 23rd Division, whose own losses amounted to less than 750, captured 11 officers and 517 other ranks, nearly all of the *360th*, *361st* and *362nd Regiments* (*4th Ersatz Division*). According to the statements of prisoners, the attack on the morning of the 8th caught the *III./360th* relieving the *I./360th*.

day ; [1] the fire of machine guns in shell-holes checked the advance of the 1/9th London (169th Brigade) and the 1/3rd London (167th Brigade) against Dewdrop and Spectrum trenches. Before midnight a general withdrawal to the starting line had been carried out, whilst the enemy, displaying great enterprise, pushed forward to Rainy Trench, which had been left unoccupied by the British.[2]

At 10 P.M. on the 8th October the Fourth Army issued orders for a renewal of the attack in order to secure all the objectives of the 7th.[3] The precise date depended upon the time for preparation needed by the XV. Corps, which had made least progress, and, rather optimistically, the 12th October was chosen.[4] The rain ceased on the morning of the 9th, and the two following days were fine but dull, the state of the ground rendering slow and difficult the very necessary reliefs of the divisions in the line. Between the 8th and the 11th October the XIV. Corps replaced the 56th and 20th Divisions by the 4th (Major-General Hon. W. Lambton) and the 6th (Major-General C. Ross) ; the 30th Division (Major-General J. S. M. Shea) took over from the 41st in the XV. Corps ; and the 9th (Major-General W. T. Furse) and the 15th Divisions (Major-General F. W. N. McCracken) relieved the 47th and 23rd in the III. Corps.

[1] The L.R.B. records that the battalion " had no notion what the " French were doing ".

According to F.O.A. iv. (iii.), pp. 194-5, no progress was made by the I. Corps on this day, the Germans making a counter-attack west of Sailly [Sketch A]. At night the IX. Corps relieved the I. Corps.

[2] In spite of the failure, about 84 prisoners were brought in. They belonged to the *31st Reserve* and *84th Reserve* (*18th Reserve Division*). According to German regimental accounts, the *86th Reserve* closed to its left in bridging the gap made by the French on the previous day, bringing the *31st Reserve* opposite the British right. " Res. Regt. No. 31 " states that the British broke in and there was close fighting before the situation was restored. A few of the L.R.B. were captured.

[3] On 7th October Br.-General J. H. Davidson, from G.H.Q., visited General Rawlinson, who told him that the next attack, probably on the 12th, would not be carried to the Loupart Wood line (see page 427) ; this was to be the objective of another operation to follow some four days later. It was thereupon arranged that the attacks upon the Loupart Wood line (Fourth Army) ; Irles (Reserve Army) ; and Serre—Gommecourt (Reserve and Third Armies attacking eastward) should be launched together four to five days after 12th October.

[4] General Foch expected to take Sailly-Saillisel on this date, and Sir D. Haig informed him that the British right should arrive within assaulting distance of the Le Transloy trenches at the same time. This would put the Allies in a suitable position for a combined attack upon the German defences which ran in front of Le Transloy and behind Sailly-Saillisel. Sailly commanded the ground over which the British would have to advance (see Sketch A).

The newcomers had little time in which to learn anything of the situation or to prepare suitable assembly trenches for the next assault, the commander of the 9th Division asking in vain for a 48 hours' postponement. The R.F.C. endeavoured to carry out as much photographic work as possible in order to locate, for the benefit of the infantry and artillery, any new German trenches ; but the light was too bad for much to be done.

12 Oct.　　Zero hour was 2.5 P.M. on the 12th, a day of heavy showers. In the 4th Division, right sector of the XIV. Corps, the 10th Brigade attacked next to the French ; and, on the extreme flank, part of the 1/R. Warwickshire advanced nearly five hundred yards and dug in south of Hazy Trench with flanks refused, but in touch with the French left.[1] In the evening a counter-attack upon this new position, called "Antelope Trench", was repulsed. The left of the Warwickshire failed, and the 1/R. Irish Fusiliers could do no better before Rainy and Dewdrop trenches north-east of Lesboeufs. The 12th Brigade endeavoured to complete the capture of Spectrum Trench, which was bombarded by Stokes mortars ; some of the 2/Duke of Wellington's, after suffering considerable loss, forced their way in and joined hands with the 2/Lancashire Fusiliers holding the northern part of the trench. An advance over the crest of the spur by men of both battalions failed before Zenith Trench.[2]

North of the Le Transloy road, Zenith Trench was attacked by the 2/York & Lancaster (16th Brigade, 6th Division) without success. Next on the left, the 9/Suffolk (71st Brigade) which held the salient formed by the continuation of Misty Trench and the eastern part of Cloudy, was not called upon to advance. The 18th Brigade, left of the 6th Division, became hotly engaged, for the 1/West Yorkshire found the task of carrying Mild Trench and the remaining portion of Cloudy too much for it, a frontal attack and a bombing attack from the right both failing with loss. On the extreme left, however, the 14/Durham

[1] The French IX. Corps tried to establish itself within assaulting distance of the German line running S.E. from Le Transloy ; it made some progress, but had to withdraw again. The XXXII. Corps had made an abortive night attack upon Sailly-Saillisel; its advance at 2.5 P.M. on the 12th was smothered by the counter-preparation of the German artillery. F.O.A. iv. (iii.), pp. 199-200.

[2] " Res. Regt. No. 31 " records close fighting and heavy losses on this part of the front.

L.I. was able to storm and occupy the remainder of 12 Oct. Rainbow Trench, bomb forward up the sunken Beaulencourt road with its numerous dug-outs, and join hands with the left of the West Yorkshire.[1]

Beyond the road, the Durham L.I. were in touch with the Newfoundland Regiment of the 88th Brigade (29th Division but attached to the 12th Division) which formed the right of the XV. Corps attack. North of Gueudecourt the Newfoundlanders, with the 1/Essex (also 88th Brigade), on their left, stormed a portion of Hilt Trench the continuation of Rainbow Trench. When the advance was resumed some of the Essex reached Grease Trench, the second objective, but neither battalion was able to gain more ground. The Essex, indeed, were ordered at 5.30 P.M. to withdraw to their starting line, their position being considered untenable, since on their left the attack of the 35th Brigade (12th Division) had failed. The Newfoundlanders, however, not only hung on to Hilt Trench but also bombed up it and secured part of the Essex objective, erecting a barricade. In front of Bayonet Trench, the 7/Suffolk and 7/Norfolk (35th Brigade) had encountered intact wire, and efforts to cut it by hand failed under heavy fire. The survivors, who lay in front of the German position until darkness came, were then obliged to fall back.[2]

In the 30th Division, left sector of the XV. Corps, the 90th Brigade attacked with the 2/R. Scots Fusiliers and 17/Manchester. The former advanced 150 yards in the face of deadly machine-gun fire and then the survivors had to withdraw. Small parties of the Manchester entered Bayonet Trench, but could not maintain themselves. The 89th Brigade set the 2/Bedfordshire to bomb up the Gird lines, where the opposition proved too strong, and all that could be secured was a small portion of Bite Trench, running north-eastward. On the left of the Bedfordshire,

---

[1] The *19th Reserve Division* had just completed the relief of the *7th Reserve Division*, except in the right sector, where the *6th Division* had taken over, also relieving the left of the *6th Bavarian Reserve Division*. Thus the *92nd Reserve Regiment* (*19th Reserve Division*) was engaged with the left of the 6th Division; its regimental history admits a loss of ground and prisoners.

[2] Nearly 150 prisoners were taken by the 88th Brigade. Most of them belonged to the *64th Regiment* (*6th Division*). The history of this regiment, which had two battalions in the line, records the loss of Hilt Trench and states that the forward troops and defences suffered heavily from the British bombardment. The left of the sector was " rolled up ", although a counter-attack checked the further advance of the British. Touch was lost with the *92nd Reserve Regiment* (*19th Reserve Division*), on the left.

12 Oct. the 17/King's failed gallantly under enfilade fire from the north-west. The British bombardment had had little effect upon the enemy machine gunners, who were described as " scattered all over the country ".[1]

The III. Corps set the 9th Division to capture first Snag Trench and then the Butte de Warlencourt and Warlencourt line. Included in these objectives was a trench, named " The Tail ", located as running back from Snag Trench towards the Butte ; also a mound, known as " The Pimple ", at the western end of Snag Trench. On the left the 15th Division, which had not ceased to push out posts and to dig advanced trenches,[2] assisted by concentrating fire upon the ultimate objectives ; No. 4 Special Company R.E. blanketed with smoke the Little Wood locality and the Butte. On the right, the 7/Seaforth Highlanders (26th Brigade) suffered heavily from machine-gun fire as soon as its advance began,[3] and, although the 10/Argyll & Sutherland pushed forward to reinforce, barely two hundred yards of ground were gained. The Highlanders dug in at night, mingling, on the left, with the South African Brigade. Of the latter, the 2nd Regiment, followed by the 4th, had been checked by long-range machine-gun fire, whilst smoke drifting from the Butte made it difficult to maintain direction. The survivors entrenched themselves half-way to Snag Trench, some parties remaining out in front until they were withdrawn next morning.[4]

The enemy, doubtless warned by the bombardment and by now accustomed to afternoon attacks, had been found ready and alert on the 12th October. The British battalions showed admirable powers of endurance, but were woefully weak in numbers[5] with many half-trained men in the ranks. Assistance from the air, so much relied upon in counter-battery work, in locating new German positions,

[1] The 30th Division was engaged with the *24th Regiment* (*6th Division*) and elements of the *16th* and *21st Bavarian Reserve* (*6th Bavarian Reserve Division*). The Bavarian accounts speak of heavy fighting, many companies being reduced to 35 rifles.

[2] Considerable ground was gained in this way, without fighting, by the 15th Division. The right was held back, being confronted by the Butte de Warlencourt on the opposite slope of the valley.

[3] The British heavy artillery was reported to be shooting short and causing casualties to the Highlanders, who complained that no bombardment fell on Snag Trench. It was agreed that the creeping barrage was good.

[4] Snag Trench was defended by the *20th Bavarian Reserve* (*6th Bavarian Reserve Division*).

[5] At this time few battalions in the Fourth Army could muster more than 400 men for an attack.

and in reporting the progress of an attack, had been severely **12-14**
limited by poor visibility.   Moreover many German machine **Oct.**
guns now appeared to be sited farther back in well concealed
positions from which they swept with deadly effect the zone
of the assault.[1]

Conscious that most of what he had planned to accomplish on the 5th October still remained to do, General
Rawlinson believed that the delays imposed by the bad
weather had given the enemy time to recover, so that his
resistance now required to be shaken by more methodical
bombardment.[2]   He proposed to attack again on the 18th
October, and this course had the approval of the Commander-in-Chief, who reckoned upon French co-operation.
Issued late on the 13th October, the Fourth Army order
emphasized the importance of preparing adequate assembly
trenches parallel to the objectives, and of improving communications to the front.   The preliminary bombardment
was to start forthwith, and be continued steadily until zero
hour.   Warning was given that certain positions must be
captured before the resumption of this general attack :
Zenith Trench, Mild Trench and the remainder of Cloudy
Trench by the XIV. Corps; the Gird lines south-east of
the Eaucourt l'Abbaye—Le Barque road by the XV. Corps;
and Snag Trench by the III. Corps.   General Rawlinson
considered that these enterprises were best carried out by
night, and announced that tanks were available if they
could be used to advantage.

In the XIV. Corps, at 6.30 P.M. on the 14th, the 2/Sea-
forth (10th Brigade, 4th Division) by a surprise attack
entered Rainy Trench and the gun-pits immediately south
of Dewdrop Trench, but a counter-attack compelled the
Highlanders to withdraw.   At the same time, the 2/R.
Dublin Fusiliers (also 10th Brigade) failed in an attempt to
secure the gun-pits in front of Hazy Trench.   Bombing
attacks down Spectrum Trench towards Dewdrop, made by

[1] Lord Cavan, commanding the XIV. Corps, pointed this out personally
to Sir Douglas Haig as one of the principal causes of failure.   He advocated
a creeping barrage to start immediately *beyond* each objective in turn ;
also free use of smoke shell to blind German observation.   The artillery,
however, had no smoke shell during the Somme offensive.

[2] Further reliefs of German troops followed the action of 12th October,
the *2nd Bavarian Division*, from Lorraine, relieving the *18th Reserve Division*
opposite the right of the Fourth Army ; the *40th Division*, from Flanders,
taking over from the *6th Bavarian Reserve Division* astride the Gird lines ;
and the *24th Division*, also from Flanders, replacing the *4th Ersatz Division*
north of Le Sars.

the 1/King's Own (12th Brigade) on the evenings of the 14th and 15th October, also accomplished nothing.   Before dawn of the 15th, however, the 2/Sherwood Foresters (71st Brigade, 6th Division) captured and held the gun-pits in front of the British portion of Cloudy Trench, securing some prisoners.   On the left of the corps the 11/Essex (18th Brigade, 6th Division) crossed Mild Trench and bombed up the Beaulencourt road, only to be driven back. In the III. Corps, after darkness fell on the 14th, the South Africans (3rd Battalion) seized the Pimple and fought their way along Snag Trench for 80 yards.

The 14th, like the 13th October, was dull and misty, the 15th brought showers with a few bright intervals, the 16th was definitely fine.   The next morning broke fair, but clouds gathered in the afternoon and rain set in again at night.[1]   The British bombardment continued steadily, with occasional bursts of intense fire, the German batteries replying with great vigour.   Zero hour had been fixed for 3.40 A.M., nearly two hours before sunrise, on the 18th October.

18 Oct.   In almost every brigade, forming-up positions had been taped out in front and careful compass bearings taken of the direction of the advance.   When the moment of assault arrived the British front positions and the approaches thereto were a maze of water-logged shell-holes and flooded trenches.   As the troops struggled forward through the darkness [2] officers and men stumbled and fell in the slippery ooze ;   rifles and Lewis guns became clogged with it so that bomb and bayonet were soon the only weapons.

The 4th Division, right of the XIV. Corps, set the 11th Brigade to carry Frosty, Hazy, Rainy and Dewdrop trenches.[3]   Parties of the 1/Rifle Brigade reached the gun-pits in front of Hazy Trench, but had to withdraw ;   the

[1] At the instance of General Foch, the French XXXII. Corps had renewed its attempts to capture Sailly.   On the evening of the 15th a fresh attack was made and fighting continued all night ;   by the morning most of the village was in French hands.   In the course of 17th October the Germans made five counter-attacks, but all were repulsed.   F.O.A. iv. (iii.), pp. 203-4.

[2] The moon, about to enter its last quarter, was obscured by heavy rain clouds.

[3] The French IX. Corps and the XXXII. Corps, on its right, did not attack until 11.45 A.M. on the 18th.   The IX. Corps was to advance to within assaulting distance of the German line running S.E. from Le Transloy, but was checked at the outset by the fire of the German machine guns. The XXXII. Corps improved its position in the northern part of Sailly. F.O.A. iv. (iii.), p. 206.

1/East Lancashire was checked in front of Dewdrop by the fire of unlocated machine guns. In Spectrum Trench the fight swayed to and fro, but the 1/King's Own (12th Brigade), bombing down towards Dewdrop, eventually gained 70 yards.[1]

In the 6th Division, which attacked Mild and Cloudy Trenches, the 9/Norfolk (71st Brigade) was shelled in its assembly positions before zero hour : owing to the mud, it could not keep up with the barrage when the advance began. Nevertheless, the north-western part of Mild Trench was taken by the battalion and held against a counter-attack delivered at nightfall.[2]

The only other success of the XIV. Corps was achieved after dark on the 19th October, when a platoon of the 1/Somerset L.I. (11th Brigade), finding Frosty Trench empty, occupied it and beat off a counter-attack.

On the 18th October the XV. Corps, made no attack from its centre, which would have had to advance over the low ground astride the Flers—Thilloy road. The 12th Division, on the right, therefore assaulted the line of Grease Trench with the 2/Hampshire and 4/Worcestershire (of the attached 88th Brigade) and the south-eastern end of Bayonet Trench with one battalion of the 35th Brigade. The Hampshire, who gave valuable aid to the Norfolk (6th Division) beyond the Gueudecourt—Beaulencourt road, captured Grease Trench with few casualties, and the Worcestershire were equally successful ; but both battalions suffered heavily in attempting a further advance.[3] The Worcestershire protected their left by a block in Hilt Trench, since the 9/Essex (35th Brigade) could make no progress; its left company entered Bayonet Trench at a point where there was no wire, but was bombed out from the flanks.

In the 30th Division, the 89th Brigade, on the right, made no attack.[4] The 2/Green Howards (21st Brigade) advanced against the western end of Bayonet Trench and

---

[1] Prisoners taken were of the *15th Bavarian Regiment* (right sector of the *2nd Bavarian Division*). Bavarian accounts state that the line was penetrated by parties of British which were driven out. The *II./15th Bavarians* lost half its numbers.

[2] Men of the *92nd Reserve Regiment* were captured. The history of the *64th Regiment (6th Division)*, next on the right, states that its *I./Bn.* lost 200 men on this day.

[3] Prisoners belonged both to the *64th* and the *396th Regiments (6th Division)*.

[4] The Special Brigade R.E. was to put down a lacrymatory barrage on this front, but the detachment found it impossible to get up into position through the mud and darkness.

18 Oct. almost reached it, but was brought to a standstill by showers of bombs, most of the officers being hit. Bombing parties of the battalion fought their way some distance up Bite Trench, but lost heavily and reinforcements could not get forward in time through the mud. Farther west, the 18/King's and 2/Wiltshire (also 21st Brigade) made a frontal attack on the Gird Lines ; but the King's were impeded by uncut wire, and the Wiltshire who entered the trenches were taken in enfilade from the left by machine-gun fire, so that very few survived.

Two tanks, held in readiness at Flers, were to be used if the night assault failed. At 8 A.M., when the fighting had died down, one machine crossed the British front line and sat at the end of Gird Trench for twenty minutes doing great execution amongst the Germans, who fled back north-eastward. The tank commander climbed out and signalled for the infantry to come on, but the front was so disorganized, the men so exhausted, and the number of surviving officers so few, that no response was possible. Driving the enemy before it, the tank then went forward alone along Gird Trench as far as the Le Barque road, and then retired by the way it had come. The second tank found the mud too great a handicap, and never reached the front line.[1]

The III. Corps made another attempt upon Snag Trench, whilst smoke and lacrymatory bombs were discharged from the front of the 15th Division in an endeavour to keep down aimed German fire from the Butte and the Warlencourt line. On the right, the 5/Cameron Highlanders (26th Brigade, 9th Division) captured the trench from the Le Barque road—where some of the 2/Wiltshire arrived—to within 200 yards of the Nose, as the junction of Snag Trench and the Tail had been named. In the afternoon a counter-attack from the right secured a footing in the trench, but the enemy was driven out again after darkness fell.[2] On the left of the Highlanders, the 1st South African Regiment had attacked with great resolution, two companies crossing Snag Trench and pressing forward beyond it. Machine-gun fire from the Butte accounted for

---

[1] The *181st Regiment* (*40th Division*), opposite the 21st Brigade, admits, in its history, that the mud was an enemy of the British, for it prevented a rapid surprise advance after rendering the preliminary bombardment comparatively ineffective.

[2] The prisoners taken belonged to the *104th Regiment* (*40th Division*). The *I.* and *II. Bns.* were holding Snag Trench and the *III. Bn.* carried out the counter-attack.

nearly all of them, but a small party clung to Snag Trench 18-20
on the left of the Camerons. At daybreak the South Oct.
Africans began to bomb along the trench from the Pimple,
but made little headway ; at 5.45 P.M. they attacked from
both flanks and made better progress ; at night, as far as
could be ascertained, the Germans held only about one
hundred yards of Snag Trench on either side of the Nose.

At dawn on the 19th, another day of rain, German
bombers, supported by *Flammenwerfer,* moved forward up
the Tail and attacked eastward along Snag Trench, driving
the South Africans back on to the 8/Black Watch which
had relieved the Camerons during the night. At the same
time another counter-attack against the right of the
Highlanders was repulsed.[1] The bombardment of the Nose
and Tail was maintained during the day, but the South
African Brigade—which had used all its available troops—
was in no condition for another effort. At night the 27th
Brigade took over the whole divisional front.[2] For all the
troops concerned the relief involved an agonizing struggle
through mud and water,[3] but the 6/K.O.S.B. (27th Brigade)
was considered to be capable of attacking at 4 P.M. on the
20th. Confused fighting followed, the Nose being taken,
evacuated, and reoccupied. At night the Borderers were
firmly established in Snag Trench and a company of the
11/Royal Scots had pushed forward up the Tail, which was
held for a distance of 250 yards.[4]

The Reserve Army, 1st–14th October

Reorganization of the Line : Battle of the Ancre Heights [5]

In preparation for the big operation which the Com- Sketch A.
mander-in-Chief hoped to see launched on or about the

[1] The counter-attacks were made by the storm detachment of the *40th
Division* : flame-throwers, machine-gun section, and picked men of *I./104th.*
Two columns advanced, but the left column failed owing to a British bullet
exploding a flame-thrower. " Regt. No. 104 ".

[2] German regimental accounts state that the *III./134th Regiment*
relieved most of the survivors of the *104th.*

[3] On their way back exhausted Highlanders discarded their sodden,
mud-covered kilts which had become a burden too great to be borne.

[4] " Regt. No. 104 " states that by the evening of the 20th, when the
trenches were nearly obliterated by shell-fire, a withdrawal was ordered
in accordance with the new O.H.L. policy to give up forward positions of
no tactical value rather than incur useless loss.

[5] The official title covers all the operations of the Reserve Army south
of the Ancre during the period 1st October-11th November.

1-12 Oct. 12th October, General Gough had begun the reorganization of the Reserve Army north of the Ancre. His object was to concentrate on that front the necessary forces for the eastward attack which was to start from the line Redan Ridge (immediately north of Beaumont Hamel)—Hébuterne.

At the beginning of October the 39th Division (Major-General G. J. Cuthbert), which held the whole sector of the V. Corps (Lieut.-General E. A. Fanshawe) from the Ancre to Hébuterne, was in process of being relieved from the left by the 2nd Division (Major-General W. G. Walker). When the 39th Division passed to the command of the II. Corps (Lieut.-General C. W. Jacob) on the 2nd, Major-General Cuthbert held the front from Redan Ridge to the river. It was General Gough's intention to thin his line astride the Ancre in the sector from which no advance was to be made when the big operation began ; so, on the 5th October, the 39th Division extended south of the river and relieved Major-General Maxse's 18th Division at Thiepval. Meanwhile, on the 4th, the XIII. Corps (Lieut.-General W. N. Congreve) [1] had taken over the extreme left of the Reserve Army line—from Hébuterne to a point 1500 yards southward—and by the 7th was holding it with the 51st Division (Major-General G. M. Harper) and 19th Division (Major-General G. T. M. Bridges). Next morning the V. Corps completed the relief of the 2nd Division in the corps line as far south as Redan Ridge by the 3rd Division (Major-General C. J. Deverell) and 63rd Division (Major-General Sir A. Paris. [2] The concentration upon the front of attack north of the Ancre was then in a fair way to completion.

Between the 4th and the 12th October, General Gough issued a series of instructions for the eastward attack which was to be made by his V. and XIII. Corps. He also arranged with G.H.Q. and the Cavalry Corps for the forward concentration of the 1st and 3rd Cavalry Divisions. Meanwhile the artillery of the V. and XIII. Corps fired steadily upon the German gun positions and communications south

---

[1] XIII. Corps headquarters had been in reserve at Domart, 24 miles W.N.W. of Albert.

[2] The 63rd (R.N.) Division was reconstituted after its arrival in France, May 1916, and then consisted of two naval brigades (188th and 189th) and the 190th Brigade composed of one Territorial battalion, two "Extra Reserve" battalions, and one New Army battalion. Most of the artillery came from the 2nd-Line Northumbrian Division (T.F.), which did not go overseas as a division.

Sketch 43.

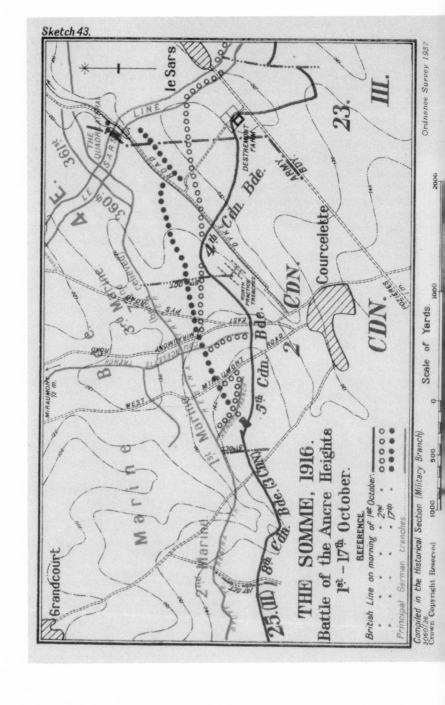

THE SOMME, 1916.
Battle of the Ancre Heights
1st – 17th October.

REFERENCE

British Line on morning of 1st October. ●●●●●
" " " " 2nd " ○○○○○
" " " " 17th " ●●●●●
Principal German trenches.

Scale of Yards.
1000   500   0   1000   2000

Compiled in the Historical Section (Military Branch).
Ordnance Survey 1937
3060/38
Crown Copyright Reserved

of the Ancre opposite the Canadian and the II. Corps, where fighting continued.[1]

South of the Ancre, at the end of September, General Gough was immediately concerned with the capture of Regina Trench in readiness for his northward advance, which was to be made from the front held by the Canadian Corps. It was also necessary to drive the enemy from the hold he still retained on Stuff Redoubt and Schwaben Redoubt.[2] Sketch 43.

On the 1st October at 3.15 P.M. the Canadian Corps endeavoured to secure that part of Regina Trench which lay on the higher ground west of Courcelette Trench.[3] From that point the Canadian line was to be established as far as Dyke Road with a defensive flank along the track to Destremont Farm. 1 Oct.

The advance of the 4th Brigade (2nd Canadian Division) east of the East Miraumont road was carried out by the 20th (Central Ontario) and 18th (W. Ontario) Battalions under spasmodic outbursts of machine-gun fire. These units dug a line which straightened the front of the brigade and represented a gain of 400 yards on the flanks.[4] There was no need to throw back the right, as the 23rd Division (III. Corps, Fourth Army) had attacked at the same hour and was in touch. The 5th Brigade, which attempted to storm 1,000 yards of Regina Trench west of the East Miraumont road, had a different experience. The enemy's barrage caught the rear waves of the 22nd (Canadien Français) Battalion on the right, his machine guns took heavy toll of the leading lines, and the few survivors who forced their way through the wire into the position were overwhelmed.

[1] On 12th October the V. and XIII. Corps carried out a feint offensive consisting of special artillery bombardments, wire-cutting, and a discharge of smoke. Retaliation by the German batteries was weak in volume and opened late. Major-General Paris, 63rd Division, was severely wounded by a shell on 12th October ; he was succeeded by Major-General C. D. Shute.

[2] See Sketch 39, Map 3.

[3] At 7.50 A.M. Major-General Turner, 2nd Canadian Division, informed both the corps and the corps R.A. that, judging by air photographs taken the previous day, he did not consider that the bombardment of Regina and Kenora trenches was sufficient. He was told that the greater part of the artillery preparation would be carried out that morning. Br.-General Elmsley (8th Brigade) reported at 12.30 P.M. that the wire in front of Regina Trench was intact : wire cutting proceeded accordingly up to zero hour.

[4] Part of the *72nd Regiment* was still in the line near the Pys road. Its regimental history says that the attack came at an unfortunate moment, as the Marines were about to take over the front.

1 Oct. In the centre, the 25th Battalion (Nova Scotia Rifles) stormed Kenora Trench and there dug in under a heavy fire, partly in enfilade, from rifles and machine guns. The 24th Battalion (Victoria Rifles) on the left, was quite successful at first ; but when the 5th C.M.R. (3rd Canadian Division), which advanced on its flank, was driven back by counter-attack, the Germans, in great strength, began to bomb down Regina Trench, and bitter fighting followed. At night, the 5th Brigade held most of Kenora Trench with advanced posts in the sunken West Miraumont road and in Courcelette Trench. These positions were handed over to the 6th Brigade before next morning.

The 8th Brigade (Major-General L. J. Lipsett's 3rd Canadian Division) attacked with the 5th and 4th C.M.R. against an alert enemy, who put a barrage on the Canadian front line just before zero hour. In spite of uncut wire and a hail of machine-gun bullets, parties of both battalions entered Regina Trench, where a bombing fight swayed to and fro. A footing west of the Courcelette—Grandcourt

2-7 Oct. road was maintained until 2 A.M. next morning, when heavy losses and a shortage of bombs compelled a retirement.[1]

Preparations to renew the attack were put in hand at once ; but here, as on the Fourth Army front, the bad weather caused great hardship and imposed delay. The next effort of the Canadian Corps was eventually postponed until the 8th October. In the meantime the artillery, which had to contend with high winds and poor visibility, continued to bombard Regina Trench and to cut the wire in front of it. On the night of the 3rd/4th October the 3rd Canadian Division relieved the 2nd,[2] and, 24 hours later, handed over the front of its left brigade to the 25th Division (Major-General E. G. T. Bainbridge) of the II. Corps. On the following night the 1st Canadian Division (Major-General A. W. Currie) took over the right of the corps with its 1st and 3rd Brigades as far as a point 700 yards east of the Pys road.

The objectives were now to include the Quadrilateral,

---

[1] Prisoners taken belonged to the *I./2nd Marine Regiment*, holding the sector astride the Courcelette—Grandcourt road, with the *I./1st Marine Regiment* on its left. The *Marine Brigade*, from the *Naval Corps* on the Belgian coast, had relieved the *8th Division* at the end of September. According to " Marine Regt. No. 2 ", the situation was not restored until after daybreak on 2nd October, when parts of the *I.* and *II. Bns.* counter-attacked. Heavy losses are admitted.

[2] The total casualties of the 2nd Canadian Division, 1st September-4th October, were returned as 6,530.

formed by the junction of the Gird lines with the Le Sars line ; [1] Regina Trench along the whole front of the corps ; and, ultimately, a German trench on the high ground between Courcelette Trench and the West Miraumont road. Good work was done by the Canadians, mostly under fire, in linking up advanced positions and digging assembly trenches, so that west of the Pys road the corps line was established about three hundred yards from Regina Trench. Farther to the right, also, an appreciable gain of ground was made in this fashion. Daily reconnaissance by infantry patrols seemed to show that the German wire was being cut systematically, but that at night the enemy was throwing out loose " concertina " wire to block the gaps.

The assault was launched in cold rain at 4.50 A.M. on the 8th October. On the right, the 4th Battalion and 3rd Battalion (Toronto Regiment) of the 1st Brigade advanced to the Le Sars line without a check, the 4th Battalion negotiating Dyke Road, which here ran in a depression 75 yards wide and 40 feet deep. South-east of the Quadrilateral gaps in the wire had to be sought for, with the result that the battalion swerved to the left and mingled with the 3rd. Nevertheless the front trench of the Le Sars line, from Dyke Road to a point 400 yards beyond the Quadrilateral was bombed clear of Germans and occupied. $\qquad$ **8 Oct.**

At 1.20 P.M. a threatened counter-attack was checked by the prompt intervention of the artillery, and preparations were made to complete the capture of the Quadrilateral. Then, covered by a heavy barrage, the Germans counter-attacked in force down the trenches from the north-east and north-west. Heavy fighting followed, with great loss to both sides, until at dusk the Canadians, greatly outnumbered and with no bombs left, were obliged to fall back to their " jumping-off " trenches.[2] After darkness fell the 4th Battalion dug a forward trench on the right to within 50 yards of the Le Sars line, and established touch with the 23rd Division (III. Corps).

In the 3rd Brigade, the 16th Battalion (Canadian Scottish) had entered Regina Trench, after forcing its way

[1] The Gird trenches (see Sketch 42) passed south of Warlencourt, Eaucourt and Little Wood to join the Le Sars line (continuation of the Flers trenches) about 1,400 yards N.W. of Le Sars.

[2] The two battalions lost 700 out of 1,100 of all ranks. They had captured 240 prisoners.

8-10 Oct. through the wire; but when the 3rd Battalion on its right withdrew, it could hold on no longer.[1] Next on the left, the 13th Battalion (Royal Highlanders) was stopped by the wire and, after suffering heavy loss from close range machine-gun fire, also withdrew as night came on.

The 3rd Canadian Division could do no better than the 1st, although its battalions attacked with equal resolution. In the 9th Brigade, the 58th Battalion tried to penetrate the wire and some of the right company found a way into Regina Trench through two sally-ports; but these parties were overwhelmed. The 43rd Battalion (Cameron Highlanders) entered Regina Trench at its junction with Courcelette Trench, but had to withdraw again. The two right companies of the Royal Canadian Regiment—right battalion of the 7th Brigade—stormed Regina Trench and began to work westward, bombing the dug-outs. They also advanced up the West Miraumont road, but repeated counter-attacks, although gallantly met, eventually forced them to relinquish all they had won.[2] On the extreme left of the assault the 49th (Edmonton) Battalion encountered new wire, and all its efforts to bomb forward up Kenora Trench failed before the fire of the German machine guns.

On the night of the 10th October the 4th Canadian Division (Major-General D. Watson)[3] began to replace the 3rd in the left sector, a preliminary to the complete relief of the Canadian Corps.[4] The heavy losses sustained by the Dominion troops bear witness to their determination and self-sacrifice under conditions as difficult and harassing as any which prevailed upon the Somme.

On the front of the II. Corps south of the Ancre, the

[1] Piper J. Richardson, 16th Battalion, played his company to the assault and continued to play, under heavy fire, when it was checked at the German wire; he then did good work as a bomber, but was eventually reported missing. He received the postumous award of the V.C.

[2] According to " Marine Regt. No. 2 ", part of its *II. Bn.* took part in this fighting. The Canadian left was engaged with the *1st Marine Regiment.*

[3] It had been formed in England and began training there in June 1916. Some battalions, broken up to provide reinforcements for the Canadian Corps after the Mount Sorrel fighting (see " 1916 " Vol. I., p. 227), had to be replaced; but the division landed in France in August, and, after some experience of trench warfare in Flanders, had just joined the corps. It brought no guns, but the brigades of the Lahore Division, which for several months had been acting as 3rd Canadian Division artillery and were covering the sector it took over, now became the divisional artillery.

[4] Casualties of the 3rd Canadian Division, 27th September-14th October, were returned as 2,969.

25th Division, which had relieved the 11th [1] in the right 1-9 Oct. sector by the morning of the 1st October, devoted its energies, in rain and mud, to the work of consolidation. The completion of the capture of Stuff Redoubt waited upon an improvement in the weather.

Meanwhile, the 55th Brigade of the 18th Division continued the struggle for complete possession of the Schwaben.[2] At 5.15 A.M. on the 2nd October the Germans counter-attacked along all the trenches between the eastern end of the redoubt and the old German front line, where they were left with a small gain of ground after bombing had continued all day.[3] The fight was renewed on the 4th October without advantage to either side. On the 5th, at 10 A.M., when the 8/Norfolk (attached from the 53rd Brigade) tried two converging bombing attacks upon the uncaptured portion of the Schwaben, movement in the mud proved very difficult and no success was achieved. On the 7th and 8th October,[4] after the 39th Division had relieved the 18th,[5] the Germans attacked at the redoubt, using *Flammenwerfer*, but were repulsed by the 16th and 17/Sherwood Foresters (117th Brigade), which took 25 prisoners.[6] At 4.30 A.M. on the 9th, the 16/Sherwood Foresters, advancing over the open since the trenches were filled with mud, made a surprise attack in the dark upon the northern face, which lay beyond the crest. The Germans were standing to arms and, although the right company of the Foresters entered the trench, it had to withdraw.

Later on this day, at 12.35 P.M., the 10/Cheshire (7th Brigade, 25th Division) stormed the northern face of Stuff Redoubt and thus completed the capture of the work, killing many Germans. Forward posts were established to the north-eastward and in the old German 2nd Position ; in the evening two counter-attacks were repulsed.[7] Fresh

---

[1] The losses of the 11th Division, 10th-30th September, were returned as 5,236.

[2] See Map 3, Sketch 39.

[3] According to "Regt. No. 66", part of its *II. Bn.* took part in this fighting. "Regt. No. 170" states that the *I./170th* had relieved the *66th* at the Schwaben. Both these regiments belonged to the *52nd Division*, but were under the orders of the *26th Reserve Division*.

[4] Br.-General P. Howell, B.G.G.S. II. Corps, was killed near Authuille by a shell on 7th October.

[5] The casualties of the 18th Division (26th September-5th October) were returned as 3,344.

[6] Of the *110th Reserve* (*28th Reserve Division*) which was relieving the *26th Reserve Division*.

[7] There were 116 prisoners of the *111th Reserve* (*28th Reserve Division*).

11-14 efforts were made by the enemy on the 11th and also on
Oct. the 12th, when, in the evening, repeated counter-attacks
towards the north-western corner of Stuff Redoubt were
driven back by the 8/Loyal N. Lancashire (7th Brigade). On
the 14th October at 2.45 P.M. this battalion attacked north-
westward from the redoubt and secured a position called
" The Mounds " which gave observation over Grandcourt.
The enemy, who had just carried out a relief, showed little
fight on this occasion, and over one hundred of the *II./111th
Reserve Regiment* were captured.

At the same hour on the 14th, the 39th Division drove
the Germans from their last hold on the Schwaben.   The
4th/5th Black Watch and 1/1st Cambridgeshire (118th
Brigade), assisted by the 17/K.R.R.C. (117th Brigade),
attacked over the open and, although the fighting continued
until 11 P.M., the enemy's discomfiture was then complete.
More than one hundred and fifty prisoners of the *II./110th
Reserve Regiment* were collected.   Meanwhile, the 1/6th
Cheshire (118th Brigade) had advanced the line on the left.
Three counter-attacks against the Schwaben, two of them
made with *Flammenwerfer*, were repulsed in the course of
the following day.

NOTE I

The French Operations South of the Somme, 10th–21st October [1]

Sketch A.   The French Tenth Army resumed its offensive on the 10th
October, and, in the course of eleven days' fighting, captured the
woods north-west of Chaulnes (4 miles south of Estrées), and made
some progress towards Pressoir, Ablaincourt and Fresnes on a
frontage extending some 3½ miles north-eastward from Chaulnes.
On the 15th October General Micheler, who was resigned to the fact
that his reserves were inadequate for a large-scale offensive, remarked
that he was " reduced to the rôle of a watch-dog for Fayolle ".[2]
The XXXIII. Corps (right of Fayolle's Sixth Army), astride the
Somme, attacked south of the river on the 18th October in order to
deal with German mining operations and to improve the French
salient at La Maisonnette (½ mile S.S.E. of Biaches).   A short advance
was made between La Maisonnette and Biaches, but on the 21st a
German counter-attack regained some ground after heavy fighting.

[1] F.O.A. iv. (iii.), pp. 205-7 and pp. 208-26.
[2] " Le Général Alfred Micheler " by Colonel E. Herbillon, p. 97.

NOTE II

The German Side, 1st–20th October [1]

The great crisis of the struggle on the Somme lasted until the middle of October. Set to defend inadequate positions constructed hastily during the course of the battle, the troops fought at a great disadvantage. General von Below, commanding the *First Army*, reported that the hostile heavy artillery " destroys our defences, " causes most losses, prevents traffic in back areas, and, by its " incessant fire, robs the fighting troops of their necessary rest ". He therefore urged that the heavy artillery reinforcements—he had the 24-cm. (9·6-inch) naval guns in mind—should be given, as their first task, the destruction of the Allied routes of ammunition supply. As a consequence of " three unpleasant blows ",[2] Gallwitz lost his trusted Chief of the Staff, Colonel Bronsart von Schellendorf, who was removed by O.H.L.

On the 5th October, O.H.L., in a letter to the German Crown Prince, said that at Verdun " every unnecessary saphead and length " of trench must be evacuated ", in order to provide troops for the Somme. During the period from the end of September to the 13th October, the six divisions in the line from Le Transloy to the Ancre were replaced by seven, and two of these were relieved in their turn. Of the nine divisions thus put in during the course of fourteen days' fighting, four (*6th, 2nd Bavarian, 19th Reserve* and *28th Reserve*) came from the German Crown Prince's Group of Armies ; two (*24th* and *40th*) from the *Sixth Army* in Crown Prince Rupprecht's Group ; two (*4th Ersatz* and *5th Ersatz*) from the *Fourth Army* in Belgium ; and one (*Marine Brigade,* equivalent to a division) from the Belgian coast. By the 20th October the comprehensive arrangements made by the new O.H.L. to reinforce the battle-front were bearing fruit : the artillery was greatly strengthened [3] and the infantry could be systematically relieved ; the additional aeroplane squadrons enabled a considerable amount of counter-battery work to be done with air observation, and " once more the infantry began to trust our flying " men ". An effective stiffening of the defence was perceptible, although attacks continued with undiminished force.

From the 7th October onward Rupprecht detected signs that, north of the Ancre, the British intended to attack eastward with considerable forces : it was anticipated that the blow would fall at any time after the middle of the month. On the 19th, O.H.L. feared that the French were about to resume the offensive at Verdun—they were indeed about to do so—and stopped the movements of reinforcements from the German Crown Prince's Group of Armies to the Somme.

---

[1] G.O.A. xi., pp. 83, 84, 87, 91 ; Ludendorff, Rupprecht, Schwarte, Gallwitz and Kuhl.

[2] Operations of the French Tenth Army, see Note I.

[3] Between 15th September and 8th October 23 more heavy batteries were sent to the *First Army* and 13½ to the Second ; and 36 worn-out batteries were replaced.

CHAPTER XVII

THE SOMME 1916

(Map 5 ; Sketches A, 44, 45)

THE SITUATION IN MID-AUTUMN AND THE CHANGE IN THE BRITISH PLANS

Oct. THE Commander-in-Chief's general view of the situation in the early days of October is contained in his report, dated the 7th, which was transmitted to the Chief of the Imperial General Staff for the information of the War Committee. He estimated that the Germans had already employed 70 divisions in the Somme battles—40 of them against the British—and had lost some 370,000 men : [1] the new defences which they had been able to construct bore no comparison either in strength or depth to the elaborate trench systems already captured from them : although bad weather increased the difficulties, a normal winter should not suffice to stop offensive operations provided the necessary means were available : the great essentials were adequate reinforcements,[2] increased supplies of ammunition, and the provision of adequate communications and troop accommodation in the devastated zone already wrested from the enemy. In conclusion, Sir Douglas Haig urged that the " utmost efforts of the Empire " should be directed towards enabling him to continue the offensive without intermission : it was not possible to say how near to breaking point the enemy might be, but there was fair prospect of far-reaching success " affording full compensation for " all that has been done to attain it " : any relaxation of

[1] According to G.O.A. x. and xi. 38 complete divisions had been engaged with the British up to the end of September. The casualties, in round figures, given month by month in the narrative amount to 335,000, but to this total the lightly wounded must be added (see the Preface to this volume).
[2] The low fighting strengths of the British battalions have been noted frequently in the narrative.

effort would, on the contrary, discount the great advantages Oct. already gained.

His hopes of carrying out the extensive operations planned at the end of September [1] were fading, although he intended to attempt all that the weather conditions allowed; and he had already settled upon the reorganization of his forces with a view to maintaining the utmost pressure upon the enemy throughout the winter. On the 7th October instructions issued by G.H.Q. fixed the strengths and composition of the Fourth and Reserve Armies, which were to become self-contained and " so organized as to be " able to carry on offensive operations when weather con- " ditions permitted ", and " to take the offensive again " energetically at the beginning of next year " : [2] the Third Army to have three divisions always training in reserve : new divisions as they arrived from England to go to the First and Second Armies : [3] one corps headquarters to remain in G.H.Q. reserve ready in case of emergency to " pick up " reserve divisions from the Second, First and Third Armies and intervene at any point on the British front. The necessary troop movements and organization were to be completed in a month.

By the middle of October conditions on and behind the battle-front were so bad as to make mere existence a severe trial of body and spirit.[4] Little could be seen from the air through the rain and mist, so counter-battery work suffered and it was often impossible to locate with accuracy the new German trenches and shell-hole positions. Objectives could not always be identified from ground level, so that it is no matter for surprise or censure that the British artillery sometimes fired short or placed its barrages too far ahead. Bursts of high-explosive were smothered in the ooze; many guns had been continuously in action for over two months and were too worn for accurate fire; in some

---

[1] See page 427.
[2] Fourth Army : 4 corps each of 4 divisions, with 3 corps in line and one training well in rear ; each corps front held by 2 divisions with 2 in close support, resting, refitting and training.

Reserve Army : 4 corps =3 of 3 divisions each and one of 4 divisions, with 3 corps in line and one training.
[3] The 3rd Australian Division, which crossed to France at the end of November, was the only one to arrive before 1917. On the other hand, the 60th Division was withdrawn from the line at the end of October and began to leave for Macedonia on 14th November (see page 460).
[4] There is a vivid description of the Somme battlefield in late autumn in " The Land-Locked Lake " (pp. 205, 210) by Lieut.-Colonel A. A. Hanbury-Sparrow, who served in the 8th Division.

Oct. partially flooded battery positions sinking platforms had to be restored with any battle débris which came to hand. The ground was so deep in mud that to move one 18-pdr. ten or twelve horses were often needed, and, to supplement the supplies brought by light-railway and pack-horse, ammunition had to be dragged up on sledges improvised of sheets of corrugated iron. The infantry, sometimes wet to the skin and almost exhausted before zero hour, were often condemned to struggle painfully forward through the mud under heavy fire against objectives vaguely defined and difficult of recognition.

After Sir Douglas Haig had consulted with Generals Rawlinson and Gough, G.H.Q. decided on the 17th October that the Third Army should now take no active part: instead of making a converging advance from both sides of Sketch A. the Ancre valley, the Reserve Army would attack astride the river, probably on the 23rd, with the co-operation of the left of the Fourth Army: the Fourth Army would attack Le Transloy on the 26th in conjunction with a French advance in the direction of Rocquigny, $1\frac{1}{4}$ miles east of Le Transloy.[1]

The situation on the 18th October, after the early morning attack of the Fourth Army had achieved such meagre results, called for another revision of the programme. Generals Foch, Rawlinson and Gough came to G.H.Q. for a conference next day, when the following operations were decided upon, " weather permitting ".

21st October: Reserve Army to attack Regina Trench (that is, complete the capture of the Thiepval ridge);

Sketch 44. 23rd October: Fourth Army to make a preliminary attack towards Le Transloy, French Sixth Army co-operating;

25th October: Reserve Army to attack astride Ancre; Fourth Army to secure spur north of Gueudecourt, also Butte de Warlencourt and the Warlencourt line beyond.

26th October: Fourth Army and French Sixth Army to deliver the Le Transloy attack.[2]

To carry out this programme proved a sheer impossi-

[1] Sir Douglas Haig, who saw General Foch on 17th October, was ready to hand over to the French Lesbœufs and the necessary road and rail communications, so that General Fayolle's Army could carry out the Le Transloy attack. General Foch was grateful but could not accept, as he was unable to transfer sufficient heavy artillery from the south side of the Somme to support such an operation.

[2] The French contemplated a progressive advance on Rocquigny and Le Mesnil, the right of the movement to be covered by the capture of St. Pierre Vaast Wood, S. of Saillisel. F.O.A. iv. (iii.), p. 229.

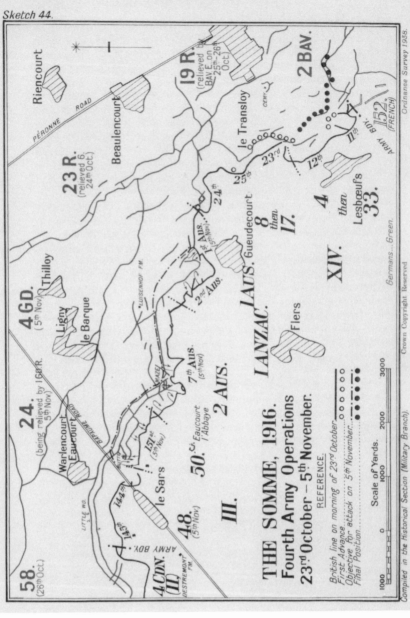

Sketch 44.

THE SOMME, 1916.
Fourth Army Operations
23rd October – 5th November.

REFERENCE.

British line on morning of 23rd October.
First Advance.
Objective for attack on 5th November.
Final Position.

Scale of Yards.

Compiled in the Historical Section (Military Branch).
Crown Copyright Reserved
Ordnance Survey 1938.
3060/38.

Riencourt

Beaulencourt

19 R. (relieved by BAV.E. on 25th–26th Oct.)

23 R. (relieved 6. 24th Oct.)

2 BAV.

le Transloy

52. (FRENCH)

PÉRONNE ROAD

Thilloy

4 GD. (5th Nov)

Ligny
le Barque

Luisenhof Fm.

2nd Aus.

3rd Aus. (5th Nov)

24th

25th

23rd

12th

11th

4. then Lesbœufs 33.

Germans.—Green.

XIV.

Gueudecourt
8 then 17.

I ANZAC.

I AUS.

Flers

7th Aus. (5th Nov)

2 AUS.

Warlencourt
Eaucourt

24. (being relieved by 16th R. 5th Nov)

Ce. Eaucourt l'Abbaye

50.

48. (5th Nov)

III.

le Sars

151st (5th Nov)

144th

143rd

58. (26th Oct.)

4 CDN. (II)

DESTREMONT Fm.

ARMY BDY.

BAPAUME ROAD

LITTLE WD.

bility.   Much rain fell on the 19th October, and after three **Oct.**
comparatively fine days a wet and stormy period super-
vened : it was not until the 3rd November that any
improvement in the weather was seen, and this proved to
be only a temporary respite.

General Joffre, who was hardly in a position to appreciate the realities of autumn warfare upon the Somme, would
have welcomed another large-scale offensive.[1]   On the
16th October he expressed to General Foch his desire that
attacks upon narrow fronts with shallow objectives should
give place to the original conception of the offensive upon
a broad front designed to carry all enemy positions which
could be effectively bombarded.   Next day he wrote to Sir
Douglas Haig in the same strain enclosing a copy of his
letter to General Foch ; and on the 18th, after he had been
informed of the revised plans for the Fourth Army, he
wrote again to the British Commander-in-Chief, urging
the resumption without delay of a powerful offensive in the
original direction, Bertincourt (3¼ miles E. of Villers)—
Bapaume—Achiet le Grand.   This letter was couched in **Sketch A.**
such terms that Sir Douglas Haig, in his reply next
day, felt obliged to repudiate the implication that he was
needlessly losing time or slackening his efforts : he also
pointed out that he was the sole judge of what the British
Armies could undertake and when they could undertake
it.[2]

Sir Douglas Haig was called on the 20th October to an
Allied conference of Ministers and their military advisers
at Boulogne, when the chief subjects for discussion were
the situation in Greece and the composition and rôle of
the Allied forces in Macedonia.[3]   The Commander-in-Chief

---

[1] As Commander-in-Chief of the French Armies (see " 1916 " Vol. I.'
p. 4) he was, to a certain extent pre-occupied with the co-ordination of
the Allied effort on all European fronts, which, at this juncture, required
grave consideration.   The Central Powers had now stabilized their front
from the Carpathians to the Pripet marshes.   In bad weather the Italians
had attacked again in the eighth battle of the Isonzo, 9th-12th October,
with small results, and were preparing to renew the offensive.   Falkenhayn
had already cleared the invading Rumanian Armies from Transylvania ;
Mackensen had defeated the Rumanians and Russians in the Dobrudja, and
on the 19th had established himself north of the Constanza—Czernavoda
railway.   In Macedonia the Franco-Serbian offensive towards Monastir
began on 12th October, but there seemed to be little hope of bringing effective
Russo-Rumanian pressure to bear upon the Bulgarians.

[2] General Joffre accepted this reminder with the utmost good humour.
He lunched at Beauquesne with Sir Douglas Haig on 23rd October, when
complete amity prevailed.

[3] See " Macedonia " Vol. I., p. 201.

Oct. was chiefly affected by the French proposals that reinforcements should be sent to Salonika, a course which the British were reluctant to approve.   On the 26th October, however, Sir Douglas Haig was ordered to send one division from France to Salonika.   He selected the 60th (2/2nd London) Division (Major-General E. S. Bulfin), fresh, well-trained and at full strength.

THE RESERVE (FIFTH) ARMY [1] : 15TH OCTOBER–12TH NOVEMBER

BATTLE OF THE ANCRE HEIGHTS (*concluded*)

Having discussed his plans with Lieut.-General Kiggell, Chief of the General Staff, on the previous day, General Gough had been able to issue an operation order for his modified offensive as early as the 15th October.   The attack, now to be made astride the Ancre, would be delivered by the II. Corps south of the river and the V. Corps, with some assistance from the XIII. Corps, on the Sketch A. north : the objectives named were the spur running north from Courcelette, Miraumont, thence to Serre ; a subsequent advance was to secure Pys and Irles.

The necessary reorganization of the battle line began at once ; for at this time it was hoped to attack on the 23rd October, after the II. Corps had captured Regina and Stuff trenches on the 19th.   North of the Ancre the XIII. Corps (Lieut.-General W. N. Congreve) parted with the 19th and 51st Divisions,[2] and by the 17th October its whole front (extending south from Hébuterne for 1,500 yards) was held by the 31st Division.   Next on the right, Lieut.-General E. A. Fanshawe's V. Corps extended its front southward as far as the river, relieving the left of the 39th Division by the 63rd Division, and bringing in the 2nd Division again.   The corps then had the 63rd, 51st, 2nd Sketch and 3rd Divisions in line from right to left.   In the II.
45. Corps, south of the Ancre, the 39th Division extended its right to Stuff Redoubt, Lieut.-General C. W. Jacob taking over the line up to the right boundary of the Fifth Army. This was accomplished by the replacement of the 1st Canadian Division by the 4th Canadian Division, the latter coming under the II. Corps when the relief of the Canadian

---

[1] General Gough's Army was renamed " Fifth " at the end of October. It will henceforward be convenient to call it so.

[2] The 19th Division went to the II. Corps, the 51st to the V. Corps.

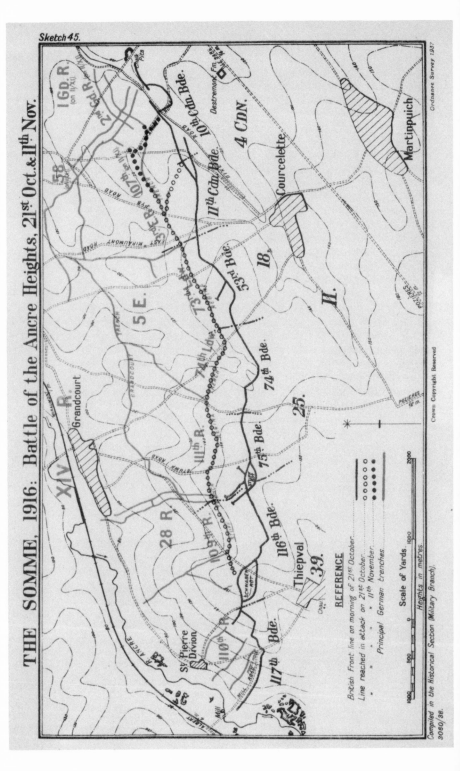

Sketch 45.

THE SOMME, 1916: Battle of the Ancre Heights, 21st Oct. & 11th Nov.

REFERENCE

British Front line on morning of 21st October.............
Line reached in attack on 21st October..............
    "   "   "   11th November...........
Principal German trenches.............

Scale of Yards

Heights in metres.

Compiled in the Historical Section (Military Branch).

3060/38.

Ordnance Survey 1937.

Crown Copyright Reserved

Corps was completed on the 17th October.[1] Between the Oct.
4th Canadian Division and the 25th was the 18th Division
which, on the 14th, had supplied a brigade to hold the left
of the Canadian sector.

It is to the credit of pilots and observers that the 5th
Brigade R.F.C. continued to provide all possible assistance
in spite of rain, high winds, mist and cold. Poor visibility
was, of course, a great hindrance to counter-battery work,
but full advantage was taken of every bright interval to
direct artillery fire and to photograph new work on the
German defences. Although the banks of the canalized
Ancre had been broken by shell-fire, so that there was much
overflow into the marshland on either side, air reconnaissance discovered no signs that the enemy had dammed
the river ; flood water seen south of Miraumont mill
was attributed to an accumulation of weeds in the river
bed.

On General Gough's application, it was arranged to
reinforce his heavy artillery by 12 siege batteries and three
divisional artilleries from the Third Army. The 1st
Cavalry Division and all the tanks available were also
to be at the disposal of the Fifth Army.[2] Unfortunately,
whilst frequent postponements gave ample time for special
reconnaissance by the tank commanders, the deep mud
threatened to make tank action impossible.

At the beginning of October tunnelling operations had
been restarted on the front opposite Beaumont Hamel—
Serre, with the object of reconditioning the Russian saps
prepared for use on the 1st July, and mining the crater
on Hawthorn Ridge, west of Beaumont Hamel, which
was in German hands.[3] The work made good progress,
although the removal of spoil and the bringing up of timber
was much impeded by the bad weather and enemy shell-
fire.[4]

At 9.45 A.M. on the 19th October, the Fifth Army
announced that the capture of Regina and Stuff trenches
was postponed for 24 hours ; following the decision

---

[1] The Canadian Corps (1st, 2nd and 3rd Divisions) departed at once to
join the First Army, but the field artillery of these divisions remained in
action under the II. Corps.

[2] Early in October 52 machines, organized in three companies, were
concentrated at Acheux, 5½ miles west of Auchonvillers (see Sketch A).
One company of 20 was sent south of the Ancre on 16th October.

[3] See " 1916 " Vol. I., p. 429, et seq.

[4] The 252nd Tunnelling Company R.E. was responsible for most of
the V. Corps work, the 174th Company operating in the Hamel sector and
in the II. Corps area south of the river.

Oct.-Nov. reached at the G.H.Q. conference,[1] a message issued at 1.30 P.M. altered the date for this attack to the 21st October and that for the main operation to the 25th. A day of rain was succeeded by sun on the 20th when a high wind dried the mud to some extent ; the next morning broke fine and cold. The II. Corps attack was duly and successfully delivered on the 21st ;[2] but, although the 22nd October was fine, a heavy mist then came down, and on the 24th rain set in once more. The main operation was repeatedly postponed, General Gough being given full discretion to do so by G.H.Q., and on the 27th the " provisional date " was fixed for the 1st November. Two days later this was altered to the 5th, and on the 3rd November the Commander-in-Chief authorized General Gough to postpone his offensive indefinitely " with the proviso that arrangements " are made to bring on the attack without delay as soon as " the weather shows signs of being more settled ".

Sir Douglas Haig came to Fifth Army headquarters on the afternoon of the 5th and suggested a smaller effort, if the state of the ground permitted, whilst the preparations for the main attack proceeded : General Gough thought that if no more rain fell the V. Corps could take the Beaucourt—Beaumont Hamel—Serre position on the 9th, the II. Corps assisting by an advance of its left. There was rain on the 6th,[3] when General Gough telephoned to G.H.Q. to say that if the weather grew no worse he could attack on the 9th with fair prospect of success : nevertheless, if the general situation permitted, he thought it wiser to delay. Sir Douglas Haig replied that, in any event, the attack must not be launched until the ground was dry enough for the infantry to advance freely and two days of fair weather were in prospect. Consequently a further postponement took place. Late on the 8th November,[4] following a visit from Lieut.-General Kiggell, General Gough conferred with his corps commanders and decided that, provided no more heavy rain fell, the attack should be launched on the 13th November. Meanwhile staff

[1] See page 458.
[2] See below.
[3] On this day Sir Douglas Haig told the Third Army to continue its attack preparations against Monchy le Preux, S.E. of Arras, which would certainly be required in the spring, if not before : for this operation improved railway communications were of particular importance.
[4] The 1st Cavalry Division, which had remained S.W. of Doullens under Fifth Army orders, marched on 8th November to rejoin the Cavalry Corps in the coastal area.

officers and patrols were sent out at short intervals to report upon the state of the ground.

On the 21st October, a fine, cold day, the II. Corps attack was delivered against Regina and Stuff trenches upon a frontage of nearly 5,000 yards. It was supported by 200 heavy guns and howitzers and the field artilleries of seven divisions.[1] As if aware that an assault was impending, the Germans delivered a counter-attack at 5 A.M., before daylight, against the northern face of Schwaben Redoubt and obtained a footing in it at two points. They were driven out, after a sharp fight, by the 17/K.R.R.C. (117th Brigade, attached 116th) and part of the 14/Hampshire (116th Brigade), leaving behind some thirty prisoners. During the morning there was considerable shelling of the corps line.

The British artillery had, at last, dealt effectively with the German wire in front of both trenches, where a methodical bombardment had wrought much havoc. Zero hour was 12.6 P.M., when the infantry of the 4th Canadian, 18th, 25th and 39th Divisions went forward behind an excellent barrage.

Advancing from the left sector of the 4th Canadian Division (Major-General D. Watson), the 87th (Canadian Grenadier Guards) and 102nd Battalions (11th Brigade) were aided by intense overhead machine-gun fire. They encountered little opposition in gaining their objective, for the enemy seemed to be taken by surprise. A defensive flank was formed by the 87th Battalion on the right, east of the Pys road, and posts were established well forward of Regina Trench. On the left the 102nd Battalion was in touch with the 10/Essex (53rd Brigade of Major-General Maxse's 18th Division), which gathered in a number of Germans who came forward to surrender, but had some sharp fighting before completing its task. The 8/Norfolk of the same brigade also overcame all resistance, although, at a point near the Courcelette—Grandcourt road, a bombing struggle persisted for some time. In this the 11/Lancashire Fusiliers, forming the right of the 25th Division attack, played a part.[2]

---

[1] Beginning at zero hour the heavy artillery fired for 40 minutes (average 23·5 rounds per gun) on Grandcourt Trench, all trenches and tracks running back to Grandcourt and Miraumont, and Grandcourt village. There were special concentrations upon trench junctions and other selected points.

[2] The junction of the 18th and 25th Divisions was almost opposite that of the *73rd* and *74th Landwehr* (*5th Ersatz Division*, which had relieved the *Marine Brigade*, 11th/12th October).

21 Oct.

Sketch 45.

21-22
Oct.
The 25th Division (Major-General E. G. T. Bainbridge) employed two brigades. On the right the 74th Brigade, with the 11/Lancashire Fusiliers, 9/Loyal N. Lancashire and 13/Cheshire in line, succeeded at slight cost, many Germans being caught unprepared and without their equipment. In the 75th Brigade, west of the Pozières—Miraumont road, the 8/Border Regiment (with one company of the 11/Cheshire attached), 8/South Lancashire and 2/South Lancashire, had an almost similar experience. The Border Regiment, which suffered casualties from hugging the barrage too closely, had to bomb a large dug-out full of recalcitrant Germans. Bombers of the 8/South Lancashire pushed on, clearing the dug-outs in Stump Road until progress was stopped by the British standing barrage.

Stuff Trench was captured by the 116th Brigade of the 39th Division (Major-General G. J. Cuthbert). The 13/R. Sussex had something of a struggle in bombing forward beyond the objective up the original German 2nd Position, where fifty yards of trench were gained ; but the 11/R. Sussex, in the centre, and a company of the 14/Hampshire, on the left, accomplished their task without much trouble. A subsidiary attack of the 117th Brigade, delivered by one company each of the 17/Sherwood Foresters and 16/Rifle Brigade, gained some ground in the vicinity of Pope's Nose.

The capture of the II. Corps objective had been accomplished in half-an-hour ; but, although the whole crest of the Thiepval ridge was now in British hands, observation of the Ancre valley at close range was still, to a considerable extent, hampered by the convex nature of the slope. The enemy appeared to anticipate a further advance, for he put down a barrage in front of the Grandcourt line. Only the Canadian left (102nd Battalion) received counter-attacks, at least three being repulsed during the afternoon; it was not until later in the day that the captured trenches were heavily shelled. As consolidation proceeded, more and more prisoners were collected, and by 5 P.M. next day 16 officers and 1,041 other ranks had been captured.[1] The infantry losses of the II. Corps averaged less than 25 per cent in the assault, but these were considerably increased by the subsequent hostile bombardment.

On the night of the 22nd October, the 18th Division

---

[1] Including representatives of every battalion but three in the *5th Ersatz Division* and *28th Reserve Division*. The latter was relieved almost at once by the *38th Division*, and on 26th October the *58th Division*, began to relieve the *5th Ersatz Division*.

extended its left to the Pozières—Miraumont road, and the 22 Oct.-
19th Division (Major-General G. T. M. Bridges) relieved the 11 Nov.
25th Division, also taking over the right sector of the 39th
as far as the western side of Schwaben Redoubt. Forty-
eight hours later the 4th Canadian Division took over from
the left of the Fourth Army as far as the chalk pits on the
Le Sars—Pys road. Next day the 44th Battalion (10th
Canadian Brigade) made a stout effort to extend by frontal
attack the Canadian occupation of Regina Trench up to
Farmer Road. The attempt was, however, foiled by the
mud, a heavy German counter-barrage, and machine-gun
fire from the right flank.

At 5 A.M. on the 26th October the Germans attacked
Stuff Redoubt east of the old German 2nd Position and
were repulsed with considerable loss by the 7/East Lancashire (56th Brigade, 19th Division) assisted by artillery fire,
an officer and 40 other Germans being captured. On the
29th the 39th Division, by a bombing enterprise, again
improved its position at Pope's Nose. The bad weather
then caused a suspension of offensive operations on the
corps front. Finer conditions on the 9th and 10th November having permitted an effective bombardment to be
carried out, the 4th Canadian Division tried again for the
eastern portion of Regina Trench at midnight on the
10th/11th November in the misty light of the moon. The
46th (S. Saskatchewan) and 47th (Br. Columbia) Battalions
(10th Brigade), with a company of the 102nd Battalion
(11th Brigade) on their left, advanced as close as possible
to the German line before zero hour when the barrage
opened ; eight minutes later it lifted and the Canadians
stormed the trench before the enemy was ready to resist.
Advanced positions were established in the centre, and
up the trenches leading north-eastward into the Le Sars—
Pys line. Several counter-attacks were repulsed and four
machine guns and 87 prisoners were captured,[1] the losses
of the Canadians amounting to about two hundred.

North of the Ancre a considerable gas operation was 28 Oct.
carried out by the Special Brigade R.E. on the 28th
October. No less than 1,126 lacrymatory bombs were fired
from 4-inch Stokes mortars into Beaumont Hamel, silencing
the German machine guns and *Minenwerfer* in two minutes.
At night 9.5-inch mortars and 2-inch Stokes mortars

---

[1] Mostly *107th Regiment* (*58th Division*) and some of the *2nd Guard
Reserve* in the right sector of the *1st Guard Reserve Division*.

28 Oct.- hurled 135 40-lb. phosgene bombs into Beaumont Hamel
7 Nov. and Y Ravine south of the village and also into the head of
the valley south-west of Serre.[1]

Active patrolling and many raids were carried out by
the V. and XIII. Corps, although these enterprises were
handicapped by the mud and by the difficulty of maintaining direction in the prevalent fog. On the night of the
31st October a patrol of the XIII. Corps entered the German
front line south-east of Hébuterne and found it unoccupied
for a distance of fifty yards. Two patrols of the V. Corps
broke in opposite Serre on the following night and penetrated to the German support line. A raid carried out at
1 A.M. on the 7th November by the 31st Division (XIII.
Corps) south-east of Hébuterne accounted for over thirty
Germans, including four prisoners, at the cost of four men
wounded. The enemy seemed to be in greater strength
and more alert near the river in the vicinity of Beaumont
Hamel.

The Fourth Army

21st October–11th November

Map 5.   Little rain fell whilst the XIV. Corps (Lieut.-General
Sketch Lord Cavan) completed its preparations for the attack of
44.
the 23rd October ; but the day of battle was so misty that,
after consultation with the French, zero hour was changed
23 Oct. from 11.30 A.M. to 2.30 P.M. in the hope that visibility
might improve. The objectives remained the same : first,
the German front defences and the establishment of a line
beyond the crest of the spur ; then a position within assaulting distance of Le Transloy. A halt of 30 minutes was to be
made on the first objective. The heavy artillery continued
to bombard the village and the cemetery ; at zero hour
a standing barrage was placed upon the first objective,
and a creeping barrage started in front of the infantry,
moving at the rate of 50 yards per minute. In this,
and in subsequent operations of the Fourth Army, the
battalions engaged were usually represented by two weak
companies.

On the right the 11th Brigade of the 4th Division
(Major-General Hon. W. Lambton) attacked with the
1/Hampshire and 2/R. Dublin Fusiliers (attached from the

[1] For further details see Major-General C. H. Foulkes's " Gas ",
p. 168, f.n. 1.

10th Brigade).   The Hampshire and the left of the French 23 Oct.
(152nd Division) were stopped almost at once by fire from
Boritska [1] Trench, their joint objective, and from machine
guns in scattered shell-holes; but, when the 1/Rifle Brigade
arrived to reinforce, posts were established north-west of
the objective.   After dark touch was obtained with the
Fusiliers, who had secured the gun-pits on their front,
and also a strongpoint beyond.[2]   The 1/R. Warwickshire
(attached from the 10th Brigade) was to advance through
the Irishmen, but the two battalions had become mixed,
and, after hand to hand fighting, all attempts to go farther
were frustrated by fire from the flanks.[3]   The 12th Brigade
failed against machine-gun fire from Dewdrop Trench
astride the Lesboeufs—Le Transloy road, a few of the
2/Essex who forced their way into the position being overwhelmed.   The 1/King's Own, however, entered the
German portion of Spectrum, north of Dewdrop, and then
pushed on.   Bombers of the 2/Duke of Wellington's lent
assistance, but in the end only Spectrum was captured.

The 8th Division (Major-General H. Hudson), which had
completed the relief of the 6th on the morning of the 20th
October,[4] had the 23rd Brigade on the right where the
2/Scottish Rifles and 2/Middlesex stormed Zenith Trench.
The Rifles pushed on into Orion, 200 yards ahead, but were
shelled out before darkness fell; on the left, the efforts
of the Middlesex to bomb northwards failed.   The 25th
Brigade frontal attack upon the northern part of Zenith met
with no success, the 2/Lincolnshire being stopped by rapid
fire; only a few small parties came forward on the right to
join hands with the Middlesex.   The 2/Rifle Brigade, next
on the left, could not carry a strongpoint situated at the
salient formed by the junction of Zenith and Eclipse
Trenches; but a line of posts was established for some
hundred and thirty yards from the British front line south-
eastward towards the strongpoint.   On the left of the
divisional front the 2/East Lancashire (24th Brigade)
stormed and consolidated most of Mild Trench and blocked

---

[1] Called " Baniska " by the French.
[2] This success was largely due to the gallant action of Sergt. R. Downie,
2/R. Dublin Fusiliers, who, after the advance had been checked, charged
a machine gun single-handed and killed its detachment.   He was awarded
the V.C.
[3] The *15th Bavarians* (*2nd Bavarian Division*) is said to have lost 200
yards of front and some prisoners, but regained ground by counter-attack
during the night.   Regimental history.
[4] From 9th-20th October, 1,863 casualties were reported by the 6th
Division.

the flanks, where bombing attacks were repulsed.[1]   Nearly fifty prisoners were captured.

24-28   A night of rain promised little chance of success for a
Oct.   renewed attack of the 25th Brigade against Zenith Trench which was delivered at 3.50 A.M. on the 24th October. Struggling through mud and water, the 2/R. Berkshire and 1/R. Irish Rifles lost the barrage and were stopped by rifle and machine-gun fire after going 70 yards.   At night began the relief of the 4th Division by Major-General R. J. Pinney's 33rd Division.[2]

On the 24th October [3] the Allied attack against Le Transloy was postponed for 48 hours ; further postponements followed, on account of the bad weather, and on the 31st General Foch asked Sir Douglas Haig for a delay until the 5th November.

Meanwhile, in accordance with General Rawlinson's orders, the XIV. Corps made fresh efforts to gain ground in the direction of Le Transloy.   On the 28th October the 33rd Division succeeded in capturing Rainy and Dewdrop trenches, north-east of Lesboeufs.   The 1/Middlesex and 4/King's (98th Brigade) advanced at 6 A.M., and, in spite of machine-gun fire, the Middlesex reached Rainy ; by 9.30 A.M. the battalion had bombed the Germans out of the southern part of Dewdrop, capturing two officers, 60 men and two machine guns.   The King's, on the left, obtained a footing in Dewdrop and cleared their portion in the same way, securing 148 prisoners, among them a battalion commander.[4]

---

[1] " Res. Regt. No. 92 " (*19th Reserve Division*) states that the British broke in on the left of the *64th Regiment* (*6th Division*) S.E. of the Gueudecourt—Beaulencourt road, causing a gap.   The right of the *92nd Reserve* was in danger of being rolled up, but the situation was restored about 5 P.M. by the reserves.   There was still a gap on the right when the *102nd Reserve* (*23rd Reserve Division*) relieved the *64th Regiment* on the night of 24th October.

" Regt. No. 64 " claims that the ground lost was regained, but companies were reduced to 20-40 men.   A difference between the French and British tactics is noted : the former bombarded in depth and attacked in small groups ; the latter shelled principally the German front positions and attacked in masses losing heavily thereby.

[2] The 4th Division reported its October casualties as just over 4,000.

[3] On this day at Verdun, under General Nivelle's direction, General Mangin attacked on the right bank of the Meuse in thick fog with 8½ divisions (3½ in first line) supported by 654 guns.   Fort Douaumont was retaken and the French line carried close to Fort Vaux, thus flattening the German salient N.E. of the city.   Fort Vaux was evacuated by the Germans on 2nd November and occupied by the French that same night. General Mangin wished to exploit the success, but General Joffre could only allot a small quantity of the artillery ammunition required.   F.O.A. iv. (iii.), pp. 361, 389-404, 422.

[4] They belonged to the *15th Bavarian Reserve* and *III./28th Ersatz,*

At dawn, 5.45 A.M., next morning the 19th Brigade 29 Oct.- (1/Cameronians and 5th/6th Scottish Rifles), in the right 3 Nov. sector, made an attack which was checked by machine-gun fire from fortified shell-holes. Some of the Scottish Rifles had a bayonet encounter in the north-western portion of Boritska Trench, but gained no ground. The next effort of the division was made on the 1st November, when the French left, " which had not been ready before ",[1] attacked in concert with the 100th Brigade. The 1/9th Highland L.I. and 2/Worcestershire were shelled before they advanced at 3.30 P.M., " up to the waist in slime ", against Boritska and the German position north-west of that trench. They had to withdraw at dusk, failure being due to machine-gun fire from Le Transloy cemetery and to the exhausted state of the troops. The French had carried most of their portion of Boritska Trench and also Tranchée de Tours, running southward from it; but they had made no effort on their extreme left.[2]

The 17th Division (Major-General P. R. Robertson), which relieved the 8th Division at the end of October,[3] captured the remainder of Zenith Trench—the south-western face of the German salient mid-way between Gueudecourt and Le Transloy—by a surprise attack at 5.30 P.M. on the 2nd November, when a detachment of the 7/Border Regiment (51st Brigade) killed a number of Germans with bayonet and bomb, and sent back some prisoners. After a counter-attack had been repulsed a block was established 150 yards up Eclipse Trench, which ran north-eastward. Next day the 7/Lincolnshire (also 51st Brigade) repulsed by fire a counter-attack upon Zenith from the north, made over the open ; in the evening, assisted by bombers of the 7/Green Howards, the battalion cleared out a " pocket " of Germans in Zenith.[4] At 4 P.M. the 1/Queen's (100th Brigade, 33rd Division) made an

---

next on the south (both of the *Bavarian Ersatz Division*, which had relieved the *19th Reserve Division* 25th/26th October) ; also to the *12th Bavarians* (*2nd Bavarian Division*).

" Bav. Regt. No. 12 " states that it had 11 companies in line, its left flank being opposite the French. The two right companies were overrun and mostly captured, as the attack penetrated a gap next to the *28th Ersatz* and effected a surprise.

[1] Since 23rd October it had been trying to progress due eastward without much success. F.O.A. iv. (iii.), pp. 241-8.

[2] By next day they were firmly established in Tranchée de Conte [600 yards N.E. of Boritska]. F.O.A. iv. (iii.), p. 246.

[3] The 8th Division showed a casualty list of nearly 2,500 for the period 23rd-29th October. There were many sick.

[4] The *15th Bavarian Reserve* (*Bavarian Ersatz Division*) was the chief sufferer in this fighting.

unsuccessful attempt on Boritska Trench, the French barrage appearing to fall beyond the objective.[1]

3-4 Nov. On the 3rd November General Rawlinson received a letter from Lord Cavan, who expressed the view, shared by his subordinate commanders, that Le Transloy ought to be attacked from the south and not from the west : he had already lost 5,320 men in attacks from the west and south-west : he was ready to sacrifice the British right rather than jeopardize the success of the French left if such was the intention, and orders had been issued for the 5th November operation : but no one who had not visited the front could really appreciate the state of exhaustion to which his troops were reduced owing to the rain and mud and the long distance over which all food, water and battle stores had to be carried.

In consequence, General Rawlinson informed G.H.Q. that he proposed to limit the scope of his next attack, and on the afternoon of the 4th the Commander-in-Chief called a conference at Fourth Army headquarters, which General Foch attended. It was then decided that the XIV. Corps should do no more than capture the nearest German positions east and north-east of Lesboeufs. The British difficulties were explained to General Foch, who expressed his complete understanding ; but, always optimistic, he pointed out that he hoped to secure St. Pierre Vaast Wood and Government Farm on the 5th and when this was accomplished the French would be holding a dangerous salient.[2] Sir Douglas Haig said that the Fourth Army would be attacking at other points on the 5th in order to exert a general pressure upon the German line. Subsequently General Rawlinson saw Lord Cavan, who undertook to ensure that the left of the French would be covered.

Oct.-Nov. On the 30th October the I. Anzac Corps (Lieut.-General Sir W. R. Birdwood) had replaced Lieut.-General Du Cane's XV. Corps in the centre of the Fourth Army front, the 1st Australian Division (Major-General H. B. Walker) relieving the 29th Division (Major-General H. de B. de Lisle).[3] The

---

[1] The French XXXII. Corps had repulsed German counter-attacks at Sailly (Sketch A) on 21st October and 1st November, and had made small advances there on 29th and 30th October. After three abortive attempts to secure the N.W. edge of St. Pierre Vaast Wood a lodgment was secured by the V. Corps on 1st November and held against a counter-attack on the 4th. F.O.A. iv. (iii.), pp. 247-50.

[2] See Sketch A. Government Farm was a mile S.E. of Saillisel.

[3] The 29th Division, which had relieved the 12th Division on the morning of 19th October, following the last attack of the XV. Corps, returned its casualties as 1,874 for the period 11th-30th October.

5th Australian Division (Major-General Hon. J. W. McCay)[1] had been in the line since the 22nd October, having then taken over from the 30th Division.[2] No attack had been launched by the centre and left corps of the Army since the 18th October, the contemplated operations waiting upon the advance of the Fifth Army. On the 30th October, however, it was decided that the German salients north of Gueudecourt and north-east of Eaucourt l'Abbaye, together with the Butte de Warlencourt, should be the objectives of an independent operation whenever the weather permitted. First fixed for the 2nd November, the date was eventually altered to the 5th to coincide with the attacks of the XIV. Corps and the French.

Map 5.
Sketch 44.

A wet night was succeeded, as day broke on the 5th November, by a heavy gale. The general zero hour was 11.10 A.M., when the assaulting battalions found great difficulty in scrambling out of their assembly trenches, still deep in mud. The " going " on open ground was, in many parts, better than might have been expected, and the barrage which, in the XIV. Corps, began to " creep " at the rate of 25 yards per minute, did not move too quickly for the infantry.

5 Nov.

In the 33rd Division, on the right next to the French,[3] the 2/Worcestershire (100th Brigade) took Boritska and Mirage trenches by a flank attack delivered from the French front.[4] The battalion joined hands with the 16/K.R.R.C. (also 100th Brigade), which had carried Hazy Trench by frontal assault.[5] Next on the left, the 2/R. Welch Fusiliers (19th Brigade) pushed forward up the Lesboeufs—Le Transloy road, but could not gain much ground owing to the failure of the fighting patrols of the 7/East Yorkshire

[1] The 5th Australian Division had fought at Fromelles. It was transferred to the I. Anzac Corps in October, its place in the II. Anzac Corps being taken by the 3rd Australian Division which arrived from the United Kingdom in November.

[2] The casualties of the 30th Division, 11th-22nd October, amounted to 2,650.

[3] The French left was checked at once by machine-gun fire. Farther to the east (see Sketch A) a little progress was made at Saillisel by the XXXII. Corps, which also penetrated St. Pierre Vaast Wood from the N.W. The advance of the V. Corps into the wood from the S.W. failed. F.O.A. iv. (iii.), pp. 260-1.

[4] The Worcestershire were rallied after a check by Lieut. E. P. Bennett, who urged on the advance with a spade in his hand. This officer, who had previously been blown up by a shell, was awarded the V.C. for his gallant leadership.

[5] Prisoners taken belonged to the *81st Reserve* (*222nd Division*), which had just relieved the *I./24th Bavarians* (*1st* attached *2nd, Bavarian Division*).

5 Nov. and 7/Green Howards (50th Brigade), advancing from the right sector of the 17th Division. The Green Howards tried again at night, with no better success.

In pouring rain at 12.30 A.M. the I. Anzac Corps had made a preliminary attack against the German salient north of Gueudecourt, the 3rd Battalion (1st Brigade, 1st Australian Division) sending forward bombing parties to enter the German front line on the eastern face and work along it in both directions. The southern party was checked by machine-gun fire, but the bombers who turned north inflicted considerable loss on the enemy [1] and joined hands with another party which had advanced north-westward along a sunken road on the right. Unfortunately all that was gained had to be relinquished, for the 1st Battalion, which advanced from the trenches of the 2nd Australian Brigade, had failed in two frontal attacks on Hilt Trench, a bombing attack meeting with the same fate. The troops were wet through and " chilled to the bone " before zero hour and, owing to the mud, found it impossible to keep up with the barrage.

As the Fourth Army operation order had said " weather " permitting ", there was much consultation in the I. Anzac and III. Corps as to the advisability of launching the main attack. Br.-General J. Paton,[2] whose 7th Brigade was to advance from the Anzac left sector,[3] wanted a postponement, but he was over-ruled.

The 7th Brigade attacked with the 27th Battalion on the right, a composite battalion in the centre,[4] and the 28th Battalion on the left, having for objectives the western end of Bayonet Trench and the Gird trenches as far as the left boundary of the corps. By a misunderstanding, some companies waited three minutes after zero hour and so lost all hope of keeping close to the barrage ; nevertheless, the 27th Battalion entered Bayonet Trench at several points and maintained the struggle until the survivors were compelled to withdraw at dusk. Some of the composite

---

[1] Prisoners belonged to the *101st Reserve* (*23rd Reserve Division*), which had relieved the *6th Division* on 24th October.

[2] He was wounded by a sniper in the morning, before the attack was launched.

[3] The 2nd Australian Division had relieved the 5th Australian Division here, but Major-General McCay continued in command till noon, 5th November.

[4] One company each of the 27th, 26th (from support) and 25th Battalions. The 25th could not get forward through the mud in time to take part as a whole, so a hasty improvisation had to be made. The leading company of the 25th arrived just in time to advance.

battalion entered the Maze, whence all efforts of the enemy 5 Nov. could not completely dislodge them. The 28th Battalion failed after two attempts ; later in the day it made a gradual withdrawal from the shell-holes it had occupied about a hundred yards from the German line.[1]

In touch with the Australians, the attack of the III. Corps (Lieut.-General Sir W. P. Pulteney) was delivered by the 1/8th, 1/6th and 1/9th Durham L.I. (151st Brigade of Major-General P. S. Wilkinson's 50th Division).[2] The 1/8th, on the right—where men had to pull each other out of the mud before they could advance—struggled on, far behind the barrage, almost to the German front line, but was then stopped by enfilade machine-gun fire from both flanks. A gradual withdrawal was carried out during the day. The 1/6th Durham L.I. suffered a similar experience, except on the left where some of the battalion entered the German position with the 1/9th. The latter broke through two lines of German trenches, reached the Butte, and established a post on the Bapaume road ; some parties even entered the Warlencourt line. Observers could see Durham men on the Butte itself so that a notable success was expected, but during the afternoon the advanced posts were driven in. Fighting continued all day, and at 10 P.M. the quarry, west of the Butte, was still held and also 500 yards of the German front line. Then, about midnight, German counter-attacks at last prevailed : the weary survivors of the Durham L.I. were forced out of the captured trenches and compelled to withdraw altogether.[3]

[1] The opponents of the Australians belonged to the *4th Guard Division* which had relieved the *40th Division*.

"Foot Gd. Regt. No. 5" relates that its line (Bayonet Trench) was entered and that local counter-attacks failed as the Australian bombers out-threw those of the Guard. The whole position was eventually restored except on the right (the Maze). On the 11th it was found that the Australians had withdrawn.

"Gd. Gren. Regt. No. 5" states that two assaults were repelled by its *II. Bn.*, the Australians (left and left centre of attack) seeking cover in shell-holes.

[2] The corps heavy artillery concentrated on the Gird lines, the Butte de Warlencourt, and the area between Warlencourt and Le Barque—Thilloy.

[3] The *1st Guard Reserve Division* was relieving the *24th Division*. "Regt. No. 179" relates how the British swarmed over the Butte and reached the Warlencourt line ; fighting continued all day, the German artillery firing on friend and foe alike. Detachments of the *I./1st Guard Reserve* and *I./179th* and *139th Regiments* (both *24th Division*) took part, and at 10.50 P.M. a converging attack eventually cleared the quarry "where the British defended themselves well".

The right and centre of the 151st Brigade had been checked by the right of the *5th Guard Grenadiers* and *93rd Reserve* (the latter in the right sector of the *4th Guard Division*).

On the 6th November General Rawlinson explained the Commander-in-Chief's future intentions to his corps commanders and their staffs. The big operation of the Fifth Army had been reduced in scope and was now expected to start on the 9th November, when the I. Anzac Corps and the III. Corps would repeat their attacks, weather permitting. In general, the Fourth Army would " undertake modified operations ", in accordance with the Allied policy which now aimed at exerting such pressure upon the Germans as to prevent them reinforcing other theatres with troops from the Western Front.

General Foch had relinquished all idea of large-scale attacks. The French XXXII. Corps continued the struggle at Saillisel on the 6th November without much success, and next day the plateau of Sailly-Saillisel and the northern part of St. Pierre Vaast Wood were named as the Sixth Army objectives. Elsewhere the French proceeded with the consolidation of the line they held.[1] The British attack upon Le Transloy was further discussed between Lord Cavan and General Rawlinson. A proposal to take over front from the French in order to attack the village from the south came to nothing owing to the bad weather, and also to the negotiations for a considerable extension of the British line of which more will be said hereafter.

NOTE I

THE LAST PHASES OF THE FIGHTING SOUTH OF THE SOMME [2]

Sketch A. On the 29th October the XXXIII. Corps (French Sixth Army) lost La Maisonnette, at the tip of the French salient south-east of Biaches ; the position was smothered and cut off by a German bombardment of high explosive, gas and lacrymatory shell. Preparations to retake La Maisonnette were delayed by the necessity of first carrying out infantry reliefs and reinforcing the artillery. The attempt was never made.

The renewed attack of the Tenth Army was delayed by bad weather until the 7th November when Bois Kratz, south-west of Pressoire, and the villages of Pressoire and Ablaincourt (respectively 3 and 2½ miles south of Estrées) were taken. All counter-attacks, including a very powerful one against Bois Kratz and Pressoire on the 15th November, were repulsed. Preparations were then begun for operations against the line Mazancourt (3 miles S.E. of Estrées)

[1] F.O.A. iv. (iii.), pp. 265-7. The capture of Saillisel was practically completed by attacks delivered on 9th, 10th, 11th November.
[2] F.O.A. iv. (iii.), pp. 251-3, 277-80, 291.

Happlincourt (on the Somme 4 miles south of Péronne)—Biaches, as a preliminary to the spring offensive planned by General Joffre. This project was abandoned when General Nivelle succeeded General Joffre in December.

NOTE II

The German Side, 21st October–11th November [1]

The French attack at Verdun on the 24th October [2] upset the programme of reliefs for the Somme front. Nevertheless, owing to the continuation of the British attacks, all seven German divisions holding the front from Le Transloy to the Ancre had to be relieved during the period 24th October-10th November ; and one of the fresh formations was relieved in its turn. Of these eight new divisions, three (*38th, 222nd* and *Bavarian Ersatz*) came from the Crown Prince's Group of Armies ; three (*4th Guard, 58th* and *1st Guard Reserve*) from the *Fourth Army* ; and two (*23rd Reserve* and *24th Reserve*) from the *Sixth Army* in Crown Prince Rupprecht's own group. Many commanders lamented the deterioration in the fighting quality of the German troops, but after the 1st November a serious reverse to the *First Army* was no longer feared by O.H.L.

On the 6th November O.H.L. ordered the formation of 13 new divisions, of which five were to be organized and equipped for mountain warfare in the Rumanian and Italian theatres.

The German success at La Maisonnette [3] on the 29th October was greeted with great satisfaction by Ludendorff and Rupprecht. After the French victory at Verdun, the *Fifth Army* complained of ammunition shortage, and supplies to the *Second* and *First Armies* were reduced accordingly ; but more artillery ammunition was expended on the Somme in October than in the previous month. Even so, on the 4th November, Below stated that his real inferiority to the enemy lay in ammunition supply rather than the number of guns in action.

After the successful attack of the British II. Corps on the 21st October Rupprecht favoured the evacuation of the salient between St. Pierre Divion and Beaumont Hamel. Ludendorff agreed, but Below, commander of the *First Army*, pointed out that a withdrawal would give up high ground with valuable observation; he considered the existing position south of the Ancre to be strong and well sited. North of the Ancre the line was reinforced by the *12th Division* (from *First Army* reserve), which began to take over the Beaumont Hamel sector between the *38th Division* (Beaucourt) and *52nd* (Serre) on the 22nd October. On the 6th November, however, Colonel von Lossberg, Below's very able Chief of the Staff, described the Ancre—Serre angle as dangerous, being exposed to concentric artillery fire ; Below, at this time, thought that a withdrawal east of Lesboeufs might be advisable. The anticipated attack by the British north of the Ancre was not expected to extend, south of the river, beyond Grandcourt in the first instance.

---

[1] G.O.A. xi., pp. 40, 43-4, 92-3, 97 ; Ludendorff, Hindenburg and Rupprecht.
[2] See page 468, f.n. 3.
[3] See Note I.

CHAPTER XVIII

THE SOMME

The Battle of the Ancre
13th–19th November,[1] 1916

(Map 6 ; Sketches 46, 47)

Final Plans and Preparations

On the night of Friday the 10th November there was still some difference of opinion as to whether the ground was dry enough to justify an attack, although there had been no rain since the 8th and colder weather had set in. Next morning General Gough, who had consulted his subordinate commanders freely, decided that his offensive should be launched on Monday the 13th.[2] After considering the advantages of a night operation—there had been a full moon on the 9th—zero hour was fixed for 5.45 a.m., an hour and a half before sunrise.

Early on the 12th, when the preliminary bombardment had already begun, Lieut.-General Kiggell came to Fifth Army headquarters to emphasize that the Commander-in-Chief " did not in any way wish to bring on a battle in " unfavourable conditions " ; but General Gough, to whom the decision was left, replied that he must either attack next day or withdraw and rest the bulk of his troops. In the afternoon Sir Douglas Haig arrived. He said that a success was much wanted, as it would have favourable repercussions upon the Russian and Rumanian fronts, and create a heartening effect at home : yet he did not desire to risk too much. After careful enquiry he was reassured,

---

[1] The official period of the battle is 13th–18th November, but the extra day may be appropriately included.

[2] Up to the end of the first week in November, brigade and battalion commanders were generally of opinion that conditions were too unfavourable for the attack to succeed. Then they became in favour of " attack " or cancellation ", as repeated postponements were not fair to the troops.

Sketch 46.

THE SOMME, 1916: 31st October.

Scale of Miles.

Compiled in the Historical Section (Military Branch).
3060/38.

Ordnance Survey 1937.

Crown Copyright Reserved.

Line at night ———
British – Red.
French – Blue.
Germans – Green.

and left General Gough to carry out his attack as already Nov.
arranged.   At 9.30 P.M. there was a corps commanders'
conference regarding subsequent action in the event of
success being obtained on the morrow.   Nothing definite
was laid down, but it was understood that if all should go
well a further advance towards Pys and Irles would be
undertaken.

The "limited operation" which now aimed at reducing the Sketch
head of the German salient between the Albert—Bapaume 46.
road and Serre, was really a modification of the first phase
of the offensive as ordered on the 15th October.[1]   Extensive
alterations to the plan of attack and to the barrage tables
were not required, but continual postponements had resulted
in a stream of orders and amendments to orders, owing to
the necessity, within the divisions, of frequent reliefs and
fresh apportionments of work in and behind the line.

The main attack was to be delivered by the V. Corps Map 6.
(Lieut.-General E. A. Fanshawe), with the 63rd, 51st, 2nd Sketch
and 3rd Divisions against the original German defences 47.
north of the Ancre which had been assaulted in vain on the
1st July.[2]   But the subsequent nineteen weeks of active
trench-warfare [3] were reckoned to have produced considerable effect upon the German powers of resistance, and in
certain localities the British line had been pushed forward
so that the average width of No Man's Land was now
reduced to less than 250 yards.   The operation was divided
into three stages.   From Beaucourt station, on the Ancre
opposite St. Pierre Divion, the first objective extended up
the Beaumont Hamel valley and round the eastern edge of
that village, then across Redan Ridge and the slope in front
of Serre, representing an average advance of 800 yards.
Three trench lines forming the German front system had
to be carried, and in places a fourth trench as well.   The
second objective, from 600 to 1,000 yards ahead on most
parts of the front, ran back from the western edge of
Beaucourt along the eastern slope of Redan Ridge, crossed
the valley south of Serre, and bent forward round the eastern
edge of that village.   Here the defensive flank was to run
back westward towards the left boundary of the V. Corps,
the XIII. Corps affording further protection by advancing
into the German trenches south-west of Star Wood.   The

[1] See page 460.
[2] See " 1916 " Vol. I., Chapter XVII.
[3] On 3rd September the 39th Division had attacked from the trenches
in front of Hamel to cover an operation south of the Ancre.   See page 279.

Nov. final objective was Beaucourt, on the Ancre, with the left thrown back along the western slope of the valley up which the road ran northward to Puisieux.

The II. Corps (Lieut.-General C. W. Jacob), south of the Ancre, was to drive the enemy from the remains of his front system between Schwaben Redoubt and St. Pierre Divion, clear the south bank of the river, and establish a line to face, roughly, north-east abreast of Beaucourt. The two principal river crossings, the road bridges by Beaucourt station and at Beaucourt mill, also had to be secured; for the Ancre, 20-30 feet wide, 3-4 feet deep, flowing in a marshy valley 200-300 yards wide, was impassable except at the bridges, which had causeways leading to them.

The reinforcement of the Fifth Army artillery enabled General Gough to prepare and support his offensive with a proportionately greater weight of metal than had been available for the Fourth Army on the 1st July.[1] The artillery plan aimed to " isolate " the area of attack. In addition to firing upon roads and approaches, the heavy guns and howitzers bombarded all villages and the principal trenches in the area, also Pys, Irles, Miraumont and Puisieux. On the II. Corps front east of the old German 2nd Position—hereafter called the Grandcourt line—a destructive bombardment was maintained although no infantry advance was intended; and at zero hour barrages were to be put on the German front defences as though an assault were about to be delivered. On the other flank the XIII. Corps batteries [2] fired on the approaches leading from the Puisieux valley to the German front.

---

[1] The details are as follows :
   V. Corps : Field artillery (2nd, 3rd, 32nd, 37th, 39th, 49th, 51st, 63rd Divisions) : 18-pdrs., 364 ; 4.5″ howitzers, 108.
      Heavy and siege artillery (8 groups) :
   Howitzers : two 15″ ; one 12″ ; twenty-eight 9.2″ ; sixteen 8″ ; fifty-six 6″. Guns : four 6″ ; forty-six 60-pdrs. ; eight 4.7″.
   II. Corps : Field artillery (11th, 17th, 18th, 19th, 25th, 1st, 2nd and 3rd Canadian Divisions ; IV. and VII. Brigades R.H.A.) : 13-pdrs., 30 ; 18-pdrs., 405 ; 4.5″ howitzers, 100.
      Heavy and siege artillery (9 groups) :
   Howitzers : two 15″ ; three 12″ ; thirty-six 9.2″ ; twenty-eight 8″ ; seventy-eight 6″. Guns : four 6″ ; sixty-six 60-pdrs. ; four 4.7″.
Roughly, the V. Corps had a field gun (or howitzer) to every 13.5 yards of front, and a heavy gun (or howitzer) to every 31 yards ; the II. Corps figures were 16.5 and 38.5, respectively, but its infantry attacked on a frontage with a field gun to every 10.25 yards. The figures for 1st July are 21 and 57 ; those for 15th September (Flers—Courcelette), 10 and 21.
[2] In addition to the guns already enumerated the V. Corps had the use of 12 howitzers (4 each, 9.2″, 8″ and 6″) and two 6″ guns, lent by the XIII. Corps for counter-battery work.

The bombardment on the front of the V. Corps was Nov. planned to effect a tactical surprise. Each morning, about thirty minutes before dawn when the night firing programme finished, the heavy artillery had been placing on the German trenches a barrage which lasted for nearly an hour, and ended with intense fire in which the field batteries joined. It was hoped that the Germans, having become accustomed to this routine, would not anticipate an infantry assault on the morning of the 13th when the crashing down of the barrage at 5.45 A.M. was to be the signal for the advance.[1] Then, whilst the barrage remained on the German front trenches, 25 per cent of the 18-pdrs. were to fire 50 yards short to cover the infantry advance into No Man's Land. Six minutes after zero hour the barrage would begin to " creep " at the rate of 100 yards every five minutes,[2] with a short pause beyond the reserve line of the German front system. The infantry was expected to be on its first objective 56 minutes after the start, and to move upon the second objective an hour later. The lifting barrage, following five minutes' silence, would open with intense fire as a signal for the renewed assault. The attack upon Beaucourt by the 63rd Division was fixed for 3 hours 20 minutes after zero, the village being bombarded first by all available artillery.

The assault of the II. Corps was to be delivered from Stuff Trench and Schwaben Redoubt, the German trench known as the Hansa Line being the objective. Thus the flank of the corps would swing forward to a position abreast of Beaucourt. On the left the attack was to be launched north-westward down the German trenches leading to the Ancre, in conjunction with an advance straight up the river valley. The corps was timed to complete its task by 7.25 A.M.

The 11th November was dull with much low cloud but no rain ; little could be seen either from the air or from ground observation posts, and heavy mist persisted upon the 12th. At 5 A.M. on this day No. 2 Special Company R.E. fired 180 lacrymatory bombs into Beaumont Hamel,

---

[1] Writing on the 28th October, Crown Prince Rupprecht comments upon these tactics and interprets them correctly.

[2] Altered from 4 minutes. Major-General C. J. Deverell (3rd Division), who had personally inspected the muddy ground on his front, asked that the rate should be 100 yards per 10 minutes, but this was considered impracticable. It was employed with success for an attack on this front in January 1917.

11-12 Nov. using 4″ mortars.   At 3.30 P.M. 47 gas drums were projected into the village and 39 into Y Ravine, causing the enemy, as was afterwards found, considerable loss.[1]   Although certain groups of tanks had moved forward from Beaussart, three miles behind the centre of the V. Corps front, on the evening of the 11th, the officer commanding the tank company felt obliged to report next day that the bad state of the ground would prevent the machines from taking part. He was therefore directed to withdraw them at night, but this was a difficult and fretful business to undertake whilst the troops were moving up, and some tanks had to be left in their forward positions.[2]

Most of the infantry had a long and trying march to the front,[3] but the spirit of the men was remarkable considering that they had spent weeks, generally cold and often wet to the skin, in muddy trenches or in poor billets and bivouacs behind the line with little respite from battle preparations and from such uncongenial tasks as scraping mud off the roads.   With the attack constantly postponed but never cancelled, all ranks had passed through a time of great tension, so that it was a relief to know that the hour was actually at hand.   Movement towards the front began in the clear light of the moon, which was still somewhere above the horizon in the early hours of the 13th November, when the whole battlefield had become shrouded in dripping fog. Their presence unsuspected by the enemy, the troops waited in close packed ranks until at 5.45 A.M. the barrage crashed down and the advance began—with some confusion and, in certain places, loss of direction, for it was impossible to see much more than 30 yards.

13TH NOVEMBER : THE II. CORPS ATTACK SOUTH OF THE ANCRE

Map 6.   Forming the right of the II. Corps attack, the 7/East
Sketch Lancashire and 7/Loyal N. Lancashire of Br.-General F. G.
47.   M. Rowley's 56th Brigade (19th Division), advanced from Stuff Trench.   These battalions were to safeguard the

---

[1] The history of the *62nd Regiment*, which held this sector, observes that " gas offensives had severely tried the regiment before the big attack ".

[2] Only one group—that with the 39th Division (II. Corps) south of the Ancre—received orders to attack.

[3] For instance, the 152nd Brigade (51st Division) left Forceville, 5 miles behind its assembly position between 9 and 10 P.M. on 12th November. There was a halt for tea or food on the way, and the battalions were not in place much before 4.30 A.M. on the 13th.

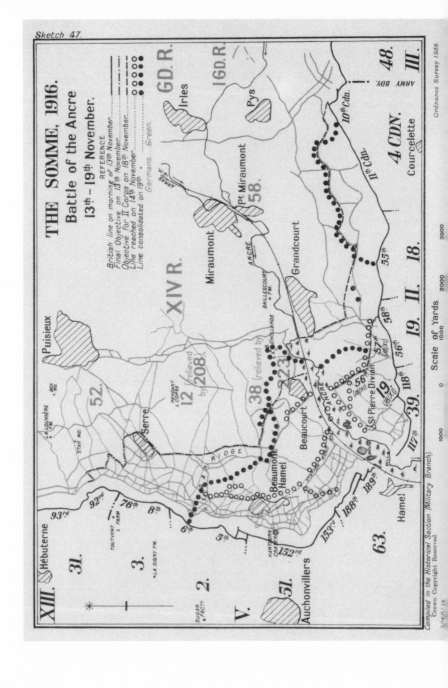

Sketch 47.

THE SOMME, 1916.
Battle of the Ancre
13th - 19th November.

REFERENCE
British line on morning of 13th November. ————
Final Objective on 13th November. – – – –
Objective for II Corps on 18th November. ● ● ● ●
Line reached on 14th November. ○ ○ ○ ○
Line consolidated on 19th. ○ ○ ○ ○
Germans Green.

Compiled in the Historical Section (Military Branch).
Crown Copyright Reserved.

Ordnance Survey 1938.

Scale of Yards.
1000   0   1000   2000   3000

flank of the 39th Division, the right of the East Lancashire pivoting upon the Grandcourt line.

Under cover of the fog the leading waves had assembled outside their front trenches, eight guns of the 56th Machine-Gun Company being sited in No Man's Land to provide close-range covering fire. The barrage was excellent, and the Germans, taken by surprise, offered little resistance. Owing to the fog the N. Lancashire, with three companies in line, overran their objective at some points, but by 8.15 A.M. were brought back to a suitable position, in touch on both flanks. The East Lancashire had already reported the success of their right; but their left, which lost its bearings, was a little later in occupying the objective. A number of prisoners were taken from the dug-outs in the sunken road called Lucky Way, which ran north-eastward through the Grandcourt line and thence down the slope into Grandcourt. This road and the trench beside it had been enfiladed by an 18-pdr. battery firing 100 yards in advance of the general barrage.

Two sections of the 81st Field Company R.E. and two companies of the 5/South Wales Borderers (Pioneers) came forward to help in the work of consolidation, but the mist thinned about noon and digging was somewhat interrupted by machine-gun fire at short range from the left front. A company of the 7/King's Own reinforced the right of the North Lancashire and posts were established beyond the new line. Farther to the right, the 6/Wiltshire (58th Brigade) had failed to effect a lodgment at Stump Road, which marked the right boundary of the division.

The total casualties in the attack amounted to less than two hundred, whilst over one hundred and fifty prisoners were taken, and the enemy's loss in killed and wounded was obviously considerable. As the day wore on German shell-fire increased, but it was very erratic, and fell partly upon the German trenches. There was no attempt to counter-attack.

The attack of the 39th Division (Major-General G. J. Cuthbert) had been planned by the corps commander. Its purpose was to clear the Germans from the slope above the Ancre as far to the north-east as the Hansa Line, which extended down to the river valley opposite the near edge of Beaucourt. Br.-General E. H. Finch-Hatton's 118th Brigade formed up clear of the Schwaben Redoubt on lines taped by the 234th Field Company R.E.; its assembly,

13 Nov. which was covered by listening posts of the 116th Brigade, appeared to be unnoticed by the enemy. On the right, the 1/1st Hertfordshire, facing north, had for objective the Hansa Line and also 500 yards of Mill Trench, which ran back along the road to St. Pierre Divion.[1] The other three battalions faced north-west, for the 1/1st Cambridgeshire was to take the remainder of Mill Trench; the 1/6th Cheshire the Strasburg Line, leading down to St. Pierre Divion, and also the village itself; and the 4th/5th Black Watch the German front and support trenches as far as the river bank.[2]

Keeping close behind the barrage, the Hertfordshire made steady progress from the start without encountering much resistance. They reached their objective soon after 7.30 A.M., and captured 150 Germans, together with four machine guns. Parties of the Cambridgeshire were in touch, but the two left companies of the battalion lost direction and were obliged to halt and reorganize. Machine guns firing from the Strasburg Line had inflicted some loss, but the Cambridgeshire reached and occupied Mill Trench, and by 10 A.M. the station crossing and Beaucourt mill were also secured. The post at the mill joined hands later in the day with men of the Hood Battalion and the H.A.C. (63rd Division) who formed the right of the V. Corps advance.

The 1/6th Cheshire and 4th/5th Black Watch found the fog a great handicap and experienced difficulty in keeping up with the barrage whilst they scrambled forward among the maze of shattered trenches. They lost direction soon after the start, and, although the adjutant of the Cheshire went forward and reorganized his battalion, confused fighting continued in and about the Strasburg Line, where German machine gunners and snipers maintained a spasmodic resistance. The Black Watch, who lost many officers, got forward very slowly along the German front trenches and, as no reports reached battalion headquarters, their commanding officer went forward later to control the advance.[3]

[1] In the centre this represented an advance of some 1,100 yards.

[2] The 116th Machine-Gun Company and the 4th Motor Machine-Gun Battery from positions beyond the river near Hamel fired in enfilade ; the 117th Machine-Gun Company supplied covering fire for the early stages of the assault ; and 8 guns of the 118th Machine-Gun Company enfiladed the German trenches north of the Ancre.

[3] Communication with the forward troops depended mainly upon runners until telephone wires were run out. The bad visibility not only prevented assistance from the air but gravely handicapped ground observers.

At 6.15 A.M., the 16/Sherwood Foresters (117th 13 Nov. Brigade) had attacked up the Ancre valley from Mill Road, near the river on the extreme left of the corps line. Although the movement was preceded by a special barrage fired by the LXXXV. Brigade R.F.A. (twelve 18-pdrs.), it appears to have come as a complete surprise to the enemy. The slope to the river terminated in a steep bank some twelve feet high which was known to contain many deep dug-outs, some of them connected by galleries. These were dealt with by two companies of the Foresters; a third company cleared the enemy from the top of the bank where the German bombers were routed with the help of the reserve company which came forward very promptly. Good progress was made along the river, the enemy who showed fight being driven into the dug-outs and confined there whilst the attack passed on.[1] A party of the Black Watch, coming down the slope from the right, emerged from the fog and joined the Foresters as they pressed forward to St. Pierre Divion, which was taken by a mixed force of Foresters, Highlanders and Cheshire at about 7.40 A.M., a battalion staff being captured in the cellars of the village.[2]

Starting from Thiepval at zero hour three tanks, each with an infantry escort, were to move north-westward, enter the German front trench near the river, and work abreast along the slope to the Strasburg Line and St. Pierre Divion. One machine stuck fast in the mud before reaching Thiepval; another developed mechanical trouble; the third reached the German front trench about 7 A.M., having lost its escort, and beat off some Germans who tried to surround it. Going on later to the support line, it crashed through a dug-out, lay immovable upon its side, and was again attacked. An appeal for help was sent off by pigeon message,[3] but meanwhile, men of the Foresters and Black Watch arrived about 9 A.M. and drove off the Germans.

The assault of the 118th Brigade had forced so many Germans down into the Ancre valley below St. Pierre Divion that by 9 A.M. the prisoners outnumbered the

[1] A small supply of White Star (gas) grenades was carried for use against defiant Germans in deep dug-outs. Very few of these grenades were expended.

[2] As the cellars and dug-outs of St. Pierre Divion were reported to be mined, a special detachment of the 225th Field Company R.E. was detailed to search for and cut the leads; but none were found.

[3] This did not reach corps headquarters till 10 A.M.

13 Nov. attackers. Br.-General R. D. F. Oldman, commanding the 117th Brigade, thereupon reinforced the 16th with the 17/Sherwood Foresters. Having heard, about 9.30 A.M. that parties of the enemy were still holding out in the German front and support trenches and in the Strasburg Line, Br.-General Finch-Hatton ordered the 14/Hampshire (attached from the 116th Brigade and waiting in the dug-outs of Schwaben Redoubt) to follow in the track of the Cheshire and Black Watch. The Hampshire advanced shortly after 11 A.M. and collected some prisoners on their way down to the Ancre valley where the fighting was now over ; the battalion was then reorganized and, in the afternoon, withdrawn. The Hertfordshire were now digging in 50 yards beyond the Hansa Line, their right in touch with the 7/Loyal N. Lancashire of the 56th Brigade. The Cambridgeshire and the Cheshire worked on Mill Trench as far back as St. Pierre Divion, which was organized for defence. A section of the 4th Motor Machine-Gun Battery came up to the village, the motor cycles, with some guns on side-cars, being driven down to the Ancre at the Mill Road crossing, and thence man-handled forward.

At noon the situation north of the Ancre was by no means clear to Lieut-General Jacob, although there was a report that Beaucourt was in British hands. By corps instructions, Major-General Cuthbert took every precaution against counter-attack. Responsibility for the defence of the ground won devolved upon the 118th Brigade, and Br.-General Finch-Hatton [1] ordered the Black Watch, who were mingled with the Cheshire, to reorganize and take over the right half of the Hansa Line. This movement could not, however, be completed until the early hours of the 14th November, for the German barrage was heavy and the ground deep in mud. Meanwhile, the Hertfordshire began the construction of a strongpoint at the junction of the Hansa Line and Mill Trench, having occupied Mill Trench for 400 yards to the south-west. The Cambridgeshire dug a support line, facing north, across the base of the Hertford-shire position, whilst the Cheshire became responsible for the St. Pierre Divion defences and the strongpoints in the river valley, besides maintaining posts at the mill 200 yards east of Beaucourt station and at the station crossing. Sappers and pioneers assisted in the work which, from

---

[1] He was taken ill in the evening, and Lieut.-Colonel G. A. McL. Sceales, 4th/5th Black Watch, assumed command of the brigade.

3.30 P.M. onwards, was somewhat hampered by a heavy hostile barrage.

At 6.45 P.M. a party of 25 Germans with five machine guns blundered on the strongpoint at the apex of the Hertfordshire line : a few of the enemy were shot and the rest captured. Later, a small bombing attack in the same vicinity was driven off by fire.

As early as 8.32 A.M., by which hour the capture of all objectives had been reported to divisional headquarters, Major-General Cuthbert gave verbal orders to his C.R.E. for the repair of the Hamel—St. Pierre Divion road. The 227th Field Company R.E. and part of the 13/Gloucestershire (Pioneers) were accordingly sent forward to begin work. Despite some interruptions by hostile artillery fire, the road was made fit for limbered transport as far as the German front line by 4 P.M. and a mud track for infantry in file and pack animals constructed into St. Pierre Divion.

The II. Corps success was by no means dearly bought, for casualties among the attacking infantry amounted to less than a thousand, mostly wounded, while the prisoners numbered 27 officers and 1,300 other ranks.[1] The enemy loss in dead and wounded was very heavy. Although the fog had caused some of the attacking battalions to lose their bearings and threw them into confusion, it concealed the scope and direction of the assault and helped to effect a tactical surprise. The enemy in the area between the Hansa Line and the river, to a great extent cut off by the destructive fire of the British artillery, proved to be in no condition to offer an organized and protracted resistance.

13TH NOVEMBER : THE V. AND XIII. CORPS ATTACK NORTH OF THE ANCRE

Immediately north of the Ancre the 63rd (R.N.) Sketch 47. Division (Major-General C. D. Shute), forming the right of the V. Corps, assembled its battalions on the forward slope facing the lower end of the Beaumont Hamel spur. The troops which were not occupying trenches formed up on specially taped lines. Next to the river the 189th Brigade (Br.-General L. F. Philips) had the Hood and Hawke

---

[1] Principally of the *I.* and *III./95th Regiment* (*38th Division*) and the *I./144th Regiment* (*223rd Division*). In the Grandcourt sector the relief of the *38th* by the *223rd Division* was proceeding at the time of the attack. Near the river, the *I.* and *III./95th* had not yet been withdrawn ; next on the east, the *I./144th* had just relieved the *I./91st Reserve* (*2nd Guard Reserve Division* but attached to the *38th Division*).

13 Nov. Battalions in front with Drake and Nelson in rear. Behind were the 1/H.A.C. and 7/Royal Fusiliers of Br.-General W. C. G. Heneker's 190th Brigade. Br.-General R. E. S. Prentice's 188th Brigade was on the left with the Howe Battalion and 1/Royal Marines in the van, and the Anson and 2/Royal Marines in second line. In rear were the 4/Bedfordshire and 10/R. Dublin Fusiliers of the 190th Brigade. A spasmodic burst of German shell-fire caused some seventy casualties whilst the troops were waiting.[1]

As the division had never before taken part in an offensive on the Western Front, orders had been meticulously framed and frequent conferences held ; movements and advances were carefully explained so that all ranks knew exactly what was expected of them. The leading battalions were to take the German front system ; those in second line were then to pass through to the first objective which ran along the top of a high bank on the eastern slope of the valley beyond the road from Beaucourt station to Beaumont Hamel. The units which led the first assault would " leap-frog " in their turn and take the second objective, Beaucourt Trench, running north-westward up the slope from the near edge of Beaucourt village.[2] Finally, the battalions in second line were to capture Beaucourt and establish a defensive flank on the left. The rôle of the 190th Brigade was to give general impetus to the later stages of the advance.

At zero hour the mass of infantry moved forward and approached the German trenches close behind the barrage. On the right, the Hood Battalion, followed by the Drake, encountered stout opposition ; enfilade machine-gun fire from the left caused considerable loss, and Lieut.-Colonel A. S. Tetley, R.M.L.I., commanding the Drake was mortally wounded. Nevertheless the German front system was captured together with 300 prisoners.[3] When dawn came, with the fog still thick, there was much confusion in the shattered German lines, for the stormers had had to advance round shell craters and up communication trenches deep in mud. On the left, parties of both battalions were still heavily engaged. Lieut.-Colonel B. C. Freyberg, com-

---

[1] Lieut.-Colonel F. J. Saunders, R.M.L.I., commanding the Anson Battalion, was killed before the assembly position was reached.

[2] Each battalion was responsible for " mopping-up " the German defence within the limits of its own advance.

[3] Mostly of the *55th Reserve* (*2nd Guard Reserve Division*, but attached *38th Division*), whose front practically coincided with that of the 63rd Division.

manding the Hood Battalion, promptly rallied what men he could for the assault of the first objective, and led them forward at the appointed time with great success, nearly four hundred more Germans being taken from the dug-outs in Station Road and at Beaucourt station.   The success of the Hood may be attributed to resolute leading, and accurate guidance by compass bearing which preserved the direction of the advance throughout.

With this detachment of the Drake and Hood were some men of the 1/H.A.C.   One company of this battalion had been detailed to cover the right of the advance by seizing "The Mound," a knoll which formed the southern extremity of the German front line north of the Ancre, and then clearing the dug-outs along the railway embankment which flanked the German front system.   This very important task was accomplished after brisk fighting in which trench mortars and machine guns provided valuable support.   So, by 6.45 A.M., the right of the 63rd Division was firmly established on its first objective, German tools and wire being used to consolidate the position ; but Lieut.-Colonel Freyberg held a frontage of barely four hundred yards, and his left flank was in the air.

On the left of the Hood and Drake, the Hawke Battalion, followed by the Nelson, encountered deadly machine-gun fire before the German front line was reached.   Heavy losses in officers [1] made reorganization difficult, but parties entered the enemy trenches to become involved in a con-fused struggle with rifle and bomb.   The 188th Brigade had a similar experience, coming under rifle and machine-gun fire from both flanks.   A small force—less than a hundred rifles—consisting of men of the Howe, Anson and Nelson battalions, under Lieut.-Commander J. M. Gilliland of the Anson, managed to fight its way forward over the spur, and reached the first objective on the farther slope of the valley.   On the extreme left of the division the 1/Royal Marines, which had every company commander killed before entering the German trenches, was only able to progress in isolated groups ; its sister battalion, which followed, also lost cohesion.   A few marines, however, were able to continue the advance in touch with the 51st Division.

Communication, by telephone through the 190th Brigade and, later, when the wire was cut, by relay runner post,

[1] Lieut.-Colonel L. O. Wilson, R.M.L.I. (Hawke) and his adjutant were wounded, and Lieut.-Colonel N. O. Burge, R.M.L.I. (Nelson) was killed.

13 Nov. had been established with Lieut.-Colonel Freyberg. On the remainder of the divisional front, the enemy was known to be holding out in various parts of his support and reserve lines, and by 6.30 A.M. it was evident that in places even the German front line had not been captured.[1] The chief centre of resistance was said to be a " strongpoint ", variously reported to be in the support and reserve line of the German front system,[2] against which the battalions of the 188th Brigade were organizing bombing attacks, and Major-General Shute now ordered the 190th Brigade to carry the advance forward. Br.-General Heneker's battalions had already followed up, and by 7.40 A.M. the 1/H.A.C., on the extreme right, was digging in along the German reserve line. The 7/Royal Fusiliers, however, was held up by fire in the German front line, as were the Bedfordshire and Dublin Fusiliers, farther north ; but parties of these three battalions had made some progress, so that the struggle in the trenches on the Beaumont Hamel spur continued with a greater admixture of units than before. In compliance with a divisional order Br.-General Heneker then called for an attempt to clear the front by pushing in behind the H.A.C. and moving north-westward ; but all his troops were already too closely engaged for this to be done.

About 7.45 A.M. Lieut.-Colonel Freyberg advanced behind the barrage to the attack of the second objective. His force comprised 300 men of the Hood and 120 of the Drake, with some of the H.A.C.,[3] and covered a frontage of about three hundred yards. The edge of Beaucourt was reached with hardly a check, but then the fire of the British heavy artillery combined with a German protective barrage to compel a slight withdrawal before the men began

---

[1] Hostile machine-gun fire still swept No Man's Land, but the German batteries were not particularly active. The light signals of the German infantry could not be seen through the fog ; and, although it was obvious that the front had been penetrated, the enemy artillery, lacking observation, was at a loss to know where to place its barrage.

[2] Although the Germans had hardly constructed a " subterranean city " in the chalk hills north of the Ancre, as has sometimes been stated, they had turned to good account the old tunnels and catacombs used as refuges during the Wars of Religion. Where their trenches intersected the tunnels it was easy to make deep dug-outs with several entrances. Often these dug-outs had access to machine-gun emplacements low-sited and designed for enfilade fire ; it was a series of such points (numbered 62, 97 and 66 on Map 6) in the German support and reserve trenches which had escaped destruction by the bombardment and had broken up the advance of the centre and left of the 63rd Division.

[3] A gun of the 189th Machine-Gun Company followed the advance.

to dig in with their " grubbers " among the shell-holes. 13 Nov. Attempts to erect German wire, of which the supply was plentiful, were interfered with by the fire of German snipers in the village.

Divisional headquarters received a report of the success soon after 9.30 A.M., and Lieut.-Colonel Freyberg, who felt confident that Beaucourt was his for the taking, stated that he proposed to attack it with half his little force. Major-General Shute informed him that the barrage would not lift for this purpose : the doubtful measure of success which had attended the efforts of the centre and left had made it advisable to attempt no more than the second objective, especially as every battalion of the division had been drawn into the fight. About 12.30 P.M. the H.A.C., which was about to bomb northward up the German reserve line, received an order to send two companies to reinforce Lieut.-Colonel Freyberg, but the movement, which would have had to be carried out under heavy rifle and machine-gun fire, was cancelled at the instance of that officer. During the afternoon he got into touch with the 1/1st Cambridgeshire (39th Division, II. Corps) at the mill beyond the river.[1] On the front of the 188th Brigade, Lieut.-Commander Gilliland's party, which had followed the barrage to the second objective, was isolated and unable to communicate with the rear. As darkness fell the little band moved to the right and eventually joined Lieut.-Colonel Freyberg.

During the day many bombing attacks had been made upon the strongpoints and the surrounding area in the German front system, and some progress was made despite the stout resistance of the German machine-gunners and snipers. A stream of prisoners trickled back to the British trenches and reports were received of the arrival of small parties of troops on the first objective. Visibility continued to be so poor that aeroplane reconnaissance was of little avail. At noon Major-General Shute ordered a five-minutes' bombardment to be followed by a general assault of the German reserve line on the 188th Brigade front, all troops which had secured a footing in the support line to take part. The guns opened twenty minutes later, but there had been no time to organize the infantry, and a similar attack which

---

[1] By arrangement between the V. and II. Corps, on Major-General Shute's suggestion, the II. Corps replenished the bomb supplies of Lieut.-Colonel Freyberg's force, by way of the river crossing at the mill, the 63rd Division having no troops available for carrying parties.

13 Nov. was to have been undertaken at 3.45 P.M. failed to start for
the same reason.

The six tanks allotted to the division had gone back to
Beaussart on the previous night, but early in the afternoon
Major-General Shute arranged for these machines to come
forward again to Auchonvillers.   There was no chance of
bringing them into action before next morning.   As infantry
reinforcement the V. Corps had already allotted to the
63rd Division two battalions of the 111th Brigade (Br.-
General R. W. R. Barnes) from the 37th Division (Major-
General H. B. Williams) [1] in corps reserve.   At 10 A.M.
these battalions began to move up from Hedauville, four
miles W.S.W. of Hamel, and in the afternoon the rest of the
brigade followed, for the whole was now to be held in
readiness to renew the attack next morning.   Verbal orders
to this effect reached the 63rd Division from the corps at
6.40 P.M.

By this time the situation on the front of the 63rd
Division was tolerably clear.   On the right was Lieut.-
Colonel Freyberg, who had received two slight wounds, with
a mixed force, principally Hood and Drake, of the 189th
Brigade; a few of the 188th Brigade; and some men
of the H.A.C. (190th Brigade).   He held a line from
the railway embankment to Railway Alley (the communication trench nearest the Ancre), just short of the second
objective.[2]   Behind him on the first objective were parts
of the H.A.C. and 7/Royal Fusiliers (190th Brigade), with
an admixture of troops of the 188th Brigade and of the
Bedfordshire and R. Dublin Fusiliers (190th Brigade)
prolonging the left as far as the communication trench called
Station Alley.[3]   In the support line of the German front
system parties of the 188th Brigade linked up on the left
with the 51st Division.   The Germans still holding out in
front of the first objective were thus in a precarious position.

The 111th Brigade (37th Division), which moved into
the battle zone after dark, was to be employed next
morning, with the 190th Brigade, to gain the second
objective of the 63rd Division and then to capture Beaucourt.   Several contradictory orders were issued ; but

---

[1] He had succeeded Major-General S. W. Scrase-Dickens, who had
fallen sick, on 9th November.
[2] By 3.30 P.M. there were two machine guns of the 189th Machine-Gun
Company here, and 11 in the first objective.
[3] At dusk six platoons of the 14/Worcestershire (Pioneers) and portions
of the 1st and 3rd Field Companies, having waited until the German
machine-gun fire died down, began to consolidate this line.

eventually it was understood that after the 111th Brigade 13 Nov. had captured the second objective by coming up on Lieut.-Colonel Freyberg's left, the 190th Brigade would pass through his line and take Beaucourt. The 13/K.R.R.C. (111th Brigade), however, was sent forward at once to support Colonel Freyberg, and about 9.30 P.M. extended his position to the left as far as the next communication trench, Redoubt Alley. About fifty Germans were captured in the process. Of the other battalions of the brigade, the 13/Royal Fusiliers and 13/Rifle Brigade arrived on the first objective about midnight, at which time the 10/Royal Fusiliers was moving forward from Hamel to the original British front line. The 190th Brigade had been ordered to reorganize, but communication was difficult and, with the exception of the H.A.C., the battalions were so scattered that little could be done before morning.

Next on the left, the 51st Division (Major-General G. M. Harper) was confronted by the Y Ravine salient, and by Beaumont Hamel in the valley east of Hawthorn Ridge. Its first objective was the far edge of the village, but, owing to the converging advance of the 63rd and 2nd Divisions on its flanks, the second objective consisted only of 250 yards of Frankfort Trench overlooking the Beaucourt valley.

On the right, Br.-General D. Campbell's 153rd Brigade had two battalions, 1/7th Gordon Highlanders and 1/6th Black Watch, in first line, with the 1/5th Gordon Highlanders in support, the 1/7th Black Watch providing carrying parties. On the left, the 152nd Brigade (Br.-General H. P. Burn) adopted a similar formation with the 1/5th Seaforth and the 1/8th Argyll & Sutherland Highlanders in front and the 1/6th Seaforth in support ; but the 1/6th Gordon Highlanders was kept in reserve. In each brigade the leading battalions were to press straight on to the first objective ; the advance to the narrow second objective was to be made by two companies of the 1/5th Gordon (153rd Brigade) and two of the 1/6th Seaforth Highlanders (152nd Brigade). Br.-General J. G. H. Hamilton's 154th Brigade was held in divisional reserve east of Forceville, nearly 3½ miles behind the front line. The tanks remained in readiness at Auchonvillers, although there seemed little prospect of using them.

The assembly was accomplished without serious hitch, and six minutes before zero hour the leading battalions

13 Nov. moved forward to get clear of the British wire. In this part of the field zero hour was signalized by the blowing of the mine at Hawthorn Crater, whence the enemy could have enfiladed the advance both to the north and south. The roar of the explosion coincided with the opening crash of the barrage.[1]

Both brigades started well.[2] On the extreme right two companies of the 1/7th Gordon Highlanders took the German front line with little trouble. Still following the barrage closely, they broke through the German front system, passed the eastern end of Y Ravine and reached the first objective at 6.45 A.M., with a small party of marines (63rd Division) on their right. Seeing Germans retiring before them, these companies continued their advance, almost due northward up the hill, and collected about forty prisoners before withdrawing to Station Road. The left of the battalion experienced hard fighting in the German front system, where machine guns and snipers had to be subdued. The extreme left, together with the 1/6th Black Watch, was held up by the Y Ravine salient, the ravine, thirty feet deep with almost perpendicular sides and connected by tunnels with the neighbouring trenches, being still a formidable stronghold.[3] Here the 1/5th Gordon Highlanders, from support, was drawn into the struggle soon after 7 A.M., success now depending upon the enterprise and determination of small parties. Some of the 1/6th Black Watch skirted the northern side of the ravine and pushed on.

Communication by runner and telephone was tolerably well maintained, although here, as elsewhere, the action after dawn was fought in the half-light of a heavy fog which made observation impossible from the usual ground stations and from the air. Reports were therefore fragmentary and apt to mislead; but by 10.30 A.M. Major-General Harper was aware that the right of the attack had reached the first

---

[1] The charge consisted of 30,000 lbs. of ammonal and effectually disposed of the Germans holding the crater, a platoon of the *III./62nd Regiment*, according to the German regimental narrative. From an adjacent dug-out a party of the 252nd Tunnelling Company R.E. collected nearly sixty prisoners, who said that each dug-out of six which were closed by the explosion held a similar number of Germans. For other mining activities on the V. Corps front see Note I at end of Chapter.

[2] They were confronted by the *III./62nd* and *I./62nd Regiment*, holding the left sector of the *12th Division*.

[3] Starting at zero hour, a field battery had enfiladed the ravine for six minutes, but the Germans had sheltered from the bombardment in large, deep, boarded dug-outs with traversed entrances and electric alarm bells.

objective. He had already ordered up the 1/4th Gordon 13 Nov.
Highlanders (from the 154th Brigade, in reserve) for the
purpose of isolating Y Ravine by bombing attacks from
north and south. Before the movement could be started,
however, the Germans in this area began to surrender
freely—on the personal summons, it is said, of Lieut.-
Colonel T. M. Booth, 1/6th Black Watch—and early in the
afternoon the 1/4th Gordon Highlanders advanced to carry
the assault down into the southern end of Beaumont
Hamel, which was entered by a mixed force of 1/4th and
1/5th Gordon Highlanders and 1/6th Black Watch.[1]

By this time the four battalions of the 152nd Brigade,
on the left, were also in the village. The 1/5th Seaforth and
1/8th Argyll & Sutherland Highlanders had been heavily
engaged in the German front system. South of Hawthorn
Crater the Seaforth lost precious time in groping for the
gaps in the wire, which were not easily seen in the ob-
scurity ; the Argyll & Sutherland, north of the Auchonvillers—Beaumont Hamel road, suffered from machine-gun
fire before the front trench was carried. The support line
was not so stoutly defended, but the attackers then
encountered deep mud and lost the barrage. Most of the
1/6th Seaforth Highlanders came in on the right to help
their brethren of the 1/5th, whilst the reserve battalion,
1/6th Gordon Highlanders, sent forward bombing parties.
After a protracted struggle, the German reserve line was
carried and the advance continued into Beaumont Hamel.

Although the German resistance was failing, it took
most of the afternoon to pass through the ruins of the
village, clear the enemy from its dug-outs and cellars,[2] and
establish a line upon its eastern edge, the first objective.[3]
Two tanks—their employment in the assault had been
suggested in a message from the Fifth Army—came forward

---

[1] " Regt. No. 62 " states that its *I. Bn.*, holding the Y Ravine salient,
maintained its resistance until the attack had got round both flanks. As
no counter-attack materialized most of the survivors of the battalion,
which was almost cut off, surrendered in the afternoon.

[2] A platoon of the Argyll and another of the 1/6th Seaforth, each led
by a subaltern, went straight for two battalion headquarters, which had
been located by a captured map, and secured the surrender of the battalion
staffs. The Seaforth party, much reduced in numbers, was obliged to
hand over its prisoners to a contingent of the 10/R. Dublin Fusiliers (63rd
Division), which had worked northward. " Regt. No. 62 " admits the
capture of the staffs of the *I.* and *III. Bns.*

[3] The booty secured in Beaumont Hamel included machine guns and
mortars, ammunition, a variety of bombs and grenades, searchlights, an
armourer's shop complete, canteen stores with a welcome stock of aërated
water, a piano, and the " incoming mail ".

13 Nov. up the road from Auchonvillers, but one was ditched between the German front and support lines, and the other met a similar fate on the northern edge of Beaumont Hamel.

At 4 P.M. the Argyll & Sutherland were ordered to push forward on the left along the sunken Wagon Road, leading northward to Serre, as far as the divisional boundary, so as to link up with the foremost troops of the 2nd Division, but the British protective barrage prevented this movement. Consolidation of the first objective proceeded, assisted by a party of the 1/8th Royal Scots (Pioneers),[1] and some reorganization was carried out. The new front was then held by the 1/4th Gordon Highlanders (154th Brigade), the 1/6th Black Watch (153rd Brigade) two companies of the 1/6th Gordon Highlanders, and the 1/8th Argyll & Sutherland (both 152nd Brigade), in touch on the left with the 2nd Division. The 1/7th Gordon Highlanders (153rd Brigade) and 1/5th and 1/6th Seaforth (152nd Brigade) were withdrawn to the reserve line of the German front system, where they were reinforced by two companies of the 1/7th Argyll & Sutherland (from the 154th Brigade, in reserve) about 9 P.M. The 1/5th Gordon Highlanders (153rd Brigade), having no knowledge of the extent of the advance of the 63rd Division, formed a defensive flank to connect with the left of that division in the German front system.[2]

Major-General W. G. Walker, commanding the 2nd Division which attacked along Redan Ridge, had Br.-General G. M. Bullen-Smith's 5th Brigade on the right, with the 2/Highland L.I. and 24/Royal Fusiliers in front, and the 17/Royal Fusiliers and 2/Oxford & Bucks L.I. in second line. On the left was the 6th Brigade (Br.-General A. C. Daly), the 13/Essex and 2/South Staffordshire being in the van, with the 1/King's and 17/Middlesex in rear. Br.-General R. O. Kellett's 99th Brigade was in divisional reserve.[3]

[1] For the most part, the sappers and pioneers were employed upon roads, tracks and communications across No Man's Land and through the German front system.

[2] " Regt. No. 62 " states that its *II. Bn.*, from reserve, was assembled in Munich Trench [about 900 yards E. of the northern end of Beaumont Hamel], after suffering heavy loss from British shell-fire. No touch could be obtained with the forward battalions. At night the *II./62nd* could only muster 300 rifles and no other troops were available in the sector. Touch was gained with the *23rd Regiment* (holding the northern sector of the *12th Division*), and patrols tried to locate the flank of the *55th Reserve*, to the south.

[3] Opposite the 2nd Division, the *23rd Regiment*, holding the north sector of the *12th Division* front, had its *I.* and *III. Battalions* in line.

As the British trenches were deep in mud, the leading 13 Nov. battalions of the 5th Brigade which were to take the first objective, Beaumont Trench, formed up in the open. The attack started spendidly, close up to the barrage. In the German front line many of the garrison, being caught as they issued from the dug-outs, surrendered freely so that more than one hundred and fifty prisoners were collected. Suffering considerable loss on the way from snipers and bursts of machine-gun fire, the Highland L.I. and 24/Royal Fusiliers then pressed on through the German front system and arrived, on time, at Beaumont Trench, which ran up the hill from the north-eastern edge of Beaumont Hamel. The Highland L.I. were not in touch on the right, for the 51st Division, as we know, did not reach the village until the afternoon ; on the left, the 24/Royal Fusiliers, assisted by the 2/Oxford & Bucks L.I., was obliged to block the trenches running north and repel spasmodic bombing attacks from that direction, for the 6th Brigade was in difficulties.[1]

Here the salient known as the Quadrilateral proved a stumbling block. In front of it, and farther north, the German wire was mostly still intact and, because of the fog, the stormers, often floundering in deep mud, could not see their way either to the gaps or to the firmer ground. The barrage lifted forward and was lost, whilst the German machine guns,[2] as they were designed to do, took most of the brigade frontage in enfilade. Some of the Essex and King's, on the extreme right, pressed on to the first objective with the 5th Brigade, and assisted to safeguard its flank by forming a block at the junction of Beaumont Trench with the communication trench called Lager Alley. The South Staffordshire and Middlesex, on the left, were inclined to swerve north-eastward ; they had been thrown into confusion by troops of the 3rd Division, next on the left, who had lost their way and came across the line of advance. This additional handicap made success impossible. Parties of all four battalions forced their way into the German front trench, but were held there by deadly bursts of machine-gun fire at close range ; others remained in shell-holes outside the enemy parapet.

At 7.30 A.M., when the battalions which had formed the

---

[1] " Regt. No. 23 " states that the remnants of its *I. Bn.* had great difficulty in withdrawing to Munich Trench and to Frankfort Trench (second and final objective on this part of the front).

[2] In the chord of the Quadrilateral, it appears—not in the first trench.

13 Nov. second line were due to assault the final objective—
Frankfort Trench, on the reverse slope of Redan Ridge—
only the 5th Brigade was in a situation to do so. The
attack was made by about 120 men of the 17/Royal
Fusiliers and the 2/Oxford & Bucks L.I., and, on the
left, a few of the Essex and King's of the 6th Brigade.
Frankfort Trench was entered in places by parties who could
not get in touch with each other, and were not in sufficient
strength to hold their own against the German snipers and
bombers. Gradually the various groups withdrew fighting,
first to Munich Trench, 200 yards back, and then, on the
right, to Wagon Road and Crater Lane—a communication
trench in the middle of the 5th Brigade front—and, on
the left, to Beaumont Trench, the first objective. On
the right, there was as yet no touch with the 51st Division ; on the left, Lager Alley was made the defensive
flank.[1]

About 9 A.M. the remnants of the 6th Brigade were
ordered to withdraw to the British front line and reorganize.
The divisional commander was anxious to renew the attack,
but Br.-General Daly reported that his battalions were
unfit for a fresh effort. At 9.30 A.M., however, a V. Corps
order for a fresh assault was received, and Major-General
Walker then called upon two battalions of the 99th Brigade
in reserve. Passing south of the Quadrilateral, they were
to assault Bow Trench [2] in conjunction with an attack by
the 3rd Division, which would fix the hour.[3] On the 6th
Brigade front the heavy artillery barrage was brought back
to Serre Trench, the first objective, and that of the field
artillery to Bow Trench.

Br.-General Kellett's 99th Brigade had begun to move
forward about 7.30 A.M., and two companies of the 23/Royal
Fusiliers were sent, two hours later, to reinforce the 5th
Brigade on the first objective. Here the left flank had
begun to give anxiety, and soon after 2 P.M. the 22/Royal
Fusiliers was ordered to move into the captured trenches
and take up a line facing almost due north with its right on

[1] According to " Regt. No. 23 ", the British advance was stayed at
Munich Trench after heavy fighting ; a counter-attack by two companies
of the *II./23rd* repulsed the British near the junction of Munich Trench
and Lager Alley (extreme right of 6th Brigade). There were no troops
available for further counter-attacks.

[2] Bow Trench ran back from the Quadrilateral into the valley S.W. of
Serre, and thence forward again to join the German front system opposite
the centre of the 8th Brigade (3rd Division).

[3] The 3rd Division, as will presently be seen, had failed in its assault.

Beaumont Trench, the first objective, and its left facing the 13 Nov.
Quadrilateral.[1]

By this time, after considering a report received from
Major-General C. J. Deverell, commanding the 3rd Division,
Lieut.-General Fanshawe had cancelled the combined attack.
At 3 P.M. the corps gave verbal orders for the 99th Brigade
(less one battalion) to attack Munich Trench, but this
operation was soon postponed to the morning of the 14th
November. At night, on the 5th Brigade front, the 17th
Royal Fusiliers was holding advanced positions in Wagon
Road and Crater Lane ; the first objective was held by the
2/Highland L.I.—now in touch with the 51st Division—
the 24/Royal Fusiliers, and two companies of the 23/Royal
Fusiliers (detached from the 99th Brigade). The 2/Oxford
& Bucks L.I. and a few of the King's and Essex (6th
Brigade) in Lager Alley, forward of the first objective, and
in Serre Trench, continuation of the first objective, covered
the left of the brigade, and the 22/Royal Fusiliers (99th
Brigade) was on its way to strengthen this flank. Two
sections of the 226th Field Company R.E. and two platoons
of the 10/Duke of Cornwall's L.I. (Pioneers) had been sent
forward to construct strongpoints in the first objective.

At 8.15 P.M. two battalions of the 112th Brigade
(Br.-General P. M. Robinson), from the 37th Division in
corps reserve, were placed under the 2nd Division. They
moved forward from Bertrancourt to Mailly Maillet (less
than a mile west of Auchonvillers) at 9 P.M.

The 3rd Division (Major-General C. J. Deverell),
forming the left of the V. Corps, had first to secure Serre
Trench, which lay across the forward slope some two hundred yards from the near end of the village. The ultimate
objective was Serre, a defensive flank having to be thrown
back westward to link up with the 31st Division of the
XIII. Corps. According to the original intention, all three
brigades were to have been employed, the centre brigade
having Serre as its objective, the others wheeling up on
right and left to complete the formation of the defensive
flank. The bad conditions of ground and weather had
resulted in a modification of this plan, amended orders
being issued by the corps on the 10th November. Major-
General Deverell then decided to attack with two brigades,
keeping the other in reserve.

[1] Facing also the *III./169th (52nd Division)*, which had secured its
southern flank. · " Regt. No. 23 ".

13 Nov.   Serre, on its little knoll, commands the whole of the slope to the west, and the fog was not so thick as to hide the British advance from the enemy.[1] There was no question of a swift assault, for the heavy loam, made friable by the incessant bombardments, dried more slowly than the chalk surface farther south, and the troops of the 3rd Division, like those of the 6th Brigade on their right, lost the battle in the mud.

Br.-General E. G. Williams's 8th Brigade was on the right, the 2/Royal Scots and 1/R. Scots Fusiliers in front having orders to go through to Serre, the second objective ; the 8/East Yorkshire and 7/K. Shropshire L.I. were in second line. On the left in the 76th Brigade (Br.-General C. L. Porter) the 10/R. Welch Fusiliers and 2/Suffolk were the leading battalions, but the 1/Gordon Highlanders and the 8/King's Own in rear were to continue the assault after the first objective, Serre Trench, had been captured. The story of the advance may be told in a few words. Starting in good order, the leading battalions were soon struggling through mud which, in places, was waist-deep ; and when the German wire was reached few gaps could be found in it. By this time the rear battalions had begun to mix with the troops in front and, the barrage being lost, groups of men forced their way into the German trenches in the face of an alert enemy, to carry on the fight as best they could.

In the 8th Brigade parties from all four battalions reached the German support line but could not maintain themselves there ; others lost direction completely and mixed in confusion with the left of the 2nd Division. The right of the 76th Brigade, Welch Fusiliers and Gordons, penetrated to Walter Trench, the German reserve line, and even to the first objective, but only in small isolated parties which were overwhelmed. On the left some of the Suffolk suffered the same fate in the support line, and a heavy barrage in No Man's Land prevented the rear waves of the King's Own from entering the German position.

The failure of the attack became known at the two brigade headquarters by 6.30 A.M. when attempts were made to collect the exhausted men and bring them back to the British front line. Some, however, held on doggedly for most of the day in shell-holes outside the German parapet. At 7.30 A.M. Major-General Deverell, who was aware that parties were still fighting in the German

---

[1] The sector (southern half of the *52nd Division* front) was held by the *169th Regiment*, with two battalions in line.

front and support lines, urged his brigades to prepare a 13 Nov.
fresh attack without delay ; in preparation for this he had
the field artillery barrage brought back to Walter Trench
and that of the heavy artillery to Serre Trench and Serre.
At 10.25 A.M. the corps informed the division of the progress
made farther to the south, also of the advance of the 31st
Division on the northern flank.   Major-General Deverell
thereupon allotted to each of the front brigades a battalion
from the 9th Brigade in reserve.   As we have seen, two
battalions of the 2nd Division were to co-operate in the
renewed assault, but the time of its delivery was to be fixed
by the 3rd Division.   This could only be " when the German
" barrage moderated ", for the front line of the division, as
well as No Man's Land, was heavily enfiladed by the German
batteries farther north.[1]   At 12.45 P.M. the division informed the corps that a new attack held little prospect of
success.

Major-General Deverell was greatly handicapped by
being deprived of direct telephone communication with the
divisions on his right and left, the wire being cut by shell-
fire about 10 A.M. and not repaired until 4.30 P.M.[2]   He
wished to join up his front line with the troops of the 31st
Division, which, as will presently be seen, were holding on
in the German front system : the 31st Division hoped he
would be able to push forward his left to the support line
of the enemy's front system.   He finally suggested an
attack at 10 P.M. " when the moon would be up ", but,
under instructions from the Fifth Army, the corps, at
4.30 P.M., cancelled all further operations.

The attack by the right of the XIII. Corps, in order to
extend the defensive flank of the 3rd Division, was made on
a frontage of 500 yards by the 92nd Brigade (Br.-General
O. de L. Williams) of Major-General R. Wanless-O'Gowan's
31st Division.   The objective on the right was the reserve
line of the German front system, and on the left the support
line ; the enemy front trench was to be blocked at the

---

[1] The German artillery was very active against the left portion of the
V. Corps front (from the centre of the 2nd Division northward) and the
right of the XIII. Corps.   Farther south, the enemy batteries were taken
more or less in enfilade by the II. Corps guns beyond the river, and could
not develop nearly so destructive a fire.   The advance of the II. Corps
and of Colonel Freyberg's detachment had some effect also, for one German
regimental account speaks of batteries retiring from the Beaucourt valley
up the road towards Miraumont.

[2] In the meantime messages had to be sent through the headquarters
of the 3rd Division artillery or by runner.

13 Nov. Touvent Farm—La Louvière Farm road. Thirty-six machine-guns [1] were sited in the area south of Hébuterne and on its south-eastern edge to cover the left and to check any German fire or movement from the vicinity of "The "Point." [2]

The two assaulting battalions 13th and 12/East Yorkshire, completed their assembly by midnight, and pushed forward snipers and Lewis guns into No Man's Land to provide close support when the advance began. At 5.45 A.M. the Yorkshiremen went forward steadily through the mist behind a good barrage, and reports soon showed that the German front line had been carried. It was, indeed, entered without difficulty through the remains of the wire, and the dug-outs were then bombed to good effect, the prisoners taken being of the *66th Regiment*.[3] Opposite John Copse, which marked the right boundary of the corps, lay an old mine crater unoccupied by the enemy ; but a post established therein to protect the right flank was destroyed by shell and machine-gun fire.

In the remains of his support trench the enemy resisted stoutly with rifle and bomb, but was overcome by sheer hard fighting. On the right some of the 13/East Yorkshire kept up with the barrage and reached the reserve line, where they held on in the vain hope of being reinforced. Only a few returned later in the day ; the rest were overwhelmed. Bombing counter-attacks up the communication trenches leading back to Star Wood developed about 8 A.M., but the Yorkshiremen in possession of the German support line stood to it grimly all the morning, although bombs ran short and heavy losses were sustained.[4]

German shell-fire was now so heavy on No Man's Land and the British front line that communication with the forward troops became wellnigh impossible. Two companies of the 11/East Yorkshire, moving forward to reinforce, were held up, and carrying parties failed to get

[1] 93rd Machine-Gun Company ; Lucknow and Sialkot Machine-Gun Squadrons, from the 1st Indian Cavalry Division.

[2] This salient in the enemy line (a mile S.E. of Hébuterne) was bombarded with smoke by No. 1 Special Company R.E. for 20 minutes beginning at zero hour. The 93rd Brigade, holding the front as far as Hébuterne, was prepared to release a smoke cloud, using " P " bombs and smoke candles, but the wind (very slight, from N.W.) proved unfavourable.

[3] The *66th Regiment*, holding the northern half of the *52nd Division* front, had two battalions in line, and it was the *I./66th* which engaged the East Yorkshire battalions. Heavy losses are admitted in the German regimental account.

[4] Pte. J. Cunningham, 12/East Yorkshire, repelled two attacks single-handed, his prowess being rewarded with the V.C.

through.[1]   About 9.30 A.M. a German counter-attack in 13 Nov.
some force was made south-westward from Star Wood, but
the machine-gun group on the left flank opened effective
fire and the enemy melted away.   This was the only
attempt he made to advance over the open.

By 8 A.M. Major-General Wanless-O'Gowan was aware
that the left of the 3rd Division had been unsuccessful.
Co-operation became difficult, for, as already noticed, direct
telephone communication between the two divisional
headquarters failed about two hours later.   It seemed
obvious that the salient held by the East Yorkshire, shelled
continuously and subjected to incessant counter-attack by
German bombers, would soon become untenable unless the
line on the right could be prolonged by a fresh advance of
the 3rd Division.   At 5.25 P.M. came a telephone message
from the corps, announcing that the 3rd Division was not
to renew its attack, and that the Fifth Army approved of
the withdrawal of the 92nd Brigade.

Heavy losses had compelled the dogged Yorkshiremen
to give up their footing in the enemy's support line about
3 P.M. and retire to his front trench.   Here they were
making a fresh stand whilst all the wounded who could be
collected were passed back to the British line.   After dark
the final withdrawal began, the last parties coming in about
9.30 P.M.   Between them, the two battalions lost nearly
800 officers and men ; but they had inflicted heavy loss on
the Germans and taken over 130 prisoners.

The day's fighting had resulted in a partial success
which there seemed a reasonable prospect of developing by
a renewed effort.   General Gough was tolerably satisfied
with the progress made astride the Ancre, and for the
moment the II. Corps, south of the river, was well placed ;
on the other flank, however, fresh forces and thorough
preparation would be needed if the attack on Serre were to
be repeated.   He judged it to be well within the capacity
of the V. Corps, next day, to capture its original objectives from Beaucourt [2] to Ten Tree Alley, on the slope

---

[1] Major-General Wanless O'Gowan asked the corps heavy artillery to
increase its counter-battery measures against the German guns in action
about Rossignol Wood (1,000 yards N. of La Louvière Farm) and on the
south side of Bucquoy (some 2,000 yards farther E.) but the enemy fire did
not lessen appreciably all day.

[2] At 6.20 P.M. General Gough had ordered patrols to be pushed into
Beaucourt " to test the enemy's strength ", the village to be occupied if
abandoned by the Germans.

13 Nov. of Redan Ridge facing Serre, a total frontage of 3,300 yards.

Definite instructions from the Army for the resumption of the attack on the morning of the 14th were received about 7.30 P.M. by the V. Corps, which was already taking the necessary measures ; a formal operation order was issued by the corps to divisions at 10 P.M. In the first phase, the left of the 63rd Division was to complete the capture of its second objective, Beaucourt Trench, whilst the 51st and 2nd Divisions took Munich Trench ; the 63rd Division was then to secure Beaucourt village and Muck Trench, its third objective, and the 51st and 2nd Divisions were to carry Frankfort Trench, their second and final objective.

NOTE I

Mining Work on the Front of the V. Corps

Map 6. Apart from the explosion of the Hawthorn mine, the efforts of
Sketch the 252nd Tunnelling Company R.E. were devoted to driving under-
47. ground communications into the German position by developing the tunnels which already existed. Owing to the frequent postpone-ments of the attack the company never knew how much time it had at its disposal ; also, particular care had to be taken to preserve secrecy, since, in the event of the failure of the attack, it was desired to keep the enemy in ignorance of the plans for mining under Beau-mont Hamel during the winter. No less than nine tunnels were opened on the front where the attack succeeded, although the majority were not connected with the German lines until the evening of the 14th November. They were not suitable for the passage of formed bodies of troops, but some runners used them, and signal wires were run through them.

On the front of the 63rd Division, where part of the work was done by the 174th Tunnelling Company R.E., Nos. 1, 3 and 4 tunnels were broken out, No. 2, at the German salient opposite the centre of the 188th Brigade front, being used to explode a small mine under the hostile trenches. In the 51st Division area there were three, the entrance to one, Sap 6 opposite Y Ravine, being blown in by a German shell before zero hour, so that a new entrance had to be made outside the British trenches ; South Street tunnel, north of the Auchonvillers—Beaumont Hamel road, was to have been opened up after the consolidation of Beaumont Hamel, but orders to do so were not given until the afternoon of the 14th. On the 2nd Division front, North Street, near the right boundary of the 5th Brigade, was opened up 25 minutes after zero hour ; Cat Street, on Redan Ridge was used to explode a mine in No Man's Land, the crater being con-nected to the gallery and eventually to the German front trenches. This work was much impeded by snipers until darkness fell on the 13th November.

NOTE II

GERMAN REINFORCEMENTS ON THE NIGHT 13TH/14TH NOVEMBER [1]

Immediate steps were taken to reinforce the sorely tried troops which had been driven from the German front system north of the Ancre. Units of the *223rd Division* not yet in the line were brought up, the *III./144th Regiment* to Beaucourt and the *III./29th Ersatz Regiment* to Ancre Trench, behind Beaucourt, facing south along the river. The remnants of the *55th Reserve Regiment*, holding Beaucourt, retired when the *III./144th* arrived, the latter taking over the defence of the village. The *II./144th* came up south of the Ancre, crossed the river about 2 A.M. on the 14th November by a rough bridge composed of trees felled for the purpose, and occupied Puisieux Trench—in the old 2nd Position—north of Ancre Trench. The Beaucourt road was a crater field and the ruins of the neighbouring villages were in flames ; in view of the uncertain situation no counter-attack could be contemplated.

Part of the *26th Reserve Division*, which was holding the Monchy au Bois sector, had also to be called upon. From Pronville, 9½ miles west of Cambrai, the *121st Reserve Regiment* was hurried through the night first in lorries and then by march route. The men could scarcely believe in the loss of Beaumont Hamel, which they had held for so long. This regiment, with portions of the *99th Reserve* and *173rd Regiments* (*223rd Division*) moved forward to stiffen the line of the *12th Division* east and north-east of Beaumont Hamel.

[1] Gerster and various regimental histories.

CHAPTER XIX

THE SOMME

THE BATTLE OF THE ANCRE
13TH–19TH NOVEMBER 1916 (*concluded*)

(Map 6 ; Sketches A, 47)

14TH NOVEMBER : RENEWED ATTACKS OF THE
V. CORPS

FOLLOWING a cold and cheerless night a thin mist spread over the battle-field in the early morning of the 14th November ; but as the day wore on the weather cleared, and air reconnaissance again became possible, British machines flying low over the German positions. A keen, drying wind from the north-east promised a betterment of conditions underfoot, although mud was still deep in the trenches and on low-lying ground.

The V. Corps heavy artillery had maintained a slow bombardment throughout the night, and German retaliation was heavy on some parts of the front. Then at 6 A.M. intense fire was opened on the first objective—Beaucourt Trench on the front of the 63rd Division, and Munich Trench, opposite the 51st and 2nd Divisions. Twelve minutes later, just before dawn, the field artillery barrage came down, and at 6.20 A.M. the infantry advanced to the assault.

Map 6. The attack of the 63rd Division against Beaucourt
Sketch Trench was made from Station Road by the 13/Royal
47. Fusiliers and 13/Rifle Brigade (111th Brigade, attached from the 37th Division), with their right on Redoubt Alley. A loss of direction at the beginning of the advance was partially corrected under machine-gun fire from Beaucourt village and Muck Trench, which now formed the second objective, but the first impetus could not be regained. Eventually part of the 13/Royal Fusiliers, which lost

504

Lieut.-Colonel G. H. Ardagh wounded on this day, extended 14 Nov. the line of the 13/K.R.R.C. north-westward for 300 yards ; farther to the left, the remainder of the Fusiliers and the 13/Rifle Brigade were checked some two hundred yards short of Beaucourt Trench.[1] Nothing more was done until the right of the division attacked Beaucourt at 7.45 A.M.

This was the task of the 190th Brigade, which had managed to collect, near Beaucourt station, 400 of the H.A.C. and about eighty of the 7/Royal Fusiliers ; as one officer recorded, " it was a great scramble to get people up " in time ". The detachment advanced at the appointed hour, but came under rifle and machine-gun fire, and halted when it reached Lieut.-Colonel Freyberg's position. It is to the credit of the local commanders, each of whom acted on his own initiative, that the assault was renewed with so little delay. Lieut.-Colonel Freyberg, although wounded again, led the mixed force in his vicinity straight into Beaucourt, whilst the 13/K.R.R.C. pressed forward south-eastward through the village. Little resistance was encountered, and nearly five hundred prisoners were collected from the cellars and dug-outs, a line being established round the eastern edge of Beaucourt. Patrols were pushed forward as far as the protective barrage permitted.[2]

The capture of Beaucourt was reported at 10.30 A.M. By this time the 13/Royal Fusiliers and 13/Rifle Brigade, having secured a fresh barrage for their renewed assault, were in possession of most of Beaucourt Trench, where, again, there was little resistance.[3] The Rifle Brigade started to bomb towards Leave Avenue on the left, but saw no sign of an advance by the 51st Division.

Meanwhile, steps had been taken to deal with the Germans still holding out in their front system. Two tanks [4] from Auchonvillers started to cross No Man's Land as soon as it was light enough for an officer of the 188th Brigade to guide them. One machine stuck fast in the mud before reaching the German front line. The other did likewise between the front and support trenches, but opened fire with its 6-pdr. gun, the Germans in and about

---

[1] Here, according to one German regimental account (" Regt. No. 62 "), was the critical point. If the British movement developed north of Beaucourt the Munich—Frankfort position could not be held.

[2] " Regt. No. 144 " states that its *III./Bn.* in Beaucourt was surrounded. The artillery did not reply to its light signals, and there was " great slaughter ", few of the battalion escaping or being captured.

[3] Prisoners of the *55th Reserve Regiment* were taken here.

[4] A third had been damaged by a chance shell before starting from the rendezvous.

14 Nov. the strongpoints then raising a white flag. Over four hundred prisoners were eventually rounded up with the help of the 10/R. Dublin Fusiliers (190th Brigade). At the same time parties of the Howe Battalion (188th Brigade) collected Germans from dug-outs and trenches as far forward as Station Road, securing another two hundred prisoners.

At 1 P.M. came reports from air and ground observers of German infantry massing near Baillescourt Farm, nearly a mile east of Beaucourt ; and, as Beaucourt was being heavily shelled,[1] a counter-attack upon the right of the 63rd Division appeared to be imminent. A special field artillery protective barrage was therefore put down, whilst the heavy artillery of the II. and V. Corps bombarded the area east of Beaucourt, and no further signs of a German reaction were seen.[2] Lieut.-Colonel Freyberg was brought back from Beaucourt in the evening, having been severely wounded by a shell. His cool and capable leadership, which had carried the advance a mile into the German lines on the 13th November and had also been displayed in the capture of Beaucourt, was fitly rewarded with the Victoria Cross.

At night the 13/K.R.R.C. (111th Brigade) and the H.A.C. (190th Brigade), assisted by a company of the 14/Worcestershire (Pioneers of the 63rd Division) and men of the 189th Brigade, consolidated the eastern edge of Beaucourt, the left being prolonged by the 13/Royal Fusiliers and 13/Rifle Brigade (111th Brigade) in occupation of Beaucourt Trench. South-east of Beaucourt the railway bridge over the river was held by the H.A.C. ; on the other flank, no touch had been obtained with the 51st Division. Major-General Shute was anxious for the 111th Brigade to secure Muck Trench as ordered, but the failure of the 51st Division to get forward had resulted in no effort being made to do so. The V. Corps contemplated, also, an attack by the 63rd Division upon Puisieux Trench, east of Bois d'Hollande, early next morning ; but this operation was postponed for the same reason. After darkness had fallen the relief of the 63rd by the 37th Division was begun.

The 152nd Brigade of the 51st Division was to have attacked Munich Trench at 6.20 A.M., when the 111th

---

[1] A situation report by pigeon message had been received by the V. Corps from Lieut.-Colonel Freyberg via the II. Corps.

[2] Whilst the *III./144th* was " being sacrificed " in Beaucourt, a well-knit defensive position had arisen astride the Ancre (Grandcourt line and, north of the river, Puisieux Trench). " Regt. No. 144 ".

Brigade made its first advance, but orders were not received **14 Nov.**
in time by the 1/7th Argyll & Sutherland Highlanders
(attached from the 154th Brigade).   All that could be done
was to push forward strong patrols and these, being stoutly
opposed, lost the barrage.   At 7.30 A.M. two companies
advanced against the southern portion of Munich Trench.
Although progress through the mud was slow, the trench
was occupied about an hour later, there being little resistance.   Frankfort Trench, 200 yards ahead, seemed to be
full of Germans.   Soon after 11 A.M., by cruel mischance,
a British heavy battery began to shell Munich Trench and
the severely tried Highlanders were obliged to fall back
some distance and take refuge in shell-holes.   A little later
a company of the 1/9th Royal Scots (also 154th Brigade)
was set to bomb forward along Leave Avenue, but this
isolated effort could not make much progress.   Nothing
more was attempted on this day, a corps order for an
attack against Frankfort Trench at 2.45 P.M. reaching the
infantry too late for compliance.

At night the 2/2nd Highland Field Company R.E. and
a company of the 1/8th Royal Scots (Pioneers) began to dig
a new line, called " New Munich Trench ", some two
hundred yards west of Munich Trench.   Unaware that
Munich Trench had been evacuated, the V. Corps issued
orders for a fresh operation on the morrow, the 152nd
Brigade being told at 9.50 P.M. that it would assault
Frankfort Trench between Leave Avenue and Glory Lane—
the original objective of the 51st Division—in conjunction
with an attack by the 2nd Division, at 9 A.M.

The 2nd Division had attacked Munich Trench at
6.20 A.M., using two battalions of the 99th Brigade,
1/K.R.R.C. and 1/R. Berkshire, which were formed up in
Beaumont Trench an hour before zero.   The barrage was
erratic and caused many casualties ; for this reason, and
also because the troops were new to the ground, direction
was lost in the mist and gloom.   On the right the Rifles
strayed into the 51st Division area and actually entered
Leave Avenue from the south, being under the impression
that it was Munich Trench.   Although the mistake was
discovered, subsequent frontal and bombing attacks failed
to penetrate as far as the objective, which was still being
shelled by the British artillery.   Parties held on in Leave
Avenue for most of the morning and then withdrew to
Wagon Road with 60 prisoners.   The Berkshire, who had
been ordered to form a defensive flank beyond Lager

14 Nov. Alley, reached Munich Trench, but not in sufficient strength ; much confusion ensued, some Germans being disposed to surrender whilst others resisted stoutly. The left of the battalion swept over Lager Alley without recognizing it, and extended the British hold on Serre Trench, which it entered from the rear, capturing a number of Germans. In the course of the morning the men in and near Munich Trench fell back on Wagon Road, where part of the 23/Royal Fusiliers, the support battalion, assisted to strengthen the line.

The barrage which covered the left of this assault proved so effective that a German counter-attack from the direction of Serre melted away. By daybreak the 22/Royal Fusiliers had come into position on the defensive flank which ran from a strongpoint constructed on the south side of the Quadrilateral to Lager Alley at a point east of the German reserve line. This position was linked up to the British trenches by the Cat Street tunnel.[1]

Another effort was fixed for 2.45 P.M. when, as we have seen, the 51st Division made no movement. The 11/R. Warwickshire and 6/Bedfordshire, of the 112th Brigade (37th Division) now lent to the 2nd Division, were hurried forward to attack Frankfort Trench under the orders of the 99th Brigade. It was not known at divisional headquarters that the previous attack upon Munich Trench had failed, and the Warwickshire, at least, expected to pass through British troops in occupation of it. Both battalions had had a tiring march to the battlefront ; and when they advanced they were soon checked by accurate and quite unexpected machine-gun fire from Munich Trench. A withdrawal was made to Wagon Road, where there was now an embarrassing mixture of units.[2]

The 5th Brigade R.F.C. took full advantage of the change in the weather which made flying possible on the

---

[1] See page 502.

[2] " Regt. No. 23 " states that all available troops were put into the Munich—Frankfort position to stop this attack. British artillery fire was so heavy on communications that supplies of bombs and ammunition could not be replenished. A shell destroyed a well in Puisieux Trench and, in default of anything better, the troops were ordered to drink the foul water from shell-holes, much sickness being caused thereby.

Other regimental accounts record that the *62nd* and *23rd Regiments*, holding the *12th Division* front (from Munich Trench to beyond Lager Alley) had been reinforced by part of the *63rd* from reserve ; by portions of the *121st Reserve* and *99th Reserve* (*26th Reserve Division*), which were put in by companies as and when required ; and also by part of the *185th Regiment*, belonging to the *208th Division*, which was coming up to relieve the *12th Division*.

14th November, and the British counter-battery work 14 Nov. benefited accordingly.   No abnormal movement or activity behind the German lines was observed on this day.

In the II. Corps, south of the Ancre, the only offensive operation was a raid carried out at dawn on the front of the 19th Division by parties of the 9/Welch (58th Brigade) and 7/South Lancashire (56th Brigade) against the German positions in the vicinity of Stump Road and Lucky Way, due south of Grandcourt.   The 9/Welch reached and bombed some dug-outs before withdrawing, but the South Lancashire were checked by wire.   Later in the day the 19th Division began to relieve the 39th by extending its left to the river line, a movement which was completed by 3.30 A.M. next morning.

On the other flank of the V. Corps the 3rd Division reorganized and, in common with the 31st Division (XIII. Corps) which was also carrying out reliefs, suffered a heavy hostile bombardment.   When the mist cleared German aeroplanes came over, but they withdrew after sighting British machines.

Upon receipt of an optimistic message telephoned from Lieut.-General Fanshawe, General Gough came to V. Corps headquarters at noon on the 14th November to hear the corps proposals for the resumption of the offensive.   Lieut.-General Fanshawe was still counting upon the capture of Munich Trench and Frankfort Trench that afternoon ; and when the 37th Division had completed the relief of the 63rd, he hoped to capture Puisieux Trench, which would give him observation over the Miraumont villages, whilst the II. Corps secured Grandcourt.   He even considered that another attempt upon Serre " with any fresh troops " which could be found ", might follow.   The Army commander agreed, and an operation order was accordingly issued at 5 P.M. for the continuance of the attack on the 15th, " on the assumption that to-day's objectives of the " V. Corps have been gained ".   The objectives of the II. Corps were Grandcourt ; those of the V. Corps were Baillescourt Farm, and Puisieux Trench and River Trench —the old German 2nd Position—as far north as Artillery Alley, that is, on a frontage of 2,200 yards.

A copy of the order was sent the same evening to the Commander-in-Chief, who was in Paris.[1]   Sir Douglas

---

[1] On his way to attend the inter-Allied military conference to be held at Chantilly on 15th and 16th November.   See Chapter XX.

Haig promptly telephoned to G.H.Q. to say that he did not wish the Fifth Army to undertake any further operation on a large scale before his return.

15TH–17TH NOVEMBER

THE PLAN FOR THE RESUMPTION OF OPERATIONS

15 Nov.   On the 15th November, after the thick mist of early morning had been dispersed by the keen north-easterly wind, extended air reconnaissance was resumed ; but still no signs of any considerable forward movement of German reserves could be detected.[1]

By 6 A.M. Br.-General E. R. Hill's 63rd Brigade (37th Division) had relieved the 189th Brigade in the Beaucourt position, and all troops of the 63rd Division were brought out of the line.[2] At noon Major-General H. B. Williams (37th Division) took over command from Major-General Shute. The latter had been chiefly concerned with linking up his left with the 51st Division ; but, although bombers of the 13/Rifle Brigade (left of the 111th Brigade) worked up Beaucourt Trench towards Munich Trench before 9 A.M., it was not until 10 P.M. that touch could be established. On the other flank, Beaucourt was shelled heavily all day.[3] At night a patrol of the 63rd Brigade found the junction of Muck and Railway trenches unoccupied by the enemy, Muck Trench, most appropriately, being reported as full of mud. The post at the railway bridge, east of Beaucourt, was abandoned under heavy shell-fire, the ground in the vicinity being too wet for digging.

On the fronts of the 51st and 2nd Divisions the combined attack was delivered at 9 A.M. on the 15th, two fresh companies of the 1/7th Argyll & Sutherland Highlanders being assembled in New Munich Trench, nearly 500 yards in advance of the 2nd Division troops in Beaumont Trench.

---

[1] Successful night bombing raids were carried out by the R.F.C. on the 14th/15th, 15th/16th, and 16th/17th, the chief objectives being the railways at Achiet le Grand and eastward towards Cambrai.

[2] The losses of the 63rd Division were, approximately, 3,500.

[3] " Regt. No. 144 " observes that it was not considered feasible to retake Beaucourt without also launching a properly prepared attack south of the Ancre against St. Pierre Divion, and there were not sufficient resources for such an operation. East of Beaucourt the admixture of units belonging to different divisions caused considerable confusion in command ; on 15th November the *III./29th Ersatz* (*223rd Division*), the *II./99th Reserve* (*26th Reserve Division*) and the newly-arrived *II./25th* (of the incoming *208th Division*) were constituted " Regiment Wangenheim ".

This difference in alignment, together with the divided
command, was largely responsible for the subsequent
failure. The Highlanders, shelled before they started, ran
into their own barrage ; and, although some parties reached
Frankfort Trench and bombed some dug-outs there, the
position was untenable and a withdrawal had to be made
to New Munich under cover of Lewis-gun fire. The 2nd
Division used the remaining battalions of the 112th Brigade
(37th Division), 10/Loyal N. Lancashire and 8/East Lancashire, under the command of the 99th Brigade. Having
only arrived in their assembly positions forty minutes
before zero hour,[1] the troops lost direction in the mist,
sustained heavy casualties in officers, and eventually fell
back to Wagon Road.[2]

Meanwhile the 22/Royal Fusiliers (99th Brigade), with
some parties of the 6th Brigade, had improved the position
of the left defensive flank by bombing forward, a strongpoint being constructed in the Quadrilateral near the crest
of Redan Ridge. Two tanks were to have lent their
assistance, but both stuck fast in the mud before they could
come into action.[3]

At 9 A.M. on the 15th November, Lieut.-General Kiggell,
Chief of the General Staff, had visited General Gough to
acquaint him with the Commander-in-Chief's disapproval
of a renewed offensive. Later in the morning the Fifth
Army commander discussed the situation with Lieut.-
Generals Jacob and Fanshawe. As a result, he telephoned
to Lieut.-General Kiggell to say that all were agreed that
the proposed operation had good prospects of success : a
further advance would improve his line and create a good
moral effect : " all ranks were keen to attack again ", and
there were no signs of the enemy putting in substantial
reinforcements : if the weather remained good, he would
like to carry out two more days of offensive operations
and could resume on the 17th if the Commander-in-Chief
would permit him to do so.

Lieut.-General Kiggell saw Sir Douglas Haig in Paris
that evening, explained the situation to him at some

---

[1] Major-General Walker had asked that the attack be deferred until
1 P.M. in order to allow time for reconnaissance, but his request was
refused by the corps.

[2] German regimental accounts state that the British entered Munich
Trench, but were bombed out again.

[3] Two battalions of the *185th Regiment* (*208th Division*) were put into
Pendant Alley, south-east of Serre, on this day to form a defensive flank.
They came under the *12th Division*. " Regt. No. 185 ".

length, and obtained his consent to General Gough's proposals as outlined in the Army operation order of 14th November.   A message to this effect was at once despatched to Fifth Army headquarters.

16 Nov.   The events of the 15th November, however, led General Gough to take a much less optimistic view of the situation when he met his corps commanders at 9 A.M. on the 16th. Munich and Frankfort trenches had not yet been taken ; more troops had been used up than had been foreseen ; sufficient forces could not be found for another attack against Serre ; the capture of Grandcourt and Puisieux Trench did not appear feasible.   In the Army operation order issued at 8 P.M. the chief task was therefore assigned to the II. Corps : west of Courcelette Trench there was to be an advance of approximately 500 yards towards Grandcourt Trench, the left securing the Grandcourt line south of Grandcourt and gaining the western edge of the village.   The V. Corps was to cover the flank by pushing forward along Ancre Trench on the northern bank of the river, occupying Bois d'Hollande and establishing a line westward to the northern outskirts of Beaucourt ; and, farther north, Frankfort Trench was to be taken.   To allow what was considered ample time for preparation, the attack was not to be launched until the 18th November at 6.10 A.M.

On the 16th November, a cold, fine day, following a frost, there was little activity before darkness fell.   Then the 8/Somerset L.I. (63rd Brigade) pushed forward up Ancre Trench and established a post at Bois d'Hollande, whilst the 10/Royal Fusiliers and 13/K.R.R.C. (111th Brigade) formed posts in Railway Trench and Muck Trench, the 152nd Field Company R.E. assisting in consolidation. Thus the 37th Division was in a fair way to complete its allotted task.

Major-General W. H. Rycroft's 32nd Division, which since the 12th November had been in reserve to the II. Corps, south of the Ancre, was now relieving the front of the 2nd Division.[1]   At dawn on the 16th November the 14th Brigade (Br.-General C. W. Compton) had taken over the northern defensive flank [2] where there was considerable doubt as to the exact situation of the front line.   On the

---

[1] The losses of the 2nd Division totalled nearly 3,000.

[2] The 3rd Division, which had extended southward in the British line to the point where it joined this flank, was transferred to the XIII. Corps on the evening of 15th November. Losses in the division, 13th-15th November, totalled 2,400.

night of the 16th/17th the 97th Brigade (Br.-General J. B. 17 Nov.
Jardine) relieved the troops of the 112th Brigade in Wagon
Road, the right linking up with the 51st Division in New
Munich Trench and Leave Avenue. During the 17th
November, another bright, frosty day, the 97th Brigade
extended its line southward in relief of the 51st Division.[1]
The 32nd Division then held the front from Leave Avenue
as far as the Quadrilateral at the western end of the defensive
flank.

The weather still permitted of extensive air reconnaissance. Reports received by the Army from the R.F.C.
up to 5.10 P.M. indicated that Puisieux Trench south of
Artillery Alley, and also the Grandcourt line south of the
river had been abandoned by the enemy. General Gough
promptly ordered the V. Corps and II. Corps to push
forward patrols, and, if possible, occupy these trenches
during the night, whilst a new operation order extended the
scope of the attack on the morrow. The II. Corps was to
take Grandcourt, crossing the Ancre to occupy Baillescourt
Farm also ; the V. Corps objectives included Puisieux
Trench and River Trench as far north as Artillery Alley.
These additions to the tasks already laid down entailed
hurried amendments to the orders of corps and lower
formations, and eleventh-hour preparations which, as
previous experience had shown over and over again, were
fatal to success. Lieut.-General Jacob, whose information
differed from that on which the Army had acted, protested
in vain. About midnight on the 17th/18th November
patrols of the 56th Brigade (19th Division) discovered
Germans working on the wire in front of the Grandcourt
line, sufficient indication that the trenches—now a maze of
shell-craters and half-frozen mounds of earth—were still
occupied.

The II. Corps operation order allowed a halt of 90
minutes on the first objective, after which the 19th Division
would attack Grandcourt and Baillescourt Farm. When
this assault was launched the 4th Canadian and 18th
Divisions, continuing their advance, were to carry Grandcourt Trench and link up with the 19th Division at the
eastern end of Grandcourt. In the V. Corps the assault of
Puisieux and River trenches was to synchronize with the
assault of the II. Corps on Grandcourt and Baillescourt
Farm.

---

[1] The 51st Division had lost nearly 2,200 officers and men.

18TH–19TH NOVEMBER

THE FINAL ATTACK OF THE II. AND V. CORPS

18 Nov.   During the night the first snow of the winter had fallen, and at 6.10 A.M. on the 18th November the assault was delivered in whirling sleet which afterwards changed to rain. More abominable conditions for active warfare are hardly to be imagined : the infantry, dark figures only visible for a short distance against the white ground, groped their way forward as best they could through half-frozen mud that was soon to dissolve into chalky slime. Little wonder that direction was often lost and with it the precious barrage, whilst the objectives, mantled in snow, were hard indeed to identify. Observation from the air was impossible ; ground observers could see little or nothing, so that the batteries, in almost as bad a plight as the infantry, were, for the most part, reduced to firing their prearranged programme, regardless of the fortunes of the advance. To the sheer determination, self-sacrifice and physical endurance of the troops must be attributed such measure of success as was won.

Map 6.   In the right sector of the II. Corps, the 4th Canadian
Sketch   Division (Major-General D. Watson) had as objectives the
47.   newly-dug German defences known as Desire [1] Trench and Desire Support Trench, the latter lying half-way down the uneven slope between Regina Trench and the next enemy position, Coulee Trench—Grandcourt Trench.

Beyond the Pys road one company of the 46th (S. Saskatchewan) Battalion and two of the 50th (Calgary) Battalion (10th Brigade, Br.-General W. St. P. Hughes) advanced to cover the eastern flank. Here the troops were confronted by a new German trench, the exact position of which was not yet known ; and, on the extreme right, some confusion was caused by the smoke of a barrage, provided by No. 2 Special Company R.E., in order to prevent German observation from the north-east. The company of the 46th Battalion lost so heavily from rifle and machine-gun fire that the survivors were obliged to withdraw, although some lay out in shell-holes until dusk. The companies of the 50th encountered little resistance, but lost touch on the left with the 11th Brigade. They captured 100 Germans and began to consolidate a little in rear of

[1] German " Dessauer ".

Desire Support Trench, when they suffered such heavy 18 Nov. losses from machine guns firing in enfilade from both flanks that a withdrawal to Regina Trench was ordered.[1]

The 11th Brigade (Br.-General V. W. Odlum), with orders to carry Desire Support Trench and entrench beyond it, attacked with two companies each of the 75th (Mississauga), 54th (Kootenay), 87th (Canadian Grenadier Guards) and 38th (Ottawa) Battalions.[2] In the blinding sleet, the 75th swung off the proper line of advance so that its right reached the objective west of the Pys road; otherwise the brigade was successful, and made many prisoners.[3] Strong patrols of the 87th and 38th pushed forward down the slope into Grandcourt Trench, where few Germans were found; and an enemy detachment emerging from Coulee Trench, on the right front, presumably to counter-attack, dropped its weapons and came forward to surrender.

The situation became known to divisional headquarters by 9.20 A.M., and half an hour later a German movement southward from Pys was broken up by artillery fire. Early in the afternoon the 10th Brigade brought up companies of its 44th and 47th (Br. Columbia) Battalions in an endeavour, with artillery support, to prolong the new front of the 11th Brigade; but the line eventually consolidated left the Germans in possession of Desire Support Trench to a point some distance west of the Pys road.

At 12.30 P.M. Major-General Watson had decided to withdraw the patrols from Grandcourt Trench, and to reorganize on the first objective, in readiness to continue the advance if required; but at 7.50 P.M. the corps cancelled the second operation. The men of the 87th and 38th Battalions in Grandcourt Trench, though " bothered by " the British barrage ", were reluctant to vacate it, and did not come back till early next morning.

At the cost of 1,250 officers and men, the 4th Canadian Division had gained the greater part of its first objective,

---

[1] These companies had been engaged with the left of the *III./107th Regiment* (left sector of the *58th Division* which was being relieved by the *56th Division*). According to German regimental accounts, the divisional storm troops and two companies of the *I./88th* (*56th Division*) restored the situation by counter-attack.

[2] The 38th Battalion was attached from the 12th Brigade.

[3] These were of the *I./106th Regiment* (centre of the *58th Division*) and of the *III./107th*, on its left. The German regimental accounts state that the *106th* was driven back to Grandcourt Trench, which was eventually held by all three battalions of the *106th*, and some of the *35th Fusiliers* (*56th Division*). " It was as much as they could do." British artillery fire prevented any attempt to counter-attack.

18 Nov. captured 620 prisoners, and inflicted heavy loss in killed and wounded. It could undoubtedly have occupied Grandcourt Trench if a fresh advance had been sanctioned. Coming into the Somme battles at a late stage, the division had worthily upheld the reputation won by the Canadian Corps at the Battle of Flers—Courcelette. That it was not relieved until the 28th November, after nearly seven weeks in the battle front, is testimony to the reliance placed upon it.

Next on the left, Major-General Maxse's 18th Division had the four battalions of the 55th Brigade (Br.-General G. D. Price) in line, 8/East Surrey, 7/R. West Kent, 7/Buffs and 7/Queen's, each on a frontage of two companies. The German barrage fell upon Regina Trench which was empty, the troops having assembled in No Man's Land, where they lay in the snow until zero hour. All started well. At 8.10 A.M. the 8/East Surrey was reported to have captured its portion of Desire Trench and to be consolidating a line beyond, in touch with the Canadian left. Seventy minutes later the 7/R. West Kent was also reported to be on its objective, but there was a gap between the companies, which a bombing attack from the right, assisted by the East Surrey, eventually closed.

Telephone communication from the East Surrey and West Kent had been established back to the advanced brigade report centre, and remained intact all day, except for brief intervals. Nothing, however, was heard of the other two battalions ; seven runners, sent forward to bring back information, all became casualties, and Germans were still sniping from shell-holes in No Man's Land.[1] At 10.46 A.M. the division was informed that the right battalion of the 19th Division, west of Stump Road, the divisional boundary, had failed. Later messages showed that the Queen's had not been able to clear the dug-outs in Stump Road, as the detachment detailed for this purpose was nearly annihilated by shell-fire before it could get in. Part of the Queen's was, however, reported to be on the objective, although few of the Buffs had advanced so far.

At the point in Desire Trench where the Courcelette—Grandcourt road crossed the Pozières—Miraumont road (known as Point 66 from its abbreviated map reference) the Germans still held out. In the afternoon a well-planned

___
[1] It was afterwards discovered that in front of Desire Trench the Germans had deepened many of the shell-holes, to which they came forward by way of previously prepared " slits " as soon as the creeping barrage lifted on to the trench. Thus they were able to open close-range fire as the stormers approached.

combined effort, by bombers of the West Kent working 18 Nov. along the trench and by riflemen of the same battalion advancing over the open, captured this centre of resistance and killed 25 of the enemy. An advance westward was then made, the Germans fleeing from the trench, and parties of the Buffs were thus enabled to occupy a portion of their objective.[1]

In the meantime the Queen's, who had overshot Desire Trench, came under deadly machine-gun fire from Stump Road[2] and from Grandcourt Trench. Few of the two front companies were seen again. Major-General Maxse, having rightly decided, in view of the failure of the 19th Division on his left, that an attack upon Grand-court Trench would not be feasible, at 5 P.M. ordered the evacuation of Desire Trench west of Point 66. Next day patrols collected 30 prisoners and a number of British wounded from this part of the trench, which was held thereafter by posts. Point 66 was consolidated with the help of a section of the 92nd Field Company R.E., a line being dug back to Regina Trench.

In the 19th Division the task of the 57th Brigade (Br.-General G. D. Jeffreys) was to capture the whole of the Grandcourt line south of Grandcourt. This involved an advance roughly north-eastward, across Battery Valley ; but, on the right, the western end of Desire Trench had to be secured by attacking northward in extension of the 18th Division assault. On the other flank, the 7/South Lanca-shire (Br.-General F. G. M. Rowley's 56th Brigade) was to advance up the Ancre valley to the western edge of Grand-court. After these objectives had been captured there would follow the assault of the village by the 56th Brigade, and the passage of the river in order to reach Baillescourt Farm, the 57th Brigade keeping pace on the right.

When the assault was launched, the 8/North Stafford-shire, right battalion of the 57th Brigade, disappeared in the blizzard and for a time its fate was unknown. Actually the greater part of it entered the German trenches west of Stump Road and penetrated to a considerable distance,

---

[1] The right and centre of the 55th Brigade had been opposed by the *120th Reserve* (*58th Division*), whose history states that the *I. Bn.* in the front line suffered severely from shell-fire before the assault, and had its left flank turned when the *III./106th* was driven back. The four com-panies were destroyed. In Grandcourt Trench the British bombardment " pinned down " the *II. Bn.*, which could do nothing.

[2] The *I./29th Ersatz* (*223rd Division*) held the German front astride Stump Road.

18 Nov. but the survivors, including Lieut.-Colonel C. L. Anderson, were cut off and captured. Only about seventy men were able to extricate themselves, and these did so later, coming back in small parties up Battery Valley, farther to the left. Next to the North Staffordshire, the 10/R. Warwickshire lost direction and then regained it ; but the right companies were checked in front of uncut wire and suffered heavy loss. A few bombers managed to enter the Grandcourt line, and some of the two left companies pressed forward mixed with the 8/Gloucestershire, which achieved a notable success. This battalion stormed the German trenches on a front of 300 yards and entered the south-western end of Grandcourt.[1] In the early stages of the advance across Battery Valley the " mopping up " detachments of the Warwickshire and Gloucestershire had dealt with the enemy still remaining in trenches, shell-holes, dug-outs and old gun positions ; but they suffered cruelly from machine-gun fire in abortive efforts to locate the main German line.

The 7/South Lancashire (56th Brigade) sent forward two companies up the St. Pierre Divion—Grandcourt road, and one platoon up the railway to join hands with the V. Corps at the eastern end of Beaucourt beyond the river. Deploying to the right of the road, where the ground was comparatively firm, the assault delivered by the two companies reached the western edge of Grandcourt, captured some Germans, and pushed forward bombing parties into the ruins of the village where touch was gained with the Gloucestershire.[2] The left linked up with the platoon which, having crossed the Ancre near Beaucourt mill, had advanced along the railway embankment to a point almost due north of the western edge of Grandcourt. The South Lancashire now prepared to bomb their way through the village, in accordance with verbal orders received just before zero hour, but the failure of the right of the 57th Brigade led to the cancellation of this enterprise. Strongpoints were constructed on the railway and on the road at the entrance to Grandcourt, a section of the 81st Field Company R.E. assisting in the work of consolidation.[3]

---

[1] Thus no impression was made upon the right of the *I./29th Ersatz* and the left of the *I./144th*, which occupied the Grandcourt line facing west ; but the right of the last-named battalion was turned. " Regt. No. 144 " states that counter-attacks only resulted in the loss of leaders.

[2] The South Lancashire had driven in the *II./29th Ersatz*, whose front joined that of the *I./144th* south of Grandcourt.

[3] Two sections of the 82nd Field Company R.E. had followed the advance, man-handling baulks of timber which were intended for bridging

Meanwhile the 7/East Lancashire (also 56th Brigade), with orders to secure Baillescourt Farm in the second stage of the attack, had already pushed forward. The battalion was organized in two companies. One reached a position in close support of the S. Lancashire and was then held up by machine-gun fire from Grandcourt, Lieut.-Colonel T. G. J. Torrie being mortally wounded. The other followed the route of the S. Lancashire platoon across the Ancre and along the railway embankment, although its progress became impeded by the British protective barrage. A patrol eventually managed to get into communication with one of the V. Corps.

A fresh effort was made by the 57th Brigade to cover the left of the 18th Division, the 9/Cheshire (attached from the 58th Brigade) being launched to the assault of Desire Trench west of Stump Road at 5 P.M. Nothing was achieved, for the battalion, brought up hurriedly and having no knowledge of the ground, lost direction at the start and failed to reach its objective. When, late in the day, the situation of the forward troops became known to divisional headquarters, the captured line was placed under the 56th Brigade. Consolidation proceeded under heavy shell-fire.

Early on the morning of the 19th November, a day of **19 Nov.** chilling rain, the 7/South Lancashire beat off by fire a German counter-attack at the western end of Grandcourt. In the afternoon Major-General Bridges ordered a new position to be dug from the Ancre up Battery Valley parallel to and about five hundred yards west of the Grandcourt line.[1] To this trench the East Lancashire, South Lancashire, Gloucestershire and Warwickshire were withdrawn at night, since the ground they had captured, overlooked as it was by the Germans still in possession of the southern end of the Grandcourt line, was, in the judgment of the Fifth Army, untenable.

North of the Ancre, on the front of the 37th Division, the **18 Nov.** 8/Somerset L.I. (63rd Brigade), moving up through Beaucourt about 1 A.M. on the 18th November, had completed

---

the Ancre. Thus heavily burdened, the sappers could not keep pace with the infantry ; they dropped behind and so lost the barrage, and, coming under machine-gun fire from the Grandcourt line, were obliged to take refuge in shell-holes and remain there.

[1] The work was done by the 5/South Wales Borderers (Pioneers) and 24/Manchester, pioneer battalion of the 7th Division which was arriving on the Fifth Army front from Flanders.

18 Nov. a line of posts from Bois d'Hollande westward across the open ground to the Puisieux Road, and southward to Ancre Trench. One company had orders to establish itself in Puisieux Trench, but its advance through the falling snow, though covered by machine-gun and Stokes-mortar fire, failed to effect an entry : hostile posts occupied shell-holes covering the German line and could not be driven in, although repeated attempts were made to do so. By dawn the 8/Lincolnshire (63rd Brigade) and the 13/K.R.R.C. and 10/Royal Fusiliers (111th Brigade) had established posts in Muck Trench nearly as far west as Leave Avenue, and were ready to bring fire to bear upon the enemy when he should be driven out of Frankfort Trench by the 32nd Division.

At zero hour the 13/K.R.R.C. pushed patrols north of Muck Trench, meeting with only slight opposition in Railway Trench, whilst on the left the 10/Royal Fusiliers sent its bombers to secure the junction of Leave Avenue and Frankfort Trench in order to link up with the 32nd Division. This movement failed because the advance of the 32nd Division had been checked.

It had been intended that the 8/Somerset L.I., supported by the 4/Middlesex (both 63rd Brigade) should attack Puisieux and River trenches when the left of the II. Corps (19th Division) assaulted Grandcourt. More time, however, was needed for preparation, consequently the hour was altered to 11 A.M. and the advance began without regard to the fortunes of the II. Corps. The Somerset L.I. were late in starting and at 11.20 A.M. their commander, Lieut.-Colonel J. W. Scott, went forward to find his men sheltering in shell-holes from the fire of the British artillery. A message was got through to the guns, and, after the assaulting companies had been reorganized, the 4/Middlesex, which had come up through Beaucourt, was called upon to take part in a combined assault at 1.30 P.M. Before that hour, however, the Somerset bombers and patrols entered Puisieux Trench south of the Miraumont road ; and, after a few spasmodic encounters with the enemy, the trench was then occupied and consolidated down to the Ancre, the Middlesex lending assistance. A patrol obtained touch with the 19th Division on the railway some distance farther back.

19 Nov. On the 19th November the 10/Royal Fusiliers made an afternoon attack, following a three-hour bombardment by heavy artillery, upon the junctions of Munich and Frankfort

trenches with Leave Avenue.   Apparently the enemy had
suffered little, for machine-gun and rifle fire checked the
advance and nothing was gained.   At night when the left
of the II. Corps (19th Division) was withdrawn from the
edge of Grandcourt, the right of the 63rd Brigade conformed
by giving up its hold on Puisieux Trench.[1]

The 32nd Division had allotted to the 97th Brigade 18 Nov.
(Br.-General J. B. Jardine) the task of capturing Munich
and Frankfort trenches between Leave Avenue and Lager
Alley, and, by the express desire of the corps, all four
battalions 17th and 16/Highland L.I., 11/Border Regiment
and 2/K.O.Y.L.I., were employed.   Their assembly, in
New Munich Trench and on tapes which extended the
alignment northward to a total frontage of 1,125 yards,
proved a tedious and difficult process.   It began soon after
darkness fell on the 17th November, but the 16/Highland
L.I. reached its position only an hour before zero, and then
reported that it was being shelled by the British artillery.

When, at 6.10 A.M. on the 18th November, the troops
went forward through the sleet the 17/Highland L.I., on
the right, was checked by rifle and machine-gun fire, the
British barrage proving ineffective.[2]   The right company
of the 16/Highland L.I. suffered a like fate ; but the other
companies, pressing on with great determination, stormed
both Munich and Frankfort trenches.   Finding themselves
isolated in the German position, a withdrawal became
imperative, and, in the course of this movement, all the
captured Germans were lost and heavy casualties suffered.
Very few men regained the British lines.   Next on the left,
the Border Regiment was also met by machine-gun fire,
and most of the parties which fought their way through to
Frankfort Trench were forced back again after a protracted
struggle.   The right of the 2/K.O.Y.L.I. was held up by
fire from a strongpoint in Munich Trench, but, reluctant to
accept defeat, the men hung on in shell-holes until dusk.
The two left companies, suffering no check, swept over the
junction of the trench with Lager Alley[3] and continued

[1] " Regt. No. 144 " admits that the regiment was " at its last gasp "
when relieved on the night of the 19th November by troops of the *50th
Reserve Division*.   The *144th* had entered the fight 3,065 strong and
mustered 1,256 of all ranks when it came out.
[2] The southern half of the Munich—Frankfort position was held by the
I. and *III./121st Reserve (26th Reserve Division)*, with Leave Avenue as a
defensive flank.
[3] North of Frankfort Trench the inter-sections of trenches on the
northern slope of Redan Ridge formed a strong centre of resistance called
by the Germans " Feste Soden ".   According to regimental accounts,

18 Nov. down the hill, almost due northward, in touch with the 2/Manchester of the 14th Brigade.

The 14th Brigade (Br.-General C. W. Compton) was to carry the defensive flank forward to the line of Ten Tree Alley, an advance of 500 yards. Already, before zero hour, the 2/Manchester had pushed eastward along Lager Alley. When the general assault was delivered the three leading companies, with their left on Serre Trench, advanced down into the valley towards Serre, accompanied by part of the K.O.Y.L.I. Most of the officers fell, and the men struggled forward in small groups, some of which even entered the village, until their effort was spent. Isolated, exhausted, with little ammunition left, the survivors were overwhelmed in the course of the afternoon.[1]

On the left of the Manchester, the 15/Highland L.I., which reckoned that the British covering barrage fell quite 600 yards ahead, endeavoured to bomb forward up the trenches. Assailed by machine-gun fire at short range, the battalion was able to make little headway.

Heavy shelling by the German batteries had cut most telephone wires, so that communication from the front was mainly confined to pigeon messages, and to runners whose progress through the mud was very slow. By 11 A.M. it was known that the 97th Brigade had failed, and the rest of the day was spent in rallying the battalions in New Munich Trench and Wagon Road.[2] The sole gain of the

---

elements of the *12th, 208th, 223rd* and *26th Reserve Divisions* were engaged here and in Frankfort Trench. There was hard fighting, many Germans being captured and then released as the British broke their way in and then were forced to withdraw. The *62nd Regiment* had " melted away to " about 250 men " when relieved on 20th November.

[1] " Regt. No. 185 " states that the situation was restored by a counter-attack in which the *169th* (left sector of *52nd Division*), the *I./185th*, and a company of the *173rd* (*223rd Division*) took part, 70 prisoners and 4 machine guns being taken.

The history of the *66th Regiment* (right sector of the *52nd Division*, north of Serre), records that the British were " driven out of Serre " by two companies of the *III./66th* advancing over the open from Pendant Trench (500 yards E. of Serre).

According to Gerster a company of German prisoners approached Feste Soden from the north, the British escort having lost its way, and were released by the *II./121st Reserve*, which captured the escort.

[2] On the morning of 21st November two men of the 11/Border Regiment reported their return from a party of 11/Border Regiment and 16/Highland L.I., comprising many wounded, still occupying, unknown to the Germans, a dug-out in Frankfort Trench. Patrols made repeated efforts to get into touch with the party that night, but failed to do so. Next morning two more men got back. Eventually an attack was made, unsuccessfully against Munich and Frankfort trenches by the 16/Lancashire Fusiliers

14th Brigade, which brought up the 1/Dorsetshire to reinforce the 15/Highland L.I. and replace the 2/Manchester in Lager Alley, was represented by a slight advance of the 15/Highland L.I. on the left flank in the neighbourhood of the Quadrilateral.

The rain which veiled the battlefield upon the 19th **19 Nov.** November effectually prevented any further offensive operation by the II. Corps and V. Corps, neither of which, indeed, was fit for one.[1] To relieve the weary divisions, put the new front into a state of defence and improve the forward communications, were the immediate tasks of the Fifth Army.

The Battle of the Ancre may be regarded as an attempt to reap the fruits of previous successes, since the capture of the Thiepval ridge, which placed the right of the Fifth Army on the flank and left rear of the Germans north of the Ancre, had created such a favourable situation for the attack of the strong Beaucourt—Serre defences that it could hardly be neglected. As we know, the Commander-in-Chief had contemplated a further development of this offensive, but the ensuing period of bad weather had forced him to abandon any such project. After weeks of postponement even the limited operation, begun on the 13th November, when the mud proved a greater handicap than the fog, did not fulfil expectations. Although Beaumont Hamel and Beaucourt fell, the enemy's desperate defence of the Munich—Frankfort position on Redan Ridge confined the area of the " break-in " to the lower slopes nearer the river.

Following the first onset, it was not surprising that limited attacks, for the most part hurriedly planned and ill co-ordinated, achieved so little. As in all other operations conducted in defiance of the unfavourable autumn weather, the volume and precision of the artillery fire, the mobility of the infantry, and the transmission of orders and reports were all grievously affected ; tanks could not be employed

---

(96th Brigade) on the afternoon of the 23rd, when the 10/Loyal N. Lancashire (112th Brigade) co-operated and slightly improved the position of the left flank of the 37th Division.

" Regt. No. 185 " mentions the existence of the party which was discovered and captured some days after the 18th November attack.

[1] The casualties of the 32nd Division, 18th-24th November, were returned as 2,524, of which more than 50 per cent were " missing ". Those of the 37th Division, 13th-24th November, totalled 2,469, but include sick as well as battle losses.

with advantage ; the use of trench mortars and machine guns in close support of the infantry was always difficult and often impossible ; the collapse of roads and tracks, under the combined effect of hostile shell-fire and heavy rain, hampered and restricted the work of the administration and supply services, thereby inflicting additional hardship upon the troops.

Both sides suffered severely—the Germans, perhaps, more than the British [1]. If the salient astride the Ancre which was won by the Fifth Army had few merits as a defensive position for the winter, it proved a distinct asset when operations towards the Bapaume—Achiet le Grand line were resumed in January 1917.

The Fourth Army during the Battle of the Ancre

The Fourth Army did all that was possible to assist General Gough's offensive astride the Ancre, although by this time it was not easy to carry out heavy and sustained bombardments owing to the increasing difficulty of conveying ammunition through the mud to the forward battery positions. Nevertheless, the German line opposite the whole front of the Army was shelled with some severity on 12-13 the 12th November. Next morning, when the Battle of Nov. Ancre opened, a " Chinese " attack was delivered at 5.45 A.M. in order to give the impression that infantry action was impending. This demonstration lasted 40 minutes, but accelerated counter-battery work continued all day whilst the light allowed.

No rain having fallen since the 8th November, General Rawlinson issued orders on the evening of the 12th for a small enterprise to be carried out by the inner flanks of the I. Anzac Corps and III. Corps astride the Eaucourt l'Abbaye —Le Barque road.[2] The objectives were the Maze and Gird Support as far as, and including, Hook Sap, which connected the Gird lines with Butte Trench, the German front line farther to the west. The 2nd Australian Division (Major-General J. G. Legge) employed Br.-General W. Holmes's 5th (N.S.W.) Brigade, which had just replaced two of its own units, almost exhausted by their tour in the

---

[1] The Fifth Army casualties are recorded weekly : the total on the whole front for the period 11th-24th November is given as 23,274, of which 6,488 are shown as " missing ". During the same period, 7,183 Germans, wounded and unwounded, were captured.

[2] See Map 5, Sketch 44.

wet trenches, with the 25th (Queensland) and 26th (Queensland & Tasmania) Battalions from the 7th Brigade ; but the 19th, one of the two battalions thus relieved, was brought back to take part in the assault. The 50th Division (Major-General P. S. Wilkinson), holding the right of the III. Corps front, called upon the 1/5th and 1/7th Northumberland Fusiliers of the 149th Brigade (Br.-General R. M. Ovens).

Although the surface of the ground had dried, trenches 14 Nov. and shell-holes were still deep in mud and water when the attack was launched at 6.45 A.M., half an hour before sunrise, on the 14th November. The 26th Battalion, which formed the Australian right, did not succeed in following close behind the creeping barrage, and failed against the German machine guns in the Maze. Most of the 25th Battalion, in the centre, could do no better for the same reason. On the left, however, the 19th Battalion, conforming to the advance of the Northumberland Fusiliers who were allowed more time to get out of their trenches and approach the barrage before it began to creep, penetrated to Gird Support. The right of the 1/5th Northumberland Fusiliers was also successful and gained touch with the Australians ; but, as Gird Support was found to be too wet and neglected to permit of consolidation, a withdrawal was made to Gird Trench which, for some five hundred yards astride the Eaucourt l'Abbaye—Le Barque road, was held by bombing posts and Lewis guns. About fifty prisoners of the *5th Guard Grenadier Regiment* were sent back.[1] The advance of the 1/7th Northumberland Fusiliers on Hook Sap appeared to have succeeded, but the Germans in Butte Trench maintained so deadly a fire that communication with these companies was impossible, and nothing more was heard of them.

As the day wore on suspected German counter-attacks were prevented by the fire of all arms. Attempts to renew the assault where it had failed met, however, with no success. Two companies of the 20th (N.S.W.) Battalion were checked by machine-gun fire when they advanced against the Maze at 4.45 P.M., whilst about midnight of the 14th/15th a detachment of the 1/4th and 1/5th Northumberland Fusiliers attacked on the other flank with the same result. In the captured position a determined

---

[1] The *III. Bn.* was holding the front attacked, and the regimental history records that immediate attempts to counter-attack were stopped by the British artillery fire.

counter-attack delivered about 11 P.M. from front and
both flanks was beaten off by the Australians and the
1/5th Northumberland Fusiliers, which had been reinforced
by some of the 1/4th Battalion.[1]

On the 15th November the Australians and the Fusiliers
tried to bomb outwards along Gird Trench, but the mud was
so great a handicap that the troops soon became exhausted.
At dusk the 19th (N.S.W.) Battalion was relieved by the
28th (W. Australia) from the 7th Australian Brigade, and
the Northumberland Fusiliers by two companies of the
1/4th East Yorkshire. Communications on the right of
the 50th Division were so difficult, owing to the mud and
to German enfilade fire, that the British troops in Gird
Trench were obliged to rely upon the Australians for supply
of rations, water and ammunition.

At 3 P.M. on the 16th a heavy German bombardment
was begun, preceding a counter-attack which came in the
gathering darkness shortly before 5 P.M. The captured
portion of Gird Trench, where casualties from German shell-
fire had been very heavy, was enveloped by strong parties
bombing in from the flanks and it was also assaulted from
the front. In a little over half an hour the remnants of
the British and Australians were forced back out of the
position, and those who were able to do so withdrew to
their own lines.[2]

Sketch A. This, the last offensive operation undertaken by the
Fourth Army in the Battles of the Somme, coincided with
the concluding attempt of the French Sixth Army to improve its position at St. Pierre Vaast Wood. A little
progress was made on the 14th November ; but next day
the Germans counter-attacked in considerable strength,
recovering a small part of Saillisel and re-establishing their
line on the north-western edge of the wood. General
Fayolle regarded the resultant situation as " critical ", but
further French effort was delayed by the bad weather and
eventually cancelled.[3]

---

[1] " Gd. Gren. Regt. No. 5 " states that most of the divisional storm
company was put in on the flanks, a company of the *I. Bn.* making the
frontal assault. The *II. Bn.* had relieved the *III. Bn.* in Gird Support.

[2] " Gd. Gren. Regt. No. 5 " claims that the counter-attack effected a
surprise. The divisional storm company again delivered the flank assaults,
detachments of the *I. Bn.* and *II. Bn.* attacking from the front.

[3] F.O.A. iv. (iii.), pp. 268-70.

NOTE

The success of the British astride the Ancre on the 13th November is called by Ludendorff " a particularly heavy blow ", for O.H.L. considered such a happening no longer possible, particularly in sectors where German troops occupied good positions.   There had been a general hope that rain would put a stop to all British operations.

In the course of the fighting, the *223rd Division* from Alsace relieved the *38th* at Grandcourt ; the *208th Division*, which arrived from Russia in October, the *12th* east of Beaumont Hamel ; the *56th Division*, from the Crown Prince's Army Group, the *58th* north of Courcelette ; and units of the *26th Reserve Division*, holding the right of the *First Army* (Monchy au Bois sector) had been used to sustain the line east of Beaumont Hamel.   The German troops suffered much from exposure, and sickness was prevalent.   Between the 19th and 23rd November the *223rd* had to be relieved in its turn by the *50th Reserve Division* from the *Sixth Army*, and the *14th Bavarian Division*, resting after withdrawal from the Verdun front, relieved the *52nd* in the Serre sector.   Opposite the Fourth Army the *Marine Brigade*, from Flanders, reinforced the *Guard Reserve Corps* on the Warlencourt front.

The German losses on the Somme front in November, up to the night of the 18th, are given as 45,000.   There was a feeling of relief when it seemed that the heavy fighting of the year was over at last. Nevertheless O.H.L. feared that the Allies, with the object of relieving the Rumanian situation, might deliver another big attack about the end of November : probably on the Somme, with smaller attacks at Arras and Verdun—St. Mihiel.

[1] G.O.A. xi., pp. 101-3, Ludendorff, Rupprecht and Schwarte ii.

CHAPTER XX

EXTENSION OF THE BRITISH FRONT

(Sketch 48)

Sept.-
Oct.
As early as the 12th September, General Joffre had intimated to the British War Committee, through Sir William Robertson that, in consequence of the heavy French losses during the past two years,[1] he saw the time coming when the British must take over more front. The question was studied in detail at G.Q.G. and mentioned later by the French Mission with G.H.Q.

The British Commander-in-Chief proved very reluctant to extend his line.   In his view, the British Army was in France to fight " not to take over trenches and act pas- " sively ".   By the end of October 1916 he was planning to carry on throughout the winter such minor operations as the weather should allow.   This he had agreed to do at the earnest request of General Joffre.   Moreover, the battle training of the British divisions—filling up as they were with raw drafts—in readiness for a large-scale offensive in the spring of 1917 was of primary importance.

On the other hand, the French had been quite as heavily engaged,[2] and they held more than four times as much of the front as the British.   Although practically half of their line—from east of St. Mihiel to Switzerland—was confronted

---

[1] F.O.A. iii., p. 602, gives 1,961,687 casualties (all but 29,636 in France) up to 31st December 1915.

F.O.A. iv. (iii.), shows (pp. 520-3) that the French losses at Verdun and the Somme together totalled 581,484 ; the total British (unadjusted) losses for the whole of the year 1916 were 607,784 (figures of the Adjutant-General, G.H.Q., France), so that, when allowance is made for the French casualties in normal trench warfare, the French losses for the year appear almost to balance those of the British.   In proportion the latter had, of course, suffered much more severely.

[2] From F.O.A. iv. (iii.), p. 271, it appears that practically all the 98 active French divisions on the Western Front fought either on the Somme or at Verdun, 30 divisions engaging in both battles.   Of the 56 British divisions, 53 took part in the Battles of the Somme ; another (61st) was engaged at Fromelles in July, but not on the Somme.

THE SOMME, 1916: 16th November.

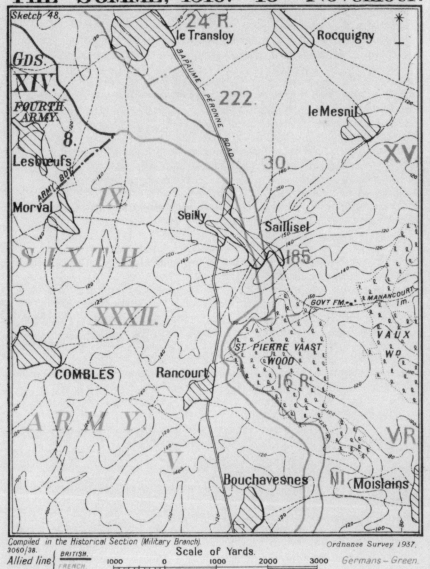

Sketch 48.

24 R.

le Transloy

Rocquigny

GDS.
XIV.

FOURTH
ARMY.

8.

222.

le Mesnil

XV

Lesbœufs

30.

IX

Morval

Sailly

Saillisel

185

SIXTH

MANANCOURT
1m.

GOVT FM.

VAUX
WOOD

XXXII.

ST PIERRE VAAST
WOOD

COMBLES

Rancourt

16 R.

A R M Y.

V R

V

Bouchavesnes

III

Moislains

Compiled in the Historical Section (Military Branch).
3060/38.

Scale of Yards.

Ordnance Survey 1937.

Allied line { BRITISH.
            { FRENCH.

1000   0   1000   2000   3000

Germans — Green.

Heights in metres.

by comparatively weak German detachments of inferior Oct.-
quality, and might be thinly held, their need for some such Nov
relief as General Joffre had in mind was real enough, and
not to be disregarded. Each Commander-in-Chief, of
course, wished to concentrate upon his preparations for the
spring, limiting as much as possible the effects of " usure "
on his Armies during the winter. The French staff study
had also considered another aspect of the question : if
sufficient French divisions were available to mount the
spring offensive on a front of about 40 km. (25 miles), it
could be launched under French direction without depending
upon the close co-operation of the British as in 1916.[1]

On the 1st November General Joffre addressed the
British Commander-in-Chief on the question of plans for
the spring offensive, suggesting an Allied attack on a
very wide front in order to exploit the situation north and
south of the Somme : the French to operate between the
valleys of the Oise and the Somme and the British from
Bapaume to Vimy ; the front between Péronne and Le
Transloy to remain upon the defensive in the first instance ;
if Sir Douglas Haig agreed, they could then " decide upon
" the division of the passive front ".[2]

Thus it was assumed that the British were able and
willing to take over more line. Sir Douglas Haig expressed
his general agreement with the above propositions on the
6th November, and on the 10th consented to take over the
front of the French Sixth Army as far as a point north-east Sketch
of Bouchavesnes, relieving thereby three French corps. 48.
He asked that, before he did so, the St. Pierre Vaast Wood
—Saillisel position should be stabilized. After considerable
correspondence it was decided on the 21st that the relief
should be completed by the middle of December ; but as
the fighting round Saillisel had ended rather unfavourably
for the French, Sir Douglas Haig had to trust them to hand
over a good line " such as they themselves would like to
" hold for the winter ".

[1] " Si nous pouvons nous-mêmes consacrer à notre offensive un nombre
" de divisions suffisant pour que notre front d'attaque ait une étendue
" d'une quarantaine de kilomètres, nous ne serons peut-être pas obligés de
" demander à nos alliés de prononcer leurs attaques — ou du moins leur
" attaque principale — en liaison immédiate avec nous ; ils pourront alors
" procéder à leur opération dans la région d'Ypres, qui semble toujours
" leur tenir au cœur. Dans le cas où celle-ci ne comporterait pas l'emploi
" de toutes leurs forces, nous exigerions que le surplus en soit utilisé à
" notre aile gauche." F.O.A. v. Annexe 22.
[2] Orders for the necessary reorganization of the French Armies had
already been issued. F.O.A. iv. (iii.), p. 32.

2 M

General Rawlinson had been informed of these negotiations by G.H.Q. on the 14th November. On the following day he had issued a warning order for adjustment of corps boundaries and the extension of the Fourth Army to the right.[1]

THE CHANTILLY CONFERENCE
15TH/16TH NOVEMBER

The conference of Allied commanders called by General Joffre and presided over by him, was held at G.Q.G. at Chantilly on the 15th and 16th November.[2] As in December 1915, the chief concern of the French Commander-in-Chief was to ensure better co-ordination of the Allied effort in the following spring, after providing such safeguards as seemed necessary to tide over the winter months.

Prospects were not unfavourable, although the operations of 1916 could hardly be said to have gone according to plan. At Verdun in February the Germans seized the initiative in an endeavour to shatter the resistance of France, but they succeeded merely in diminishing the French contribution to the Allied offensive on the Somme. Italian attacks upon the Isonzo front in March had little result beyond provoking strong Austrian reactions. In May the Austrian thrust from South Tirol, which came almost as a surprise to the Italian High Command, anticipated the resumption of Italian operations upon the Isonzo. Three weeks later the balance was more than restored by the launching of the Brusilov offensive : the Russian Armies, attacking on a front of nearly two hundred miles, overran Volhynia and Bukovina and reached the Carpathian passes.[3] Thus relieved from Austrian pressure, the Italians launched a counter-offensive which recovered about half the ground lost in the Trentino ; early in August they passed again to the attack upon the Isonzo and

[1] The relief by British troops of the French Territorials holding about half a mile of front in the Boesinghe sector, between the British and Belgians, was arranged to be completed by 1st December.
[2] The chief representatives were General Joffre, with General de Castelnau, his Chief of the Staff ; Sir Douglas Haig, Sir William Robertson and Major-General F. B. Maurice, D.M.O. ; General Porro, C.G.S. Italian Army ; General Wielemans, C.G.S. Belgian Army ; General Palitzine, Russia ; Colonel Rudeanu, Rumania ; General Rachitch, Serbia. Lieut.-Colonel Nogai attended on behalf of Japan.
[3] See G.O.A. x. and xi., Schwarte ii. and iv., Ludendorff and Falkenhayn for the German accounts ; and " A Soldier's Notebook 1914–18 ", the English translation of the memoirs of General A. A. Brusilov, for the Russian side.

captured Gorizia.[1] Moreover, before the end of August, the Rumanians had entered the War and begun their advance into Hungary through the passes of the Transylvanian Alps. By this time, on the Western Front, the Somme offensive had stabilized the situation at Verdun, where the French were enabled to pass to the offensive in their turn ; it had also, in some measure, supported the later stages of the Russian effort. Although the Germans in the West succeeded in maintaining their defence, their powers and resources were extended to the utmost, for O.H.L. was compelled to divert sufficient strength to prevent an Austrian collapse on the Russian front, and to find troops for the urgent counter-offensive against Rumania. It was against Rumania that the Central Powers achieved their one positive success of the year ; Russian assistance failed to save the newest Ally, who was defeated in the autumn.[2] In Macedonia, however, a Bulgarian advance had been checked, and French and Serbian forces after heavy fighting, were about to enter Monastir.[3]

In the matter of man-power the Central Powers were at a decided disadvantage, for they had nothing to compare with the numbers still available in Great Britain, Italy and Russia. Russia, too, was now better equipped and better supplied than ever before, although none realized until later how much it had cost her to maintain her summer offensive. The material resources of the Allies, who had most of the world to draw upon at need, far transcended those of their enemies. To the British blockade Germany could only oppose the submarine which was, indeed, taking heavy toll of Allied tonnage ; yet it promised no decisive effect without recourse to the politically doubtful expedient of unrestricted warfare.[4] In August 1914 Germany had counted

---

[1] The operations were continued until November, albeit with limited success. For the Austrian and Italian operations of 1916 see the Official Accounts, iv. and v. (Austrian) and iii. and iv. (Italian).

[2] The defeat of Rumania was accomplished by German, Austrian, Bulgarian and Turkish forces under Mackensen and Falkenhayn which invaded Wallachia from south and north, after Falkenhayn had crushed the Rumanian offensive. The fighting in September and October decided the issue, although Bucharest was not occupied until 6th December. See G.O.A. xi., Falkenhayn's " Der Feldzug der 9. Armee," and the Austrian Official Account (v.).

[3] Monastir was entered by the Allies on 19th November. See " Macedonia " Vol. I.

[4] Unrestricted submarine warfare was begun on 1st February 1917, and on the 3rd the United States of America severed diplomatic relations with Germany, eventually declaring war on 6th April.

upon a speedy triumph ; now, after over two years of war, Ludendorff saw no more than a " possibility " of victory.[1]

Nov. In this rather hopeful atmosphere the Chantilly Conference assembled. General Joffre was already in agreement with Sir Douglas Haig and Sir William Robertson regarding future Franco-British action on the Western Front, so here it will suffice to record the general decisions arrived at on the second day : [2]

(a) During the winter 1916–17, offensive operations actually in progress on each front will be continued to the fullest extent permitted by climatic conditions.

(b) In order to be prepared for all eventualities, especially to prevent the enemy from regaining the initiative, the Allies will be ready to undertake combined offensives from the first fortnight of February 1917 with all the means at their disposal.

(c) From the time when the Armies are ready to attack, the commanders-in-chief will act, respectively, according to the situation of the moment.

(d) If circumstances do not prevent it, the combined offensives, carried out with all the means which each army is able to employ, will be launched on all fronts as soon as they can be synchronized, at dates to be fixed by common accord between the commanders-in-chief.[3]

(e) To achieve a common accord in these diverse hypotheses, commanders-in-chief will not cease to maintain close contact with each other.

In addition, the principle of mutual support was reaffirmed. If one Power were attacked the others would come to its aid immediately with all their means : indirectly by attacking in localities previously selected ; directly by the despatch of troops, where communications permitted, to the threatened front. The problems of the transportation and employment of combined forces were to be studied by the French, British and Italian staffs.

These decisions formed, for the most part, a restatement of the policy outlined at the Chantilly Conference in December 1915,[4] but the situation in the Balkans now demanded special consideration and called for prompt action. The decisive defeat of the Bulgarians was to be

[1] Ludendorff i., p. 308.

[2] The " Notes " prepared by G.Q.G. for the Conference are reproduced in F.O.A. v. (i.), Annexes 104, 114, 115 ; the decisions are given in Annexe 119.

[3] It was agreed that synchronization would be realized if there did not ensue a delay of more than three weeks between the initial dates of the offensives launched on the various fronts.

[4] See "1916" Vol. I., pp. 4-9.

sought by Russo-Rumanian forces acting from the north Nov.
in co-operation with the Salonika Army advancing from the
south, the latter to be increased to 23 divisions for the
purpose.[1]

General Joffre was much pleased at the results of the
conference,[2] and on the 16th November the members were
entertained to luncheon by M. Briand, the French Premier
(President of the Council) and Foreign Minister, and to
dinner by the President of the Republic. But if the
soldiers were in complete accord, their proceedings were
not viewed with satisfaction by certain statesmen, notably
Mr. Lloyd George, British Secretary of State for War,
although none was more eager than he for the ardent
prosecution of the struggle. Since July 1916, when he
went to the War Office, he had become increasingly dissatisfied with the strategy and general policy of the Allies.
In his eyes the offensive on the Somme had been persisted
in too long, and its results were a bitter and costly disappointment ; he possessed no confidence in a renewed
offensive on the Western Front. In answer to his demand
for an estimate as to the probable duration of the War, Sir
William Robertson, as was not surprising, had confessed
his inability to make such a forecast ; and the recommenda-
tion, contained in a General Staff memorandum dated the
26th October, " that our forces in France should be at the
" greatest possible strength by next spring, and that all
" the resources of the Empire, and all demands for men for
" whatever purpose, should be examined from that point of
" view ", proved extremely unpalatable to the Minister.
He had visions of an " encirclement " of Germany, the
chief enemy, by an offensive from the East,[3] and, at his
instigation, the War Committee arranged a preliminary

---

[1] Made up of seven British, six French, three Italian and six Serbian
divisions, with one Russian division. It was decided that the Serbs could
be brought up to this strength by voluntary enlistment of Serb nationals
who had been obliged to serve in the Austro-Hungarian forces and were
now prisoners in Italy and Russia.

[2] " . . . il ne faisait pas de doute que les fruits que nous avions fait
" mûrir par notre union en 1916, nous les cueillerions en 1917 ". Joffre ii.,
p. 365.

[3] At the beginning of 1915, whilst Chancellor of the Exchequer, Mr.
Lloyd George had submitted to the War Council a long memorandum
which advocated the landing of 600,000 men at Salonika or on the
Dalmatian coast, for an advance in conjunction with the Serbs, Rumanians
and Greeks, through the Balkans into Austria. It was thus that he would
have employed our New Armies, then in the making, and during the
following years nothing shook his faith in this or a similar plan. See
" War Memoirs ", p. 320.

Nov. meeting in Paris of the representatives of the Allied Governments who—without reference to their principal " expert advisers ", intent upon seeking victory in the West—would study the whole situation and consider anew the future conduct of the War. This meeting was intended to be followed by another, which would be held at the headquarters of the Russian Armies, and attended by the military representatives. Definite strategic plans could then be formulated.

An attempt to secure a postponement of the Chantilly conference until after the Paris deliberations did not succeed, so whilst the soldiers were in conclave at G.Q.G. the statesmen were assembled in the French capital.[1] Here, on the first day, the principle was affirmed that the general conduct of the War remained the responsibility of the Allied Governments and was not to be determined by their military advisers ; it was also agreed that the proposed conference should be held in Russia. On the following afternoon, the 16th November, the decisions of the Chantilly conference were available, and Generals Joffre, Haig, Robertson and Porro were present. An animated discussion ensued regarding the maximum force which could be based on Salonika, but nothing which was said could shake the military opinion that shipping facilities and the character of the land communications would not permit the concentration of more than the total of 23 divisions fixed upon at Chantilly.

Thus the Paris conference effected nothing, nor did a fundamental change of policy result from the events of the following month, which saw General Nivelle supersede General Joffre as Commander-in-Chief of the French Armies,[2] and Mr. Lloyd George replace Mr. Asquith as Prime Minister of Great Britain. Henceforward the increasing divergence of views between Mr. Lloyd George and Generals Haig and Robertson should be borne in mind. The soldiers, in line with the preponderance of French

---

[1] There were present Mr. H. H. Asquith, Prime Minister, Mr. D. Lloyd George, Secretary of State for War, and Sir M. Hankey ; M. Briand, French Premier and Foreign Minister, Admiral Lacaze, Minister of Marine, and also M. de Margerie ; the Russian and Italian Ambassadors ; and two other Italian Ministers.

[2] For the circumstances under which General Joffre was superseded by General Nivelle who became commander of the " Armies of the North and North-East " (Western Front) see F.O.A. v. (i.), pp. 146 *et seq.* The change was made by M. Briand, President of the Council, to placate the French Radical-Socialists who were bent upon securing greater political control of the direction of the War.

opinion, were convinced that the main effort must still be made against the chief enemy in the West. The statesman, who had never been in sympathy with the Chief of the Imperial General Staff, remained firm in his belief that an adventure on a large scale in Eastern Europe, whilst remaining on the defensive in the West, was a cheaper recipe for victory.

Situation on the Somme, November 1916

The monthly conference of Army commanders, which Nov. had been suspended during the battles of the Somme, was resumed on the 18th November when the Commander-in-Chief had returned from Paris. Sir Douglas Haig laid down the general policy for the winter : if attacked, the British Armies would hold their ground and not allow their future plans to be upset ; if an Ally were attacked a British attack would be launched in its turn, and, in any case, methodical pressure would be maintained " in order to " prevent the recovery of the enemy " ; preparations would continue for a general combined offensive in the spring, and all was to be in readiness by the 1st February 1917. More specifically, he said, the Fourth and Fifth Armies would continue offensive operations to a limited extent, " as far as resources and weather permitted ", and the Second Army might be called upon to attack the Spanbroekmolen spur, west of the Messines—Wytschaete ridge.

General Rawlinson had written to the Commander-in-Chief on the 7th November to point out that his battle-weary divisions required rest and were all in urgent need of the opportunity to assimilate their new drafts and to train for future operations. He now observed that the Fourth Army would find it difficult to be ready by the beginning of February : the battle had barely died down and all his defences required to be reconstructed, whilst the improvement of his communications—a vital necessity—was hampered by lack of road metal. General Allenby said that the Third Army wanted road metal and also ballast for railway extensions. General Horne was most concerned with the incessant mining and trench-mortar activity of the Germans opposite the First Army front, and the very heavy work upon the maintenance of defences entailed thereby : in consequence, he was making some parts of the third line his line of resistance, holding the first and second as outpost

Nov. positions : he required another division in order to carry out the reliefs necessary to his programme of rest and battle training. For the Second Army, General Plumer said the preparations for his Messines attack were well advanced, but he was counting upon divisions being brought up to establishment.

The question of reinforcements was taken up strongly by the Commander-in-Chief in his report to the Chief of the Imperial General Staff, dated the 21st November. He pointed out that on the 17th of the month the 55 British and Dominion divisions on the Western Front [1] showed an infantry strength of 576,079 against an establishment of 689,480 : there were 22,881 reinforcements at the base, so the actual shortage amounted to 90,500 ; but, in order to provide for a 10 per cent surplus with units, the wastage of the winter months, and adequate drafts to be available at the base on the 1st March 1917, 302,500 infantry were required.[2]

The appalling conditions under which the Fourth and Fifth Armies had fought during the later phases of the Somme offensive, and were now facing the third winter of the War, were revealed by Sir Douglas Haig in the following words :

" The ground, sodden with rain and broken up every-
" where by innumerable shell-holes, can only be described
" as a morass, almost bottomless in places : between the
" lines and for many thousands of yards behind them it is
" almost—and in some localities, quite—impassable. The
" supply of food and ammunition is carried out with the
" greatest difficulty and immense labour, and the men are
" so much worn out by this and by the maintenance and
" construction of trenches that frequent reliefs—carried out
" under exhausting conditions—are unavoidable ".[3]

In the front trenches there had been no opportunity to provide adequate cover against either fire or weather.

---

[1] The 60th Division had just left for Macedonia, so the number of divisions in France was now 55.

[2] The details are as follows : deficit, 90,500 ; 10 per cent surplus, 69,000 ; available at base, 30,000 ; replacements of winter wastage (estimated), 113,000 ; total, 302,500. An estimate of requirements up to the end of October 1917 was also sent ; this reckoned on a battle wastage (March-October inclusive) of 800,000 and asked for a total provision of 1,500,000 in infantry alone. The British Government, it may here be noted, decided for National Service on 19th December.

[3] From the Commander-in-Chief's report to the C.I.G.S., dated 21st November.

Between the front and the reserve positions on the reverse slopes of the Bazentin ridge—Ginchy, Guillemont, Longueval, the Bazentins, Pozières—stretched a sea of mud more than two miles in extent, and the valley of the Ancre was a veritable slough of despond. Movement across these wastes was by way of duckboard tracks which, exposed as they were to hostile shell-fire and the disintegrating action of the mud and rain, could only be maintained and extended by arduous and unending labour. Stretcher-bearers, with never less than four men to a stretcher, made the journey down from the regimental aid posts through mud which no wheeled carrier could negotiate : but all that man could do was done to get the sick and wounded away with the minimum of exposure and suffering.[1]

Sickness had begun to take a steady toll, and although the precautions—proved by the experience of the previous winters—against trench-foot were now adopted as a matter of routine, it was not easy for men who stood or waded for days at a time in mud and water to keep their feet dry and their blood in brisk circulation.[2] Frost-bite and trench-foot cases—the figures for each separately are not available —admitted to medical units from the whole of the British forces on the Western Front amounted in 1916 to 16,955, as against 22,718 in the previous year. There were 707 admissions to hospital from this cause during the week ended 28th October, the total rising to 1,099 and 1,417 in the two succeeding weeks : for the five weeks ended on the 30th December, the number was 9,370.[3]

[1] The bearers of the field ambulances were often reinforced by pioneers, men from the divisional trains, and others who could be spared. Prisoners on their way down from the front also assisted. The " carry " from Gueudecourt to Longueval, where the wounded were transferred to a tramway, was about 3,500 yards, divided into three stages.

[2] The usual procedure consisted of a periodical rubbing of the feet with whale-oil and a change to dry socks. These were sometimes sent up to the line in waterproof bags. Men often used sandbags to replace puttees which restricted circulation in the legs.

[3] See the Official History : " Medical Services : Casualties and Medical " Statistics ", which shows (p. 155) that the chief causes of admission to hospital from disease, apart from venereal disease, during 1916 were :

	per 1,000 of ration strength
Trench-foot and frostbite	12.82
Nephritis	7.42
Dysentery	4.37
Rubella (German measles)	4.15

As regards nephritis, " it seems feasible to suggest that the predisposing " causes are cold and humidity, hard work and overloading the soldier with " heavy equipment ". *Idem*, p. 90.

Nov.   Some officers, speaking from experience of both offensives, are of opinion that the conditions on the Somme in the
late autumn of 1916 were as bad as, if not worse than, those
at Passchendaele a year later of which the public were to
hear so much more.   Certain it is that the troops of all
arms were tried almost to the limit of their endurance, and
bore the ordeal with admirable patience and courage.
None gave more proof of these qualities than the Australians,
who were experiencing for the first time the rigours of a
winter in Northern Europe, and that not in well-constructed
trenches but amid the devastation of the battlefield.

The Germans were in like case as far as their front
defences and the approaches thereto were concerned.   Their
regimental accounts contain ample testimony to the miseries
of life on the Somme at the end of 1916.   Farther to the
rear, however, lay no such devastated stretch of ground as
that across which they had been driven.   Although continuous bombardment had wrought much damage and
caused heavy loss, the villages still in enemy occupation
were not yet reduced to heaps of rubble, and wheeled
traffic could still negotiate the country roads.   So billets
could be found for the troops, and forward transit from
railhead was comparatively easy.   On the other hand, the
Germans in and behind the line were not so well fed or
equipped as their opponents ; they were exposed to a
greater volume of shell-fire, and were less frequently relieved.

As soon as the battle died down, work was begun upon
the permanent consolidation of the line to be held for the
winter by the Fourth and Fifth Armies.   In the forward
trenches the construction of dug-outs and shelters was
taken in hand ; farther in rear the German dug-outs and
the cellars in the captured villages were cleared of débris
and adapted for the accommodation of troops, signal
centres, and various headquarters.   The captured tunnels
and underground works on the slopes of Thiepval ridge and
around Beaumont Hamel proved a great acquisition, but
considerable engineer and pioneer effort had to be expended
in maintaining the Ancre crossings and in work on the river
banks.   Much was done to improve accommodation and
facilities at battery positions and wagon lines.

The progressive clearing of the battlefield was carried
out by burial parties [1] working under corps arrangements,

---

[1] Dumps of quicklime had to be provided, for hostile shelling frequently
uncovered the bodies of men and animals.

and by the divisions which undertook the salvage of arms, Nov. equipment, clothing and stores of almost every description, both British and German. One valuable item was signal cable, so often abandoned when badly damaged and replaced by a fresh line. There was no approved establishment for divisional salvage companies, but, following the example of the 3rd Division,[1] such were formed, suitable personnel being drawn from the units and increased or decreased as circumstances required. Transport was provided by the divisional trains, and the salvage, after being gathered into dumps, was mostly handed over to the Ordnance service. Some divisions, however, partially refitted themselves from the gleanings of the battle areas. Salvage work soon took on a competitive aspect; it was systematically continued until the end of the War and saved millions of pounds.

The arrangements for the supply of water during the Somme offensive—a corps responsibility in the forward areas—have been outlined in the preceding volume.[2] By the 1st July 1916 over 100 power pumps had been installed in the Fourth Army area, and nearly 120 miles of water-pipes had been laid. As fast as the progress of the Armies permitted, pipes laid down from the advanced pumping stations already established [3] were extended to forward water-points in the vicinities of Bernafay Wood, Fricourt, Contalmaison, Pozières cemetery, Mouquet Farm, and Thiepval crucifix. At Fricourt a water-point was opened within 12 hours of the capture of the village. The steady development of this system in the Fourth Army area eventually brought the pipes across the Bazentin ridge to seven water-points, with distributing branches, almost up to a line drawn from Saillisel to Le Sars. Progress was governed by the capacity of the pumping plants; the rate of supply of material; the amount of labour, skilled and unskilled, available; and the degree of enemy interference,

[1] The 4th Division had organized some salvage work during " Second Ypres " in May 1915. Major-General J. A. L. Haldane formed the salvage company of the 3rd Division a month later. The Q.M.G. enquired for particulars of his system in July 1915, and in February 1917 control was given to corps, each division in the corps to have one salvage section (18 other ranks of " Permanent Base " medical category). The total establishment of permanent salvage personnel in France was then fixed at 50 officers and 1,330 other ranks.

[2] " 1916 " Vol. I., pp. 275-6. For the technical study in detail, see " The Work of the R.E. in the European War 1914–19 : Water Supply— " France ".

[3] There were seven of these behind the front from Suzanne (on the Somme) to Thiepval Wood.

Nov. for pipe-lines were frequently damaged by hostile bombardment.

The boring plants with the Armies tapped fresh sources of supply and the wells in the captured villages were cleared and developed ; yet the water tank columns were fully employed up to the end of October.[1] At the height of the offensive water was provided for about 300,000 men and 150,000 animals ; at one time 1,250,000 gallons per day were supplied by pumping, whilst 100,000 gallons per day were being carried by road. Thus were met the needs of the baths and wash-houses established on the rearward fringe of the battle area, of the artillery and supply column horses and mules, which drank from troughs at a system of water-points farther forward, and of troops in support and reserve who drew from stand-pipes and tanks in their particular areas. Water reached the men in the line in two-gallon petrol tins carried up by hand.

Along the Somme and the Ancre all villages had been allotted between billeting areas, and the measures taken beforehand for the accommodation of the divisions in reserve were extended as the advance proceeded.[2] Provision was made in the Fourth Army for a general line of hutted camps from Bray to Albert, and construction started in September with the material available. The improvised bivouacs and camps for the reserves of divisions in the line gradually gave place to huts wherever the sites were secure from enemy ground observation. Six men could erect two Nissen huts [3] per day, but it was impossible to push on with the work quickly whilst those employed upon it had to be brought up daily from billets far in rear. Meanwhile, in the back areas of the corps much building was in progress : baths and wash-houses, establishments for drying and disinfecting clothing, canteens, and cinemas. All these contributed to restore the health and well-being of the troops when they came into reserve.

The eight groups, each of two casualty clearing stations, formed for the offensive [4] had been slightly augmented at

[1] In October the Fourth Army had 408 vehicles and the Fifth (Reserve) Army, 211, each with 80 additional regimental water-carts and one set of clarifying and de-poisoning plant (30 vehicles) attached.

[2] See " 1916 " Vol. I., p. 278.

[3] This portable semi-cylindrical hut, the type most generally used, had been designed in April 1916, with a view to the winter, by Captain (later Lieut.-Colonel) P. N. Nissen, a Canadian civil engineer serving with the R.E. It was 27′ × 15′, covered with corrugated iron sheets on bent wrought-iron angle frames, and housed 40 men. It could be carried on a lorry.

[4] See " 1916 " Vol. I., p. 281.

the end of the first week of July, and some were pushed Nov.
forward as the railways extended. By November the
Fourth Army had three groups at Grovetown (between
Maricourt and Dernancourt) ; three at Edgehill (north of
Dernancourt) ; two at Heilly ; one each at Albert, Corbie
and Allonville ; and a stationary hospital at Amiens. The
Fifth Army had three at Varennes ; two at Contay ; two
each at Puchevillers and Gézaincourt ; one at Recmenil
Farm ; and at Doullens two stationary hospitals, one of
which had been lent by the Third Army for the Ancre operations. There was no increase in the total hospital accommodation during 1916, heavy evacuations to England being
carried out whenever a large influx of wounded was expected.

The R.E. and pioneers of a division in the line not only
assisted the infantry to consolidate its battle positions and
constructed rear defences, but were responsible for all work
within their divisional area. The keeping of tracks and
tramways in repair, the maintenance of dumps of R.E.
stores, the building of huts, the construction of horse-
standings, were only some of their tasks, and demands for
assistance from "resting" infantry were heavy and
frequent. To corps areas the Armies allotted the R.E. and
labour units [1] at their disposal, a tunnelling company being
regarded as a "prize" by a corps Chief Engineer when the
making of deep dug-outs or similar work was on hand.
The cavalry supplied large working parties for burying
signal cable and water-pipes ; on the 17th November,
G.H.Q. ordered the Cavalry Corps to furnish by the 20th,
four pioneer battalions—each 850 to 870 strong—to the
Fourth Army and two to the Fifth Army.

The bad state of communications hampered every form
of activity. Strenuous efforts were made, by using any
débris available, to maintain the wagon tracks leading to
the field battery positions. Ammunition wagons and
limbers, forced to pick their way carefully or be hopelessly
bogged, had to come up by daylight, in spite of hostile
bombardment. So far as material and labour permitted,

---

[1] The following units were working in the two Army areas on the dates
specified :

| | Fourth Army | | Fifth Army | |
	12th Oct.	3rd Dec.	12th Oct.	3rd Dec.
Siege Coys., R.E. .	..	..	2	2
Army Troops Coys., R.E. .	15	17	8	9
Tunnelling Coys, R.E. . .	2	6	2	4
Labour bns., R.E. . .	2	3	1	2
Labour bns., infantry . .	6	6	2	2

Nov. light railways or " foreway " tramways, were constructed [1] in the battle areas for the carriage of ammunition, rations and stores, and the evacuation of the wounded. Usually the trucks were horse-drawn or pushed by hand, a slow process entailing many stoppages and considerable damage to the track.[2] The Fourth Army had only 20 mechanized tractors for its 60-cm. tramways in October 1916.

Farther in rear, motor and horse traffic on the roads was maintained under ever-increasing difficulties, with constant blocks, break-downs, and delays.[3] Previous to the opening of the offensive, the Engineer-in-Chief (Major-General S. R. Rice) and the Chief Engineer of the Fourth Army (Major-General R. U. H. Buckland) had both urged the vital importance of keeping the roads in repair ; at the outset, however, General Rawlinson had given ammunition the preference over road metal on the railways, for he " hoped to get forward on to good roads ". In any case, the capacity of the railways proved insufficient to deliver both ammunition and road metal in sufficient quantities, even if there had been no shortage of the latter. From an engineer's point of view, " the chief anxiety from the 1st " July onward was the deplorable state of the roads. . . . " It was a continual problem of getting stone up to a rail- " head at which it could be off-loaded without holding up " Q's work (food and ammunition), securing transport to " take it where it was badly wanted, and getting a working " party from a resting (and consequently tired) division to " lay it on a road congested with traffic ".[4]

Road metal was in urgent demand for the yards (" cours ") of new railway sidings and stations, and for the approaches to new camps and dumps which, in many cases, threatened to become isolated in a sea of mud. The supply of stone improved with the development of the quarries in the Calais-Boulogne area. By October these were providing nearly 2,400 tons per day, and sufficient timber was then available for the building of log, slab and plank roads.[5] Motor transport to carry the material

---

[1] See " 1916 " Vol. I., p. 275.

[2] In October the Fourth Army ordered that the personnel of the Heavy Artillery, most of whom had been in action since the opening of the offensive, were not to be used to push up ammunition.

[3] See " 1916 " Vol. I., pp. 276-8.

[4] Major-General R. U. H. Buckland in " The Royal Engineers Journal ", September 1917.

[5] See " 1916 " Vol. I., p. 277, f.ns. 1, 2. Towards the end of July a party of Canadian lumbermen, sent up specially, made a corduroy wagon-road through Mametz Wood.

forward from railhead had still to be borrowed from Nov. formations, so that delivery was irregular and unsatisfactory. As regards labour, the chief need was for officers and men with road-making experience.

In the course of the battle there had been some development of railway communications. To serve the right flank of the British front the Dernancourt—Loop metre-gauge line was extended from the Loop to Maricourt and Trônes Wood.[1] In the centre, a new line branching off from the Dernancourt—Loop line ran via Fricourt and Bazentin le Grand to Longueval. On the left, the Candas—Acheux line was extended to Aveluy on the main Albert—Arras line, and a further extension, running eastward from Aveluy, was under construction. Nevertheless, existing facilities, although supplemented by motor transport on the roads, were woefully inadequate : to cross the wastes of mud which led forward towards the front line only light railways were practicable. Events had made inoperative the original policy of the Q.M.G., which anticipated no such hiatus between the advanced railheads and the transport of the fighting troops.[2]

TRENCH WARFARE—JULY TO NOVEMBER 1916

Whilst the struggle on the Somme proceeded, the three July-Armies holding the front from Hébuterne to Boesinghe (3 Nov. miles north of Ypres) endured an ever-increasing strain.[3] Not only had they to feed the main battle by exchanging fresh for battle-weary divisions, and supplying commanders and staff officers, guns and ammunition, and material of all descriptions ; they were also called upon to wear down the enemy formations opposed to them, and, by initiating such demonstrations and minor enterprises as their means allowed, to prevent the free reinforcement of the Germans on the Somme. Every British division in France except two was used in turn for the main offensive, some several times. It followed that active trench-warfare on the " quiet " fronts was eventually conducted almost entirely by divisions from the Somme, whose depleted ranks had been only partially filled, and that with ill-trained drafts.

[1] See Sketch 17, " 1916 " Vol. I.
[2] See " 1916 " Vol. I., p. 275.
[3] Third Army (General Sir E. Allenby) : Hébuterne—Vimy Ridge.
First Army (General Sir C. Monro to 13th September ; then Lieut.-General Sir R. Haking to 30th September ; then General H. S. Horne) : Vimy Ridge—Laventie.
Second Army (General Sir H. Plumer) : Laventie—Boesinghe.

July-
Nov.

Ammunition supplies were strictly limited, but feints, wire-cutting, and special destructive bombardments were carried out systematically by the artillery, which also played its part in the frequent raids upon the German trenches. Apart from the general policy of harrying the enemy, identification of German units was of particular importance, and during the twenty weeks from the opening of the offensive on the 1st July until the middle of November the hostile trenches opposite the fronts of these three Armies were raided on no less than 310 occasions.[1] The troops employed varied from two platoons to two companies, often with parties of engineers attached for demolition work. Thus, although the only operation of greater importance was that of Fromelles on the 19th and 20th July,[2] life in the thinly held trench line was arduous and harassing. There was much work to do on the defences, and sometimes gas cylinders to be installed or removed, whilst the relief of a division was generally the prelude to a period of intensive training in preparation for its move to the Somme front.

In August, and again in September and October, G.H.Q. reminded Army commanders that there were ample supplies of gas available and urged its frequent use : there was no better means of causing casualties to the German potential reserves for the main battle. The Special Brigade R.E., under Colonel C. H. Foulkes, R.E., which often had to overcome the prejudices of local commanders before it could secure freedom of action, discharged cloud gas—sometimes combined with smoke—on 26 occasions during this period, mostly from points in the line which experience had shown to be most advantageous for gas operations. These localities were astride the Lys in front of Armentières and in the northern part of the Ypres salient (Second Army) ; the Loos salient (First Army) ; and around Arras (Third Army). In most cases the enemy sustained considerable

---

[1] Third Army : 40 raids (26 reported successful) ; First Army : 166 (102 reported successful) ; Second Army : 104 (76 reported successful). During the same period the Germans made 7 raids (5 successful) on the Third Army front ; 37 (10 successful) against the First Army ; and 21 (7 successful) against the Second Army.

[2] See Chapter V. It may here be mentioned that in the early morning of 30th June two battalions of the 39th Division had attempted to reduce the German salient south of Neuve Chapelle known as " The Boar's Head " : the trenches were taken, but had to be evacuated two hours later under concentrated artillery and machine-gun fire, losses amounting to 950. The operation " looked upon as a raid ", was considered by the corps commander to have been successful.

loss as was subsequently proved by German testimony.[1]
The only German gas attack worthy of note is that delivered
south of Ypres against the VIII. Corps on the night of the
8th/9th August. It was combined with a heavy bombardment and an infantry raid which failed, but the effects of
the gas were felt as far back as Poperinghe.

In spite of the increase in the number of tunnelling
companies,[2] there were not enough tunnellers, so that
officers and men had few chances of rest. They worked
subject to frequent interruptions by bombardment and gas
alarm, and their operations were also liable to be held up
while the infantry carried out a raid ; but sometimes mines
were blown in co-operation with infantry action. On the
Third Army front (Lieut.-Colonel F. G. Hyland, R.E.,
Controller of Mines) tunnelling under the German salient
at Gommecourt continued steadily, and there was much
mining activity south-east of Arras and at Vimy Ridge.
The First Army tunnellers, under Lieut.-Colonel G. C.
Williams, R.E., were engaged at the north end of Vimy
Ridge and also in the Loos salient and north of the La
Bassée canal, two localities where the workings were shallow
and mining operations had become an essential part of
trench warfare.[3] To mention one incident, at Hill 70, near
Loos, a gas-filled gallery was charged and tamped and, on
the 18th September, "blown" by the First Army Mine
Rescue School, just anticipating the German miners who
were ready to "blow" the British front line.

Preparations, under Lieut.-Colonel A. G. Stevenson,
R.E., for the deep-mining offensive of the Second Army
against the Messines—Wytschaete ridge had been in
progress since early in the year.[4] On the front from
Ploegsteert to Hill 60 six of the twenty mines had been
charged before the 1st July and ten more were ready by the
middle of November. Underground fighting was frequent,
for the Germans blew camouflets to destroy the British
galleries and, by the same means, the enemy defensive work

---

[1] See " Gas : The Story of the Special Brigade R.E." by Major-General
C. H. Foulkes. Chapter VIII. gives details of the big gas attacks at Monchy
(30th August) and Hulluch (5th October). In the Hulluch sector the *54th
Reserve Division*, which had only arrived from the Somme at the end of
September, was taken out of the line after 10 days, owing to gas casualties.

[2] See " 1916 " Vol. I., pp. 76-7.

[3] From 1st July to the middle of November 196 small mines and camouflets were blown on the fronts of the three Armies, the Germans exploding
151. By far the largest number of these were on the front of the First
Army.

[4] See " 1916 " Vol. I., pp. 31-2, 200, 265.

was kept in check by the British. Here, as elsewhere, the British tunneller proved himself vastly superior to his German opponent, both in enterprise and " footage ".

By the continual bombing of important points behind the German front, the Royal Flying Corps forced the enemy to divert part of his air strength from the Somme in order to protect his communications farther north. In addition to its reconnaissance and artillery work, the III. Brigade (Br.-General J. F. A. Higgins) [1] frequently attacked the stations, sidings and aerodromes of Douai and Valenciennes and also participated in the main battle. For instance, it bombed the billeting areas and railways around Bapaume, and in August by the same means attacked the German gun positions in the valleys running from Irles to Warlencourt and thence to Courcelette. Lille was an important objective of the I. and II. Brigades and the I. Brigade attacked, time after time, the railways running south-eastward to Cambrai behind the German battle front. In the air, as on the ground, the greatest pressure was brought to bear upon the enemy during September. Thereafter flying was restricted more and more by the bad weather.[2]

From the beginning of July to the middle of November the casualties reported by the Third Army averaged, in round figures, 400 per week ; [3] those by the First Army, nearly 1,000 ; and by the Second Army rather less than 2,000.

THE TRANSPORTATION PROBLEM [4]

Prior to the landing of the British Expeditionary Force in France in 1914, it was arranged that the French railways would meet all its requirements, and during the first two years of the War this plan had been followed, under ever-increasing difficulties. The Chemins de Fer du Nord Company had lost some of its personnel on mobilization, whilst a considerable amount of rolling-stock and many workshops had fallen into German hands in 1914. By the middle of 1916 two years' wastage had depleted the resources of the company to a very serious extent, but it

[1] Attached to the Third Army. The I. and II. Brigades (Br.-Generals D. Le G. Pitcher and T. I. Webb-Bowen) were with the First and Second Armies, respectively.
[2] See " The War in the Air " Vol. II., pp. 325-34.
[3] Exclusive of the losses sustained by the VII. Corps on 1st July ; see ".1916 " Vol. I., p. 474.
[4] Acknowledgements are due to the official " Transportation on the Western Front 1914–1918 ", compiled by Colonel A. M. Henniker, C.B.E., late R.E.

continued to operate a truncated system between points and over routes hastily adapted to meet the needs of the British Armies.

Traffic essential to the life of the country had also to be maintained with this inadequate lay-out, depleted personnel and deteriorating equipment, so that it is no matter for surprise that as time passed congestion and delay became more and more frequent, not only on the railways but at the base ports. The ever increasing quantities of munitions, stores and equipment shipped across the Channel and from other parts of the world to meet the essential needs of the Armies began to overwhelm the facilities for their reception. At the quayside there was insufficient labour to handle them and a lack of storage accommodation; on the railways there was a shortage of engines and rolling-stock, whilst the necessary duplication and extension of tracks could not be carried out for want of skilled operatives, and labour and material.

As early as June 1916 an enquiry was held by the Shipping Control Board into the detention of tonnage at the French ports, and the War Office expressed its grave concern at a situation which threatened to jeopardize the maintenance and supply of the British Armies in France. The matter engaged the earnest attention of Mr. Lloyd George, former Minister of Munitions, when he became Secretary of State for War in July, and in August he sent Sir Eric Geddes [1] to France to confer with the Commander-in-Chief.

Sir Douglas Haig received his visitor with great goodwill, being only too well aware that the transportation service in France was being starved of many essentials which the resources of the Empire could have, and should have, supplied. At this time the efficient maintenance and supply of the Fourth and Reserve Armies during their Somme offensive, as well as of the static portion of the British line, was the urgent need; beyond loomed the problem of providing such a railway system as would permit the rapid concentration of troops and artillery, ammunition, stores and supplies, in any locality selected for an offensive upon a grand scale. [2]

---

[1] Sir Eric Geddes had worked under Mr. Lloyd George in the Ministry of Munitions. A former manager of the North-Eastern Railway, he was a lieut.-colonel in the long-established Engineer & Railway Staff Corps, which consisted mainly of higher officials of the principal British railways, and distinguished civil engineers and contractors.

[2] " ' Dans le cas très improbable d'une guerre . . . les vrais généraux, " ' ce seraient les chefs de gare ? ' " Anatole France in " Le Lys Rouge ".

At the end of the month Sir Eric Geddes paid a more extended visit to the Western Front. In company with a staff of civilian and military experts he examined the problem thoroughly and advocated a reorganization which involved new railway construction on an extensive scale; his proposals for the control of transportation resembled in outline those made by Br.-General Sir Percy Girouard when sent by Lord Kitchener to report upon the problem nearly two years before. The new scheme contemplated arrangements at the ports and inland depôts for the reception of 250,000 tons per week ; and, in order to provide for delivery at the front, a service which would maintain the roads in a fit state for motor and horse transport and establish a network of light railways. Although their construction could not keep pace with a rapid advance or a war of movement, light railways were well adapted for the needs of trench-warfare and could be used to great advantage during such gradual progress as was being made in the summer of 1916. They became indispensable under the conditions of mud and rain which prevailed in the late autumn on the Somme.

On the 18th September the Army Council had approved of the appointment of Sir Eric Geddes as Director-General of Military Railways under the Q.M.G. at the War Office ; [1] and, on Sir Douglas Haig's suggestion, he was also appointed, on the 19th October, Director-General of Transportation in France with direct access to the Commander-in-Chief, such as the Chief of the General Staff, the Adjutant-General and the Quartermaster-General enjoyed. In France there were under him no less than five directorates : Ports ; Broad-Gauge Railways ; Narrow-Gauge Railways ; Inland Water Transport ; and Roads.[2] His deputy was Sir Philip Nash, formerly of the Great Northern and East Indian Railways, who eventually succeeded him for a time. All but one of his directorates were working before the 1st January 1917.

Mr. Lloyd George hoped that " Geddes would have a

[1] In January 1917 the Director of Movements was made responsible to the D.G.M.R., and the latter, ceasing to be a deputy of the Q.M.G., became a member of the Army Council. His status was then that of Inspector-General of Transportation for all theatres of war.

[2] At the beginning of December the Inspector-General of Communications (Major-General Sir F. T. Clayton) ceased to function, the control previously exercised by him over administrative services and departments being transferred to the Q.M.G. Command of personnel, etc., on the L. of C. was assigned to Lieut.-General J. J. Asser, appointed Commander Lines of Communication Areas.

" free hand on both sides of the Channel " ; but reorganization, really transfer and expansion, was, of necessity, gradual. That it was effected with so little friction was largely due to the personal interest and tactful attitude of the Commander-in-Chief. The first, and most important, effect of the new régime was that the requisite quantities of equipment and material, and also adequate numbers of operatives skilled in transportation work, previously refused by the War Committee and the Government Departments concerned, were now supplied without question. The excellent work, carried out with insufficient resources and personnel, and under ever-increasing difficulties, which had been performed up to this time by the Directors of Transport (Br.-General W. G. B. Boyce), of Railways (Br.-General J. H. Twiss), and of Works (Major-General A. M. Stuart), and their staffs, has been generally overlooked.

Sir Eric Geddes reviewed the railway situation at the Army Commanders' conference on the 18th November. He mentioned the shortage of steel, of which 500,000 tons were wanted and only 20,000 were immediately available without robbing some other service : he had already placed orders for steel sufficient for 1,000 miles of 60-cm. track, which should all be received by mid-summer 1917, and was making arrangements to get 600 miles of the 1,400 miles of broad-gauge track required by pulling up rails in England, Ireland and Canada, although these could not arrive before March or April : he considered that the serious shortage of broad-gauge wagons would best be met by producing wagons with wooden frames in England, and shipping them over in bulk for assembly in France : [1] it was difficult to see how the normal supply of rails and material could be appreciably increased before March.

The great shortage of labour at the ports and upon the lines of communication was eventually overcome in 1917 by the employment of prisoners of war and by the importation of Chinese.[2]

As early as February 1916 the French had asked for

---

[1] Actually, this type of wagon represented only about 5 per cent of the total number subsequently imported. See below for the demands of the French as regards rolling stock, etc.

[2] A West Indies labour contingent had been working in the Fourth Army area, within range of the German artillery, during the Somme offensive. Several battalions of the South African Native Labour Contingent had also arrived in 1916, and were employed, chiefly, at ammunition depôts. A newly-formed Directorate of Labour took over control, administration and allotment of all labour—except R.E. technical units—at the beginning of 1917.

2,500 railway wagons, and in May suggested that the British should provide the whole of the wagons required for British traffic in France and Belgium. In November General Joffre asked for locomotives and wagons, together with shops for their maintenance, also for assistance in carrying out railway construction work. Hitherto, the French had jealously retained the general responsibility for the railway service, as settled by the pre-War agreement, but their continued requests for assistance eventually amounted to the demand that the British should provide and do everything necessary for the working of their own traffic. Apart from this additional burden, which could only be assumed by degrees, the transportation services, incomplete in personnel and equipment, were confronted at the end of 1916 by an exceedingly difficult task in providing for current necessities and, at the same time, preparing for an offensive in the early spring.

In November the Shipping Control Board had informed the War Office that the shipping situation [1] made it imperative to reduce the tonnage required for oats and forage.[2] Since it was now impossible to reduce the forage ration, which had already been cut down, the War Office suggested to the Commander-in-Chief either that some portion of the cavalry should be sent home for the winter or that local purchase should be extended. Sir Douglas Haig, who refused to consider any further reduction in cavalry establishments—some small economies had previously been effected—was all against the first course. He insisted that the cavalry must be thoroughly trained as such throughout the winter, and this could be carried out better in France than in England; and he showed that the tonnage required for transporting the cavalry home and out again would offset that required for forage. By the 21st November he had arranged with the French to billet the cavalry for the winter in the Department of the Orne (north of Le Mans), where all forage could be bought locally.

[1] British tonnage sunk by German submarines amounted to 104,572 in September; 176,248 in October; 168,809 in November; and 182,292 in December.
[2] From 9th August 1914 to 10th November 1918 the dead-weight of oats and forage shipped to France exceeded that of ammunition.

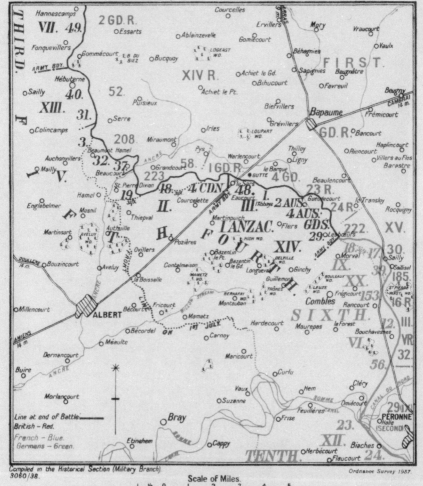

Sketch 49.

THE SOMME, 1916: The end of the Battle.

Line at end of Battle:
British – Red.
French – Blue.
Germans – Green.

Compiled in the Historical Section (Military Branch).
3060/38.

Ordnance Survey 1937.

Scale of Miles.
½ 0 1 2 3 4 5

CHAPTER XXI

Retrospect

(Sketch 49)

It has been urged insistently that in 1916 the chief military effort of Great Britain should have been made elsewhere than on the Western Front; that, once launched, the Somme offensive was conducted with little skill and no imagination; that it was persisted in too long; and that in the " battle of attrition " the British and French armies were worn down by losses far greater than those of the Germans with whom the advantage remained.

At the beginning of 1916 the German Army was still very strong: a formidable fighting machine which had never yet been taxed to the utmost. On the Eastern Front it had won great, if somewhat easy, successes, whilst repulsing all attempts to break its front in the West. Thus the German Supreme Command was in no mood to make peace: and no peace acceptable to the Entente could be assured whilst the enemy remained in possession of so large an area of France and Belgium. After some openly expressed doubts the French assumed without question that Britain's increasing military strength would be used to assist in the defeat of the invader on the Western Front, and the British Government was committed absolutely to this policy, which constituted the very basis of the Entente.

To penetrate the strongly fortified German lines stretching from Switzerland to the sea was, indeed, a tremendous task; yet there was no " way round ". The employment of the bulk of the British armies farther east, either on the Italian or the Balkan front, was a physical impossibility: railway facilities and shipping resources were inadequate for the transport and maintenance of such large numbers. The same reasons forbade an extensive development of the effort against Turkey. Moreover no quick decision was to be gained either among the Julian Alps or in the Trentino;

and certainly not in the difficult country of the Balkans where communications towards the Austrian frontier were bad and could only be improved to a very small extent.[1] Finally the Germans, having the advantage of interior lines and land communications, could always come to the support of their Allies more quickly than the Entente could concentrate to attack them ; [2] so that wherever else in Europe and its confines the Entente might choose to send their main forces, these would be confronted by the troops of the Central Powers, strongly entrenched and in equal if not superior numbers.

Thus the transference of the British main effort to Eastern Europe or beyond, even if it had been possible, could hardly have produced any better result than another deadlock under conditions still more favourable to the enemy.   Meanwhile the diminished forces of the Entente upon the Western Front would have been exposed to very grave risk.   Many German authorities, notably General von Gallwitz, have shown that the employment of British divisions elsewhere than in France was always welcomed by Germany.   Her leaders had no doubt as to which was the decisive theatre of war.[3]

The policy adopted at the Chantilly Conference in December 1915 [4] may therefore be regarded as sound strategy : namely to seek a decision by co-ordinated offensives with maximum forces, British and French, Russian, and Italian, in the three principal theatres of war where the enemy's main strength was assembled ; commitments in secondary theatres to be strictly limited.

The development of the Franco-British plans for the Somme offensive will presently be traced ; also, the conditions under which the British delivered battle in 1916, the difficulties of their task, and the tactical methods employed will be discussed in some detail.

With regard to Sir Douglas Haig's persistence in maintaining his offensive despite the autumn rain and mud, the narrative of operations has shown that the British Commander-in-Chief was acting in loyal acceptance of General Joffre's policy to harry the sorely battered enemy until offensive action should be no longer possible.   Even so,

---

[1] This point is emphasized in both the German and Austrian Official Accounts of the Balkan campaigns.

[2] See " 1916 " Vol. I., p. 7, for a comparison of the speed of railway and sea transport.

[3] See " 1918 " Vol. II., p. 468 ; also Ludendorff i., pp. 173-4, 255.

[4] See " 1916 " Vol. I., pp. 5-9.

French opinion blamed the British, as predominant partner in the struggle, for breaking off the battle too soon. Mortified, perhaps, at being denied another chance of encompassing the defeat of Germany, General Joffre has even stated that decisive victory could have been won if the British had persevered.[1]

In estimating the losses of the belligerents fresh data are available, for the published French and German official accounts now cover the whole period of the offensive. Careful calculation shows that the total German casualties on the Somme are in the region of 660,000, and may, perhaps, amount to as many as 680,000. On the other hand, the combined casualties of the British and French may fairly be reckoned at less than 630,000, so that it is clear that the Allies inflicted greater losses in killed, wounded, captured and missing than they received.[2] That the Germans engaged with the British suffered as much as, if not more than, those who confronted the French is shown by the table of losses by divisions published in the German official account, and confirmed by reference to the German regimental histories which make no secret of their sacrifices on the Somme.

When the Somme offensive was about to be launched the immediate necessity was to bring relief to the French at Verdun, and this was speedily accomplished. A strict limitation of German offensive action on the Meuse followed the opening of the preliminary bombardment on the Somme : Falkenhayn ordered the " strict defensive " at Verdun ten days after the Franco-British assault was launched. So hard-pressed were the Germans on the Somme that the initiative eventually passed to the French at Verdun where, on the 24th October and again on the 15th December, they won considerable victories.[3]

But the French and British Armies on the Somme were expected to make an important contribution to the common effort of the Allied Powers in 1916. By the 1st July large

---

[1] " Il n'était pas en mon pouvoir de contraindre nos alliés à marcher " malgré eux. . . . Force m'était donc de m'incliner devant une nécessité " qui sauvait — pour un temps — nos ennemis d'une complète défaite." Joffre ii., pp. 263-4.

[2] For details see the Preface to this volume.

[3] See page 468, f.n. 3. On 15th December the French, under General Mangin, attacked again at Verdun with four divisions and four in second line. After four days' fighting, in very bad weather, their line was advanced to Bezonvaux—Côte du Poivre (see " 1916 " Vol. I., Sketch 3), the Germans sustaining very heavy loss including more than 11,000 prisoners and 115 guns captured or destroyed.

forces of Russians and Italians were already engaged, and an Allied offensive in the West was due, if not overdue, in order to exert such pressure upon the Germans as to prevent them from despatching important reinforcements to the other principal theatres of war. As the Russian effort declined, that of the Italians grew ; and, with the entry of Rumania into the War at the end of August, there was more need than ever to persist in the battle on the Western Front. The Allied purpose seems to have been accomplished to a very considerable degree ; one French authority has no doubt whatever that the British and French played their parts to the full.[1]

Actually, in addition to a certain amount of heavy artillery, some technical troops, cavalry, and unbrigaded formations such as *Landsturm* battalions, twenty complete divisions were despatched from Germany or France to other theatres whilst the Battles of the Somme were in progress, and six were sent from Russia to the Western Front.[2] Of those divisions sent from West to East nine had sustained heavy losses on the Somme or at Verdun, and nine were new formations constituted by " milking " regiments from existing divisions, incorporating *Jäger* battalions, forming new regiments of recruits of the 1917 and 1918 classes, and drawing upon returned sick and wounded. Other such divisions were constituted in Russia, or formed for service

---

[1] " On peut dire, en définitive, que les armées franco-britanniques, " immobilisant devant elles plus des deux meilleurs tiers des forces alle- " mandes et leur infligeant une usure matérielle et morale sans précédent, " ont tenu au delà des engagements qu'elles avaient souscrits et bien " mérité de la Coalition ". Oemichen, pp. 29-30.

[2] The German official record of train movements gives the following particulars :

Month	Divisions	Direction
July 1916	*121st, †1st, *123rd, ‡195th, ‡197th	Western Front to Russia
August 1916	‡199th, *10th Bavarian, *117th, *3rd Guard	Western Front to Russia
	187th	Western Front to Rumania
September 1916	‡208th, ‡Alpine Corps	Western Front to Rumania
October 1916	‡12th Bavarian, *8th Bavarian Reserve	Western Front to Rumania
	‡202nd, ‡203rd	Germany to Russia
	208th, 199th	Russia to Western Front
November 1916	‡215th, *15th, *53rd Reserve, 16th	Western Front to Russia
	43rd Reserve, 19th, 20th, 3rd Guard	Russia to Western Front

* Previously engaged on Somme.
† Previously engaged at Verdun.
‡ Newly formed division.

on the Western Front, where there were actually more German divisions in November 1916 than there had been in July.[1] The Somme had used up the strength of $95\frac{1}{2}$ divisions, $43\frac{1}{2}$ being employed twice and four, three times.[2] Germany was, indeed, hard put to it to find the forces necessary to sustain the struggle upon all fronts, and only just managed to do so. On the 21st August, before Rumania entered the War, Falkenhayn wrote to the Chancellor : " Beneath the enormous pressure which now " rests on us we have no superfluity of strength. Every " removal in one direction leads eventually to dangerous " weakness in another place which may lead to our " destruction if even the least adjustment in the enemy's " dispositions is made ".[3] Ludendorff states that when the 1916 fighting concluded " the German Army had been fought " to a standstill and was utterly worn out ".[4] On the 9th January 1917 at the conference which decided upon unrestricted U-boat warfare Hindenburg said, " We must " save the men from a second Somme battle."[5]

The rapid expansion forced upon the German Army reduced considerably the average fighting power of its divisions, the more so that many of the best of the surviving officers were required for new staffs and formations.[6] The losses suffered were irreplaceable. In the preceding volume [7] will be found ample and indisputable testimony that the old, highly-trained body of the German Army—officers, non-commissioned officers and men—largely disappeared in the carnage of the Somme. A German writer who fought on the Somme admits that " in its results the first " material-battle of the World War turned to the disadvan- " tage of the victorious (*sic*) Germans, for no art of the " commander could give them back the trained soldiery " which had been destroyed ".[8]

The Somme offensive produced another result of deep significance. If at the beginning of 1916 Falkenhayn had

[1] Gehre gives the following figures :

    1st July : Western Front,   112 ⎫ 164
             Eastern Front,   52 ⎭
    15th Nov. : Western Front,   121 ⎫ 197
              Russia and Rumania, 76 ⎭

[2] G.O.A. xi., pp. 103-4.
[3] G.O.A. x., pp. 675-6.
[4] Ludendorff i., p. 304.
[5] G.O.A. xi., p. 470.
[6] G.O.A. xi., p. 188.
[7] " 1916 " Vol. I., pp. 494-5.
[8] " Somme " by Hans Henning Freiherr Grote, p. 163.

doubts of the eventual victory of the Central Powers, his subordinate commanders and the regimental officers and men were still convinced of the power and invincibility of the German Army. The struggle on the Somme shattered that illusion. Some German writers have since used the phrase " die Material-Schlacht " in disparagement of the tactics employed by the British ; in 1916 it bore a very bitter meaning to the German soldier. " The immense " material superiority of the enemy did not fail to have its " psychological effect on the German combatants ".[1]

So went the old confidence in German might. Falkenhayn was superseded after the first two months of the Somme, and on the 17th September, in the midst of the Battle of Flers—Courcelette, two " Group " (corps) commanders, Marschall and Kirchbach, were replaced. Such changes on the German side only followed upon marked failure.[2] Of less importance was the extent of the ground yielded, although it must be remembered that the retreat of the Germans early in 1917, a direct result of the losses they had sustained on the Somme, had great influence upon the future course of events.[3] The triumph of the Entente could only be assured by the disintegration in defeat of the German Army, and this was not to be accomplished until two more years had passed and many mistakes had been committed and many a set-back suffered ; but in Picardy during the summer and autumn of 1916 the foundations of the final victory were laid.

Sketch 49.

It is said that in striving to co-ordinate the efforts of the Allied Powers—a harassing task for one who, having no supreme authority, was obliged to depend upon his prestige and powers of diplomacy—General Joffre originally contemplated a break-through (" rupture ") upon both the Russian and Western Fronts : he was convinced that this could be done if each offensive were sufficiently powerful and sustained.[4] As regards the Western Front, he dis-

---

[1] Colonel Hierl. See " 1916 " Vol. I., p. 495.

[2] For instance, Moltke, C.G.S., after the Marne 1914 when the chance of speedy victory had disappeared. At Verdun in December 1916, following the French success, the commanders of the *Fifth Army* (Lochow), *VII. Reserve Corps* (Zwehl) and *39th Bavarian Reserve Division* were removed, whilst court-martial proceedings were taken against other leaders. See G.O.A. xi., pp. 72, 165.

[3] See " 1916 " Vol. I., p. xi.

[4] F.O.A. iv. (i.), p. 6. This, however, is at variance with the French President's view when, in December 1915, he credited Joffre with simply having in mind a war of attrition to be carried out chiefly by England,

closed to Sir Douglas Haig at the end of 1915 a plan for a
Franco-British offensive between Lassigny and Arras as
part of a general scheme which included the preparation of
attacks from various parts of the French front. He also
desired the relief by the British of the French Tenth Army,
which held the line from Ransart to Lens between the
British Third and First Armies.

In January 1916, however, General Joffre strongly urged
that the British should make preliminary attacks upon a
large scale north of the Somme during April and May in
order to wear down the Germans by engaging their reserves.
This was beyond the capacity of the British if they were
to play their part in the main operation, but the French
Tenth Army was relieved in March. Meanwhile, on the 14th
February, at a conference between the two Commanders-in-
Chief it had been agreed that the British should deliver a
preliminary attack in the La Bassée—Ypres area a week or
two before the combined offensive which would be launched
about the 1st July.[1]

The French, advancing with their left astride the Somme,
were to reduce the German salient between the Somme and
the Oise, whilst the British attacked between Maricourt
and Gommecourt or Monchy au Bois, the total frontage
extending over seventy kilometres or nearly forty-four
miles.[2] No strategic aim appears to have been mentioned.
A frontage which included the point of junction of French
and British was the obvious one to choose if the Allies were
to attack in close co-operation. In this region, however,
the enemy's lines were exceedingly strong, for he had been
able to work upon them, with little interference, during the
greater part of two years ; and the defence possessed many
natural advantages. One French writer observes that it
was " un terrain tourmenté, d'accès difficile ", whereas the
open ground of the Santerre plateau, in the French zone
south of the Somme, was favourable for offensive operations.[3] Moreover, only a very substantial success—the

---

Russia and Italy. M. Poincaré believed that the French commanders, not
excepting Foch, had lost faith in an offensive. See " 1916 " Vol. I., p. 33,
f.n. p. 34, and p. 44.

[1] All idea of preliminary attacks was abandoned as a result of the
German offensive which was launched at Verdun on 21st February. The
development of the Allied plans for the Somme offensive is described
in detail in " 1916 " Vol. I., pp. 25-51.

[2] F.O.A. iv. (i.), p. 62.

[3] " La Bataille de la Somme en 1916 " by General G. Girard, pp. 32,
41, 42.

rapid exploitation of a break-through on a wide front—
could threaten the German communications. Mezières lies
nearly ninety miles east of Roye. Yet, in spite of these
disadvantages, General Joffre decided that the British
ought to attack in the Somme area " because, as a whole, it
" is more advantageous than the others, for the reason that
" it is the nearest to the sectors of attack of the Armies of
" the North."[1]

Even after the Germans had seized the initiative by
opening their attack at Verdun on the 21st February,
General Joffre assumed that the French would play the
decisive rôle, for he aimed at using the utmost economy of
means in the defence of the fortress in order to be as strong
as possible for the Somme. In his letter addressed to Sir
Douglas Haig on the 27th March, Lassigny—Hébuterne
was defined as the front of attack, the British portion
Maricourt—Hébuterne, being about half the extent of the
French, Lassigny—Maricourt. Success was to be exploited
" in an easterly direction ". No change in intention is to
be observed in his letter of the 14th April, when he named
the French objective as the Ham—Péronne—Bapaume
road, in order to " threaten the German communications ",
and assigned to the British the task of covering the French
during the passage of the Somme, by attacking from the
front previously selected.

As the defence of Verdun continued to absorb more and
more men, guns and ammunition, it became inevitable that
the British should play the leading part in the offensive
which must have, as its primary purpose, the relief of the
French from German pressure on the Meuse. General
Joffre then began to anticipate a more protracted struggle.[2]
At the conference held at the end of May, a fortnight after
the Austrian offensive in the Trentino was launched, he said
that if the Franco-British effort did not obtain a decision,
a long battle of attrition must be undertaken by all the
Allies until the enemy was weakened beyond recovery.[3]
It was at this stage that General Joffre mentioned the
possibility of a fresh German attack, perhaps in Champagne,

---

[1] F.O.A. iv. (i.), p. 55, quoting from a G.Q.G. Note dated 18th December
1915. At the same time, General Joffre attempted to obtain " the sub-
" ordination of the British Command in France to the French Command ",
an idea his own Government declined to entertain. F.O.A. iv. (i.), p. 67.
[2] " . . . la réduction importante de l'effort de l'armée française semble
" écarter une décision rapide sur la Somme ". F.O.A. iv. (ii.), p. 183.
[3] " Joffre et la Guerre d'Usure 1915–16 " by General M. Daille, pp.
390-1.

which might result in the British having to undertake the offensive alone, assisted by such " material " as the French could spare.

In writing to Sir Douglas Haig on the 6th June, two days after the Russians had struck, the French Commander-in-Chief, with more confidence, defined the object of the Somme offensive as the defeat (" mise hors de cause ") of the German forces on the Western Front, or at least of an important part of them. The rôle of the French was now reduced to covering the British right by an attack astride the Somme [1]—there was no longer any question of capturing the Roye salient—and, in the same letter, General Joffre said that it did not seem possible, at this stage, to settle the way in which success should be exploited after the three German defensive positions had been carried. He emphasized that the offensive must be of a " caractère de " continuité et de durée prolongée ".[2]

In loyal co-operation, Sir Douglas Haig had subordinated his own wishes to those of the French, in so far as his responsibility as Commander-in-Chief of the British Armies permitted. The choice of the Somme region for the offensive was not his : he would have preferred to attack in the La Bassée—Ypres area, where success offered important strategic advantages. He submitted to the inconvenience of sharing the Maricourt salient, north of the Somme, with a French corps ; [3] he deferred to French wishes as regards the date of the offensive, although he would have liked six more weeks for preparation, and even as regards the hour for launching the first assault ; and he agreed to a prolonged preliminary bombardment when he would have preferred a short, sharp one. In addition, he maintained very active trench-warfare on his front during the first six months of the year [4] and relieved, at considerable inconvenience, the French Tenth Army. It must be remembered that during this period, with many new formations and batteries arriving in France, he had to press on with the work of organizing and training the British Armies

----

[1] The French frontage of attack was to extend from the Amiens—St. Quentin road to Maricourt, divided into two by the marshes of the Somme between Frise and Curlu. This frontage was about half that of the British, Maricourt—Hébuterne.

[2] On 21st June G.Q.G. forwarded to Sir Douglas Haig a somewhat academic " Instruction " which defined the object of the offensive as " to " place a mass of manœuvre on the junction of the enemy's lines of com-" munication marked by Cambrai—Le Cateau—Maubeuge, etc."

[3] See " 1916 " Vol. I., p. 264.

[4] See " 1916 " Vol. I.

in readiness for the great effort presently to be required of them. One of the penalties of Great Britain's novitiate as a military Power on the Continental model was that her policy was subordinated to that of the French ; as a result, her growing Armies on the Western Front were always liable to be called upon to do more—either by taking over more of the front or by launching an offensive—than their state of readiness seemed to justify.

In formulating his own plans for the Somme—he had alternatives in mind, notably the Messines—Wytschaete attack, for which preparations were in hand—the British Commander-in-Chief aimed from the outset at a definite " break-through " as a preliminary to rolling up the enemy front northwards, not to a vague exploitation eastward. When he attacked on the 1st July he hoped for rapid progress, but calculated that it might take a week, or even more, for the Fourth Army to penetrate the three German positions and establish a defensive flank from Ginchy to Bapaume ; then the northward movement from Bapaume —Miraumont to roll up the German line, and, in conjunction with an attack eastward by the Third Army, to clear the enemy from the Arras—Bapaume—Serre region, was to follow after the shortest possible interval.[1]

It would have been in accordance with the tactical principles of " siege-warfare in the field " if Sir Douglas Haig had stopped his attacks after the limited success of the 1st July and proceeded to try elsewhere. Unfortunately such a course was not possible. The French were relying upon the close co-operation of the British on the Somme, where all available British resources were concentrated ; and in any case lateral communications behind the line did not permit of the transfer, within a reasonable time, of a great mass of artillery and its ammunition to another part of the front.[2] So, despite the disappointing results of the opening day of the battle, the British continued their slow and costly advance throughout July and August ; but the same end was always kept in view by the Commander-in-Chief. As we know, at the beginning of August he regarded himself as in the middle of a " wearing out " battle which would

[1] See " 1916 " Vol. I., pp. 308-9.
[2] Ludendorff in 1918, after full preparation, required a minimum of 14 days to move his " battering train " elsewhere for a subsidiary attack, and a month for a major offensive. The locations and the opening dates of his offensives in 1918 were as follows : Picardy, 21st March ; Lys, 9th April ; Chemin des Dames, 27th May ; Matz, 9th June ; Marne, 15th July.

probably reach its crisis in the last half of September ; and the Battle of Flers—Courcelette, which began on the 15th of that month, was planned with much the same objectives as those originally named.

In war the issue between two antagonists who are more or less evenly matched must ultimately be decided by battle ; but sound strategy may often limit—it can hardly abolish altogether—the necessity of " wearing down " an opponent by sheer hard fighting. It could not do this in 1916 on the Western Front where a continuous front, making manœuvre impossible, stretched from neutral Switzerland to the sea, and the character and temper of the German resistance made inevitable a " battle of attrition ". How long such a struggle would have to be maintained could hardly be gauged before the first onset. General Joffre cherished some hopes that it would end in the decisive defeat of the enemy before the end of the year, whilst Sir Douglas Haig aimed at a definite tactical success of considerable proportions. This optimism, manifested in different ways, of the two Commanders-in-Chief was not shared by many of their subordinate commanders : it arose partly from an under-estimation of a brave and tenacious enemy, and partly from an inadequate conception of the conditions under which the offensive battle would have to be waged.

German official opinion is that Falkenhayn, also, underrated his opponents and had no proper appreciation of his difficulties when making his plans for 1916.[1]

General Joffre's conception of the offensive battle was based upon the experience gained by the French during the autumn of 1915 in Artois and Champagne.[2] The German method of attack at Verdun tended to confirm the soundness of his theory, which was followed, in principle, by the British.

A broad front of attack was considered essential in order to minimize the effect of enemy action from the flanks and prevent the defensive concentration of fire and reserves : a succession of heavy blows must be delivered at the shortest possible intervals, so that the enemy would have little or no respite : at each stage the objective must be limited to the depth—estimated at from $1\frac{1}{4}$ to $2\frac{1}{2}$ miles—which could

[1] G.O.A. x., pp. 664, 666.
[2] See F.O.A. iv. (i.), pp. 43-52, and iv. (ii.), pp. 220-1 ; also General Foch's " La Bataille Offensive ", 20th April 1916, F.O.A. iv. (ii.), Annexe 2.

be bombarded effectively by the heavy artillery. In this methodical fashion a way was to be battered through the enemy's defensive positions, including such new lines as he might contrive to construct during the offensive.

The value of surprise was not ignored. As the elaborate preparations for such an offensive could hardly escape notice, similar preparations were to be made on other parts of the front : thus the enemy would be kept under constant threat of attack in several localities, and thereby induced to retain the greatest possible force in the West, whilst the Allies would be able to take the initiative at any time at one or more of a number of points, with good hopes of effecting a tactical surprise. To carry out such a policy on an extensive scale required a preponderance of strength greater than the Allies possessed in 1916, even if the Germans had not seized the initiative by attacking at Verdun ; but the activities of the British Third, First and Second Armies during the preparations for the Somme offensive certainly left Falkenhayn and Crown Prince Rupprecht in doubt as to where the main blow would fall.[1]

Co-operation between British and French was as satisfactory as could be expected. Occasional misunderstandings or clashes of opinion there were bound to be, considering the differences in temperament and in military usage ; but when necessary, by personal contact, the two Commanders-in-Chief smoothed away dissension and reached agreement. Sir Douglas Haig's loyal adherence to the main purpose of the offensive did not prevent him from preserving his tactical freedom of action if the French plans were not prejudiced thereby.

The actual frontage of attack upon the 1st July was about half that originally suggested by the French Commander-in-Chief, and, as the principal rôle was that of the British, it largely depended upon Sir Douglas Haig as to whether this frontage could be preserved as the operations proceeded. When the initial failure of his centre and left caused him to concentrate upon his right—he had not the resources for a renewal of the assault along the whole line as General Joffre desired—the French Commander-in-Chief sought to maintain his own principle by developing the French action south of the Somme.· Then the success of the British attack at dawn on the 14th July encouraged the renewed effort of the French on their left, north of the river.

[1] See Note: " German Intelligence as Regards the Somme Offensive ", " 1916 " Vol. I., p. 316.

General Joffre's anxiety, in August, to anticipate Rumania's entry into the War by another attack upon the grand scale is as easy to understand as is Sir Douglas Haig's reluctance to co-operate before he felt ready to do so without prejudice to his chances of success. It was none the less unfortunate that when the British assault was delivered on the 15th September the French, who had launched their attack upon the 3rd and renewed it upon the 12th, should not have been in a state to provide substantial support.

The intermediate attacks upon narrow fronts, to which General Joffre objected so strongly throughout, were the natural corollaries of the partial successes so often won. After each main attack there usually remained in enemy possession one or more localities which had to be carried in order to secure a favourable line from which to start the next big phase of the offensive ; and the French local commanders were as ready as their British confrères to engage in these minor struggles for the purpose of obtaining a good " base de départ ". Such operations, it must be admitted, were often hastily conceived, and as often failed ; if ill-prepared they were costly in men and munitions and consumed more time than they were designed to save.

As regards delivering a number of heavy blows in quick succession, the weather itself prevented such a procedure. Destructive bombardments had to wait on many occasions for a clear day when accurate air and ground observation of fire was possible ; mud often hampered the deployment of heavy artillery in forward positions when a fresh phase of the offensive was due to begin. A new problem arose when the Germans were forced to rely upon a defensive conducted by snipers and machine gunners ensconced in shell-holes : whilst seeking to crush all such opposition in the forward zone—an almost impossible task—the bombardment was apt to lack the prescribed depth.[1]

It was upon their heavy artillery that the French, in the main, relied. " L'artillerie dévaste, l'infanterie submerge ", an absolute reversal of their tactics of August 1914, when all was staked upon the élan of the infantry. The destruction of the enemy's defences was to be accomplished, not

[1] See F.O.A. iv. (ii.), pp. 273, 287, for comment upon the comparative failure of the French VII. and XX. Corps on 30th July. General Daille, in " Joffre et la Guerre d'Usure ", p. 399, states that, on one occasion, General Fayolle saw with satisfaction that the Germans were digging a new trench line. He said to General Foch : " At least we shall know " where they are, and shall be able to regulate our fire accordingly ".

by a general bombardment—fire on " zones " was always to be avoided if possible—but by concentrating on machine-gun emplacements, observation posts, redoubts, places of assembly, headquarters, and other points of tactical importance.[1] Due provision having been made for counter-battery work which went on unceasingly throughout the offensive, for harassing fire, and for the engagement of special long-range targets, the extent of front to be attacked depended upon the amount of heavy artillery—the 155-mm. " court ", equivalent to the British 6-inch howitzer, was the unit—available for the destructive bombardment.[2] Possessing less heavy artillery, the British did not use the number of 6-inch howitzers available as a yard-stick to determine their frontage of attack.[3] General destructive bombardments of the German trench lines were combined with concentrations of fire upon such tactical points as had been located ; but the policy of relying " à fond " upon the effect of heavy artillery was not pursued after the results of the 1st July.[4] So the British commanders came to expect more of the infantry than did the French.[5] French doctrine considered it wrong to call upon the infantry to take a position " at all costs " ; such an order was by no means unknown in the British Armies.

In order to obtain the full effect of their destructive bombardment the French set great value upon good day-light observation during the concluding stage, so their infantry seldom attacked at dawn.[6] On the other hand, the British, even before their experience of the 1st July when they conformed to the wishes of the French,[7] appreciated the

[1] On 11th July, in a " Note " to his corps commanders, General Fayolle complained that the fire of the artillery had become " as bad as possible ". Owing to lack of proper observation, it was falling anywhere but on the proper targets. He said that it was better not to fire at all than to waste valuable ammunition in giving the infantry a false impression of security. F.O.A. iv. (i.), Annexe 2255.

[2] On 1st July the French had one heavy gun or howitzer to about every 21 yards of front, whilst the British, on their main front of attack from Maricourt to opposite Serre, averaged one to every 50 yards.

[3] Nearly three months before the offensive was launched Sir Douglas Haig was told by his Artillery Adviser that he was " stretching " his artillery too much, but the warning had no effect. See " 1916 " Vol. I., pp. 251-2.

[4] Previously it had been assumed that " the infantry would only have " to walk over and take possession ". " 1916 " Vol. I., p. 288.

[5] When, however, Fayolle's VII. Corps failed in its attack between Maurepas and the Somme on 24th August, he was disposed to blame, as he had done before, the subordination of manœuvre to artillery action. F.O.A. iv. (ii.), p. 296.

[6] See " 1916 " Vol. I., p. 251, f.n.

[7] Idem, p. 484.

advantage of moving to the assault before daylight could reveal the intention to the enemy. Subsequently, the dawn attack of the Fourth Army on the 14th July, following a night advance, effected a tactical surprise and was a revelation to the French, whose disbelief in its success was partly founded upon the arrangements for artillery support which, according to their standards, were insufficient. Later the British came to recognize the value, as a variation of method, of devoting the morning hours to observation of the bombardment, and attacking in the afternoon. This was done at the Battle of Morval when the assembled British divisions waited for many hours in full daylight without attracting heavy fire; and after the objective had been won consolidation was favoured by the gathering dusk.

Between the 1st January and the 3rd July the British Armies were reinforced by 17 divisions from England and Egypt, whilst at the beginning of the year two Territorial divisions had been reassembled in France where their battalions, attached to Regular brigades, were already serving.[1] In January the heavy artillery at the Commander-in-Chief's disposal comprised 324 guns and howitzers, by the 1st July the number had increased to 714, and 1,127 were available when the offensive was drawing to its close.[2] Technical units—corps, Army and lines of communication troops—also showed a great increase.

This expansion of the forces under Sir Douglas Haig's command involved a drastic re-organization which had to proceed concurrently with the training of all arms and the general preparations for an offensive upon an unprecedented scale; also with the taking over of 22 miles of front from the French. Commanders and staffs for the many new heavy artillery groups had to be found; new corps headquarters were needed; and one new Army, the Fourth, was formed. When, at the beginning of the sixth week of the Somme, Britain entered upon the third year of the War she was still paying the price of her unpreparedness for war on such a scale.

---

[1] See " 1916 " Vol. I., p. 24.

[2] Appendix 30 shows the distribution of artillery with the British Armies in France at various dates from July to November 1916. Early in 1916 Sir Douglas Haig had submitted to the War Office his programme of the additional artillery required. This was based upon what was known of German establishments, and aimed at securing a permanent superiority over the enemy. His requirements were only partly met in 1916, and never completely fulfilled.

The Somme was an artillery battle, but British artillery tactics underwent no important development during its course. Counter-battery work,[1] the systematic bombardment of the hostile defences, harassing fire upon communications and approaches, and wire-cutting were all standing tasks. An artillery commander who was both gunner and tactician could sometimes cause considerable loss and embarrassment to the enemy by a surprise concentration of fire ; but it was necessary to be prepared for and to seek such opportunities, which were not often found although the general collection and distribution of artillery Intelligence became more systematic as the offensive continued. To cut wire effectively was never easy. It was a task for the field artillery since the explosion of heavy shell among the entanglements formed craters which constituted a fresh obstacle. Good ground observation was essential, and often required the assistance of infantry patrols, whilst an instantaneous fuze was lacking.[2] When, as the advance progressed, batteries were hurried forward and had to complete their task in a limited time whatever the weather conditions, the difficulties were greater still.

Although the Field Survey battalions R.E., in addition to their "flash-spotting" groups and sound-ranging sections, began to lend valuable aid, registration by fire and observation was meticulously carried out by all batteries before each attack was launched, little reliance being placed upon what is now called "predicted fire".[3] Some artillery officers considered that registration was over-done and that the sudden opening of fire "by the map" at the beginning of an attack would sometimes have lost little in accuracy and brought better results. In any case, the importance attached in 1916 to the preliminary destructive bombard-

---

[1] The standard had steadily improved since the autumn of 1915 and during the Battles of the Somme special counter-battery staffs were formed. Although the destruction of the enemy's guns was sought they could be "neutralized" or silenced by inflicting casualties upon their personnel, by forcing detachments to keep under cover away from the guns, or by obstructing the ammunition supply. Only by continuous action, with air observation and strict control of fire, could good results be obtained. To destroy one well-protected gun-pit it was estimated that at least 100 rounds of 6″ howitzer ammunition were required ; alternatively, 80 rounds of 8″, or 60 rounds of 9.2″. Less might be needed if a battery position, with pits not far apart, could be taken in enfilade.

[2] See also "1916" Vol. I., pp. 294-7.

[3] That is, fire without previous registration. The relative positions of guns and targets can now be fixed with great accuracy by survey methods, which were in their infancy in 1916. These methods were first used for a big attack in November 1917 at Cambrai.

ment always precluded the possibility of a major surprise, but the enemy could sometimes be kept in suspense as to the hour, if not the day, of a fresh infantry assault. Intensification of fire as a signal for the infantry to advance gave warning of the intention, and the practice was abandoned.

The artillery fire plan for each major attack followed conventional and rigid lines, being based upon an estimate of the destructive and protective power of the guns and the offensive capacity of the infantry. Subordinate artillery commanders were allowed little initiative ; some, who were eager to adapt their training to every necessity of modern battle and to extend, if possible, the field of artillery achievement, grew to regard their brigades as " mere barrage " machines ". The length of time for which the heavy and field artillery barrages were to be kept on each objective in succession was fixed to the minute, as was the progress of the infantry assault. When there were checks and the advance fell behind the time-table, as only too frequently occurred, the necessary alteration in the times of the barrage lifts or the bringing back of a barrage after range had been increased, had to be effected with the least possible delay. Everything then depended upon good observation from ground and air, and the prompt receipt of accurate reports from the front.

There was little fault to be found with the British system of artillery command and few changes proved to be necessary : before the end of the offensive the artillery advisers with corps headquarters became commanders in practice as well as in name, each corps with a heavy artillery commander under its G.O.C. Royal Artillery.[1] The organization of the heavy artillery into mixed " groups ", each of four or five batteries, worked well. Four, or at most five, groups were allotted to each corps, whose artillery commander could interchange batteries between groups as the nature of the artillery tasks required.

The permanent allotment of all field artillery to divisions proved most unsatisfactory. For one thing, the infantry of a division engaged in battle required to be relieved much sooner than its batteries ; for another, to reinforce the field artillery on any portion of the battlefront meant dislocating a division elsewhere. Besides the administrative difficulties which ensued, the time spent by artillery on the march to or from its own division represented a distinct loss of gun-

[1] See " 1916 " Vol. I., p. 60.

power. After the Somme battles one field artillery brigade was taken from each division to become an " Army " brigade, thus providing a " fluid " reinforcement for field artillery in action.[1] In November G.H.Q. asked the War Office to provide 34 additional batteries to form into Army brigades.[2]

Although many batteries of both field and heavy artillery were new units and had never been in action before, the standard of gunnery was better than might have been expected, and improved as the battle went on. It became increasingly difficult, however, to find sufficient battery commanders for the R.F.A., which sustained the heavier losses, and it was sought to solve the problem by converting the four-gun 18-pdr. batteries of the New Army and Territorial divisions into six-gun batteries.[3] This expedient was not altogether a success, for the command of the larger battery required a considerably higher standard of knowledge and experience.

The hurried expansion of the munitions industry involved considerable sacrifice of quality to quantity. Even so, at various times during the offensive the reserves of guns and howitzers of nearly all calibres were not sufficient to replace casualties without some delay ; and lack of spare parts prevented the Armies from keeping all units up to strength. Only by the constant husbanding of ammunition could the operations be kept going, and on the 31st October the War Office was asked to double the estimate of requirements previously made.[4] There were many defects both in guns and ammunition.[5] Early in the operations the 4.5-inch howitzers had frequent prematures, and when, in September, this trouble seemed over it recurred with the 18-pdrs. It is not surprising that in the later stages of the offensive, the cause was sometimes traced to dirty ammunition.

Apart from faults, such as the poor quality of the firing

---

[1] There was a corresponding reduction of each divisional ammunition column in order to form Army field artillery brigade ammunition columns.

[2] Early in November, too, the Germans decided to provide " fluid " reinforcements of field artillery and proceeded to form " Army field artillery reserves ". G.O.A. xi., pp. 95-6.

[3] Divisional artillery eventually consisted of two brigades, each of three 6-gun 18-pdr. batteries and one 6-gun 4.5″ howitzer battery. This reorganization was completed early in 1917.

[4] From 30th June to 30th September 1916 the average expenditure per 18-pdr. gun per day was 50 rounds, the highest of any such period during the whole War. The quarterly receipts and expenditure of gun ammunition by the British Armies in France during the period of the Somme offensive are shown in Appendix 31.

[5] See " 1916 " Vol. I., pp. 122-4.

tubes in some of the heavier pieces and weak buffer-springs in the 18-pdrs., the " life " of every gun and howitzer was, of course, limited ; [1] and for re-lining they had to be sent back to England.

For counter-battery fire and for use against such objectives as High Wood, Delville Wood and the Combles ravine, lethal gas shell would have been invaluable, but it was still in the experimental stage and only a very limited quantity was available for the British artillery. No smoke shell was received until November.

Mounted on a scale and waged with an intensity unprecedented, continued for month after month, the Somme was a new and searching experience for the British leaders. " Of the corps commanders on the 1st July, only " two had commanded as much as a division in peace time, " and of the 23 divisional commanders in the field only " three had commanded as much as a brigade before the " War." [2] Their great problem was how to retain control of the battle once the assault was launched. A corps headquarters, although admirably located for quick communication with Army headquarters and with the corps on its flanks, was always too far back to keep in close touch with the shifting phases of the battle and to deal with them as they arose. There was little, indeed, that a corps commander could do except facilitate the forward flow of reserves, ammunition, battle stores and supplies as these were needed. Divisional commanders were in a much better position to " fight " the battle, but, as a general rule, too little initiative was allowed them. Divisions were sometimes forbidden to engage their reserve brigades without corps authority, and the extent to which they could influence artillery action was limited. Much dissatisfaction was naturally aroused in lower formations, such as brigades, when, by corps order, they were detached from their own division to reinforce another which was already engaged ; but the practice had much to commend it. Often the only alternative during an action was to relieve a divisional commander and his staff, who were conversant with the situation and knew the ground, by newcomers who did not possess these advantages.[3] In any case, to employ reserves and reinforcements with success corps and

---

[1] For example, the average life of the 18-pdr. was 20,000 rounds, fired with full charge ; of the 6″ gun (Mk. VII.), 1,500 rounds ; and of the 6″ howitzer (26 cwt.), 10,000 rounds.

[2] " 1916 " Vol. I., p. 491.

[3] See below for the German view of this problem.

divisional commanders required to possess a fair appreciation of what British infantry could and could not do: they were then unlikely to order the impossible or to cry halt when all was going well.

How far in rear of the front line the brigade headquarters should be located, and when, if ever, brigade commanders were justified in going forward to bring their personal influence to bear, were other questions not easy to decide. In any case effective control throughout the chain of command depended to a very great extent upon the efficiency of communications and the work of the staffs.

Owing to the dearth of trained officers, the staffs of corps, divisions and brigades included many young Regular[1] and New Army officers who had to learn the duties of their branch in the heat of battle. In some cases over-anxious staff officers " nursed " inexperienced brigade and battalion commanders too much, thereby curbing and discouraging initiative ; on the other hand, proper guidance and help from the staff were not always forthcoming when most needed. To regulate movement to and from the battle-front so that the fighting troops might be fed and watered, reliefs carried out, the flow of ammunition and battle stores maintained and the wounded evacuated, called for the best efforts of all branches of the staff. The congested roads, tracks and trenches steadily deteriorated through much usage and the combined effect of bad weather and hostile fire, so that confusion and delay were at times inevitable. One of the worst features was that battalions coming forward to take part in an attack often had to spend hours on the way and arrived in their assembly positions in an almost exhausted state, with little time left in which to make ready for action.

The perfunctory battle training of the troops was based upon tactical principles sound for the most part, but lacking in some essential details and in a proper anticipation of the difficulties with which the infantry would have to contend. For instance, despite the results of the fighting in 1915, the power of the enemy machine gun in defence was not fully realized throughout the higher commands. As the offensive proceeded British Intelligence, which did admirable work, secured much information regarding German defensive tactics, but too little use was made of it.

---

[1] Quite a number who had arrived from Sandhurst to join their units on the Aisne in 1914 filled junior appointments on corps and divisional staffs and were brigade-majors or staff captains in 1916.

Generally speaking, the new British infantry, unlike that of the old Regular Army, had not been taught to combine fire and movement to the best advantage ; it had begun to rely too little upon the rifle and too much upon the bomb ; it was not well practised in the use of ground ; and, whilst inclined to be unduly sensitive as regards its own flanks, did not sufficiently appreciate the necessity of helping adjacent formations. Loss of direction during the advance, a frequent cause of failure, was only to be expected when inexperienced troops encountered the havoc wrought by bombardment which destroyed landmarks and often created fresh obstacles.

There remained in the Armies few battalions possessed of the deep grounded knowledge and battle discipline which react instinctively to an unexpected situation and deal effectively with it. In circumstances where the training manuals provided no guidance, an admirable anxiety to do the right thing too often foundered in ignorance of what was the right thing to do. Even the Regular and the older Territorial divisions contained a large number of new enlistments, and many junior officers who had nearly everything to learn. In those formations which had fought at Loos the presence of the comparatively few veterans was not enough to leaven the inexperience of the new-comers. Moreover, owing to the protracted nature of the struggle, divisions brought out for rest and reconstitution had to return to the fight too soon, their ranks filled by new drafts which there had been no time to assimilate and train. Many officers who proved themselves capable commanders in action were not so successful out of the line when the reconstitution and training of their battalions, companies, or platoons became the vital need. Yet natural leaders there were in plenty, and the gallantry and spirit of officers and men were beyond all praise ; the pity of it was that they should have had to learn their business in the hard school of the Somme.[1]

[1] The question of the lack of trained and experienced officers to command battalions had been taken up by G.H.Q. and considered by the War Office before the end of July 1916. At this time Army schools in France were giving a short course of instruction to a limited number of suitable officers, but the demand could not be met in this way. In October G.H.Q. appointed Br.-General A. Solly-Flood to organize at Auxi le Château (11 miles N.W. of Doullens) instructional classes for lieut.-colonels and majors. At the beginning of 1917 this officer was brought to G.H.Q. to inaugurate a Training Directorate for all arms and services in France. This provided for the co-ordination of all training, whether carried out under G.H.Q., the Armies, the corps, or the divisions. (See "1915" Vol. I.,

Sir Douglas Haig had suggested on the 15th June that lightly equipped fighting patrols should lead the advance ; [1] but the infantry assault in waves of successive lines was persisted in throughout the offensive. Even so late as September 1916 some battalions took pride in preserving their " dressing " whilst advancing to the assault, regardless of the fact that lines of men formed ideal targets for machine guns firing in enfilade. The best formation, as was proved later in the War, consisted of small groups each trained to use ground and covering fire to the best advantage, and to work on its own initiative whilst affording support and assistance to other groups. Doubtless it was generally considered that the standard of training amongst the rank and file and the junior leaders was not high enough for such tactics to succeed in 1916 ; yet some such alternative would have saved the great sacrifice of life which so often occurred when an assault was delivered against an unsubdued machine-gun defence. Actually, if the advancing lines were not almost annihilated, great gaps were torn in them by heavy casualties ; and, as the survivors were obliged to break formation in order to avoid shell-holes and seek passages through the wire, they had generally split into small parties by the time they sought to enter the hostile position. These parties, however, were pitifully few and lacked cohesion and leadership.

The great lesson of the 1st July was that the infantry must break in before the machine-gun defence could come into action : this meant that the shortest possible interval must elapse between the lift of the barrage and the arrival of the stormers. It was the evolution of the creeping barrage,[2] and the education of the infantry in keeping as close as possible to it, which provided a solution to this problem. The pace of the assault could not be quickened : in " battle-order ",[3] an infantryman could only proceed at a

---

p. 12, f.n. 1.) At home a Senior Officers School was established at Alder-shot, the commandant, Br.-General R. J. Kentish, and the instructors being supplied from France. The first course began on 16th October ; it lasted 2½ months and was attended by 120 selected infantry officers withdrawn from service on the Western Front.

[1] See " 1916 " Vol. I., p. 290 ; also, for a corps commander's views, Appendix 14 of this volume.

[2] See " 1916 " Vol. I.

[3] In the assault each man generally carried 120 rounds (or more) S.A.A. ; 4 sandbags ; an iron ration and the unconsumed portion of the day's ration ; respirator ; a flare ; and 2 bombs. Also 50 per cent of the troops would have a pick or a shovel. " Specialists " were differently equipped,

walk, so the rate of the barrage had to conform. Eventually, when the ground was particularly bad for movement, it sometimes " crept " as slowly as 25 yards per minute, the leading infantry always striving to keep within 50 yards of it.[1]

It remained a debatable question as to whether the lines or small columns following in support and reserve of the leading waves—perhaps to go through them and attack a farther objective—should close up in order to escape the almost inevitable German barrage which fell in No Man's Land and on the departure trenches, or should preserve their distance and so avoid confusion and loss of control. What may be called the " forward " policy answered well in some cases. Experience proved that, if possible, infantry should not be called upon to cover more than 200-250 yards in its advance to the assault : a greater distance increased the risk of heavy casualties and the danger of losing direction, besides imposing an undue physical strain upon the troops. If the opposing trenches were closer together the British front line, as a rule, had to be cleared for the final bombardment which was liable to cause disorganization at the critical time.

There were occasions when ground was gained at little or no cost by advancing at night and digging in, and this might have been done more frequently. After a successful attack the enterprise of patrols was, as a rule, discouraged if not prohibited by the " protective barrage ".[3]

The Fourth Army had emphasized the fact that the Lewis gun was in reality an automatic rifle,[3] but some battalion and company commanders were slow to take full advantage of its mobility and its capacity for accurate fire without fixed emplacement. Similarly, the value of the Vickers gun for covering and supporting fire was only realized by degrees, although brigades were quicker in making this weapon the framework of the defence of a

---

but bore as heavy a burden. In 1904–5 the Japanese infantry had adopted a light assault equipment consisting of a long narrow bag worn en banderole.

[1] The French on the Somme gradually adopted the same method. The " barrage précurseur " or " barrage roulant " does not seem to have been employed by them at Verdun before October. See F.O.A. iv. (iii.), Annexes 612, 968, 1065.

[2] In October G.H.Q. instructed that the protective barrage should be lifted " as soon as possible " so that patrols might exploit success to the utmost by pushing on in advance of the objective.

[3] See " Fourth Army : Tactical Notes ", " 1916 " Vol. I., Appendix 18.

captured position. There were always difficulties in man-handling Vickers guns over bad ground with the very limited personnel available ; likewise, the use of Stokes mortars in the offensive was limited by the reluctance of some commanders to sacrifice rifle strength in order to provide parties to carry the bulky ammunition which was so rapidly consumed by this weapon.

The action of the tanks, as we have seen,[1] was extremely limited in effect. Nothing of significance was achieved by minor close-support weapons such as the blazing oil projector. The elaborate installation needed for the dis-charge of cloud gas prohibited its employment in the course of the offensive. Smoke barrages, provided by mortars firing bombs—there was no smoke shell for the artillery—were used on too small a scale to yield important results.

Reference has already been made to the importance of the rapid transmission of reports, orders and intelligence. The maintenance of reliable means of communication always presented, a difficult problem, as, indeed, it does to-day. No signal system yet devised was, or is, infallible under a heavy bombardment. Deep-buried cables, which are the least vulnerable, cannot be extended quickly, but every effort was made to run out lighter cables and to keep them in repair. All forms of visual signalling—disc, shutter, fan, flag and lamp—were tried in the forward areas when conditions permitted. Communication between infantry and aeroplane by means of flares and ground panels—the airmen calling on the troops, by Klaxon horns, to show their positions at stated times—became an accepted pro-cedure, but infantry parties were liable to show such signals from localities not permanently occupied by them. Carrier pigeons were used freely, although there was often con-siderable delay in the arrival of the birds at report centres in rear ; they could not, of course, be employed in the reverse direction. Wireless, apart from R.F.C. establish-ments, was relied upon to a limited extent, but practically no reserve of trained operators existed, whilst many of the sets in use were not of a design which functioned easily under battle conditions. Much, therefore, still depended upon the courage and devotion of the despatch runner. One result of the Somme offensive was the eventual res-toration of the battalion signals officer to the infantry establishment, but first there came an increase in the

[1] See page 364.

personnel of divisional signal companies and of artillery signal staffs.[1]

The tasks which devolved upon the field companies R.E. were as heavy as they were diversified, and the semi-skilled work of the pioneer battalions was indispensable. Fortunately the practice of sending forward sections of R.E. with the assaulting infantry fell out of favour, but sappers were often employed with very little discrimination in the consolidation of captured positions. " Strongpoints ", which, as one engineer officer remarked, " looked well in operation " orders and on the maps ", became rather an obsession. R.E. personnel wasted much strenuous effort, and suffered heavy loss by shell and machine-gun fire, whilst endeavouring, under divisional orders, to construct these works. When they were completed the fighting troops were sometimes unaware of their precise location and therefore failed to utilize them ; sometimes they proved to be of no tactical value owing to the shifting phases of the action. In any case, the truest service which the engineers can render the infantry is the maintenance and improvement of communications so that reinforcements, ammunition and supplies can reach the battlefront with the minimum of trouble and delay. Infantry, without engineer assistance, should be capable of digging such defences as are required as an insurance against counter-attack in the course of an action.

In the preceding volume [2] there has been noted the tendency of the higher command to regard the assault of strong field-fortifications as more or less analogous to the climax of the infantry attack in open warfare. This may account for the fact that the slower and surer methods of siege warfare by parallel, sap and mine were so little employed.[3] After the 1st July [4] mining played little part in the offensive. Russian saps [5] proved of use at several points on the first day, but, as tunnels, there were not enough of them to ease the problem of communication across No Man's Land, even if the fighting troops in general

---

[1] See also " 1916 " Vol. I., pp. 67 *et seq.*, and " The Work of the R.E. " in the European War 1914–19 : The Signal Service (France) ".

[2] See " 1916 " Vol. I., p. 487.

[3] It is worthy of note that the quickest recorded progress made by tunnellers in chalk soil is 62′ × 6′ 6″ × 3′ 6″ in 24 hours, this length of gallery being fully timbered in the time.'

[4] When 8 large and 11 small mines were fired. See " 1916 " Vol. I., p. 286.

[5] See " 1916 " Vol. I.

had been familiar with their location. Where these saps were opened up as straight trenches it required much time and labour to construct traverses in them.

Tunnelling officers who saw their companies employed upon roads, mined dug-outs, and water-supply duties often felt that they might have been used to better purpose.[1] If the " nibbling " tactics of the Reserve Army throughout August and during the greater part of September against the Thiepval ridge had been supplemented by mining operations the subsequent infantry assault might have been less costly and more quickly successful, and much gun ammunition saved. The difficulties of getting up material and of disposing of the very conspicuous chalk " spoil " could have been overcome despite the excellent observation enjoyed by the enemy in the Thiepval sector.

The part played by the Royal Flying Corps is only to be judged by the record of the corps as a whole : from June onwards all its activities had a distinct bearing upon the Somme battles.[2] It is difficult to over-estimate the value of aeroplane co-operation upon which the accuracy of artillery fire so largely depended ; the aeroplane photograph became an almost indispensable aid to the mapping sections ; and British superiority in the air had a remarkable moral effect upon the troops. On many occasions airmen joined in the fighting by swooping low along the enemy trenches and opening machine-gun fire. The policy of engaging the German machines over their own territory was so successful that, for the greater part of the offensive, artillery and photographic work was carried on without any interference from the enemy. Also, for the first $2\frac{1}{2}$ months he was prevented from doing any such work, and thereafter accomplished comparatively little.

The R.F.C. assisted to register 8,612 targets for the artillery and took more than 19,000 photographs, over 420,000 prints being made. By the middle of November there were 542 wireless ground stations at work, and 306 aeroplanes using wireless. In 298 bombing raids on points of tactical importance there were dropped 176,000 bombs, a total weight of 292 tons.

To maintain such a vigorous offensive in the air con-

---

[1] One officer remarked that " some commanders have a prejudice " against mining as they have against gas ". Crater fighting was certainly loathed by the troops on both sides.

[2] See " The War in the Air ", Vol. II.

siderable losses had to be accepted and promptly replaced, as the following figures will show :

Machines available 1st July . . .	410
,, ,, 17th November . .	550
Wastage	782 [1]
Pilots available 1st July	426
,, ,, 17th November . .	585
Casualties	576 [2]

The number of hostile aircraft destroyed was 164, and 205 were driven down damaged : a proportionately greater loss. It must also be remembered that the combats in the air occurred, almost without exception, behind the German lines.

The Germans were obliged to concentrate upon the problems of the defensive battle. It was not, however, until the later stages of the Somme offensive, when the crises of September had passed and sufficient troops, artillery and ammunition were available, that the maintenance of resistance at all costs, by extemporized measures, could give place to properly planned methods.

Falkenhayn's order, issued on the 2nd July, that not one foot of ground must be abandoned, and that ground, if lost, must be retaken at all costs,[3] committed the troops to a rigid defence which was bound to involve heavy casualties and the greatest hardship and suffering. With the advent of Hindenburg and Ludendorff loss of ground came to be accepted as inevitable in some circumstances ; but until the end of the offensive the voluntary evacuation of a position was not supposed to occur without the authority of the Army commander.

Protection from bombardment became the first consideration when new positions in rear had to be constructed in all haste. Hence the reverse slope, with the disadvantage of limited observation and small field of fire, was generally chosen. As there was no time to put out broad obstacles in front of the trenches deep mined dug-outs gave way to small shelters from which troops could emerge quickly and easily. The great lesson, however, was that a prolonged

[1] Wrecked, shot to pieces in the air, or worn out, 592 ; missing, 190.
[2] Battle casualties to pilots, 308 ; in addition, 109 observers were killed, wounded or missing.
[3] G.O.A. x., p. 355.

2 P

resistance to the attack of superior forces could only be offered by a defence organized in considerable depth.[1]

A new doctrine for the defensive battle was compiled at O.H.L. and issued in December. Ludendorff favoured an active and elastic defence conducted in a battle zone—a belt of fortified localities—extending, probably, to 2,000 yards in depth. " It was of course intended that the " position should remain in our hands at the end of the " battle, but the infantryman need no longer say to him- " self: ' Here I must stand or fall '." The fighting was to take place not *in*, but *for* the front line.[2] Lost positions were to be recovered by local counter-attacks; if these failed the task would fall upon counter-attack divisions.

It was realized that such freedom of action could only be accorded with safety to well-trained troops of good morale, and this consideration weighed heavily with many German commanders, who felt doubtful of the quality of the reinforcements, mostly very young and inexperienced, which replaced the well-trained soldiery lost on the Somme and at Verdun.[3] The result was seen in a new training manual based upon the conclusions of General Fritz von Below, commanding the *First Army*, and Colonel von Lossberg, his Chief of the Staff.[4] In the battle zone, with every trench organized for defence, the front line was to be held lightly, but supports were to be kept close at hand: the havoc caused by the hostile bombardment was liable to leave the defenders to face the assault in shell-holes or in isolated lengths of trench, but voluntary evacuation of a position must only take place by permission of the higher commanders: good, well-trained troops might, however, temporarily evacuate a very heavily shelled position by moving forward: excellent results had been obtained on

---

[1] G.O.A. xi., pp. 108, 112.

[2] G.O.A. xi., p. 107-8 ; Ludendorff i., p. 387. Compare F.S.R. ii. (1935), p. 137, para. 4.

[3] Compensation for the deterioration of the fighting value of the German division was sought by increasing its fire power. Three, and later three more, light machine guns were added to each infantry company ; also, by the end of January 1917, each battalion was to receive 18 heavy machine guns, this number to be doubled when the output of the armament works permitted. G.O.A. xi., p. 508.

[4] " Erfahrungen der I. Armee in die Sommeschlacht 1916 ", dated from Army Headquarters, 30th January 1917. This and other relevant documents did not fall into the hands of the Intelligence Branch at G.H.Q. until after the Battles of Arras had begun in the spring of 1917 ; but valuable information regarding the lessons learnt by the Germans at Verdun was received in February.

the Somme by obliging every man to fight at the post where he was stationed and " the enemy's advance could only be " over his dead body ".

After three months of fighting on the Somme it became recognized that the control of the battle inevitably passed from Armies and " Groups " (or corps) to the divisional commanders. The Group commanders were then chiefly concerned in the co-operation of divisions for the purpose of counter-attack and in the sending forward of reinforcements and supplies as they were required. It was important that each divisional commander should control the fire of the artillery in his sector, but difficulty arose when a new division came in, the field and heavy batteries being already in position. In September O.H.L. issued an order that all artillery in a divisional sector should be placed under the tactical command of the division, but General von Below found himself unable to comply: he placed all field artillery under the divisional commander and kept the heavy artillery under the Group, with close liaison between the two artillery headquarters. This plan proved, perhaps, more effective, for it facilitated the employment of the heavy artillery fire on other divisional sectors when required.[1]

During 1917 the theory of the defensive battle continued to occupy the close attention of German commanders and staffs, and German defensive tactics underwent further developments. The results will be seen in the volumes which deal with the fighting in that year.

[1] G.O.A. xi., pp. 107-9.

GENERAL INDEX

INDEX TO
ARMS, FORMATIONS AND UNITS

592

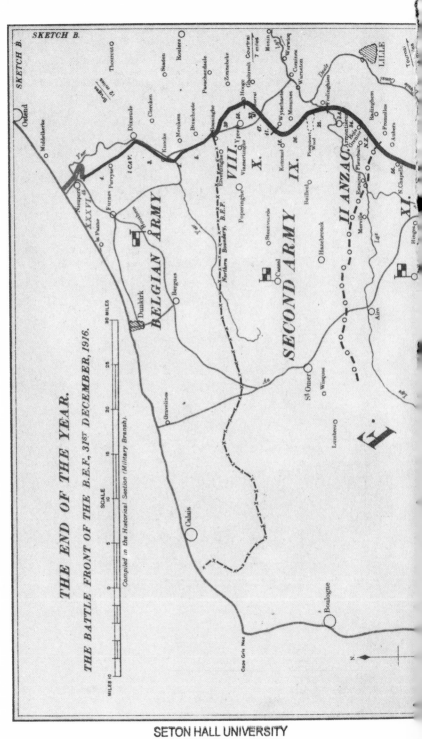

THE END OF THE YEAR.

THE BATTLE FRONT OF THE B.E.F., 31ST DECEMBER, 1916.

SKETCH B.

SCALE

Compiled in the Historical Section (Military Branch).